Robert H. Lieshout is Emeritus Professor of International Relations at Radboud University in the Netherlands. He has published widely on the theory and history of international relations, including two major works of political science: *Between Anarchy and Hierarchy: A Theory of International Politics and Foreign Policy* (1995) and *The Struggle for the Organization of Europe: The Foundations of the European Union* (1999). He was President of the Dutch Political Science Association from 1999 until 2003.

'An important window into the nuances of the British "official mind" in the Middle East during one of the most turbulent and significant phases of modern history'

Warren Dockter, author of *Churchill and the Islamic World: Orientalism, Empire and Diplomacy in the Middle East* (I.B.Tauris, 2015)

ROBERT H. LIESHOUT

BRITAIN AND THE ARAB MIDDLE EAST

WORLD WAR I AND ITS AFTERMATH

Published in 2016 by
I.B.Tauris & Co. Ltd
London • New York
www.ibtauris.com

Copyright © 2016 Robert H. Lieshout

The right of Robert H. Lieshout to be identified as the author of this work has been asserted by the author in accordance with the Copyright, Designs and Patents Act 1988.

All rights reserved. Except for brief quotations in a review, this book, or any part thereof, may not be reproduced, stored in or introduced into a retrieval system, or transmitted, in any form or by any means, electronic, mechanical, photocopying, recording or otherwise, without the prior written permission of the publisher.

Every attempt has been made to gain permission for the use of the images and documents in this book. Any omissions will be rectified in future editions.

ISBN: 978 1 78453 583 4
eISBN: 978 0 85772 933 0
ePDF: 978 0 85772 729 9

A full CIP record for this book is available from the British Library
A full CIP record is available from the Library of Congress

Library of Congress Catalog Card Number: available

Typeset by Riverside Publishing Solutions, Salisbury, SP4 6NQ
Printed and bound by CPI Group (UK) Ltd, Croydon, CR0 4YY

To Renée

The part played by the British has had the tendency to make people believe that they are playing a very deep game, with a very definite aim which will only be revealed at the right moment.

William Yale, Report #3, 12 November 1917, Library of Congress

I suppose that in this, as in most investigations of British foreign policy, the true reason is not to be found in far-sighted views or large conceptions or great schemes. A Minister beset with the administrative work of a great Office must often be astounded to read of the carefully laid plans, the deep unrevealed motives that critics or admirers attribute to him. Onlookers free from responsibility have time to invent, and they attribute to Ministers many things that Ministers have no time to invent themselves, even if they are clever enough to be able to do it. If all secrets were known it would probably be found that British Foreign Ministers have been guided by what seemed to them to be the immediate interests of this country without making elaborate calculations for the future.

Viscount Grey of Fallodon, *Twenty-Five Years* (London, 1926), Vol. I, p. 6

CONTENTS

List of Maps		xi
Preface		xiii
Introduction		1
Part I	**The Asquith Governments 1914–16**	
1	I Suppose the I.O. Know How This Can be Done	13
2	Keeping Better Educated Moslems Busy	33
3	We Have Got to Keep in with Our Infernal Allies	57
4	The Whole Subject is Becoming Entangled	83
5	Rabegh Has Been a Perfect Nuisance	123
Part II	**The Lloyd George Government 1916–19**	
6	Taking the Sherif into the Fullest Confidence Possible	165
7	Up Against a Big Thing	189
8	A Whole Crowd of Weeds Growing Around Us	233
9	Since I Am So Early Done For, I Wonder What I Was Begun For!	275
10	Getting Out of This Syrian Tangle	321
11	We Regard Palestine as Being Absolutely Exceptional	381

| Conclusion | 417 |

| Biographical Notes: British Officials, Politicians and Soldiers Connected with British Foreign Policy towards the Arab Middle East, 1914–19 | 425 |

| Bibliography | 435 |

| Notes | 441 |

| Index of Names | 493 |

| Index of Subjects | 503 |

LIST OF MAPS

2.1	The Western Arab Middle East (Source: Wavell, *The Palestine Campaign*)	32
4.1	The Anglo–French–Russian Agreement of 1916	82
5.1	Medina, Rabegh and Mecca	122
9.1	Occupied Enemy Territory, Administrative Zones (Source: Falls, *Military Operations* Vol. II)	274
11.1	Palestine, as Claimed by the Advisory Committee on Palestine, November 1918 (Source: Jewish Virtual Library)	380
11.2	Palestine's Northern Border, 1919–23 (adapted from *IBRU Boundary Security Bulletin* 2000–1, p. 74)	416

PREFACE

It cannot be denied that this study has known a long period of gestation. It all started in the autumn of 1977, shortly after I had obtained my master's degree in Political and Social Sciences from the University of Amsterdam, when I submitted an application for a research grant to the Dutch Organisation for the Advancement of Pure Research (ZWO). My application was successful and, in August 1978, I started my PhD project on British foreign policy towards the Middle East 1914-19. In the early spring of 1984, my supervisor and I reached the conclusion that a successful defence of my thesis did not require that I cover the whole period up to and until the end of 1919, and that my analysis of the years of the Asquith governments, from the autumn of 1914 until the end of 1916, could stand on its own and be presented to the manuscript committee for examination. After the successful public defence of my thesis *Without Making Elaborate Calculations for the Future: Great Britain and the Arab Question 1914-1916* in December 1984, it was my intention to complete the second part of my study but in the meantime, I had become a Lecturer in International Relations and my research interests began to drift more and more towards other subjects. In the first instance, these included the development of a general theory of international relations and foreign policy making, which resulted in my book *Between Anarchy and Hierarchy*, published in 1995, and after that the history of the early years of the West European integration process, which led in 1999 to the publication of *The Struggle for the Organization of Europe*, for which a thoroughly revised and much enlarged Dutch edition was published in 2004. At the beginning of 2012, I was set free from all administrative and teaching obligations at the university and decided, after I had convinced myself that I still had a feel for the subject, to tackle the years of the Lloyd George government and at last bring my thesis up to the end of 1919.

As a student, I had been much impressed by Graham Allison's *Essence of Decision*, in particular his exposition of the Organisational Process Model and the Governmental Politics Model, as well as his application of these models to the Cuban missile crisis of 1962. It appeared from Allison's book that, in spite of the evident irrationality of a nuclear war of destruction, we can never disregard the possibility that, through the execution of organisational routines or the fighting out of bureaucratic conflicts, states will somehow end up in such an irrational war. Foreign policy makers are not coolly calculating people guided by a shared and clear concept of the national interest; instead, they are people, calculating to be sure, but enmeshed in standard operating procedures and bureaucratic infighting, justifying their positions by appeals to a national interest as they see it. Simply put (and admittedly a bit exaggerated), foreign policy is not the triumph of rationality, but a mess. The central objective in my research proposal was to find out whether Allison's depiction of foreign policy making also applied to Great Britain's foreign policy towards the Middle East during the period 1914–19, which, in view of the enormous extension of Britain's influence in the Arab-speaking Middle East in the course of those years, was generally regarded as the epitome of successful power politics. I believe that the story I present in Chapters 1 to 11 can lead to no other conclusion than that it does apply, and how!

I am indebted to the late Professor Frits de Jong Edz., as without his willingness to put his signature under my application for a research grant, nothing would have come of all this. I am also grateful to my PhD supervisor, Professor Johan K. De Vree. I remember with great warmth our long and intense discussions on the role that power plays in decision-making processes (the academic world included!). I also owe a great debt to the late R.R. Mellor of the Public Record Office, London, who helped me decipher the handwriting of ministers, soldiers and officials involved in British Middle Eastern policy making. Without his help, many a passage would have remained a mystery to me. Lesley Forbes, former Keeper of Oriental Books at the Oriental Section of the University Library, Durham, lent me great assistance during my researches of the Wingate and Clayton papers. I am also grateful for the help of the staffs of the Public Record Office, the India Office Library and Records, the Bodleian Library, the British Library, Churchill College, the House of Lords Public Record Office, the National Archives of Scotland, St Anthony's College and Cambridge University Library.

Several people read parts of the manuscript. During the early 1980s, they included Professors Jan van Deth and Jacques Thomassen, Aleid Truijens and in particular Don Westerheijden. In recent years I profited from comments by Professors Jehuda Reinharz, Jonathan Schneer and Bernard Wasserstein, Bill Mathew and especially Bob Reinalda. I very much appreciate their willingness to take the time to read my work.

I dedicated my doctoral thesis, the first part of the present book, to my first wife Marieke, who sadly died in 2002. Shortly thereafter, Renée, who had introduced Marieke to me in 1974 in the first place, re-entered my life, and we have been together ever since. It gives me great satisfaction to dedicate *Britain and the Arab Middle East* to her. I am very grateful to both for their unwavering love and support.

INTRODUCTION

Taking Nonsense Seriously

Edwin Montagu, MP, was appointed secretary of state for India on 17 July 1917. In this capacity he was responsible for British relations with the Trucial Chiefs on the coast of the Persian Gulf, the emirs of Kuwait and Mohammerah, the sultans of Nejd, Muscat and Oman, Aden and its hinterland, Iman Yahya of Yemen and the Idrisi of Asir. Sir Percy Cox, chief political officer with the British forces that had occupied the southern part of Mesopotamia, including Baghdad, also reported to him. Almost one month after his appointment, Montagu received a letter from Sir Mark Sykes, civil assistant secretary to the War Cabinet, and generally regarded an expert on the Middle East. In his letter, Sykes set out to educate Montagu on the 'fundamental factors which divide the moderately well-to-do East from the moderately well-to-do West'. According to Sir Mark, the mentality of the West resulted from four:

> Big historical influences which are absent from the East –
>
> i. Roman law and the theory of order and authority based on order.
> ii. Medieval Christianity with the corollary of 'chivalry' based on sacrifice and respect for women.
> iii. Baconian science and the reformation, viz.: material progress and the theory of individual judgment.
> iv. The French Revolution and the development of the constitutional democratic idea.

Sykes contrasted this heritage with that of the East, which had been shaped by three 'physical factors', to wit:

i. Malaria.
ii. Harem life, leading to early masturbation say at the age of 6 or 7 and thence to sodomy, bestiality etc., etc., as tolerable things.
iii. Completely disorderly domestic habits.

Sir Mark subsequently invited Montagu to contemplate what would happen if 'a youth influenced by the last three factors' was introduced to the Western heritage 'through alien and not very competent channels'. He further added that what you then got was 'this devastating intelligentsia of parrots, who cheat, kill, bomb, peculate or chatter as the evil spirit moves them'.[1]

I have been unable to trace Montagu's reaction to Sykes's letter, if he ever sent one. I also have not come across a book or an article in which it is quoted. This brings me to what I believe crucially distinguishes this study on British foreign policy towards the Middle East 1914–19 from the many, many others that have dealt with the subject. It is my guess that scholars who visited St Anthony's College in Oxford in the course of their researches and read this letter did not take it seriously, were even embarrassed by it, and decided to ignore it. They simply could not imagine that fanciful notions like these might have played a role in such a weighty matter as the formulation of British Middle East policy. The approach I have adopted in this book, however, which follows from the theoretical considerations I shall elucidate in the next section, entails that letters of this kind are taken seriously, and allows for the possibility that notions like those of Sykes might very well have guided the ministers, officials and soldiers who were responsible for formulating British foreign policy towards the Middle East in the period 1914–19.

Another distinguishing characteristic of this study consists in its comprehensive treatment of the subject. Naturally, thousands of articles and books dealing with British Middle East policy have been published in the course of the years, but these always focus on the actions of certain individuals, or the coming about of certain events, and almost without exception have been written against the background of the tragic developments that have occurred since then. This book is different. I try to cover the whole range of subjects with which the most important British policy makers who dealt with the Middle East busied themselves during these years. This history has been written from their perspective. This means that I also address subjects that with hindsight seem hardly to have mattered but at the time certainly preoccupied them. A perspective like this is sensitive to bureaucratic infighting, routine, mistakes, dead ends, carelessness, prejudice and, as we have just seen, even outright nonsense.

A Bureaucratic-Politics Perspective

When I studied the public and private papers with respect to British foreign policy towards the Middle East 1914–19, time and again I came across memoranda, reports, minutes, letters and telegrams that stood out from the rest because of the 'quality' of the arguments their authors employed in defending or attacking a certain policy. The reasons they advanced in support of their position and the conclusions they arrived at constituted a consistent whole and, with the benefit of hindsight, I was able to say, also agreed with the facts. At the same time, I noticed that only very rarely did these sound proposals win out. Again and again, these 'technically' superior recommendations were ignored in favour of proposals formulated by others, who clearly did not bother to think through their ideas very carefully, advocated policies based on observations that did not correspond with the facts, and who sometimes even seemed to have had their way without using any arguments worthy of the name at all. In this section, I present some theoretical observations that have helped me to resolve this puzzling phenomenon, and have guided my efforts to find my way through the enormous wealth of material collected in public and private archives, as well as to write this book.

When we put ourselves in the place of the most important decision makers who were involved in formulating British Middle East policy 1914–19, and try to understand why they acted like they did, the most fundamental and helpful insight is that almost without exception these men had made their careers in a bureaucratic-political environment, and that their rise to prominence would not have been possible had they not mastered to a sufficient extent what matters in such an environment and the ways in which it functions.[2] In particular, they must have acquired an adequate feel for the fact that in bureaucratic and political decision making everything turns on a decision maker's credibility, his effectiveness (that is to say, his reputation for getting things done), as well as the rule that the higher the credibility of a bureaucrat or politician, the more readily other bureaucrats and politicians will act according to his wishes. They must have grasped, either consciously or unconsciously, that in a bureaucratic-political world, of the three sources of power traditionally distinguished, the capacity to use violence is irrelevant, economic gain can never be more than a side payment, but credibility is all decisive.

Theoretically speaking, credibility has three aspects. The first I have already mentioned, and concerns a decision maker's 'effectiveness', his or her reputation for being able and willing to execute threats and to fulfil promises. The second relates to his or her reputation for playing by the rules, while the third refers to his or her reputation for speaking the truth (or perhaps more correctly, for not having publicly been caught out telling lies). The first of these aspects is the most important by far. This description also makes clear that, although one can certainly say that a certain decision maker possesses a high or a low credibility, this 'possession' is not a very tangible one. It only exists in the eye of the beholder, in this case his or her fellow decision makers, and their perceptions of this decision maker's reputation can be way off the mark, to the latter's advantage or disadvantage. It is precisely for this reason that Hans Morgenthau, in his *Politics Among Nations*, defined political power as a 'psychological relation between those who exercise it and those over whom it is exercised. It gives the former control over certain actions of the latter through the impact which the former exert on the latter's minds'.[3]

Relations between decision makers in a bureaucratic-political environment are consequently highly 'psychological' or, if you wish, 'theoretical' in character. It is no easy task for the individual decision maker to establish whether another decision maker's reputation for getting things done corresponds with reality or not. This task only becomes more complicated when decision makers interact very frequently and the pace of the decision processes in which they participate (i.e. the frequency with which they are confronted with deadlines, as in times of crisis) is such that it does not permit them to find out (provided they would like to do so) whether the other decision makers are actually capable of fulfilling the promises and executing the threats that seem to be involved in their attempts to influence one another's behaviour. Under such circumstances, guessing at the guesses of the other decision makers becomes increasingly important, and it is easy to see that these guesses can begin to lead a life of their own, with the result that the relationship between the decision makers' reputations for power and their 'real' positions of power can become more and more tenuous.

In the course of their bureaucratic or political careers, decision makers have gradually come to understand that their advancement stands or falls with the successful protection and strengthening of their credibility. This means that their credibility has gradually become *the* criterion with the help of which they assess the importance of verbal or written messages about developments, not only in the world outside, but also, and perhaps even more importantly, in the bureaucratic-political environment in which they operate. They have learned that their reaction to such messages should depend on whether their credibility is threatened by them or, on the contrary, strengthened, or that these have no consequences for their credibility. If they reach the conclusion that their credibility is indeed at stake, either positively or negatively (and, in the latter case, also have come to the conclusion that the message cannot be swept under the carpet), then they will, in reaction, attempt to influence the behaviour or points of view of other decision makers. But, if they decide that their credibility is not at stake, then they will not act on this message (they will ignore it).

An important consequence is that decision makers will not be all that interested in whether the facts presented in a certain telegram, letter or memorandum correspond with reality, or whether the quality of the arguments employed meet certain standards. They will be not so much concerned with the content of the message, as with the messenger who brings it – where the messenger gains in importance at the expense of the message's content to the degree that according to decision makers their credibility seems to be more at stake. In addition, the more relevant for their credibility the message appears to be – the more it promises to strengthen their credibility or the more it threatens to harm it – the less value decision makers will attach to facts and arguments as a means to profit from this promise or to avert this threat. A decision maker will only be prepared to let a problem be resolved by means of argument in the case where they consider it to be a rather unimportant, esoteric, 'technical' question. It is also only with respect to questions of this type that they will be able and willing to change their point of view. In all other cases, arguments mainly serve to legitimise the position they take up with respect to the possible solution of a certain problem; they will stick to this position irrespective of the arguments put forward by the other participants in the decision-making process, and they will only add new arguments if these appear to strengthen their position.

Conferences and meetings do not provide an atmosphere in which the participants in a decision-making process freely discuss the validity of one another's arguments, are prepared to learn from each other, to adopt an attitude, as Karl Popper has phrased it, of '*I may be wrong and you may be right, and by an effort, we may get nearer to the truth*',[4] but only provide an opportunity to ventilate arguments that have been put forward before. This also means that in the majority of cases in which decision makers are confronted with an issue in which they take up conflicting positions, they will be less interested in the arguments that are advanced to solve this issue than in the reputation of power of those who bring them up. Another implication is that the higher a decision maker's credibility, the less attention other decision makers will pay to the quality, in terms of internal and external consistency, of his or her arguments. This also suggests that, in a situation where there are conflicting proposals regarding how to resolve a particular problem, the higher the level to which this conflict has escalated with respect to the solution of the problem, and the more of their credibility that adversaries in consequence have invested, the less value they will attach to arguments as a means to resolve it.

In contrast to the less powerful members of a political party and junior bureaucrats, the leaders of a political party, as well as senior bureaucrats, need to invest less of their time and energy inventing arguments in support of a solution to a problem advanced by them. They also need to pay comparatively less attention to the quality of their arguments. It is also easy to see that, in contrast to the less powerful, they would have less time available to do so. Their time is to a great extent taken up by attempts by the latter to win them over to their proposed solution to a certain problem. After all, the powerful members are the ones with the reputation for getting things done. Their amount of available time moreover will only become less to the extent that the pace of the decision-making processes in which they take part becomes faster. Conversely, it will be clear that, comparatively speaking, the less powerful have more time to invent arguments for or against a particular solution of a certain problem, and to pay attention to the quality of these arguments. This can only lead to the conclusion that, the less powerful the proponents of a particular proposal for the solution of a certain problem *vis-à-vis* the other decision makers participating in the decision-making process, the more time and energy, as compared to the latter, they will employ in inventing arguments in support of the solution advanced by them, and the less likely it becomes that this solution will be adopted. This conclusion provides the solution to the puzzle I introduced at the beginning of this section. The superior argument, in terms of internal and external consistency, time and again loses out because it is advanced by the less powerful participants in the decision-making process, while the inferior argument succeeds because it is put forward by the more powerful ones.

Now what does this admittedly rather abstruse reasoning mean for the study of British Middle East policy during the years 1914–19? It means that one should not be surprised to find that, in the autumn of 1914, the Foreign Office in a period of a few weeks first instructed the authorities in Cairo to encourage the Arab movement in every way possible and subsequently that they should refrain from giving it any encouragement (Chapter 1). That Sir Edward Grey and the officials at the Foreign Office had no thought-out conception of what British Middle East policy should be, but judged developments in that area on the basis of the simple rule that nothing should be done that might arouse France's susceptibilities with respect to Syria (Chapters 1 to 5). That in the summer of 1915 the Foreign Office without much discussion exchanged a policy of restraint in regard to exploiting Arab nationalist sentiment as advocated by the India Office and the Government of India for a more active pro-Arab policy urged by the authorities in Cairo and Khartoum, and authorised High Commissioner Sir Henry McMahon to react favourably to the overtures made by Abdullah, the second son of Sharif Husayn, the Emir of Mecca (Chapter 2). That the negotiations between Great Britain and France on the settlement of British and French spheres of direct and indirect influence in the Arab Middle East in 1915–16, which started in the wake of the British negotiations with Husayn on the conditions under which 'the' Arabs would rise against their Turkish overlords, continued even after it had become clear that the Arabs were too weak to start a revolt on their own and that Husayn could not be regarded as the spokesman of 'the Arab nation' (Chapters 3 and 4). That during the various discussions in the War Committee and, subsequently, the War Cabinet in the autumn of 1916 with regard to the sending of a brigade to Rabegh on the coast of the Hijaz in order to prevent the Arab revolt from collapsing, the last thing on the participants' minds was to find out whether Turkish troops were actually advancing on Mecca or not (Chapter 5). That the objective of the Sykes–Picot mission in the spring of 1917 imperceptibly shifted from advising Sir Archibald Murray on relations with the Arabs in light of the Sykes–Picot agreement to informing

King Husayn on the content of that agreement (Chapter 6). That Foreign Secretary Arthur Balfour hardly exerted himself to get the proposal adopted that the British government issue a declaration of sympathy with Zionist aims (Chapter 7). That on the eve of General Allenby's offensive into Syria, the Eastern Committee overruled the Foreign Office and agreed with Allenby that military considerations prevented François Georges-Picot becoming his chief political officer with respect to areas of special interest to France under the terms of the Sykes–Picot agreement (Chapter 8). That Lord George Curzon, who as chairman of the Eastern Committee had fought very hard in 1918 to establish that committee's pre-eminence over the Foreign Office, the India Office and the War Office as far as British Middle East policy was concerned, immediately proposed to disband it when it became clear that he would be appointed acting secretary of state for foreign affairs in January 1919 (Chapter 9). That the settlement of the Syrian question during the Paris peace conference turned into a highly personal affair between prime ministers David Lloyd George and Georges Clemenceau and was held up by them for months when to all others involved it was clear what should be done, and led to the biggest row they had as a result of Clemenceau's repeated accusations of bad faith on Lloyd George's part (Chapter 10). That the warnings by the British military authorities in Palestine that the existing resistance under the great majority of the Arab population, both Muslims and Christians, against the execution of a pro-Zionist policy might lead to violent protests and endanger the British position in Palestine, did not deflect the British authorities in London and Paris from their pro-Zionist course (Chapter 11). In short, that it should not surprise us that during these years, British policy makers took decisions that had momentous consequences, which reverberate to this very day, without making elaborate calculations for the future.

Not Complete, No Polemic

Although I have claimed in the first section of this introduction that this book contains the most comprehensive treatment of British foreign policy towards the Middle East 1914–19 that has yet been published, I readily admit that it is far from complete. The book's size may easily give rise to a different impression, but most of the material I gathered over the years, I have left out. Subjects I have decided not to deal with in this book include, for instance, British attempts to create an Arab Legion, to forge an alliance between Arabs, Jews and Armenians, the relations between Sharif Husayn and, respectively, the Imam Yahya, the Idrisi and Ibn Rashid, British declarations regarding the inviolability of the holy places, Franco-Italian rivalry in Palestine, the Lebanon delegation at the Paris peace conference, the conflict between Sir Percy Cox and Sir Stanley Maude about the administration of Mesopotamia, T.E. Lawrence's exploits in the desert, the formation of a Jewish regiment, British secret negotiations for a separate peace with the Ottoman Empire, the settlement of claims for compensation by British subjects, offers to put houses at the disposal of the advancing British troops in Mesopotamia, the Egyptian attitude towards the Arab revolt, the attempts by the Zionists to remove Ronald Storrs from his post as governor of Jerusalem, the Long–Bérenger agreement, the Mesopotamian authorities' refusal to allow Mesopotamian officers from Faysal's army to return to their home country, as well as the scheme to land British troops at Yenbo to prevent a Turkish advance on Mecca. I have not dealt with these subjects because they had hardly any impact, or no impact at all on the outcome of the issues that preoccupied British decision makers at the time as far as Middle East policy was concerned.

When I started writing this book back in the early 1980s, I took one crucial decision with respect to the way in which it had to be written. I had reached the conclusion that nothing so much hampered a sound understanding of British foreign policy towards the Middle East 1914–19 as the polemical attitude taken up by the great majority of the authors who published on the subject. Almost without exception, authors were out to prove a point and to prove other authors wrong (a tendency that seems to have diminished greatly in the more recent literature). I therefore decided that I, as the author, should not directly intervene in the main body of the historical chapters, but only present the historical material. From this it followed that I should not comment on what happens in these chapters, demonstrate that I know better or that the protagonists could have known better, enter into discussions with other authors on the correct interpretation of certain events, and also not speculate on how things must have been. It is only in the notes that I critically discuss the findings of other historians, remark on the empirical validity of observations made by ministers, officials and soldiers at the time, or speculate on what must have been the reason or reasons why someone was successful or failed. This does not mean that I for one moment believe that history speaks for itself. I have worked very hard to make it speak. My intervention has, however, been indirect, and based on the theoretical considerations I have developed in the previous section on what matters in decision making in a bureaucratic-political environment. These have guided me in my selection of the historical facts that have been included in this study as well as the manner in which I present the historical narrative.

PART I

THE ASQUITH GOVERNMENTS 1914–16

1 I SUPPOSE THE I.O. KNOW HOW THIS CAN BE DONE

Introduction

On the eve of the war with the Ottoman Empire, the Foreign Office was convinced that because it lacked the necessary expertise, it had to defer to the India Office and the Government of India when it came to exploiting existing Arab discontent with their Turkish masters. The India Office and the Foreign Office were agreed that it would be greatly advantageous to induce the Arabs to side with Great Britain, but the Government of India was very much against any policy initiative that might give the Muslim population of India the impression that Britain actively tried to set Muslims against Muslims. The Foreign Office, moreover, was very keen not to offend French susceptibilities with respect to Syria, which France considered her *domaine reservé*. Despite the Arabs' great potential to weaken the Ottoman Empire's war effort, Indian Muslim anxieties and French–Syrian ambitions dictated a very cautious response to Arab nationalist overtures to gain Britain's support for their schemes to revolt against Turkey.

The British authorities in Cairo had far fewer scruples about exploiting Arab nationalist sentiment. The appointment of Lord Kitchener, the British agent and consul-general in Egypt, as secretary of state for war at the beginning of August 1914, provided an excellent opportunity to push through their views. Together with Foreign Secretary Sir Edward Grey, Kitchener drew up a telegram informing Cairo that the Arab movement should be encouraged in every way possible. Kitchener also drafted a message, approved by Grey, to Sharif Abdullah, the second son of the Emir of Mecca, guaranteeing support for the Arabs if they assisted Britain in the war against Turkey. These initiatives bore no fruit, however, and when the India Office and the Government of India found out about them, they strongly protested, stressing their deleterious effects on Indian Muslim feeling and relations with France. The officials at the Foreign Office shared these misgivings. At the beginning of January 1915, the policy of restraint with respect to the Arab Middle East was again in the ascendant.

Arab Potential and Indian Muslim Susceptibilities

Grey and the Foreign Office officials involved in formulating British policy towards the Middle East in the late summer of 1914 were agreed on one thing at least. The discontent with the rule by the Committee of Union and Progress (CUP) that existed under the Arab-speaking part of the population of the Ottoman Empire was a major factor in the possible war with that state. On the one hand, a rapprochement between the Arabs and their Turkish overlords might encourage the latter 'to engage in the war we wish to avoid',[1] while on the other hand, if this reconciliation did not take place and Turkey sided with Germany nevertheless, then 'probably one of the most effective weapons would be support and organisation of an Arab movement either openly or indirectly'.[2] They were at the same time convinced that they did not have the expertise and contacts to exploit Arab discontent. In their opinion, the India Office, which, through the Government of India, was responsible for relations with the semi-autonomous Arab rulers along the coast of the Persian Gulf and in the neighbourhood of Aden, was far better placed to do this. Sir Edward observed that 'directly Turkey joins Germany we should at once give every support and encouragement to the Arabs to possess themselves of Arabia and the holy places. I suppose the I.O. know how this can be done from Aden and elsewhere and by what means.'[3] George Clerk, head of the War Department in the Foreign Office, noted that in case of war 'we should leave the policy and strategy mainly to the Government of India'.[4]

This understanding of its own limitations made the Foreign Office conform to the priorities that according to the India Office and the Government of India obtained in a war against the Ottoman Empire.

These were very clear to Secretary of State for India Lord Crewe and his officials. They fully appreciated the importance of the Arabs having a sympathetic attitude, as 'with Arab support we should be absolutely safe in Egypt against any Turkish action',[5] but it was far more important to avoid all actions that might try the loyalty of the Muslim population of India. For the sake of peace and tranquility in India, nothing should be done that could be interpreted by Indian Muslims as an attempt by Britain to set Muslims against one another.[6] It was this maxim that guided the thinking of the India Office and the Government of India in their dealings with the Middle East. In this connection, Lord Hardinge, viceroy of India, had telegraphed that he intended to announce, simultaneously with the declaration of war, that 'no attack would be made by British forces or those of Allies on the holy places [...] provided that no hindrance is placed on arrival of pilgrims from India'. As Hardinge explained to Crewe, 'the assurance of freedom of the holy places from molestation is a very important factor in the views of Indian Mohammadans and may make all the difference in their attitude in the event of a war with Turkey'.[7] The Foreign Office and the India Office approved the proposal without delay.

In a further telegram, the viceroy expressed his satisfaction with this decision. However, he remained silent on a proposal advanced by the India Office and the Foreign Office that aimed to lure the Arabs away from the Turks.[8] In his covering letter with Hardinge's first telegram, Sir Arthur Hirtzel, head of the Political Department in the India Office, had suggested to Clerk that:

> An assurance as the viceroy wishes to give would not prevent us – in the event of war with Turkey – giving an assurance to the Arabs that if they rise and eject the Turks from the holy places we will after the war maintain them as custodians of the holy places – or something of this kind?

This suggestion was in line with the role the Foreign Office believed the Arabs might play. Sir Arthur Nicolson, permanent under-secretary at the Foreign Office, accordingly observed on Hirtzel's suggestion that 'if Turkey does go with our enemies I do not think we should delay encouraging the Arabs to rise'.[9] When Hardinge finally made clear that he opposed this assurance, because 'an unfavourable impression might be caused among Mohamedan communities if we were to identify ourselves with open encouragement of Arabs to this end',[10] the Foreign Office and the India Office dropped their proposal.

The Creation of Force 'D' and the Occupation of Basra

In June 1914, the British government had taken a majority share in the Anglo–Persian Oil Company (APOC). After the outbreak of the war, Vice-Admiral Sir Edmond Slade, one of the two government representatives on the board of APOC, started to press for the dispatch of an expeditionary force to Fao (at the mouth of the Shatt al-'Arab), to defend the oil refinery on Abadan Island against a possible Turkish attack.[11]

The viceroy was against this project. His first line of argument was that a shortage of troops prevented India from dispatching the necessary force,[12] unless the sixth (Poona) division, which was on the point of leaving for France, should go to Fao instead. At an interdepartmental meeting of the Foreign Office, the India Office and the Admiralty on 26 September 1914, it became clear that the War Office could agree to Hardinge's proposal. It also appeared that the Foreign Office and the India Office were not so much in favour of the scheme in order to protect the oil installations as 'to show Bin Saud and the Arabs that we were ready to meet any Turkish movement against us'.[13] The Cabinet subsequently instructed the viceroy to take the necessary measures so that the first contingent was ready to leave for the Persian Gulf on 10 October. In reaction, Hardinge objected to the sending of any troops at all. The dispatch of an expeditionary force might be interpreted by Indian Muslims as an act of aggression against the Ottoman Empire. A policy of wait and see might lead to the loss of the oil works, but the viceroy doubted 'their value being so great as to outweigh the consequences of an apparent attack by us on Turkey'.[14] This time, Hardinge's opposition was not sufficient reason for the India Office and Foreign Office to drop the plan. Crewe wrote to Hardinge that the primary motive for sending an expeditionary force was 'the moral effect on the Arab Chiefs'. The viceroy should moreover keep things in perspective, 'Turkey's conduct about the Goeben has been so monstrous that she deserves no sort of consideration for her beaux yeux'. There remained to Hardinge little else than to wash his hands of the whole affair. On 15 October, he informed Crewe that the expeditionary force had started, but that he personally had 'never been much in favour of this expedition to the Persian Gulf unless we were in a state of war with Turkey [...] The danger, in my opinion, is that we may provoke war.'15

Fifteen days later, the Entente powers severed diplomatic relations with the Ottoman Empire. On 31 October, Force 'D', as the expeditionary force had been named, was instructed to proceed to the Shatt al-'Arab at once, and on 6 November, one day after Britain's declaration of war against Turkey, Fao was occupied. After it had become clear that the Turks were unable to put up any resistance, the troops advanced upon Basra, which was captured on 22 November 1914.

Lord Kitchener Intervenes

Herbert Henry Asquith had combined the office of prime minister with that of secretary of state for war since March 1914, but once the war had broken out it was obvious that this arrangement could not continue. On 5 August, Asquith decided, 'believing that none of his colleagues were suitable for the post [...] on the "hazardous experiment" of appointing Kitchener as Secretary of State. The latter reluctantly accepted.'16 Field-Marshal the Earl Kitchener of Khartoum had been British agent and consul-general in Egypt since 1911. His appointment put him in an excellent position, in particular considering his daily conferences with Asquith and Grey on the progress of the war, to influence British policy towards the Middle East, the more so as the Foreign Office soon started to send Kitchener files on Middle East matters for his inspection and advice.

One of the first files forwarded to Kitchener contained a note on a conversation by Captain R.E.M. Russell with Aziz Ali al-Masri. The latter reported that he had been deputed:

> By a Central Committee at Baghdad to ascertain the attitude of the British government towards their propaganda for forming a united Arabian state, independent of Turkey, and every other power except England, whose tutelage and control of foreign affairs they invite.17

Al-Masri's claim that he was a representative of a nationalist Arab movement came as no surprise to the Foreign Office and Kitchener. On 9 February 1914, al-Masri, a major in the Turkish army, had been arrested by order of Enver Pasha, the Turkish minister of war. Al-Masri's brother-in-law, the governor of Cairo, had subsequently approached Kitchener to intervene on al-Masri's behalf. The British agent had requested Sir Louis Mallet, the British ambassador at Constantinople, to make representations. After conversations with the minister of the interior and the Grand Vizier, Mallet had informed the Foreign Office and Kitchener that the position of Aziz Ali was rather precarious, since:

> There is no doubt that Aziz Ali Bey has been one of the leading spirits in a group of young Arabs, officers, and others, who are dissatisfied with the present Turkish government. It is difficult to gauge the importance of this group, but it has come to my knowledge that some at least of them are identified with more or less definite schemes for organising a movement which would aim at releasing the whole region from Mosul to the Persian Gulf from Turkish domination.[18]

Aziz Ali had been condemned to death in the middle of March. When this sentence had become known, it had provoked great agitation in Egypt as well as an international press campaign for his release. After a couple of weeks, al-Masri had been pardoned, and had left for Egypt on 22 April.[19]

The interview with Russell had been Aziz Ali's second contact with the British authorities in Cairo within a month. He had earlier informed Captain Gilbert F. Clayton, the Sudan agent and director of intelligence of the Egyptian army, that the Turks had been intriguing against British rule in Egypt and the Sudan for a considerable time. Al-Masri had suggested as a countermeasure, so Cairo had wired, that 'we should lend him our help to lead the Arab tribes of Irak and Syria against the Turks'.

The difference in reaction by the officials of the Foreign Office to this telegram (which was neither forwarded to Kitchener nor submitted to Grey) and Kitchener to the note on Russell's conversation was striking. While the Foreign Office simply instructed Milne Cheetham, who substituted for Kitchener, to 'impress strongly on El Mazri the need for him to keep quiet and to leave the Arabs alone',[20] Kitchener was sympathetic to Aziz Ali's schemes. According to him 'all depends on how Turkey acts [...] if Turkey breaks out, action in Arabia under our auspices would naturally follow'.[21]

The terse reply by the officials of the Foreign Office was not so much induced by concerns for Indian Muslim susceptibilities, as by worries that British encouragement of Arab nationalist projects might upset relations with France. Arab nationalist schemes that involved Syria clashed with the traditional French claims on that country. Foreign Office officials were anxious to avoid a deterioration in British and French relations like the one that had occurred at the close of 1912 as a consequence of French suspicions of British intrigues in Syria. At the time, the collapse of the CUP had seemed imminent as a result of the loss of Tripoli and the Cyrenaica to Italy after the Tripoli war, as well as the rapid defeats of the Ottoman army in the first weeks of the first Balkan war. The situation in Syria had become more and more unsettled. The impression had gained ground that the CUP had lost their willingness to maintain law and order, and stories about possible intervention had been rife. The majority of Syrians, both Muslim and Christian, had apparently been in favour of a British intervention, as opposed to a French one, and one of the schemes that had been widely discussed called for the annexation of Syria by British-controlled Egypt. These developments had resulted in a vehement campaign in the French press, in particular directed against Kitchener and his staff at Cairo. They were accused of actively encouraging the pro-British sentiments of the Syrian population. Although the Foreign Office had summarily dismissed the charges in the French papers as inventions, Grey and his officials had at the same time considered it desirable to spare French susceptibilities with respect to Syria. When, on 5 December 1912, French ambassador Paul Cambon had had an interview with Grey, the latter had taken the opportunity to inform him that Britain had no designs on Syria. The next day, Cambon had asked Sir Edward whether Raymond Poincaré, the French prime minister and foreign minister, could make this assurance public. After he had consulted Asquith, and pointed out to Cambon that it concerned British political aspirations only, Grey had assented. Poincaré had subsequently delivered a speech to the French Senate on 21 December, in which he had voiced the government's determination to uphold French interests in Syria, and in this connection he had quoted Grey's assurance.[22]

Although Kitchener had denied all charges, this episode had nevertheless earned the Cairo authorities the reputation of favouring Arab nationalist schemes. This was even to the extent that G.H. Fitzmaurice, chief dragoman of the British embassy at Constantinople, observed in a memorandum that to encourage the Arab nationalist movement in case of war, would be 'exceedingly embarrassing' to the Turks, but that such a project was dependent on 'harmonising the French and Cairo points of view'.[23]

On 12 October, the Foreign Office received telegrams from the British consuls at Beirut, Damascus and Jerusalem, giving their assessment of how the indigenous population would react in the case of a war between the Entente and the Ottoman Empire. Syrians and Palestinians were not averse to a British occupation, but a French intervention would meet with resistance. As A.H. Cumberbatch, the British consul-general at Beirut, observed, the Muslims of Syria were 'at heart well disposed towards Great Britain, though they may deplore her support of France, of whose intentions regarding Syria they are as apprehensive as ever'.[24] In view of Fitzmaurice's memorandum and these telegrams, Lancelot Oliphant, clerk in the Foreign Office, suggested that 'if Syria is to be taken in hand, French cooperation should be sought without delay, in order to be forewarned and prepared for joint action'.[25]

Sir Edward did not fall in with Oliphant's suggestion. Precisely at this time, Kitchener's influence made itself felt. Cheetham twice inquired about a declaration, to be communicated to suitable Arabs, on Great Britain's attitude towards the Arabs in a war against the Ottoman Empire. Both times a telegram was personally drafted by Kitchener and Grey, without the latter consulting his department. Their first telegram, to be sure, did not clash all that much with the policy of restraint pursued by the Foreign Office – it contained no more than a vaguely worded declaration of British–Arab friendship – but this certainly did not apply to the second one, which seemed to leave it at Cairo's discretion to do everything necessary to encourage the Arab nationalists to revolt against Turkey, without making any reservations regarding French claims on Syria.

On 17 October, Cheetham wired that from conversations with two Muslim Syrians 'of good standing', it had become clear that 'it might be desirable to give some indication to the ruling chiefs of Arabia [...] of attitude of the British government in case of attack by Turkey'. Kitchener drafted a reply, which was sent in Grey's name the following day. Cheetham could inform the two Syrians that:

> Great Britain had no quarrel with the Arabs, and even if the Turkish government forced by Germany, commits acts of aggression against us which necessitate acts of war, England will not consider that the Arabs are involved in this war, unless they by overt acts take part in assisting German-Turkish forces which we have the utmost confidence they will not do even under coercion.[26]

After the outbreak of war, Cheetham again approached the Foreign Office on the subject. Kitchener's earlier declaration was too vague to reassure the Arabs, but an:

> Excellent effect would be produced by a definite statement on the part of British government that there was no intention to undertake any military or naval operations in Arabia, except for protection of Arab interests against Turkish or other aggression or in support of attempt by Arabs to free themselves from Turkish rule.

Grey and Kitchener had not the slightest difficulty with a declaration of this kind. They replied the next day that 'you can give the assurance you suggest in name of British government'.[27] This was not all, however. On 26 October, Clayton had conducted another interview with Aziz Ali, in the course of which the latter had observed that:

> The only way in which the Pan-Arabian programme could be carried out successfully and the country freed from Turkish domination was an organised revolution backed by a comparatively small but well-equipped force. The nucleus of this force could be obtained from the Mesopotamian Army, in which the seeds of disloyalty had been sown for some time past.[28]

Cheetham therefore also wished to know whether there was 'any further action now desirable here in connection with Arab movement as a whole?' He added that al-Masri planned 'to start a revolution in Mesopotamia backed by a small but well-equipped force'. Kitchener and Grey again were very definite in their reply:

> The Arab movement should be encouraged in every way possible. Aziz Bey might be sent to organise with a sum of £2,000, or thereabouts, if you think it would be useful. He can report results to the [Cairo] agency, and then further support might be given to any movement he was able to initiate among the Arabs.

This telegram, which completely disregarded Indian Muslim suscep-tibilities and French Syrian pretensions, clearly demonstrated Kichener's personal influence on Grey. When Clerk had minuted on Cheetham's telegram that the Foreign Office should await the views of the Admiralty and the India Office, Sir Edward had noted that 'there should be no delay', and together with Kitchener had proceeded to draw up the telegram.[29]

On 15 November, the India Office asked the viceroy for his opinion on Cheetham's telegram. Not surprisingly, Hardinge objected to the proposed assurance, because it went 'too far and might prove embarrassing, since we are already taking military action in Mesopotamia'.[30] The viceroy remained silent on the scheme to send Aziz Ali to Mesopotamia. A further telegram on this subject was sent to Hardinge on 19 November, but again the viceroy failed to reply.[31] Eight days later, Sir John Maxwell, the general officer commanding-in-chief, Egypt, telegraphed to Kitchener the proposal to let Aziz Ali go to Basra, in particular because 'he and his party seem anxious as regards our ultimate intentions as to Bagdad and Basra'.[32] Kitchener informed Crewe of this proposal, and the latter – after he had expressed the hope that 'Maxwell will not let him go until we have concurrence: he might be rather a bore to our people on the spot'[33] – dispatched yet another telegram to the viceroy to elicit a reply:

> El Mazri is now ready to start, but we are asking Cheetham to keep him back until I receive your views as to how his mission will fit in with situation as it now exists. Please telegraph as soon as possible. Cheetham says El Mazri and his party show anxiety as to our ultimate intentions as to Basra and Bagdad.[34]

The project to send al-Masri to Basra was finally abandoned at the beginning of December. The India Office first received a copy of Clayton's report of his interview with Aziz Ali on 26 October. It prompted Hirtzel to observe that the whole scheme 'was entirely irreconcilable with our military operations and was intended by El Masri to be so. It is to be hoped that we shall hear no more of it.'[35] A few days later, it also received a telegram from the viceroy, in which he reported a conversation between Sir Percy Cox, the chief political officer with Force 'D', and Nuri as-Sa'id. The latter was an officer in the Ottoman army, who had been taken prisoner at Basra, and according to al-Masri was involved in the Arab nationalist movement. Hardinge concluded from Sir Percy's account that Arab nationalism counted for little, 'both owing to quality of leaders and because tribes and Sheikhs concerned are too backward to pay attention to "Young Arab" propaganda'. The India Office observed in a covering letter that 'had Captain Clayton's letter of 30th October [...] been available at an earlier stage', Lord Crewe 'would have deprecated any action on El Masri scheme'. Foreign Office officials agreed. Oliphant minuted that as the India Office did 'not approve of the employment of el Masri [...] it was better to pursue the matter no further'. Little more than a month after a Foreign Office telegram had informed the Agency that it should support Aziz Ali in his efforts to organise an Arab movement, another was sent in which the Foreign Office stated that 'you should therefore refrain for the present from giving any definite encouragement to Aziz Ali'. This reversal of policy drew no comment from either Grey or Kitchener.[36]

Overture to Sharif Husayn, the Emir of Mecca

According to Mallet, one of the reasons why he found himself in a difficult position to intervene on al-Masri's behalf was that the 'visit of Shereef of Mecca's son to Cairo [was] causing suspicion of our good faith in regard to Arab movement'.[37] Mallet referred to Abdullah, the second son of Sharif Husayn, the Emir of Mecca,[38] who had visited Cairo at the beginning of February, on his way to Constantinople to discuss the problems that had recently arisen between his father and the Turkish government. He called on Kitchener on 5 February 1914, and informed the latter that:

> Affairs in the Hedjaz were not going on as well as could be wished owing to the recent appointment of a new Turkish Vali who combined civil and military functions and who is not in sympathy with the people and does not act harmoniously with his father in the conduct of the internal affairs of the holy places as well as for the comfort and security of the Moslem pilgrims from all parts of the world for which his father as Sherif has been so long responsible.

In this connection Abdullah was anxious to know what the attitude of Great Britain would be:

> In case this friction became acute and an attempt was made by the Turkish government to dismiss his father [...] He stated very decidedly that, if the

Turkish government dismissed his father, the Arab tribes of the Hedjaz would fight for the Sherif and a state of war against Turkish troops would ensue. He hoped in such circumstances that the British government would not allow reinforcements to be sent by sea for the purpose of preventing the Arabs from exercising the rights which they have enjoyed from time immemorial in their own country around the holy places.

Kitchener reported in conclusion that Abdullah had asked 'whether you would send his father some message', but that he had replied that he 'thought it would be improbable that you would do so'.[39]

Mallet instructed his staff to draw up a memorandum on Sharif Husayn, which was forwarded to the Foreign Office on 18 March 1914. It explained that:

> The position of the Grand Sherif of Mecca differs considerably from that of other Arab potentates in as much as he is always invested with his authority by the Sultan's firman, and is in close touch with the capital, where several members of his family ordinarily reside. Any given Grand Sherif might quite conceivably put himself at the head of an Arab movement, and, if he wished to do so, his alleged descent from the Prophet, and membership of the Koreish tribe would doubtless be a valuable asset; but in order to gain any widespread influence he would have to start almost from the beginning.

The memorandum continued with a sketch of Husayn's career since being appointed Emir of Mecca in 1908. He had been rather successful in consolidating his own power, not only in relation to the other Arab rulers on the peninsula – as a result of military actions undertaken in the name of the Turkish government – but also *vis-à-vis* Constantinople, in consequence of a succession of valis 'of little account'. Relations with the CUP were strained, and the Young Turks 'may fear that his aggrandisement has gone too far'. Under these circumstances it was easy to see 'how anxiously Hussein Pasha must have viewed the advent of a young and possibly energetic vali', and this anxiety 'doubtless explains him sending Abdullah Bey to Lord Kitchener'.[40]

The arrival of the new vali Vehib Bey had been accompanied by disturbances. S. Abdurrahman, the acting consul at Jedda, had reported on 11 March that:

> It is an open secret that the cause of all this disturbance is the Grand Shereef himself. He was, up to the arrival of the new Vali, the sole monarch of the Hedjaz and his word was law in this country. The Grand Shereef is naturally opposed to any reform and wants that everything should run in ancient rut. All departments in Mecca and Jeddah were under the authoritative guidance of the Shereef and the Turkish government was only in name.
>
> The Turkish government, it appears, is in a different mood now [...] The new Vali has confiscated all authority from the Grand Shereef and wishes to do away with this dual government.
>
> Naturally the Grand Shereef, seeing this change of policy on the part of the Turkish government and knowing this will be a death-blow to his interests, has instigated the Bedouins, whose object is one with the Shereef as far as the construction of the railway is concerned.[41]

Abdurrahman's claim that Husayn was the instigator of the unrest in the Hijaz, and that the Bedouin were his natural allies, was confirmed by a report from G.P. Devey, the British consul at Damascus. According to the latter, 'the Sherif is inciting the Arabs around about Mecca to insurrection on the pretext of protesting that they will allow no railway to be made to Mecca because it will lessen their camel transport profits'.[42] Kitchener agreed. The Bedouin objected to 'the proposal to push forward railway communications [because it] would cause great pecuniary loss to the Arabs who live on their camel hire'.[43]

The conflict between Husayn and the vali did not last long. On 3 April, Devey added a postscript that 'a completed reconciliation has been effected between the Vali and the Grand Sherif and Wahab Bey will remain at Mecca. The Sherif is to be allowed a free hand.'[44] According to Abdurrahman, some in the Hijaz were 'still sceptic and doubtful about the correctness of this news and believe that the government, on account of its unpreparedness, have displayed this time-serving policy, and in the near future they are sure of the dismissal of the present Grand Shereef, who is opposed to the interests of the Turkish government in this country'.[45] Indeed, while Abdullah was on his way back to Mecca, he had 'somewhat unexpectedly' turned up again in Cairo on 18 April. He explained to Ronald Storrs, the oriental secretary of the Agency, that 'on his first interview with the Grand Vizier he learnt that the extension of the railway was regarded by the Porte as essential', and that the Turkish government had not been prepared to reconsider their decision. In view of this development, Abdullah had been instructed by his father to approach the Agency 'with a view to obtaining with the British government an agreement similar to that existing between the Amir of Afghanistan and the Government of India, in order to maintain the status quo in the Arabian Peninsula and to do away with the danger of wanton Turkish aggression'. The next day, however, after he had consulted Kitchener, Storrs told Abdullah that he 'could not expect any encouragement from the British government [...] that we had in principle not the smallest wish to interfere in the government or the administration of the holy cities, which only concerned us in so far as they affected the safety and comfort of British pilgrims'.[46]

Storrs later related in his memoirs that he, at the end of summer 1914:

> Could not forget how the Sharif Abdallah had unlocked his heart during his visit to Cairo that same spring. I therefore submitted a short note, suggesting that by timely consultation with Mecca we might secure not only the neutrality but the alliance of Arabia in the event of Ottoman aggression. But [...] for one reason and another days passed into weeks without my proposal being even discussed.

Luckily for him, Storrs found a kindred spirit in Clayton, who 'actively condoned my proposed irregularity of urging it upon Lord Kitchener in a private letter, which I accordingly dispatched'.[47] Storrs's letter arrived in London about the same time as an *Appreciation of Situation in Arabia* drawn up by Clayton's staff. In this memorandum it was argued that:

> For some years past the Turkish government in Arabia has had great difficulty in keeping the country quiet, and Turkish authority has been steadily on the decline.
>
> There seems little doubt that there has been a distinct tendency towards combination on the part of the more powerful chiefs such as: Ibn Sa'ud of Nejd, the Idrisi of Asir, the Sherif of Mecca and possibly also Ibn Rashid, with a view to throwing off the Turkish domination and working towards an Arabia for the Arabs.

This propitious development considering a possible war against Turkey had however come to a halt, because:

> Immediately prior to and since the outbreak of war in Europe, the Turkish government had made great efforts to come to an arrangement

with the principal chiefs in Arabia in order to secure, if not their active assistance, at least their friendly neutrality, and it appears probable that considerable success is attending their efforts. In any case, it seems almost certain that the Sherif of Mecca has now definitely thrown in his lot with Turkey.

This appreciation drew no comments from Foreign Office officials, and was not submitted to Grey. The file was, however, forwarded to Kitchener, and the latter reacted immediately. He got in touch with Grey, who afterwards minuted that 'this paper is very important: it should have been sent to me as well as to Lord Kitchener. I have only seen it now because Lord Kitchener has sent it me.'[48] That same day, 24 September, a telegram was sent to Cairo, which was neither drafted by a Foreign Office official, nor submitted to the India Office:

> Following from Lord Kitchener.
> Intelligence report 6th September statement regarding attitude of Sherif of Mecca. Tell Storrs to send secret and carefully chosen messenger from me to Sherif Abdullah to ascertain whether 'should present armed German influence at Constantinople coerce khalif against his will and Sublime Porte to acts of aggression and war against Great Britain, he and his father and Arabs of Hedjaz would be with us or against us'.[49]

On 30 October, the messenger returned from Mecca with a letter from Abdullah. A summary was telegraphed to Grey the next day:

> Communication is guarded, but friendly and favourable. Desires 'closer union' with Great Britain, but expects and 'is awaiting written promise that Great Britain will abstain from internal intervention in Arabia and guarantee Emir against foreign and Ottoman aggression'.
> The Shereef himself, in a secret conversation with the messenger, expressed himself more freely and openly, saying 'Stretch out to us a helping hand and we will never aid these oppressors'.
> Reply is being prepared subject to your approval disclaiming all intention of internal intervention and guaranteeing, against external aggression only, independence of Shereefate.

Messenger must leave Monday morning or week will be lost. Please instruct me at once.

Less than five hours after the telegram had been received in London, a reply was sent to Cairo, drafted by Kitchener, and approved by Grey:

Following from Lord Kitchener.
Lord Kitchener's salaam to the Shereef Abdalla. Germany has bought the Turkish government with gold notwithstanding that England, France and Russia guaranteed the integrity of the Ottoman Empire if Turkey remained neutral in this war [...] If the Arab Nation assist England in this war that has been forced upon us by Turkey, England will guarantee that no internal intervention takes place in Arabia and will give the Arabs every assistance against external foreign aggression.
It may be that an Arab of the true race will assume the caliphate at Mecca or Medina and so good may come by the help of God out of all the evil which is now occurring.[50]

By sending this telegram, Kitchener and Grey ignored the advice of Andrew Ryan, acting first dragoman at the Constantinople embassy, which had been submitted to both of them. According to Ryan:

Taking the future into consideration [...] it would be unwise to associate ourselves with any movement in the Red Sea provinces (i.e. the Hedjaz and Yemen). To destroy the Sultan's real though incomplete authority in the Hedjaz would be a challenge to the Moslem world, if done openly. Even if done secretly, it would create scandals in that world and raise issues, which we should not raise unless we are prepared, and confidently prepared, with a concrete and positive programme for their solution [...] So far as one can see at present, it would be better from our point of view that the Sultan of Turkey, even a reduced Turkey, should continue to be in theory at least sovereign of the holy cities.

Clerk had minuted that it would be rather difficult to leave the Hijaz and Yemen completely out of the British sphere of action, if only because 'the Turks are stirring up the Arabs in the Hedjaz against Eygpt', but he had agreed that a separation of the caliphate from the sultanate 'must be brought about, if at all, by the Moslems themselves without any outside interference'.[51]

Not unexpectedly, the India Office had fully subscribed to a policy of non-intervention:

> The separation of the khalifate from the sultanate raises great political questions, and Lord Crewe would regard the creation of a powerful politico-religious entity in Arabia with serious misgivings. He therefore agrees that the matter must be left to the Moslems themselves, but for his own part, he would not encourage it even indirectly.[52]

This consensus had, however, not prevented Grey and Kitchener from sending their telegram of 31 October.

On 11 November 1914, Kitchener wrote a letter to Sir Edward, in which he brought the various strands of his proposed Middle East policy together:

> Supposing that the Arabs took up arms against the Turks, I think it would be our policy to recognise a new khalif at Mecca or Medina of the proper race, and guarantee the holy places from foreign aggression as well as from all internal interference. If this were done, there appears to me to be a possibility for allowing Syria to be organised as an Arab state under the khalif, but also under European consular control and European guidance as regards government.
>
> France would be greatly weakened by having Syria which is not a remunerative possession and which from its geographical position must lead France astray from her real objective: Tunis, Algeria, Morocco. I believe it is more sentiment than anything else that induces France to keep up her influence in Syria and if we frankly said, we do not want Syria, they would probably say the same and allow the formation of an Arab state that would enable the new khalifate to have sufficient revenue to exist on.

But Kitchener's exposition was not well received either in the Foreign Office or the India Office. The objections were predictable. Anglo–French relations should not be burdened with the question of Syria, and Great Britain should have nothing to do with a policy that would set Muslim against Muslim. Grey minuted that 'we cannot act as regards Syria',[53] while Crewe noted that 'surely it would not be possible to negotiate with the Arabs behind the back of the French?' It was left to Hardinge to deliver the final blow to all ideas of a forward policy in the Middle East (Sir Edward: 'this view of the viceroy is conclusive against any action at present'):

Kitchener's suggestion is based on a hypothesis which has not materialised so far. The Arabs have not taken up arms against the Turks but even cooperated with them at Sheikh Syed and on Shatt-el-Arab. It is possible that their attitude may change in the future, but there is nothing that could make us more unpopular with them and the Mohammedan world generally than an attempt on our part to meddle with the pretence of a new khalif.

I share the views of the Foreign Office as to the likelihood of serious difficulty with France over the proposed organisation of Syria as an Arab state under the Kalif. French interests in Syria are not purely sentimental. Much French capital has been sunk in railways and other enterprises in Syria. France is regarded as the natural protector of all classes of native Christians, and her *clientèle* and influence are spreading everywhere. In an Arabic Syrian state, the reactionary Turk would simply be replaced by the unenterprising Arab.

For the above reason, I would strongly deprecate any announcement to the Arabs for the present and would recommend that we should await developments before deciding upon any definite policy for the future khalifate and Arabia.[54]

The result was that Crewe could complacently write to the viceroy on 4 December:

It does not look at present as though anything like a real Arab rising against Turkey is imminent. I have always thought that there are two sides to any such outburst, one of them rather inconvenient. So I shall not lament if they do not now do anything very active, so long as they are friendly and unsuspicious. For one thing, I quite share the doubt which you expressed about the notion of a new caliphate including Syria. Shades of Coeur de Lion and Saint Louis![55]

Crewe's satisfaction with the course events had taken seemed fully justified, but only a week later India Office officials were startled by the receipt of a letter from the Foreign Office, enclosing a copy of a telegram by Cheetham, in which the latter reported on the results of the messenger's second visit to Mecca in consequence of Grey's and Kitchener's telegram of 31 October, as well as copies of the telegrams exchanged in connection with Kitchener's first message to Abdullah.

This was the first time that the India Office was informed of Kitchener's contacts with Abdullah. Hirtzel considered it 'a very dangerous correspondence', especially in view of 'the hint to the Arabs to assume the caliphate at Mecca and Medina [that] does the very thing this Office has understood H.M.G. would not do'. However, since it appeared from Cheetham's telegram that Husayn had indicated that 'his position in the world of Islam and present political situation in the Hedjaz made it impossible for him to break with Turks immediately', and after having established that it concerned 'a private communication of Lord Kitchener's', and not 'a guarantee for which the Indian Government is responsible', the India Office was prepared to regard the Foreign Office's failure to keep it informed with equanimity.[56]

A further indication that, with respect to British Middle East policy, the priorities of the India Office and the Government of India once again prevailed, was the way in which the Foreign Office handled a dispatch from Cheetham, which arrived on 28 December. It contained an account of yet another conversation with al-Masri, this time conducted with Captain Philip Graves. According to the latter, Aziz Ali had offered to do all in his power to assist Great Britain 'on the condition [...] that we did not intend to annex Mesopotamia, but intended to make some kind of buffer state British occupied for many years to come'. At first Grey minuted 'send to the I.O. that we should reply favourably to this', but Oliphant hesitated 'to act on Sir E. Grey's minute without calling attention to the India Office views expressed in (81700) [The India Office depreciation of 'any action on El Masri scheme'; see previous section 'Lord Kitchener Intervenes'] which may have escaped Sir E. Grey's memory'. Nicolson subsequently concluded that 'we had perhaps better leave it alone', and Grey concurred: 'I withdraw send it to the I.O. without comment'.[57]

At the beginning of 1915, everything seemed to indicate that the proponents of a policy of restraint with respect to the Middle East were again in the ascendancy. Barely eight months later, the Foreign Office nevertheless authorised Sir Henry McMahon,[58] the British high commissioner in Egypt, to enter into negotiations with the Emir of Mecca on the conditions upon which the Arabs were prepared to revolt against Ottoman rule. But this time this change of policy was not the result of Kitchener's personal interventions with Grey, and the India Office was unable to reverse it.

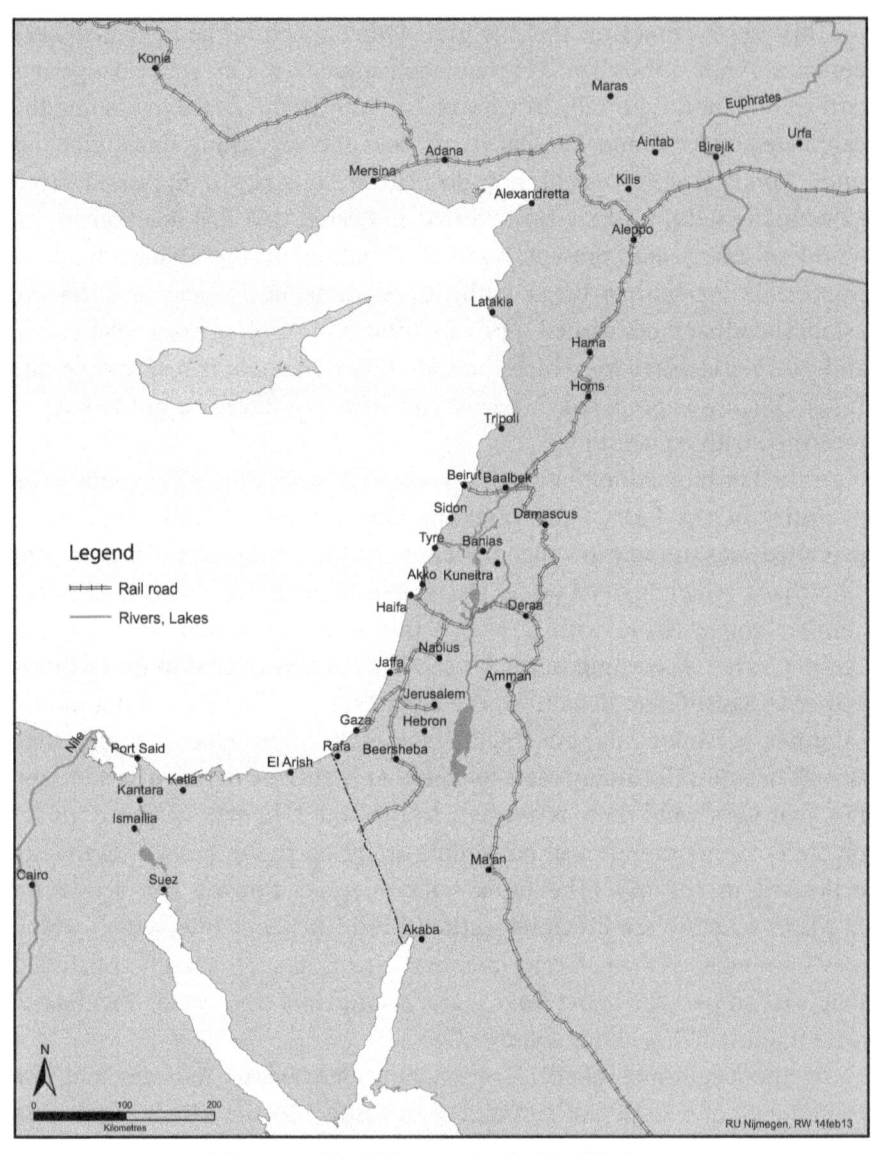

Map 2.1 The Western Arab Middle East
(Source: Wavell, *The Palestine Campaign*)

2 KEEPING BETTER EDUCATED MOSLEMS BUSY

Introduction

The British policy of restraint with respect to the Middle East was a source of constant concern for the authorities in Cairo and Khartoum. Their anxiety was strengthened by the fact that the Germans and Turks seemed to be very much alive to the vital importance for the progress of the war of definitely estranging the Arabs from the British. It appeared to them that the central powers would not hesitate to use whatever means at their disposal to bring this about, and to their minds the adoption of an active, pro-Arab policy constituted the only adequate answer to these 'Turco–German machinations'. But such a policy could only be initiated if they were able to overcome the existing obstacles of French Syrian pretensions and Indian worries about Muslim susceptibilities. During the first eight months of 1915, they made several attempts to do so. These were singularly unsuccessful as far as French aspirations were concerned. Sir Edward Grey and his officials were not prepared to jeopardise relations with France to win the support of the Arabs. They did, however, meet with success regarding the objections of the India Office and the Government of India to actively exploiting Arab discontent with Ottoman rule. This had the result that the Foreign Office was prepared to respond favourably to the Emir of Mecca's overtures at the end of August 1915, India Office protests notwithstanding.

The Alexandretta Project and the Syrian Question

On 1 January 1915, the Chancellor of the Exchequer, David Lloyd George circulated a memorandum to his colleagues in the Cabinet containing 'some suggestions as to the military position'. One of these was that Great Britain would be well-advised not to interfere with Turkish preparations for an invasion of Egypt, but the moment the Turks began their attack on the Suez Canal, to land 'a force of 100,000 [...] in Syria to cut them off'. In this manner, 'a force of 80,000 Turks would be wiped out and the whole of Syria would fall into our hands'. Lloyd George concluded by observing that 'unless we are prepared for some project of this character, I frankly despair of our achieving any success in this war' (Map 2.1).[1]

The British authorities in Cairo were convinced that a landing in Syria was of vital importance to the defence of Egypt. On 7 January, Milne Cheetham dispatched a telegram to London containing a summary of a note written by Gilbert Clayton. He favoured Alexandretta as a possible landing place. He also once again pointed out the drawbacks of a policy of acquiescence in French pretensions with regard to Syria considering the anti-French attitude of the majority of the Syrian population. Precisely as the British consuls in Syria and Palestine had done in October 1914 (see Chapter 1, section 'Lord Kitchener Intervenes'), Clayton stated that 'a large proportion of the population of Syria and Palestine would welcome the advent of British force, and might even afford active assistance provided they were assured that the occupation of their country would be permanent', but that there was 'evidence that similar feelings are not entertained with regard to the advent of the French or Russians, except among the Maronites of the Lebanon, who are pro-French'. Only a British force would reap the full benefits of a landing at Alexandretta but, admittedly, such a scheme could not be executed before 'some definite understanding with our allies' on Syria had been reached.

The reactions by the officials of the Foreign Office sounded rather familiar. They did not doubt that Clayton's observations were correct but, in view of the paramount importance of cordial relations with France, they could make precious little use of them. Lancelot Oliphant minuted that 'all this is here and, I think, generally recognised (including the unpopularity of the French). To act, however, independently of our allies is out of the question', and Sir Arthur Nicolson agreed.[2] During a meeting of the War Council on 8 January, it appeared that Sir Edward Grey also attached more weight to friendly relations with France than to the possible difficulties that might ensue from British acquiescence in French pretensions. As far as a landing at Alexandretta was concerned, 'it was important not to lose sight of the political considerations involved in an expedition of this kind [...] a permanent occupation would probably secure the support of the civil population, but there then would arise the possibility of friction with France'.[3]

The Turkish offensive against the Suez Canal turned out to be a failure. After some skirmishes at the canal, the Turks were forced to retreat to positions in the Sinai desert. This turn of events made a landing at Alexandretta less urgent. However, a solution to the 'Syrian question', as Sir Henry McMahon designated the clash between French and Arab nationalist aspirations, remained as urgent as ever. According to the high commissioner, the question had even reached 'an acute phase' due to 'the arrival in Egypt of the French military mission and to the general supposition that it has been sent to further French interests in Syria'. As a solution to this Syrian question, Sir Henry again trotted out the old idea of establishing Egyptian sovereignty over Syria under a British protectorate. Whatever the merits of this scheme, the existing unrest under Syrians and pan-Arab nationalists had made one thing abundantly clear. Some 'definite conclusion as to our future policy is no longer avoidable, and [...] a complete understanding as to that policy between France and ourselves is not only desirable but essential'.

McMahon's dispatch did not stir the Foreign Office into action. Although it was judged important enough to be printed and circulated to the members of the Cabinet, and George Clerk observed that it raised 'in some ways, the most difficult issue of the whole war', it would nevertheless 'be a mistake to open it with France until the attack on the Dardanelles has reached its end' (see section 'The Expedition to the Dardanelles and the Partition of the Ottoman Empire', below). Nicholson also knew only one solution to the Syrian question. It 'must remain dormant for the present. France would hardly be disposed to renounce her aspirations.'[4] Grey for his part deemed it advisable to send a private telegram to the new high commissioner, in which he urged Sir Henry not to lose sight of the order of priorities in the Syrian question. It was:

> Perhaps well to say at once that it would mean a break with France if we put forward any claims in Syria and to claim it for Egypt would be the equivalent to claim it for ourselves. You must be careful therefore not to arouse the

susceptibilities of France about Syria; if this was done, our relations with France could be impaired in a way that would be most unfortunate while we are prosecuting war in common.⁵

On the same day this telegram was sent, McMahon dispatched a letter to Nicolson. He pointed out that, however much the authorities in Cairo exerted themselves not to offend French Syrian susceptibilities, it just could not be denied that there was an 'increasing weight of evidence to prove that no one, not even the Maronites, want the French to go there', but his warning was wasted on the permanent under-secretary. McMahon should learn to live with the fact that 'the French are exceedingly sensitive in relation to Syria and always fear that we may be inclined to attempt to get some influence there'. Sir Henry could take comfort in the thought that 'we need not touch upon these questions during the war, nor indeed, till it has been decided by the Powers as to what is to be the future of Ottoman rule in Asia'.⁶ The renewed attempts by the British authorities in Cairo to induce Grey and his officials to reconsider their pro-French policy with respect to Syria had also come to nothing.

Sir Reginald Wingate Starts his Correspondence

On 16 November 1914, an interdepartmental meeting between the Foreign Office, India Office and Admiralty had been held to discuss Cheetham's telegram no. 264 of 13 November (see also Chapter 1, section 'Lord Kitchener Intervenes'). One of the subjects concerned the safeguarding of British shipping in the Red Sea. In this connection it had been decided that the resident at Aden 'should get hold of Saïd Idris [the Idrisi of Asir; R.H.L.], who will want money'.⁷ In a telegram of 5 January 1915, the resident informed the viceroy that these instructions had been carried out but that there were 'other agencies at work […] in the Red Sea Littoral. Unless the Arabian Littoral policy is directed from Aden or some well concerted programme is agreed upon there is likely to be considerable confusion.' Lord Hardinge fully agreed. In a telegram to the India Office sent two days later, the viceroy argued that it would be 'more convenient if all such action were arranged in consultation with Resident at Aden', and that he accordingly deprecated 'independent action in this quarter by other agencies as being only likely to cause confusion and failure'. Lancelot Oliphant concurred. This would 'lead to terrible confusion if not stopped at once'. On 12 January he drafted a telegram to McMahon informing the latter that 'Resident at Aden should be kept fully informed of any intelligence received by Egyptian authorities', and that the resident alone should conduct negotiations with the Idrisi.[8]

Sir Reginald Wingate – the governor-general of the Sudan and sirdar (commander in chief) of the Egyptian army – had already been aware of the activities developed by Aden in the Red Sea littoral before the Foreign Office telegram reached Cairo. He had not been particularly pleased. He had already written on 9 January to Clayton that he was somewhat worried:

> About our interfering in Arabian politics [...] You will understand, and I am sure Sir J. Maxwell will agree with me, that we had much better cry 'hands off' in matters in which it may be thought we can do no good. Of course I have my own views that we might be able to do just as well as India in these affairs, and geographically and ethnographically we are perhaps better placed, but, like most things in our Empire, there is a general want of direction from a central head as well as cooperation and coordination.

The contents of the Foreign Office telegram of 12 January had induced Wingate to write yet another letter to Clayton in which he had expressed his fear that an 'Arab policy run on the lines indicated [...] is bound to result in failure'. It seemed that McMahon had 'a strong case for suggesting that he should deal with it, and I hope he will adopt this line'.[9]

From his telegram of 24 January it appeared that Sir Henry was not prepared to accept the decision of the home authorities without question, especially because the Idrisi had 'much more intimate relations with Egypt than with Aden'. He proposed to divide the Arabian Peninsula into a sphere of influence for Cairo, and one for the Government of India, where Cairo was to be responsible for the Hijaz, Ibn Rashid and the Idrisi, and the Government of India for the remaining Arab rulers.[10]

In his reply to Wingate's letter, Clayton predicted that the Foreign Office would not agree to Sir Henry's proposals. The Sudan agent assumed that in spite of the fact that the Sudan was 'far more closely in touch with Arabia in every way than anywhere else', the India Office 'probably do not feel much inclined to relinquish the Idrisi to us [...] and it looks probable that the government will hesitate to change the control at this juncture'.[11] He was right. The India Office agreed that it was 'convenient' to divide the Red Sea into two sections, but the Idrisi had to remain the resident's responsibility. The Foreign Office sent a telegram in this sense to McMahon three days later.[12]

Understandably enough, Wingate regarded this decision as 'not altogether satisfactory', but he quite saw, so he explained to Clayton, that 'it is useless to go on pushing just at present'. It nevertheless remained rather disappointing, as he wrote in a subsequent letter, that 'in spite of my position in Egypt and the Sudan and the number of years I have been in the country, little use has been made of my experience in this, or in other matters connected with the situation'.[13] The Sudan agent could very well imagine Wingate's disappointment. On 3 March, he wrote to the sirdar that he regretted 'the manner in which you have been treated and the way in which your unique experience of this country and its problems have been made no use of', but it just could not be helped, 'the Arab question […] seems now to be definitely placed in the hands of the Indian Government'.[14] A few days before, however, Sir Reginald had reached the conclusion that the battle had not definitively been lost and decided to abandon his, as he described it to Clayton, 'dog-in-the-manger attitude'.[15]

At the beginning of February, Clayton had sent the sirdar a memorandum written by sheikh Rashid Rida – one of the best known leaders of the pan-Arab movement in Egypt – at the request of the Sudan agent. Clayton had observed in his covering letter that the sheikh realised that his scheme for an independent Arab empire was 'unlikely to be fulfilled in his lifetime – the practical elements being wanting', and that it accordingly was 'only a sort of Utopia which cannot be reached except by very gradual stages'.[16] Wingate was at least as sceptical regarding Rida's pan-Arab ambitions. He had nevertheless thought it a good idea to send a copy of the memorandum to Lord Cromer, with whom he maintained a correspondence. Moreover, on 27 February, he dispatched letters to Hardinge, McMahon and Grey, enclosing a memorandum on British policy in Arabia written by his private secretary, Captain Stewart Symes. This change of heart, as the sirdar explained to Clayton, had been due to the fact that after he had 'been thinking over the matter seriously', he had reached the conclusion that 'we ought not – at the present juncture – to keep entirely to ourselves information and views which may be helpful to those who will have the responsibility of settling this momentous question'. Wingate was especially hopeful that Hardinge and Grey, 'as I know them both well', would 'read the somewhat lengthy but admirable note compiled by Symes'.[17]

Four Memoranda

Symes stated in his memorandum that the 'impending collapse of the Turkish Empire' was a cause of great unrest under the Muslims, as 'the majority of Moslems share the opinion that the future welfare and dignity of Islam is inseparable from its perpetuation as an independent political system, as opposed to a creed or a mere school of ethics'. He had been given to understand by 'a prominent member of the "young Arab" party, a man of education and a professed Anglo-phil', that Muslims feared nothing more than that 'the future state of the Moslems will be that of the Jews – namely complete political dependency'. At the same time, many of them realised only too well that the Ottoman Empire in consequence of its siding with the central powers in the war was bound to be dismembered. With this prospect, 'the thoughts of many Moslems turn, not unnaturally, to the glory of the former Arabian empire and the possibility of its revival under a new Arab Khalifa'. The British promises made thus far had not been very inspiring to these Muslims. Symes therefore deemed it desirable that Great Britain 'at the first favourable opportunity' issued a formal proclamation that should be more explicit respecting these 'two most vital questions in the minds of Moslems at the present time – A. the Khalifate, and B. Arabian independence'. With regard to the first, Symes observed that:

> It is clear that anything like intervention or direct suggestion by a Christian Power in a matter of this kind must be avoided, and it would probably be impolitic officially to undertake more than to protect the embryo from outside interference and thus permit the Arabian peoples to work out their own salvation undisturbed.
>
> If an undertaking of this kind were given, and stress laid on the traditional claims of the Arabs (Koreish) to the Sceptre of Islam, the destruction of the temporal dominion of Turkey might assume, in Arab and Anglo-phil Moslem eyes, the character of a blow struck on behalf of the rightful protectors of Islam (the Arabs) against the Turkish Usurper of the Khalifate.

As to the second question, an independent Arab empire covered more than the Arabian Peninsula. It was 'bounded on the north by Kurdistan, on the west by the Mediterranean, on the south by the Red and Arabian seas, and on the east by the Persian Gulf'. Arab ambitions therefore clearly clashed with the well-known French and Russian claims to parts of that area, and together with the British advance in Mesopotamia and the declaration of a British protectorate over Egypt, these conflicts of interests made the powers of the Entente 'increasingly suspect'. Symes suggested that the proclamation could remove Arab suspicions by declaring that 'military operations against Turco–German forces on the coasts of Arabia and in Mesopotamia, undertaken in support of the Arabs' cause, imply no intention of entering into possession of, or alienating from their lawful owners, the Arabian lands which are the rightful heritage of Islam'. A proclamation along these lines would make it clear that Britain sympathised with Arab aspirations and might turn 'the present difficult situation [...] to our advantage and may well prove an important land-mark in the history of British relations with Islam'.[18]

In spite of the supposedly great benefits that Great Britain stood to gain from the proposed proclamation, reactions were not encouraging. Both McMahon and Grey did not bother to reply, and while Hardinge took the trouble to do so, he had no sympathy for Symes's arguments. He merely repeated the Indian adage that 'our wisest course seems to me to be to let the Arabs in Arabia work out their own salvation'.[19]

Wingate had also sent a copy of the memorandum to Clayton. His reaction was also rather disheartening. The Sudan agent wrote that he 'entirely agreed' with the memorandum's conclusions, but England could not issue the suggested proclamation without running the risk of being accused of a breach of promise in the future. To him it looked 'very much as though we had agreed to leave Syria to France', and he seriously doubted 'whether our government (urged by the Indian authorities) would consent to forego territorial acquisition in Mesopotamia'. If he was right, then 'a declaration such as suggested would be impossible, as subsequent action would lay us open to a just charge of breach of faith'.[20]

Without waiting for their replies to his first letter, Wingate again dispatched letters to Grey, McMahon and Hardinge on 11 March, enclosing a copy of a letter 'from one prominent member of the Arab party to another member'.[21] The responses to this letter again were not particularly hopeful. Although this time Sir Edward, as opposed to Sir Henry, took the trouble to answer, he limited himself to observing that 'your two notes which you sent me on the subject of the Arab question [...] are extremely interesting and are of great value at this time when we are trying to find a solution to this most difficult question'.[22] Hardinge for his part insisted that it was too dangerous for Great Britain to have anything to do with the question of the caliphate.[23]

Although the results of his correspondence had been rather disappointing thus far, Wingate did not lose confidence. He again sent a memorandum on the Arab question to Grey, McMahon and Hardinge on 27 March. This time, the memorandum had been written by the grand kadi of the Sudan, Muhammad Mustafa al-Maraghi. Four days later, he also sent this memorandum, as well as the one by Symes, to Lord Cromer.[24]

It seemed that, thanks to the grand kadi's memorandum, Wingate's efforts finally began to bear fruit. Although the grand kadi discussed the same theme as Symes had done in his note, the regeneration of an Arab empire under an Arab caliph, his memorandum did elicit a reaction from the Foreign Office. On 14 April, a telegram was sent to McMahon instructing him that he:

> Should inform Wingate that I authorise him to let it be known, if he thinks it desirable, that His Majesty's Government will make it an essential condition in any terms of peace that the Arabian peninsula and its Moslem Holy places should remain in the hands of an independent Sovereign Moslem State.
>
> Exactly how much territory should be included in this State is not possible to define at this stage.
>
> His Majesty's Government feel that the question of the Khalifate is one which must be decided by Moslems without interference from non-Moslem Powers. Should Moslems decide for an Arab Khalifate, that decision would naturally therefore be respected by His Majesty's Government, but the decision is for Moslems to make.[25]

Grey, moreover, took the trouble to notify Wingate that this telegram had been sent.[26] Although this message did not go as far as the proclamation Wingate had wished for (especially with respect to Arab territorial ambitions) in his next letter to Sir Edward the sirdar nevertheless characterised the telegram as 'most helpful'. He had at once informed the grand kadi and 'some of the principal religious Chiefs of the Sudan and the replies are most appreciative of this important assurance of the British government'.[27]

The viceroy, in his reply, concentrated on the point that the grand kadi had suggested that 'there should be no sort of partition of any part of Arabia, and that Arabia intact should be handed over to the Arabs'.[28] Already on 2 December 1914, only ten days after its occupation, Hardinge had written to Crewe that he was 'strongly of opinion that we ought never to give up

Basrah again', because 'if we hold Basrah [...] our position in the Persian Gulf will be absolutely secure for ever'.[29] From that moment on, the viceroy had been pressing the secretary of state for some private intimation that the British government agreed that Basra should be retained permanently. The 'complete and permanent' occupation of the vilayet of Basra would not suffice, however. Basra was not secure, economically or strategically, unless 'a stable and friendly administration' was created at Baghdad. For this reason, Great Britain should also establish 'some form of protectorate over the province of Baghdad'.[30] Hardinge had therefore taken exception to the phrase in Symes's proposed proclamation that military operations in Mesopotamia implied 'no intention of entering into possession of, or alienating from their lawful owners, the Arabian lands which are the rightful heritage of Islam'. The Government of India felt that it was 'absolutely necessary to safeguard the future of our position in the Persian Gulf, and that this can only be done by holding Basrah permanently'.[31] In his observations on the grand kadi's memorandum, Hardinge more forcefully returned to this point. The grand kadi's wish that Basra would form part of the new Arab empire was:

> Hardly practicable, for our interests in the Persian Gulf secured during the past 150 years by our trade and enterprise have of late years been seriously endangered by the Germans under Turkish protection. This is a situation which it would be folly on our part to allow to recur, and it is of no use for the Arabs to say that this would not happen under their rule, for it is always possible that it might, and Arabs have not a great reputation for honesty. My own view is that having by lucky chance obtained possession of Basra, which dominates the Persian gulf, we should under no circumstances ever surrender it.

From Cromer's reply to the memoranda by Symes and the grand kadi, it appeared that the former British agent in Egypt was at least as suspicious as the viceroy of the Arabs and their ambitions. Cromer had thought it a good idea to forward the two memoranda to Lord Curzon, and enclosed the latter's reaction for Wingate's information. Curzon evidently was not impressed:

> The Arabs are now opening their mouths very wide, and appear to want a new Arabian state and Khalifate from the Persian Gulf to Egypt and from Egypt to Syria (which it is to include). What evidence have they shown of

their capacity to organise or administer such a state? Where is the new man of the Koreish tribe whom they all will accept? Where is to be his seat of government? [...] How futile it would be to declare the formation of a new state, without territory, without capital and without ruler!

Apparently too we are to prejudge all the issues of the war by at once promising to give up Busrah, Lower Mesopotamia and the places where we are spending much money and life to a people (the Arabs) who are at this moment fighting against us as hard as they can, and are known to be in the pay of the Germans!

According to Cromer, these observations were 'very forcible'. Something could naturally be done 'to allay the uneasiness which is undoubtedly felt as regards our intentions in the Moslem world, more especially in the direction of indicating our views as regards the Khalifate', but Wingate's proposal to encourage the Arabs to realise their aim of an independent Arab empire was not practicable. As far as Cromer knew, 'the ordinary Arab cares for two things, (1) his religion, (2) his piastres, and I am not at all sure that he does not care for his piastres more than he cares for his religion'.[32]

Curzon's question 'where is the new man of the Koreish tribe whom they all will accept?' earned him an underlining and a question mark in the margin on Wingate's copy of Curzon's letter. To Wingate this was an odd question. The Emir of Mecca naturally was that man. The next memorandum he sent to Grey, McMahon, Hardinge and Cromer left no doubt about that. The author was the sayyid Ali al-Mirghani, according to Wingate 'the man of more religious influence in the Sudan than anyone else'. The sayyid showed himself to be a strong advocate of the nomination of Sharif Husayn for the caliphate:

> The present Sharif or Emir of Mecca is the most suitable man for this dignified position, owing to his religious importance in the Hedjaz which comprises the 'Haramein El Sherifein' (the Holy Places) so much venerated and respected by all Moslems throughout the whole world. We may add that the Sherif or Emir of Mecca is a man very closely related to the Prophet and highly honoured by all Mohammedans, a fact which should give him the necessary precedence due to the honour of his position.

In his covering letters, Wingate at the same time tried to meet the two major objections of his correspondents against an active, pro-Arab policy, namely that the Arab striving for an Arab caliphate was no more than a chimera, and that pan-Arab territorial ambitions clashed with British interests in the Middle East. He observed to Grey that he was well aware that:

> It may be considered futile to talk of the formation of a new State without territory, without Capital and without ruler, but however Utopian it may be, there can be no doubt that, when the psychological moment comes, all Moslem eyes will be turned to Great Britain to whom they look for support in this – perhaps the supreme crisis – in their religious and national existence.[33]

In his letter to Cromer, Wingate moreover tried to explain why he was prepared to entertain these pan-Arab schemes. Of course, 'all these plans for the formation of an independent Arab Sovereign State and Khalifate are […] Utopian at the present stage', but the thing that mattered was that 'there is undoubted unrest in the minds of thinking Moslems and something must be done to satisfy them'. Seen in this light it should be obvious that 'the more we can keep the better educated Moslems busy with plans for their Utopian Kingdom and Khalifate, the less likely are they to imbibe the vile lies and poisonous propaganda of Sheikh Shawish and his Teutonic supporters'. Sir Reginald also made an attempt to put Cromer at ease as to the territorial claims of the pan-Arab nationalists. The sirdar explained that with regard to Mesopotamia, he had gathered from conversations that 'they now quite realise these districts are essential to British interests in the Persian gulf and of course we must have them, but they hope Baghdad will be left to the New State'. With respect to Syria and Palestine, his interlocutors now also realised that, 'much as they dislike the idea […] that portions of these districts must also be left outside the New State'.[34]

McMahon again failed to reply, but from their answers it appeared that Hardinge and Cromer had become less dismissive of the sirdar's wish for an active, pro-Arab policy. The viceroy observed that he quite shared Wingate's view that 'the present Sharif of Mecca would be a most suitable successor to the Sultan of Turkey as Caliph. From all accounts, he is a very ambitious man, hates the Turks and is anxious to be free of them.' Hardinge nevertheless persisted in his objections against a British initiative in these matters. In any case, it was:

> Satisfactory to hear that you had further talks with the Moslem leaders about certain portions of Mesopotamia being incorporated in the British

Empire. I am glad to think that they are reasonable upon this point, for I do not think that we can possibly recede from the position we now occupy in and around Busrah without betrayal of all our friends.

Cromer admitted that Wingate's arguments with respect to the importance of an active, pro-Arab policy were strong, but he kept his doubts in view of the risks involved, 'unless we intervene nothing satisfactory will be done. But, on the other hand, if we intervene we shall probably make a mess of it by reason of the jealousy there is in respect to Christian interference in these matters.'

Cromer had once again forwarded Wingate's letter to Curzon, and enclosed the latter's reply. Wingate's letters had convinced Curzon that 'we ought to know more about this Sherif of Mecca. His family and position are impeccable. But what of the man?' This had the result that Cromer asked Wingate if he knew anything about the Emir of Mecca, 'what sort of man he is, whether he has any authority outside his immediate circle, etc?'[35] The result of this question was yet another question mark in the margin and yet another memorandum, this time again composed by Symes. On 20 July, Wingate dispatched it to his correspondents. Before he did so, something had happened that had considerably increased its importance. On 12 July, a messenger of Sharif Husayn had arrived in the Sudan, 'apparently with a view to ascertain if British government is prepared to assist the Sherif and his Arab supporters with arms and ammunition'.[36] A few days later, Wingate confided to Clayton that he 'had an interesting talk with "the man from Mecca"', and that he trusted that 'in due course something may come of it'.[37]

Wingate did not refer to the messenger's visit in his covering letter with Symes's memorandum to Grey, but opined that he 'should not altogether be surprised if the Sherif himself does not secretly seek our assistance, and should he do so, I earnestly trust he may be helped'. He also drew Grey's attention to the fact that, from his correspondence with Hardinge, he had gathered that the latter agreed that 'when the house of Othman disappears from the scene', the Sherif of Mecca was 'the most likely candidate' for the caliphate.

Symes's memorandum was based on a statement by a 'well educated intelligent member of a famous (Sherifian) family who left Mecca seven months ago'. The latter's information was 'naturally biased in favour of the family', but Wingate nevertheless considered it trustworthy. It agreed with 'a good deal of independent evidence'. The statement was most of all a panegyric on the Emir of Mecca:

> Sherif Hussein is described to be of a very mild and generous character. He is well educated and is of exceptional ability in religious matters and Mohammedan literature [...] He is very generous, kind-hearted and liberal, and he has never shown any signs of pride in consideration of the feelings of others, no matter how low they might be on the scale of civilisation [...] He is very just and merciful, and the Arabs prefer him to all his predecessors of the Ashraf who ruled Mecca, and greatly respect him.

With respect to Abdullah, the informant stated that Husayn's second son was 'in a very great measure the "power behind the throne" of the Sherif of Mecca'. Both Husayn and Abdullah aspired to the independence of the Hijaz, but to the latter this independence was no more than a 'preliminary to his larger schemes'. To what extent the Sharif shared these 'secret aspirations of his son in regard to the assumption of the khalifate, the informant professes to be uncertain'. In any case, it seemed that Husayn and Abdullah were agreed that independence could only be brought about 'by force of arms, which, informant states, the Sherif would gladly accept secretly at the hands of His Majesty's Government'.[38]

Before Wingate could receive any answer, the pace of events quickened. On 12 August, Clayton telegraphed to Wingate that 'an Arab Sheikh from the Hedjaz' was on his way to Suez, 'bearing important letters for the British Oriental Secretary Cairo from the Sherif of Mecca which have to be delivered personally'.[39] Sir Reginald replied the same day. The first draft of his telegram had read, 'I trust messenger will bring corroborative evidence', but he had thought better of it, and changed it into a more guarded 'this messenger will probably bring corroborative evidence of the Sherif's anxiety for secret British assistance'.[40]

The Expedition to the Dardanelles and the Partition of the Ottoman Empire

Although Grey sent only one letter in reply, his lukewarm response was no indication that Wingate's letters had no effect on the Foreign Office point of view as to the policy that should be pursued in the Middle East. Symes's first memorandum had arrived at a crucial time. On 2 January 1915,

Russia had requested her allies to make a demonstration against Turkey. After negotiations with France, the War Council had approved a proposal strongly advocated by the First Lord of the Admiralty, Winston Churchill. After the shelling of the Gallipoli Peninsula, marines would take possession of the peninsula, with the occupation of Constantinople as their ultimate object.[41] The attack, which had started on 19 February, eventually ended in failure, but on 4 March there had been no prospect of this. That day, the Russian government had notified France and England that any solution to the question of Constantinople and the Straits would be 'insufficient and precarious' if the city of Constantinople, the west coast of the Bosporus, the Sea of Marmara and the Dardanelles, as well as the Ottoman part of Thrace were not incorporated into the Russian Empire. Strategic considerations further required that a part of the east coast of the Bosporus, the islands in the Sea of Marmara and the islands of Imbros and Tenedos were incorporated as well. If France and England agreed to these demands, so the Russian government assured its allies, their designs on other parts of the Ottoman Empire would be treated in the same sympathetic spirit.[42]

After two meetings on 9 and 10 March, the War Council decided to accept the Russian claims, 'subject to the war being prosecuted to a victorious conclusion, and to Great Britain realising the desiderata referred to in the last sentence of the Russian aide-mémoire. These desiderata will be put forward by the British and French government as soon as there had been time to consider them.'[43]

When Symes's memorandum reached Clerk's desk, the decision-making process to determine British desiderata was still underway. It was therefore 'well worth consideration at the present moment, especially if read in connection with Sir T. Morison's paper on Indian Moslem feeling'.[44]

Sir Theodore, a member of the Council of India, drew attention to the existing unrest under the Muslims of India. Like Symes, he was of the opinion that it emanated from the existing fear that the war might lead to the destruction of the Ottoman Empire, the last stronghold of Islam, and that as a result the Muslims would become 'like the Jews, a people without a country of (their) own'. The best thing to do to take away this fear was to conclude a separate peace with Turkey as soon as possible. However, such a policy stood little chance of success, considering the present Turkish attitude. The creation of an independent Arab kingdom constituted a good alternative. It would have to include not only the Arabian Peninsula, but also Syria and Mesopotamia, because only 'when these are included it becomes a state in which Muhammadan patriotism can take a legitimate pride'.⁴⁵

The two central themes in the memoranda by Symes and Morison – Islam was not just a religion, and it was in Britain's interest to encourage the re-establishment of an Arab empire – made an impression on Clerk. He minuted that 'Islam, to the Moslem, is not merely a creed, but a definite political system, which must exist in an independent state or perish. It is this which makes the Moslem so dread the impending fall of Constantinople', and although an Arab kingdom comprising the Arabian Peninsula as well as the Fertile Crescent 'cuts right across any views of British possession of Mesopotamia […] and comes into conflict with French and Russian "reversions" […] it deserves serious consideration', especially in view of the British desideratum that 'if Turkish rule in Mesopotamia disappears, the inheritance falls to us', which implied that Britain 'should also hold Alexandretta, the natural outlet to the West, and the key to the direct route between the Mediterranean, the Persian Gulf and India'. It was therefore very desirable to consider:

> Whether we cannot achieve the essential part of the Mesopotamia–Alexandretta policy in another way, that is, by encouraging the idea of a Moslem State which shall include those regions, while we, in return are accorded definite recognition of our special position in the Persian Gulf up to Basrah […] and a free port at Alexandretta.
>
> Even so, the difficulties of negotiations are great enough, but we shall at least show the Moslems that we respect and sympathise with their aspirations, and approach the French with a better grace and an easier cause than if we have to claim Alexandretta for ourselves.⁴⁶

At the meeting of the War Council devoted to the discussion of the partition of the Ottoman Empire in Asia, it became evident that Grey had also been impressed by the main strands in the two memoranda. According to him, the War Council should first agree on the answer to a 'great question of principle': 'ought we not to take into account the very strong feeling in the Moslem world that Mohammedanism ought to have a political as well as religious existence?' If this question was answered in the affirmative, then 'Arabia, Syria, and Mesopotamia were the only possible territories for an Arab Empire. If we took this standpoint we could say to our Moslem subjects that, as Turkey had handed itself over to the Germans, we had set up a new and independent Moslem State.' The War Council were receptive to Grey's argument. He was authorised to send a reply to Petrograd stating:

> That after the Straits have been forced, and Constantinople has passed into the hands of the Allies, our first desideratum would be the establishment of a Moslem entity. It would have to include Arabia, and the question would arise as to what was to go with it. In the meantime, it would be premature to discuss the partition of Turkey.[47]

The grand kadi's memorandum led Grey to draft a telegram giving Wingate permission to make public the War Council's position that to Great Britain it was 'an essential condition in any terms of peace that the Moslem Holy Places should remain in the hands of an independent Sovereign State' (see previous section 'Four Memoranda'). Crewe, however, pointed out that the Arab empire envisaged by the grand kadi comprised Sunni as well as Shia holy places, but that:

> Kerbela and Nejef, the two first in consideration of the Shia Holy Places, are not within Arabia as ordinarily understood, although I do not know that the exact boundary of Arabia on that side has ever been formally defined. There is also a Moslem place of much sanctity at Jerusalem. So we ought not to arouse too many hopes in the mind of the Kadi.

A sentence was therefore added at the end of the telegram to avoid possible misunderstanding on this score (as Prime Minister Asquith minuted, 'I understand that the telegram is purposely so worded as to exclude the Shia Holy Places'), which stated that 'Wingate will understand that the Shia Holy Places would have to receive separate treatment, and I have worded our promise so as not to commit us with regard to them'.[48]

In Wingate's letter of 30 April 1915, in which the sirdar informed the foreign secretary of the reception of Grey's telegram in the Sudan, he also mentioned that the religious leaders of the country would like to 'spread the news urbe et orbi', but that he had adopted a method that would give the telegram's contents a very wide confidential circulation. In this manner, Wingate continued, the way was prepared 'for an official statement which I hope H.B.M.'s Govt. may be in a position to make at the psychological moment which would seem to be when Constantinople falls'.[49] On 20 May, after consultations with Crewe, Grey sent a telegram to McMahon in which he observed that 'if you and Wingate think it desirable you can at any time or place you think opportune make a public announcement about Arabian Peninsula, Holy Places and Khalifate in the terms of my telegram to you, no 173 of April 14'.[50] When, on 23 June, the viceroy complained about a proclamation 'issued to Arabs in Arabia, Sudan and Western Desert on 13th June, presumably under the orders of the High Commissioner of Egypt', Oliphant naturally assumed this proclamation was based on Grey's telegrams of 14 April and 20 May.[51] McMahon, however, when asked for an explanation, replied that 'nothing in the shape of formal proclamation has been issued'. Instead, an 'unsigned leaflet in Arabic' had been distributed, in which the War Council's decision had been interpreted to mean that it was Britain's intention that:

> When this war ends it shall be laid down in the terms of peace as a necessary condition, that Arabian Peninsula and its Mahometan holy places shall remain independent. We shall not annex one foot of land in it, nor suffer any other Power to do so. Your independence of all foreign control is assured, and with such guarantees the lands of Arabia will, please God, return along the paths of freedom to their ancient prosperity.[52]

It was this paragraph that the viceroy had found quite exceptionable. It appeared 'to go much further than was ever intended. Expression "Arabian Peninsula" is open to serious misinterpretation and might be held to tie our hands in Oman and even to indicate an intention to withdraw from Aden'.[53] The India Office also protested. The clause 'we shall not annex one single foot of land in it', surely did not apply to 'the tribes who have taken or who take up arms against Great Britain and her Allies?'[54] This time, however, the objections of the viceroy and the India Office did not lead to anxious reactions by Foreign Office officials. The attitude they took with respect to these complaints against the policy pursued by Cairo bore a strong resemblance to their attitude with regard to Cairo's warnings of impending trouble as a result of French claims on Syria. They did not question the correctness of the observations, but things could not be as bad as these were made out to be. The best course was to let the matter rest. Clerk minuted that 'the passage marked is unfortunately open to a wide interpretation and certainly goes further than anything we have authorised, but I do not think it involves any such consequences as the viceroy fears'. Nicolson admitted that the leaflet was 'not a happy production', but he was 'inclined to leave matters as they are'. This new attitude was perhaps best put into words by Crewe – no longer secretary of state for India, but lord president of the council – who deputised for Grey while the latter was on leave to rest his weak eyes, when he minuted that it was 'wise to take no further step at present; but I do not apprehend any ill consequences from this proclamation'.[55]

In his memorandum, al-Mirhgani had not only claimed that Husayn was the most suitable candidate for the caliphate, but also put forward a scheme to increase the probability that the Emir of Mecca was actually selected:

> A Khalif must be powerful enough to justify the responsibility thrown upon his shoulders by his post. It is beyond doubt that Great Britain is the most competent Power to render to the Khalif this assistance and support. Such assistance, however, should be rendered secretly or behind a very thick veil in accordance with conditions and circumstances, and to do this Great Britain could utilise the services of some of the Mohammedan Emirs, Sultans and Chiefs who are under her control and protection, and whom she could trust. Such assistance, if it comes directly from such Chiefs to the Grand Emir (Khalif) will be of very great advantage.

Wingate had stated in his covering letter that it was worth exploring this proposal further. Sir Edward had agreed, and before he went on leave had left instructions to discuss the matter with the India Office.[56] Grey's concurrence was remarkable, because al-Mirghani's proposal completely clashed with the established policy of non-interference in the question of the caliphate. Not surprisingly, the India Office objected strongly to it. It reiterated that the caliphate was a question 'Moslems should decide for themselves without interference from the Powers'. It was 'desirable to leave the Arabs to manage their own affairs as much as possible, and to avoid an adventurous policy in the interior'. Although Nicolson considered 'the views of the I.O. [...] eminently sound', they did not induce the Foreign Office to warn Wingate to be more circumspect in his future dealings with pan-Arab nationalists. The officials in the Foreign Office did not even bother to inform the authorities at Cairo and Khartoum that they still adhered to a policy of non-intervention with respect to the caliphate. They merely forwarded without comment a copy of the India Office letter to McMahon, together with a copy of al-Mirghani's memorandum, requesting the high commissioner's views on the proposed scheme.[57]

Sharif Husayn's Opening Bid

On 18 August, the messenger from Mecca arrived in Alexandria. He carried with him a note and a covering letter addressed to Storrs. According to the latter, the note as well as the letter were 'in the writing of the Sherif Abdalla [...] probably at the dictation of his father'.[58] In the letter, Abdullah entrusted Storrs with ensuring, 'as you know how to, the acceptance of the enclosed note which contains our proposals and conditions'.[59] The contents of the note were no surprise to people like Storrs and Clayton. The oriental secretary observed that there was 'a curiously exact resemblance between the terms herein proposed, and the views frequently expressed by Shaykh Rashid Rida, especially in regard to frontiers'.[60]

On behalf of 'the Arab nation', Abdullah declared that it was in Great Britain's interest to support the Arabs in their endeavours to gain independence, and that the Arabs, 'in view of the well-known attitude of the Government of Great Britain', would gladly accept Britain's assistance, provided she accepted, within 30 days of the receipt of the note, the following conditions:

1. Great Britain recognises the independence of the Arab countries which are bounded: on the north by the line Mersin–Adana to parallel 37° N and thence along the line Birejik–Urfa–Mardin–Midiat–Jazirat (ibn 'Umar)–Amadia to the Persian frontier; on the east, by the Persian frontier down to the Persian Gulf; on the south, by the Indian Ocean (with the exclusion of Aden whose status will remain as at present); on the west, by the Red Sea and the Mediterranean Sea back to Mersin.
2. Great Britain will agree to the proclamation of an Arab caliphate for Islam.[61]

However familiar these conditions sounded to people like Clayton and Storrs, they nevertheless considered them excessive. It was one thing in the battle against 'Turco–German Jehad propaganda' to sympathise vaguely with Arab nationalist pretensions, even to encourage them, but it was quite another actually to accept such precisely worded proposals as those of Abdullah. In March, Clayton had already opposed the proclamation favoured by Wingate and Symes, not only because such a proclamation laid Great Britain open to a charge of breach of faith (see section 'Four Memoranda', above), but also because he could not see 'any practical possibility of the formation of an Arab Empire'. The idea was 'an attractive one but the necessary elements appear to me to be lacking'.[62] Now it seemed, so Clayton explained to Wingate in a hurried letter on 21 August, that 'the High Commissioner will have to send a vague reply saying that it is early days to begin negotiating agreements, the first thing being to oust the Turks from Arabia'.[63] Storrs shared Clayton's point of view. The Sharif had 'received no sort of mandate from other potentates. He knows he is demanding, possibly as a basis of negotiation, far more than he has the right, the hope or the power to expect.'[64] Sir Henry agreed with his advisers. On 22 August he telegraphed to London that Husayn:

> Has of course at present no mandate beyond Hedjaz. His pretensions are in every way exaggerated, no doubt considerably beyond his hope of acceptance, but it seems very difficult to treat with them in detail without seriously discouraging him.
> I propose following reply:
> 'Gratification at his declaration of identity of British and Arab interests: confirmation of His Majesty's Government's friendly sentiments and promises as expressed in Lord Kitchener's communication of last November. Discussion of boundary details however premature during the war, Turks not having yet been expelled from much of the area in question: and His Majesty's Government having observed with surprise and regret that Arabs in some parts are still neglecting this supreme opportunity and are working for Turks and Germans.'[65]

McMahon's telegram induced Clerk to study the memorandum by Symes that Wingate had sent to London on 20 July. He reached the conclusion that it was 'quite interesting, and it shews the need of great care in our relations with the Sherif'.[66] Such care Grey certainly did not observe in his relations with the India Office. While Oliphant got in touch with Hirtzel 'in view of the interests of the India Office in this matter', Grey without further consultation drafted a telegram in which the answer proposed by McMahon was approved. Oliphant, however, took the liberty to defer the dispatch of this telegram pending receipt of the India Office's reaction.[67]

Hirtzel had already informed Oliphant that the India Office were 'not inclined at first sight entirely to share Sir H. McMahon's view', and the next day this was confirmed in an official letter. Husayn's proposals appeared 'to be dictated by extreme Pan-Arab aspirations (and) are obviously unacceptable as they stand'. It would be wrong, however, to give an evasive reply to such definite proposals, as this might 'lead him to think that we were not serious in our overtures'. If Grey wanted to answer at all, then an addition had to be made in the sense that Great Britain was prepared 'to negotiate a preliminary agreement for securing the independence, rights and privileges of the Sheriffate, if he will send his son Abdullah – or some other plenipotentiary – to Egypt for the purpose'. Should Husayn agree to this, then it would become possible 'to reduce (his proposals) to reasonable dimensions'. The India Office finally considered it necessary 'to give some answer to this question about the Khalifate', and suggested that this might take the form of 'a reference to the penultimate sentence of Lord Kitchener's message of November last [actually the last sentence of this message: see Chapter 1, section 'Overture to Sharif Husayn, the Emir of Mecca'; R.H.L.], with the addition that he must consult his co-religionists as to whether he should proclaim himself Khalifa'.

The Foreign Office again was not prepared to meet the objections raised by the India Office. According to Clerk:

> Sir H. McMahon and his advisers are in a better position than anyone else to gauge the Sherif's sentiments; and I should prefer the reply suggested in 117236 [Grey's draft; R.H.L.] [...] If however it is considered better to make the addition proposed by the I.O. [...] I would suggest that it should be left to Sir H. McMahon's discretion.

He drafted a new telegram to McMahon, which the same afternoon (Sir Arthur Nicolson: 'this matter is very urgent') was approved by Nicolson, Austen Chamberlain (Crewe's successor as secretary of state for India), Kitchener and Grey:

> Proposed reply to Sherif of Mecca approved.
> If you think it advisable, you may add a private message to the effect:–
> 'His Majesty's Government are prepared to discuss a preliminary agreement for securing the independence, rights and privileges of the Sheriffate, if the Sherif will send his son Abdullah, or some other plenipotentiary, to Egypt for the purpose.
> As regards the Khalifate, if the Sherif, with the consent of his co-religionists, is proclaimed Khalif, he may rest assured that His Majesty's Government will welcome the assumption of the Khalifate by an Arab of their race, as already indicated in Lord Kitchener's communication of last November'.[68]

Sir Henry availed himself of the discretion left to him to omit the proposed private message, because he believed that the moment had:

> Not arrived when we can usefully discuss even a preliminary agreement, and it might at this stage injure the Sherif's chances of the Khalifate to advertise his dealings with us by sending a son or other notable to treat with us.
>
> I have also omitted any explicit mention of the Sherif as the future Kaliph as the terms of my message will be sufficiently clear to him on this point. To do so moreover might limit the extent to which he might otherwise make use of my letter.[69]

These arguments drew no further comments from Nicolson, Grey and Kitchener. The India Office did not object to McMahon's decision, although both Holderness and Chamberlain thought the high commissioner 'went quite far enough'.[70]

In his reply to Clayton's hurried letter of 21 August, Wingate made no bones about his disappointment at the cool reception Husayn's proposals had received in Cairo. The reply advocated by Clayton seemed to indicate that:

> The negotiations with the Sherif are likely to fall flat. To my mind this is a thousand pities and I cannot too strongly urge that some more definite encouragement should be given than that indicated in your letter. However, I suppose our various legislators both in India and at home have their own views, and it may be a matter of some difficulty to convert them to our way of thinking. The future will show which would have been the best course to take.[71]

It remained hidden from the relative outsider, Wingate, that his attempts to convert 'the various legislators at home' had already been more or less successful. He had been the major influence in the Foreign Office's conversion to a more favourable attitude towards a policy of exploiting pan-Arab sentiments in the war against the Ottoman Empire. In the first months of 1915, Grey and his officials had accepted the India Office's ascendancy in Middle East policy, if only because the 'I.O. know how this can be done'. In consequence, they had as a matter of course been averse to proposals to exploit the supposed Arab striving for the restoration of an Arab caliphate. Wingate's letters and memoranda had, however, made them familiar with the idea that the Emir of Mecca was not just another Arab potentate, but the likely successor to the caliphate, and the future ruler of an empire consisting of the Arabian Peninsula and the Fertile Crescent. This had the result that, when in August 1915 Husayn's proposal for an Anglo–Arab alliance reached the Foreign Office, it was regarded as less presumptuous than the India Office made them out to be. For this reason it seemed unwise to reject these out of hand, however strongly the India Office urged the Foreign Office to do so. The India Office and the Government of India had lost, permanently, as later events were to show, their predominant position in the circle of the Foreign Office's advisers on the formulation of British Middle East policy.

3 WE HAVE GOT TO KEEP IN WITH OUR INFERNAL ALLIES

Introduction

The Cairo military authorities believed that the desertion of an Arab officer from the Turkish army at Gallipoli, who claimed to represent an organisation of Arab officers in the Turkish army in contact with the Arab chiefs, combined with Sharif Husayn's reply to Sir Henry McMahon's letter of 30 August, provided a golden opportunity to spur the home authorities into action regarding the Arab question. Lord Kitchener and Sir Edward Grey were receptive to the promptings from Cairo. At the same time, Grey and the officials at the Foreign Office realised that the boundaries claimed by the Arabs clashed with French ambitions in Syria, as well as those of the Government of India in Mesopotamia. An obvious way out of this problem seemed to them to be to sacrifice Indian interests in Mesopotamia in order to persuade the French to be more accommodating in Syria. McMahon was authorised to react favourably to Husayn's territorial claims in as far as Britain was free to act without detriment to the interests of France. For the Foreign Office, the time had now arrived to open negotiations with the French on the extent of their claims in Syria. The Government of India and the India Office strongly protested against the disregard of India's territorial ambitions in Mesopotamia, but they got nowhere with Sir Edward. The only comfort he could give them was that, in view of the weakness of the Arabs, nothing would come of these schemes.

When the British cabinet decided to evacuate Gallipoli, Kitchener warned that this would prevent the Arabs from siding with the Entente. He strongly advocated a landing at Alexandretta as a countermeasure. The French, however, refused to entertain this proposal, and the project was subsequently dropped. On the eve of the negotiations with the French on the boundaries of the future Arab state, Grey and the officials in the Foreign Office realised that, unless the Entente intervened with military force in the Middle East, there was no prospect of the Arabs rising against the Turks. At the same time they insisted that French claims on Syria precluded such an intervention taking place without French permission and active participation.

The Military Authorities in Cairo Take the Opportunity to Rub It In

When the attempts by the British–French fleet to destroy the Turkish forts commanding the Narrows of the Dardanelles had threatened to end in failure, the War Council had decided to launch a combined attack by army and navy on the Gallipoli Peninsula. On 25 April 1916, a British division had landed at the southern tip of the peninsula, while two divisions of the Australian and New Zealand Army Corps (Anzac) had been put ashore on the west coast. These landings had also proved to be unsuccessful. A deadlock had resulted, which the attackers were unable to break, despite considerable reinforcements and a new landing at the beginning of August – this time at Suvla Bay – by two divisions from Kitchener's New Army. These latest attempts to force a breakthrough were still continuing when, on 20 August, as Sir Ian Hamilton (General Officer Commanding-in-Chief [GOC-in-C], Mediterranean Expeditionary Force [MEF]) reported to the War Office five days later, 'an officer of the Turkish army (an Arab) named Sherif El Faroki, came into the British lines' to surrender. The officer claimed to belong to:

> An organisation, the head of which is Aziz el Masri [...] That under the organisation of Aziz a propaganda amongst the officers of the Turkish Army has been and still is being carried on. It is intended that these officers should desert to us, and then returning to Syria, raise the standard of revolt in that province against Turkey.

The War Office forwarded Hamilton's letter to the Foreign Office on 9 September. There, officials initially reacted rather coolly to Faruqi's assertions. Clayton should first of all ascertain 'what credence is to be given to this proposal', while Hamilton should particularly be careful 'not [to] commit H.M.Govt. in any negotiations with deserters or emissaries without first consulting the W.O. and the F.O'.[1] For, as George Clerk minuted on a subsequent letter from the War Office, 'there may be some truth in this, but there is nothing tangible'.[2]

The reactions by the authorities in Cairo were quite the opposite. On 9 October, Gilbert Clayton wrote to Sir Reginald Wingate that Faruqi had been sent to Cairo, and that Sir John Maxwell had told him:

> To prepare a note on the officer's views [...] I shall take the opportunity of rubbing this fact in that if we definitely refuse to consider the aspirations of the Arabs, we are running a grave risk of throwing them into the arms of our enemies which would mean that the Jehad which so far has been a failure would probably become a reality.

'Many golden opportunities' had already been lost. The Arab question moreover was an issue of 'life and death'. If Great Britain failed to win the Arabs, then 'our Empire [would shake] to its very base', but he rather doubted whether this was 'realised to the full at home'.[3]

The day after Clayton had written to Wingate, a messenger from Sharif Husayn arrived at Port Sudan carrying the latter's answer to McMahon's letter of 30 August (see Chapter 2, section 'Sharif Husayn's Opening Bid'). Cyril E. Wilson, the governor of the Red Sea Province, immediately cabled a summary to Cairo, from which it appeared that the Emir of Mecca:

> Declares his sincerity towards Great Britain in spite of his feelings at his essential point re boundaries not being considered now, and he wishes explanation of the doubt and hesitation shown concerning this question of boundaries: also wishes to know policy of Great Britain regarding this question: he says the result of negotiations in this matter is anxiously awaited by Mohammedans generally.[4]

Clayton was able to incorporate Husayn's emphasis on an early settlement of the boundary question in his assessment of Faruqi's statements, which he drew up in close consultation with Ronald Storrs. The latter wrote to Oswald Fitzgerald, Kitchener's private secretary:

> The Arab question is reaching an acute stage.

> I gather from the Sherif, as does Clayton from Faroki that they feel, rightly or wrongly, that their time has come to choose between us and Germany […] I have thrashed the thing out at great length with Clayton, and beg you to give all possible prominence to the note being sent by the G.O.C. in this week's bag.[5]

On 12 October, both Maxwell and McMahon dispatched Clayton's memorandum to London. Sir John also sent a telegram to Kitchener that same day, in which he summarised the memorandum's contents, and in which he emphasised the importance and the urgency of the matter:

> I am forwarding by mail a memorandum on the Arab question which is now very pressing.
>
> A powerful organisation with considerable influence in the Army and among Arab Chiefs […] appears to have made up its mind that the moment for action has arrived. The Turks and the Germans are already in negotiation with them and spending money to win their support. The Arab party however is strongly inclined towards England but what they ask is a definite statement of sympathy and support even if their complete programme cannot be accepted.
>
> Sherif of Mecca, who is in communication with the Arab party, also seems uneasy and is pressing for a declaration of policy on the part of England.
>
> If their overtures are rejected or a reply is delayed any longer the Arab party will go over to the enemy and work with them, which would mean stirring up religious feeling at once and might well result in a genuine Jehad. On the other hand, the active assistance which the Arabs would render in return for our support would be of the greatest value in Arabia, Mesopotamia, Syria and Palestine.

Kitchener replied the next day that 'the government are most desirous of dealing with the Arab question in a manner satisfactory to the Arabs. Please telegraph to me the headings of what they want and discuss the matter with McMahon. You must do your best to prevent alienation of the Arabs' traditional loyalty to England.' However, Maxwell's telegram caused considerably less excitement in the Foreign Office. Clerk merely minuted that the question could 'not usefully be discussed until the memo is received'.[6]

Maxwell's reply to Kitchener on 16 October was more or less a repetition of his earlier telegram. The general explained that 'behind all the Arab potentates there is a large and influential Arab party actually in the Turkish army who are sworn to the cause'. The proposals of the Emir of Mecca had actually been the proposals of this Arab party. It was both 'necessary and urgent to waste no time, otherwise they and the potentates will throw in their lot with the Turks [...] [U]nless we make definite and agreeable proposal to the Shereef at once, we may have a united Islam against us.'

Maxwell also discussed the question of the conditions upon which 'the Arab party' was prepared to side with the Entente powers:

> The proposals set forth in McMahon's telegram [of 22 August, see Chapter 2, section 'Sharif Husayn's Opening Bid'] represent the total demands, but we have reason to believe that they would accept considerable modification in negotiation with Great Britain. The time is past in my opinion for vague generalities, and our best course seems to me to be to eliminate what we cannot and will not allow, and to treat the rest as a basis for negotiation. But we must bear in mind in so doing that, even if we insist on retaining the Vilayet (of Basra) as British, the rest of Mesopotamia must be included in the negotiations; likewise, on the west, the Arab party will, I think, insist on Homs, Aleppo, Hama, and Damascus being in their sphere.[7]

Two days later, the Foreign Office received a telegram from McMahon containing a résumé of Sharif Husayn's second letter. The high commissioner stated that the Emir was:

> Disturbed by our statement that discussion of territorial limits of the Arab power is useless while the countries involved are still in enemy hands. Though it may be necessary to settle the Arab boundaries with more than one Power, and that only after the war, the matter is all the same one of life and death for the Arab people. On this point they are united and must discuss the question with Great Britain, the one Power they trust.
>
> Shereef [...] dismisses the idea that we hesitate to admit the Arab demands because some of their people are still defending Turkish interests. We may rest assured that all Arabs, even those obeying Turco–German orders are only waiting for the result of the present negotiations. This result depends on our refusal or acceptance of their territorial proposals and our declaration to safeguard their religion and their rights.

Sir Henry did not mention, in complete agreement with Husayn's letter, that a reply was urgently required. This led Clerk to conclude that 'the question has two aspects, military and political, of which the military side is urgent'. He continued:

> We are told that not only the Arabs in Arabia, but also the Arab officers and men in the Turkish army are ready to work against the C.U.P. and the Turks, if we will accept their pretensions, while if we cannot come to terms they will definitely side with the Germans and Turks against us.
>
> Politically, the first thing is to settle whether we are prepared to accept in principle the idea of Arabia – even an exaggerated Arabia such as the Sherif proposes – for the Arabs. If I may express my own view, it is, as I have held since the war began, that the best solution is an independent Arabia, looking to Great Britain as its founder and protector, and provided with territory rich and wide enough to furnish adequate revenues.
>
> There are however two important limitations to the creation of such a state:
>
> i. French claims and ambitions.
> ii. Our own advance in Mesopotamia.
>
> i. It is difficult to challenge the position which France claims, and has to some extent secured by acquiring special interests, in the north-western portion of Arabia as now defined by the Arabs. But we cannot win the Arabs unless we can reconcile French and Arab claims, and the position must be clearly understood from both the French and the Arab side from the outset, or we shall be heading straight for serious trouble. It seems to me that the line to work on is, first, to impress on our Allies the urgency of the situation and to get them to accept us as our mouthpiece, at the same time impressing on the Arabs that we speak for the Allies as a whole; and, secondly, to be ready to recognise the priority of French commercial interests in the north-west.
>
> ii. Mesopotamia is primarily a question for India, but I do not think that a solution, which would provide for Arab independence and yet safeguard our vital interests is necessarily impossible. Moreover, we shall have to be ready to resign acquisition of territory in Mesopotamia if we are to get the French to give up their Syrian dreams.[8]

Clerk's minute signalled a further change in the value the Foreign Office attached to the interests of the India Office and the Government of India with regard to the Arab question. Only a year before, these interests had taken priority over schemes to induce the Arabs to revolt against their Turkish masters, and in the summer of 1915 they had at least figured prominently in Foreign Office considerations. But now these interests were reduced to the status of a *quid pro quo* in negotiations with the French on the terms of an Arab revolt. For the moment, however, the India Office and the Government of India were unaware of this shift in Foreign Office priorities. They had not been informed of the telegrams that had been sent by Maxwell, Kitchener and McMahon.

Sir Henry McMahon's Letter of 24 October 1915

On 19 October, yet another telegram from McMahon arrived in London. It was for the most part a repetition of Maxwell's telegram of 16 October. Sir Henry now also claimed that the question was urgent. From further conversations with Faruqi it appeared 'evident that Arab party are at parting of the ways and unless we can give them immediate assurance of nature to satisfy them they will throw themselves into the hands of Germany'. A satisfactory assurance should contain a statement that:

> England accepts principle of independent Arabia under British guidance and control within limits propounded by Sherif of Mecca, in so far as England is free to act without detriment to the interests of her present Allies (this refers to French in regard to whom see remarks on modification of north west limits of Arabia).

With respect to the latter question, McMahon observed that 'Faroki thinks Arabs would accept modification leaving in Arabia, purely Arab districts of Aleppo, Damascus, Hama and Homs, whose occupation by the French they would oppose by force of arms', while he at the same time accepted 'that British interests necessitate special measures of British control in Basrah Vilayet'.

The high commissioner's telegram was not, however, a completely slavish copy of Maxwell's telegram. McMahon also indicated two possible objections against the whole scheme. The first was that, within the limits of the proposed Arab state, 'Arabs will recognise British and no other influence', and the second that 'unless care is taken it is quite possible that young Arab party may eventually prove as troublesome as young Turks'.[9]

McMahon's second telegram became the starting point for Grey's draft of a reply to the high commissioner, which he wrote during a session of the Cabinet. From this draft it appeared that Grey was anxious to protect French interests in the Middle East, and quite prepared to disregard the interests of the India Office and the Government of India:

> You can give assurance on the lines, and with the reserve about our Allies, proposed by you. Stipulations that Arabs will recognise British interests as paramount and work under British guidance etc., should not be included unless it is necessary to secure Arab consent, as this might give impression in France that we were not only endeavouring to secure Arab interests, but to establish our own in Syria at expense of France.
>
> There is no difficulty in speaking without reserve about the Arab Peninsula and Holy Places. The general reserve you propose is however necessary more especially for North Western Boundaries.

Grey passed this draft to Kitchener with the question, 'Lord Kitchener. Will this do?' The latter believed it would: 'Yes, I think it might start "you can give warm assurance".'[10] However, Austen Chamberlain intervened before the telegram was sent. McMahon's second telegram, too, had not been forwarded to the India Office, but the Foreign Office had circulated it to the members of the Cabinet, and in this capacity Chamberlain had received a copy. As he explained to Hardinge two days later:

> In this connection I ought to refer to the exchange of telegrams between Grey and McMahon about the attitude of the Arabs. They are being sent to you, together with some communications passing between Egypt and the War Office, of which we, in the India Office, only became accidentally aware at the last moment. I was most anxious to consult you before Grey sent his answer, but he urged so strongly the need for an immediate decision that all I could do was to ask Grey to introduce some word to safeguard what I may call Indian interests [...] We have asked that, in future, all such telegrams shall be repeated to you, so that you may have early information of what is passing.[11]

Sir Thomas Holderness drafted the rider meant to safeguard India's interests. It was to the effect that 'as regards Mesopotamia proposed sphere of British control, namely Basra Vilayet, will need extension in view of British interests in Baghdad province and area actually in our occupation'. In a covering note, Holderness observed that 'this would come at the end of the telegram',[12] but Grey thought better of it. Without further consultation, at least according to Chamberlain,[13] he added yet another two sentences, in which he stressed what ought to take precedence, and left the high commissioner a large measure of discretion:

> But the important thing is to give our assurances that will prevent Arabs from being alienated, and I must leave you discretion in the matter as it is urgent and there is not time to discuss an exact formula.
> The simplest plan would be to give an assurance of Arab independence saying that we will proceed at once to discuss boundaries if they will send representatives for that purpose, but if something more precise than this is required you can give it.[14]

The 'area actually in our occupation' referred to in Holderness's proposed rider had greatly expanded since the occupation of Basra in November 1914. Strategic considerations, put forward with much adroitness by Sir Percy Cox and the successive commanders of Force 'D', had cleared the way for an advance on Baghdad, the viceroy's doubts notwithstanding. They had successfully argued that Basra could not be defended without first occupying Qurnah, and after the occupation of that town, the occupation of 'Amara had become inevitable, while the possession of 'Amara had unavoidably led to the occupation of Nasiriya, for the defence of which town soon the possession of Kut al-'Amara had appeared to be indispensable. Sir John Nixon, GOC-in-C, Force 'D', had entered that town on 29 September 1915. Four days later, Nixon had informed the home authorities that he considered his forces strong enough to occupy Baghdad.[15]

The Cabinet believed that the occupation of Baghdad was desirable for political reasons, provided Nixon's forces were sufficient to occupy and hold the town. According to the viceroy this was not the case. Without reinforcements Nixon would have to remain at Kut. These would, moreover, have to come from the Indian divisions stationed in France, because there were no troops available in India. The War Office and the Admiralty were not prepared to meet this demand. In a joint memorandum, Sir Henry Jackson, the first sea lord, and Sir Archibald Murray, the Chief of the Imperial General Staff (CIGS), argued that 'under no circumstances must troops […] be diverted from the primary theatre of war for the purpose of conducting a campaign which cannot appreciably influence the decision as between the armies of the Allied and those of the central powers'.[16]

It was on the basis of this memorandum that the Dardanelles Committee discussed the advance on Baghdad on 21 October. During this meeting it became clear that Kitchener, ignoring Murray's point of view, was prepared to send two Indian divisions to Mesopotamia. At the same time he was opposed to the occupation of Baghdad. The Turks would do everything in their power to recapture that city, and 'the city would be far more difficult to hold than a position at Kut-al-Amara', a town that the Turks were moreover less likely to attack. According to Kitchener, the best thing to do was 'making a raid and taking away everything of military value'. Sir Edward for his part asked the members of the Dardanelles Committee:

> Whether it were worth while to take Baghdad and hold it for four or six months. One point he wished to bring forward, which was a very important one, was that the Arabs seemed to be at the parting of the ways whether to act with the Turks or against them, and that now was the critical moment for us to make an offer to bring in the Arabs with us. He had telegraphed to Sir H. McMahon authorising him to approach the Arabs and offer them an independent Arabia, in the hopes that they might break finally with the Turks [...] He himself thought that the offer of Baghdad might decide them.

In the course of the discussion, Sir Edward reiterated that he attached:

> Great importance to the point of bringing in the Arabs. If we did that we might effect a great coup. The balance of the argument round the table seemed to be against an advance. At present we were practically bankrupt of prestige in the East, and our position could hardly be worse, and it was of great importance to us to regain our prestige, even for four or five months. He personally, therefore, favoured an advance.

The members of the Dardanelles Committee felt unable to settle the question, and decided that Chamberlain, in consultation with Kitchener, Grey and Balfour, should draft a telegram to the viceroy, asking for his advice.[17] Maurice Hankey, secretary to the Dardanelles Committee, noted in his diary:

> Cabinet War Ctee. in morning to consider advance on Bagdad [...] the usual shilly-shallying, no grip, no courage [...] Lunched alone with Sir Edward

Grey […] Urged strongly that we should push on to Bagdad without delay, and on arrival issue a proclamation that we had occupied the city temporarily and for military reasons only, and that we were favourably disposed towards the formation of an Arab Empire independent of Ottoman rule, to which Bagdad may be handed over. Grey agreed and my view found echo in the telegram sent to the viceroy.[18]

Hardinge's reply arrived in London on 23 October. That same day it was discussed at an informal meeting of the four ministers who had drafted the telegram to the viceroy. They decided to authorise Nixon to advance upon Baghdad.[19]

The next day, McMahon dispatched his answer to Husayn. The contents of this letter and Grey's telegram of 20 October led to mutual congratulations between Clayton and Wingate. The Sudan agent confessed that he had been rather unprepared for 'the speed with which H.M.G. acted – or rather allowed action to be taken – at this last moment', but that the high commissioner had come out of it rather well:

Taking the responsibility upon himself of replying to the Sherif without further reference. The F.O. telegram certainly gave him a free hand but, in their usual way, they left several openings for making a scapegoat in the event of necessity, and there is many a man who would have fumbled it.

I expect the way in which you have paved the way with Sir E. Grey has had a lot to do with the ready manner in which they acquiesced.

Clayton also expressed the hope that 'the question will march now. It is just a question whether we are not too late but, if we are in time, I am inclined to think […] that we have struck the exact psychological moment when the effect will be the greatest. It is a near thing.'[20] The sirdar was equally content, 'as you rightly say, it is very much to the High Commissioner's credit that he boldly took the responsibility on himself of replying to the Sherif without further reference', and he returned Clayton's compliment by observing that he had 'no doubt that our combined work of the past year in this Arab question has gone a long way to prepare the ground'.[21]

On 26 October, McMahon sent a telegram to London summarising the contents of his reply to Sharif Husayn:

After reference to his last letter I stated that the districts of Mersina and Alexandretta and portions of Syria west of the districts of Damascus,

Hama, Homs and Aleppo cannot be regarded as purely Arab and should be excluded from the area proposed by him.

I said that we accepted those boundaries (with the above modification and without prejudice to existing arrangements with Arab Chiefs) and as regards the territories therein in which Great Britain is free to act without detriment to the interests of France, I gave the following assurances:

Great Britain will (1) within the above limits recognise and support the independence of Arabs: (2) guarantee the Holy Places against aggression: (3) advise and assist Arabs in the establishment of the most suitable form of government when the proper time comes, it being understood that Arabs desire that advisers and officials should be British.

Arabs on their part will recognise that the position and interests of Great Britain necessitate special measures (?of) administrative control in the Vilayets of Bagdad and Basra.[22]

McMahon dispatched the full text of his letter the same day. In his covering letter he justified his decision to avail himself 'of the authority to act without further reference, accorded to me' by pointing out that 'the matter appeared to me to admit of no delay'. He also explained the purpose of the general proviso regarding French claims. As he had not been aware of 'the extent of French claims in Syria, nor of how far His Majesty's Government has agreed to recognise them',[23] he had decided:

While recognising the towns of Damascus, Hama, Homs and Aleppo as being within the circle of Arab countries [...] to provide for possible French pretensions to those places by a general modification to the effect the His Majesty's Government can only give assurance to those territories 'in which she can act without detriment to the interests of her ally France'.[24]

McMahon believed that he had just as scrupulously dealt with Indian interests. In his covering letter to Hardinge with his letter to the Sharif and his dispatch to the Foreign Office, he observed:

As you will have seen they left the formulation of the terms to the Arab party almost entirely to my discretion, and it had to be done in the shortest possible time, it was a difficult and delicate task. I have endeavoured to safeguard our interests in Mesopotamia and trust I have succeeded.[25]

Four Towns and Two Vilayets

The high commissioner's wording of his promise to Husayn drew no comment from Foreign Office officials, Grey or Kitchener. Clerk merely minuted that he did 'not see that much can be done here until we learn how the Sherif, Faroki, and Abd-el-Aziz regard the assurances contained in Sir H. McMahon's reply', after which he returned to the point that there ought to be 'an early decision as to taking French military opinion into consultation, for it seems to me that we can best tackle the question with France from that side'. Kitchener noted that he had already taken action in that direction. He had asked Etienne Millerand, his French counterpart, 'to send over a competent officer or civilian from Paris to discuss this matter. He promised to do so but no one has yet come probably political position in France has delayed matters.' (The Viviani government was replaced by the Briand government on 30 October.) Sir Edward added in passing that he had 'also urged this matter on M. Cambon some days ago'.[26]

The Foreign Office learned more about Grey's conversation with the French ambassador when the foreign secretary drafted a telegram in reply to a private telegram from Sir Henry in which the high commissioner had voiced his concern about the fact that the French minister at Cairo had apparently got wind 'of recent interchange of messages between Mecca and ourselves on the Arab question'. From Sir Edward's reply, it appeared that he had informed Cambon 'in fairly general terms' of the British point of view that:

> We were in favour of an independent Arab State in order to avoid any possible accusation of bad faith on the part of our French allies and I have suggested that French government should send an expert here to discuss boundaries of a possible Arab State, saying that we could not settle such a project without consulting with French. No mention has been made to French of Grand Sherif of Mecca. I have spoken generally of giving assurances to Arabs.

Possible French interference clearly worried McMahon. Even before Grey's reply could have arrived, he sent yet another telegram, explaining that he had 'no high opinion of either his [i.e. Albert Defrance, the French minister at Cairo; R.H.L.] ability or discretion and would not willingly recommend taking him into our full confidence regarding Arab question'. McMahon suggested that 'Paris might give him a hint to restrain dual activities in this matter'. Sir Edward adopted this suggestion in a telegram to Lord Bertie, the British ambassador in Paris, which was repeated to the High Commissioner:

> I hear French representative at Cairo is in communication with Arabs. You should ask French government [...] to discourage any activity of French representative at Cairo in this very delicate matter. Great harm may be done and Arabs thrown entirely into hands of Turks by any precipitate action and on no account should any mention be made of the Khalifate as the whole Mahommedan World would resent any initiative or interference of a non-Mussulman Power in this matter.[27]

McMahon replied three days later that 'in conversation with French Minister today, I referred to Arab question on lines indicated in your telegrams and I think with desired effect. Incidentally, I alluded to importance attached by Arabs to Aleppo, Hama, Homs and Damascus.'[28]

That the Arabs attached great value to the possession of these four towns was also emphasised in a memorandum that Captain Aubrey Herbert, MP, had written after conversations with Clayton,[29] and subsequently forwarded to Grey. Herbert had been wounded at Gallipoli, and thereafter transferred to Cairo. When he had arrived in that city:

> About ten days ago, the Arab question had reached a crisis. I saw the General [presumably Sir John Maxwell; R.H.L.], Clayton, Cheatham, and the High Commissioner. They all agreed that it was of almost supreme importance to get the Arabs in with us, that the opportunity would be lost if this was not done soon, and that while the Arabs would accept modifications in the frontiers which they were asking, Homs, Hama, Damascus and Aleppo were essential to them. If this estimate of the situation is correct, it is vital to reconcile the French to making the large concessions involved.

Herbert admitted that the obstacles to be overcome before the French would be prepared to make these concessions were quite formidable, as it implied 'a bitter disappointment to French aspirations', but this was 'not a time when dreams can outweigh strategy. It is after all the partial sacrifice of territory which is not yet hers, that is asked of France.'[30] Such strong language appealed to Grey. On 4 November, he wrote to Kitchener that:

> Aubrey Herbert who has just come back from Egypt says that all that is necessary to get the Arabs is to promise definitely the four towns of Damascus, Aleppo, Homs and Hama.

As we are risking our Eastern empire to help the French in a Balkan expedition [a combined Anglo–French force had landed at Salonika at the beginning of November; R.H.L.] against our better judgement I think the French ought to agree to this. If you are seeing the French expert will you concentrate on this point and I will do the same with Cambon.[31]

In his last sentence, Grey referred to Kitchener's coming visit to Paris, on his way to Gallipoli. The offensive during the months of August and September had not resulted in a breakthrough, and with the approaching winter disaster threatened the forces on the peninsula. On 14 October, it had been decided to replace Hamilton by Sir Charles Monro. The latter had arrived at Moudhros, the British headquarters on the island of Lemnos, on 27 October, and had telegraphed to London four days later that withdrawal was inevitable. Kitchener was completely opposed to this, and ministers finally decided that he personally should go to Gallipoli to study the desirability of an evacuation on the spot.

Kitchener left for Paris on the evening of 4 November. The next day he had an interview with the new French prime minister, Aristide Briand, and minister of war Joseph Gallieni. The Arab question was also discussed. According to Kitchener the position of the French government was one of moderation. His interlocutors 'quite agreed in pushing it on but had no troops to help it forward. They spoke of maintaining French sentimental rights in Syria but not with any view of stopping an Arab movement there.'[32]

With respect to his side of the negotiations, Grey sent a telegram to McMahon in which he informed the latter that 'a French expert is expected here next week to discuss possible boundaries of an independent Arab State'.[33] Grey proposed during these negotiations 'to concentrate on getting French consent to inclusion of Damascus, Hama, Homs and Aleppo in Arab boundaries'. In that case, however, Great Britain ought to be prepared 'to sacrifice provision that Arabs are to seek the advice and guidance of Great Britain only and that all European advisers and officials are to be British'. He therefore wanted to know whether this clause had been inserted 'to secure our interests or to please the Arabs?' for it was not 'our primary and vital object […] to secure a new sphere of British influence, but to get Arabs on our side against Turks'.[34]

In his reply, McMahon emphasised anew that 'Arabs attach very great importance to inclusion of Damascus, Hama, Homs and Aleppo in Arab boundaries'. With respect to the provision that 'Arabs are to seek guidance of Great Britain only', Sir Henry pointed out that it had been inserted 'at express request of Arabs', but that it applied:

> To those portions only of Arab territory wherein Great Britain is free to act without detriment to the interests of her ally, France.
>
> I regard the provision as very important to safeguard, not only our own present interests especially in Mesopotamia, but to prevent Arabia becoming a future source of trouble and danger.
>
> There is nothing in my assurance to prevent some similar understanding between France and the Arabs regarding the hinterland of Syria, i.e. Aleppo, etc., but for the future peace of Arabia if it is not possible to avoid such hinterland altogether, it would be wise to restrict it to the smallest limits possible.

McMahon's telegram made Oliphant comment that he feared that the latter was 'unjustifiably optimistic as regards the future peace of Arabia in any circumstances [...] there will inevitably be disorder, trouble and danger'. But, according to Grey, he missed the whole point. The only thing that mattered was that 'we want [...] Arab help now against the Turks'.[35]

Both the India Office and the Government of India took strong exception to the contents of McMahon's second letter to Sharif Husayn. On 27 October, the day after the receipt of Sir Henry's telegram summarising this letter, Chamberlain had an interview with Grey, in the course of which he strongly protested against the manner in which McMahon had thought fit to handle India's interests. Grey had not been sympathetic. Chamberlain informed Hirtzel and Holderness that 'the best comfort he could give me was that the whole thing was a castle in the air which would never materialise'.[36]

On 4 November, the viceroy sent a telegram to the India Office and the high commissioner in which he complained that McMahon had exercised the discretion left to him 'without due regard to Indian interests, by the inclusion of provinces of Baghdad and Bussorah in the proposed independent Arab state, only "special measure of advanced administrative control" in these two vilayetis being reserved to H.M. Govt. or the Govt. of India'. He continued that:

> We have always contemplated as a minimum eventual annexation of Bussorah vilayat and some form of native administration in Baghdad vilayat under our close political control. McMahon guarantees apparently putting

annexation out of the question. By surrendering Bussorah vilayat to Arab Govt. of any kind, we shall not only be preparing trouble for ourselves at the head, and along southern littoral of the Gulf, but shall be giving up main fruits of hard won victories in Mesopotamia [...] We sincerely trust that formula may be amended so as to admit of H.M. Govt. having free hand in eventual disposal of Bussorah and Baghdad vilayats, which have been won at such a cost.[37]

The high commissioner's defence arrived in London the following day. He explained that 'in framing reply to the Sherif I kept special interests of India fully in mind'. Indeed, the formula he had chosen:

Was intended to give us everything short of definite and open annexation i.e. a free hand regarding military measures, internal administration as well as developments and commercial and industrial enterprise.

Read in conjunction with preceding clause ['Arabs are to seek guidance of Great Britain only': R.H.L.] it practically amounts to our monopoly of all administration and control in those Vilayets and was interpreted in that sense by Arab representatives here.

Grey minuted on McMahon's telegram that Chamberlain had again spoken to him on this subject, and that the latter would 'draft a telegram, to which I should perhaps add something, to be sent to Sir H. McMahon'.[38] Chamberlain's draft took the form of a memorandum. He naturally criticised Sir Henry's promises, but above all took exception to the idea that Great Britain was negotiating these matters with people like the Emir of Mecca and Faruqi:

I cannot decide here what weight attaches to information as to Arab feeling collected in Egypt but my information is that Grand Shereef is a nonentity without power to carry out his proposals, that Arabs are without unity and with no possibility of uniting and I disbelieve in reality and efficacy of suggested Arab revolt in Army and elsewhere.

Seen in this light, it was highly necessary that it was made clear to Sharif Husayn and Faruqi that 'promises made by McMahon are dependent on immediate action by them in sense of their offers and will not be binding on us unless they do their part at once'.

Nicolson believed that Chamberlain's depiction of the situation represented 'the true state of the case', but he did not see how the Foreign Office could have acted otherwise than to respond 'in friendly terms to the Shereef's requests'. Perhaps McMahon had gone further than was desirable, but then again, 'so long as nothing is published or proclaimed, I doubt if much harm will have been done'. Grey decided to telegraph the text of Chamberlain's memorandum to Cairo in full. He made it clear in his observations at the end of the telegram that he accepted the secretary of state for India's additional condition that 'in the next communication made to them we should state that they should act at once', and that he shared Chamberlain's doubts 'as to chances of securing this movement'. He nevertheless insisted that 'an effective Arab Movement against Turks, would be worth the future inconvenience as regards Bagdad', but this did not prevent Chamberlain from concurring in the text of the telegram before it was sent off.[39]

In a letter to Hardinge, the secretary of state for India showed himself to be rather pleased with the invention of the additional clause:

> You will, I think, approve my memorandum and feel that I was right to make an effort to bring to immediate proof the ability and willingness of the Grand Sherif and Faruji to carry out their promises and to press that it should be made clear that, unless they acted at once on the lines contemplated, we should not be bound by McMahon's offer.[40]

Chamberlain, however, had scarcely expressed his satisfaction with the turn events had taken, when he set eyes on a dispatch from Grey to Bertie, in which Sir Edward reported a conversation with the French ambassador on the Arab question. Grey had informed Cambon that Great Britain attached great importance to effecting a separation between the Arabs and the Turks, and that Great Britain and France therefore should be prepared to sacrifice existing or future interests in the Middle East, but had failed to mention Chamberlain's proviso.[41] Chamberlain accordingly felt obliged to write a second memorandum:

> I am afraid that this conversation leaves some ambiguity in our position.
>
> I have already said that I regret the offer made by Sir H. McMahon, but this offer was not merely conditional on 'a separation' between the Arabs and the Turks but on the <u>immediate active cooperation</u> of the Arabs with us against the Turks.

I venture to urge that it is of the first importance that this should be made clear to the French as well as to the Arabs, and that Monsieur Cambon should be told that it is only on this condition that McMahon's offer is binding on us or that we seek the assent of the French government to the proposal regarding Syria.

Grey however did not oblige. He merely minuted 'let me have this when Cambon comes in Monday' and left it at that.[42] Chamberlain did not return to the subject.

Clerk had observed with regard to McMahon's telegram of 5 November that 'we can see if this mollifies the Government of India',[43] but from the viceroy's telegram of 11 November it appeared that the opposite was true:

We find nothing in McMahon's telegram of 5th November to palliate in any way position he has brought about, and fact remains that although he could apparently, without imperilling the negotiations, safeguard other interests at Alexandretta, Mersina and Syria, he yet found it necessary to guarantee to Arabs the rendition of territories in Mesopotamia won by our arms in face not only of Turkish but also of Arab opposition, without which Turks alone would have been of small account [...] The possession of Basra is in our opinion essential for the protection of Abadan and the security of our interests in oil-fields. We are still in dark as to actual *quid pro quo* to be given by Arabs in return for those sweeping assurances, but trust it may be of sufficiently definite character to enable us, if Arabs fail to perform their part, to repudiate those assurances – at any rate as far as Mesopotamia is concerned.

The viceroy's angry reaction nevertheless caused little consternation in the Foreign Office. Clerk merely observed that 'this can be considered at tomorrow's conference'.[44] He referred to a meeting of an interdepartmental committee to discuss the British position in the negotiations with France on the future Arab state, in preparation for the coming visit of the French representative François Georges-Picot. Nicolson had suggested to Grey that the India Office and the War Office should take part in these preparations. Grey had agreed, provided 'the discussion should be kept if possible to the four towns Damascus, Homs, Hama and Aleppo. That is what we want the government [of] France to concede.'[45]

From Clerk's minutes it appeared that the interdepartmental meeting had resulted in a compromise between the Foreign Office and the India Office. On the one hand, Georges-Picot should be informed of 'the negotiations with the Sherif of Mecca and the disposition of the Arabs in the Turkish army, as stated by El Farughi', and 'the danger of the present situation' made clear to him, but, on the other hand, also that 'all promises to the Arabs depended on the Arabs at once giving serious proof of their break from Turkey'. Finally, the French government 'should be asked to resign their immediate hopes of Damascus, just as we were ready to give back Basra etc., if the Arabs came in'.

Clerk's minutes prompted Grey to write down once again what ought to have the highest priority in these negotiations:

> Make it clear that we have told the Arabs we cannot make promises about Syria irrespective of our Allies: that we have no intention of standing in the way of the French there or pushing claims of our own: that the sole origin is to detach the Arabs from Turks and unless this is done Egypt or Soudan may be endangered and the trouble will extend to the whole of North Africa.[46]

That the whole scheme depended upon the Arabs' capacity to act at once, as the India Office had stipulated and the interdepartmental meeting had agreed to, the foreign secretary again failed to mention.

Alexandretta Once Again

The Foreign Office telegram containing Chamberlain's memorandum on the negotiations with Sharif Husayn arrived in Cairo just after McMahon and Maxwell had left for Moudhros to discuss with Kitchener the possible consequences of an evacuation of Gallipoli. The contents of the telegram took Clayton by surprise, so he wrote to Wingate on the evening of 12 November. The Sudan agent had rather 'hoped from the viceroy's letter to you that they would have assumed a more favourable attitude'.[47] He telegraphed Chamberlain's memorandum to Wingate the next day. Its contents made the sirdar quite angry. With respect to the proviso, he wrote in the margin of the telegram with big letters 'Rot',[48] and in a letter to Clayton he gave vent to his indignation:

I am lost in wonderment at the attitude of the Home Authorities who would hold a pistol at the wretched Sherif's head unless he rises instantly in revolt – how can he rise when he is neither prepared as to money, arms, ammunition and other necessaries which go to make a revolt successful? I hope most devoutly this altogether unfair attitude will be abandoned once and for all and that a benevolent acquiescence in the Sherif's requests will be shown. After all what harm can our acceptance of his proposals do? [...] If the Arab State becomes a reality, we have quite sufficient safeguards to control it [...] In other words the cards seem to be in our hands and we have only to play them carefully, but to throw down our hands in disgust – such as holding a pistol at the Sherif's head means – would be, to my mind, the height of folly and I earnestly hope it may not be entertained for a moment.[49]

As appeared from his reply to McMahon's letter of 24 October, Husayn was also averse to 'speedy action', because 'premature action might give rise among Moslems who do not as yet appreciate the realities of the situation, to the criticism that, by proclaiming a revolt, we are seeking the disruption of Islam'.[50] Storrs and Clayton nevertheless concluded that the Emir of Mecca proclaimed that, provided four conditions were met, the Arabs 'will come in at once'. They were doubtless encouraged to do so by the statement by Husayn's messenger that Abdullah in conversation had impressed upon him 'the readiness and intentions of the Arabs to begin "work" at once', and 'the point that the restrictions contained in his written reply should not be taken too seriously'.[51] Their summary of Husayn's letter, which Clayton wired to Maxwell that same evening, and McMahon forwarded to the Foreign Office on 14 November, ran as follows:

Letter is long and requires careful translation to ascertain full meaning but main points are as follows:–

First he agrees to exclusion of Mersina and Minisandria [sic? Alexandretta].

Secondly he maintains that vilayets of Beirut and Aleppo are both Arab and should be under Arab Mohammedan government.

Thirdly he maintains that Mesopotamia is also Arab but as Great Britain has special interests there, it may be left out of discussion for the present.

Meanwhile he asks for subsidy for what he terms 'the Arab Kingdom'.

Fourthly he expresses fear lest European peace should leave Arabs at the mercy of Turks and wishes Great Britain to bind herself not to abandon Arabs.

On these four conditions they will come in at once.

Clerk's reaction was that 'we must now get to grips with the French, and meanwhile ask the Sherif what is "the Arab Kingdom", what subsidy he wants, and what active steps he proposes to take'. He drafted a telegram to McMahon in this sense. The telegram was, however, held up.[52] A subsequent telegram from Cairo, which McMahon forwarded on 16 November, did mention Husayn's objections against immediate action. The high commissioner also explained more fully Husayn's proposal respecting the settlement of the Mesopotamian question. The Emir was prepared 'to leave under British Administration for a short time those districts now occupied by British troops against a suitable sum paid as compensation to Arab Kingdom for period of occupation'. This made Oliphant observe that 'for sheer insolence it would be difficult to find any passage to equal' it. Nicolson for his part drew the conclusion that Husayn 'like others, will sit on the fence for a time – and if they think that (events are) not moving in our favour, they will come down on the other side'. Crewe, who deputised for Grey, regarded this prospect 'not at all hopeful [...] for the proposals are absurd'. Eventually a telegram was sent to McMahon in which he was simply informed that the Foreign Office awaited his views on the latest proposals of the Emir of Mecca. Clerk's three questions were left out, because, so Nicolson minuted, they could give McMahon the impression that 'we are quite ready to entertain the Sherif's demands and accepted his uncertain attitude'.[53]

Crewe acted as deputy for Grey because the latter was in Paris, together with, among others, Asquith, Lloyd George and Balfour for a conference with the French to discuss the Alexandretta project, which had been reanimated by Kitchener. One of the reasons why the latter had been opposed to a withdrawal from Gallipoli had been that this would 'also block effectively the Arab movement that we are doing all in our power to develop'.[54] An inspection of the position on the Gallipoli Peninsula had, however, convinced him that an evacuation was unavoidable, and he had proposed a landing at Alexandretta as a countermeasure. This proposal had been discussed at a meeting of the War Committee on 13 November. During this meeting, Murray had reported that the French military attaché had visited him that morning, and that he had left a note on the subject in which it was observed that:

> French public opinion could not be indifferent to anything that would be attempted in a country that they consider already as being intended to become a part of the future Syria, and they would require of the French government that, not only no military operation in this particular country could be undertaken before it has been concerted between the Allies, but even that, in the case of such an action being taken, the greater part of the task would be entrusted to the French troops and the Generals commanding them.[55]

The War Committee had decided that French anxiety on this score had to be removed, and it had approved a telegram drafted by Grey,[56] which had been sent to Bertie that same day:

> You should inform French government that we have come to no decision that operations in Syria or even the Eastern Shore of Asia Minor would be desirable, though they have been discussed in connection with projects for defence of Egypt.
>
> If we do come to a decision that military operations in that region are desirable we shall at once consult with the French.
>
> I am well aware of French feeling about Syria and we have no intention of disregarding it.[57]

On the evening of 13 November, a further telegram from Kitchener had arrived, in which he had once again urged a landing at Alexandretta, as otherwise 'the effect in the East of [...] a possible evacuation of our position in Gallipoli [...] will be enormous and will have far-reaching result by throwing the Arabs into German hands and thereby uniting them against us'.[58] Two days later, he had stressed that 'if another position in the neighbourhood of Alexandretta were occupied, where Turkish movements eastwards would be effectively stopped, the realisation of the German objective against Egypt and the East would be prevented'.[59] These arguments counted for little at the Anglo–French conference, however. The Alexandretta project was 'dismissed almost in a word'.[60] Kitchener had to resign himself to the inevitable, but not before pointing out that this implied 'the failure of any attempt to detach Arabs from Turks'.[61]

In London, Lieut.-Colonel Alfred Parker, who had recently arrived from Egypt and been nominated one of the two War Office representatives in the British delegation to negotiate with Georges-Picot, was one of the advocates of the Alexandretta scheme. Parker explained in a letter to Clayton that he had discussed the matter with Sir Charles Callwell, the director of military operations (DMO), and had pointed out that:

> Our interests entirely outweighed the French, not necessarily as regards the purely local question at Alexandretta, Aleppo, etc., but as a spot that was essential to us to
> (1) Block Turkish-German reinforcements to Baghdad.
> (2) To block ditto towards Egypt.
> (3) To probably bring in all the Arabs with us.
> He agreed, but said 'We have got to keep in with our infernal Allies'.[62]

On 21 November, Parker produced a note that was circulated to the members of the interdepartmental committee. He dissociated himself from 'a feeling in London that the Arab movement is unreal, shadowy, and vague; and that it cannot, on account of its incoherence, be of any value to us'. He claimed that 'the reality and possible force of the movement is not doubted by any person of experience in the near east'. Everything, however, hinged on the point that 'all await some move on our part to convince them of our sincerity and to give them protection whilst they organise'. This could be accomplished most advantageously 'by one single operation: the seizing of Alexandretta and Aleppo'.[63]

Kitchener's and Parker's arguments did not lead to a landing at Alexandretta, but they did manage to leave Grey and his officials with the impression that negotiations with the Arabs were pointless, unless the Entente Powers intervened by force of arms. Clerk minuted on 20 November that 'the whole thing hinges on a decision to give active support at Alexandretta',[64] while a few days later he observed that 'all Arab discussion is futile unless we (and the French) are prepared to give armed support in force'.[65] Grey concurred. He minuted on a telegram from McMahon that 'nothing will move the Arabs in our favour except military action giving them protection against the Turks. Unless we can effect this, negotiations and promises will be useless and embarrassing'.[66]

One of Clayton's 'golden opportunities' again seemed to slip away. Not because the Foreign Office did not realise how important it was to bring the

Arabs over to the side of the Entente – thanks to the incessant lobbying by Wingate, Clayton, Storrs, Maxwell, McMahon and Kitchener, it had become thoroughly aware of that – not because the India Office and the Government of India had been successful in obstructing initiatives in this direction, but because Kitchener and the authorities in Cairo and Khartoum once again faced a far more formidable obstacle: the Foreign Office's refusal even to think of a Middle East policy not based on a sympathetic attitude towards French ambitions in Syria.

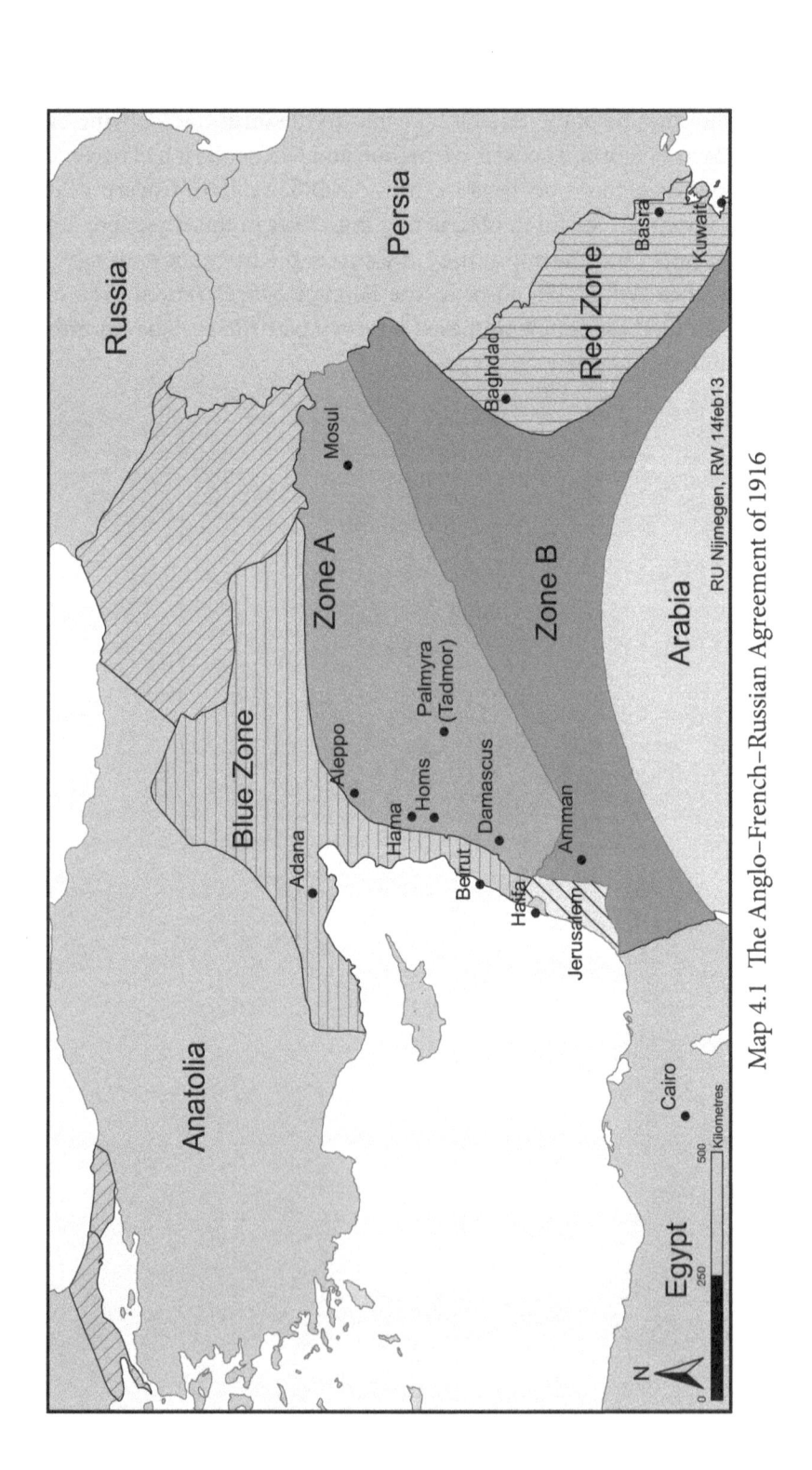

Map 4.1 The Anglo–French–Russian Agreement of 1916

4 THE WHOLE SUBJECT IS BECOMING ENTANGLED

Introduction

This chapter mainly deals with the negotiations between the British and the French, and subsequently the British, the French and the Russians, to settle their claims on the Asiatic part of the Ottoman Empire. The Foreign Office started these negotiations because it considered that they had to be brought to a successful conclusion before the Emir of Mecca could again be approached regarding the terms under which the Arabs would be prepared to side with the Entente. A settlement should also secure French consent to a military intervention on the coast of Syria, providing a screen behind which the Arabs would rise against the Turks. During the negotiations, which started at the end of November 1915 and finally came to an end in the middle of May 1916, Sir Edward Grey and his officials again and again stipulated that an agreement only held good if the active cooperation of the Arabs was secured. At the same time they were well aware that, after the British and French governments had decided at the end of December 1915 to concentrate their forces on the Western front and that the amount of troops on the other fronts should be reduced to the barest minimum, a military intervention on the Syrian coast was out of the question and Arab active assistance consequently would never materialise. This had at least the advantage that critics of the negotiations could easily be disarmed by pointing out that nothing would ever come of all this. Not three weeks after an exchange of letters between Grey and French ambassador Paul Cambon had finalised what would become known as the

Sykes–Picot agreement, Sharif Husayn started his revolt against his Turkish masters. That the Emir revolted without waiting for a fresh round of negotiations or a military intervention by the Entente drew no comments from Grey and his officials.

A second topic in this chapter concerns the attempts by the Cairo authorities to impress on the Foreign Office that the object of the negotiations with Husayn was not to gain the Arabs' active assistance, but rather their passive support in order to prevent a jihad. They also tried to make clear to the home authorities that Arab opposition to French ambitions in Syria was real and could not be ignored, that there were divisions in the Arab nationalist camp, and that as a result of a rapprochement between the Turkish opposition parties and the Arab nationalists, it was inopportune to divulge the terms of the Sykes–Picot agreement to Husayn. The main result of these efforts to educate Grey and his officials on the true state of Arab feeling was that the latter grew heartily tired of the whole affair.

Georges-Picot's Opening Bid and McMahon's Third Letter

The first meeting of the British interdepartmental committee headed by Sir Arthur Nicolson with François Georges-Picot took place on 23 November 1915. The French representative was not convinced of the importance of inducing the Emir of Mecca and the Arab nationalists to side with the Entente. Austen Chamberlain reported to Lord Hardinge that Picot had 'expressed complete incredulity as to the projected Arab kingdom, said that the Sheikh had no big Arab chiefs with him, that the Arabs were incapable of combining, and that the whole scheme was visionary'. The secretary of state for India was very pleased. It seemed that the French delegate 'knows his Arab well. I expect he has sized up the Sheikh's scheme pretty accurately. I doubt if it has any element of solidity or that any promise will have weight with the Arabs until they are absolutely convinced that we are winning.'[1]

Moreover, French demands – which according to Picot the French were obliged to make as 'no French government would stand for a day which made any surrender of French claims in Syria' – were rather excessive. Picot informed the Nicolson committee that France claimed the:

> Possession (nominally, a protectorate) of land starting from where the Taurus Mts approach the sea in Cilicia, following the Taurus Mountains and

the mountains further East, so as to include Diabekr, Mosul and Kerbela, and then returning to Deir Zor on the Euphrates and from there southwards along the desert border, finishing eventually at the Egyptian frontier.

Picot, however, added that he was prepared 'to propose to the French government to throw Mosul into the Arab pool, if we did so in the case of Bagdad'. In amplification, Nicolson minuted that Picot had:

> Intimated his readiness to proceed to Paris to explain personally our view – and the Arab desiderata. M. Cambon told me that he had objected to this visit, on the ground that he would not be well received at the Quai d'Orsay were he to carry with him such unpalatable proposals as he had suggested. M. Picot would, therefore, communicate with Quai d'Orsay in writing. We must, therefore, await the reply.[2]

The French reply had not yet been received when a telegram from Sir Henry McMahon arrived on 30 November. In this telegram the high commissioner gave his considered opinion on Husayn's letter of 5 November, and at the same time took the opportunity to defend himself against Chamberlain's charges. He observed that the Emir's letter was:

> Satisfactory as showing a desire for mutual understanding on reasonable lines. It also affords an opportunity of meeting the wishes of the Government of India with regard to Mesopotamia by some change of formula, but I cannot personally think of any formula on that subject more favourable to Indian interests than the one employed in my former letter, without raising Arab suspicions.
> With regard to nonentity of Shereef [...] Everything would tend to prove that he is of sufficient commanding importance, by position descent and personality, to be the only possible central rallying point for Arab cause, and sufficiently anti-Turkish to be in great personal danger at Turkish hands.

McMahon did not fail to point out that his negotiations with Husayn were in a quandary thanks to the policy 'of awaiting in Egypt the threatened Turco–German advance'. It jeopardised 'any attempt to secure Arab cooperation', and made it 'appear unwise urging Arabs into premature activity which through want of our support and fear of Turkish retaliation might hasten their abandonment of our cause'. At the same time it rendered 'alienation of Arab assistance from Turks a matter of great importance, and we must make every effort to enlist the sympathy and assistance, even though passive, of Arab people'. In view of this difficult situation, McMahon proposed to reply to Husayn along the following lines:

1. Acknowledge his exclusion of Adana and Mersina from Arab sphere. [...]
2. Agree that with the exception of tract around Marash and Aintab, vilayets of Beirut Aleppo are inhabited by Arabs but in these vilayets as elsewhere in Syria our ally France has considerable interests, to safeguard with some special arrangements will be necessary and as this is a matter for the French government we cannot say more now than assure the Shereef of our earnest wish that satisfactory settlement may be arrived at.
3. With regard to the vilayets of Basra and Baghdad some such arrangement as he suggests would provide suitable solution, i.e. that these vilayets which have been taken by us from the Turks by force of arms should remain under British administration until such time as a satisfactory mutual arrangement can be made.
4. Assurance of the Shereef that Great Britain has no intention to conclude peace in terms of which freedom of Arabs from Turkish domination does not form essential condition. (On some assurance of this nature sole hope of successful understanding depends).
5. Appreciation of Shereef's desire for caution and disclaim wish to urge him to hasty action jeopardising Arab projects but in the meantime he must spare no effort to attach Arab peoples to our cause and prevent them assisting the enemy, as it is of the success of these efforts and on active measures which the Arabs may hereafter take in our cause when the time comes that permanency of present arrangement must depend.

McMahon concluded by expressing the hope that the Foreign Office would be able to reply 'without undue delay', but, as George Clerk minuted, the Foreign Office could not answer until they had received 'the views of the Government of India [...] an Alexandretta expedition has been finally decided, one way or the other, [and] having prepared a reply [...] get the concurrence of the French government'. It was 'therefore of little use discussing Sir H. McMahon's views now'.

The India Office reacted first. Sir Arthur Hirtzel observed that the India Office:

Agree with Sir H. McMahon that for the success of these negotiations some display of force is necessary to which the Arabs can rally.

Whether such is possible, and, if so, where and how, are questions for the British and French governments and their military advisers.

If it is <u>not</u> possible, we doubt whether there is any real use in pursuing these negotiations. But if it is considered expedient for the sake of appearances to do so, they should be as vague as possible regarding future commitments.

Apart from a few minor modifications, Hirtzel approved the proposed reply, even the suggestion to 'disclaim wish to urge him to hasty action'. The India Office also qualified Chamberlain's earlier proviso that McMahon's promises only held good if the Arabs acted at once (see Chapter 3, section 'Four Towns and Two Vilayets'). This no longer applied in case 'there is to be <u>no</u> display of force. But, if there is, Arab assistance must be immediate and universal.'[3]

A French reply was not forthcoming. On 10 December, Nicolson decided to wait no longer. If the Foreign Office kept on waiting:

We shall lose much valuable time – and it is essential to send a reply to the Shereef as soon as possible. In regard to Syria, McMahon can say that as the interests of others are involved he must consider the point carefully. I think a further communication […] will be sent later – he can then proceed to reply on all the other points. Would you draw a telegram embodying I.O.'s views and the viceroy's wishes – and we should get I.O. concurrence and Lord Crewe's the sooner we can get of this telegram the better.

After it had been approved by Chamberlain and Crewe, a telegram was sent to Cairo the same day:

Importance of display of British or Allied force round which Arabs can rally is fully recognised here, but you will realise that present situation at Gallipoli and Salonica makes it out of the question for the moment to embark on any other expedition.

Attitude of French government in regard to Syria is also very difficult and we have little hope of obtaining from them any assurance that will really satisfy Arabs.

On the other hand, we must try to keep the negotiations with the Sherif in being, and you are authorised to reply to him as follows: -

Points 1 and 2, as you propose.

As regards point 3, you should say that as the interests of others are involved, the point requires careful consideration by His Majesty's Government and a further communication in regard to it will be sent later.

Point 4. We should prefer to say that His Majesty's Government are, as the Sherif knows, disposed to give a guarantee to assist and protect the proposed Arab Kingdom as far as may be within their power, but their interests demand, as the Sherif has recognised, a friendly administration in the Vilayet of Bagdad and the safeguarding of these interests call for much fuller and more detailed consideration of the future of Mesopotamia than the present situation and the urgency of the negotiations permit.

Point 5. The first [...] assurance you propose.

Point 6 [...] As you suggest.[4]

In anticipation of the Foreign Office telegram, McMahon wrote a private letter to Hardinge on 4 December in which he tried to justify his actions with regard to the negotiations with Husayn. He claimed that the viceroy took 'the idea of a future strong united independent Arab State [...] too seriously', as 'the conditions of Arabia do not and will not for a very long time to come, lend themselves to such a thing'. Sir Henry moreover did 'not for one moment go to the length of imagining that the present negotiations will go far to shape the future form of Arabia or to either establish our rights or to bind our hands in that country. The situation and its elements are much too nebulous for that.' His only objective had been 'to tempt the Arab people into the right path, detach them from the enemy and bring them on our side'. As far as Britain was concerned, this was 'at present largely a matter of words and to succeed we must use persuasive terms and abstain from academic haggling over conditions – whether about Baghdad or elsewhere'.[5]

McMahon also sought the support of the sirdar. Wingate was honoured with a letter for the first time. McMahon excused his negligence in answering Wingate's letters by explaining that he was 'a poor correspondent at the best of times', and that a correspondence also was not really necessary as Clayton kept them both fully informed of each other's ideas and views. After this apology, he proceeded to complain about 'the curious and, to me, mistaken attitude which India is taking in the matter', as well as 'the unreasonable and uncompromising attitude of France in regard not only to Syria but an indefinitely large hinterland in which she will not recognise Arab interests'. Indian and French opposition, combined with Britain's 'failure to hold out a hand to the Arabs by putting a force into Cilicia', made it likely that Britain would 'lose all chance of Arab cooperation and sympathy and drive them into the enemies hands against us'.[6]

McMahon was familiar with the French position because Alfred Parker had forwarded a report on Picot's meeting with the Nicolson committee to Clayton. The latter had circulated this report, with a covering note, to Maxwell, McMahon and Wingate. In this note, Clayton observed that the result of the meeting was 'only what might have been expected with M. Picot as the representative of the French government', considering that Picot was 'well known as being extreme in his ideas, and completely saturated with the vision of a great French possession in the Eastern Mediterranean'. Clayton took the opportunity to emphasise why he was in favour of negotiations with the Arabs. These were important, not because they might result in the Arabs actively supporting the Entente in the war against the Ottoman Empire – which after the dismissal of the Alexandretta scheme was out of the question anyway – but because they might prevent the Arabs from joining the Turks and Germans. If the latter happened, then the call for the jihad would become effective. The great gain resulting from a successful conclusion of these negotiations was that Britain secured the passive support of the Arabs:

> In considering the Arab movement, too much attention has been given to its possible offensive value, and it has to some extent been forgotten that the chief advantage to be gained is a defensive one, in that we should secure on their part a hostile attitude towards the Turks, even though it might be only passively hostile, and rob our enemies of the incalculable moral and material assistance which they would gain were they to succeed in uniting against the Allies the Arab races and, through them, Islam.[7]

McMahon incorporated Clayton's note into a telegram on the Arab question that was sent to London three days later. He informed Grey that 'selection of Picot as their representative on recent committee on this question is discouraging indication of French attitude'. The French delegate was 'a notorious fanatic on Syrian question and quite incapable of assisting any mutual settlement on reasonable common sense grounds which present situation requires'. As far as the negotiations with the Arabs were concerned, 'conditions of Arabia never justified expectation of active or organised assistance such as some people think is object of our proposed mutual understanding. What we want is material advantage of even passive Arab sympathy and assistance on our side instead of their active cooperation with enemy.'

Clerk quite agreed with McMahon's opinion of Picot. The latter had 'been particularly chosen, for his very fanaticism'. All in all, things could no longer go on in this fashion:

> The question is so serious that I think it must be treated between government and government, and no longer between M. Picot and this department. This is a matter for consideration by the War Committee and I would venture to urge that that body should hear the views of Sir Mark Sykes, who is not only highly qualified to speak from the point of view of our interests, but who understands the French position in Syria today – and in a sense sympathises with it – better probably than anyone.

Nicolson and Crewe concurred in this suggestion. Two days later, Prime Minister Asquith informed the Foreign Office that 'Sir M. Sykes might be invited the next meeting of the War Committee. The India Office shall also be represented.'[8]

Enter Sir Mark Sykes

Wingate and Clayton regarded Lieut.-Colonel Sir Mark Sykes, Bart., MP as their champion in the London battle for an active, pro-Arab policy. On 9 December, Wingate wrote to Sir John Maxwell that Sykes, 'should be a powerful ally in regard to Arab policy', while the next day, in a letter to Clayton, he expressed the hope that 'Mark Sykes's arrival in London on the 8th will mean that a definite Near Eastern Policy will be adopted without more hovering'. The Sudan agent for his part believed that now 'Lord K. is at home again and also Sykes [...] things may have gone better recently'.[9]

Sir Mark's involvement with the Middle East dated from 1890, when he, at eleven years old, had accompanied his father on a journey through Palestine, Syria and Lebanon. This was the first of five prolonged travels in which he ranged the Fertile Crescent. Inspired by his travels, Sykes had written two books – *Through Five Turkish Provinces* and *Dar-ul-Islam* – which had established his reputation as an expert on the Middle East, even though his knowledge of Arabic was limited seeing that he could neither read nor write the language. At the end of 1904, Sykes had been appointed honorary attaché at the Constantinople embassy. He had occupied this post up to the end of 1906. Most of his stay had been taken up with another bout of travelling through the Middle East, but he had also developed intimate relations with Gerald Fitzmaurice, the chief dragoman, Aubrey Herbert, George Lloyd and Lancelot Oliphant.[10]

It had been Oliphant who had introduced Sykes to Oswald Fitzgerald, early in September 1914. On that occasion, Sir Mark had offered his services.[11] This offer had not been accepted straight away, and for the time being he had been forced to stay with his territorial battalion at Newcastle. In a letter to his wife Edith, Sykes had given voice to his disappointment 'not to be where I could be most useful, i.e., in the Mediterranean. Is it not ridiculous the haphazard way we do things!'[12] However, Sykes had finally been ordered to come to London in March 1915, and was 'appointed at the personal request of Lord Kitchener as a member of the Committee formed to ascertain British desiderata in Asiatic Turkey'.[13]

Besides Sykes, this committee consisted of representatives from the Foreign Office, the India Office, the Admiralty and the Board of Trade. It was chaired by Sir Maurice De Bunsen, until the outbreak of war, British ambassador at Vienna. During 13 meetings, from 12 April to 28 May 1915, the commission busied itself with determining British desiderata with respect to the future of the Asiatic part of the Ottoman Empire. These deliberations resulted in a voluminous report, which was presented to the Cabinet on 30 June.

In its 'preliminary considerations' the committee stated that 'our Empire is wide enough already, and our task is to consolidate the possessions we already have, to make firm and lasting the position we already hold, and to pass on to those who come after an inheritance that stands four-square to the world'. Against this background, the committee opted for a scheme in which, 'subject to certain necessary territorial exceptions' – Basra, Smyrna and the Asiatic part of Constantinople would have to be ceded, respectively, to Britain, Greece and Russia – the independence of the Ottoman Empire was maintained, 'but the form of government to be modified by decentralisation on federal lines', while Arab chiefs would be granted 'complete administrative autonomy' under Turkish sovereignty.[14]

Sykes was unable to append his signature to the report, because he left England at the beginning of June. The War Office had instructed him to discuss the committee's findings with the British authorities in the Near and Middle East, and at the same time to study the situation on the spot. He successively visited Athens, Gallipoli, Sofia, Cairo, Aden and again Cairo. Sir Mark subsequently sailed for India. There he gained but a poor opinion of the capacities of the Indian authorities, and was angered by their attitude towards the Muslims. It seemed that the only thing they could think of was not upsetting 'religious susceptibilities, a phrase which is beginning to get on my nerves'.[15] Sykes's visit nevertheless passed off rather smoothly. His subsequent visit to Mesopotamia was not without incidents. Nine months later, Lloyd explained to Clayton that Sykes seemed 'to have been amazingly tactless, and not only to have rather blustered everyone but also to have decried openly everything Indian, in a manner which was bound to cause some resentment'.[16] Arnold T. Wilson, at the time assistant political officer, Force 'D' (see Chapter 1, section 'The Creation of Force "D" and the Occupation of Basra'), observed in his memoirs:

> He was too short a time in Mesopotamia to gather more than fragmentary impressions. He had come with his mind made up, and he set himself to discover facts in favour of his preconceived notions, rather than to survey the local situation with an impartial eye. Whatever we were doing to change the Turkish regime, or to better the lot of the Armenian, Jew and Sabaean minorities, had his cordial approval – for the rest, we must do justice to Arab ambitions and satisfy France![17]

Shortly after the receipt of Husayn's third letter, Sykes was back in Cairo. During his third stay at the Egyptian capital within six months, Sykes dispatched a number of telegrams to General Callwell. To a large extent these telegrams echoed Cairo's point of view with regard to the Arab question: the matter was urgent and a decision had to be taken as soon as possible; a sympathetic attitude by the Arabs towards the Entente was of the utmost importance, if only to prevent the dreaded jihad; a settlement of the conflicting French and Arab claims was feasible, as was a formula protecting Indian interests in Basra and Baghdad; and, finally, the Arabs would not act before a landing at Alexandretta had taken place. On 20 November, after an interview with Faruqi, Sykes telegraphed to London, that he:

> Anticipating French difficulty, discussed the situation with him with that in view. Following is best I could get, but seems to me to meet the situation

both with regard to France and Great Britain. Arabs would agree to accept as approximate northern frontier Alexandretta-Aintab-Birijik-Urfa-Midiat-Zakho-Rowanduz. Arabs would agree to convention with France granting her monopoly of all concessionary enterprise in Syria and Palestine, Syria being defined as bounded by Euphrates as far south as Deir Zor, and from there to Deraa and along Hedjaz Railway to Maan.

Sykes also informed the DMO that Faruqi insisted that the whole scheme depended on 'Entente landing troops at a point between Mersina and Alexandretta, and making good Amanus Pass or Cilician gates. He further stipulated that Shereef should not take action until this had been done.' Sykes added that he agreed with Faruqi. It was 'out of the question [...] to call on Shereef or Arabs to take action until we had made above mentioned passes secure'.[18] The day before, Sykes had sent off another telegram in which he had suggested possible solutions to the territorial aspects of the Arab question. A far as the vilayets of Baghdad and Basra were concerned, these were 'incapable of self-government and a new and weak state could not administer them owing to Shiah and Sunni dissension. We might agree with Arabs to administer these provinces on their behalf allocating certain revenues to their exchequer [...] (this corresponding to their demand for subsidy).' At the end of this telegram, Sykes had explained that he made his suggestions because he believed that:

> The situation is critical. I feel that Arab nationalism as such presents no danger for India now or in future unless we confine ourselves to the canal defensive and let Turk and German masses assemble in Syria and northern Mesopotamia and re-establish their prestige and so work a real Jehad with Arab support.[19]

Small wonder Wingate and Clayton looked forward with confidence to Sir Mark's return to London. Sykes did not let them down, witness the statement on the Arab question he made to the War Committee on 16 December. After an exposition in which he stressed that the Arab nationalists were averse to revolutionary ideologies, tolerant of other religions and favourably disposed towards Great Britain, he observed that, with respect to the Arab question:

> If I may say so, the chief difficulty seems to me to be the French difficulty, and the root of that, I think, to speak frankly, lies in Franco-Levantine finance.

Vitali represents the French group which used to be at Constantinople, who is in touch with M. Hugenin, who is a Swiss, and he is in touch with the Bagdad railway, and they have a great many relations with Javid. They have obtained the Syrian railways, and that very big loan of 1914, which gave them immense concessions all over Turkey. Now that party, I feel, is working through two agencies, and is checking the *Entente* policy in the Near East. One is the French cleric which is sentiment.

When Asquith interjected 'What is that?', Sykes added in clarification that he was referring to the French nationalist party:

Which is sentimental, bearing in mind the crusades. I think that that financial group works upon a perfectly honest sentiment. On the other side, they work on the fears of the French colonial party of an Arab Khalifate, which will have a common language with the Arabs in Tunis, Algeria, and Morocco […] I think at the back of all this, the influence that is moving them, is sinister.

Sykes considered the French financiers 'a very evil force working two honest forces, which are unconscious of the real purport of it'. He proposed that Britain should pursue a policy consisting of three steps. First:

We ought to settle with France as soon as possible, and get a definite understanding about Syria. Secondly, to organise a powerful army in Egypt which is capable of taking the offensive; and, thirdly, to coordinate our Eastern operations. Get that as one machine, and one definite problem: link up Aden, Mesopotamia – the whole of that as one definite problem for the duration of the war. If we had that I think it is worth backing the Arabs, no matter what ground we may have lost to the north of Haifa.

Asked by Asquith how he would come to terms with the French, Sykes stated that:

I think that we have those two assets. I think we can play on the French colonial if we work it well: get into the French colonial's head what a Committee of Union and Progress Sherif means, and point out what they have done in India and what they might do elsewhere. I think the French clerical is quite capable of being influenced by reason of the danger to his one asset in Syria, and if you rob the occult French financial force of its two agencies, then, I think you are on the high road to a settlement.

In answer to a question by Lloyd George, Sykes repeated his opinion that the Arab question should first have to be settled with France before any military action could be contemplated. With respect to that, he observed that Egyptian military opinion 'strongly [held] the idea of making a landing at Alexandretta', which was confirmed by Kitchener.[20]

In the course of the subsequent discussion, Asquith wondered what military value attached to the Arabs. Echoing Clayton, Sykes replied that their value was mainly negative. The Arabs were 'bad if they are against us, because they add to the enemy's forces, and if they are on our side there is so much less for the enemy and a little more for us, but I do not like to count upon them as a positive force to us'. To Balfour the situation was clear: 'If we decide to do nothing, first of all we shall lose the Sherif, and after him we shall lose the Arabs, and lose them forever'. However, Lloyd George and Crewe – again deputising for Grey – first wanted to know whether or not a landing at Alexandretta was feasible, because, as Crewe argued: 'it is no good starting on any proposals with France until we have made up our mind that a big military effort is possible'.

Before Sykes withdrew, he was given the opportunity to emphasise once again that:

> The question is very urgent: it is important that a decision should be given quickly. Every day that we delay we lose more and more Arabs from our side, and every day that we put off brings us nearer to the day when there will be many Turks in Syria.

After he had left, the members of the War Committee further discussed the Arab question. Kitchener once again repeated that 'the offensive-defensive' – as Balfour put it – was indeed the best way to defend Egypt. Balfour proposed that the French send troops, although not to Alexandretta, but to Ayas Bay. Kitchener concurred, as 'the Turks expect us at Alexandretta, which has been entrenched, but there are no entrenchments at Ayas'. Asquith believed that this was 'an attractive programme'. At the suggestion of Crewe, it was decided first to consult Bertie before approaching the French government.[21]

Crewe dispatched a letter to Bertie the next day. He acquainted the ambassador with the views, Sykes had expressed before the War Committee. As far as the 'offensive-defensive' was concerned, Crewe fully realised that 'then we come up against French susceptibilities and claims, and any discussion becomes exceedingly delicate, because the French always seem to talk as though Syria and even Palestine were as completely theirs as Normandy'. The War Committee therefore believed that 'it might be advisable for Mark Sykes to go over to Paris, accompanied, perhaps, by someone like Fitzmaurice, in order to talk to some of the French Ministers. He could press his own views upon them without committing us to any particular movement.' Bertie, however, opposed 'the Sykes expedition to Paris'. He argued that:

> However intelligent Sir Mark Sykes may be, and however good his arguments, I do not think that his coming to Paris to talk to some of the French Ministers would be in the least useful. However much he might press his views as his own views, they would be regarded as the views of the British government; for otherwise, why should he come?

The ambassador was prepared to sound Briand personally on 'a possible joint expedition somewhat north of Egypt', but warned that 'contrary to Kitchener's persistent contention, they hold that Salonica and the *possibility* of an expedition somewhere not defined will prevent the Germans starting any considerable Turkish or Turco–German force for a march to Egypt'.[22]

On 28 December 1915, the War Committee indirectly decided to shelve the whole project. It accepted the recommendations on military policy for 1916 made by Lieut.-General Sir William Robertson, Murray's successor as CIGS.[23] These were based on the decision taken at an inter-allied conference at Chantilly on 8 December that the war could only be won on the Russian, French and Italian fronts, and that the number of troops on the other fronts should be reduced to the barest minimum. Consequently, an 'offensive-defensive' policy for the defence of Egypt was out of the question, at least for 1916. In his memoirs, Hankey observed that:

> Robertson must have come away from the meeting of December 28th well satisfied. He had obtained the adoption of his main principle that the western front was the main theatre of war and he had been authorised to prepare for a great offensive there. He had also secured the application of the principle of a defensive role to the Egyptian and Mesopotamian campaigns.[24]

Sir Mark Sykes and François Georges-Picot Come to an Agreement

The second meeting between the Nicolson Committee and Georges-Picot took place on 21 December 1915. Picot informed the British delegation that 'after great difficulties, he had obtained permission from his government to agree to the towns of Aleppo, Hama, Homs, and Damascus being included in the Arab dominions to be administered by the Arabs'.[25] The discussion then turned to the boundaries of the area that should come under direct French administration, as well as the question of which part of the future Arab state would fall within the French sphere of influence. With respect to the latter, it was agreed that the Arab state should be 'divided between England and France into spheres of commercial and administrative interest, the actual line of demarcation to be reserved, but [...] that it should pivot on Deir el Zor eastward and westward'. It was also decided that the Lebanon, which 'should comprise Beirut and the anti-Lebanon', and an enclave around Jerusalem should be excluded from the Arab territories.

Two points were reserved for further discussion: 'the allocation of the Mosul Vilayet [and] the position of Haifa and Acre as an outlet for Great Britain on Mediterranean for Mesopotamia'.[26] This fresh delay made Nicolson complain to Hardinge that 'our discussions with the French in regard to the Arab negotiations are proceeding exceedingly slowly, and I cannot say that I see much prospect of our coming to an agreement'.[27] Sykes on the other hand was rather sanguine. On 28 December, he informed Clayton that he had 'been given the Picot negotiations. I have prepared to concede Mosul and the land north of the lesser Zab if Haifa and Acre are conceded to us.' Sykes expected that it would not take him 'above 3 weeks' to solve the last problems with the 'Picot negotiations'.[28]

Sykes's optimism turned out to be justified. Within a week he came to an understanding with Georges-Picot. The terms of the proposed agreement were laid down in a memorandum that reached the Foreign Office on 5 January. Sykes and Picot claimed that three parties were involved in a settlement of the Arab question – France, the Arabs and Great Britain – and that each cherished territorial, economic and political ambitions that could not be satisfied without coming into conflict with those of the other two. From this it followed that 'to arrive at a satisfactory settlement, the three principal parties must observe a spirit of compromise'. This settlement would, moreover, have 'to be worked in with an arrangement satisfactory to the conscientious desires of Christianity, Judaeism, and Mahommedanism in regard to the status of Jerusalem and the neighbouring shrines'. In the light of these considerations, they had arrived at the following proposal (see Map 4.1):

1. *Arabs.* – That France and Great Britain should be prepared to recognise and protect a confederation of Arab States in the areas (*a*) and (*b*) under the suzerainty of an Arabian chief. That in area (*a*) France, and in area (*b*) Great Britain, should have priority of right of enterprise and local loans. That in area (*a*) France, and in area (*b*) Great Britain, should alone supply advisers or foreign functionaries at the request of the Arab confederation.
2. That in the blue area France, and in the red area Great Britain, should be allowed to establish such direct or indirect administration or control as they desire.
3. That in the brown area [which covered the greater part of Palestine; R.H.L] there should be established an international administration, the form of which is to be decided upon after consultation with Russia, and subsequently in consultation with Russia, Italy, and the representatives of Islam.
4. That Great Britain be accorded (1) the ports of Haifa and Acre, (2) guarantee of a given supply of water from area (*a*) for irrigation in area (*b*). (3) That an agreement be made between France and Great Britain regarding the commercial status of Alexandretta, and the construction of a railway connecting Bagdad with Alexandretta.
5. That Great Britain have the right to build, administer, and be sole owner of a railway connecting Haifa or Acre with area (*b*), and that Great Britain should have a perpetual right to transport troops along such a line at all times.

On the same day, Nicolson circulated copies of the memorandum to Holderness, Brigadier-General George Macdonogh, director of military intelligence (DMI), and Captain Hall, director of the intelligence division (DID) at the Admiralty. In his covering letter he stated that, although 'of course the agreement merely represents the personal views of Sir Mark Sykes and M. Picot', he believed that it presented 'a fair solution of the problem'.[29]

Only the India Office agreed with Nicolson's conclusion. The loss of Mosul would clearly be 'a serious sacrifice for us', but, on the other hand, it would force the French 'to be very accommodating elsewhere, e.g. Haifa'.

The India Office should like to see some modifications in the proposed terms, but on the whole the memorandum, as Hirtzel noted, 'represents a considerable abatement on M. Picot's original claim, and we are under a great obligation to Sir Mark Sykes'.[30] Macdonogh and Hall were considerably more critical. They accepted that an early settlement of the Arab question was important to prevent a jihad, but questioned the assumption that an agreement with France had to be reached first, before the Arabs could be dealt with. Macdonogh argued that:

> To me it appears that the one point of importance is to get the Arabs in on our side as early as possible. I would therefore suggest that all that is necessary at the moment is that we should be in a position to inform the Sheikh what are the approximate limits of the country which we and the French propose to let him rule over. This may involve an agreement as to the respective British and French spheres of influence in that district, but I hope that its discussion will not be allowed to delay the settlement of the main question.[31]

Hall, for his part, doubted whether it was 'necessary to have some agreement with the French about Syria and Mesopotamia, in order that such action may be taken as may avert a combination between the Turco–German forces and the Arabs, the result of which would produce something like a serious general Moslem *jehad* against us'. According to the DID, 'action, which will convince the Arabs of our effective power, is very necessary'. Indeed, 'force is the best Arab propaganda', and it was therefore very desirable that a concerted naval or military action be undertaken that would 'result in cutting off the Arabs from the Turks by an occupying force and so screening the former', but precisely 'no such action on the part of the French, or on our part with their good-will and furtherance is a term of the agreement'. The proposed agreement was moreover unsatisfactory considering the assurances Husayn had asked for:

(*a*) That the Arabs shall not be deserted by the Allies in any peace which may be made; and
(*b*) That all territories properly considered as inhabited by Arabs shall (with certain exceptions) be part of an independent Arab State, guaranteed by the Allies. He does not appear ever to have been willing to exclude Syria, and more especially the Arab centre of Beirout, from the Arab State.

Further, he and other Arab leaders in touch with the British have, on several occasions expressed themselves very emphatically against their being placed under any obligation to accept French advisers locally, whereas they stated that they were prepared to welcome British.

These considerations led Hall to the conclusion that 'the only advantage' of the proposed agreement that 'would at present be gained seems to me the possibility of giving definiteness to the assurances which would in themselves be unsatisfactory'.[32] Finally, both Macdonogh and Hall could not help thinking that, as the former put it, 'we are rather in the position of the hunters who divided up the skin of the bear before they had killed it'.[33] Pending Picot's return from Paris, the observations by Hirtzel, Macdonogh and Hall drew no comments from Grey or his officials.

On 16 January 1916, Sykes informed the Foreign Office that he had spoken to Picot, and that the latter had informed him that 'at Paris he had much difficulty, but that he believed that it would be possible to come to an agreement on the lines of the memorandum'.[34] Nicolson convened a further meeting of the interdepartmental committee on 21 January. During that meeting, 'the criticisms of the various Departments on the Sykes-Picot Memorandum were considered and no insurmountable difficulty to the scheme was put forward in any of them'. Nicolson impressed upon the other delegates that it was 'essential to take France in our confidence before we embarked on final negotiations with the Arabs', and it was again laid down that 'if the Arab scheme fails the whole scheme will also fail and the French and British governments would then be free to make any new claims'. Sykes was authorised to inform Picot of the results of the meeting, as well as that 'H.M.G. would feel compelled to consult the Russian government after agreement with the French' on the northern frontier of the blue area.

As a result of this meeting, the Foreign Office drew up a draft agreement. Its conditional character was emphasised by adding a preamble stating that 'should the negotiations with the Grand Shereef of Mecca fail to secure the active cooperation of the Arabs on the side of the Allies the whole proposals in regard to all spheres whether of administration or of influence will lapse automatically'. The India Office and the DMI concurred with the draft agreement. Holderness commented that it was 'in accordance with the conclusions reached by the Committee on Friday', while Macdonogh 'quite agree[d] with its contents'. Hall, however, protested anew against the absence of a 'stipulation for French cooperation in, or consent to, any concerted plan of action against the Germans and Turks as a condition of the agreement'.³⁵

The Foreign Office completed the final draft on 2 February. It was circulated to the Cabinet that same evening, with a covering letter in which Nicolson explained the reasons for negotiating this agreement with France. It had been 'found at the outset impossible to discuss the northern limits of the future Arab State or Arab Confederation, unless the French desiderata in Syria were also examined, as M. Picot was unable to separate the two questions'. Eventually, it had been agreed that 'the four towns of Homs, Hama, Aleppo and Damascus will be included in the Arab State or Confederation, though in the area where the French will have priority of enterprise, etc'. Nicolson did not fail to point out that the preamble was intended to lay down 'with sufficient precision' that 'the proposals in regard to the Blue area, as well as the Red area are contingent on the fulfilment of certain essential conditions', and that Russia should be given full opportunity to have a say in the final settlement of the question.³⁶

The War Committee considered the matter the following day. It was decided on the suggestion of Sir Edward that 'the whole Arab Question should be discussed at a meeting between Mr Bonar Law [the secretary of state for the colonies; R.H.L.], Mr Chamberlain, and Lord Kitchener, and that the French should be informed if we agreed to their proposals'.³⁷ This meeting took place the next day. Crewe and Nicolson were present, as well as Holderness and Hirtzel; 'a representative of the Admiralty was also present, but was not in a position to give an opinion on the merits of the scheme'. Those who were decided that:

> M. Picot may inform his government that the acceptance of the whole project would entail the abdication of considerable British interests, but provided that the cooperation of the Arabs is secured, and that the Arabs fulfil the conditions and obtain the towns of Homs, Hama, Damascus and Aleppo, the British government would not object to the arrangement. But, as the Blue Area extends so far eastwards, and affects Russian interests, it would be absolutely essential that, before anything was concluded, the consent of Russia was obtained.

On the evening of 4 February, Sir Arthur informed Georges-Picot of the British decision. He minuted afterwards that he had laid 'emphatic stress on the absolute necessity of nothing whatever being considered settled until the Russian consent had been obtained – and [...] that we should say nothing to the Arabs until that consent has been obtained'.[38] Five days later, Cambon told Nicolson that 'the French government are in accord with the proposals concerning the Arab question'.[39] Sykes and Picot were entrusted with the task to inform the Russian authorities of the contents of the agreement.

The Arab Question Becomes a Regular Quicksand

Foreign Office officials had little time to savour the successful conclusion of the negotiations with the French on the Arab question. On 5 February, Oliphant and Nicolson occupied themselves with Husayn's reply to McMahon's letter of 14 December 1915 (see section 'Georges-Picot's Opening Bid and McMahon's Third Letter', above). This letter, dated 1 January 1916, had been received by the Foreign Office on 2 February. The high commissioner had declared in a telegram of 26 January that the letter was 'of friendly and satisfactory nature',[40] but after they had studied it both Oliphant and Nicolson disagreed. The former minuted that he could not 'regard the Sherif's letter as very satisfactory, though it is at least outspoken and frank', while the latter observed that he did not:

> Consider this letter at all satisfactory as regards the Sherif's remarks respecting the French and I wish in his telegram [...] Sir H. McMahon had given us some indication of this – He made no mention of the northern parts in his telegram – and we have had to believe that the Shereef had not taken serious notice of them while on the contrary he employs rather ominous language in regard to them.

With regard to the Emir's position on these 'northern parts', McMahon explained in his covering dispatch that:

> Satisfactory as it may be to note his general acceptance for the time being of the proposed relations of France with Arabia, his reference to the future of those relations adumbrates a source of trouble which it will be wise not to ignore.
>
> I have on more than one occasion brought to the notice of His Majesty's Government the deep antipathy with which the Arabs regard the prospect of French Administration of any portion of Arab territory.

> In this lies considerable danger to our future relations with France, because difficult and even impossible though it may be to convince France of her mistake, if we do not endeavour to do so by warning her of the real state of Arab feeling, we may hereafter be accused of instigating or encouraging the opposition to the French, which the Arabs now threaten and will assuredly give.[41]

McMahon's observations reflected Clayton's anxieties, which the latter had voiced in two letters to Wingate. The Sudan agent considered 'the Sherif's answer [...] on the whole satisfactory', but taken together with the results of the second meeting with Picot on 21 December, he feared that the British could not go on 'negotiating much longer, without laying ourselves open to a charge of breach of faith, unless we honestly tell the Arabs that we have made Syria over to the French'. A problem that was the more important since:

> Some of our Syrian friends seem to have an inkling that we have handed Syria over to the French and I foresee some trouble. The time has nearly arrived when we shall have to tell them so straight out and hand them over to the French to settle with – otherwise we shall risk giving rise to the very friction with France that we have sacrificed so much to avoid.[42]

Wingate was more optimistic. According to him the results of the meeting were:

> On the whole not quite so unsatisfactory as I had expected, and I think I see in the general trend of the discussion, the possibility of coming to an arrangement which may satisfy all parties – indeed I do not see that even if French demands are conceded in their entirety, that we can be accused of any serious breach of faith – it is true the Arabs will not get all they wanted, but they will achieve a great deal and in any circumstances, I should think that further discussions will result in a certain modification of the French demand.[43]

However, Clayton, in a further letter, confessed that he did not 'share these hopes'. He enclosed copies of McMahon's covering dispatch with Husayn's fourth letter, and the reply the latter intended to send 'without waiting for formal approval'. Clayton explained that it had not been an easy assignment 'having only a couple of hours to do it in, and [having] to steer clear of the various quicksands and yet to say something which would satisfy the Sherif'.[44] Clayton could have spared himself the trouble as far as Grey was concerned. To him the Arab question already was 'a regular quicksand'.[45]

Cambon was rather more sanguine. In view of McMahon's suggestion to warn the French 'of the real state of Arab feeling', the India Office had expressed the desire that the Foreign Office should do so. Of course, it was 'not unlikely that they will not take the statement seriously. But Mr Chamberlain apprehends that His Majesty's Government may hereafter be under some suspicion of bad faith if, with the information before them, they allow the negotiations to proceed without warning the other party.' Grey had consequently instructed the department to mention the matter to Cambon.[46] As the India Office had predicted, the latter did not take the matter very seriously. He cheerfully remarked to Nicolson that 'the Shereef would not be an Arab if he did not say something of that kind'.[47]

Sykes, meanwhile, acted as advisor to the British ambassador at Petrograd, Sir George Buchanan, during the latter's negotiations on the frontiers of the blue area with the Russian minister for foreign affairs, Sazonov, and the French ambassador, Paléologue, who was assisted by Georges-Picot. Grey had observed in his instructions that Britain had 'no desire whatever to urge the Russian government to make concessions in the districts which are of direct interest to them if they have any objections to doing so'.[48] Sazonov indeed objected. At the first meeting of the three parties he showed 'very plainly he did not like extension of the blue area so far eastward'.[49] However, a compromise was reached within two days, to the effect that the most eastern part of the blue area would become part of the area under direct Russian administration, while France would be compensated for the loss of this region 'by enlarging her blue area to the north of Marash'.[50]

On 17 March, Buchanan telegraphed that the Russian government had decided to accept the compromise.[51] At a meeting of the War Committee six days later, it appeared that Balfour, Kitchener and Asquith objected to the proposed scheme, albeit on different grounds. Each time, Grey tried to neutralise their objections by emphasising that 'the whole arrangement was provisional on the Arabs coming in. Unless they did, there would be no break up of Asia Minor,' and that, accordingly, 'he thought that nothing would come of all this, [and] Asia Minor would never be divided'.[52] Eventually, it was decided that 'His Majesty's Government would raise no objections to the proposed arrangement between France and Russia'.[53]

Despite this progress, negotiations again could not be brought to a conclusion. Fresh problems arose with respect to 'all concessions for railway construction and other advantages such as religious missions granted to the French by the Turks in any territory that Russia may acquire'.[54] The result was that, on 3 April 1916, 171 days after Maxwell had telegraphed that 'time is of the greatest importance, and that unless we make definite and agreeable proposal to the Shereef at once, we may have a united Islam against us', and 110 days after Sykes had testified before the War Committee that 'the question is very urgent: it is important that a decision should be given quickly. Every day that we delay we lose more and more Arabs from our side', Buchanan still had to impress on Sazonov the importance of a speedy conclusion of the negotiations in order that Britain would be 'able to clinch matters with Arabs at once'.[55]

Sir Mark had indicated some weeks before that two potential dangers threatened the Arab revolt: '1. Peninsula nomads moving before intellectual Syrians are prepared and scheme failing through want of organisation. 2. Of intellectual Syrians failing to combine with intellectual Mosul and Irak Arabs to join in movement owing to doubt as to our designs on Irak'. With respect to the latter, Sykes had suggested sending 'Arab and Kurd officers now Turkish prisoners of war in India to Egypt and letting Colonel Clayton sound those committed to Arab cause and select best to work with Masri and Faruki'. Although Oliphant had minuted that he could not 'conceal my scepticism as to the success of the scheme', Sykes's telegram had been repeated to Cairo. The next day, yet another telegram had been sent to McMahon, in which he had been informed that 'no action whatever should be taken on it' (i.e. Sykes's telegram), but that the Foreign Office would 'be glad of your observations on it'.[56] McMahon considered it wiser to send Aziz Ali and Faruqi to Mesopotamia and there to get in touch with 'the Arab element in the Turkish Army'. There was, however, the problem that they:

> Demand for themselves and Arab military element whom they would have to approach some definite assurance of British policy towards Arabia. They consider this essential to the success of any effort to win over Arab element in the Army.

They would be tolerably content with the assurances already given to the Shereef. Their tendency at present is to demand less from us with regard to Mesopotamia than would have been acceptable before.

Oliphant supported McMahon's 'suggestion that these two men should go'. Grey and Kitchener, too, were in favour of the proposal. Together they drafted – 'at the Cabinet this morning' – a telegram in which the high commissioner was authorised, provided Clayton did not object, to send Faruqi and Aziz Ali to Mesopotamia. They also gave Sir Henry permission 'to give assurances, if necessary, but you should be very careful not to exceed in any way the limits of the assurances already given to the Shereef'.[57]

Copies of both telegrams were forwarded to the India Office. Chamberlain was not amused. The India Office drew the Foreign Office's attention to Husayn's letter of July 1915, in which the Emir:

> Purported to speak for the 'Arab Kingdom of the Shereef', while in that of 1st January he expressly stated that his procedure was not personal, but the result of the decisions and desires of his peoples of which he was only the transmitter and executant. There is no clear evidence as to how far this claim accords with facts, but it has not, so far as Mr Chamberlain is aware, been questioned by His Majesty's Government. If the claim is well founded, it is a point for consideration whether independent assurances should be given to other, and ex hypothesi less responsible Arabs.

Oliphant minuted that the telegram to Sir Henry 'was not a departmental draft', and proceeded to draft a telegram in the sense of the India Office letter. Nicolson was clearly embarrassed by the letter, although he 'understood that Sir E. Grey and Lord Kitchener consulted M. Chamberlain before the telegram was despatched'. He admitted that there was 'a good deal of force in the concluding remarks of the I.O. letter', but the text of Oliphant's draft 'rather clashes with the telegram sent in 54229 [the one drawn up by Grey and Kitchener; R.H.L.] – and would possibly confuse Sir H. McMahon'.[58]

Two days later, the Foreign Office received another letter from the India Office, enclosing a telegram from General Sir Percy Lake, GOC-in-C, Force 'D'. The latter was opposed to McMahon's suggestion. It was:

> Not considered possible that either of the above individuals could themselves pass over from occupied territory to the sphere of the Turkish

troops opposed to us on the Tigris or Euphrates, or could be of any practical use to us if they did. From the political standpoint it appears to us that their political views and schemes are much too advanced to be safe pabula for the communities of occupied territories and their presence in any of the towns of Irak would be in our opinion undesirable and inconvenient.[59]

Lake's telegram had been repeated to Cairo and McMahon promptly reacted. He explained that 'it was not intended that Al Masri and others should pass over to Turkish lines'. All that had been envisaged was that 'presence of one or two prominent and carefully selected members of the Arab party in our ranks would afford Arab elements in Turkish army much required guarantee of our unity of interest and good faith'. He moreover warned that the decision not to send Aziz Ali and Faruqi would:

> Produce disappointment and rumours of danger being ascribed either to our mistrust in their loyalty, or to our unwillingness, if not inability, to carry out our assurances, and this may not be without effect on Shereef. An impression is gained that there is visible limit to the patience of those in whom we have raised feelings of expectation nor is it possible to guarantee that present favourable attitude of certain individuals can be counted on later.

McMahon therefore trusted that he might 'continue to give all guarantees short of definite action and within the limits approved by you to those who have now committed their destinies to us'.

This telegram induced Chamberlain to compose a very biting memorandum:

> I do not find this telegram very easy to understand.
>
> The decision to which it refers is that El Faruki and El Masri should proceed to Mesopotamia. As it now appears that Sir H. McMahon never contemplated that they should pass over to the Turkish lines (as was supposed here), it is not clear of what use he thought they could be. It is not believed that either of them have any influence in Irak. How is 'practical use' to be made of them?
>
> 'An impression is gained', Sir Henry telegraphs, 'that there is visible limit to the patience of those in whom we have raised feelings of expectation'. This is the severest criticism I have seen of Sir H. McMahon's policy. He raised the expectations. We have given assurances by his mouth much wider than

we at home intended: We have given money and arms and promised more. The Sherif has done nothing, and we are now to be told by Sir H. McMahon that it is <u>we who</u> fail to fulfil the expectations we have raised! Will Sir Henry ever realise that there are two sides to a bargain and that the Shereef has his part to play and that it is now 'up to' him the Shereef to make the next move?

What does he mean by 'continuing to give all guarantees short of definitive action?' He has given guarantees as already stated in excess of our intentions. He safeguarded French freedom of action in Syria but not ours in Mesopotamia. But by his declarations we hold ourselves bound and there has been no suggestion that we should recede from them. If he only desires to repeat himself, he has authority to do so, but does he mean that he is to give further assurances, and if so what?

I am very uneasy about the whole handling of the question by Egypt.

Grey's reaction to Chamberlain's complaint was very characteristic. He did not enter into a discussion on the merits of the latter's arguments. He confined himself to a brief note to Nicolson:

You will see what Mr Chamberlain says. I am disposed simply to telegraph to Sir H. McMahon that I do not understand his difficulty about assurances that he can repeat assurances already given but must not go beyond them, that we are I believe giving arms and money and the sole question is whether and when the Arabs will do their part.

A telegram in this sense was dispatched to Cairo on 5 April 1916.[60]

Sykes, the man whose suggestion had started this controversy, had in the meantime returned to London. There he set himself to solving the problem that according to McMahon constituted the biggest threat to a satisfactory solution to the Arab question, 'the deep antipathy with which the Arabs regard the prospect of French administration of any portion of Arab territory'. In a telegram sent from Petrograd on 16 March, Sykes had already declared that 'with regard to Arabs our greatest danger lies in their falling out with the French', but that 'if I can get Picot and Faroki or Aziz Ali into a room together, I believe I can manage to patch up a bargain between them'. He had therefore advised:

Get El Masri or Faruki or both to London where I could enter into formal discussion with them and when ground was prepared bring them into contact with Picot. I suggest this as I fear French and Arab discussions in Cairo leading to intrigues and quarrels and Picot would like this arrangement. If Arabs reach London April 7th, I believe by May 8th ground would be clear of Arab French question.[61]

In spite of this hopeful prospect, the Foreign Office had not acted on Sykes's suggestion. This did not prevent Sir Mark from submitting to the Foreign Office a telegram to Clayton in which he asked the latter's opinion on this scheme. After consultations with Macdonogh, the telegram was finally sent off on 14 April. Sykes first informed Clayton on the situation with respect to the Anglo–French–Russian negotiations in Petrograd, as well as the compromise that had been reached as to the limits of the blue area, and continued:

The crux of the difficulty is that at present French theoretically concede no outlet to Arab State on Syrian littoral. They intend to negotiate this point with Arabs themselves. Negotiations on this point through any medium in Cairo will precipitate the Maronite versus Anglophil controversy. In my mind it is essential that French should have become practical before Picot goes to Egypt. I advise therefore following procedure which I have got Picots approval of, i.e. that you send here to London 2 Arab officers representative of intellectual Syrian Moslem Arab mind, that when I have got their point of view that I compare it with Picots, that when Picot has been got into right frame of mind I bring them together and they have informal talk, Picot then gets Paris to make concession of principle of Arab State outlet on Syrian littoral in the form of Aide-Memoire to H.M.G. [...] Objection was taken to this procedure in London on ground that Arab officers would not be representative and that negotiations would be being conducted in two places at once. I wish to make it clear that suggestion is not to negotiate but to examine, and that official status of Arab officers is not important as long as they are mentally representative.[62]

Unfortunately for Sykes, Clayton was opposed to the scheme. However much he agreed with Sir Mark that Picot's presence in Egypt would be undesirable at the present juncture, he did not see how 'presence in London of any Arab officers with whom we are at present in touch would in any way assist you'. According to Clayton, it would moreover 'be most impolitic to raise now with Arabs Syrian question which is quiescent for the moment. To do so would, I am convinced, be contrary to interests both of ourselves and French, who have everything to gain by delay.'

There was the added problem that at the moment there seemed to take place a 'certain rapprochement' between the Arabs and the Turkish opposition (the 'Turkish decentralisation parties', as Clayton called them) – a development that McMahon would explain in a further telegram – and this meant that 'an attractive offer by such Turkish parties would be in serious competition to any proposals Allies can put forward'. Against this background, Clayton also did not think it very advisable to disclose the results of the Anglo–French–Russian negotiations on the future of the Ottoman Empire. Of course:

> Any agreement on main principles between Allies is all to the good, but to divulge it at present and to insist on any particular programme would I am convinced be to raise considerable feeling, to strengthen Arab-Turkish rapprochement, and possibly to affect injuriously political and military situation of Allies in Turkey at a moment when true attitude of Arabs is not quite clear.[63]

As Clayton's telegram was addressed to Sykes, Foreign Office officials did not comment on it, but they did, and in very strong terms, comment on McMahon's telegram when it arrived two days later. The high commissioner repeated Clayton's objections to raising the Syrian question at the present moment. He also confessed that he was 'unaware whether proposals outlined by Sir M. Sykes have received the approval of three governments concerned or whether they are merely suggestions as a result of his and Picot's conversations in Petrograd'. McMahon hoped that the latter was the case, as there were indications that 'Turkish parties in opposition to Committee of Union and Progress are already considering peace terms which, in certain circumstances, it might suit the Allies to consider'. The Petrograd compromise moreover appeared 'to ignore existence of Turkey and necessity, under any circumstances of providing an adequate home for remnants of that nation if defeated'.

In their minutes, Oliphant and Nicolson gave vent to their feelings of frustration with the manner in which the Arab question developed. Oliphant's minute could have been written by Hirtzel or Chamberlain:

I venture to think that this telegram is by no means satisfactory. It shows that there is considerable confusion in Sir H. McMahon's mind and that matters are merely drifting [...]

1. To state that the future of the Turks is ignored is erroneous [...] The Vilayets of Brusa, Smyrna, Angora, Konia, Kustammi and Eskisher – an area as large as France and the only districts inhabited by an Ottoman Turk majority are not touched by the agreement in question, which were from the outset drafted on the basis of ethnographic interests.
2. The arrangements were devised to fall in with Turkish liberal views if the Turkish liberals are strong enough to oust the C.U.P.

    Obviously the Turkish liberals if in power, would have to approach Russia in the final instance. As regards Turkish parties we know Sherif Pasha and Saba ed Din are in Paris and some may be in Egypt [Sherif Pasha and Prince Sabah-al-Din acted as spokesmen for the Turkish opposition; R.H.L.]. But Enver is in Constantinople and the Sherif in Mecca.

It seemed to Nicolson that there was no end to fresh complications. He minuted that he was 'afraid that the whole subject is becoming entangled', and that at the very moment that 'we, Russia and France are now quite clear and in accord as to our interests and aspirations in the Ottoman Empire'. As far as the proposals of the Turkish opposition were concerned, these were 'merely empty talk'. The permanent under-secretary concluded that the Foreign Office should 'let Sir H. McMahon fully know the present position and our arrangements with Russia and France as regards Asiatic Turkey and also inform him of our attitude towards the irresponsible and unofficial overtures made to us by Prince Sabadeddin and others'. Crewe agreed, and a telegram in the sense of Oliphant's and Nicolson's minutes was sent to Cairo on 27 April.[64]

In his reply of 4 May, McMahon voiced his disappointment with the Foreign Office attitude towards the Turkish 'liberal and anti-committee parties', especially as the 'situation as far as we can gauge it here, does not yet appear one in which we can afford to disregard potential value of this disintegrating factor in Turkey'. He also observed that:

Although there is nothing in arrangement agreed on between France and Russia and ourselves as defined in your telegram that conflicts with any agreements made with or assurances given to Shereef and other Arab parties, I am of opinion it would be better if possible not to divulge details of that arrangement to Arab parties at present.

Moment has not yet arrived when we can safely do so without some risk of possible misinterpretation by Arabs.

Grey personally drafted a telegram to Cairo in which he agreed that 'details of arrangement should not be divulged'.[65]

In his minute on Sir Henry's telegram of 22 April, Oliphant had also submitted that in order:

To avoid further confusion [...] a meeting between Sir M. Sykes, M. Picot, and Col. Clayton would be helpful not in Egypt as M. Picot's presence there is obviously inopportune. But perhaps at Rome or even Paris: at any rate somewhere within reach of London. So that eventually decision can be derived at here, and the details worked out at Cairo.[66]

On 3 May, Clerk reported that Sykes was in favour of a meeting between him, Picot and Clayton, perhaps at Paris. Nicolson saw no objection, but Kitchener doubted whether Clayton could be spared from Egypt.[67] This seemed to be the end of Oliphant's suggestion, but in a memorandum on a conversation with Georges-Picot, who had returned from Russia, Sykes again raised the subject. He reported that the French and Russian governments had settled their part of the arrangement on the Middle East by means of a mutual exchange of letters between Paléologue and Sazonov, and that the French government wished that Grey and Cambon should follow the same procedure. Sykes urged the importance of an early exchange of these letters, also because 'exchange of notes is an essential prelude to a conference between M. Georges-Picot and Colonel Clayton on Franco–British Arab policy. Such a conference M. Georges-Picot earnestly desires.'[68]

In spite of Sykes's plea for a speedy settlement, an exchange of letters between Grey and Cambon did not take place immediately. Grey first wanted to make sure whether the French were fully aware of 'the point of its being conditional upon action taken by the Arabs'. During an interview with Grey, Cambon assured him that 'it was well understood that it was dependent upon an agreement with the Sherif of Mecca and that this provisional character was already in writing'.[69] There was also the point whether or not the French government, in those areas that would 'become entirely French, or in which French interests are recognised as predominant', would respect 'any existing British concessions, rights of navigation or development, and the rights and privileges of any British religious, scholastic or medical institutions'. A letter to this effect was sent to the French ambassador on 15 May. In his reply, which reached the Foreign Office the following day, Cambon confirmed that France would maintain existing British rights, privileges and concessions, whereupon Grey dispatched a letter to the French ambassador that same day that contained the terms of what would go down in history as the Sykes–Picot agreement.[70]

Now that this obstacle was out of the way, Clerk once again pressed for a meeting between Picot, Sykes and Clayton 'as soon as possible'.[71] McMahon was not averse to the proposed conference, but found it 'extremely inconvenient to General Clayton until the return of members of Arab Bureau and Storrs which should be in ten days time'. It was also 'desirable that Clayton should be able to take home "first hand" information with regard to result of their mission'.[72]

Ronald Storrs, accompanied by Captain Kinahan Cornwallis and Commander David Hogarth, had left Cairo for the Hijaz. The object of their mission was to meet Abdullah, at the latter's request. However, Abdullah was unable to make it to the rendezvous. On 6 June 1916, the British delegation instead spoke with Zeid, the youngest of Husayn's sons. In his report, Hogarth observed that the British delegates had feared that 'the substitution of Zeid for Abdullah had rendered it unlikely that [...] we should be in a position to appreciate the actual situation and future policy of the Sherif',[73] but they were in for a surprise. Zeid informed the British delegation that the day before, Ali and Feysal, Husayn's two other sons, had started hostilities against the Turkish garrison at Medina. The revolt of Sharif Husayn, Emir of Mecca, against his Turkish masters had begun.

Preliminaries to Sharif Husayn's Revolt

It was not so much the fact that Husayn revolted that came as a surprise to the British authorities at Cairo and Khartoum, as the moment he chose to do so. On 16 February 1916, Husayn had sent a letter to McMahon in which he not only unfolded his plan of action, but also asked for arms and money. Oliphant and Nicolson hesitated to grant these demands, because, as Oliphant argued, to do so might lead the Emir to think that Great Britain considered herself to be definitely committed to him. Sir Arthur agreed. He was:

Anxious lest the Shereef should consider by our sending him the additional £20,000 he may regard his agreement with us as definitely concluded, and that we are bound to meet all his desiderata. I consider that Sir H. McMahon should make it quite clear to the Shereef that we are providing him with the sums for which he has asked as an evidence of our friendly feelings towards him and that we let him know later when we consider that the opportune moment has arrived for his taking [undecipherable; R.H.L.] action as will lead to the revolt of the Arabs against Turkish rule – and which will result in the discomfiture of the Ottoman Empire in the regions where Arab interests are predominant and where it is desired to establish Arab independence – we should telegraph Sir H. McMahon in above sense.

Lord Kitchener might be shown this before it is dispatched – and I.O. concurrence obtained.

Neither Chamberlain nor Kitchener had a good word to say for the proposed telegram. The former scathingly minuted:

I have not thought it very probable that the Grand Sheriff would take any definite action, Sir H. McMahon seemed to me to have succeeded in giving him the impression than we were in much more need of him than he of us.

But now the unexpected happens. The Sheriff declares that the time for action has come – and we propose to wet blanket his enthusiasm!

Subject to military opinion [...] I should <u>pay the money and encourage him to go ahead</u>.

We have warned France that she must obtain the acquiescence of Russia. We have warned the Sheriff that we cannot speak for our allies. What more has either of them a right to expect from us and why should we discourage a potential ally?

I am not sure of the Sheriff's good faith, but at least we can now test it by taking him at his word.

Kitchener concurred. He had 'no idea there would be any hesitation in paying the money and accepting the Sherif's proposed help. I hope the proposed telegram may be modified and sent without delay.' Nicolson rather timidly minuted that 'in view of their opinion, I am afraid that we can only telegraph to Sir H. McMahon to send the money and accept the Sherif's proposals'. A telegram in this sense was dispatched the same day.[74]

Wingate regarded this telegram as a signal success, witness his letter to McMahon of 17 March in which he confirmed the receipt of the latter's telegram:

> Giving me the welcome news that the British government has finally approved of the Sherif's demands and that everything is 'en train' [...] I am full of hope that the Arab Policy which we initiated so long ago is really going to materialise. Of course there is naturally some risk that things may not go quite as we hope and expect they will, but in this, as in most operations of the sort, it is a case of 'Nothing venture nothing have' and in this matter especially I think the game is well worth the candle.[75]

McMahon reported in a telegram of 21 March that a messenger from Husayn had arrived at Port Sudan, carrying yet another letter. Cyril Wilson had telegraphed a summary to Cairo. On the basis of this summary, Sir Henry drew the conclusion that the 'Shereef appears to have made up his mind definitively to side actively with us and his last two letters make no further reference to political matters so that he would seem to be satisfied with assurances we have given him and to require nothing further in this respect', and that Husayn had decided that 'rising will begin at end of coming Arabic month or at beginning of month after'. At the Foreign Office, this news impressed no one. Oliphant minuted that McMahon's telegram struck him as 'very optimistic', while other officials, as well as Grey, merely initialled it.[76]

On 24 May, Sir Henry sent a telegram to the Foreign Office in which he reported that 'Storrs is urgently required by Abdullah Shereef's son to meet him on Arabian coast. Shereef is asking for £50,000 and Abdullah for £10,000.' He strongly recommended complying with these requests without delay 'as (?matter) appears to have reached point at which we must not fail to give it every encouragement'. Clerk's reaction showed that the various quicksands and entanglements that seemed to inhere in the Arab question had also not failed to make an impression on him. He minuted that 'this may be encouraging, but there is another interpretation, which is that fair words cost nothing and are well worth £60,000'. He suggested:

> To send Mr Storrs across at once to hear what Abdulla has to say; meanwhile collect the money at Port Sudan, and if Mr Storrs' report is favourable, hand

it over. Mr Storrs can always explain that it takes a little time to get £60,000 together, and that he has come across in advance, so as to lose no time.

It took five days before a telegram in this sense was sent to Cairo.[77] On the evening of 28 May, without waiting any longer for Foreign Office authorisation, Storrs and his companions left for the Hijaz. McMahon telegraphed that day that 'they will proceed to Port Soudan, pick up Sherif's messenger and go to Hedjaz coast to meet Abdullah. They take £10,000 for latter but sending of £50,000 for Sherif must await your sanction'. The Foreign Office acquiesced to the high commissioner's decision to send the £10,000, while the 'payment of £50,000 to Sherif is sanctioned if there is a real rising'.[78]

A telegram from McMahon transmitting Storrs's report of his meeting with Zeid arrived in London on 9 June. It stated that 'rising began yesterday [5 June 1916; R.H.L.] at Medina but all communications in Hedjaz are cut no news. Other towns to rise on Saturday.' It was left to Sykes to comment upon this event. Just like the Foreign Office officials, he was rather wary. True, if Husayn's revolt was successful, it constituted a serious threat to the central powers but, if it was not, then the repercussions for Britain would be very serious indeed. It seemed to him that, now that Husayn had burned his boats, Britain had no other option but to support him and 'failure to support the movement adequately will be disastrous to our prestige such as it is and react to our permanent detriment in India, Egypt, and the Persian Gulf'.[79] That the chances of Husayn failing were very real became clear from a further telegram from McMahon. He informed the Foreign Office of his fear that 'both in organisation and armament of forces too much has been left to the last moment and to luck'. Although Clerk considered this telegram 'not altogether reassuring', he nevertheless spotted a ray of hope, 'we may remember that the Turks have often found it a heavy task to quell the Arabs when circumstances were much easier for the Porte'.[80]

Nobody in the Foreign Office commented on the fact that Husayn had started his revolt without awaiting the results of the negotiations between Great Britain, France and Russia, on the basis of which, as Nicolson had written to Hardinge on 16 February 1916, 'we shall really have to come to some decision as to further conversations with the Grand Shereef'.[81] The Emir of Mecca as yet was unaware of the agreement that, according to Grey and his officials, had to be concluded before the Arabs could again be approached on the conditions under which they would be prepared to revolt against their Turkish overlords.

The Arab Bureau

In the course of his mission to the Middle East, Sykes became convinced that, if Britain did not want to lose the war, then it was of vital importance that the activities of the various agencies involved in the Middle East be coordinated. As he formulated it in a speech to the House of Commons after his return, 'if we muddle, if we go on muddling, and if we are content to allow muddling, it will not be a question of a draw, but the War will be lost'.[82]

After his visit to Aden in July 1915, Sykes reported to Callwell that he was greatly worried about 'the want of co-ordination in our Arabian policy'. He was 'well aware of the departmental difficulties which lie in the way, but at the present moment the necessity of co-ordination is of great importance especially in view of the fact that our enemy is working [...] from one centre of political and military influence'.[83] He also voiced his worries in a private letter to Clerk:

> We live in watertight compartments, if we are to do any good we should have a special committee with one F.O. and one Government of India Representative under a person of grasp, that is a committee of 3, established in Cairo charged with running anti-Jehad policy – working all the Anglophil influences and anti-C.U.P. and revolutionary influences and formulating a policy and working it, not merely reporting [...] there must be organisation and co-ordination.[84]

On his way back from Mesopotamia, Sykes wrote a long private letter on the subject to Lord Robert Cecil, the parliamentary under-secretary of state for foreign affairs. He explained that:

> The thing which remains first and last in my mind, in fact is ever present, is the want of co-ordination which runs through the whole of our organisation between the Balkans and Basra – which is opposed to the German scheme of things which is highly co-ordinated, though evidently well decentralised. Thus in Afghanistan, Persia, Mesopotamia, Southern Arabia, the Balkans, and Egypt you find the [undecipherable;

R.H.L.] committee machine working armies, agents, and policies with one definite purpose in accordance with a general plan, our opposition to this consists of different parties putting up a local offensive or defensive on almost independent lines, and quite oblivious of what the others are doing. This let me say is no fault of any individual but the result of our traditional way of letting various officers run their own shows, which was all right in the past when each sector dealt with varying problems which were not related, but is bad now that each sector is dealing in reality with a common enemy.

To counteract these centrifugal forces, Sir Mark suggested that:

It would be worth considering whether a new department under a secretary or under-secretary of state should not be started, this would be the department of the Near East and would be responsible for policy and administration of Egypt, Arabia, and Mesopotamia [...] You will notice that the area I suggest is one in language and practically in race and its unification under one department would give the government of the day an engine to deal with the Arab situation both national, strategic, and economic, a personelle of side and intimate acquaintance with the problems, and consequently give English statesmen an opportunity of following a consistent line.[85]

Sykes subsequently unfolded a much less ambitious scheme in a telegram to Callwell of 9 October. He reiterated that he was impressed by the necessity:

For the coordination of our policy in regard to the Ottoman Empire, Arabian people and the Mahometan opinion in the British Empire. A means of ameliorating the position which suggests itself to me would be to authorise me [...] to complete my mission by establishing in Cairo a Bureau under your department which should receive copies of all telegrams giving available information regarding our enemies, Islamic propaganda and methods and effect thereof, as well as tendency of popular opinion, from intelligence and political officers in Mesopotamia, and Persian Gulf, Indian Criminal Investigation Department, Soudan Intelligence Department, Chief Intelligence Officer, Mediterranean Expeditionary Force, Intelligence Officer, Athens. I could then from time to time transmit to you for the use of the

Cabinet a general appreciation. I suggest Egypt as the place for the Bureau owing to its central situation and the local touch with the Islamic world.

The Foreign Office received both Sykes's private letter to Clerk and his telegram to Callwell on 12 October. Clerk considered Sir Mark's scheme of a special committee under 'a person of grasp' a good suggestion, and Nicolson concurred – 'the Bureau seems to me a good idea', but they were of the opinion that this project could not usefully be discussed before Sykes returned to London. For the moment, Clerk did no more than inform Hirtzel of Sykes's idea.[86]

Sykes also raised the subject of want of co-ordination in his statement before the War Committee on 16 December (see section 'Enter Sir Mark Sykes', above). Twelve days later, he informed Clayton on the way things were going with, as he now called it, the 'Arab Bureau'. It seemed that:

We are confronted with a difficult problem. The W.O., F.O. and I.O. are slow and the Admiralty has barged in and seized me and the Bureau [...] The Admiralty want to annex the Bureau as part of their immense network, and keep me in an office in London, they object to my organisation and say all that must be left to you, this is merely a cliché, but they refuse to transmit any suggestion of mine to you. The objection to the Admiralty is that it is discredited, with the more staid departments, and cannot carry the day where policy is involved. The merit of the Admiralty is that it alone achieves anything, has large funds and does things. Fitzgerald is of opinion that the Bureau should be nominally under the F.O. but in fact in close touch with the D.I.D. and able to use its codes, agents, and machinery. I have therefore to try and pull this off but the difficulties are immense.[87]

Sir Mark's proposals on the constitution and functions of the Arab Bureau were discussed at an interdepartmental conference on 7 January 1916, with representatives of the Foreign Office, the War Office, the India Office and the Admiralty, as well as Sykes, being present. The participants agreed that the establishment of an Arab Bureau was desirable, and concurred with Sykes's suggestions with respect to its functions:

The first function of the Bureau will be to harmonise British political activity in the Near East, and to keep the Foreign Office, the India Office, the Committee of Imperial Defence, the War Office, the Admiralty, and the

Government of India simultaneously informed of the general tendency of Germano-Turkish policy.

The second function will be to coordinate propaganda in favour of Great Britain and the Entente among non-Indian Moslems without clashing with the susceptibilities of Indian Moslems and the *Entente* Powers.

The bureau, however, should not, as opposed to what Sykes had suggested, become a new, independent agency 'nominally under the F.O.'. The DID had its way. It was decided that the bureau 'should be organised as a section of the existing Soudan Intelligence Department in Cairo, and that it should make its reports through the High Commissioner of Egypt to the Foreign Office'.[88] This implied that 'Mark Sykes drops out', as Hirtzel wrote to Grant of the Indian Foreign Department the same day.[89] This was quite a relief to Hardinge. He confessed to Nicolson that he had at first been opposed to the whole scheme, 'because we considered that the composition was radically bad, for we have no faith in Mark Sykes [...] Now that Colonel Clayton is to be head of the bureau, we accept the position gladly, and we intend to depute a really first class officer to represent Indian views.'[90]

As far as the Government of India was concerned, matters were still not settled. They were anxious lest the first function of the Arab Bureau – to harmonise political activity in the Near East – gave the bureau too wide powers. The bureau's functions should be confined to the collection and distribution of information for the benefit of the relevant departments, and a shared responsibility with regard to propaganda. The viceroy therefore asked the India Office for assurance that 'our political officers will not be called upon to act at dictation of bureau without consulting Government of India'. The India Office had no difficulty in giving it, and the Foreign Office concurred with the India Office's suggested reply.[91]

In the next three months the Government of India succeeded in further and further reducing the Arab Bureau's possible influence on developments in Mesopotamia. First, the India Office and the Foreign Office decided, at the suggestion of Sir Percy Lake, that with respect to 'Arab propaganda in the East', the Arab Bureau should do no more than to lay down principles, and that the GOC-in-C, Force 'D' 'should be left to make his own arrangements as a matter of local detail',[92] while shortly afterwards, this time at the request of Sir Percy Cox, the Foreign Office and the India Office agreed that liaison officers sent to Mesopotamia by the Arab Bureau should not directly report to Cairo, but through Cox and Lake. As Hardinge explained to Chamberlain, it was only in this manner that co-ordination between the Arab Bureau and the political officers, Force 'D', could be secured.[93]

By the end of May 1916, the Arab Bureau, instead of the 'committee of 3, established in Cairo charged with formulating a policy and working it' that Sykes had envisaged in September 1915, had pretty much turned into one of those 'water tight compartments' charged with 'merely reporting' that Sir Mark, by means of his proposals, had wanted to abolish.[94]

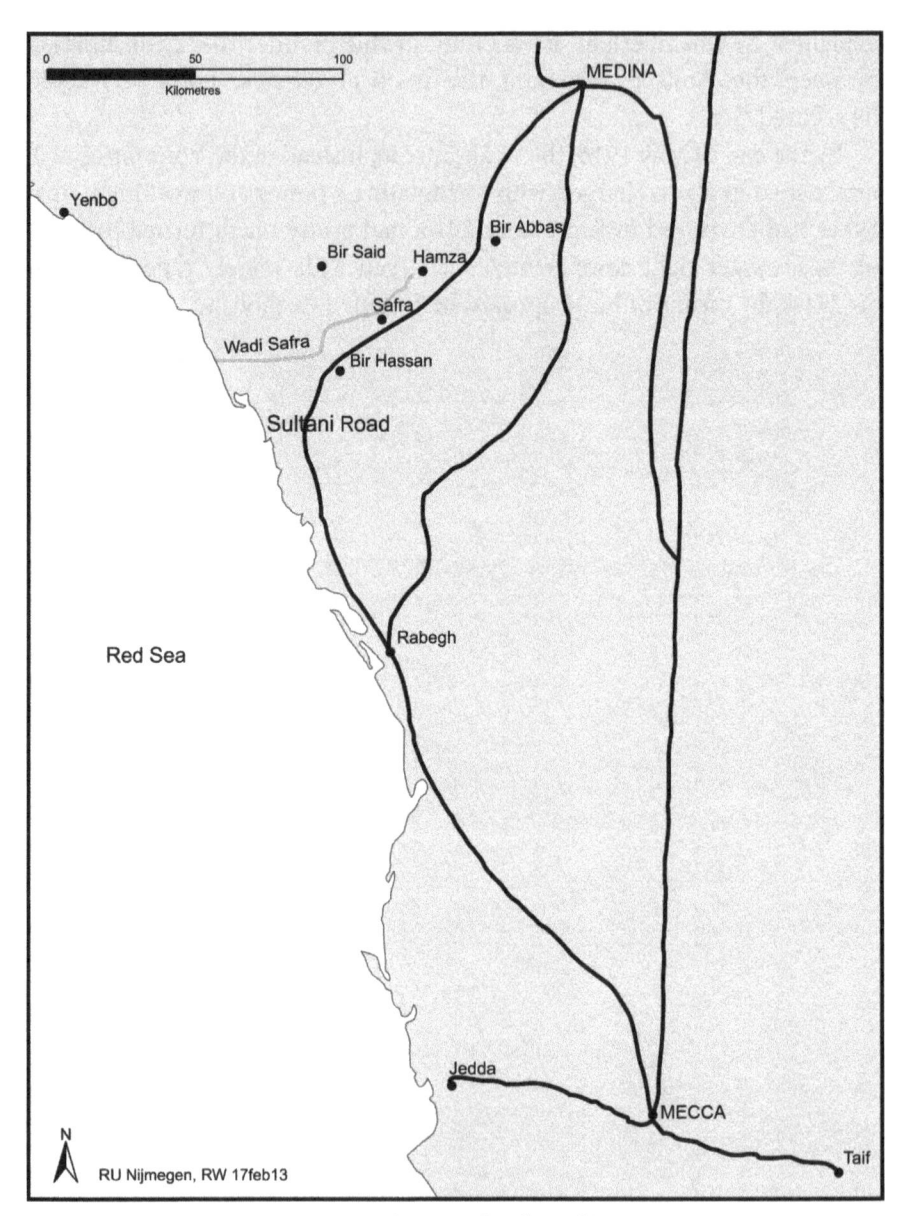

Map 5.1 Medina, Rabegh and Mecca

5 RABEGH HAS BEEN A PERFECT NUISANCE

Introduction

This chapter is mainly concerned with the various crises that erupted in London from September 1916 to January 1917 as a result of a series of requests by the authorities in Cairo and Khartoum to send a British brigade to the town of Rabegh on the coast of the Hijaz to prevent the Turks from advancing on Mecca and crushing Sharif Husayn's revolt. These requests offered ministers dissatisfied with the manner in which the war was being conducted the opportunity to challenge the established military policy of concentrating all available forces on the Western front in France. However, to overthrow this policy was quite another matter. At times, the War Committee hovered on the brink, but in the end it always decided to postpone the decision, even when it had been decided to take a decision. When in December the newly created War Cabinet decided to delegate the responsibility for sending the brigade to Sir Reginald Wingate, the latter, although he had been the most ardent advocate of the scheme, promptly shifted it onto Husayn, who in the meantime had been proclaimed 'King of the Arab Nation', his precarious position notwithstanding. By the middle of January 1917, it was evident that Husayn would not permit British troops to land in the Hijaz. This proved to Wingate's own satisfaction that, if the Arab revolt collapsed, the blame lay firmly on Husayn's shoulders. There would be no further Rabegh scares.

Cairo, Ismailia and Khartoum Wrestle for Political and Military Control

The Foreign Office received Ronald Storrs's report on his mission to the Hijaz on 21 June 1916. George Clerk minuted two days later that:

> When the Turks do begin a serious operation against the Sherif, we should be expected to do more than pay out doles of £50,000 [McMahon had asked on Husayn's behalf for another £50,000 three days before; R.H.L.] at a time. Unless we are in a position to threaten to cut off the Turkish forces from the neighbourhood of Akaba and Ma'an, the Arabs will very likely collapse.

According to Clerk this, however, was 'a question for the War Committee'. Sir Edward Grey concurred.[1]

McMahon, too, was of the opinion that the Turks crushing the Emir's revolt could be prevented by landing a British force at Akaba, but he also realised that such an expedition clashed with established military policy that assigned a purely defensive role to Egypt.[2] This was confirmed by a telegraphic exchange between Sir Archibald Murray (who had succeeded Sir John Maxwell as GOC-in-C, Egypt) and Sir William Robertson. They agreed that military assistance 'must for the present be confined to provision of munitions and supplies'.[3] Robertson did not wish to rule out 'a forward movement to Akaba and El Arish' altogether, but this did not need to be decided before October.[4] This point of view found its way into a General Staff memorandum drawn up for the benefit of the War Committee, suggesting that it might be desirable to undertake an offensive to threaten the Turkish lines of communication, and Murray therefore 'should make all possible preparation for the occupation of El Arish and Akaba'. At the same time, 'climatic conditions' rendered it unlikely that these operations could start before October, and the practicability of such an operation should then be considered anew.[5] After a brief discussion, in the course of which Arthur Balfour stressed the importance of these operations, and Robertson the difficulties involved, the War Committee accepted the General Staff's position.[6]

Two weeks before, on 22 June, Wingate had written a letter to Robertson in which the sirdar impressed on Sir William 'the immense effect that a successful movement of this sort would have throughout the whole Islamic world and how seriously it would upset the nefarious and lying propaganda of our Turco–German enemies'. Wingate naturally was well aware that 'the real settlement must be made on the Western Front', and fully realised 'how difficult it is to be able to spare troops for these projects', but he nevertheless advocated 'allied action in the direction of Alexandretta, or somewhere in that neighbourhood', to cut Turkish communications and to bring about 'a complete debacle of the Turkish armies'.[7]

He also favoured another scheme. In a telegram to McMahon of 4 July, he observed that 'we should be prepared to offer Sherif cooperation of a British or Indian force on Arabian coast – the acceptance or refusal of this offer, in view of drawback of previous landing of foreigners in proximity to holy places to be left entirely at his discretion'.[8] The major advantage of this project, so he explained in a letter to David Hogarth, was that the responsibility for success or failure of Husayn's revolt, if the Turks were able to threaten his position at Mecca, would be put firmly on the Emir's shoulders:

> When the Sherif is faced with [...] an advance on Mecca by the Turks. He will probably then have to choose between accepting an offer by us to despatch a military expedition and almost certain defeat. It is on this account that I so strongly urged that the offer be made him; should he refuse, then we are exonerated from all blame for the failure of his movement.[9]

Murray, meanwhile, was not prepared to resign himself to the haphazard way in which Cairo, Ismailia (Murray's headquarters) and Khartoum had until then had to react to events in the Hijaz. He confessed to McMahon on 19 June that he did 'not know who is supervising this campaign of the Sherif's against the Turks', and that he would be glad if the latter would send him 'a line to tell me who is supervising, or controlling, the action of the Sherif, if anyone'.[10] Sir Henry's reply was characteristic. He gave Murray to understand that control and supervision were two different things, and that 'as regards control, no one can be said to be doing this except the Sherif himself [...] As regards supervision, this is naturally limited to watching the course of events, and this I do by the means of the wireless messages sent me by our warships off Jeddah'.[11] Murray was not put off by this reply. On 25 June, he dispatched a telegram to Wingate in which he stated that he believed that 'some controlling organisation must be set up so as to keep the threads together and to avoid friction', and in this connection he wished to know whether Sir Reginald had any suggestions to make.[12]

Murray repeated his telegram to McMahon, as a result of which Sir Henry, too, sent a telegram to the sirdar. He explained that, as far as he was concerned, 'the coordination of military matters concerning these operations can best be carried out by Sir Archibald Murray', while he had to 'retain direction of political matters as hitherto'.[13] Small wonder that Wingate in his reply to both could think of no other suggestion than that 'a careful coordinated scheme should be devised as soon as possible'.[14]

McMahon and Murray discussed the question on 28 June. The same day, the former telegraphed the result of their deliberations to Wingate. They had agreed that 'it is preferable that the general direction of military matters connected with our assistance to the Sherif should rest with you. I trust that you will kindly undertake this.' Wingate replied that he could not accept the proposal as it stood. He also hinted that he was only prepared to accept military responsibility if he also became responsible for the political aspect of Husayn's revolt, 'unless I am given full discretionary powers and I am assured that my recommendations will meet with immediate consideration, little benefit and possibly more confusion than exists at present will result from proposed changes'. McMahon refused to reconsider his position. Sir Reginald's responsibilities were to be confined to 'general military supervision'. Wingate pointed out in a subsequent telegram that under these conditions 'my utility and capacity to assist would almost be nullified'. He therefore asked McMahon to re-examine the question, and to authorise him 'to enter into direct communication with Sherif', and to give him 'full discretionary powers'.

Sir Henry was not prepared to yield. He had:

> Carefully considered question of political control of Hedjaz matters raised in your recent telegrams and it has become increasingly evident that this must remain in my hands.
>
> I thought for a time that our assistance to Sherif might develop on lines which would make it depend more and more on Sudan for native personnel troops, supplies etc, and that Port Sudan would be base of operations, but my supposition has proved incorrect. Suez is now chief base for supplies, munitions etc.
>
> Moreover [...] any active military assistance must be outside Hedjaz and that if given will be rendered by British troops.
>
> There is nothing therefore to weaken former objections to transfer of political control, but a good deal to strengthen them and I do not now propose to raise the question with His Majesty's Government.

There remained to Wingate little option other than to put on a brave face. It was 'a great satisfaction to me to know that necessity of operations outside Hedjaz is now appreciated by H.M.G.' McMahon could rest assured that the sirdar would 'do all I can in so far as resources at my disposal will allow to assist in making the Sherif's movement a success'. In view of these 'satisfactory' developments it was, however, impossible for him to accept military responsibility. This 'obviously' should rest with 'Sir A. Murray, as military authority from whose base operations are contemplated and who will supply troops and other military requirements'.[15]

In the meantime, the position of the man whose downfall 'would be disastrous to our prestige and would gravely complicate our future relations with Mohammedan peoples',[16] remained very precarious. After two months of fighting, the insurgents could boast few military successes. Jedda had been captured on 16 June, after the town had been shelled by British warships. The Turkish garrison at Mecca had surrendered 14 days later, after the arrival of a battery of field artillery of the Egyptian army (dispatched by Wingate) had decided the battle for that city in Husayn's favour. Yenbo had been occupied on 25 July, again after British warships had bombarded the town. The siege of Taif, led by Abdullah, had, however, as yet been unsuccessful, while the attack on Medina by the Sherifian main force, headed by Ali and Faysal, had ended in failure. Moreover, after the arrival of reinforcements from Damascus, Fakhri Pasha, the commander of the Turkish garrison at Medina, had started a counter-attack. Little by little, Faysal was forced to retreat along the Sultani Road in the direction of Mecca (see Map 5.1).

Wingate was very worried lest Husayn's revolt be crushed. He warned Clayton that if the British authorities persisted in their passive attitude, then the consequences would be disastrous. Husayn's collapse would 'be for the British government in the eyes of its Moslem subjects an even greater blow than the Gallipoli evacuation or the Kut el Amara surrender'. It was high time that the powers that be shook off their apathy, 'the nettle must be grasped, the ostrich policy abandoned, and the whole matter taken firmly in hand, otherwise I cannot see how the wretched Sherif is to succeed. If not, if the Sherif is allowed to go to the wall [then] the verdict of history will be dead against the policy which brings about that catastrophe'.[17] Murray repeated Wingate's words in a letter to Robertson:

> I do not in the least wish to be an alarmist, but both Reginald Wingate and myself are most anxious that the operations of the Sherif should be a success. It is very difficult to see how, from a military point of view, we can assist him, but I am convinced that if the Sherif fails the verdict of history will be dead against the policy which brings about that catastrophe.

Robertson was not impressed. He explained to Murray that:

> What we have got to bear in mind is whether the operations will pay us, and I am afraid we cannot attach too much importance to what the verdict of history may be.
>
> One never knows where these little expeditions may not lead us, and I am dead against undertaking any which do not promise us a good return in close connection with the main operations.[18]

When writing this letter, Robertson was still unaware of the request Faysal had made the day before in the course of an interview with Cyril Wilson (who had become British representative at Jedda). This request would very severely put to the test his firm conviction that the war could only be won on the western front and that no troops were available for side shows. On 30 August 1916, McMahon telegraphed to the Foreign Office that Faysal had requested that 'about 3,000 trained soldiers sent to him, even if they remain at Yenbo they would show Arabs that Great Britain was helping them, put heart into them and give Faysal a sense of security'.

The Rabegh Question: The First Round

Wilson had urged that 'at least 1,000 Mohammedan troops (if 3,000 are not available) be sent to Yenbo as soon as possible'. McMahon hesitated to support this demand 'owing to views of Indian Government and to those of Sultan'. Clerk concurred and Lord Hardinge, who had returned to the Foreign Office and had taken up his old post of permanent under-secretary, also believed that 'the proposal to send troops seems out of the question, certainly from India'. However, the views of Foreign Office officials would not matter much in the Rabegh question. That would be the War Committee's province. Lancelot Oliphant's minute on McMahon's telegram was symbolic, 'this being up for the War Committee, no further action taken here'.[19]

On 1 September 1916, the War Committee discussed McMahon's telegram, together with a telegram from Wingate, which Sir Henry had forwarded to London. The sirdar had offered 'to send as many Moslem troops as I can spare safely from Khartoum district and from Egypt on condition that their place is taken in the Sudan by a brigade of British troops'.[20] Lord Crewe thought this a good suggestion, but Sir Mark Sykes advised against sending troops. He explained that 'the thing that would pay would be to supply everything in the way of arms etc. in the Hedjaz, and elsewhere confine ourselves to naval bombardments'. The War Committee accepted this advice.[21] McMahon was instructed to inform Faysal that the British government was 'unable to send Mohammedan troops to the latter at Yenbo', but had 'issued orders for 20,000 more rifles and adequate ammunition to be collected and sent to Egypt for Shereef', and was prepared to 'supply six more Maxims and as many hand-grenades as may be required'.[22]

Wilson, this time accompanied by Alfred Parker, had another interview with Faysal on 9 September. Faysal emphasised again that he would be unable to prevent the Turks from advancing on Mecca unless regular troops were put at his disposal, which should be encamped near the coastal town of Rabegh. Wilson wired McMahon that:

> If two batallions with maxims and field batteries all British troops with at least two aeroplanes could be sent to Rabeg Sherm now, the moral effect would be enormous. They would not go inland and Sherif has no objections. Such a force (which would be withdrawn when the situation clears) would be complete proof that Great Britain is really backing the Arab cause.[23]

Wilson sent his telegram from HMS *Dufferin*, which carried him to Egypt to attend a conference to discuss the various problems that had arisen since the beginning of Husayn's revolt. This conference had been called by McMahon at Murray's request. With the exception of Wingate and Hogarth, all the central figures involved in Hijaz affairs were present at Ismailia on 12 September: McMahon, Murray, Sir Rosslyn Wemyss (C.-in-C., East Indies and Egypt Station), Clayton, Cornwallis, Storrs and Wilson. The latter explained that he primarily advocated the dispatch of British troops to raise the morale of the Arabs:

> What the Arabs want is some tangible evidence that the English government is not going to let them be crushed, and give them not only money, rifles and that sort of thing. What Feisal and the Arabs are very keen on is to see some regular troops. These could be landed, not for use inland, but to safeguard their road to Mecca [...] The immediate necessity to make this revolt a success is that some trained troops should be sent down to Rabegh.

Wilson considered that a brigade would suffice for the purpose. McMahon emphasised that 'we are absolutely forced to do something drastic and soon to produce the moral effect which will avert a big military disaster'. He also introduced two arguments to refute the War Office's objections to the sending of British troops to Rabegh. The first was that the costs of the proposed operation were incomparably smaller than the costs Britain would incur if Husayn failed. It would:

> Effect the Mohammedans throughout the world. The effect in India would be enormous; I do not know how many troops it would take to clear that up. In other parts of the world like Abyssinia and Somaliland, it would mean a very very serious situation indeed, which would cause very serious military trouble and would, I imagine, result in pulling off a good many troops from various places – a great deal more than the General or the War Office would wish for.

His second argument was that, if Great Britain was not prepared to assist the Emir of Mecca, then he saw no other option than to allow France to do so. The French no doubt would eagerly seize this opportunity to abolish British supremacy in the Red Sea, but 'if I cannot get these troops from the British government I am reduced to getting them from the French'.[24]

Murray had been strengthened in his opposition to the dispatch of troops by Robertson's letter, which had 'arrived on the 10th most opportunely [...] I thank you very much for the straight lead you have given me'.[25] He took a hard line:

> We are absolutely clear at the War Office as to our line of policy, as are all the Allied nations. We have made up our minds that we will concentrate in the West every single man we possibly can, and that we shall allow the secondary theatres of war to struggle on with the minimum of troops, and that we will on no consideration undertake fresh campaigns or fresh liabilities [...] There is no good telling me that you only want this and that. From the experience of war, and experience of recent campaigns it is absolutely clear that you start and you grow.

The only concession Sir Archibald was prepared to make was that, immediately after he had received an official request from McMahon for the dispatch of troops to Rabegh, he would send a telegram to the War Office, in which he would state that 'from the point of the local theatre of operations it does seem necessary that you should have support there and that you should have what you ask for', but that he would have to add that he could not 'supply them without a direct order from the War Office in which case it would seriously interfere with my operations both east and west of Egypt'.[26]

It was decided to follow this course of action. Sir Henry addressed a memorandum to Sir Archibald in which he explained the reasons why he felt obliged to request a brigade for Rabegh. Both Murray and McMahon telegraphed the memorandum to London the next day. In the memorandum Sir Henry stated that:

> We should offer Shereef to send an infantry brigade to Rabegh to give Faisal the moral support which he so urgently demands and, if Shereef accepts, troops should be sent without delay. It should be clearly pointed out that no advance will be made beyond Rabegh in any circumstances, that a brigade absolute maximum and that it will be withdrawn immediately present crisis is over [...]. If we do not send troops, I know French government is ready to offer to send French Moslem troops to Hedjaz and this I greatly deprecate, as it will rob us of very great political advantages which Shereef's success will hereafter give us.[27]

Robertson and Lord Grey were not impressed by McMahon's arguments in favour of an expedition to Rabegh.[28] Sir William wrote to Grey that McMahon seemed 'to present an exaggerated view of the situation'. He also took exception to the idea that 'the brigade should only give moral support to Faisal and under no circumstances beyond Rabegh'. It was 'useless to send troops to any theatre unless they are intended to fight and defeat the enemy'. He also opined that 'such dispersions of force as here proposed invariably develop into far greater and more dangerous and costly enterprises'. Grey replied that he personally admitted the strength of the military objections against sending an expeditionary force to the Hijaz, and that 'the decision of the War Committee is certain to be in the negative'. He also enclosed the text of a telegram to McMahon for Robertson's approval. The latter concurred, and the telegram was sent the same day:

> On September 2nd. War Committee considered proposal to send Sudanese troops to Hedjaz and replace them by British troops from Egypt and were decidedly of opinion that latter could not be spared. This decision would

equally apply to sending British troops to Hedjaz. I cannot hold out any hope that objections of military authorities, which appear to me on military grounds to be well-founded, can be overcome.

But this being so we cannot object and must facilitate assistance which the French may be able to send, if and when such is forthcoming.[29]

On 18 September, the War Committee discussed the telegrams from McMahon and Murray, as well as Sir Henry's reply to Grey's telegram, in which he urged that in any event 'a flight or even half flight of aeroplanes' would be sent 'to keep up spirits of Arabs'.[30] During the discussion the outlines began to emerge of the dispute with regard to Rabegh. On the one side, there were Curzon, Chamberlain, Lloyd George and Grey, who all, with greater or lesser insistence, advocated the view that, in the light of political considerations, Husayn must be supported, if need be with British troops. On the other side, there was Robertson who, without denying the political desirability of supporting the Emir of Mecca, stuck to his view that there were no troops available for an expedition to Rabegh. Finally, there was Balfour, who subscribed to the position that a small ally like Husayn must be supported, but claimed that the Admiralty, and not the War Office, should take care of this.

Robertson defended the general staff's point of view with the same two arguments he had employed in his letter to Grey four days before. He doubted the urgency of the matter, as there was 'always trouble going on in that country', and pointed out that, although it was true that the request was for no more than a brigade, the experiences of the Gallipoli and Mesopotamia campaigns had taught them that it was highly unlikely that this would be all, 'one cannot forecast what an expedition of this sort might lead up to. Commencement with a brigade might end in many divisions.'

In consequence of Robertson's unyielding attitude, the discussion soon resulted in deadlock. None of his opponents wanted to push things to extremes, even though it concerned, according to Lloyd George,[31] 'a matter of first class importance to help the Sherif if we could. Otherwise our prestige would go.' It was eventually decided that first Robertson, after consultations with the Admiralty war staff, should report to the War Committee as soon as possible which actions, if any, could be taken to prevent Sharif Husayn's downfall. In this connection, Grey 'particularly asked that the Chief of the Imperial General Staff would consider the possibility of complying with the High Commissioner's request for the dispatch of aeroplanes for Rabegh'. Second, Sir William should ask Sir Archibald 'without in any way prejudicing the final decision […] what troops he could best spare' if the government 'should decide that the political importance of the Sherif was sufficient to justify the dispatch of a brigade to Rabegh'. Third, the Admiralty 'should at once take steps to dispatch a naval force to cooperate with the Sherif'.[32]

Robertson had already completed the desired memorandum two days later. The CIGS once again presented all his objections to the dispatch of a force to Rabegh. The first was that there were no troops available, and even if there were, then they must be employed on the western front, and not in the Hijaz, as 'the only way to win this war is to beat the German armies'. His second objection applied to the complications that would result from landing Christian troops in the Hijaz. In this connection, Robertson referred to a note by Sykes in which the latter reported a conversation with Ernest Weakley 'who is a first-rate authority on the Hejaz Arabs'. According to Weakley it 'was rash in the extreme to introduce British troops into such a place […] British troops landing would be enough to send the whole of the Arabs against the Shereef'. Sir William's third objection concerned the danger that more and more troops would have to be sent: 'we may land a force at Rabegh with the intention of refusing to advance inland, of sending no further troops and of withdrawing as soon as possible', but the Dardanelles and Mesopotamia expeditions had taught that circumstances or enemy action might 'compel us, in order to avert disaster, to send more and yet more troops […] to the detriment of the main theatre of war'. Robertson finally argued that it would take some time before a brigade could be sent off, time that apparently was not available in light of McMahon's recent telegrams claiming that 'immediate action is required'.

Sir William's counterproposal consisted of two elements. Instead of sending troops to Rabegh, 'our assistance should for the time being be limited to such as the Navy can supply, and to the provision of munitions, money and supplies'. At the same time, Wingate should be authorised 'to raise and train a force of Sudanese Moslems to be paid and equipped at Imperial expense'.[33]

The Rabegh question was again on the agenda of the War Committee on 25 September. Robertson drew attention to the news that three days before, after a siege of almost four months, Taif had finally fallen. He claimed that this 'was an important matter', as 'it relieved the troops who had been besieging it'. Curzon and Chamberlain emphasised in turn the enormous consequences that would result from Husayn's downfall. The Lord Privy Seal argued that the repercussions of the Emir's failure for British prestige and the situation in India would be such that 'it might be better to run the risk of putting British troops into the Hedjaz than to allow the Sherif to go down'. The secretary of state for India confirmed that 'if the Sherif was wiped out it would have a serious effect on India [...] If we were to let the Sherif go down, it would not be only one brigade that would be required.' Balfour disputed Robertson's argument that the dispatch of a brigade inevitably involved the sending of more troops. He declared that:

> If all we said was that it was to prevent the Turks from taking Rabegh, he could not believe that we could not send it [...] If the proposal to send an expedition would involve us in a second Mesopotamia, that was a strong argument against it. But if the intention was only to hold Rabegh, he could not think that we could be involved in anything bigger.

When Asquith thereupon asked Robertson 'what he had to say to that', the latter could think of nothing else than that 'it was a difficult question to discuss across the table. His views of the whole business had been expressed in his paper. He could not answer Mr Balfour's queries.'

The CIGS was saved from his plight by Sykes. He invited Weakley, who had been sent for, to 'say what he thought about landing British troops'. The latter emphasised the difficulties involved in the dispatch of Christian troops, although he admitted that 'it would be different if the Sherif asked for it'. However, this qualification had far less impact than his observation that 'there were several routes from Mecca to Medina, three or four, and that the Rabegh route was always used when the other lines were used and caravans were held up by the tribes'. After Weakley had withdrawn, Grey stated that 'he was impressed by the fact that Rabegh was not the only route to Mecca', to which Asquith added that 'it was not even the best route'. Bonar Law turned into an opponent of the project, considering that 'there were several other routes besides through Rabegh'.

Weakley's information provided the War Committee a good way out of the impasse. If the Turks need not pass through Rabegh during their advance on Mecca, the dispatch of troops seemed useless. It appeared that Robertson would have his way, until Chamberlain observed that naturally 'none of them could argue the military question as against the Staff. He presumed the Germans argued in the same way, nevertheless that did not prevent them from sending troops and arms and agents for stirring the Arabs up.' This sparked a fresh round of arguments, questions and suggestions, in the course of which Lloyd George observed that 'they had to work off Turkey as well as Germany to finish the war', and that 'by attacking the Turks in Arabia, we were saving Turks from assisting the Germans in Europe'. Grey reverted to his old position that 'the military importance of sending a brigade seemed small beside the political importance of saving the Sherif. He therefore would send a brigade.' Even if this meant that 'this would be the first time that there had been a question of overruling military opinion'. The War Committee was, however, not prepared to let things go as far as that. Such a momentous decision could only be taken after more information had been obtained. Balfour proposed to ask Vice-Admiral Wemyss whether he would be able to defend Rabegh without military assistance. It was also decided, on the suggestion of Curzon, to telegraph Wilson in order to establish whether the 'position of the Shereef' was indeed one of 'real danger'.[34]

Robertson had had enough. He told Sir Maurice Hankey the next day 'to give a hint to the P.M. that he would not stand War Committee's present interference in regard to his rejection of a proposal to send a brigade to Rabegh on the coast of the Hedjaz'.[35] There was no need to carry out his threat. Two days later, during the next meeting of the War Committee, Balfour read out a telegram from Wemyss stating that 'Rabegh is now held by a force of 5,000 or 6,000 well-armed Arabs, and that with the extra protection which could be given from men-of-war there should be no question of this port falling into the hands of the enemy'. Admiral Jackson added that 'he had ascertained that, though there were other routes from Medina to Mecca, the route through Rabegh appeared to be the only one practicable for an army'.[36] The matter was definitively settled when McMahon telegraphed that same day that Wilson believed that Husayn for the moment was not in real danger. He confirmed Wilson's assessment three days later.[37]

The Rabegh question seemed a thing of the past. On 16 October, Robertson wrote to Murray that he:

> Had great difficulty in knocking out the Rabegh proposal. It gave me a great deal of trouble. It would undoubtedly have been strategy gone mad [...] My sole object is to win the war and we shall not do that in the Hedjaz nor in the Sudan [...] Our military policy is perfectly clear and simple, and it has the approval of the government, and we cannot change it every day in the

week. The policy is offensive on the Western Front and therefore defensive everywhere else.[38]

The Rabegh Question: The Second Round

Even though the immediate threat of having to send a brigade to Rabegh had been averted, Robertson considered it better that the War Office no longer be responsible, not even in part, for events in the Hijaz. On 3 October, he proposed to the War Committee to relieve Murray from his responsibilities with respect to the provision of personnel and supplies to Husayn. According to Sir William, 'the whole thing should be placed in the hands of the sirdar'. (Wingate, as sirdar, came under the high commissioner, and therefore the Foreign Office.) After Grey had expressed his agreement, the War Committee accepted Robertson's suggestion without further discussion.[39]

McMahon was informed of the War Committee's decision the same day.[40] He regretted it very much:

> For strong reason that proposed arrangement has already been given full trial and found impracticable [...] Arrangement after some weeks had to be abandoned, much to the relief of the sirdar and myself as it led to endless correspondence, overlapping and confusion without any compensating advantage.
> I trust therefore that decision may be reconsidered or at least held in abeyance pending the views of the sirdar whom I am consulting.[41]

When doing so, McMahon had given Wingate to understand that as far as he was concerned the 'arrangement under present conditions would be even more confusing and troublesome than when we tried it last July'.[42] This time the sirdar was less susceptible to the pressure exerted by the high commissioner. He agreed that under the present circumstance it was best to leave things as they were, but:

> I must however point out and ask you to correct the mis-statement in your telegram [...] to the Foreign Office that proposed arrangement had been given full trial for some weeks and found quite impracticable. The arrangement was never tried because I fully realised that 'The political and military aspects of the question were so intermixed' that to separate

them would have meant hopeless confusion. You pointed out that you must control politics and I therefore declined military control without local political control which you found impossible to give me.

Wingate also urged McMahon, 'in fairness to myself', that 'telegraphic correspondence on the subject should be submitted to the War Council in order that it may not be thought that I have shirked responsibility in a matter in which I am deeply concerned and which is of such vital importance not only to the Soudan but to the whole Empire'.[43]

Murray wholeheartedly sided with Wingate. He wired to Robertson that:

Unless a large measure of political control were allowed to devolve on him, I do not think that the Sirdar could assume military control and supervision of arrangements for assisting Sherif. In my opinion he would have a very difficult task without such devolution.

Undoubtedly, the sirdar is the best man for the military control, and to conduct political control from Cairo and military control from the Soudan seems to me unworkable.[44]

In the telegram forwarding Wingate's reply, McMahon tried to refute the sirdar's implicit accusation. He also was not above questioning Sir Reginald's motives. According to Sir Henry, it appeared from their earlier correspondence on the subject that:

Far from shirking any responsibility, sirdar showed a generous disposition to assume both political and military responsibilities which in my opinion his geographic position and dearth of military resources rendered him and still renders him incapable of discharging with full advantage to the cause in which we are all interested.

McMahon, however, fought a losing battle. With regard to Wingate's reply, Hardinge observed that the sirdar 'makes out a good case for having political control also',[45] and on 9 October, after Robertson had pointed out that Murray agreed with the sirdar that 'he must have the necessary powers', the War Committee accepted Grey's suggestion that 'Sir Henry [...] must ensure that the sirdar be given whatever political powers were necessary'.[46] The struggle for political and military control of Hijaz operations had finally been decided in Wingate's favour.

Sir Reginald promptly used his freshly acquired powers to request Sir Archibald to make all necessary preparations for the transport of the brigade to Rabegh in case of an emergency. He fully realised 'objection to troops, and necessary transport remaining in suspense', but only when the Arabs were 'assured that Rabegh is secure' would they 'operate with greater boldness against the Turkish main force'.[47] McMahon forwarded Wingate's request to the Foreign Office the following day. In reaction, Grey drafted a reply to Sir Reginald in which the latter was informed that the 'War Committee, after careful consideration, had already decided that it was impossible to spare a brigade for Rabegh or to send one to Sudan to replace a brigade sent from there. Demands to assist Roumania [a combined German–Bulgarian attack threatened to crush the Romanian army; R.H.L.] have made it more than ever impossible to spare a brigade for Rabegh.'[48]

Grey's reply had not yet arrived in Cairo when McMahon dispatched another telegram to London, forwarding a telegram from Wilson, in which the latter stated that Husayn had requested the British government 'to send troops [...] to Rabegh at once'. Wilson accordingly suggested that, provided the troops were available, 'they should be sent to hold Rabegh now'. Unaware of Grey's firm rejection of Wingate's proposal, he requested that, in view of his coming meeting with Abdullah on 16 October, 'a definite decision be arrived at by that date as to whether His Majesty's Government will or will not guarantee safety of Rabegh in the event of any serious advance by Turks on that place'.[49] Wingate, who also was still ignorant of Grey's reply, supported Wilson's request. He telegraphed to McMahon that 'in keeping Wilson, the Shereef and his sons in suspense on the question of the defense of Rabegh we are incurring a very serious responsibility'. Wilson's telegram had only strengthened him in his opinion that the dispatch of British troops to Rabegh 'should be at once sanctioned by War Office and Foreign Office'.

In London, Clerk was unreceptive. He minuted that once Wingate and Wilson had received Grey's telegram of 13 October, it should be clear to them that the dispatch of British troops was 'out of the question'. Their telegrams 'should go to the War Committee, but I do not think that they require other action'.[50]

During the War Committee's meeting of 17 October it was evident that its members were not prepared to reconsider their decision on the basis of Wingate's and Wilson's telegrams, while some of them complained about the sirdar's methods. According to Robertson, 'the people out there were either disregarding the War Committee's conclusion, or did not know it', and Curzon regretted that 'the entire management of affairs had been put in the hands of the sirdar', as the latter 'had gone over to be an advocate of sending troops to Rabegh, and was reviving old alarms'. Grey was of the opinion that it would suffice 'to say to the sirdar that a British brigade could not be sent because it could not be spared', and he proposed to send a telegram in this sense.[51] After Robertson and Holderness had concurred regarding its contents, the telegram was sent to Cairo on 19 October:

> Following for sirdar.
> 'Decision of His Majesty's Government is that neither a British nor a Soudanese Infantry Brigade can be sent to Rabegh. Even if on general military grounds it was desirable to send a brigade there are political objections to sending British troops or British officers. But you have full discretion to arrange with Commander-in-Chief in Egypt to send aeroplanes, guns and supplies of all kinds that are really required and can be spared'.[52]

The Rabegh Question: The Third Round

On 1 November 1916, McMahon wired to the Foreign Office that in the course of consultations on board HMS *Dufferin*, Aziz Ali and Sharif Ali had informed the commander that 'the Turks are seriously advancing not only by Sultani Road but also by inland road', and that, 'if seriously attacked [...] they cannot hold Rabegh and request assistance as soon as possible, guns and machine-guns especially, complete with British crews'.[53] The news did not cause a stir in Khartoum. Wingate explained to Wemyss that it was 'not impossible, having regard to unreliability of Arab reports, that Turkish strength and immediate intention are exaggerated and misrepresented', but even 'if news of immediate Turkish advance in force is true, it is quite impossible for additional guns and assistance to get to Rabegh in time'. Little else could be done than 'to arrange rapid assembly of war and other ships off Rabegh to give a measure of moral support to Arabs; and perhaps to the Turks the impression that an expeditionary force is arriving'.[54]

At the War Committee's meeting of 2 November, McMahon's telegram caused considerable excitement, Prime Minster Asquith's suggestion that 'the whole thing might be exaggerated' notwithstanding. Both Chamberlain and Curzon thought that the telegram afforded a good opportunity to renew the struggle with Robertson. The former declared that he still favoured the sending of troops. He believed that 'it would be a perfect disaster if the Turks took Rabegh'. Not to send troops 'was courting disaster and reproach'. Curzon added that he 'thought we ought to run the risk of sending troops'. He proposed to send all available troops, be they French, British or Egyptian, to Rabegh at once. He also asked Robertson how matters stood with respect to the brigade, but Sir William did not budge. He 'had nothing to do with Egypt, but he did not think they had any brigade available'. On the suggestion of Grey it was decided that Wingate should consult Wemyss.[55] If the vice-admiral no longer adhered to his opinion that the Arabs could hold Rabegh with naval assistance, then Wingate 'should send to Rabegh whatever French, British and Soudanese military assistance which is immediately available'.[56]

Robertson interpreted the War Committee's decision in a rather surprising manner in a telegram to Murray. According to the CIGS:

> You should understand these instructions are not intended to extend to the despatch of any troops from your command to Rabegh or to that of any troops to replace those, if any, which may be sent by the sirdar [...] In other respects you will do your best to assist him. I do not know if he will ask you for assistance but in any case there is no question of sending anything of the nature of an expeditionary force or such other forces as may involve us in still another campaign.[57]

As yet unaware of this proviso, Wingate judged 'the decision I got in the middle of the night [...] all to the good',[58] the more so – as appeared from a telegram from Wilson of 2 November – that 'report of Turkish advance has little foundation in fact'.[59] It seemed that there existed a breathing space during which it was possible 'to put up a good defence of Rabegh if the Turks make up their minds to attack'.[60] Sir Reginald, however, did not remain ignorant of Robertson's proviso for long. On 3 November he informed the Foreign Office that he was 'asking General Murray to hold (?brigade) of British troops in readiness to proceed to Rabegh if immediately available'.[61] In reply, Murray sent Wingate Robertson's telegram, to which he added that, in view of these instructions, he did 'not feel justified in sending a brigade to Rabegh', but that Wingate could rely on him 'within the instructions above quoted to give every help I can and to act in full sympathy with you in your difficult task'.[62] Sir Reginald resignedly wrote to Wilson that:

It is rather typical of our Home Authorities to tell me that I can use British, French and Sudanese troops if available, and when the question of their being available is gone into, it is found that they cannot come – however, we must do the best we can in circumstances and I am delighted the Admiral is coming here with Lawrence [Captain T.E. Lawrence; R.H.L.] – they are due this afternoon and a good talk over the whole situation with them, should clear the atmosphere considerably.[63]

Clerk and Hardinge had meanwhile reached the conclusion that a Turkish advance on Rabegh was only a matter of time. They therefore thought it highly desirable that the necessary measures would at last be taken to enable Wingate to get the town's defence on a sound footing. In any case, so Clerk observed, 'we want to avoid both another scare of this sort, and the hurried action which we are consequently rushed into'. According to him:

We must first of all recognise that we can only make Rabegh safe if we have there a proportion of trained Christian officers and men. We were ready to send them there in a hurry, on the chance of saving Rabegh, and we should do so again. I take it, in similar circumstances, the principle of allowing no Christians on Hedjaz soil has in fact to go when it is a case of saving Mecca.

Wingate should impress upon Husayn that 'if he wishes to protect Rabegh and the road to Mecca', then it was necessary that the Emir should 'give the strictest orders for complete facilities for British and French units at Rabegh, for if there are any difficulties those units will have to be withdrawn entirely'. Hardinge agreed. He minuted that 'this course seems right. Draft telegrams accordingly.'[64]

On 7 November, Wingate reported to the Foreign Office on his conference with Wemyss and Lawrence. The three of them had reached the conclusion that the 'Rabegh position if strongly attacked by the Turks would not be tenable even with Naval assistance', and that the alternatives to avert this danger were '(a) at least a brigade of regular troops with artillery could arrive there by sea in time, or (b) a trained Arab force of about 5,000 men, with artillery, was available for the defence'. However, option (a) was 'ruled out by the War Office decision that troops are not available', while option (b) would clearly take some time before it could be realised. For the time being, there remained little else to do but to keep 'the most important group of tribesmen (viz:– those hitherto operating under the Emir Feisal) in the field'. Wingate and Wemyss therefore suggested providing Faysal's forces with all the necessary 'moral and material support (aeroplanes, guns, machine-guns)' enabling them 'to continue their defensive in the hills, and their attempts on the Hedjaz railway'.[65]

The Foreign Office forwarded Wingate's telegram to Robertson. The latter drew up a reply in which he studiously avoided discussing the possibility that the War Committee might reconsider its decision and put a brigade at the sirdar's disposal. This induced Hardinge to write a letter to Grey in which he put on record his objections to Sir William's handling of the Rabegh affair:

> It seems to me that Gen. Robertson in his fear of our being involved in a serious affair, which may develop into something on a much bigger scale at Rabegh, ignores absolutely the very serious political effect that may arise if the Sherif is defeated by the Turks [...] My belief is that the effect will be disastrous throughout the East, and will gravely affect our military operations in Mesopotamia and our position at Aden, in Persia, and on the N.W. frontier of India.
>
> My impression is that there are at present more than 100,000 troops in Egypt; surely 4,000 could be spared to uphold the Shereef?
>
> I feel so strongly the deplorable effect of a possible defeat of the Shereef that I venture to put these views before you.[66]

Rabegh was again on the agenda of the War Committee on 10 November.[67] As Robertson observed in his memoirs, 'the majority of the War Committee were by this time heartily tired of the whole question, and they decided to refer it to a committee'.[68] This committee, consisting of Grey, Chamberlain, Curzon and Robertson, met the same day. Chamberlain and Curzon employed the same argument as Hardinge, 'the General Staff were making a great fuss about a small matter – one infantry brigade'.[69] Sir William replied that a brigade was 'too small a force' if it was decided to deny Rabegh to the Turks. He insisted that 'we must not repeat the mistake of the Dardanelles or of Mesopotamia by attempting an object with a force insufficient to secure it'.[70] However, this argument failed to dissuade Grey, Chamberlain and Curzon. After a 'long and rather unpleasant discussion',[71] the ministers agreed that they were 'prepared to take the responsibility for deciding that

Rabegh should be secured. It was therefore decided that Sir W. Robertson should report to the War Committee what force he considered necessary to send'.[72]

Robertson dispatched a telegram to Wingate the same day. He asked whether the latter could agree with him that if the Turks intended 'making a really determined effort to seize [Rabegh], it would be possible for them to advance with about sixteen thousand men and twelve guns'. Not that the CIGS had received fresh information about an imminent Turkish attack, but 'if any Imperial troops are sent there, they must be sufficiently strong and possess enough mobility to defeat such a force as that mentioned'. Sir Reginald replied that 'our information of the Turkish force intended for the advance south is practically identical with that mentioned in your telegram'. He nevertheless agreed with the 'local authorities' that 'a brigade of imperial troops at Rabegh, well supplied with artillery and with the support of the fire of naval ships in the harbour, would be sufficient to hold that place against any force the Turks could send against it'.[73] Robertson could not understand Wingate's estimate of the number of troops necessary to secure Rabegh. He found it incomprehensible, so he wrote to Hankey, that Wingate concurred with him as to the strength of the Turkish force and at the same time subscribed to the view of the 'local authorities' that a brigade was sufficient to defend Rabegh.[74]

In his memorandum for the War Committee, Robertson returned in detail to the subject that a far larger force than a brigade was needed for the defence of Rabegh. After he had explained that he still adhered to his objections to the dispatch of an expeditionary force to Rabegh as stated in his memorandum of 20 September (see section 'The Rabegh Question: The First Round', above), Robertson proceeded to formulate four additional arguments against the scheme. The first concerned the number of troops necessary to secure Rabegh:

> We have had sufficient experience in this war of the folly of embarking upon expeditions with *minimum* forces, and I cannot advise the Committee to send less troops than are sufficient to defeat the *maximum* force which the enemy can employ. I put the force necessary to meet and defeat a Turkish attack by 16,000 men at two brigades of infantry, two companies of camel corps and two brigades (six batteries) of field artillery. These with the requisite administrative units […] bring the force up to about 15,000 men.

And even such a large force was really no guarantee at all, as the Turks without doubt 'have troops available for a much larger expedition, provided they can be maintained'. Robertson's second argument was that the dispatch of such a force reduced the strength of Murray's forces 'to below what is required for his advance on El Arish, which has been ordered by the War Committee' (see Chapter 6, section 'The British Offensive in the Sinai and the Sykes–Picot Mission'); consequently, 'it will be necessary [...] to reverse the previous decision and to abandon El Arish operations'. The War Committee should moreover realise that a host of practical problems had to be overcome before the proposed force could be landed, which meant – and this was Robertson's third argument – that 'if the orders are now given', the force would be at Rabegh 'about the middle of December, and before then the Turks may be in Rabegh'. The CIGS finally argued that 'in war some risks must be taken if a dissemination of force such as makes victory very difficult if not impossible is to be avoided'. He concluded by summing up his position:

> Nothing would give the Germans greater pleasure than to see us frittering away our troops in secondary operations, and that of itself is almost sufficient reason for not embarking on still another campaign. I admit, of course, that if we do not send the force, the Turks may reach Rabegh but I consider that the Committee would be not only justified in accepting this risk, but that they ought to take it as otherwise they will commit a very serious military mistake.[75]

The War Committee again discussed the Rabegh question on 16 November. Asquith, Lloyd George and Robertson were not present owing to an inter-allied conference in Paris. Bonar Law therefore raised the point whether it was 'possible or desirable to discuss the Rabegh question', especially as Sir William 'had such strong opinions on the subject'. However, Grey, supported by Hardinge, argued that the matter admitted no further delay. He regarded:

> Time as of the utmost importance, and therefore he thought the question must be discussed on that day. [...]
> The conference at the Foreign Office had decided that it was of the highest importance to save Rabegh. Let the War Committee confirm the decision that Rabegh must be saved, and let them leave it to the Military

Authorities to say how is should be done: otherwise he feared that Rabegh might fall.

Balfour believed that 'it was impossible that these questions should be left to the Military Authorities to decide'. He turned Robertson's argument that in war some risks must be taken, against the CIGS. Indeed, 'a risk must be taken somewhere', and, for this very reason, 'he disputed the necessity of accepting the Chief of the Imperial General Staff's estimate of 15,000 men stated to be required to make Rabegh <u>absolutely</u> secure. He thought it would be sufficient if a smaller force were sent which would make the place <u>practically</u> safe.' Chamberlain added that, although 'the crushing of the Sherif would blacken our faces irretrievably', Robertson apparently was prepared 'to accept that and <u>any</u> risk, sooner than divert troops to Rabegh'.

Curzon agreed with Grey that the meeting of 10 November had been intended to arrive at a 'definite' decision, and 'it only remained for the War Committee to confirm that decision: it was quite unnecessary for the whole thing to be discussed over again'. However, when it appeared that Bonar Law would not stand for 'any measures which went beyond asking for further information', Curzon suggested that the War Committee for the moment should refrain from taking a definitive decision. He proposed that a telegram be sent to Murray with several practical questions relating to the dispatch of a brigade. After a long discussion, this compromise was eventually accepted.[76]

The next day, Murray sent a telegram to Robertson in which he drew the latter's attention to a telegram he was sending to the DMI 'although the question of the advisability or otherwise of sending British or foreign troops is out of my province'. This telegram contained a report by Lawrence on his recent visit to the Hijaz. According to Lawrence, this 'violent memorandum on the whole subject' had rather pleased both Clayton and Murray.[77] In his telegraphic summary, Murray explained to Robertson that Lawrence's:

> Strongly expressed opinion that no British or foreign force should be sent to Hedjaz is strongly supported by civilian and soldier residents in this country who are intimately acquainted with the delicate nature of the Sherif's position as a religious chief and the peculiar feelings of the Arabian Moslems towards foreigners.
>
> Shortly put the views held by the Moslem experts who have spoken to me on the subject entirely confirm Lawrence's views that the Sherif as a

religious chief ceases to exist the moment foreign troops land in Arabia and that the occupation of Rabegh force acting on the defensive is useless.[78]

After he had sent this telegram, Murray also dispatched a telegram to Wingate. He informed the sirdar that he had just seen Lawrence, and that he had gathered that Wingate concurred in Lawrence's strong objections 'against white troops to Arabia'. He therefore suggested that 'Chief London should at once be informed', the more so as it appeared from the latest telegrams that 'question sending British troops to Rabegh is once more under consideration in London'. Wingate surely agreed with him that 'if any recent developments in Arabia have indicated the inadvisability of sending white troops there, Chief London should be informed?'[79]

After the War Committee's meeting of 16 November, the Admiralty had asked Wemyss for his opinion on the feasibility of landing a force of 15,000 men at Rabegh.[80] Sir Rosslyn had replied that:

> Operation presents no difficulty whatever from naval point of view provided water is arranged for, but I submit I look upon the policy of landing Christian troops in large numbers in the Hedjaz, except as very last resource, as highly dangerous to the success of the Shereef's cause owing to fanatical prejudice of Arabs against the presence of Christians in the Hedjaz.[81]

In contrast to Murray, the vice-admiral informed Wingate of the contents of his telegram. Sir Reginald had in the meantime replied to Sir Archibald that, as far as he was concerned, 'both Chief London and F.O. have the true facts of the situation before them and to further complicate them now by such remarks as Lawrence seems to suggest would, in my opinion be highly undesirable. If Lawrence is still in Cairo, please tell him how matter stands.' He also requested that Murray and Wemyss get in touch with one another, as it was 'very important we should all represent identical views as far as possible'.[82]

The objections Lawrence and Wemyss had voiced against the sending of troops to the Hijaz also served to 'knock out' another proposal. On 16 November, the French government had offered to provide Husayn with the necessary 'support and material', now that Britain was unable to do so. This offer was totally unacceptable to the Foreign Office. According to Hardinge:

> To adopt such a proposal would be disastrous, since it would imply the reversal of our policy of the last 100 years which has aimed at the exclusion of

foreign influence on the shores of the Red Sea. The establishment of France at Djibouti has been a thorn in our sides almost from the moment it took place, and to allow the French to establish their influence in the Hedjaz as predominant over our's will be to abdicate the position that we have always held in the Muslim world.[83]

However, 'if we decided not to send a brigade because we had not one', so Grey explained to the War Committee on 20 November, 'we could not prevent the French from sending one'. Luckily, Lawrence's and Wemyss's assertions offered a nice way out of this dilemma seeing that 'the mere fact of sending a European force would entail the collapse of the hill tribes'.

Bonar Law and Robertson for their part argued that Husayn until then had never personally asked for the dispatch of a brigade. Chamberlain complained that the War Committee 'got opinions from so many points that they did not know what value to attach to them. He supposed that the sirdar was the man who knew most about it, and they ought to know his views.' Grey wished to know whether Lawrence's and Wemyss's objections also obtained if the French sent Algerian troops. It was decided to dispatch telegrams to Wemyss and Wingate to determine whether the objections applied equally to the landing of French Muslim troops. Sir Reginald was also requested to inform the War Committee of his views on Lawrence's report.[84]

Wemyss confirmed that the Arabs objected to the landing of any considerable number of foreign troops, 'whatever may be their religion or nationality', as it would 'arouse the prejudices and suspicions of the tribes of Arabia, who are hardly less prejudiced against people of a foreign nationality than they are against men of the Christian religion'.[85] Wingate sent two long telegrams in which he mainly tried to justify the position he had taken up in the Rabegh question thus far. He did not directly answer Grey's question as to whether or not Muslim troops, instead of Christian troops, could be landed in the Hijaz, but did not deny that Lawrence 'is probably quite correct in warning us of the danger of landing Christian troops in any large numbers in the Hedjaz'. For this reason the sirdar had advocated a policy to postpone the dispatch of British or French troops 'as long as we possibly can'. Wingate repeated his 'carefully considered opinion that neither British nor French brigades should be sent to Rabegh until true facts of enemy's situation and intentions are clearer, but that preparations for an emergency should be made'.[86]

The third Rabegh crisis had also not produced the outcome Wingate had wished for, but the sirdar was not yet ready to give up. In a letter to Wilson he applied the same argument he had already used in his letter to Hogarth at the beginning of July. Lawrence appeared:

> To have omitted the one and important essential, and that is that the Arabs have no more desire to come under the heel of the Turks again than has the Sherif himself, and when it comes to a matter of almost certain defeat, the Arabs will, in my opinion, welcome any steps taken to save them, just as a drowning man catches at a straw, only in this case, I hope that the straw, in the shape of a British or French brigade, will prove to be a very solid plank which will save him.[87]

It seemed that Wingate, in his efforts to provide Husayn with the military support he considered essential to save the latter's revolt, possessed the same personality trait that enabled Robertson to resist them. The latter observed in a letter to Murray that Rabegh had 'been a perfect nuisance during the last few weeks but I have been as stubborn as a donkey and so far I have succeeded in getting my way'.[88]

The Rabegh Question: The Fourth Round

On 6 December 1916, Wingate sent a telegram to the Foreign Office that contained indications of a fresh Rabegh crisis. He had received telegraphic reports that Djemal Pasha, the commander-in-chief of the Turkish fourth army, had arrived in Medina, and that Turkish troops had begun to advance on Rabegh simultaneously. Wingate thought it still too early to say 'whether Turkish menace is sufficiently grave to necessitate immediate consideration of emergency measures', but he reminded the Foreign Office that his 'opinion regarding desirability of preventing at all costs the capture of Rabegh by Turks is unchanged'.[89]

According to Wilson, a crisis was imminent, although he admitted to Wingate that 'lack of accurate intelligence makes it extremely difficult to estimate degree of emergency'. In any case, 'at least a brigade of troops [...] should be held ready for immediate embarkation at Suez'.[90] Wingate telegraphed a summary of Wilson's observations to London on 7 December, and added that a Turkish offensive 'having regard to the nature of Arab forces now in the field, would almost certainly result in the entry of a Turkish force into Mecca (with all its grave political and military consequences) within a space of a few weeks'.[91]

Six days earlier, a government crisis had broken out in London. On 1 December, Lloyd George had more or less delivered an ultimatum to Asquith by demanding the reconstitution of the government in order to increase the efficiency of the British war effort. The events that followed culminated in Lloyd George being asked to form a government on 6 December, a task he successfully completed within a day.[92]

The reorganisation of the government that was carried out in the next couple of days included, among other things, the creation of two new government bodies. The first was the War Cabinet. Beside Lloyd George, it consisted of the following ministers: Lord Alfred Milner, Curzon, Bonar Law and Arthur Henderson (as the representative of Labour). With the exception of Bonar Law, who also held the post of chancellor of the exchequer, the members of the War Cabinet were ministers without portfolio (although Curzon was also lord president of the council and leader of the House of Lords). Ministers in charge of a department, in the future, could only attend cabinet meetings if matters were under consideration that involved their department. In such a case, they took part in the discussion on an equal footing with the members of the War Cabinet, and were equally responsible for the decisions taken. The second innovation was the creation of a War Cabinet Secretariat, headed by Hankey. The secretariat was responsible for the agenda, the preparation and the minutes of the War Cabinet's meetings, and also for informing the relevant departments of the War Cabinet's decisions.[93]

Grey did not return in the new government. His successor was Balfour.[94] Cecil stayed on as parliamentary under-secretary and became responsible for Middle Eastern affairs. Chamberlain continued as secretary of state for India. On 7 December, he sent a letter to Lloyd George in which he urged the latter, with reference to Wingate's telegrams, to settle the Rabegh question right away.[95] Robertson remained chief of the Imperial General Staff. On 8 December, he wrote a memorandum in which he expressed the hope that he had heard the last of the Rabegh affair:

> We need to keep our attention on the big things and not brood and waste brainpower over such petty matters as Rabegh, Persia, etc. It is really pitiable sometimes to see the worried and pessimistic looks of certain people because of some temporary set-back which matters not at all. I hope you

will not mind my saying that some members of the late government never had any proper perspective of the war. They lived from telegram to telegram and attached so much importance to a few scallywags in Arabia as I imagine they did to the German attack on Ypres two years ago.[96]

The War Cabinet met for the first time on 9 December 1916. Two days earlier, Murray had handed Robertson yet another weapon in the battle against the sending of a force to Rabegh, by explaining that the water supply there was not sufficient to support a brigade.[97] Rabegh was discussed 'at considerable length' with Chamberlain in attendance. Although long, the discussion did not yield any new point of view. The change of government had not resulted in breaking the Rabegh deadlock. This time, again, the decision was to postpone the decision pending further information, and to instruct the authorities in Egypt and the Sudan to take the necessary precautionary measures in case, 'in the last resort' troops had to be dispatched to Rabegh. The Foreign Office was further instructed to ask the French government whether they had decided to send a brigade, 'and if so, what troops they proposed to send and when they will be ready'. It was also directed to inform Wingate to take 'any action possible with a view to the preparation of a military position at Rabegh, in readiness for occupation by the Allied forces on their arrival'. The War Office was instructed 'to prepare a brigade for the use of the sirdar if ordered', while the Admiralty, pending the French reply, 'should examine into the question of water supply at Rabegh'.[98]

That same day, Sir Reginald dispatched a telegram to London in which he stated that he had 'little doubt that the Turks really mean business'. Given that 'all military opinions' agreed that the Arab forces at Rabegh 'even with naval assistance are incapable of defending this base against a determined attack by the Turks', there were:

Only two alternatives open to us.

1. To despatch at least one brigade of regular troops with the necessary artillery from Egypt to Rabegh. I gather that French troops in sufficient numbers are not available there so British troops would have to be sent. If the Turks go first to Yenbo these troops might still arrive in time to put Rabegh into a state of defence and deny it to the Turks. Or,
2. Preparation to evacuate foreign, British and Egyptian personnel, aeroplanes and stores from Rabegh as soon as information is received that Turkish advance to this base has actually begun.

The effect of those preparations on the moral of the Arabs will be naturally very bad.⁹⁹

Wingate remained silent on which alternative he favoured, but in a letter to Clayton he was less reticent. It seemed 'almost inevitable that a brigade be sent to Rabegh […] if the Turks really mean coming south after having pushed Feisal and Co. aside, then an effort must be made to stop them – the question is can we do it in time?'¹⁰⁰

On 10 December, Sir Reginald instructed Wilson to tell Husayn that it was 'the considered opinion of the British military advisers that the local Arab troops, even with naval assistance, are totally inadequate to oppose with success a resolute attack on Rabegh by the Turks'. If Husayn was prepared to 'make a formal request, which must be confirmed in writing under his own signature', then Wingate would 'represent to His Majesty's Government the necessity to despatch as soon as possible from Egypt a brigade of European troops with the necessary artillery'. The sirdar naturally could not guarantee that these troops were 'immediately available nor that they will be sent', but he had good hopes that 'on the formal request by the Sherif, and with the latter's assurance that every facility will be given us by the Arab leaders at Rabegh for the defence of that place by European troops, His Majesty's Government may be disposed to reconsider their previous decision in this connection'.¹⁰¹

The next days witnessed a dispute involving the War Cabinet, Wingate and Husayn, in which they took turns in trying, in more or less subtle ways, to shift the responsibility for the decision of whether or not to send troops to Rabegh, and above all its possibly fatal consequences, onto one another. Sir Reginald telegraphed the Foreign Office on 11 December that Wilson had received a letter from Husayn, in which the latter had stated that 'owing to present war circumstances it is necessary to bring six battalions of regular troops. If it is possible for His Majesty's Government to bring Moslem troops it will be good, if not there is no objection if European troops are brought.'¹⁰² No sooner had the sirdar sent this telegram, than he received yet another from Wilson, in which the latter cancelled his previous one. Wilson had reached the conclusion, after a long conversation with Husayn, that the latter did not wish for British troops to land in the Hijaz just yet. Husayn greatly feared 'the effect on Moslem opinion if Christian troops are landed in Hedjaz'.¹⁰³ In his reply, Wingate made it very clear who was to blame if the revolt collapsed:

Shereef is aware that nature and scope of military assistance we have hitherto rendered to Arab cause has been greatly restricted by our desire not to offend Moslem susceptibilities.

His present decision therefore inasmuch it affirms the necessity to maintain the present restrictions, also clearly admits this responsibility for its military consequences.[104]

When the War Cabinet discussed the situation on 12 December, only Wilson's first telegram had been received. Unaware of the latest developments, it decided to send a telegram to the sirdar in which the decision to send troops was left at his discretion. The War Cabinet did 'not wish to land troops in the Hedjaz except in the last extremity', but 'the Shereef must be saved from destruction, if possible'. Sir Reginald was therefore authorised 'to despatch these troops whenever you think the moment has come', provided that there was still time to prepare an entrenched position, that a brigade would suffice, and that it could 'be supplied with water and all necessities'.[105]

The Foreign Office, however, refrained from dispatching the telegram as it stood, because shortly after the War Cabinet's meeting it had received Wilson's second telegram. Hardinge feared that, in view of Husayn's cancellation, the text of the War Cabinet telegram was open to misapprehension. He therefore limited Wingate's discretion by substituting 'receive a request from Sherif in this sense' for the original 'think the moment has come'.[106]

Cyril Wilson had yet another interview with Husayn on the evening of 11 December. During this conversation, Husayn again opposed the landing of Christian troops. Wingate's telegram containing Wilson's report of this meeting induced Clerk to minute in exasperation that 'the Sherif is hopeless. My opinion is that, if we can, we should try to save him in spite of himself, for the consequences of his collapse may be most serious for us, and when it is too late he will beg for British troops.'[107] Wingate came to the same conclusion. He telegraphed to the Foreign Office the next day that 'the Shereef and his Arabs' would have to be saved 'in spite of themselves'. British assistance would have to consist of regular troops. The sirdar saw 'no alternative or practical means of assisting Arabs and of saving the Shereef's movement from collapse'. He therefore suggested that the War Cabinet should authorise him to 'send necessary troops at once as if enemy advances as we think he may one day, there is no time to be lost'.[108] The War Cabinet saw through Wingate's attempt to shift the responsibility for the decision back to the War Cabinet. The result of its discussion of the Rabegh question on 15 December was to instruct the Foreign Office to send a telegram to Sir Reginald in which the sirdar was given to understand that, although the War Cabinet fully realised that 'the responsibility of the collapse of the Shereef's movement, if it should unfortunately occur, will rest with him owing to his final refusal of British military assistance', the decision whether or not to send troops was entirely Wingate's. He had the authority 'to take necessary steps to send British brigade [...] if you are satisfied as to conditions named in our earlier telegrams'.[109] 'This is now in the sirdar's own hands', so Hardinge summarised the situation.[110]

Wingate decided not to avail himself of the War Cabinet's authorisation to save the Arabs in spite of themselves. He telegraphed to the Foreign Office on 16 December that he proposed to inform Husayn that the latter should decide 'whether or not he requires a European force to be landed at Rabegh in the course of the next fortnight. If his reply is in the negative he must understand that we shall regard his refusal as final, and that our present offer will not be repeated.'[111] The next day, Sir Reginald, in a letter to Wilson, gave vent to his disappointment with the turn events had taken:

> I don't think there ever was a more difficult and unsatisfactory position. To think that after all our efforts to get our government to send troops and now they are not acceptable??
>
> The S[harif] is absolutely wrong and I fear he will realise it too late.
>
> I have always said the drowning man will catch at the proverbial straw – but this time I fear the straw will not save him. Turks and Germans will play Old Harry with his embryonic Kingdom [see section 'The Emir of Mecca is recognised as King of the Hijaz', below] and no man ever had a better chance, or more whole-hearted support – and now has he used it?[112]

Clerk was not particularly pleased with Wingate's solution. It was with the utmost diffidence that he put forward any views on the question, 'as one never knows which way the pendulum is swinging at the moment', but he was still in favour of sending troops to Rabegh, and 'risk the explosion of Moslem feeling'. Sir Ronald Graham agreed.[113] Experience showed that 'the "explosions of feeling" on such occasions are not usually so violent as is anticipated. They protest much, but accept the "fait accompli".' What mattered was that 'the collapse of the Sherif's movement would be a disaster to us throughout the East'.[114] At this time, again, the views of Foreign Office officials did not matter much. Although the War Cabinet rejected Wingate's latest invention on 19 December, it accepted it the next day. The Foreign Office was instructed to send a telegram to Sir Reginald 'to the effect that His Majesty's Government approved his suggestion, and he should inform the Sherif as proposed'.[115]

The fear of being saddled with responsibility for the wrong decision also settled the fourth Rabegh crisis, by taking the decision not to take a decision. Proponents of radical solutions had second thoughts the moment they were given the opportunity to carry them out. When the chips were down, the parties involved preferred to gamble on the chance that, as Wingate had put it in his telegram of 16 December, 'Turkish lack of initiative coupled with nervousness regarding their communications might still deter them from undertaking an offensive of sufficient force to overwhelm native Arab levies', even though this chance was 'a very small one'.[116]

The Rabegh Question: The Fifth and Final Flare Up

In the last weeks of 1916, Wingate and Husayn continued to argue about who was responsible if the Turks yet succeeded in crushing Husayn's revolt. The latter wrote to Sir Reginald that 'the substance of the rise and fall of the Arab Kingdom, pardon my saying so, comes back upon the honour and prestige of he who has guaranteed the independence and continued existence'. The sirdar replied that he regretted Husayn's decision not to permit Christian troops to land in the Hijaz, and that, in consequence, 'the responsibility for preventing the Turks from retaking Mecca definitively' devolved on him.[117] Husayn's reaction to this message from Wingate resulted in a last, short-lived crisis with respect to Rabegh.

On 3 January 1917, Pearson, who deputised for Wilson while the latter was away from Jedda, telegraphed to Wingate that he had received a message from Husayn, signed by Fu'ad al-Khatib, to the effect that the king, in view of Wingate's claim that 'the despatch of the force would fulfil the purpose and prevent the risk', authorised the landing of British troops.[118] Sir Reginald considered this formula satisfactory enough to take action. He decided to send a brigade to Rabegh. In a memorandum for Murray, which he dictated to Clayton, he expounded his motives for this decision:

> My instructions and my object are to prevent the collapse of the Sherif's revolt and consequent recapture of Mecca at all costs.

The forces at disposal are:–
(a) the Arab tribesmen now in the field.
(b) A British brigade, which I have been authorised to use if I consider it necessary.

The Arab tribesmen cannot prevent a Turkish advance on Mecca, which is therefore at the mercy of the Turks if they can organise the requisite transport and supply.

Moreover, the Arab tribesmen may at any time lose confidence and disperse, without the feeling of security which a backing of trained troops will give. After weighing advantages and disadvantages I have decided to send the brigade to Rabegh, as the course best calculated to maintain the Arabs' cause and protect Mecca, in so far as possible, with the means at my disposal.[119]

Wingate's decision was a great disappointment to Murray. In his reply he made no attempt to hide it, 'I need hardly say what a blow your letter and the Sherif's telegrams are to me. It is not for me to criticise your actions or views in this matter, but I do consider that the Sherif has been more or less obliged to accept the assistance.'[120] Murray at the same time dispatched a telegram to Robertson, in which he informed Sir William of the latest developments and requested 'covering sanction'.[121] Wingate refrained from informing the Foreign Office of the latest developments until 6 January. He reported that, with reference to a 'formal application by the Shereef that a British force may be landed at Rabegh for the defence of that place against a possible Turkish attack', he had started the necessary preparations. One of these had been to ask Husayn 'to notify me as soon as possible of general line of his propaganda to explain arrival of Christian troops in Hedjaz'.[122]

How much weight could be attached to a message that had only been signed by Fu'ad al-Khatib? None whatsoever, as far as Wilson was concerned. A request like the one contained in the message, with such far-reaching consequences, ought to be made in the king's own handwriting. Besides, had it not been decided in December that no troops were available? Wilson instructed Pearson to request Wingate to reply to the message in this sense.[123] After his return to Jedda, Wilson, in a subsequent telegram to Wingate, added the observation that Husayn in his request must accept full responsibility for the consequences if British troops were landed, but, with the way in which Fu'ad al-Khatib's message had been worded, this responsibility was completely put on Wingate's shoulders.[124]

Small wonder that the receipt of a further telegram from Wingate, instructing Wilson to inform Husayn that 'we are acting on his application [...] and that a British brigade will sail for Rabegh from Suez as soon as possible', came as an unpleasant surprise. Wilson telegraphed on 7 January that he much regretted:

> This decision without conditions stated in my telegram W. 118 Jan. 6th being complied with, and consider the sending of British troops to Hedjaz on strength of a telephonic message from an official of the Arab government, a most dangerous proceeding. The Sheriff can easily repudiate the message in whole or in part. I also consider that before the landing of British troops at Rabegh, sufficient time should be given Sheriff to make his propaganda. This he cannot do if troops leave in next few days, and I consider the Sheriff should be consulted as to how long he requires.[125]

Someone from the Arab Bureau passed Wilson's telegram on to Murray, who decided to employ the 'Lawrence-procedure' once more. He forwarded Wilson's telegram, without consulting Wingate, to the War Office, although this time Wingate did receive a copy.[126] Sir Reginald reacted at once. He telegraphed to Wilson that the latter's telegram and his own had apparently crossed. Wingate naturally agreed that 'the application [...] must be confirmed by Sherif in writing', but considered that 'this general assurance in this connection will suffice, taking into account the urgent requirements of the military situation, the Sherif's character and the course of recent negotiations'.[127] Wingate also dispatched a telegram to the Foreign Office, in which he explained that he had already instructed Wilson that 'before landing of British troops in Hedjaz can be sanctioned, Shereef must (a) confirm in writing application in a cipher telegram to me [...] (b) give written assurance in regard to reception of Christian troops by Arab commanders and tribesmen.' He nevertheless recommended the 'despatch of British troops to Rabegh immediately the formal confirmation of Shereef's application to me is received'.[128]

Wingate's telegram arrived in London too late to be discussed during the meeting of the War Cabinet on 8 January. Lloyd George, Milner and Robertson did not attend. Sir Frederick Maurice, DMO, deputised for the latter. Chamberlain completely agreed with Wilson. He regretted that Husayn in his message 'appeared to throw the responsibility for the landing of Christian troops on Sir R. Wingate', and he believed that it was:

> Essential that the King should ask for this assistance in writing, and at the same time he should issue a manifesto over his own signature, in terms approved by Sir R. Wingate, explaining exactly why he had urged us to send troops, and taking full responsibility upon himself, in order to allay any suspicions of Moslems in general and Indian Moslems in particular in regard to our interference in Hedjaz affairs.
>
> After some discussion it was decided that:
>
> The Chief of the Imperial General Staff, in consultation with the Foreign Office, and the India Office, should send a telegram to the High Commissioner in the sense that no troops should be despatched to Rabegh until a written communication had been received from the King of the Hedjaz definitely asking for troops and accepting full responsibility for such action, and further, that the King of the Hedjaz should be required to send the draft of a manifesto explaining his action for the approval of His Majesty's Government.[129]

General Maurice drafted a telegram in this sense. After it had been approved by the India Office and the Foreign Office, it was sent to Cairo the same day.[130] That evening it became clear that it was highly unlikely that Husayn would be prepared to fulfil these conditions. Fu'ad al-Khatib informed Wilson by telephone that 'Sharif requests us to delay embarkation and despatch of troops until necessity arises. Full particulars follow. The Sherif obviously does not wish to confirm telephonic request for troops at present in writing'.[131]

Wingate wrote to Murray that 'we must see what the "particulars" are – but, if it means a return to the old system of procrastination and hesitancy, I shall then instruct him [Cyril Wilson; R.H.L.] to tell the Sherif that he can no longer count on British troops being sent'.[132] Sir Reginald also dispatched a telegram in this sense to London the next day.[133] His scepticism turned out to be well founded. Two days later, he telegraphed to the Foreign Office that:

> Letters from Shereef have been received at Jeddah to the effect that he does not desire us to land British troops at Hedjaz at present. He realises that this decision entails the removal of the brigade now at Suez and that he cannot

count upon British assistance being forthcoming should he apply for it at future date.[134]

The Rabegh question was definitely a thing of the past. After Husayn's decision not to permit the landing of British troops in the Hijaz, the military situation there changed as if by magic. Faysal's troops until then had been regarded as a defensive force that would not be able to prevent a Turkish advance on Mecca, but from this point on they were believed to be capable of seriously threatening the Turkish position at Medina. In view of this 'more satisfactory state of Arab military situation as shown by latest Hedjaz reports', Wingate looked favourably upon Murray's request to withdraw the brigade from Suez. He proposed that the Foreign Office consent to it, especially as 'recent letters and telegrams' between him and Husayn had 'made it clear that His Majesty's Government cannot now be charged with breach of faith in the event of movement collapsing'.[135] It seemed that Sir Reginald was finally satisfied that the responsibility for the possible collapse of the Arab revolt rested with Husayn alone, and that 'we are exonerated from all blame for the failure of his movement'.[136]

The Emir of Mecca is Recognised as King of the Hijaz

On Sunday 29 October 1916, the Foreign Office was informed by telegram that 'the notables and ulemas of the country' and all 'all classes of the populations' had 'unanimously' recognised Sharif Husayn as 'King of the Arab Nation'. The telegram was signed by Sharif Abdullah in his new capacity of foreign minister of the Arab government. Two days later, Clerk minuted that this was 'rather a bomb', and that 'we really cannot recognise the Sherif as "King of the Arab Nation" yet a while'. He suggested approaching the French government and informing them that the British government intended to reply that Husayn's title not only was 'an unwarrantable intervention in the internal affairs of Arabia', but also would do 'incalculable harm to the Sherif's cause. The time is not yet ripe for such a proceeding.' Hardinge, however, did not want to commit the Foreign Office just yet. He suggested that 'the views of the French government' should first be sought, but Grey agreed with Clerk: 'let us make up our own minds and then tell the French what we propose to do' – after all, 'the Sherif is our own affair'.[137]

The Foreign Office's advisers in Jedda, Cairo and Khartoum had also been taken by surprise. Wilson regarded Husayn's newly acquired regal dignity 'somewhat premature',[138] while McMahon observed that 'Shereef's action appears ill-advised and premature'.[139] Wingate, for his part, stated that Husayn's title 'would appear to be hardly in accord with the Sherif's own declaration regarding the complete independence within their own territories of other Arab chiefs'.[140] McMahon proposed to Wingate that Wilson should be instructed to inform Husayn that the high commissioner deprecated 'an announcement of this nature which seems most inadvisable at a time when Sherif is not in a position to substantiate fully such claims made on his behalf'. Sir Henry, in any case, felt sure that the British government would 'be unable at present to make public recognition of Shereef as more than ruler of Hedjaz and champion of Arab people against Turkish oppression'.[141]

McMahon and Wingate at the same time considered it undesirable to discourage Husayn unduly. The high commissioner explained in a telegram to the Foreign Office that, although 'in view of extent to which Shereef owes his present position and even existence to our aid and support we could be justified in withholding any recognition of his present action which has been taken without consulting us', and that 'this action is likely to prejudice his position in the eyes of certain Moslem countries where his motives and policy are still regarded with distrust', he nevertheless recommended that 'we might conclude by reiterating determination of His Majesty's Government to continue efforts to bring about and support independence of Arab nation'.[142] The sirdar concurred with the insertion of some such clause in the message to Husayn, as it would 'show that while we are doubtful of the political wisdom of his action it in no way affects our support of him and of the Arabs' cause'.[143] McMahon and Wingate also agreed on the title that should be conferred on Husayn. Sir Henry suggested that 'considering the limited extent of his dominion and having regard to our treaties acknowledging independence of Arab Chiefs such as Bin Saud etc. most that we could under existing conditions would be to recognise Shereef as "Malik" [i.e. "King": R.H.L.] of Hedjaz'. Sir Reginald, for his part, proposed that 'King of the Arabs in the Hedjaz' was 'a suitable address, as far as we are concerned, for the present'.[144]

Wilson had meanwhile been informed that a 'coronation takes place November 4th or November 5th', and even though Clerk thought the whole affair 'fantastic',[145] '*some* notice of the Sherif's elevation' had nevertheless to be taken. A telegram was sent to McMahon on 3 November, in which the latter was instructed to tell Wilson, 'if there is still time', to inform Husayn that:

> He had been instructed to offer sincere congratulations on the auspicious occasion. He should add that His Majesty's Government are in consultation with their Allies on the question of a joint official recognition of His Highness' new position, but as the enemy is not yet completely defeated and a premature recognition might do great harm to His Highness' cause in Arabia and the whole Moslem world, there may be some delay.[146]

Husayn was duly crowned as 'King of the Arabs' at Mecca on 4 November 1916. There was a simultaneous ceremony at Jedda, which Wilson did not attend.[147]

The Foreign Office submitted a draft reply to Abdullah's telegram to Sir Reginald on 6 November. This agreed, in the main, with McMahon's and Wingate's previous observations:

> Attention of Sherif should firstly be called to inopportuneness of his announcement and he should then be told that H.M. Government and governments of France and Russia though they regard and will continue to regard His Highness as titular head of Arab peoples in their revolt against Turkish misrepresentation and are glad further to recognise him as lawful and de facto ruler of the Hedjaz are unable to recognise assumption by him of any sovereign title which might provoke disunion among Arabs at present moment and thus prejudice final political settlement of Arabia on a satisfactory basis. That settlement to be durable must be come to with general assent of other Arab rulers of which at present there is no evidence and must follow rather than precede military success.[148]

One week later, the Foreign Office repeated to Wingate a telegram from Bertie in which the ambassador stated that the French government agreed with 'general terms proposed for reply to Sherif of Mecca'.[149] It would take another 11 days before Grey could inform Wingate that the Russian government also concurred, and that he might authorise Wilson 'to reply to Sherif in terms of my telegrams'.[150]

The problem of the Emir's new title still remained. After consultations with the French government, the India Office, the high commissioner and the sirdar, the Foreign Office finally wired Wingate on 11 December that, 'after consideration His Majesty's Government have decided that most suitable title would be "Malik-el-Hejaz" [i.e. "King of the Hijaz"; R.H.L.] with honourific style "Siyada" [i.e. "his Lordship"; R.H.L.], and that "unofficially" they had been informed that the French government "probably" would do the same'.[151]

PART II

THE LLOYD GEORGE GOVERNMENT 1916–19

6 TAKING THE SHERIF INTO THE FULLEST CONFIDENCE POSSIBLE

Introduction

This chapter deals with two subjects: the mission of Sir Mark Sykes and François Georges-Picot to the Hijaz in May 1917 and the complications surrounding Britain's monthly subsidy to King Husayn. The Sykes–Picot mission was intended to safeguard Anglo–French relations when British troops entered the area covered by the Sykes–Picot agreement, but when the Egyptian Expeditionary Force (EEF) failed to capture Gaza, the Cairo authorities decided that it should be used to acquaint the King of the Hijaz with the terms of the agreement. After a series of interviews, Sykes managed to convince the king that he could safely assent to a formula to the effect that the French would pursue the same policy in Syria as the British in Baghdad. Husayn had apparently gained the impression that Baghdad would be part of the Arab state, and afterwards showed himself to be very pleased that he had tricked Picot into giving Syria away. According to the Sykes–Picot agreement, however, Baghdad would be 'practically British', in which case the king had unwittingly agreed to Syria being 'practically French'. It did not take long before the Foreign Office received the first reports indicating that, as far as informing King Husayn of the terms of the Sykes–Picot agreement was concerned, the Sykes–Picot mission had been a signal failure.

In the section on Husayn's subsidy it becomes clear that the London and Cairo authorities time and again reacted positively to the king's requests, ignoring indications that Husayn might not spend the British gold on the objects for which it was intended. Husayn's apparent financial ineptitude was regrettable, but did not weigh against the political importance of his revolt succeeding.

The British Offensive in the Sinai and the Sykes–Picot Mission

On 14 December 1916, Sir William Robertson observed in a note for the War Cabinet that Murray's attack on El Arish was imminent, and that after the occupation of that town the latter intended to advance on Rafa. He believed that Sir Archibald should have the liberty to pursue the possibly demoralised Turkish troops in the area that, according to the Sykes–Picot agreement, came under international administration. However, this might easily lead to difficulties with the French 'in view of their well known susceptibilities in regard to Syria'. For this reason, the CIGS considered it desirable to inform the French government in advance that 'our sole object is to defeat the Turks, and that we should welcome their political cooperation both in the international sphere and in any negotiations which may become necessary in the French sphere of direct control, and in that of commercial and political interest'. During the meeting of the War Cabinet the following day, Sykes mentioned another reason why it was important to obtain French political cooperation. He explained that 'if the forthcoming operations proved successful, it was possible that the tribes east of the Medina Railway would rise, and the headquarters of these tribes were in the French sphere'. The War Cabinet agreed that it was desirable to prevent unnecessary French suspicion. The Foreign Office was instructed to inform the French government that Great Britain should welcome French political cooperation.[1]

The British campaign in the Sinai subsequently was one of the subjects for discussion at an Anglo–French conference held at London from 26 to 28 December. On the last day, Alexandre Ribot, the French minister of finance, raised the point that 'the French government were ready to attach a French battalion from Jibuti to the British forces in order to show the French flag'. Lloyd George promised that 'when the British troops entered Palestine, which might be in six weeks or two months, they would be ready to accept the offer', whereupon Lord Robert Cecil suggested that 'a French political officer should be attached to General Murray, because the tribes in the British sphere had headquarters in the French sphere, and it was therefore necessary to constitute some form of liaison'.[2]

Lloyd George had something completely different in mind with respect to the Sinai campaign than Robertson. According to Hankey, Lloyd George, when they had lunched together on 11 December, had 'discoursed mainly on his plans for a big military coup in Syria'.[3] Sir William, however, was as unwilling to accept this side show as any other. As far as he was concerned, Murray's mission was completed the moment the latter had cleared the Turks from the Sinai. A real offensive into Palestine was out of the question. Robertson telegraphed to Murray on 9 December, that:

> Today Prime Minister mentioned to me desirability of making your operations as successful as possible. I am in entire agreement. Wire précis of action proposed beyond El Arish, stating what additional troops you would require for advance, if any. I cannot help thinking that in view of importance of achieving big success on Eastern front, and the effects this will have, you might risk having fewer troops on Western [the Egyptian western front; R.H.L.]. A success is badly needed, and your operations promise well.

Murray interpreted 'beyond El Arish' rather liberally. In his reply, he observed that he had 'always thought important results might be secured by an advance by us from Arish into Syria'. The best thing to do after the occupation of Rafa was to attack Beersheba, 'where enemy's main concentration appears to be'. From Beersheba, moreover, Murray's aircraft were able to attack the Hijaz railway, while the occupation of that town 'would result in a rising of Arab population in southern Syria, who are known to be very disaffected towards Turks'. If his operations progressed as he hoped, he would need, however, two extra divisions on a temporary basis, perhaps from Mesopotamia, as Sir Archibald fully realised the 'undesirability of taking troops from main theatre'.

Robertson's reaction to Murray's telegram was again not formulated in unequivocal terms. After stating that it was the Prime Minister 'who wishes you to make the maximum possible effort during the winter', Sir William only referred to the problematic aspects of Murray's request. However, such subtleties were wasted on Sir Archibald. In a subsequent telegram, he merely stated further arguments in favour of putting two extra divisions at his disposal. Consequently, 'in order that any possibility of misunderstanding may be removed', Robertson telegraphed to Murray on 15 December that:

> Notwithstanding the instructions recently sent to you to the effect that you should make your maximum effort during the winter, your primary mission remains unchanged, that is to say, it is the defence of Egypt. You will be informed if and when the War Cabinet changes this policy.
>
> In the meantime you should be as aggressive as possible with the troops at your disposal subject to your main mission of defending Egypt.[4]

The War Cabinet was not prepared to overrule the CIGS. Ministers, as ever, shrank from openly intervening in strategic affairs. The day after Lloyd George had told the French delegation that it would be a matter of six weeks or two months before British troops would enter Palestine, Robertson wrote a note explaining that a campaign in Palestine during the winter was out of the question. Without denying the great advantages of the occupation of that country, it would be unsound to start an invasion under the present conditions, as this contravened 'fundamental principles of strategy'. Also, for the year 1917, the maxim obtained that 'our commitments in the minor theatres should be reduced to the minimum in order that our maximum effort may be made in France'. The only concession he was prepared to make was that 'we should complete our preparations in Egypt for an offensive in Syria in the autumn of 1917'.[5] The War Cabinet acquiesced in Robertson's point of view. On 2 January, it accepted the note 'in principle'.[6]

After the occupation of El Arish on 21 December, and the occupation of Rafa on 9 January, the EEF's advance came to a standstill a few miles from the border with Palestine. As the rising of the tribes east of the Hijaz railway failed to materialise, there seemed to be no need for the detachment of a French political officer, but preparations nevertheless continued. The War Cabinet decided on 31 January that a British political officer should also be attached to Murray's staff, and that the latter's instructions should be settled between the Foreign Office, the General Staff and Sykes.[7]

As Georges-Picot had been chosen by the French government to act as the French representative with the EEF, he was invited to come to London to take part in these discussions in order that the instructions to the British political officer tallied with those to his French counterpart. On 13 February, these consultations led to a satisfactory conclusion. The instructions constituted a careful elaboration of the Sykes–Picot agreement:

1. The C.P.O. will act as adviser to the G.O.C. on political relations with native elements in the theatre of operations of the G.O.C. in C. Egypt beyond the Egyptian frontier.
2. The French Commissioner is accredited to the G.O.C. in C. Egypt as the political representative of the French government in all negotiations that may be necessary in the theatre of operations of the Egyptian force beyond the Egyptian frontier.
3. The G.O.C. will communicate with the French Commissioner through the C.P.O. and the French Commissioner will communicate with the G.O.C. through the C.P.O.
4. The G.O.C. will use the C.P.O. or his delegate, and the French Commissioner or his delegate, as his joint representatives in negotiations between the representatives of native elements in areas A and B and himself.
5. The French Commissioner or his delegate will act alone, and on his own responsibility, in any negotiations with native elements in the Blue area subject to the exigencies of the military situation for which the Military Commander alone is responsible. He will keep the G.O.C. apprised of all these negotiations through the medium of the C.P.O. But, in the event of any part of the Blue area coming within the theatre of operations of the Egyptian Force, the French Commissioner will act jointly with the C.P.O. in negotiations with native elements inhabiting that part of the area.
6. The French Commissioner and the C.P.O. will act jointly in any communications that may be necessary with the King of the Hedjaz, but through the medium and with the approval of the High Commissioner in Egypt, G.O.C. in the Hedjaz.
7. The C.P.O. will keep the French Commissioner apprised of any negotiations with the military or political officers with the Mesopotamian force may enter into with native elements in area A.
8. With regard to the Brown area, no political negotiations shall be directly entered into with native elements in this area until it is actually occupied.

Balfour approved the temporary appointment of Sykes as chief political officer with the EEF in the middle of February.[8]

On 22 February, Sir Mark wrote a letter to Sir Reginald Wingate informing the latter of his appointment. He observed that he considered it his 'main job [...] to keep the Franco–British situation clear'. In this connection, Sykes and Georges-Picot thought it a good idea when three or five Arab delegates and a representative of King Husayn were attached to their mission. The latter 'should be [...] a venerable but amenable person who will not want to ride or take much exercise', while the Arab delegates 'should be of sufficient capacity to carry weight with the urban elements of areas A and B, and have behind them the support of the Arab Committees in Cairo by whom they should be ostensibly elected'.[9] Gilbert Clayton objected to this, as 'no Arab Central Committee exists in a form capable of putting forward definite proposals'. Undoubtedly, there were:

> Representatives of many shades of Arab opinion in Cairo [...] but none of them are men who could do more than give a guide as to the sentiments of the party to which they belong, nor could they speak with any authority or as representatives. Moreover, none of these men are sufficiently influential to sit as delegates without exciting jealousy and opposition among their colleagues and rivals.

With Husayn's representative there was the additional problem that the king as yet was not familiar with the contents of the Sykes–Picot agreement. Clayton wondered whether the king should not first be informed on 'the general lines of that agreement before asking him to send a representative to assist in the deliberations of the mission'. There naturally was the alternative 'to treat the mission as a body assembled to consider the whole problem "de novo" keeping the terms of the agreement secret and merely a guide for the British and French members of the mission', but this clearly entailed the risk that eventually it would come out that 'an agreement had already been come to between ourselves and the French before the mission started its deliberations'. All in all, the mission was 'bound to cause considerable discussion and to lead to much intrigue and speculation which might create considerable difficulties'.[10]

On 12 March, Wingate telegraphed a summary of Clayton's note to the Foreign Office. Sir Ronald Graham was not particularly impressed by the problems raised. He drafted a reply in which these were played down. With respect to the Arab delegates, all that was required was to find 'a few men of good standing to represent Syrian Moslem point of view, sign manifestoes and approve any local arrangements made'. Surely the Arab Bureau 'should be able to secure a suitable party of from 3 to 5'? At the same time there was no reason why:

> King Hussain should be given impression that future of Syria is to be considered 'de novo'. His Highness need only be informed that British and French political officers have been appointed to act under General Murray, to assist him in his relations with population beyond Egyptian frontier and be requested to select a representative to accompany the political staff.[11]

Clayton also sent a copy of his note to Cyril Wilson. In his covering letter he observed that, as far as the Sykes–Picot agreement was concerned, it was 'difficult to decide, on the present slight data, how far, if at all, the Sherif should be informed at the present moment'. It would have been better to delay telling Husayn anything at all, but 'on the whole' Wingate considered that:

> The Sherif should be told in general terms of what is contemplated and the following is the formula which he would like you to adopt in conveying this information to the Sherif.
>
> 'H.M.G. agreed with the French government to send to Egypt within a month or six weeks, a joint commission to discuss and examine the question of the eventual settlement of the Arab territories of the Ottoman Empire when the Turks have been finally defeated and expelled from those territories. For this purpose H.M.G. and the French government have each detailed a Commissioner to proceed to Cairo'.

Wilson should refrain from communicating this message until he received definite instructions from the high commissioner.[12] In view of Graham's reply, this was not an excessively precautionary measure. In accordance with the Foreign Office telegram, the message was subsequently pruned of all references to the settlement of territorial claims, and merely mentioned the military reasons for the mission.[13]

On 17 March, Wilson telegraphed that he was rather unhappy with the new formula. It would 'probably make Sherif suspicious, and, under the circumstances, I personally recommend that Sherif be taken into the fullest confidence possible regarding the Commission's real object'. In a following telegram, he suggested sticking to the original formula, but to add the words 'thus continuing our former negotiations' at the end of the opening sentence. Husayn, after all, already knew that Homs, Hama, Aleppo and Damascus 'are to be independent and was informed area east of the line of these towns was reserved for future discussion between the French and the Arabs; the commission thus naturally fits in as being the instrument for negotiations'. Wingate, however, felt unable to adopt Wilson's suggestion. He explained that the latter's instructions had been drafted by the Foreign Office, and that 'you must, therefore, carry out these instructions'.[14]

In a letter to Clayton of 21 March, Wilson made it abundantly clear that he was not particularly pleased with the way things were going. As long as Husayn was left in the dark as to the real purpose of the Sykes–Picot mission, he foresaw the greatest possible difficulties:

> It appears fairly obvious that the Sherif thinks the Commission will deal with the future of Syria etc., and I understand from your secret private letter of 10th March that this is really the case and if the eventual settlement of the Arab territories of the Ottoman Empire is to be the business of the Commission, I would most strongly urge that the Sherif be taken into our complete confidence and be informed of the actual object of the Commission.
>
> What I feel very strongly is that the settlement of Syria etc., should not be arranged behind his back so to speak [...] and I feel sure we shall greatly regret it in the future if we are not quite open and frank with him now over the whole matter.[15]

Considering the EEF's advance had stopped at the border with Palestine, it seemed that Clayton's and Wilson's worries were purely academic, but this might change if Sir Archibald's plan for a *coup de main* on Gaza was successful. The capture of that town was very desirable with an eye to the coming autumn offensive. The chances that such an operation would succeed considerably increased when on 15 March the Turkish Eighth Army abandoned the last forward position from which it could have threatened the right flank of the EEF, and retreated to the line Gaza–Beersheba. Eleven days later the battle for Gaza began.

The Turks were able to repulse the EEF's attack. In his telegraphic report of 28 March, however, Murray made it appear as if the occupation of the Wadi el Ghazze (a wadi that ran a few miles south of Gaza), and not the occupation of Gaza, had been the object of his attack, and that this had been secured, while the enemy had incurred heavy losses.[16] On the basis of this information, the War Cabinet approved Robertson's proposal to instruct Murray 'to develop his recent success to the fullest possible extent and to adopt a more offensive rôle in general'.[17]

Robertson wired Murray's new instructions that same day: as a result of Sir Archibald's recent success, 'your immediate objective should be the defeat of the Turkish forces south of Jerusalem and the occupation of that town'. After his defeat, however, Murray was no longer so anxious to take the offensive. Now it was his turn to see only problems. He emphasised in his reply that however much he wanted to capture Jerusalem, an operation of that kind entailed heavy losses. The progress of such an undertaking, moreover, was completely dependent on the rate of construction of the railway, and Murray doubted whether much more could be achieved than 20 miles a month.[18] The War Cabinet were not prepared to let this opportunity for an offensive in Palestine slip through their fingers, not even when it became clear from a subsequent telegram from Sir Archibald – after Robertson had asked for more details – that his success on the Wadi el Ghazze had actually been an unsuccessful attempt to capture Gaza.[19] For the edification of Murray, the War Cabinet during its meeting of 2 April 1917 laid great stress on 'the moral and political' advantages that were to be expected from the occupation of Jerusalem. A feat of arms of this kind:

> Would be hailed with the utmost satisfaction in all parts of the country. From this point of view a success in Palestine would have a very considerable importance quite apart from its purely military aspects. There was every probability that in the course of the next few months there would be a very considerable increase in the strain on the people of this country due to the war, and it was of the first importance that there should be military successes to counteract the depressing influences of a difficult economic situation. Nowhere did success appear easier to realise than against Turkey.
>
> Some of Sir Archibald Murray's communications tended to show that in his appreciation of the purely military and strategical aspects of the war, he had rather lost sight of the moral importance of a victory such as he might reasonably hope to achieve in Palestine and Syria.

Murray's instructions remained 'to exploit the successes already achieved to the utmost possible extent, and to capture Jerusalem'. At the same time, the

War Cabinet decided that Sykes, who was about to leave for Egypt, 'should report to them in person the action he proposed to take, and should receive their instructions'.[20]

The following afternoon, Sykes had an interview with Lloyd George and Curzon. It did not go very smoothly. When Sir Mark elucidated the relationship between his instructions and the Sykes–Picot agreement, Curzon could not keep from observing that, by this agreement, 'the French had got much the best of the bargain'.[21] When Sykes disclosed his scheme 'to open up relations with the various tribes [...] and, if possible, to raise an Arab rebellion further north in the region of the Jebel Druse with a view to attacks on the Turkish lines of communication', Lloyd George and Curzon 'laid great stress on the importance of not committing the British government to any agreement with the tribes which would be prejudicial to British interests'. Moreover, the region of Jabal al-Druze was largely in the proposed French sphere of influence, and in view of French susceptibilities, Sykes's scheme might easily lead to difficulties with the French. According to both, 'the attachment of a French Commissioner and of two French battalions to General Sir A. Murray's force [which battalions together constituted the Détachement Français de Palestine; R.H.L.] was a clear indication that the French wished to have a considerable voice in the disposal of the conquered territories'. The Prime Minister ended the interview by again impressing on Sykes 'the importance of using great caution and reporting fully to the War Cabinet'.[22]

The Visit by Sir Mark Sykes and François Georges-Picot to the Hijaz

When Sykes arrived in Cairo, Murray's second attack on Gaza, from 17 to 19 April 1917, had also failed. In expectation of things to come, Sykes and Georges-Picot met three times with '3 delegates representative of Moslem Syrian feeling'. On 30 April, Sir Mark telegraphed an account of these meetings to Sir Ronald Graham. The three delegates:

> Were agreed on the following points.
> (1) that they desired that Great Britain and France should be prepared to contemplate the establishment an Arab State or confederation in an area approximating to areas A and B.
> (2) that such a State or confederation would be obliged to rely on France and Great Britain for defence and protection.

(3) that France and Great Britain should have in return for (?this) financial and political advisors in that state or confederation.

Sykes in conclusion explained that during these talks the main difficulty had been 'to manoeuvre the delegates into asking for what we are ready to give them without showing them a map or letting them know that there was an actual geographical or detailed agreement'.[23]

No representative of King Husayn had participated in the talks, but this was no indication of a lack of interest; on the contrary, the 'advent of Picots mission to Egypt evidently caused Sheriff of Mecca considerable anxiety'.[24] No doubt, according to Clayton, because 'knowing as he does, that some arrangement has been made with the French, and unaware of the exact terms thereof, he is fearing the worst and thinks that we have given everything away'.[25] The king wanted to see Sykes in person. In view of the present lull in the fighting at Gaza, the Cairo authorities believed that the king's wish should be met. On 27 April, Wingate wired to the Foreign Office that:

> Sheriff of Mecca having expressed strong desire to see him, Sir Mark Sykes will leave [...] for Jeddah where meeting will take place. I consider very necessary that Sheriff of Mecca be now informed of general lines of our agreement with French regarding Syria and unless you see an objection I will instruct Sir Mark Sykes (who will be accompanied by a member of Picots mission) to undertake this.[26]

Hopefully, so Wingate continued, this explanation would remove the king's apprehensions with regard to the Sykes–Picot agreement. This was not only sound policy, but also, as he observed in a private letter to Graham, the right thing to do. It was 'only fair to the old man that this should be done and I am very hopeful that the effect will be satisfactory'.[27] Clayton, too, considered it a good thing to enlighten the king on the terms of the Sykes–Picot agreement, in particular, so he explained to Wilson, because 'when you see exactly how matters stand, you will think that they are a good deal better than we thought at one time, and it is not impossible that the Sherif may be rather relieved at finding the arrangement much more favourable than he had feared'.[28] On 28 April, the Foreign Office informed Wingate that there were no objections to Sykes's proposed mission.[29]

If the first objective of Sykes's mission was to reassure the King of the Hijaz, it also served another purpose, which seemed to be in complete contradiction, as it certainly would not help in restoring Husayn's peace of mind. Sir Mark had also been instructed, so Clayton informed Wilson, to remove possible misconceptions in the king's mind on the proclamation that Lieut.-General Sir Stanley Maude had issued on the occasion of the occupation of Baghdad in March 1917.[30]

Townshend's defeat at Ctesiphon had led to a reorganisation of the Mesopotamian campaign. In February 1916, on the recommendation of Robertson, the War Office had become responsible for the Indian Army. That same month, Sir John Nixon had relinquished his command. His successor had been Sir Percy Lake, but in August 1916, Lake, in his turn, had been replaced by Maude, who was Robertson's choice. Under Lake, the first steps had been taken towards the necessary reorganisation of the Mesopotamian Expeditionary Force (MEF), as Force 'D' had been renamed. Lake had also supervised three attempts to relieve the garrison at Kut al 'Amara, but each had failed. Townshend had eventually surrendered on 29 April 1916. The next day, the CIGS had wired to Lake that he attached no importance whatsoever to the recapture of Kut or the occupation of Baghdad. In Mesopotamia, too, defence was to be the primary mission. The manner in which Robertson had formulated his instructions – 'maintain as forward a position as can be made secure tactically' – had, however, left Maude some leeway to initiate offensive actions. This had the result that, in December 1916, British troops had once again begun to advance on Baghdad. Thanks to the various reforms, Maude had at his disposal a force four times larger than that of Townshend. Manoeuvring very cautiously, without incurring heavy casualties, the MEF had advanced along the borders of the Tigris in the direction of Kut al 'Amara, which had been reoccupied on 12 February 1917. Four days later, the War Cabinet had instructed Maude, overruling Robertson's objections, to exploit his success to the utmost. On 11 March, British troops entered Baghdad, the Turks having evacuated the town the night before.[31]

In Maude's proclamation, authorised by the War Cabinet, it had been stated, among other things:

> But you people of Baghdad, whose commercial prosperity and whose safety from oppression and invasion must ever be a matter of the closest concern

to the British government, are not to understand that it is the wish of the British government to impose upon you alien institutions. It is the hope of the British government that the aspirations of your philosophers and writers shall be realised and that once again the people of Baghdad shall flourish, enjoying their wealth and substance under institutions which are in consonance with their sacred laws and racial ideals.

Therefore I am commanded to invite you, through your nobles and elders and representatives, to participate in the management of your civil affairs in collaboration with the political representatives of Great Britain who accompany the British Army, so that you may be united with your kinsmen in North, East, South and West in realising the aspirations of your race.[32]

This proclamation was susceptible to various interpretations, and it certainly could be reconciled with the status that had been assigned to Baghdad in the Sykes–Picot agreement. It was now up to Sir Mark, according to Clayton, 'to indicate gently that we must take special measures as regards Baghdad, where our interests are vital, and that military and political predominance must be ensured in those territories, at any rate for a considerable time'. Clayton fully realised that the subject of the future status of Baghdad might lead to difficulties with the king, but then again, one ought not to mistake pretence for reality. Why should the outsider Husayn, even though he was referred to as 'the spokesman of the Arab Nation', have a say in the settlement of the political future of Baghdad? The king could hardly deny that 'the Arab movement as represented by himself, cuts no ice whatever in Mesopotamia, and that therefore it is quite out of the question to force it upon them'. To make this clear to Husayn naturally had to be done with the utmost care, but Clayton believed that Sykes knew 'well how to do it'.[33]

On 2 May 1917, Sykes had a meeting with Faysal at Wejh. Wingate informed the Foreign Office five days later that, 'after much argument', Faysal had accepted the 'principle of Anglo-French agreement regarding Arab confederation', and 'seemed satisfied'. Sir Mark subsequently had an interview with Husayn at Jedda. It went off very satisfactorily. The future status of Baghdad was not specifically discussed. The king and Sykes mainly occupied themselves with appraising in a general sense the implications of the Sykes–Picot agreement for the 'Arab confederation or state'. Husayn, in particular, laid stress on the following points:

1. That, unless Arab independence is assured, he feared that posterity would charge him with assisting in the overthrow of last Islamic power without setting up another in its place.
2. That, if France annexed Syria, he would be open to a charge of breaking faith with the Moslems of Syria by having lead them into a rebellion against the Turk in order to hand them over to a Christian power.

Thanks to Sykes's exposition of the agreement, the king now understood that 'if realised (it) disposes of these two points'. At the same time, Sir Mark impressed on Husayn the importance of a settlement of French and Arab claims with respect to Syria, and 'at last got him to admit that it was essential to the Arab development in Syria'. In view of this satisfactory result, and seeing that the king expressed an 'earnest desire' to see Georges-Picot, Sykes took the liberty to arrange an interview for the latter with King Husayn on 19 May.[34]

On their way to Jedda, Sykes and Georges-Picot called at Wejh, where Faysal embarked to join them for the last two days of their journey. During these days, several conferences were held on the Sykes–Picot agreement. From his earlier interview with Faysal, Sykes had come away with the impression that he had been able to satisfy the Emir, but these discussions showed that he had been mistaken: 'very little progress was made beyond establishing relations between Monsieur Picot and Faisal'.[35]

During the journey, Sykes and Georges-Picot also put the finishing touches to a memorandum with recommendations as to the policy the Entente should pursue in the Middle East. After a 'careful study of the situation', they had concluded that if Great Britain and France wanted to achieve their 'economic, political and strategic desiderata', then it was imperative that they 'should both agree to pursue a permanent, identical, and cooperative policy in their respective spheres of control and interest'. Above all, it had to be avoided that both powers became 'the instruments of Arab political elements, and so being involved in an undesirable rivalry', as it 'should be remembered that Arab politicians and leaders of all grades of development are particularly versed in the arts of promoting dissension and partisanship'. Only if both powers made it very plain to the Arabs that they were 'united and impartial' would they not run the risk that the Arabs would be 'tempted to endeavour to play one power off against another'.[36]

According to Sykes's report, the king opened the first interview with Georges-Picot, in the presence of Sir Mark, Faysal and Fu'ad al Khatib, by also emphasising the importance of 'French and British union and necessity for their close cooperation in realisation of Arab aspirations and incapacity of Arabs to achieve anything without their united help'. Husayn's benevolent attitude, however, was of short duration, especially after Georges-Picot had expressed the hope that in the future France should be in a position 'to assist on Syrian littoral by military action like British in Mesopotamia'. This statement led to a lengthy argument between Husayn and Picot in the course of which the king repeatedly stated that 'he could not be a party to proceeding purposing to hand over Moslems to direct rule of non-Moslem State'. The ensuing discussion on the status of French and British advisers in Syria and Iraq did not exactly help to clear the air. Sir Mark might very well argue that it was necessary that European advisers had 'executive authority: if not Arab rule would be helpless and corrupt and old story of sham Turkish reforms would begin again', but Husayn 'naturally disliked idea, and Fuadd said that would be the end of Arab independence'. All in all, the interview ended 'most inconclusively. Monsieur Picot being unfavourably impressed by the King'.[37]

On their way back to the residence of the British representative at Jedda, Sykes told Wilson that it seemed that Georges-Picot did not wish the Arab movement to succeed. Wilson got the impression from Sir Mark that 'things were not going at all well owing to Picot's attitude and that if the latter was not materially altered, it appeared hopeless to try and bring France and the Sherif together'.[38] At the beginning of the next meeting, the following day, the king nevertheless requested Fu'ad al Khatib to read out a statement that:

> His Majesty, the King of the Hedjaz, learned with satisfaction that the French government approve Arab national aspirations that as he had confidence in Great Britain he would be content if French government pursued same policy towards Arab aspirations on Moslem Syrian littoral as British did in Bagdad.

According to Sir Mark, Georges-Picot received this statement 'very well and relations became cordial'.

Sir Ronald Graham was rather pleased with the result of the talks with Husayn. Sykes's report showed only too clearly 'how dependent the French are upon us in establishing any relations at all with the Arabs'.[39] Wilson, who had been present at the second meeting, was frankly stupefied. Afterwards, Sykes had asked him whether he was satisfied with the outcome of the discussions. He had replied that 'as all were agreed I supposed it was satisfactory but I would have liked more said about our position in Baghdad'. In his opinion, so he explained to Clayton, 'we have not been as open and frank as we should have been'. It had, for instance, not become clear to him, and very probably also not to Picot and Husayn, 'whether Syria i.e. including Damascus etc. is meant; or merely the Syrian coast claimed by France: one may have meant Syria, the other only the Syrian coast'. It was all very awkward:

> Special representatives of Great Britain and France came expressly to fix things up with the Sherif and when the latter agreed to France having the same status in Syria as we are to have in Iraq surely the main points of our agreement re Iraq should have been stated to prevent all chance of a misunderstanding which might have far reaching consequences.
>
> What made me feel that the Sherif and Picot had different ideas as to what the position of France in Syria was to be was:
>
> 1. That the Sherif agreed to France in Syria being in same position as we in Iraq.
> 2. That Picot was so obviously delighted at getting the Sherif to verbally agree to this.
>
> From George Lloyd I gather that Baghdad will almost certainly be practically British, if this is so then I consider that we have not played a straight forward game with a courteous old man who is as Sykes agrees, one of Great Britain's most sincere and loyal admirers, for it means that the Sherif verbally [?agreed; R.H.L.] to Syria being practically French which I feel sure he never meant to do.[40]

After the second meeting, Newcombe had told Wilson that Fu'ad al Khatib had explained to him that Sykes was responsible for this surprising turn of events. Fu'ad had related how, during the first interview, Georges-Picot had repeatedly suggested to Husayn to 'let us have the same in Syria as the English in Baghdad', but that the king had refused to accept this suggestion. That same evening, however, Sykes had summoned Fu'ad, and had adjured the latter to get the king to agree to this formula. Fu'ad had promised to do his best. It had taken him three hours before Husayn finally assented to the formula: 'that the relations between the Arab government and France should be the same in Syria as that between the King and the British in

Baghdad'. The king stated as his reason for this decision that 'he trusted what the British Commissioner says: He knows that Sir Mark Sykes can fight for the Arabs better than he can himself in political matters and knows that Sir Mark Sykes speaks with the authority of the British government and therefore will be able to carry out his promises'. To avoid possible misunderstanding, Fu'ad had added that in his opinion the king had approved the formula only because the latter thought that 'Baghdad is entirely his'.[41]

On the eve of Sir Mark's visit to the Hijaz, Clayton had been confident that Sykes would be able to enlighten the king on the British position with respect to Baghdad without endangering existing cordial relations. Indeed, relations with Husayn had not deteriorated. However, in view of Fu'ad al-Khatib's account of the events that took place during the evening of 19 May and the morning of 20 May, in particular his explanation of why Husayn had finally assented to 'the formula', it seemed that Sykes had refrained from making clear to the king that the British 'in Bagdad and district whilst desirous of promoting Arab culture and prosperity [...] will retain that position of military and political predominance which our strategical and commercial interests require'.[42]

More Future Trouble

On 5 June 1917, the Foreign Office recalled Sykes, and two days later the French government was requested to do the same with Georges-Picot (see Chapter 8, section 'The Failure of the "Projet d'Arrangement"').[43] The Sykes–Picot mission had come to an end, even before Sykes and Picot had been able to occupy themselves with its primary objective; that is, to advise Murray on 'political relations with native elements', as well as in 'all negotiations that may be necessary in the theatre of operations of the Egyptian force beyond the Egyptian frontier'. It was in order to facilitate the achievement of this objective that Sykes and Georges-Picot had desired that three to five 'delegates', and a representative of King Husayn would be attached to their mission. However, the EEF's defeats at Gaza, together with the fears the authorities in Cairo entertained as to the possible adverse effects the mission might have on the Arab nationalist movement, saw to it that, once in Egypt, the mission's objective changed completely. At the onset it was, above all, intended as an instrument to ease Franco–British relations with respect to the Middle East. As Sykes had explained to Wingate, his 'main job (was) to keep the Franco-British situation clear'. The forced inactivity resulting from the failure of Murray's offensive, however, meant that Sykes and Georges-Picot had all the time in the world to busy themselves with other matters, such as trying to meet the objections others entertained with regard to their mission. The Sykes–Picot memorandum of 17 May, which dealt with the necessity to maintain close British–French cooperation in the Middle East, showed that this shift in objectives went almost unnoticed. One of its results was that the Sykes–Picot agreement turned from a guide for discussions with the local population beyond the Egyptian border, into a subject of discussion with the Sherifians and their British advisers, if only to set their minds at ease.

It thus came about that the main objective of the mission became to acquaint the King of the Hijaz with the terms of the Sykes–Picot agreement, an objective quite different from the original one. Regarding this new objective, the mission had moreover been a failure. Shortly afterwards, during a visit to England, David Hogarth wrote a note on the Sykes–Picot agreement, in which he explained that the authorities in Cairo 'had ample evidence [...] that the King of the Hejaz, if he had ever really understood what the commissioners said to him, was in no way minded to observe either the letter or the spirit of the agreement to which he was understood to have consented'.[44] A few weeks later, Clayton reported to Sir Mark that he had gathered from conversations with Fu'ad al Khatib that 'the Sherif did not at all understand the situation, as put before him in regard to Syria and Mesopotamia at your joint meeting with him in Jeddah – or at least he is determined not to understand it and to put his own interpretation on the result of the interview'.[45] King Husayn, finally, showed himself to Captain Lawrence to be:

> Extremely pleased to have trapped M. Picot into the admission that France will be satisfied in Syria with the position Great Britain desires in Iraq. That, he says, means a temporary occupation of the country for strategical and political reasons (with probably an annual grant to the Sherif in compensation and recognition) and concessions in the way of public works.
>
> In conclusion the Sherif remarked on the shortness and informality of conversations, the absence of written documents, and the fact that the only change in the situation caused by the meeting was the French renunciation of the ideas of annexation, permanent occupation or suzerainty of any part of Syria – 'but this we did not embody in a formal treaty, as the war is not

TAKING THE SHERIF INTO THE FULLEST CONFIDENCE POSSIBLE 183

finished. I merely read out my acceptance of the formula "<u>as the British in IRAQ</u>" proposed to me by M. Picot, since Sir Mark Sykes assured me that it would put a satisfactory conclusion to the discussion'.

The reactions by Clerk, Graham and Sykes to Lawrence's report were symptomatic. While Clerk gloomily minuted 'more future trouble', Graham took it all much more light-heartedly, 'sooner or later we must enlighten the King as to the true facts of the situation'. Sykes, the man who four months earlier had reported to the Foreign Office that he had completed this task to his satisfaction, and when doing so had never mentioned this alleged renunciation of French claims by Georges-Picot, preferred to remain silent, and merely initialled the report.[46]

Husayn's Monthly Subsidy

McMahon telegraphed to the Foreign Office on 30 June 1916 that Husayn had asked for a subsidy of £125,000 per month 'to pay and feed his forces and friendly tribes'. The high commissioner urged that Husayn 'be assisted to this extent for the next four months by end of which time we shall know better his future needs'. Hardinge minuted that this matter should be settled by the War Committee, but that '£125,000 strikes me as enormous for the pay and feeding of Arabs [...] Although he must be treated generously, I should have thought £50,000 would have been a more suitable figure.' Grey agreed. The sum was 'excessive'.[47] Clayton, who was in London for consultations with Georges-Picot and Sykes, explained to the War Committee on 6 July that it was not. After all, the revolt meant that Husayn 'would have to take over the support of the holy places from a pecuniary point of view', and that he 'used to get a large subsidy from the Turks for the upkeep of the holy places, and this has now ceased, and he was proposing that we should take this over'. Lord Curzon concurred: 'we should guarantee the Sherif exactly what the Sultan gave'. The War Committee eventually agreed on the text of a telegram,[48] in which Sir Henry was informed that £50,000 per month should be sufficient, but if Husayn was:

> Able to state definitely that more is required to replace the former Turkish subsidy that he received and that it is essential for the upkeep of the holy places and the pilgrimage, we would be ready to meet his views on these lines and to give him additional money for these purposes.

It was, however, added that the sum of £125,000, 'even for all these purposes', remained 'somewhat large'. When Sir Henry urged that the full amount for the next four months be sanctioned, Grey, after having consulted the War Committee, wired this sanction on 12 July.[49]

McMahon subsequently telegraphed on 14 August that since he had suggested a period of four months:

> Matters have considerably progressed in Hedjaz. Shereef's prospects of ultimate success have greatly increased and in like ratio wide importance to us of his success and necessary measures to ensure have also increased. I beg that I may be authorised to substitute [...] for words 'for a period of 4 months' the words 'for the present'.

Clerk considered that this request was 'difficult to refuse', and Hardinge agreed. On 15 August, McMahon was authorised to make the requested change. The Treasury was not informed of this decision.[50]

One month later, it became clear that the Emir of Mecca rather preferred to keep the subsidy for himself than spend it on feeding his forces and bribing the tribes in the neighbourhood of Medina. Clayton informed Wingate that Husayn had:

> Confessed to Wilson that he had saved about £200,000 out of the first two consignments of £125,000 sent to him, and Faisal was exceedingly angry at the difficulty he had in getting money out of his father for himself and Ali [...] £100,000 golden sovereigns sent to Feisal and Ali a couple of months ago would have done wonders. Wilson has spoken very seriously to the Sherif and is going to do so again and warn him that he is jeopardising his success by his parsimony.[51]

On 10 April 1917, Wingate telegraphed to the Foreign Office that Husayn had requested that his monthly subsidy be raised. According to the high commissioner, the king deplored the fact that he had to make this request, especially in view of 'his heavy financial and other obligations to His Majesty's Government', but then again, from his revolt 'serious political and military benefits' had accrued to Great Britain. Sir Reginald added that Husayn would use the extra money 'to secure the adhesion of chiefs of northern tribes and thereby to achieve that semblance of national cohesion which can (?justify) his revolt [...] in the eyes of the Moslem world'. In view of the latter, in particular, it seemed to Wingate to 'be bad and possibly dangerous policy on our part to withhold additional financial backing which he requires at a time when tribal elements east of the Jordan can render effectual assistance to our own military operations in Palestine'. He therefore did not hesitate to recommend strongly the granting of Husayn's request. At the Foreign Office, Oliphant minuted that 'in view of the present situation it would, I submit, be unwise and an expensive economy, not to meet this request'. Hardinge concurred: 'the Shereef's success has so far been very cheap at the price, and as there is every likelihood of his achieving further successes we should press for further financial assistance for him'. Lord Robert Cecil agreed 'entirely'.

Harold Nicolson was under the impression that it was the War Cabinet, and not the Foreign Office that had to decide this question. Graham disagreed, because 'financial assistance to the King of the Hejaz has been sanctioned in principle'. The Foreign Office could approach the Treasury without reference to the War Cabinet.[52] As the Treasury had not been informed of the decision to change 'for a period of 4 months' into 'for the present', the Foreign Office letter requesting permission to raise Husayn's subsidy caused some confusion there. A.P. Waterfield asked Nicolson to 'ascertain exactly how much is involved in Wingate's proposal. There is at present no "subsidy" being paid regularly.' Perhaps the high commissioner could throw some light on this matter?[53] Sir Reginald certainly could. In his reply to the Foreign Office telegram containing Waterfield's question, the high commissioner stated that he had referred to the sum of £125,000, which had been transmitted monthly to the Sharif as authorised by Foreign Office telegram no. 678 of 15 August 1916. His present proposal was to the effect that this monthly subsidy 'should be increased to a total sum of £200,000 a month, and when Medina has fallen for five months following that event, to a total sum of £225,000.[54]

The Treasury was not directly prepared to acquiesce in the fact that the Foreign Office had made its decision without seeking the Treasury's authorisation. Nicolson proposed to tell the Treasury that the telegram in question had been sent in consequence of a decision by the War Cabinet, but 'it was not quite clear [...] whether the decision was actually laid before them'. Hardinge thought it was. He was 'almost certain that the words "for the present" were authorised by the War Cabinet. Otherwise, I would not have drafted the tel. to Sir H. McMahon.' Just to make sure, he gave instructions that Hankey should be approached to enquire whether the latter could remember the War Cabinet's decision. Colonel Dally Jones, on behalf of the War Cabinet Secretariat, replied that the minutes of the War Committee unfortunately contained nothing 'to show that [they] ever sanctioned the Sherif's subsidy being increased to £125,000 for more than 4 months'.[55] This was rather embarrassing for Hardinge, but fortunately the Treasury was inclined to let the matter drop, provided the Foreign Office wrote an official letter of apology. As Waterfield explained to Oliphant, 'so we feel a trifle hurt, and are inclined to stipulate as Koko might have said to Poohbah, "No grovel, no money"!' (Ko-Ko and Pooh-Bah are central characters in the Gilbert and Sullivan comic opera 'The Mikado'.) On 11 May, the Foreign Office sent the desired letter to the Treasury. The following day, the Treasury replied that it would not object to the raise in Husayn's subsidy, 'if Lord Robert Cecil is able to assure […] that it is imperative on grounds of high policy'.[56]

Naturally, this did not mean the end of all the complications and entanglements that seemed to go with the subsidy to the King of the Hijaz. In its letter of 12 May, the Treasury also observed that it shared the high commissioner's feelings of 'considerable anxiety' with respect to Husayn's wish that the subsidy be paid in gold alone. According to Sir Reginald this imposed an unacceptable burden on the Egyptian treasury. The Treasury nevertheless refused to lend a hand. Eventually, it suggested – unofficially – that India should do so. Not surprisingly, this proposal was resolutely turned down by the Government of India, with the result that, for the time being, Egypt undertook to provide the gold on its own, on the assumption that in view of the existing trade between Egypt and the Hijaz at least some of the gold would flow back to the Egyptian treasury. The gold, however, did not return to Egypt. According to Nicolson this was partly due to 'the incapacity of the Mecca government to understand, much less to initiate, a regular banking system', but as far as Clerk was concerned, there was nothing more to it than that 'all the gold we have poured into the Hejaz has been hoarded'.[57] As he put it some months later, the gold was 'simply being drained away in the sands of Arabia'.[58]

During the summer and autumn of 1917, officials of the Foreign Office, the India Office, the War Office and the Treasury met regularly to discuss the situation, while Sir Reginald time and again tried to force the issue. On 18 June, Wingate urged that Husayn's 'monetary requirements' be met to prevent unfortunate political effects 'on Arab military operations', and one month later he stated that not meeting Husayn's demands 'would be little short of disastrous and effect on Arab military operations hardly less so'.[59] The Arab revolt, however, still continued when on 10 October the Treasury finally agreed to place £400,000 in gold at the disposal of the Egyptian treasury.[60]

This matter had hardly been settled when Sir Reginald asked permission that 'additional £25,000 a month which has already been promised to Shereef for 5 months after fall of Medina be given him now, and that it be continued for a maximum period of 5 months irrespective of date on which Medina may fall'. The high commissioner fully realised that 'Shereef's method of administering his finances is by no means beyond criticism', but the situation in the Hijaz once again was 'critical', and it was Wingate's considered opinion that Great Britain should not, 'for the sake of a relatively small sum of money, lose the full fruits of a policy which I venture to think has fully justified itself both from a military political and financial point of view'. This was exactly what was bothering Clerk. He doubted very much 'if another £25,000 a month is going to keep the Arabs together, supposing they are in the condition Sir R. Wingate describes'. He wondered whether the time had not arrived that 'we should rely on our own forces and refuse to be a milk cow for King Hussein'. Graham had no difficulty with the proposal, as it was the high commissioner's responsibility, but he agreed with Clerk that 'the Arab movement must be very unstable if £25,000 a month makes all the difference to it!'[61]

7 UP AGAINST A BIG THING

Introduction

This chapter deals with the preliminary moves and the ways in which the difficulties that stood in the way of the War Cabinet approving a public statement of support for the aspirations of the Zionist movement were surmounted. It starts with Herbert Samuel's failed attempts at the beginning of the war to win over his Cabinet colleagues to the idea of a British protectorate over Palestine in order to restore that country to the Jews. The question of a Jewish return to Palestine under the aegis of Great Britain subsequently remained the province of the Foreign Office, which did not attach much importance to it. Things changed with the advent of the Lloyd George government in December 1916. David Lloyd George and Arthur Balfour, Lord Grey's successor at the Foreign Office, were both strongly pro-Zionist. The new prime minister was moreover determined that Palestine would become British. He realised that this clashed with French ambitions, but believed that the French would have to give in after the British offensive in Palestine had created facts on the ground.

At the beginning of June 1917, the French government wrote an official letter of sympathy with the Zionist cause. The Zionists urged the British government to make a comparable gesture. The president of the English Zionist Federation, Chaim Weizmann, further increased the pressure by claiming that the German government was making overtures to the Zionist movement. After some hesitation, Balfour asked Weizmann and Lord Rothschild to produce a formula, which would be submitted to the War Cabinet. When the secretary of state for India, Edwin Montagu, set eyes on it, he wrote a memorandum in which he vehemently expressed his opposition to Zionism. Lord Milner proposed an alternative formula that strongly watered down the British commitment to the Zionist ideal. The War Cabinet discussed it on 3 September, but felt unable to come to a decision. One month later the issue was again before the War Cabinet. It appeared that Lord Curzon also opposed a declaration in support of the Zionist movement. Milner subsequently produced yet another formula designed to meet both Montagu's and Curzon's objections. When the War Cabinet discussed the declaration for the last time on 31 October, Montagu had sailed for India, while Curzon explained that he, although he stood by his objections, accepted the force of the diplomatic and political arguments in favour of a declaration. The declaration was approved, and communicated by Balfour to Rothschild on 2 November.

The Egyptian authorities wanted to forestall the international administration of the brown area laid down in the Sykes–Picot agreement. The best way to do this was to proclaim martial law for as long as military operations continued. The War Office concurred. An implication of this policy, in which the Foreign Office acquiesced for the moment, was that the Zionists should not be permitted to undertake in Palestine any activities in pursuance of the Balfour Declaration.

Sympathy and Incredulity

On 9 November 1914, only four days after Britain's declaration of war against Turkey, Samuel, at the time president of the Local Government Board, and the only Jew with a seat in the Cabinet, called on Grey. Samuel suggested that now 'perhaps the opportunity might arise for the fulfilment of the ancient aspirations of the Jewish people, and the restoration [in Palestine] of a Jewish state', and that in view of its proximity to the Suez Canal and Egypt 'British influence ought to play a considerable part in the formation of such a state'. Grey was sympathetic – 'Zionism had always had a strong sentimental attraction for him', and 'he would be prepared to work for it if the opportunity arose'.[1] That same day, Samuel also had a brief talk with Lloyd George. The latter confessed that he was 'very keen to see a Jewish State established'.[2]

A month later, Samuel was visited by Weizmann, vice president of the English Zionist Federation. Weizmann was a Russian Jew by origin. He had been born in a village near Pinsk, in the heart of the Pale of Settlement, studied chemistry in Germany and Switzerland, and had been appointed lecturer at the University of Manchester in 1904. In 1910, he had been naturalised as a British subject. Weizmann was pleasantly surprised by Samuel's positive attitude towards Zionism. He wrote to his wife afterwards that 'Messianic times have really come. It turns out that he knew a great deal about Zionism [...] Now, until the military situation becomes clear, he cannot do anything, but later, as soon as everything is clarified – and he is confident in England's success – he will set to work [...] He thinks that the whole Cabinet are of the same opinion.'[3]

However, Samuel's assessment of the cabinet's attitude turned out to be mistaken. At the end of January, Samuel forwarded a memorandum on 'The Future of Palestine' to Grey. Turkish entry into the war had opened:

> A prospect of a change, at the end of the war, in the status of Palestine. Already there is a stirring among the twelve million Jews scattered throughout the countries of the world. A feeling is spreading with great rapidity that now, at last, some advance may be made, in some way, towards the fulfilment of the hope and desire, held with unshakeable tenacity for 1,800 years, for the restoration of the Jews to the land to which they are attached by ties almost as ancient as history itself.

Samuel advocated a British protectorate over Palestine, as this would 'enable England to fulfil in yet another sphere her historic part of the civiliser of the backward countries'.[4] In his covering letter, Samuel mentioned that he had not yet sent the memorandum to Prime Minister Asquith, and expressed the hope that Grey would see no objection to Samuel circulating the memorandum to the members of the Cabinet.[5] Grey did not object, but to Asquith the memorandum was something of a shock. He noted in his diary that Samuel 'goes on to argue, at considerable length and with some vehemence, in favour of the British annexation of Palestine, a country the size of Wales, much of it barren mountain and part of it waterless [...] I confess I am not attracted by this proposed addition to our responsibilities.'[6]

Lord Bertie, the British ambassador in Paris, had been equally perplexed when Weizmann had visited him on 25 January, 'to "talk" about what *I* think an absurd scheme, though they say that it has the approval of Grey, Lloyd George, Samuel and Crewe [...] It contemplates the formation of Palestine into an Israelite State, under the protectorate of England, France or Russia, preferably England: they did not think that Russia or France would raise objections!' The ambassador had told 'the scheme-maker' that England did 'not want to have a protectorate, and that France would object to Russia, and that Russia would object to France'.[7] It also turned out that Grey, when Samuel had a further conversation with the foreign secretary on 5 February, while still 'favourable to Zionist ideas', certainly did not approve of a British protectorate. He was 'opposed to Britain's assuming any fresh military and diplomatic responsibilities'.[8]

Undaunted by these negative reactions, Samuel produced a second version of his memorandum in early March 1915. It opened with the question, 'if the war results in the break up of the Turkish Empire in Asia, what is to be the future of Palestine?', and proceeded to discuss five possible answers. The first four – annexation by France, to remain part of the Ottoman Empire, internationalisation and a Jewish state – Samuel rejected one by one. Only the last answer, a British protectorate, he considered viable, and it was moreover strategically sound. Basing himself on Cheetham's telegram of 7 January 1915 (see Chapter 2, section 'The Alexandretta Project and the Syrian Question'), Samuel also claimed that a British protectorate 'would be welcomed by a large proportion of the present population' in Palestine, while Zionists and non-Zionists alike had assured him that this outcome was 'by far the most welcome to the Jews throughout the world', and would lead to the formation in the USA, 'where they number about 2,000,000, and in all the other lands where they are scattered, [of] a body of opinion whose bias [...] would be favourable to the British Empire'.[9]

Montagu, the chancellor of the Duchy of Lancaster, and 'one of the most intimate of Asquith's political associates',[10] as well as Samuel's cousin, attacked the latter's scheme in a confidential memorandum. He was 'very strongly convinced that this would be a disastrous policy'.[11] Asquith, again, had not been impressed. On 13 March, he had written to his confidante, Venetia Stanley, that Samuel had produced:

> An almost dithyrambic memorandum urging that in the carving up of the Turks' Asiatic dominions, we should take Palestine, into which the scattered Jews could in time swarm back from all the quarters of the globe, and in due course obtain Home Rule. (What an attractive community!) Curiously enough, the only other partisan of this proposal is Lloyd George, who, I need not say, does not care a damn for the Jews or their past or their future, but thinks it will be an outrage to let the Christian holy places – Bethlehem,

Mount of Olives, Jerusalem etc. – pass into the possession or under the protectorate of 'Agnostic, Atheistic France'![12]

During the War Council of 19 March, which was partly devoted to a discussion of the partition of Turkey in Asia (see Chapter 3, section 'Alexandretta Once Again'), it appeared that the majority were none too eager to take up fresh responsibilities. The general feeling around the table was that 'we have already as much territory as we are able to hold'. It was therefore far better when none of the Great Powers took anything.[13] This had the result that Weizmann reported to C.P. Scott on 23 March that he had gathered from Samuel that the British cabinet were 'sympathetic towards the Palestinian aspirations of the Jews', but 'would not like to be involved into any responsibilities'.[14] Samuel, moreover, declined to receive Weizmann a second time.[15] The first attempt to get the ear of the British government had failed.

The Wolf Formula

The question of the possible return of the Jews to Palestine reverted to being the sole province of Foreign Office officials, who were inclined to take the matter not too seriously. Their regular contact was Lucien Wolf, the secretary of the Conjoint Foreign Committee, which had been established in 1878 by the Board of Deputies of British Jews and the Anglo-Jewish Association. It was dedicated to furthering the political rights and living conditions of Jews in foreign countries, especially in Russia, and time and again tried to enlist the support of the Foreign Office to that end. Wolf also regularly reported on developments affecting the position of Jews abroad, as well as the Committee's standpoint on these developments. It was in this context that Wolf wrote a letter to Lancelot Oliphant, enclosing his account and assessment of a meeting that had taken place on 14 April 1915 between Zionist representatives from England and abroad (Weizmann not among them), and leading members of the Conjoint Committee. The Zionists had hoped to come to an agreement on future cooperation, but to the Conjoint Committee the Zionist programme was unacceptable. Both parties agreed that Palestine could not sustain more than a minority of world Jewry. To the Conjoint Committee this meant that the establishment of a Jewish home there would bring no relief for the Jewish masses in Eastern Europe, and might even worsen their situation because it would only strengthen existing doubts about their loyalty. The Conjoint Committee especially objected to 'the scheme of a chartered company empowered to offer Jewish colonists privileges not extended to the rest of the population', because 'nothing could be more detrimental to the struggle for Jewish liberties all over the world [...] How could we continue to ask for equal rights for the Jews in Russia and Rumania if we claimed special rights for the Jews in Palestine?' Oliphant's minute was characteristic of the Foreign Office attitude. After noting that Wolf's report threw 'an interesting sidelight on Zionism showing how hopelessly impracticable the Zionists are', he light-heartedly added that, 'Mr Wolf's charge against the Zionists of intending to go "the whole hog" seems a trifle severe from one Jew to another'.[16]

Although Weizmann managed to have an interview with Lord Robert Cecil on 18 August 1915, which the latter had found 'weighty and serious', so Weizmann learned afterwards,[17] for the Foreign Office the Zionist aspirations were a non-issue. This only changed for a short while when Wolf submitted a memorandum to Cecil in the middle of February 1916. Wolf admitted that he was not a Zionist, and that he deeply deplored the Jewish national movement, but 'the facts cannot be ignored, and in any bid for Jewish sympathies today very serious account must be taken of the Zionist movement'. It had not escaped Wolf that 'what the Zionists would especially like to know is that Great Britain will become mistress of Palestine', and he understood that this might be problematic 'in view of French claims [...] in regard to the whole of Syria, which is held in Paris to include Palestine'. An assurance that the allies 'thoroughly understand and sympathise with Jewish aspirations in regard to Palestine, and that when the destiny of the country comes to be considered, these aspirations will be taken into account' would however skirt this difficulty.[18]

On 3 March 1916, Wolf submitted a formula that he believed might do:

> In the event of Palestine coming within the spheres of influence of Great Britain or France at the close of the war, the governments of those powers will not fail to take account of the historic interest that country possesses for the Jewish community. The Jewish population will be secured in the enjoyment of civil and religious liberty, equal political rights with the rest of the population, reasonable facilities for immigration and colonisation, and such municipal privileges in the towns and colonies inhabited by them as may be shown to be necessary.

Sir Arthur Nicolson saw 'no harm in the proposed "formula"', but before 'giving our imprimatur to it we should consult the French government, or in any case that I should inform M. Cambon to ask for his view'.[19] It was clear that 'we must [...] consult our Allies – especially in view of the fact that we are discussing the future of Palestine at Petrograd' [Sykes and Georges-Picot were in the Russian capital to negotiate the terms under which the Russian authorities were prepared to assent to the Sykes–Picot agreement; see Chapter 4, sections 'Sir Mark Sykes and François Georges-Picot Come to an Agreement' and 'The Arab Question Becomes a Regular Quicksand']. He therefore proposed that 'we might ask Paris and Petrograd whether they see any objection to the formula pointing out to both the advantages [...] by securing a sympathetic attitude on the part of the Jews'. Lord Crewe agreed. He realised that Jewish opinion was 'considerably divided about it', and Wolf could not 'be taken as the spokesman of the whole community', but 'we ought to pursue the subject, since the advantage of securing Jewish good will in the Levant and in America can hardly be overestimated'. On 11 March, a telegram was sent to Bertie and Buchanan containing Wolf's formula. The ambassadors were informed that the Foreign Office considered the formula 'unobjectionable', and believed that:

> The scheme might be made far more attractive to the majority of Jews if it held out to them the prospect that when in course of time the Jewish colonists in Palestine grow strong enough to cope with the Arab population they may be allowed to take the management of the internal affairs of Palestine (with the exception of Jerusalem and the holy places) into their own hands.[20]

Buchanan replied three days later. He sent two telegrams. The first transmitted Sykes's observations on the proposed formula. Sir George had communicated it to him, and Sykes had subsequently discussed it with Picot who, 'on hearing the sense of telegram made loud exclamations and spoke of pogroms in Paris. He grew calmer but maintained France would grow excited.' When in Cairo in November, Sykes had moreover been told that 'Arab Christians and Moslems alike would fight in the matter to the last man against Jewish Dominion in Palestine'. Picot had 'reluctantly admitted' the 'inestimable advantages to allied cause of active friendship of Jews of the World'. The Zionists should, however, 'give some demonstration of their power; accentuation of German financial straits and glow of pro-allied sentiment in certain hitherto anti-ally neutral papers would be sufficient indication'. Sykes, referring to Samuel's memorandum, agreed that an international protectorate was unacceptable to the Zionists, but the French 'would never consent to England having temporary or provisional charge of Palestine […] They seem hardly normal on this subject and any reference seems to excite memories of all grievances from Joan of Arc to Fashoda'. Sykes nevertheless deemed the problem 'soluble', and proposed the creation of an Arab Sultanate of Palestine under French and British protection, with perhaps one of Husayn's sons as sultan.

However inventive Sykes's proposal, officials at the Foreign Office were not impressed. Harold Nicolson noted that the whole purpose of the Wolf formula was 'to dazzle Jewish opinion – and I much doubt whether an Arab sultanate would have that effect'. Oliphant agreed, 'the Arab sultan would certainly wreck the scheme'. O'Beirne felt that Sykes should not have discussed the matter with Picot, and suggested a telegram in that sense to Buchanan. Grey concurred, and added that Buchanan should tell Sykes 'to obliterate from his memory that Mr Samuel's Cabinet memorandum made any mention of a British protectorate and that I told Mr Samuel at the time that a British protectorate was quite out of the question and Sir M. Sykes should never mention the subject without making this clear'.[21]

In a further telegram sent two days later, Sykes, not yet aware of the Foreign Office reprimand, reiterated that with regard to the Arabs and Zionists the 'greatest caution' was 'requisite as a slip in either direction might imperil scheme'. He was nevertheless confident that the British could get the Zionists full colonising facilities coupled with their rights in an enlarged Palestine'. What Britain definitely could not do, was to 'get them either political control of Jerusalem within the walls of the city nor any scheme tending thereto'. This only led O'Beirne to express the hope that 'our telegram of March 16 [49669] will have a quieting effect on Sir M. Sykes', and to point out that 'nobody proposes to give the Jews "political control" of Jerusalem'.[22]

Buchanan's second telegram reported his conversation with Sazonov. The latter had raised 'no objection to the scheme in principle but sees great difficulties in the way of its execution. Though Russian government would welcome migration of Jews to Palestine, he doubts whether any considerable number of them would care to settle there.' The Russian foreign minister had promised to send Buchanan a definitive answer 'after a thorough examination of the question'. There remained nothing else other than to await this further communication.[23]

Bertie telegraphed the result of his meeting with French prime minister Briand a week later. The latter had rather doubted 'whether scheme would really have the influence on Jewish community which is anticipated'. The proposal moreover presented 'serious difficulties and […] would run particular risk of awakening susceptibilities of Arabs whom it is advisable to treat with caution'. All in all, Briand thought that it was not useful to take up this scheme 'until after question of creation of Arab Empire has been solved'. Oliphant agreed that the formula's effect would be limited, but O'Beirne insisted that 'the Zionist scheme' appealed to a 'large and influential section of the Jews throughout the world'. He, however, accepted 'the Arab objection'. If 'the Arabs knew that we were contemplating an extensive Jewish colonisation scheme in Palestine (with the possible prospect of eventual Jewish self-government) this might have a very chilling effect'.[24]

There the matter rested for more than three months. At the end of June, Oliphant produced an overview of the state of affairs, because Wolf was 'pressing for some reply'. He submitted that in view of the Arab question it was 'unwise to commit ourselves at present', and that 'even though the formula originated with Mr Wolf we cannot regard him as speaking for all Jews'. George Clerk (O'Beirne had drowned with Kitchener on board HMS *Hampshire*) suggested informing Wolf orally that the Allies had 'not yet concluded their discussions as to the future of Palestine', and that the 'present time, when the Arabs have risen against the Turks […] would in the interests of the Jews themselves, be badly chosen for the publication of any formula such as that suggested'. Hardinge sympathised with Wolf but the latter could only be told that 'the present moment is inopportune for making any announcement'. Grey added that Wolf could also be informed of the sense of Bertie's telegram that the French government had 'pointed out certain difficulties, one being that the Jews are not agreed about it (as a matter of fact Mr Samuel and Mr Montagu I believe do not agree)'. It was left to Oliphant to communicate the Foreign Office's negative decision. On 4 July, four months after Wolf had submitted his formula, Oliphant minuted that he had handed Wolf the reply suggested by Hardinge, and that he had 'added a sentence orally in accordance with Sir E. Grey's minute'.[25]

Zionist Ambitions and the French Difficulty

On 12 November 1916, Weizmann wrote to Dorothy de Rothschild, wife of James de Rothschild and an avid supporter of the Zionist cause, in a very depressed state of mind. In Zionist affairs, 'which began in such a promising way', he could 'not see much hope. The upheaval in the world has roused everybody except the Jews'. Zionist activists were 'nice, well-meaning', but their activism was limited to their spare time. 'No wonder', so Weizmann continued, that 'all we do now is disjointed, haphazard, looks more like an adventure, than like an organised conscious effort of a people struggling for better days'. He admitted that he was 'sometimes driven to despair and one's own efforts appear almost like an irony, like the attempt of the fool who tried to empty the sea with a bucket'.[26] However, everything changed radically with the advent of the Lloyd George government in December 1916.

Weizmann had never managed to have an interview with Asquith or Grey,[27] but he personally knew the new prime minister and minister of foreign affairs. He had breakfasted with Lloyd George on 15 January 1915, and had had several meetings with the minister for munitions since then, although mostly in connection with his work as 'Chemical Advisor to the Ministry of Munitions on Acetone Supplies'.[28]

Weizmann had met Balfour for the first time on 9 January 1906. During their conversation, Weizmann had emphasised 'the spiritual side of Zionism', which meant that 'nothing but a deep religious conviction expressed in modern political terms could keep the movement alive, and that this conviction had to be based on Palestine and Palestine alone'. Balfour, who in Weizmann's opinion had 'only the most naïve and rudimentary notion of the movement', had been impressed and had asked Weizmann: 'are there many Jews who think like you?' The latter had answered that he spoke 'the mind of millions of Jews whom you will never see and who cannot speak for themselves, but with whom I could pave the streets of the country I come from'.[29] Their second meeting had taken place two days after Weizmann's conversation with Samuel in December 1914. Afterwards, Weizmann had written to his friend and mentor Ahad Ha'am that Balfour had said to him that he believed that '*you may get your things done much quicker after the war*', and that the Jewish question 'would remain insoluble until either the Jews here become entirely assimilated, or there was a normal Jewish community in Palestine'. Balfour had been very moved – 'I assure you, to *tears*' – by Weizmann's exposition of the suffering that was involved in Jewish attempts to assimilate into the communities of Western Europe, and when Balfour had seen him out into the street, he had said, 'very warmly: "*Mind you come again to see me, I am deeply moved and interested, it is not a dream, it is a great cause and I understand it'*.[30]

Another favourable development for Zionist aspirations was the appointment of Sykes as one of the civil assistant secretaries for political affairs to the War Cabinet (the other was Leopold Amery, MP). At the end of January 1917, he was occupied with drafting the instructions for the chief political officer to be attached to Sir Archibald Murray, and in this connection wished to consult Zionist leaders. Via James Malcolm, a leading figure in the Armenian community in touch with British officials, Sykes came into contact with Weizmann. They had two conversations, on 28 and 30 January. During the second, Sir Mark requested 'a larger meeting with Zionist leaders together with Herbert Samuel'.[31] In preparation for this meeting, which was scheduled for 7 February, on 31 January Rabbi Gaster sent Sykes the Zionist programmatic statement, which thereafter came to be known as 'The Demands'. The Zionists had been working on this document since September 1916, and it had only been completed at the very end of January. It concluded with the following summary of Zionist desiderata:

> Palestine is to be recognised as the Jewish National Home. Jews of all countries to be accorded full liberty of immigration. Jews to enjoy full national, political and civic rights according to their place of residence in Palestine. A Charter to be granted to a Jewish Company for the development of Palestine. The Hebrew language to be recognised as the official language of the Jewish Province.[32]

'The Demands' made no mention of a British protectorate. As Gaster explained to Sykes in his covering letter, the British Zionists were 'only too anxious to be under British protectorate', but Sir Mark had to understand that the Zionist movement was 'not an English movement; it has to a certain extent an international character, and the Zionists in the enemy countries may take strong umbrage at our putting all our eggs into one basket'.[33] During the meeting of 7 February, the Zionist delegation made very sure that Sykes did get the right impression. One after the other, the Zionist representatives hammered at the absolute necessity of a British protectorate over Palestine, and their total rejection of a condominium. Gaster opened the meeting by proclaiming that 'there must be no condominium or internationalisation in Palestine, as that would be fatal. What Zionists in England and everywhere desired was a British protectorate with full rights to the Jews to develop a national life.' Lord Rothschild followed up by emphasising that he was 'irreconcilably opposed to any form of condominium. Great Britain must annex Palestine.' Nahum Sokolow, representative of the World Zionist Organisation, claimed that 'the Jews of the whole world [...] all desired that England should annex Palestine'.

Sykes started his exposition by emphasising that 'the soldiers [...] would soon find themselves in Palestine, even though they might not think so. Time was pressing.' He continued that the 'idea of a Jewish Palestine had his full sympathy', but that he saw four 'difficulties' that had to be overcome before this objective could be realised: Russia, the Arabs, Italy and France. Sykes argued that the first three could be managed, but 'France was the serious difficulty. He could not understand French policy. The French wanted all Syria and a great say in Palestine. What was their motive? Was it sentimental, that is clerical or colonial ambition?' He suggested that 'the Zionists should approach M. Picot, the French delegate, and convince French'. Pressed by James de Rothschild on this point, Sykes reassured the Zionist leadership that the British had given the French 'no pledge in Palestine. The French have no particular position in Palestine and are not entitled to anything there.'[34] Sykes subsequently started to define the area in which the Jewish chartered company proposed by the Zionists could be active. The northern limit would be from Acre in a straight line to the Jordan, which meant that the Hauran and the greater part of Galilee were excluded. While the southern border 'could be arranged with the British government', Sir Mark also excluded the 'islands' of Jerusalem, Jaffa and 'a belt from Jerusalem to the sea along the Jaffa railway [...] because the Russian pilgrims came along this route'. The Zionists were appalled. The suggested frontier:

> Would exclude much of Galilee with its Jewish colonies and much of the Hauran which the Jews could not surrender, because with it would go the hope of an extensive population, as for the islands, Jerusalem was a Jewish city, most of the Jewish colonies lay along the Jaffa railway, the whole government of Palestine would become impossible.

Samuel 'was particularly emphatic in driving home these objections'. James de Rothschild again 'desired to know whether any pledge had been given about Palestine'. Sir Mark replied that 'with great difficulty the British government had managed to keep the question of Palestine open'.[35] He refrained from discussing the arguments the Zionists had brought forward against his delimitation of Palestine. Sykes merely reiterated his proposal to 'appoint someone to put the Jewish views' before Georges-Picot. At the suggestion of James de Rothschild, it was decided that Sokolow should be entrusted with this task, and with this the conference came to a close.[36]

The next day, Sokolow met with Picot. In the course of their conversation Sokolow observed that the Zionists desired that Palestine should become a British protectorate. Picot refused to be drawn, and only mentioned that this was a question for the Entente to decide. When Sykes intervened, Picot added that French ambitions could not be ignored. He was nevertheless prepared to discuss the Zionist programme with his superiors in Paris.[37] Picot and Sokolow had a further meeting the following day, which went off more smoothly. The subject of a British protectorate was not touched upon, and the discussion turned to such questions as whether the Jews constituted one of the smaller nations 'struggling for liberty', and whether it would be wise to grant special privileges to the Jews in Palestine. All in all, Sykes was very pleased with the result of the two conversations: 'it was a valuable thing that Mr Picot had an opportunity of informing himself to the Zionist demands'.[38]

A few weeks later, after 'a long interview' with Sokolow, Sir Mark was less sanguine regarding the prospects of solving the French difficulty. On 28 February, he wrote to Picot that the 'question of finding a (suzerain?) power or powers in this region is especially beset with difficulties. To propose it to be either British or French is to my mind only asking for trouble,' while the alternative of an international regime would 'inevitably drift into a condition of chaos and dissension'. He had therefore broached with Sokolow the subject of introducing the USA as the protecting power. Sykes did not inform Georges-Picot what Sokolow thought of this solution, but at the end of his letter he laid great stress on the absolute necessity of France reconsidering her rigid stance on Palestine. He submitted to Picot, for his:

> Earnest consideration the importance of coming to some satisfactory conclusion in this matter. If the great force of Judaism feels that its aspirations are not only considered but in a fair way towards realisation, then there is hope of an ordered and developed Arabia and Middle East. On the other hand, if that force feels that its aspirations will be thwarted by circumstance and are doomed to remain only a painful longing, then I see little or no prospect of our own future hopes.

You will find that we shall be hampered at every turn by intangible hindrances which it will beyond our power to remove.[39]

On 20 March 1917, Weizmann reported to Scott that he had understood that 'the French people have not yet fully formulated their claims, they have not yet said whether they would press some claims for the north of Palestine', and that Sir Mark believed that 'this may still adjust itself'. Weizmann, moreover, was 'perfectly convinced that it could be easily arranged if the British assert their claims', which he thought they would do, 'with some force when the country is occupied by British troops'.[40] It was therefore an unpleasant surprise for him that, when he had an interview with Balfour two days later, the latter had suggested that 'there may be difficulties with France and Italy', and that he would perhaps 'have to resort to the internationalisation of this part of the world as an extreme measure'. Like Sykes, Balfour believed that a role of the USA in the future administration of Palestine offered an attractive prospect. He wished to know Weizmann's views on 'an Anglo–American Protectorate over Palestine'.[41] The latter was far from enthusiastic about this 'rather startling suggestion'.[42] Such a project was 'always fraught with the danger that there are two masters and we do not know yet how far the Americans would agree with the British on general principles of administration'. Weizmann also pointed out that the Prime Minister and he were at one on 'the great importance to Great Britain to protect Palestine', upon which Balfour 'suggested that I should see Mr Lloyd George and even added that "You may tell the Prime Minister that I wanted you to see him".'[43]

On 3 April 1917, Weizmann, in the company of Scott, breakfasted with Lloyd George and discussed the question of Palestine. Scott recorded in his diary that the Prime Minister said that the Palestine campaign was 'the one really interesting part of the war', and that he 'was altogether opposed to a condominium with France'. He also wanted to know Weizmann's position on an internationalised Palestine. The latter replied that this was 'even a shade worse' than an Anglo–French condominium. Lloyd George subsequently sounded Weizmann on Balfour's proposal for an Anglo–American condominium. This time, Weizmann was less critical, 'he said he could accept that. The two countries would pull together.'[44]

That same afternoon Sir Mark had an interview with Lloyd George and Curzon (see also Chapter 6, section 'The British Offensive in the Sinai and the Sykes–Picot Mission'). Both impressed on Sykes 'the importance of not prejudicing the Zionist movement and the possibility of its development under

British auspices'. Lloyd George 'suggested that the Jews might be able to render us more assistance than the Arabs'. Sykes agreed, but also pointed out that 'it was important not to stir up any movement in rear of Turkish lines which might lead to a Turkish massacre of the Jews'. Although the Prime Minister had not referred to a British protectorate over Palestine in his interview with Weizmann, he now was emphatic 'on the importance, if possible, of securing the addition of Palestine to the British area'. Sir Mark therefore should 'not [...] enter into any political pledges to the Arabs, and particularly none in regard to Palestine'.[45]

In accordance with these instructions, the first thing Sykes did when he arrived in Paris was to have a conversation with Georges-Picot, in which he strongly expressed his 'opinion [...] that it would be advantageous to prepare French mind for idea of British suzerainty in Palestine by International consent'. He pointed out to that 'our preponderant military effort [...] coupled with general bias of Zionists in favour of British suzerainty, tended to make such a solution the only stable one'. Picot, however, could give Sykes little hope, as 'gross ignorance prevailed in circles formative of political opinion in France and that the average politician regarded Palestine as being the greater part of Syria instead of one seventh'.[46]

In view of Picot's reaction, Sykes thought it wise to try and temper expectations at home. He wrote to Hankey that he had to contend with great difficulties, and that he hoped the Prime Minister understood that 'the French public think that Palestine is Syria, and do not realise how small a part of the coast-line it occupies'.[47] The next day, he informed Balfour that 'the French are most hostile to the idea of the USA being the patron of Palestine', and that 'the great mass of Frenchmen interested in Syria, mean Palestine when they say Syria'. Still, 'as regards Zionism itself, the French are beginning to realise that they are up against a big thing'. Sykes also believed that when the French started 'to recognise Jewish Nationalism and all that it carries with it as a Palestinian political factor [this] will tend to pave the way to Great Britain being the appointed Patron of Palestine'.[48]

A first indication that the French might indeed have begun to realise that they were 'up against a big thing' was the outcome of a meeting that took place on 9 April between Sokolow, Paul Cambon, his brother Jules (secretary-general at the Quai d'Orsay), as well as Georges-Picot at the Quai d'Orsay. Sir Mark reported to Balfour the same day that 'Zionist aspirations (had been) recognised as legitimate by the French'.[49] In a separate telegram to Graham, Sykes noted that 'at interview question of future suzerain power in Palestine was avoided',[50] but he did not attach much weight to this.

Sokolow had assured him that 'the bulk of the Zionists desire British Suzerainty only'. Naturally, the moment was 'not ripe for such a proposal [...] but provided things go well the situation should be more favourable to British suzerainty with a recognised Jewish voice in favour of it'.[51] Bertie did not share Sykes's optimism at all. He explained to Sir Ronald Graham that:

> In dealing with the question of Syria and Palestine it must be remembered that the French uninformed general Public imagine that France has special prescriptive rights in Syria and Palestine. The influence of France is that of the Roman Catholic Church exercised through French Priests, and schools conducted by them [...] Monsieur Ribot [French prime minister and minister of foreign affairs; R.H.L.] is of the French Protestant Faith which in the eyes of the French Catholics as a body is abhorred next unto the Jewish Faith. Even if M. Ribot were convinced of the justice of our pretensions in regard to Palestine, would he be willing to face the certain combined opposition of the French Chauvinists, the French uninformed general Public and the Roman Catholic Priests and their Flocks?[52]

Sykes admitted the difficulty with the 'Syrian party in Paris' in a letter to Graham of 15 April. He observed that 'what is important is that this gang will work without let or hindrance in Picot's absence [...] The backing behind this is Political-Financial-Religious – a most sinister combination.'[53] He also telegraphed this assessment to Balfour the same day (the foreign secretary, however, was away on a goodwill mission to the USA, and during his absence, Cecil was acting secretary of state for foreign affairs). Sir Mark stated that the 'Syrian party in France' was 'noisy strong anti-British and "intransigeant"' and that he had 'private information that they consider M. Picot has betrayed them by giving away Haifa'. Sir Ronald began to have second thoughts about the whole scheme. He feared that 'the idea that the French will ever be disposed to hand over the whole administration of Palestine to us is utopian, and yet the Zionist hopes are based on this hypothesis. We should not go too far in the encouragement of these hopes, for if they are disappointed the blame will inevitably fall upon us.'[54] In a letter to Sykes of 19 April, he subsequently observed that it was 'somewhat disquieting to see how entirely the Zionist plans and ideas are based on a British Palestine'.[55]

That day, Lloyd George was in Saint Jean-de-Maurienne for a conference (without any representative of the Foreign Office being present) with the

French and the Italians on Italian ambitions in Asia Minor. The conference was a direct consequence of what had been agreed in Article 9 of the Treaty of London of 26 April 1915. In this treaty, which contained the terms under which Italy was prepared to side with the Entente powers, France, Russia and England had 'recognised that Italy is interested in the maintenance of equilibrium in the Mediterranean, and that, in the event of the total or partial partition of Turkey in Asia, she should obtain an equitable share in the Mediterranean region in the neighbourhood of the province of Adalia'. In the preceding weeks an attempt had been made to delimit the Italian sphere, but this attempt had failed 'mainly owing to the irreconcilable nature of the French and Italian *desiderata*'. In preparation for the conference, Lloyd George had drawn up a compromise proposal that Ribot found acceptable. Italian foreign minister Baron Sidney Sonnino, however, 'began to make difficulties and to increase his demands'. What Sonnino 'foresaw was that Great Britain, France and Russia had a reasonable chance of realising their aspirations in Mesopotamia, Syria, and Armenia, respectively, but that Italy was not likely to be so fortunate in Asia Minor'. He therefore demanded compensation elsewhere in case Italy failed to acquire the province of Adalia. Eventually, the participants agreed on the formula that, 'if at the time when peace is declared the total or partial possession of territories contemplated in the agreements come to between France, Great Britain, Italy, and Russia, as to the disposal of part of the Ottoman Empire cannot be fully accorded to any one or more of those Powers, then the interests of the Powers concerned will be again taken into equitable consideration'.[56]

On his way back to London, Lloyd George had an interview with Bertie in Paris. When the conversation turned to Palestine, the Prime Minister insisted that 'the French will have to accept our Protectorate: we shall be there by conquest and shall remain'.[57] At a War Cabinet five days later, however, Lloyd George had to admit that when during the conference he had 'hinted that the British government considered that Palestine should come under British control, (this) proposal had been very coldly received'.[58]

The Demise of the Conjoint Committee and the Success of Sokolow's Mission

On 21 April, Wolf, who had got wind of Sokolow's activities in Paris,[59] wrote to Oliphant that 'in the opinion of the Presidents of the Conjoint Committee a great injustice would be done to the Anglo-Jewish community, and very serious mischief might result, if an agreement on the Palestine Question were concluded without their participation, more especially as the gentlemen with whom His Majesty's Government have so far been in negotiation are all foreign Jews'. Although Graham proposed to reply to Wolf that 'H.M. Government are sincerely anxious to act in all matters affecting the Jewish community not only in its best interests but with a due regard to the wishes and opinions of all its sections,'[60] Anglo-Jewish opposition to Zionism was no real concern for him. What kept on troubling him was the irreconcilability of French claims to Palestine and the Zionist desire for a British protectorate. As he explained in a note to Hardinge:

> His Majesty's Government are now committed to support Zionist aspirations. Sir Mark Sykes has received instructions on the subject from the Prime Minister.
>
> However admirable the Zionist idea may be and however rightly anxious His Majesty's Government are to encourage it, there is one aspect of the situation to which attention should be drawn. Every Zionist with whom I have discussed the question […] insists that the Zionist idea is based entirely on a British Palestine. They are unanimous in the opinion that their project would break down were Palestine to be 'internationalised'.
>
> Are we justified in encouraging them in so great a measure when the prospect of Palestine being internationalised is distinctly stronger than the prospect of the country coming under our protection? I know that the Prime Minister insists that we must obtain Palestine and that Sir Mark Sykes proceeded on his mission with these instructions. But those who are best qualified to gauge French opinion, including Lord Bertie, are convinced that the French will never abandon their sentimental claims to Palestine.

Hardinge heartily agreed. He could not 'help feeling that this Zionist movement and its consequences have not so far been sufficiently considered. It appears that it is inseparable from a British Palestine, and this seems at present unrealisable. Are we wise in giving encouragement to a movement based on a condition which we cannot enforce?' Cecil felt obliged to admit 'the very great difficulty of carrying out the Zionist policy involving as it does a strong preference for a British protectorate over Palestine'. He proposed to send the telegram to Buchanan that had been prepared in the department on his earlier suggestion that the latter should be consulted 'as to whether he thinks that a declaration by the Entente of sympathy for Jewish Nationalist aspirations would help or not'.[61] The telegram was sent on 24 April.[62] Buchanan's reaction was not encouraging. He claimed that there was 'no great enthusiasm for Zionism among Jews in Russia more especially since overthrow of the old regime'. He doubted 'very much whether an expression of sympathy for Jewish national aspirations would help'. The Jewish question was 'always a delicate one and one has to be so careful as to what one says at present moment that the less said about Jews the better'.[63] This advice was accepted by the Foreign Office officials in London. Oliphant minuted that in view of Buchanan's reply 'we had better mark time at present', while Graham noted that the idea of a declaration had 'been dropped'.[64] Cecil had to follow suit, so he explained to William Ormsby Gore (parliamentary secretary to Lord Milner and recently appointed assistant secretary to the War Cabinet) a few weeks later. Although he did not agree with Buchanan, it was 'very difficult to go against his advice in such a matter at such a time'.[65]

In his note to Hardinge of 21 April, Graham had observed that under the Sykes–Picot agreement the brown area would be internationalised, but that 'we cannot, of course, inform the Zionists of this Agreement'. When Sir Ronald put these words to paper, however, Weizmann had already been informed on the provisions in the Sykes–Picot agreement with respect to Palestine. On 12 April, C.P. Scott had had an interview with Viscount Robert de Caix, the foreign editor of the French newspaper *Journal des Débats*, and 'obviously in close touch with the French government'. The latter had assured him – so Scott wrote to Weizmann four days later – first, that it 'had been "settled" that France was to have not only northern Syria but Palestine down to a line from St. Jean d'Acre to Lake Tiberias and including the Hauran', and second, that 'the rest of Palestine was to be "internationalised"'.[66] As a result of Scott's letter, Weizmann 'closely' questioned James Malcolm, who had accompanied Sokolow to Paris and had recently returned to London, on the subject. From what Malcolm told him, Weizmann gathered that there was 'no doubt that some sort of arrangement has been arrived at for a considerable time and the nature of this arrangement as explained by de Caix seems substantially correct'. What remained uncertain, however, was 'whether the arrangement is binding or whether it is flexible and whether there is a clear possibility of reopening the whole question'. Weizmann subsequently saw Graham on 24 April, and confronted the latter with what he had found out. Sir Ronald claimed that he had only learned about the agreement after his return to the Foreign Office, and admitted that it was unsatisfactory, and had created an 'ambiguous' situation. He also arranged an interview for Weizmann with Cecil the following day.[67] When Weizmann called on Lord Robert, he was, according to Ormsby Gore, 'in a fine rage'.[68] He objected in the strongest terms against the cutting up of Palestine and the internationalisation of the remaining part. He claimed that 'Galilea and Judea were both parts of the same country, and ought to be kept together. But he did not attach very great importance to that, because he said that it would take some time for the Zionists to colonise Judea; and when they had done so, and desired to extend, they would have a very strong case for "over-running" (as he put it) Galilea.' With respect to the internationalisation of Judea, Weizmann explained that 'international government was the worst in the world'. A Judea under sole French protection was at least as bad – 'Zionists throughout the world would regard a French administration in Palestine as a great disaster: "a third destruction of the Temple"'.[69]

The next day, Weizmann reported to Scott his version of the conversation with Lord Robert. He observed that it seemed to him that the matter had 'to be carried a little further and brought before the Prime Minister',[70] but he failed to get an interview with Lloyd George. Cecil took no further action. The Zionist scheme once again seemed to have lost momentum. Of its most important sympathisers in London, Lloyd George had hinted at a British protectorate over Palestine at Saint Jean-de-Maurienne, but had encountered French and Italian opposition, Sykes was away in Egypt and the Hijaz, Balfour was in the USA, and Cecil did not dare go against the advice of Buchanan, Hardinge and Graham. It took, however, only a few weeks before Zionist aspirations received a fresh impetus, with the demise of the Conjoint Committee and the unexpected success of Sokolow's mission in Paris. It seemed that the Jewish difficulty – Anglo–Jewish opposition to the Zionism – and the French difficulty – French ambitions in Palestine – could finally be disposed of.

In continuation of his letter of 21 April, Wolf wrote to Oliphant on 2 May that the Conjoint Committee were 'not contemplating any public polemic with the Zionists', but that the Foreign Office should understand that 'with regard to the negotiations now pending between His Majesty's Government and the Zionists, a statement of the views of the Conjoint Committee will certainly be necessary at some time or other'. He felt obliged to warn that the whole question would probably be discussed at the Committee's next meeting, in which case 'a polemic of the nature deprecated by Lord Robert Cecil will be inevitable'.[71] This warning certainly made an impression, and Wolf was received by Lord Robert on 8 May. According to Cecil's account of the meeting, Wolf had first been eager to 'impress upon (him) the fact that the Zionists were a very small minority of the Jewish community', but had also been very anxious to find out whether 'no definite arrangement with the Zionists had been made at present, and that none would be concluded without consulting all sections of Jewish opinion'. With regard to these two points, Cecil had assured Wolf that 'certainly no arrangement with the Zionists had been concluded at present', and that 'the British government would certainly never make such an arrangement without taking into account, if not consulting, the whole of Jewish opinion'.[72]

On 17 May 1917, the Conjoint Committee met and decided, so Wolf informed Oliphant the following day, 'to issue a public statement of their attitude on the Zionist question'. They felt that it was 'clearly their duty to give such guidance to the community as is in their power'. The statement had been drawn up 'there and then', with 'only two dissentients'. Wolf added that the statement was 'a very conciliatory one', and in case Lord Robert 'would like to see a copy of the statement before it is published, I shall be very happy to show it to him and discuss it with him'. Six days later the Foreign Office sent a letter to Wolf that Cecil would be glad to avail himself of this offer,[73] but that morning the statement had already been published in *The Times*. What had forced the Conjoint Committee's hand and why they decided to go to the press before they had received the Foreign Office's *nihil obstat*, so Wolf explained in a letter to Hardinge on 25 May, was that 'owing to some breach of faith, the fact that such a Statement was about to be issued was communicated to the Zionists, and was made the excuse for a most unscrupulous attempt to discredit the Conjoint Committee'.[74]

In their letter to the editor, the presidents of the Conjoint Committee, David L. Alexander and Claude Montefiore, 'strongly and earnestly' protested against the 'Zionist theory' that regarded 'all the Jewish communities of the world as constituting one homeless nationality, incapable of complete social and political identification with the nations among which they dwell', and claimed that 'for this homeless nationality a political centre and an always available homeland in Palestine are necessary'. They warned that 'a Jewish nationality in Palestine founded on this theory of Jewish homelessness, must have the effect throughout the world of stamping the Jews as strangers in their native lands, and of undermining their hard-won position as citizens and nationals of those lands'. They also protested against the Zionist proposal 'to invest the Jewish settlers in Palestine with certain special rights in excess of those enjoyed by the rest of the population, these rights to be administered by a Jewish Chartered Company'. According to them:

> Any such action would prove a veritable calamity for the whole Jewish people. In all the countries in which they live the principle of equal rights for all religious denominations is vital for them. Were they to set an example in Palestine of disregarding this principle they would convict themselves of having appealed to it for purely selfish motives. In the countries in which they are still struggling for equal rights they would find themselves hopelessly compromised, while in other countries, where these rights have been secured, they would have great difficulty in defending them.

They concluded by stating that 'if the Conjoint Committee can be satisfied on these points they will be prepared to cooperate in securing for the Zionist organisation the united support of Jewry'.[75]

Officials in the Foreign Office took no offence that the statement had been published before they had been consulted, and Harold Nicolson considered it 'perfectly harmless'. In his letter to Hardinge, Wolf reiterated that the statement had been 'drawn up in the most conciliatory terms', and expressed the hope that 'it might well serve as a starting point for fresh negotiations, and as a basis for a compromise',[76] but this was not to be. *The Times* reported on 25 May that they had 'received more letters than we can find room for from Jewish correspondents taking strong exception to the statement published yesterday'. One of the letters they did print was from Mr S. Gilbert, a member of the Board of Deputies, which spelled the demise of the Conjoint Committee. According to Gilbert, the Board of Deputies had:

> Never been consulted on the question of whether such a declaration should be issued [...] But today it finds that, without warning and without any attempt to gain its sanction, a manifesto has been issued in its name. From these facts you will gather the precise amount of authority which attaches to this declaration.[77]

The Anglo–Jewish Association was the first to discuss the Conjoint Committee's declaration. On 4 June, Wolf informed Oliphant that a vote of censure had been rejected by a large majority.[78] A fortnight later, he had, however, to report that during the meeting of the Board of Deputies on 17 June, 'a vote of censure on the Committee was carried by 56 votes to 51'. As Montagu explained to Cecil almost three months later, the letter to *The Times* had been criticised on two grounds, 'namely, that it opposed the national idea which is the foundation of Zionism, and that the Joint Committee in issuing it on its own responsibility exceeded its rights as a mere executive committee'. The vote of censure had 'obviously enlisted the support of Zionists, but also of those who felt the force of this latter criticism, and in the discussion the second point played a very large part'.[79] Wolf in his letter to Oliphant optimistically claimed that 'the effect of yesterday's voting on the constitution of the Conjoint Committee will not be to disturb existing arrangements', but Sir Ronald minuted that 'this is a very different opinion to that held by the Zionists. The Board of Deputies was regarded as the stronghold of the anti-Zionists and I believe that this vote signifies the dissolution of the Conjoint Committee.'[80] It was Graham who was right. Alexander resigned as president of the Board of Deputies in consequence of the vote of censure, and was succeeded by Sir Stuart Samuel, Herbert Samuel's brother, while Lord Rothschild became one of the vice presidents. The Conjoint Committee was eventually abolished on 9 September 1917.[81] The 'Jewish difficulty' appeared to have been solved. It would, however, resurface one last time in the course of August, when Montagu, who became secretary of state for India in the middle of July,[82] intervened (see section 'The Struggle for the Balfour Declaration', below).

After his visit to Paris, Sykes had travelled on to Rome. On 14 April, Sykes wrote to Graham that he had been received by Monsignor Eugenio Pacelli, the Vatican's assistant under-secretary for foreign affairs. Sir Mark had gained the impression that 'the idea of British patronage of the holy places was not distasteful to Vatican policy. The French I could see did not strike them as ideal in any way'. Sykes had also 'prepared the way for Zionism by explaining what the purpose and ideals of the Zionists were'. Naturally, 'one could not expect the Vatican to be enthusiastic about this movement, but he was most interested and expressed a wish to see Sokolow when he should come to Rome'. Sykes, who had to leave for Egypt, had therefore left a letter for Sokolow in preparation of his conversations with the Vatican.[83] Sir Mark explained that he had been:

> Careful to impress that the main object of Zionism was to evolve a self-supporting Jewish community which should raise, not only the racial self-respect of the Jewish people, but should also be a proof to the non-Jewish peoples of the world of the capacity of Jews to produce a virtuous and simple agrarian population, and that by achieving these two results, to strike at the roots of those material difficulties which have been productive of so much unhappiness in the past.

He had further 'pointed out that Zionist aims in no way clashed with Christian desiderata in general and Catholic desiderata in particular', and strongly advised Sokolow 'if you see fit (to) have an audience with His Holiness'.[84] Sokolow was granted an audience on 6 May, which went very satisfactorily. The Pope declared that he sympathised with 'Jewish efforts of establishing national home in Palestine', and that he saw 'no obstacle whatever from the point of view of his religious interests'. He also spoke 'most sympathetically of Great Britain's intentions'. According to Sokolov the length of his audience and the 'tenor of conversation' revealed a 'most favourable attitude'.[85]

A few days later, Sokolow had an interview with Italian prime minister Paolo Boselli, who indicated that Italy would not actively support a Zionist initiative in Palestine, but also would not oppose it.[86] At the end of the month, Sokolow returned to Paris and continued his conversations with the French authorities. He was received by Ribot and by Jules Cambon. After some days, Sokolow succeeded in obtaining a message of French support for the Zionist cause. On 4 June Cambon wrote to him that:

> You consider that when circumstances permit and the independence of the holy places is secured, it would be an act of justice and reparation to assist with the renaissance, through the protection of the Allied Powers, of the Jewish nationality on that territory from which the Jewish people have been chased many centuries ago.
>
> The French government, who have entered the present war to defend a people unjustly attacked, and pursue the fight to ensure the triumph of right over might, cannot feel but sympathy for your cause the triumph of which is tied to that of the Allies.[87]

Sokolow telegraphed two days later to Israel Rosov, a leading Russian Zionist, that he had 'happily succeeded in obtaining desired official document'. That the French government had addressed him officially, and had recognised the Zionist claim to Palestine, Sokolow considered 'the greatest moral victory our idea ever attained'. However, the French letter did not change his views on the desirability of a British protectorate. According to Sokolov, 'we are agreeable to consider British protection as the ideal solution. Practically this will be the case, at all events particularly after fait accompli, but formally phrased Entente protection is still current in diplomatic quarters.' This depiction of the state of affairs drew no comments from Foreign Office officials.[88]

The Struggle for the Balfour Declaration

On 12 June 1917, Weizmann called on Graham, and gave him 'some information of considerable interest'. The German government was intensifying its attempts to win the Zionist movement for a peace initiative. In this connection 'a prominent Zionist, who has lived a long time in Constantinople, and who is fully acquainted with the diplomatic world and also with the Committee of Union and Progress' had been received by Arthur Zimmermann, the German foreign minister. Weizmann also drew Graham's attention to the fact that in the last two or three months 'a number of articles have [...] begun to appear in the German papers all dealing with the great importance of the Zionist movement [...] and the considerable danger which a Jewish Palestine under British protection would represent to the Central Powers'. According to Weizmann there could 'be no doubt that a complete change of front on the part of the German government has taken place and that orders have been given to treat Zionism as an important political factor in the policy of the Central Empires'. He went on to sum up all the successes the Zionists had scored in the Entente countries in the last weeks, 'even in France, which was considered the stronghold of Jewish opposition to Zionism'. Weizmann 'concluded by urging very strongly that it was desirable from every point of view that His Majesty's Government should give an open expression of their sympathy with, and support of, Zionist aims and should publicly recognise the justice of Jewish claims on Palestine'.

It was Sir Ronald's position that 'in view of the sympathy towards the Zionist movement which has already been expressed by the Prime Minister, Mr Balfour, Lord R. Cecil, and other statesmen, we are committed to support it'. In his view 'the moment has come when we might meet the wishes of the Zionists [...] Such a step would be well justified by the international political results it would secure.'[89] However, Balfour felt that his hands were tied: 'how can H.M.G. announce their intention of "protecting" Palestine without first consulting our Allies? And how can we discuss dismembering the Turkish Empire till the Turks are beaten?' He was moreover 'personally' still in favour of American participation 'in the protectorate should we succeed in securing it'.[90] The foreign secretary, however, set his doubts aside after he had spoken with Rothschild and Weizmann on 19 June, and read a minute that Sir Ronald had composed that same day.

Balfour's interview with Rothschild and Weizmann took place at the request of Rothschild, who wanted 'to prove to [Balfour] that the majority of Jews are in favour of Zionism'.[91] In his minute, Graham pointed out that he 'had never meant to suggest that the question of the "Protection" should be raised at all. This would be most inopportune in view of French susceptibilities', and the Zionists did not 'ask for any pronouncement on this head'. What they wanted was 'a formal repetition, if possible in writing, of the general assurances of sympathy which they have already received from members of H.M. Government verbally'. What he proposed was that 'we should give them something on the lines of the French assurance – which would satisfy them'. Balfour subsequently noted that he had 'asked Lord Rothschild and Professor Weizmann to submit a formula', to which Lord Robert could not help adding that he had 'wanted to do this several weeks ago but was deterred by the advice of Sir G. Buchanan'.[92]

As Weizmann would be away for a few weeks for a meeting with Henry Morgenthau, the former US ambassador in Constantinople, at Gibraltar at the beginning of July,[93] he left for the guidance of Sokolow and the other members of the London Zionist Political Committee a rough draft of a declaration. The British government should declare 'its conviction, its desire or its intention to support Zionist aims for the creation of a Jewish national home in Palestine; no reference must be made I think to the question of the Suzerain Power because that would land the British into difficulties with the French; it must be a Zionist declaration'.[94] The wording of the formula led to a struggle for several weeks between the 'maximalists', headed by Harry Sacher, on the one hand, and the 'politicians', headed by Sokolow, on the other hand. Sacher wanted the Zionists to ask 'for as much as possible',[95] but Sokolow warned that 'if we want too much we shall get nothing'.[96] It was not until 17 July that Sokolow was able to carry the day, although Sacher was the main author of the formula.[97] Lord Rothschild transmitted it to Balfour the following day:

1. His Majesty's Government accepts the principle that Palestine should be reconstituted as the National Home of the Jewish people.
2. His Majesty's Government will use its best endeavours to secure the achievement of this object and will discuss the necessary methods and means with the Zionist Organisation.

Balfour replied the next day. He would 'have the formula you sent me carefully considered but the matter is of course of the highest importance and I fear it may be necessary to refer it to the Cabinet. I shall not therefore be able to let you have an answer as soon as I should otherwise have wished to.' The wheels of bureaucracy also took their toll. The process of careful consideration was held up for a fortnight due to, so Graham explained on 1 August, 'the French assurance having been mislaid'.[98]

The Foreign Office accepted the first part of the Rothschild formula (except for a minor linguistic alteration, 'accept' instead of 'accepts'), but re-worded the second in a more passive sense. The initiative to discuss the 'necessary methods and means' should not lie with the British government, but with the Zionists. The government would 'be ready to consider any suggestions on the subject which the Zionist Organisation may desire to lay before them'. The draft declaration was subsequently sent to the War Cabinet secretariat, and then bureaucracy struck again. On 17 August, Nicolson enquired whether the War Cabinet had already taken a decision on the text, but Cyril Longhurst informed him three days later that 'we received some time back four copies of the draft reply [...] but you did not say at the time whether you wished us to put the question on the waiting list of subjects for consideration by the War Cabinet'. Longhurst should appreciate it if Nicolson would let him know 'if you wish the question brought up'.[99]

Ormsby Gore had in the meantime picked up the subject. On 18 August he submitted to Hankey that with respect to the second paragraph of the Foreign Office text, 'some amendment is desirable'. The 'great thing to guard against is the appearance of Christian power "forcing" the realisation of Zionist aims. Such forcing would arouse a conflict with Arab population of Palestine at once, and would upset a certain section of non-Zionist Jews.' The work of 'practical Zionism' must be 'carried out by the Jews themselves and not by Great Britain'. He therefore proposed to substitute 'to facilitate the achievement' for 'to secure', and to add 'by the Jewish people'.¹⁰⁰

Copies of the Rothschild formula and the proposed Foreign Office reply were also circulated to Montagu.¹⁰¹ When this prominent representative of 'a certain section of non-Zionist Jews' laid eyes on these documents, he became very upset, and the next day he submitted to the War Cabinet a memorandum on 'The Anti-Semitism of the Present Government'. He began by explaining that he had chosen this title 'not in any hostile sense', but because he wished 'to place on record my view that the policy of His Majesty's Government is anti-Semitic in result and will prove a rallying ground for Anti-Semites in every country in the world'. He also felt that 'as the one Jewish Minister in the government', he might 'be allowed by my colleagues an opportunity of expressing views which may be peculiar to myself, but which I hold very strongly and which I must ask permission to express when opportunity affords'. Montagu continued that Zionism had always seemed to him 'a mischievous political creed, untenable by any patriotic citizen of the United Kingdom', and that he had:

> Always understood that those who indulged in this creed were largely animated by the restrictions upon and refusal of liberty to Jews in Russia. But at the very time when these Jews have been acknowledged as Jewish Russians and given all liberties, it seems to be inconceivable that Zionism should be officially recognised by the British government.

He laid down 'with emphasis' four principles: one, 'there is not a Jewish nation'; two, 'to bring the Jews back to form a nation in the country from which they were dispersed would require Divine leadership'; three, 'there are three times as many Jews in the world as could possibly get into Palestine if you drove out all the population that remains there now. *So that only one-third will get back at the most, and what will happen to the remainder?*'; four, 'when the Jew has a national home, surely it follows that the impetus to deprive us of the rights of British citizenship must be enormously increased. Palestine will become the world's Ghetto [...] All Jews will be foreign Jews, inhabitants of the great country of Palestine.'¹⁰² The Jewish problem had re-emerged with a vengeance.

That same day, Ormsby Gore wrote to Colonel Swinton of the War Cabinet Secretariat that Lord Milner 'would like the proposed "Zionist" declaration brought before the Cabinet as soon as possible'. He also submitted an alternative draft. Milner thought the word 'reconstituted [...] much too strong', and agreed with Ormsby Gore's objections against 'to secure', but there were two other significant changes, which further watered down Britain's commitment to the Zionist cause. The Milner–Ormsby Gore formula referred to 'a home for the Jewish people', instead of 'the National Home of the Jewish people', and to 'the Zionist organisations', instead of 'the Zionist Organisation':

> His Majesty's Government accepts the principle that every opportunity should be afforded for the establishment of a home for the Jewish people in Palestine, and will use its best endeavours to facilitate the achievement of this object, and will be ready to consider any suggestions on the subject which the Zionist organisations may desire to lay before them.[103]

The matter finally came before the War Cabinet on 3 September 1917. Lloyd George, Balfour, as well as Lord Curzon, did not attend, but Milner, Cecil and Montagu did. A first conclusion was that 'a question raising such important issues as to the future of Palestine ought, in the first instance, to be discussed with our Allies, and more particularly with the United States'. The discussion then turned on 'Lord Milner's draft for the consideration of the United States government'. Montagu protested against the phrase 'the home of the Jewish people', which evidently was not in the Milner draft, but nobody seemed to notice this, and the protagonists turned to their familiar arguments. Where Montagu urged that 'the position of every Jew elsewhere' would be 'vitally' prejudiced, Cecil and Milner expressed the view that, 'while a small influential section of English Jews were opposed to the idea, large numbers were sympathetic of it'.[104] It was suggested that 'the matter might be postponed', but Lord Robert 'pointed out that this was a question on which the Foreign Office had been very strongly pressed for a long time past'. The War Cabinet decided that 'the views of President Wilson should be obtained before any declaration was made', and requested Cecil to inform the President that the British government 'were being pressed to make a declaration in sympathy with the Zionist movement, and to ascertain [his] views as to the advisability of such a declaration'.[105] A telegram in this sense was sent the same day, but with a slight twist. Lord Robert asked Colonel House if he 'felt able to ascertain whether the President favours such a declaration'.[106] He was in for a disappointment. On 11 September, House telegraphed that in the opinion of Wilson 'the time is not yet opportune for any definite statement further perhaps than one of sympathy provided it can be made without conveying real commitment'.[107] It seemed that a new 'American difficulty' had arisen, but the next day Weizmann had already undertaken steps to get that out of the way. After having been informed by Amery and Ormsby Gore that a telegram had been sent to House, he telegraphed to Louis Brandeis, leader of the American Zionists, judge at the Supreme Court and confidant of President Wilson, the text of the Rothschild formula – Weizmann was not aware of the changes the Foreign Office had made in the second paragraph, and the alternative text proposed by Milner and Ormsby Gore – and added that he expected 'opposition from assimilationist quarters'. It would consequently 'greatly help if President Wilson and yourself would support text. Matter most urgent'.[108]

Montagu felt encouraged by House's reply to write a letter to Cecil, in which he not only tried to correct the latter's suggestion that the views he had expressed during the meeting of the cabinet 'were almost peculiar to myself and a few other eccentric individuals', but also to exploit the American difficulty:

> What can be the motive for our government, in the midst of its great preoccupations and perplexities, doing anything in this matter? To help the Allied cause in America was one of the reasons given in the Cabinet discussion. I did not see the terms of the telegram which you sent to America, but it is obvious that President Wilson does not wish for a definite statement conveying any real commitment at present. This motive then goes by the board, and therefore I am impelled to urge once more that no form of words should be used by any spokesman of the British government which implies that there is a Jewish people in the political sense.[109]

On 19 September, Weizmann at last had an interview with Balfour, who had returned from an extended holiday five days before. Weizmann reported to Kerr that the foreign secretary had acquainted him with the fate that had befallen the 'declaration', and declared that it was 'all beyond me and I cannot possibly understand why – if everybody is sympathetic – and Mr Balfour was emphatic on that point it should be all hung up'. Balfour had promised to see Lloyd George when the latter returned to London, and Weizmann heartily requested Kerr 'to put the matter' before the Prime Minister. He ended on a desperate note, 'is it at all possible to see the P.M.?

Do drop me a line. I feel we have reached a critical point and I feel I am not making an appeal in vain to you. Do help us!'[110]

The Foreign Office took action the next day. Oliphant asked Hankey 'whether any decision has yet been taken by the Cabinet on the matter?' Ormsby Gore replied that 'a preliminary discussion took place at War Cabinet [...] and I expect the subject will come up again when the Prime Minister returns from North Wales'.[111] Rothschild also managed to see Balfour, and in a letter he sent to the latter the following day, he reiterated the argument that Weizmann had employed to good effect in his interview with Sir Ronald on 12 June: the German government were making overtures to the Zionists. Rothschild observed that during recent weeks there had appeared in the 'Official and Semi-Official German newspapers' many statements, 'all to the effect that in the Peace Negotiations the Central Powers must make a condition for Palestine to be a Jewish settlement under German protection. I therefore think it important that the British declaration should forestall any such move'.[112]

Lloyd George returned to London on 23 September. The following day the War Cabinet Secretariat put the question again on the waiting list. Sir Ronald believed that the time was ripe to address yet another note to Hardinge on 'Zionist Aspirations'. Graham regarded with 'some concern the delay that is taking place in giving the Zionists some assurance of sympathy', and drew Hardinge's attention to the 'organised campaign, evidently inspired [...] now proceeding in the German Press in favour of Jewish claims to Palestine'. There was 'a danger of Zionist feeling, which should be on the side of the Allies, becoming divided, and this would be especially the case if the Germans induced the Turks to make concessions to Zionism'. He also pointed out that the French government had 'already given the Zionists a somewhat vague letter of sympathy which, however, appears to satisfy them', and he did 'not see why we should not go as far as the French in the matter'. As to the Anglo-Jewish opposition to the Zionist movement, this concerned 'a small group of eminent and influential Jews', who based themselves 'on unfounded apprehensions with regard to the effect of the movement on Jews who desire to remain entirely British', while 'abroad and in America the anti-Zionist forces are recruited from the Jewry of international finance which, if not hostile to the Allies, has never been strongly in our favour'. It was in the British political interest to encourage the Zionists. Hardinge agreed – 'we might and ought to go as far as the French' – and so did Balfour, but the latter also noted that 'as this question was (in my absence) decided by the Cabinet against the Zionists I cannot do anything till the decision is reversed'. In the end, so Graham recorded, Balfour nevertheless decided to 'raise the matter again'.[113]

The Zionist declaration gained further momentum when Brandeis's reply was finally received on 27 September. Weizmann immediately passed it on to the War Cabinet Secretariat and the Foreign Office. It seemed completely to dispose of the American difficulty. Brandeis related that 'from talks I have had with the President and from expressions of opinion given to closest advisers, I feel I can answer you that he is in entire sympathy with declaration'.[114] Weizmann also managed to have '2–3 minutes' with Lloyd George the next day,[115] and 'George, on Weizmann's representations of urgency, told Sutherland [one of the Prime Minister's private secretaries; R.H.L.] to put down "Palestine" for the next War Cabinet'.[116]

It took, in fact, another three War Cabinets before the declaration was finally discussed. In preparation for this meeting and in an attempt to stiffen the foreign secretary's resolve, Rothschild sent a letter to Balfour, enclosing an appeal to the War Cabinet signed by Weizmann and himself. Both Rothschild's letter and the appeal mainly concentrated on discrediting Montagu. According to the appeal, Jewish opponents of Zionism were 'represented by a small minority of so-called assimilated Cosmopolitan Jews mostly belonging to the *Haute* finance who have lost contact with the development of Jewish life and ideas'. The Jewish masses saw themselves as a nation – whether they were 'scientifically' justified in so doing was a 'mere academic question' – and they would persist, 'whatever some few Jewish assimilants may decree to the contrary'. Rothschild in his covering letter assured Balfour 'once more' that the 'Anti-Zionist group for whom Mr Montagu and my cousins speak, is only a minute fraction (some 80–120 thousand people) of the 12 million Jews of the world'.[117]

The War Cabinet met on 4 October, this time with Lloyd George in the chair, and was attended by Balfour, Curzon, Milner and Montagu. The foreign secretary opened the discussion by stating that the 'German government were making great efforts to capture the sympathy of the Zionist movement', and that this movement, 'though opposed by a number of wealthy Jews in this country, had behind it the support of a majority of Jews, at all events in Russia and America'. What was 'at the back of the Zionist Movement was the intense national consciousness by certain members of the Jewish race [...] and these Jews had a passionate longing to regain once more this ancient national home'. Balfour concluded his statement by reading out 'a very sympathetic declaration by the French government which had been conveyed to the Zionists', and claiming that 'President Wilson was extremely favourable to the Movement'. This claim was right away called into question in view of 'the contradictory telegrams received from Colonel House and Justice Brandeis'. Montagu subsequently repeated his argument against 'any declaration in which it was stated that Palestine was the "national home" of the Jewish people', because it might endanger 'the civil rights of Jews as nationals in the country in which they were born', and once again pointed out that the declaration was opposed by 'most English-born Jews', and supported by 'foreign-born Jews'. He ended by submitting that the Cabinet's first duty was to English Jews, and that 'Colonel House had declared that President Wilson is opposed to a declaration now'.

Curzon joined the fray. On 8 September he had already written to Montagu that he agreed with the latter 'about the absurdity of shunting the Jews back to Palestine, a tiny country which has lost its fertility and only supports meager herds of sheep and goats with occasional terraced plots of cultivation'. He also shared Montagu's nightmare that Palestine would become 'the world's Ghetto'. Curzon could not 'conceive a worst bondage to which to relegate an advanced and intellectual community than to exile in Palestine'.[118] At the Cabinet meeting he repeated these arguments. Palestine was 'for the most part, barren and desolate […] a less propitious seat for the future Jewish race could not be imagined'. The return of the Jews to Palestine 'on a large scale' he regarded as 'sentimental idealism, which would never be realised', and the government 'should have nothing to do with it'.

Deadlock threatened, when Milner intervened. Amery later recorded in his memoirs how half an hour before the meeting Milner had asked him whether he 'could draft something which would go a reasonable distance to meeting the objectors, both Jewish and pro-Arab without impairing the substance of the proposed declaration?' The latter 'sat down and quickly produced' a text,[119] which Milner now read out to the War Cabinet:

> His Majesty's Government views with favour the establishment in Palestine of a National Home for the Jewish Race, and will use its best endeavours to facilitate the achievement of this object; it being clearly understood that nothing shall be done which may prejudice the civil and religious rights of the existing non-Jewish communities in Palestine, or the rights and political status enjoyed in any other country by such Jews who are fully contented with their existing nationality and citizenship.

The War Cabinet subsequently decided that 'before coming to a decision', President Wilson, leaders of the Zionist movement, as well as representatives of the Anglo–Jewish community should be consulted on the text submitted by Milner.[120]

Although he might have taken heart from Curzon's opposition to the declaration, Montagu realised that the game was up. He was due to depart for India at the end of the month on a mission to investigate on the spot the possibilities of constitutional reforms that would increase Indian participation in the administration of the country. After the meeting of the War Cabinet he wrote to Lloyd George in a very despondent mood. He felt very sorry to have found himself in opposition to the Prime Minister that morning, and hoped that the latter did 'not resent my expression with all the vigour I was capable of views which I cannot but hold'. He appreciated Lloyd George's 'motives – your generosity and desire to take up the cudgels for the oppressed', but he simply did not 'believe in a Jewish Nation', and it was a 'matter of deep regret' that the Prime Minister was 'being misled by a foreigner, a dreamer, an idealist, who […] sweeps aside all practical difficulties with a view to enlisting your sympathy on behalf of his cause'. He found himself in an impossible situation. He could resign, of course, but resigning over 'something wholly unconnected with India at all' surely would not be understood, especially in view of his outspoken position on, and accepted responsibility for dealing with the momentous challenges that faced India. He therefore assured Lloyd George that he did not 'want to make difficulties. Among your many colleagues you have no colleague more devoted than myself. Among your many colleagues you have none more desirous of serving.' He ended his letter by asking the Prime Minister 'most respectfully to give me your advice in the difficult circumstances in which I find myself'.[121] Montagu's ferocious opposition had turned into a personal tragedy. The Jewish difficulty was on the verge of crumbling.

On 5 October, Ormsby Gore reported to Hankey that he had spoken with Montagu and Sir Lionel Abrahams and that they had agreed on Sir Stuart Samuel, Leonard Cohen, Claude Montefiore and Sir Philip Magnus, MP, as the representatives of the 'non-Zionists'. He had then seen Weizmann, who had submitted the names of Hertz, the Chief Rabbi, Lord Rothschild, Sokolow and himself as representing the Zionists.[122] It was subsequently decided to add Herbert Samuel to balance Montagu. A telegram to House was sent on 6 October. It explained that 'in view of reports that the German government are making great efforts to capture the Zionist movement, the question of a message of sympathy with the movement [...] has again been considered by the Cabinet'. It then gave the Milner–Amery formula, and continued that 'before taking any decision the Cabinet [...] would be most grateful if you found it possible to ascertain the opinion of the President with regard to the formula'.[123]

Although Amery himself was quite taken with his formula, 'this judicious blend',[124] for Weizmann it was a bitter blow. It constituted 'a painful recession from what the government itself was prepared to offer', especially because it introduced 'the subject of the "civic and religious rights of the existing non-Jewish communities" in such a fashion as to impute possible oppressive intentions to the Jews, and can be interpreted to mean such limitations on our work as completely to cripple it'.[125] However, there was little else to do than put a brave face on it. In his reply he claimed that 'the declaration framed by His Majesty's Government will, when announced, be received with joy and gratitude by the vast majority of the Jewish people all over the world'. After he had once again dismissed 'our opponents' as 'Jews who by education and social connections have lost touch with the real spirit animating the Jewish people as a whole', he suggested three alterations to the proposed declaration, which were also suggested by Sokolow in the latter's separate answer. First, he preferred 're-establishment' to 'establishment', to indicate 'the historical connection with the ancient tradition'. Second, he wished to replace the last lines with 'the rights and political status enjoyed by Jews in any other country of which they are loyal citizens', and third, to substitute 'Jewish people' for 'Jewish race'. The Chief Rabbi for his part proposed that the last phrase be shortened to 'or the rights and political status enjoyed by the Jews in any other country'. Although he was one of Montagu's and Abraham's choices to represent the non-Zionists, Sir Stuart Samuel thought that 'Jews resident in Great Britain are by a large majority favourable to the establishment of a national home for Jews in Palestine'. He, too, felt uneasy about the last phrase of the Milner–Amery draft, because 'Jews who are not "fully contented with their existing citizenship" are not protected by the proposed formula'. Herbert Samuel and Lord Rothschild refrained from proposing corrections, and merely welcomed the declaration.

In their letters, Magnus, Montefiore and Cohen rehearsed the familiar arguments of the Anglo-Jewish community. The Jews did not constitute a nation, 'ever since the conquest of Palestine by the Romans, (the Jews) have ceased to be a body politic'. Any 'privileges granted to the Jews' in Palestine 'should be shared by their fellow-citizens of other creeds'. The establishment of a national home in Palestine would stimulate anti-semitism, and was unnecessary now the Russian Jews had been emancipated, and, finally, the declaration would be strongly opposed by the Palestine population. They were united in objecting to the last phrase of the Milner–Amery draft, but differed on the text of an alternative. Each submitted a different formula.[126]

On 16 October, Sir William Wiseman telegraphed to Sir Eric Drummond that House had 'put formula before President who approves of it but asks that no mention of his approval shall be made when His Majesty's Government makes formula public, as he has arranged that American Jews shall then ask him for his approval which he will give publicly here'. The American difficulty no longer existed, and Sir George Clerk minuted that 'there seems no reason why the formula should not be given to Lord Rothschild', but Balfour cautioned 'formula not yet approved by Cabinet',[127] and it would be more than a week before the question was again discussed.

Hankey informed the War Cabinet on 25 October that he was being pressed by the Foreign Office to bring forward the question of Zionism, an early settlement of which was regarded of great importance', but that Curzon had explained that 'he had a memorandum on the subject in preparation', and the question was therefore adjourned until the following week.[128] Sir Ronald had learned that further delay threatened, and on 24 October he had already written a note to Balfour to warn against it. In this note he mustered all the arguments in favour of the declaration. The delay caused the British government to be looked upon with growing suspicion, and Graham reminded the foreign secretary that 'we might at any moment be confronted by a German move on the Zionist question and it must be remembered that Zionism was originally if not a German at any rate an Austrian idea'. Moreover, the French, the Italians, the Vatican and President Wilson were all sympathetic, and 'information from every quarter shows the very important role which the Jews are now playing in the Russian political situation'. Considering that 'almost every Jew in Russia is a Zionist and if they can be made to realise that the success of Zionist aspirations depends on the support of the Allies and the expulsion of the Turks from Palestine we shall enlist a most powerful element in our favour'.[129] Graham earnestly trusted that 'unless there is very good reason to the contrary the assurance from His Majesty's Government should be given at once'.[130] Balfour wrote to Lloyd George the next day that 'the question of the assurance to be given to the Zionists should be finally decided by the

Cabinet as soon as possible', and enclosed Graham's note, as well as 'a list of dates, showing that the Zionists have reasonable ground for complaint as to the delay which has occurred in coming to a decision'.[131]

Curzon's memorandum 'The Future of Palestine' was circulated on 26 October. He started by distancing himself from the dispute between the Zionists and Anglo-Jewry. He was only interested in the 'more immediately practical questions: (a) What is the meaning of the phrase "a National Home for the Jewish Race in Palestine" [...] (b) If such a policy be pursued what are the chances of its successful realisation?' Regarding the first question, Curzon merely drew attention to the fact that there were different opinions on what the phrase meant exactly, ranging from a fully fledged state to a merely spiritual centre for the Jews. The second question was his main concern, 'Palestine would appear to be incapacitated by physical and other conditions from ever becoming in any real sense the national home of the Jewish people'. Considering that the Jews numbered 12,000,000, and assuming that 'Palestine' meant 'the old Scriptural Palestine, extending from Dan to Beersheba', it was a country 'not much bigger than Wales', and Wales only supported 'a population of 2,000,000 persons', while 'after the devastation wrought by the War it will be many decades before we can contemplate a population that will even remotely approximate to that of Wales'. There arose the further question:

> What is to become of the people of this country [...] There are over a half million of these, Syrian Arabs – a mixed community with Arab, Hebrew, Canaanite, Greek, Egyptian, and possibly Crusaders' blood. They and their forefathers have occupied the country for the best part of 1500 years. They own the soil, which belongs either to individual landowners or to village communities. They profess the Mohammedan faith. They will not be content either to be expropriated for Jewish immigrants, or to act merely as hewers of wood and drawers of water to the latter.

If Zionism merely meant that the Jews – but not the Jews alone – would secure in Palestine equal civil and religious rights with the other elements in the population, and to 'arrange as far as possible for land purchase and settlement of returning Jews', then he saw no reason 'why we should not all be Zionists', but in his judgement this was 'a policy very widely removed from the romantic and idealistic aspirations of the Zionist leaders whose literature I have studied'.[132]

Sykes prepared a note to refute Curzon's arguments. Drummond wrote to Balfour that Sir Mark was 'of course anxious that his name should not appear, but hopes you will have time to look through it before the discussion'. Sykes opened by stating that 'the resources of Palestine are very apt to be under-estimated or misunderstood'. It had taken 'the Turks and all their men to keep the country a desert before the war', but the region of Jaffa produced oranges, olive oil and wine, the Jordan valley was 'a gigantic natural hothouse [...] Intensive cultivation [...] would certainly produce 3 crops a year', while the area of Galilee was 'extraordinarily fertile'. As someone who had 'known Palestine since 1886', it was Sykes's estimate that the population of Palestine, 'with energy and expenditure' could be 'quadrupled and quintupled within 40 years'.[133]

The final discussion in the War Cabinet took place on 31 October, Montagu did not attend, as he had sailed for India. It was something of an anti-climax. From his opening statement it appeared that Balfour had taken the notes by Graham and Sykes to heart. He submitted that 'everyone was now agreed that, from a purely diplomatic and political view, it was desirable that some declaration favourable to the aspirations of the Jewish nationalists should now be made'. Because the 'vast majority of Jews in Russia and America' and in the world favoured Zionism, 'a declaration favourable to such an ideal' would free the way for an 'extremely useful propaganda both in Russia and America'. Balfour distinguished two kinds of objection to the scheme. Palestine was too poor a country to sustain large-scale Jewish immigration, and it endangered 'the future position of Jews in Western countries'. As to the first, experts seemed to differ, but he had been 'informed that, if Palestine were scientifically developed, a very much larger population could be sustained than had existed during the period of Turkish misrule'. With respect to the second objection, he 'felt that, so far from Zionism hindering the process of assimilation in western countries, the truer parallel was to be found in the position of an Englishman who leaves his country to establish a permanent home in the United States'. Curzon 'admitted the force of the diplomatic arguments in favour of expressing sympathy, and agreed that the bulk of the Jews held Zionist rather than anti-Zionist opinions'. He stood by the observations in his memorandum, but 'recognised that some expression of sympathy with Jewish aspirations would be a valuable adjunct to our propaganda'. The struggle for the declaration was finally over. Curzon did warn that 'we should be guarded in the language used', and the Milner–Amery draft was revised in three places. The War

Cabinet accepted Weizmann's suggestion to substitute 'Jewish people' for 'Jewish race', referred to 'civil and religious rights of existing non-Jewish communities', instead of 'the existing', and replaced the phrase 'the rights and political status enjoyed in any other country by such Jews who are fully contented with their existing nationality and citizenship' (to which all Jews – both Zionists and non-Zionists – had taken exception) with Hertz's proposed alternative, 'the rights and political status enjoyed by the Jews in any other country'. Balfour was authorised 'to take a suitable opportunity' to make a 'declaration of sympathy with the Zionist aspirations'.[134]

It was fitting that it was left to Sir Ronald to put the finishing touches to the letter to Rothschild and the formula:

Dear Lord Rothschild,
   I have much pleasure in conveying to you, on behalf of His Majesty's Government, the following declaration of sympathy with Jewish Zionist aspirations which has been submitted to, and approved by, the Cabinet.
   'His Majesty's Government view with favour the establishment in Palestine of a national home for the Jewish people, and will use their best endeavours to facilitate the achievement of this object, it being clearly understood that nothing shall be done which may prejudice the civil and religious rights of existing non-Jewish communities in Palestine, or the rights and political status enjoyed by Jews in any other country'.
   I should be grateful if you would bring this declaration to the knowledge of the Zionist Federation.[135]

The Capture of Jerusalem and Martial Law

On 29 June 1917, General Sir Edmund Allenby had succeeded Sir Archibald Murray as commander-in-chief of the EEF. After an inspection of the front, Allenby had accepted the plan developed by Lieut.-General Sir Philip Chetwode for the third battle of Gaza, which involved first attacking Beersheba, at the eastern tip of the Turkish front, and, after taking Beersheba, turning west to Gaza, rolling up the Turkish front in the process. On 12 July he had reported his plan of attack to the War Office, and stated that, to be successful, he required two extra infantry divisions. At an Anglo–French conference at the end of July, after much wrangling, it had been decided that one British division would be transferred from the Salonika front to Palestine. One implication of this decision had been that Allenby's offensive had to be postponed from September until the end of October. On 10 August the War Cabinet had instructed Allenby to 'strike the Turks as hard as possible'. No geographical objective was set – 'as a goal to the Force […] Allenby was simply enjoined to defeat the Turks opposed to him, to follow up his success vigorously, and to continue to press them to the limit of his resources'.[136]

The attack on Beersheba started on 31 October 1917. The town was captured the same day. The offensive against Gaza began in the night from 1 to 2 November. Due to water shortages, the advance on Gaza was slowed down, and British troops only entered the town on 7 November. In the following days, Jaffa was captured, and British troops slowly advanced on Jerusalem. The final attack on that city began on 30 November, and the mayor of Jerusalem surrendered the city nine days later. The Turkish troops had again managed to escape. Allenby's official entry took place on 11 December, when at 12 o'clock he entered Jerusalem on foot through the Jaffa gate.

In the middle of October, Clayton had already observed to Wingate that, if Allenby's offensive succeeded, he foresaw 'proposals for an international Gendarmerie and even perhaps an international provisional government for Palestine etc. etc.' To his mind, 'these can best be countered by the C-in-C saying that he has a military administration of occupied enemy territory, working in accordance with the "Laws and Usages of War", and that […] is the only system which he can permit while military operations are in progress'.[137]

Georges-Picot was due to arrive in Cairo on 25 November to take up his position as French commissioner with Allenby. This time, Sykes would not be his counterpart. The latter had been replaced by Clayton, who had been appointed Chief Political Officer at the beginning of August.[138] Clayton understood that Picot wanted to join Allenby, but saw 'every objection. If any political people go in it will at once break down the military rampart which we have been at such pains to erect.'[139] On 24 November, Wingate telegraphed to Balfour very urgently that Picot had received instructions 'to take part in the official entry into Jerusalem'. Wingate – and Allenby shared his opinion – considered this undesirable. He was 'anxious to keep matters in Palestine on an exclusively military basis', a course that was 'both necessary from a military and expedient from a political point of view'. He therefore proposed that Picot should not proceed to Jerusalem 'until after the official entry', which could be achieved by instructing Clayton 'not to attend the official entry in which case M. Picot could not very well press his claims'.

After his arrival in Cairo, Georges-Picot immediately saw Clayton, and the latter informed him that they would visit Jerusalem on a later date. In a subsequent interview with Sir Reginald, Picot expressed his 'dissatisfaction with these arrangements, which he considered would be strongly resented in France'. Picot claimed that 'over a year ago it was agreed between the British and French governments that, pending the final settlement of the Peace terms, any conquered portions of Palestine should be jointly administered by us and the French, exclusive of Italians or other nationalities'. As he was unaware of such an agreement, Wingate submitted that Allenby 'should be informed telegraphically of the facts, and be given definite instructions as to the line he should take with Picot'. Robertson sent a telegram to Allenby the very next day. The excuse Clayton and Wingate had concocted to prevent Picot entering Jerusalem together with Allenby was rejected. The latter was instructed that 'as French Commissioner and representative Picot should join you at once and enter Jerusalem with you'. Robertson, however, agreed that the administration of Palestine ought to be in military hands as long as military operations were in progress. Allenby therefore 'should not entertain any ideas of joint administration', but at the same time 'should avoid any impression being gained by Picot that annexation of Palestine is contemplated by British'. Sir Edmund also should receive Picot's 'ideas sympathetically but you should remember his role is purely consultative and not executive'. On 29 November, Wingate reported to Hardinge that Clayton and Picot had left for Allenby's headquarters, and that it had been left to the latter 'to break it gently to M. Picot that a joint Anglo–French Administration of the conquered territory cannot be permitted'.[140] Clayton wrote to Wingate on 8 December that Picot was 'grumbling rather and insinuating that we are not acting up to our obligations by refusing to allow French participation in the temporary administration of Palestine',[141] but, as he explained to Gertrude Bell in another letter that same day, 'whatever the subsequent settlement may be we cannot possibly have political considerations interfering with military operations, which would inevitably be the case were any joint civil administration set up'.[142]

Clayton's manoeuvring to sidetrack Picot also held negative consequences for the Zionist programme. On 28 November, Clayton had already telegraphed to Sykes that:

> Announcement made to Jews should suffice for the present and further concessions should be made with utmost caution. It will be specially dangerous to permit any general union of Jewish repatriation or colonisation in Palestine just now. In any case military situation precludes it today and will probably continue to do so for some time to come.[143]

On the day of Allenby's entry into Jerusalem, Sykes and Graham nevertheless drafted a telegram to Clayton in Balfour's name, in which they explained that 'Zionists who are being criticised for inaction in regard to Palestine' were anxious to publish a statement in the press that 'as soon as military situation permits, a Commission composed of delegates of Zionist organisation will proceed to Palestine to assist Military authorities in dealing with problems connected with the position of the Jewish settlements in Palestine'. They proposed 'to authorise publication unless you see strong objections', and at the same time reminded Clayton that 'the despatch of such a commission is inevitable as a natural development of Zionist movement which is achieving considerable political results'.[144] But three days later Clayton replied that he deprecated 'publication of press notice proposed. Military situation at present demands that no one be allowed to proceed to Palestine and the longer this prohibition is maintained simpler political situation will remain.'[145] Clayton elucidated his objections in a letter to Sykes the next day. He was not:

> Fully aware of the weight which Zionists carry, especially in America and Russia, and of the consequent necessity of giving them everything for which they ask, but I must point out that, by pushing as hard as we appear to be doing, we are risking the possibility of Arab unity becoming something like an accomplished fact and being ranged against us.

He urged Sykes to face the fact that the Arab:

> In practice finds that the Jews with whom he comes into contact is a far better businessman than himself and prone to extract his pound of flesh. This is a root fact which no amount of public declarations can get over. We have therefore to consider whether the situation demands out and out support of Zionism at the risk of alienating the Arabs at a critical moment.[146]

Wingate fully agreed, as he wrote to Allenby on 16 December, 'Mark Sykes is a bit carried away with "the exuberance of his own verbosity" in regard to Zionism and unless he goes a bit slower he may quite unintentionally upset the applecart. However Clayton has written him an excellent letter which, I hope, may have an anodyne effect.'[147]

Unaware of Clayton's and Wingate's opposition, on 17 December Weizmann submitted a short memorandum on why a Zionist commission, headed by him, should go to Palestine 'as soon as possible'. Turning around the argument Clayton had used in his telegram to Balfour, he claimed that, 'the later we go out, the more difficult it may become to arrange the complicated questions which necessarily arise now both with regard to the Arabs, and perhaps also to the French'. Moreover, the arrival of the commission in Palestine 'would give a clear indication to the Jews that the Declaration of H.M. Government is being put into effect, and so help to keep up the enthusiasm which is at present existing, and I am sure it would have a far reaching effect, especially in Russia'. However, a commission acting in the limelight was something the Foreign Office wished to avoid. Clerk minuted that 'both the High Commissioner and General Allenby are shy of a "Commission", and that the suggestion now is to let Dr Weizmann and one or two others go, but in an unofficial capacity'. Graham added that he had discussed this with Sykes and Weizmann, and that they had reached the conclusion that a small committee of three, possibly assisted by Ormsby Gore, should go and that the committee's objectives, as formulated by Weizmann, required modification.[148]

In London, the Zionists and their supporters had won the struggle for a public declaration of British sympathy with the aim of establishing a national home for the Jewish people in Palestine, but in Palestine, the struggle with the British military authorities that they 'use their best endeavours to facilitate the achievement of this object' had only just begun.

8 A WHOLE CROWD OF WEEDS GROWING AROUND US

Introduction

This chapter deals with several – to a greater or lesser extent – interconnected issues: British–French rivalry in the Hijaz; the British attempt to get the French government to recognise Britain's predominance on the Arabian Peninsula; the conflict between King Husayn and Ibn Sa'ud, the Sultan of Najd; the British handling of the French desire to take part in the administration of Palestine; as well as the ways in which the British authorities, in London and on the spot, tried to manage French, Syrian, Zionist and Hashemite ambitions regarding Syria and Palestine. It has two major underlying themes. The first is the rapid erosion of Sir Mark Sykes's authority with respect to Middle Eastern affairs in the months from December 1917 to August 1918. His proposed solutions for the disentanglement of the mass of knotty problems with which Britain was confronted found less and less favour, and were increasingly ignored or rejected. At the end of this period, Sir Mark stood more or less on the sidelines of the decision-making process regarding the Middle East. There is quite some irony here, as Sykes, at his own request, had moved to the Foreign Office at the beginning of January 1918 in an attempt to become the directing actor in British Middle East policy. The second underlying theme concerns the concomitant undermining of the Foreign Office doctrine that no effort should be spared to accommodate French susceptibilities with respect to Syria. In Cairo and in Palestine, Sir Reginald Wingate, Gilbert Clayton and General Allenby championed the cause of the Arabs, sheltering behind military exigencies, while in London, Arthur Balfour and Lord Robert Cecil failed to put their stamp on the decision making within the inter-departmental Eastern Committee chaired by Lord Curzon.

The Brémond Mission

On 1 September 1916, a French mission arrived at Alexandria on its way to the Hijaz. It was headed by Colonel Edouard Brémond, according to T.E. Lawrence 'a practising light in native warfare' who had been 'a success in French Africa'.[1] However, it was not as a soldier that Brémond would establish a reputation in the Hijaz. He did not conceal from his British interlocutors that Husayn's revolt should not grow into something bigger than the local affair that it was. Cyril Wilson reported to Wingate on 24 October that Brémond believed that 'the longer the Arabs take to capture Medina the better for Great Britain and France owing to the Syrian question probably then becoming acute'.[2] At that moment, there was naturally not the slightest chance that Husayn's forces would capture Medina. The chances were far greater that Britain and France would have to intervene militarily to prop up Husayn's tottering regime. Regarding the Rabegh question, Brémond was in favour of sending a Franco–British force. According to Lawrence, however, this was not as a means to save the sherif's revolt, but because the landing of Christian troops would make Husayn's position untenable in Muslim eyes. In the same memorandum that Murray and Robertson so eagerly seized on to torpedo the plans to send troops to Rabegh (see Chapter 5, section 'The Rabegh Question: The Third Round'), Lawrence also observed that Brémond considered it vital that 'the Arabs must not take Medina. This can be assured if an Allied force landed at Rabegh. The tribal contingents will go home, and we will be the sole bulwark of the Sherif in Mecca. At the end of the war we give him Medina as his reward.'[3]

Lawrence found a sympathetic ear for his observations with Sir Henry McMahon, Sir Archibald Murray and Wingate. Each of them approached the home authorities on the matter. McMahon wrote to Lord Hardinge that Brémond had confided to Lawrence that the French object with the brigade 'was to thus disintegrate Arab effort, as they by no means wished to see them turn the Turks out of Medina any sooner than could be avoided [...] It is of course always the old question of Syria'.[4] Murray for his part warned Sir William Robertson that the French attitude towards Husayn's revolt was based on the 'fear that if the Sherif is successful in turning the Turks out of the Hijaz they will find that the Arabs propose to operate in Syria. This would not suit them.'[5] Wingate wired to the Foreign Office that the French worried about Husayn's possible capture of Medina 'in view of their future Syrian policy'. The occupation of Medina would lead to the 'active support of all Arab tribes in the Syrian hinterland who have sworn to rise in Shereef's favour immediately Medina is in his hands'.[6]

These telegrams, reports and letters, however, did not initiate a policy revision with respect to French ambitions in Syria. The machinations of the head of the French mission in the Hijaz were completely irrelevant in view of the supreme aim of preserving cordial relations with France. Lawrence's observation that Brémond favoured a landing at Rabegh in order to discredit Husayn was completely ignored during the meeting of the War Committee on 20 November, where his report and person were extensively discussed. Lawrence's remarks on Brémond were moreover deleted from the report that George Clerk compiled at the request of the War Committee for the benefit of the French government,[7] not only out of consideration for French feelings, but also, as Clerk minuted on Wingate's telegram the next day, because 'we have little evidence to support the theory that the French do not want the Sherif to take Medina, I find it hard to credit'.[8]

The source of these messages was, moreover, considered suspect. Sykes's reaction to a report by Wilson was typical. Wilson related that a member of the British mission at Jedda had been informed that during a conversation between members of the French mission and Rashid Rida, the latter had told the French that 'everybody in Egypt loathes the British and how overjoyed the Syrians were at the French joining the Arab movement as their Friend, etc.' This made Sykes burst out in anger. In a letter to Hardinge he railed against the type of Englishmen who permitted the French ally to be spied on. This he blamed on the fact that 'our people in Egypt, still think that there is a chance of getting Syria'. It was high time they realised that to the Arab cause 'cooperation between French and British is more important than Rabegh'. Sykes suggested that 'a very definite instruction should go to the sirdar urging him to see to frank and trustful cooperation among the officers of the two missions'. Wingate was accordingly informed that 'it would seem desirable to impress upon your subordinates the need for the most loyal cooperation with the French whom His Majesty's Government do not suspect of ulterior designs in the Hijaz'.[9] This was the end of the affair as far as the Foreign Office was concerned.

After this reprimand, Wingate and Wilson did not return to this subject other than Wingate transmitting Wilson's assurance that he was 'well aware of the necessity for loyal cooperation and that this policy will be scrupulously adhered to by me'.¹⁰ A report by Lawrence on a conversation between Faysal and Brémond, however, provided a good opportunity to make a fresh attempt to open the home authorities' eyes to the problem. Brémond had observed to Faysal that he should not forget that 'the firmness and strength of the present bonds between the allies did not blind them to the knowledge that these alliances were only temporary and that between England and France, England and Russia, lay such deep and rooted seeds of discord that no permanent friendship could be looked for'. Who exactly, so Wingate wrote to Balfour, was jeopardising the all important British–French cooperation? The people in Cairo, who 'loyally observed the policy of "hands off" in matters Syrian', and scrupulously saw to it that 'our policy and that of the French are, and will remain closely coordinated', or Colonel Brémond, who 'in conversation with the Arab leaders, has not scrupled to convey to them a contrary impression'?

This time the Cairo authorities did not confine themselves to dispatching letters. On the suggestion of Wilson it was decided to send Captain George Lloyd, MP, to London. Lloyd, who had served in the Hijaz in the previous months, was entrusted with the task to explain that Brémond and his staff were responsible for the recurring problems in the Hijaz, *and* that more was at stake than a purely local affair. The Foreign Office again refused to take the matter very seriously. Although Hardinge was now prepared to admit that Brémond had shown himself to be 'unreliable and untrustful', the forthcoming mission by Sykes and Georges-Picot would soon set matters right, the more so as Picot had told Sir Ronald Graham that he intended to assume control of affairs in the Hijaz.

The instructions of Sykes and Georges-Picot constituted a faithful reflection of the Foreign Office's policy towards the Middle East, with which Sir Mark completely identified. Everything turned on cordial relations between France and Britain. British diplomacy should spare no effort to accommodate French susceptibilities, whether these were justified or not. This was the reasoning behind McMahon's convoluted formulations in his letters to Husayn in the autumn of 1915. This also explained the procedure of first coming to an agreement with France before the negotiations with Husayn could be finalised. This did not mean that Grey, Sykes and Foreign Office officials were blind to the problems that this policy entailed, but these counted for little compared to the all-important objective of good relations with France. Balfour's minute on Wingate's dispatch on Brémond's machinations, however, indicated that he was less attached to this orthodoxy: 'I think if the French intrigues go on in the Hedjaz we shall have to take a strong line. They may find us interfering in Syria if they insist on interfering in Arabia.'[11]

Balfour's minute constituted a first indication that British Middle East policy would change after Grey had left the Foreign Office. This was for the greater part due to the increasing meddling in foreign affairs by members of the War Cabinet, Prime Minister Lloyd George in particular, as well as the establishment of the interdepartmental Middle East Committee, subsequently the Eastern Committee, chaired by Curzon.[12] Balfour dominated British foreign policy making to a far lesser extent than Grey had done in his days. In the early spring of 1917, matters still hung in the balance. For the time being Brémond could continue to make a nuisance of himself in the Hijaz.

The Failure of the 'Projet d'Arrangement'

Sykes's arrival in Egypt heralded the reversal of the Foreign Office's attitude towards the complaints from Cairo about the French mission. From that moment on these were no longer treated as utterances by biased men on the spot who tried to blow up incidents to further their own Syrian ambitions. On 8 May 1917, Sykes – who at the beginning of March had already written to Wingate that he had 'seen the George Lloyd correspondence and George Lloyd, truly Bremond's performances have been disgusting'[13] – telegraphed to Graham that after a careful investigation he had reached the conclusion that 'the sooner French Military Mission is removed from Hedjaz the better'. The 'deliberately perverse attitude and policy' on the part of Brémond and his staff constituted the main obstacle in the way of Sir Mark's attempts to improve relations between the French and the Arabs. These men were:

> Without exception anti-Arab and only serve to promote dissension [...] Their line is to crab British operations to Arabs, throw cold water on all Arab actions and make light of the King to both. They do not attempt to disguise that they desire Arab failure. Without assistance I do not believe Picot will be strong enough to carry the day [...] I suggest therefore that His Majesty's Government make representations that French military mission

in Hedjaz has now fulfilled its purpose […] and that it should be brought to an end.

Sir Mark's recommendation was not ignored by the Foreign Office. Four days later, Lord Bertie was instructed to impress on the French government that the mission to the Hijaz be withdrawn in view of the open enmity Brémond and his staff displayed towards the Arab cause, which 'cannot but prejudice Allied relations and policy in the Hedjaz and may even affect whole future of French relations with the Arabs'.[14]

It took almost a fortnight before Bertie received a reply. In the meantime, the Foreign Office was informed of the instructions given to Si Mustapha Cherchali, an Algerian notable who was to leave for the Hijaz on a mission principally concerned with 'purely Muslim affairs'. These confirmed that more was at stake than some local incidents. Besides instructions concerning the mission's primary objective, there were instructions of a more general political nature. These were 'of much greater importance and raise whole question of Franco–British relations in Arabia', as they made clear that 'French now desire to limit their recognition of our special position in Arabia to an admission of our preponderant commercial interests':

> France, in agreement with England, desires only to maintain on the one hand the independence of the Sherif, and on the other hand the integrity of his possessions. We feel as do our Allies, that no European Power should exercise a dominant or even preponderating influence in the holy places of Islam and we are resolved not to intervene in political questions affecting the Arabian Peninsula. We feel, moreover, in full accord with our Allies, that no European government should acquire a new foothold (établissement) in Arabia.
>
> While feeling that no Power should obtain either new territory or political prestige in Arabia, the French government recognise that the proximity of Egypt and the Persian Gulf creates a situation in favour of the commercial interests of the English Allies which you should bear in mind.

It was in particular this last sentence that Graham found unacceptable. If the French position was not challenged, then the door was wide open to, as Hardinge had formulated it in November 1916 (see Chapter 5, section 'The Rabegh Question: The Third Round'), 'the reversal of our policy of the last

100 years which has aimed at the exclusion of foreign influence on the shores of the Red Sea'. According to Sir Ronald:

> We can admit that no European Power should exercise a predominant influence in the holy places. But the French note goes much further than this in laying down that no Power is to obtain new territory or political prestige in Arabia and in limiting French recognition of our special position there to commercial interests. Hitherto the French have always recognised our special political position [...] I fear we must conclude that the French desire to go back on this attitude and to claim an equality of political position with us in Arabia – when they had no position at all and owe any improvement that they have latterly achieved in this respect entirely to our help and influence. Such a submission, which is a poor return for our rapport, must be strongly resisted.

Graham proposed to consult Wingate on Cherchali's instructions, as well as the most appropriate reaction. Cecil agreed, but cautioned that the reply had to be formulated with the greatest care, as 'it will be a definite statement of Franco–British relations in Arabia'.[15]

Wingate's reaction to Cherchali's instructions was along the same lines as Graham's minute. He also believed that 'we must insist on formal recognition by French government of our preponderant position in Arabia'. The French apparently threatened to forget that 'only by our support military as well as diplomatic, can they expect to realise their present aims in Near East and, in particular, that our continued good offices with King Hussein and Syrian Moslems will be essential to an amicable settlement of Syrian question'.

Sykes, for his part, proposed his customary solution, to let Georges-Picot and him work out an arrangement. Lancelot Oliphant and Graham were not sure. According to Oliphant, Sykes in any case should 'cease to be a free lancer', and as far as Picot was concerned, he was 'far from easy in my own mind as to the extent that M. Picot speaks for his own government (or even for himself) in talking to Sir M. Sykes'. Sir Ronald doubted 'whether M. Picot exerts such a beneficent influence in the French government as Sir M. Sykes represents'. However that may be, there was 'little prospect of their doing anything more where they are at present'. Sykes was accordingly instructed on 5 June 'to proceed to London without stopping in Paris'. Two days later, the French government was requested also to recall Georges-Picot for further consultations.[16]

In a dispatch to Balfour, dated 11 June 1917, Wingate returned to the subject. The Sykes–Picot agreement was 'unsatisfactory and inadequate in one, to my mind, all-important point of strategy'. It had not settled the British position in the Red Sea, while 'our position here must be unassailable or we run the risk of creating a "Baghdad Railway" question in the Red Sea the development of which may gravely impair our relations with France and Italy and even menace the security of our imperial system'. Wingate's remedy had two aspects, which he had most succinctly formulated in a telegram sent the day before:

> Our policy should be to obtain French recognition of our predominant position in Arabian Peninsula as a preliminary to concluding a treaty with King Hussein which, whilst not impairing his independence *vis-à-vis* of Moslem world, will prevent any foreign power under guise of pilgrim interest from acquiring rights and privileges detrimental to our special political and economic interests in the Hedjaz.[17]

According to Sir Reginald, Husayn at the end of the day was no more than one of the many chiefs on the Arabian Peninsula. It was 'very necessary to make a clear distinction between practical politics and propaganda'. He therefore did not see, 'in view of the fact that we have created, directed and financed the Arab revolt', why it would not be possible to conclude a treaty like the one he proposed. Naturally, 'we must be careful to create and preserve, for as long as may be necessary, the facade of an independent Arab Empire', as 'an Arab caliph or imam buried away in the sands of the Arabian desert (would) appeal to Moslems nowhere', but this did not imply that with the king no agreement could be signed 'differing little from those we have made with the Trucial Chiefs'.[18] To Sykes, however, it was unthinkable that Husayn would be treated on the same footing as the other rulers on the Arabian Peninsula. He argued that 'if there is to be a King of Hejaz he must be independent of all foreign control otherwise he has no value or influence and is only a danger'. When Britain would 'reduce him to the position of a feudatory chief in our pay, then we not only destroy the Arab movement but we throw the whole control of the Moslem world into the hands of the Turks, the pan-islamists, the seditionists and the Egyptian revolutionary nationalists'.[19]

Graham voiced the same argument in less alarmist terms in a minute on a further telegram by Wingate, in which the latter again urged a revision of the Sykes–Picot agreement in order 'to eliminate present southern boundary of Area B'. Sir Ronald believed that it was not in the interest of Great Britain 'to assume publicly anything in the nature of a sort of British Protectorate over the holy places and the Shereef, who may well be caliph some day. To do so would destroy or at any rate weaken his position and land us in an embarrassing situation in the future.' The revision advocated by Wingate was moreover completely unnecessary, since 'our presence in Egypt close by, the great number of British native pilgrims as compared with those of any other State and our intimate existing relations with the Sherif and his family – financial and political – render it inevitable that we should enjoy a special position with him and in the Hedjaz'. Britain's policy should be to get the other powers to give an undertaking that they would refrain from intervening in the internal affairs of the Hijaz. Hardinge concurred. Provided that 'no foreign Power is allowed to obtain a preponderating influence in the Hedjaz we may regard with serenity the fact that it is not our protectorate [...] We shall in the end by force of circumstances obtain a very strong position in the Hedjaz as the main support of the Sheriff'.[20]

After Harold Nicolson had completed a first draft for a reply to the French memorandum with Cherchali's instructions on 14 June, the question was referred to the Mesopotamian Administration Committee (MAC).[21] This committee had been established by the War Cabinet on 16 March 1917. Besides Curzon as chairman and Sykes as secretary, it consisted of Lord Alfred Milner, Hardinge, Sir Arthur Hirtzel, Sir Thomas Holderness, Graham and Clerk. Sir Henry McMahon also became a member. The MAC had initially only dealt with the organisation of the administration of the occupied territories in Mesopotamia, but it had soon been felt that it should have greater authority. The occasion had been Wingate's dispatch of 11 June. On 7 July, Sir Eric Drummond wrote to Sir Maurice Hankey that Balfour wanted an extension of the MAC's powers, 'so as to enable it to deal with other questions such as Arabia, Hedjaz, etc. The idea is I believe to form a Committee of which the S. of S. for F.A. and the S. of S. for India will be permanent members in order to decide all Middle Eastern matters. It is a good scheme.'[22] The War Cabinet accepted Balfour's proposal a week later. At this meeting, Milner relinquished his seat, and the DMI was appointed as the military representative on the committee.[23] It was also decided to change the committee's name into the Middle East Committee (MEC).

On 23 August, Hardinge submitted to Cecil a new draft reply. It was in line with a memorandum written by Curzon. As 'the matter is urgent, and has already been subject to much delay', Hardinge proposed to settle the question right away. Cecil, however, hesitated to 'authorise this draft in the absence of Mr Balfour', but it was finally approved, with some minor revisions, on 28 August.[24]

Sykes did not like the approved reply at all. He complained to Graham that:

> It is very ridiculous to adopt a 1960 A.D. policy in India and a 1887 A.D. policy in the Red Sea. We certainly do not require any rights in HEJAZ over and above those to be enjoyed by our allies. The HEJAZ must be a completely independent state if we are to defeat the Turks. It will never be independent if we have a special position there, and the Sherif will always be our dependant and therefore out of the running for the caliphate; which is contrary to our interests because it fastens the caliphate for good and all onto the Turks.

It was his opinion that the best thing would be, as always, to let Picot and him settle the matter. But Clerk, who substituted for Graham, was not entirely convinced of this. It was one thing to show consideration for French ambitions, but it was quite another to give up British interests without getting anything in return:

> Throughout these Asia Minor and Arabian negotiations it has seemed to me that Sir Mark Sykes, while quite rightly endeavouring to reach an understanding with the French which shall be free from all suspicion and misunderstanding, has gone to work on the wrong principle. He appears to think that the way to get rid of suspicion is always to recognise what the other party claims and to give up, when asked, our claims. For many years our relations with Germany were run on those lines. My own belief is that the right course is to be as accommodating as possible, and ready to recognise the legitimate claims of other people, but to be both frank and tenacious about those things which are held to be vitally necessary to the existence of the British Empire.

Hardinge fully agreed. There was nothing in Sykes's letter to modify the approved note, and 'thanks to the Sykes–Picot agreement our position is already a bad one in connection with Asiatic Turkey and Arabia, and for heaven's sake let us not make it even worse'.[25] The British memorandum on Cherchali's instructions was handed to Cambon on 29 August.

Although Graham considered the French reply of 18 September 'not altogether clear', British claims were recognised in principle, and accordingly it 'foreshadows an agreement which may prove satisfactory'. Hardinge believed that 'the note is on the whole better than might have been expected'. His disparaging remark several weeks before notwithstanding, Hardinge accepted Graham's suggestion to send Sykes to Paris in order 'to draw up an agreement "ad referendum"', be it with 'definite instructions'. These were telegraphed to Bertie on 26 September. Sir Mark was directed to draw up a draft agreement 'respecting future status of the Hejaz and Arabia'. The most important British desiderata in this agreement were:

a. That [it] is essential to obtain explicit recognition by France of British political supremacy in Arabia as a whole with the exception of the Hedjaz.
b. That the limits of the Hedjaz shall be defined.
c. That within those limits Hedjaz shall be recognised as a sovereign, independent State but that the existing arrangements for dealing with King Hussein and the Arabs shall hold good for the duration of the war.
d. That France on her part shall undertake to enter in no Agreement with the King or Government of Hedjaz on any matter concerning the Arabian Peninsula or the Red Area or Area B (Anglo–French Agreement of May 1916) without the knowledge and consent of Great Britain.
e. That Great Britain on her part shall undertake to enter into no Agreement with the King or Government of Hedjaz on any matter concerning either the Blue Area or Area A (Anglo–French Agreement of May 1916) without the knowledge and consent of France.[26]

Even though these instructions evidently reflected the accursed spirit of '1887 A.D.', within a week Sykes and Picot managed to complete a draft agreement (Projet d'Arrangement) that, in the words of Clerk, 'seems to cover the instructions sent to M. Sykes pretty well'. The most important point was that the French government were finally prepared explicitly to recognise Britain's special interests in the Arabian Peninsula, and confirmed its intention 'not to seek any political influence in these regions'. Hardinge noted with satisfaction that the French were 'ready to accept our political supremacy in the Arabian Peninsula, with the exception of the Hedjaz', which was 'a point gained'. Especially when one took into account that regarding the Hijaz, 'owing to the close connection of the holy places with Egypt, Aden and Mesopotamia [there should] be no difficulty for us in acquiring and eventually asserting a position of predominance there also'.[27]

Apart from a few minor points that needed modification, the desired supplement to the Sykes–Picot agreement with respect to the Arabian Peninsula seemed finally to be within reach. The French government, however, failed to ratify the draft agreement. Although the Quai d'Orsay time and again confirmed that the Council of Ministers could approve the arrangement any moment, they failed to do so. On 4 December, the Foreign Office replied to Wingate, after the latter had enquired how matters stood, that 'exchange of notes has not yet actually taken place, but it is hoped to complete arrangement within the next fortnight'.[28] However, this hope, too, was dashed. On 17 December, Hardinge instructed Sykes 'to ascertain the situation in regard to the proposed Anglo–French Agreement on the subject of the Hedjaz and Arabia, and to take steps to expedite its conclusion'.[29] In his report on his visit to Paris, Sykes did not touch upon this topic.[30] In the middle of January 1918, the India Office also wanted to know how things stood with the agreement. Sir Mark minuted that, as far as he knew, approval was imminent. Hardinge decided to enquire of Bertie whether the French government had perhaps approved the agreement without informing London about it.[31] The ambassador had to disappoint the permanent under-secretary, 'French government have not yet approved agreement negotiated by Sir M. Sykes regarding Anglo–French interests in Arabia'.[32]

In the subsequent weeks, the officials and ministers involved rather lost interest in the attempt to amend the Sykes–Picot agreement by securing French recognition of British predominance in Arabia. In view of the course events took, in particular Allenby's successful advance into Palestine, they started to direct their attention to proposals that aimed at a far more fundamental revision of the Sykes–Picot agreement, or even its abolishment (see Chapters 7 and 9). Sykes also favoured a comprehensive revision of the agreement, but his opinion would count for less and less after 1917. The failure of the Projet d'Arrangement was a blemish on his reputation. Sykes himself tried to play down this failure, for instance by predicting to Lloyd that it would not matter, 'as it is ten to one that all agreements will be nullified by later events, peace conference and the like'.[33] However, the failure of his standard solution to British–French problems regarding the Middle East ('let Picot and me set matters straight'), which had more or less remained concealed with respect to the Sykes–Picot mission but was now clear to see for all involved, signified a serious and, as it turned out, permanent weakening of his position *vis-à-vis* other British decision makers dealing with Middle East policy.

The Hogarth Mission

After the meeting of 20 May 1917, at the opening of which King Husayn had assented to 'the formula' (see Chapter 6, section 'The Visit by Sir Mark Sykes and François Georges-Picot to the Hijaz'), Faysal approached Sykes with a request from his father that showed that Husayn perhaps was less worried about his good name and reputation in view of French ambitions in the Lebanon and Syria than the realisation of his ambitions *vis-à-vis* the other chiefs on the Arabian Peninsula, in particular Abd al-Aziz ibn Sa'ud (usually referred to as Ibn Sa'ud), the Sultan of Najd and leader of the Wahhabite movement. According to Wilson, 'Faysal said that the Sherif was most anxious for both the above (the other chief being the Idrisi of Asir) to acknowledge him as King and that as the Sherif had done what we wanted as regards Syria could not we make the above Chiefs recognise the Sherif'. Sykes left it to Wilson to answer, who explained that 'we had agreements with both Chiefs and that it was up to the Sherif to induce Arab Chiefs to recognise him overlord but that personally [he] thought that if the large majority of Chiefs recognises the Sherif as Suzerain the two above named Chiefs would soon follow suit'.[34] Sykes nevertheless complied with Husayn's request. Two days later he sent a telegram to Sir Percy Cox in which he claimed that the king 'and his son are really very moderate in their views', and suggested that 'if Ibn Saud could by some means convey to Sherif that he regards him as the titular leader of Arab cause without in anyway committing his own local position I believe much good would result'.[35] Cox, however, declined to approach Ibn Sa'ud on the subject. He telegraphed to the India Office that he did not see his way to comply with Sykes's request without Ibn Sa'ud questioning his 'bona fides'.[36]

On 26 December 1915, Cox had concluded the Treaty of Darin with Ibn Sa'ud. In this treaty Great Britain recognised the Najd's independence, promised assistance in case it was attacked by a foreign power, and granted Ibn Sa'ud a subsidy for his military campaign against Ibn Rashid, the Emir of Ha'il, who was loyal to the Turks. On the day of the signing of the treaty, Ibn Sa'ud had characterised Husayn to Cox as 'essentially unstable, trivial, undependable'.[37] A few weeks later, Lawrence had noted that 'the Wahabis are too weak at present to cause the Sherif any apprehension', but that there was 'little doubt, however, that there will be a clash between them again, if Ibn Saoud grows really strong'.[38] After Husayn had started his revolt, Cox had reported that Ibn Sa'ud had been 'pleased to get [the news] because it meant in any case a severe blow to Turks', but that he had been rather worried by the official communiqué as this referred 'to "the Arabs" as a whole'. He therefore had felt obliged to remind Sir Percy that there had been 'a feud between him and Sherif for years on account of Sherif's persevering endeavours to interfere amongst tribes and settlements of Nejd'.[39] Since then, relations had deteriorated to such an extent that in May 1917 it had been decided to send Ronald Storrs, who had joined Cox's staff a couple of weeks before, on a mission to Ibn Sa'ud to set the latter's mind at ease as to Husayn's intentions. Storrs had, however, suffered from sun stroke, and had had to abandon his mission. The rivalry between the two chiefs continued to deepen throughout the year. According to Lawrence, it all turned on the allegiance of the Ateiba and Meteir tribes,[40] which occupied the territory between the Hijaz and Najd, and in this struggle, so Wingate explained to Balfour some months later, Ibn Sa'ud 'is fanning the flames of Wahabite zealotry as a necessary but dangerous counterpoise to Sherifial gold and ordnance'.[41]

At the end of September 1917, Sir Percy proposed a new mission to reduce the tension between Husayn and Ibn Sa'ud. This time, however, the mission would be a more complicated affair. Both the Foreign Office and the India Office would select a representative. The India Office delegated this task to Cox, who appointed Harry St John Bridger Philby,[42] a member of his staff, while the Foreign Office appointed Storrs, who was on leave in London. The plan was that Storrs would travel via Cairo to Jedda to discuss matters with Husayn, after which he would journey overland to Ryadh, to meet Philby and Ibn Sa'ud. Storrs 'would then explain position to Bin Saud and would endeavour to induce him to send a representative on a friendly mission to the King of the Hedjaz. He would then travel back with the delegate, leaving him to proceed to Mecca and himself returning to London via Jeddah and Cairo.'[43] On 12 November, Wingate reported that 'after some difficulty' he had 'obtained from King promise of safe conduct through Hedjaz and convoy for Storrs',[44] but nine days later he had to inform the Foreign Office that Husayn had revoked his approval. Sir Reginald offered no suggestion as to how this fresh problem could be resolved.[45]

While Storrs was still preparing for his journey to Husayn – it had been decided that he would first go to Jerusalem and from there to Jeddah by aeroplane – Philby had already arrived at Ryadh. After conversations with Ibn Sa'ud, he reported to Sir Percy that the ruler of Najd displayed a 'consuming jealousy of Sherif whose assumption in correspondence of title "King of the Arab Countries" galls him to distraction, while at the back of his mind is the suspicion that Sherif's attitude in this connection is based on some secret understanding with us', and that he wanted a 'greater equality of treatment both politically and financially'.[46] After his interviews, Philby decided to travel to Jedda overland.[47] On 27 December, Wingate telegraphed that Philby had arrived in Taif, and would proceed to Jeddah. He also explained that, as Storrs had unexpectedly been appointed military governor of Jerusalem,[48] he would send David Hogarth to Jedda in his stead, and that he had 'informed King it would be most desirable he should visit Jedda while Philby and Hogarth are there'.[49] Hogarth left for Jedda on 2 January. The next day, Sir Reginald confided to Clayton that he regarded the situation 'distinctly dangerous' and that, if Husayn and Ibn Sa'ud quarrelled, 'it will be nuts to the Turkish party [...] I wish I could spare someone to return to Baghdad with Philby and endeavour to make Cox understand the situation. He evidently thinks that we are rather running the Hedjaz against Nejd and Mesopotamia, but of course this is by no means the case – all we want to do is to try and preserve the unity of the Arabs and prevent them from making fools of themselves'.[50]

Wingate also believed that Husayn would certainly ask how matters stood with respect to 'the formula', especially in view of the Balfour Declaration. He therefore considered 'it very necessary at present juncture that we should make a communication to Shereef on these subjects'. He submitted the 'following formulas' to the Foreign Office for approval:

1. Jews must be accepted by Arabs in reservations (or colonies) in parts of Palestine to be settled at Peace Conference. Rest of Syria to be Arab but precise status to be left to peace conference. If Syrians demand it we should welcome (a) King Hussein's overlordship if local autonomy secured and (b) Feisal at Damascus but French must be consulted as chiefly interested.
2. That Bagdad is to be Arab under British protection but its precise government must await wishes of inhabitants and result of Peace Conference.

The Foreign Office replied on 4 January 1918. The telegram had mainly been drafted by Sykes, who had considerably rephrased Wingate's proposed formulas. With respect to Palestine, it sounded determined and clear:

Since the Jewish opinion of the world is in favour of a return of Jews to Palestine and inasmuch as this opinion must remain a constant factor, and further as His Majesty's Government view with favour the realisation of this aspiration, His Majesty's Government are determined that in so far as is compatible with the freedom of the existing population both economic and political, no obstacle should be put in the way of the realisation of this ideal. In this matter it should be pointed out to the King that the friendship of world Jewry to the Arab cause is equivalent to support in all States where Jews have political influence.

With regard to the future status of Baghdad and Syria, however, the telegram was very vague. It merely stated that 'the Entente Powers are determined that the Arab race shall be given full opportunity of once again forming a nation in the world. That this can only be achieved by the Arabs themselves uniting, and that Great Britain and her Allies will pursue a policy with this ultimate unity in view.' Sykes had wanted to be more specific, and formulated a clause with respect to the future status of Syria and Mesopotamia stating that 'the Entente Powers will only approve of measures and forms of government […] which put no obstacle in the way of ultimate unity', but Hardinge had deleted it, since 'we must be particularly careful to give no handle to any scheme by which our hold on Busra would be affected'.[51]

Hogarth arrived in Jedda on 6 January 1918. Two days later he had a first meeting with Husayn, in the presence of Philby and Lieut.-Colonel J.R. Bassett, who was substituting for Wilson (having fallen ill, Wilson had returned to Egypt to convalesce). The relationship between Husayn and Ibn Sa'ud was discussed at the second meeting, while the Foreign Office formulas were conveyed during the third. Altogether, Hogarth had ten meetings with the king, at two of which Philby was present. Both Hogarth and Philby reported on Husayn's attitude towards Ibn Sa'ud. Hogarth did not deny that to Husayn 'Arab unity' meant 'very little […] except as a means to his personal aggrandisement', but saw some merit in Husayn's point of view in the question of his title. The king was moreover too weak to risk an armed conflict with Ibn Sa'ud:

He both fears Ibn Sa'ud as a centre of a religious movement, dangerous to the HEJAZ, and hates him as irreconcilable to his own pretensions to be 'King of the Arabs'. This latter title is the King's dearest ambition, partly no doubt, in the interest of Arab unity, which he constantly says, with some reason, can never be realised until focused on a central personality. He apposes to our argument that he cannot be 'King of the Arabs' till the Arabs in general desire him to be so, the counter-argument that they will never so desire till he is so called [...] The resultant situation, however, is that the King is very unlikely to provoke a conflict with Ibn Sa'ud while the European War lasts.

He is not easy in his mind either about Central Arabia or about the loyalty of his own Hejaz people [...] He is quite firm in his friendship to us, but none too firm on his throne.[52]

Philby judged Husayn altogether more harshly, and failed to see any merit in the latter's arguments:

In all matters relating Saud, King utterly impossible and unreasonable, though unable substantiate single accusation or grievance. Basic principle of King's policy seems to me determination to prevent any Arab potentate sharing in bounty of Britain, lest his difficulties in establishing unjustifiable claims of Kingship of all Arab countries be thereby increased. Unable, however, openly profess such policy he talks vaguely of conscientious necessity for concentrating all material resources [...] to operations Sherifian forces, no other object being worth serious consideration.[53]

At a conference to evaluate the situation, which took place at the Residency in Cairo on 21 January, Philby emphasised that the conflict first of all must be seen as a local one. Ibn Sa'ud objected to Husayn's pretensions to be more than one of the potentates on the Arabian Peninsula. The former was 'quite prepared to recognise King Hussein as King of the Hedjaz, but no more grandiose title'. Philby moreover had no doubt that Ibn Sa'ud wished 'himself to be styled King of Nejd (including Hail) although he has never put forward any specific claim to this'. According to Sir Reginald, everybody in the room agreed on the local origins of the conflict. In line with Lawrence's and his own earlier observations, Wingate claimed that 'the most important bone of contention appeared to be the control of the Ataibah whom Abdalla wooed with British gold and Saud with the more dangerous and subtle weapon of Wahabite propaganda'. What made matters worse was that it was 'impossible to define a hard and fast boundary between Sherifial and Nejdian control of the Ateibah in view of the wide peregrinations of the latter'. Accordingly, the conflict 'would be insoluble without a display of good-will and consideration by both parties to the dispute'. Failing that, all the authorities in Cairo and Baghdad could do 'during the war and for long as possible afterwards', was to 'impress on their respective protégés the necessity for a policy of "hands off"' the other's vital interests'.[54]

Hogarth mentioned in his report on the Syrian question that Husayn had 'some hope of forcing France's hand when it comes to the point, and expects us to back him [...] He listened to my protestation of our perfect accord with France, and of the latter's good intentions towards the Arabs, with politeness, but lack of conviction.'[55] Husayn was apparently confident of ultimate success, but Wingate was less sure in view of the vague formula on Allied support for ultimate Arab unity in the Foreign Office telegram of 4 January. Turkish propaganda exploiting the contents of the Sykes–Picot agreement, which the Bolshevik revolutionaries had made public soon after they had seized power in Petrograd at the end of October 1917, seemed to provide a good opportunity to force the hand of the Foreign Office. Less than a fortnight after Hogarth had conveyed the Foreign Office formulas to Husayn, Wingate telegraphed that there was 'evidence that Turk propaganda based on recent revelations in Russian press is producing growing uneasiness amongst Arabs about Entente's intentions for Arab countries [...] Latest example is an urgent appeal to me by Emir Abdulla for definite refutation of Jemal Pasha's assertions, that Palestine and Irak are to be received by British and Syria by French.' He pointed out that 'in present critical state of Arab feeling [...] vague or general assurances about Arab future are not only ineffectual, but harmful, and that explicit denials of enemy assertions are necessary to restore confidence in Entente's good intentions'. Wingate therefore urgently requested – 'the matter presses if enemy propaganda is to be checked' – the Foreign Office's sanction to notify Husayn officially:

1. That His Majesty's Government is still determined to secure Arab independence and to fulfil promises made through him at the beginning of the Hedjaz revolt.
2. That His Majesty's Government will countenance no permanent foreign or European occupation of Palestine, Irak, (except for province of Basrah) or Syria after the war.
3. That these districts will be in possession of their natives and that foreign interference with Arab countries will be restricted to assistance and protection.[56]

Wingate's request was referred to the MEC. Before taking a decision, it wanted to receive Sir Percy's 'considered opinion on the whole question of future policy in Mesopotamia'.[57] The latter rather doubted the necessity 'to make any fresh declaration of our intentions', but if such a declaration had to be made, then he strongly urged that Mesopotamia was not again, 'as in the negotiations of 1915 [...] treated as a pawn in our negotiations or relations with young Arabs of Egypt and the Sherif, whose comprehensive ambitions in direction of Kingship of all Arabia, have been sufficiently demonstrated in the recent telegraphic correspondence regarding Nejd'.[58] During the Committee's meeting on 2 February, Lord Islington, parliamentary under-secretary for India, strongly supported Cox's objections against any 'new assurances specifically to Irak', while Sir Mark explained that 'the real apprehension at the back of King Hussein's mind was the accusation which might be cast against him by Moslems, that by his action and cooperation with England he had brought about the replacement of the Moslem by the Christian flag in Arab countries'. The Committee instructed Sykes to draft a reply, which should not be sent before it had been approved by Curzon, Balfour and the India Office.[59] The telegram was dispatched on 4 February 1918. Although it referred to promises made to Husayn in line with Wingate's first clause, it did not contain any specific reference to Palestine, Syria or Iraq as future Arab countries. On top of that, although Sykes had wished to state that 'liberation and not annexation is the policy of H.M.G.', Hardinge's Indian reflexes had prevented the words 'and not annexation' being included in the telegram. Wingate could transmit the following message to Husayn:

> The Turkish policy is evidently to sow distrust between the Powers of the Entente and the Arabs [...] by suggesting to the Arabs that the Entente Powers desire Arab territory, and to the Powers of the Entente that the Arabs can be turned from their purpose of self liberation [...] H.M.G. along with their Allies stand for the Cause of the liberation of the oppressed nations [...] H.M.G. reaffirm their former pledges to H.H. in regard to the freeing of the Arab peoples. Liberation is the policy H.M.G. have pursued and intend to pursue with unswerving determination by protecting such Arabs as are already liberated from the danger of reconquest and assisting such Arabs as are still under the yoke of the oppressor to obtain their freedom.[60]

On 11 February, Wingate wired that Husayn had begged him 'to convey his profound thanks for this expression of sentiments and policy of

His Majesty's Government towards Arab cause'.[61] He refrained from commenting on the merits of the message, but two weeks later he could not help complaining to Bassett about 'the great difficulty the French and British governments have in even adumbrating a clear cut policy'.[62] Bassett for his part had already indicated that Husayn surely would 'be well satisfied by the re-affirmation by His Majesty's Government of their former "pledge"', but, as Sir Reginald very well knew, the king had 'read into the terms of that "pledge" very wide territorial boundaries, and professes the most implicit trust in the intention and ability of Great Britain to redeem the "pledge" as he reads it'.[63]

French Participation in the Administration of Palestine

On 1 January 1918, Sykes submitted a memorandum on 'The Palestine and West Arabia Situation', in which he noted that 'a whole crowd of weeds are growing around us', such as '(1) Arab unrest in regard to Zionism. (2) French jealousy in regard to our position in Palestine. (3) Syrian–Hedjaz friction among the Arabs. (4) Franco–Italian jealousy' and, finally, the accursed 'Cairo Fashoda spirit'. What caused these weeds to grow up (and here Sykes returned to one of his favourite themes) was that there did not exist in London 'an executive capable of taking immediate action, guiding policy, and directing and following events under the Secretary of State for Foreign Affairs subject to the War Cabinet'. Hardinge, who as viceroy had done his utmost to undermine Sykes's earlier co-ordination schemes, now, as permanent under-secretary at the Foreign Office, agreed with 'some of Sir M. Sykes recriminations' and that it was 'desirable that some person with knowledge should have charge of problems relating to Palestine and the Hedjaz here in London'. He welcomed 'the suggestion that Sir M. Sykes should be that person'. Cecil assented,[64] while Hankey saw no objections to Sykes's transfer from the War Cabinet secretariat to the Foreign Office.[65] His appointment as acting adviser on Arabian and Palestine Affairs was subsequently finalised in the middle of January.

Sykes's ambition to become the 'executive capable of taking immediate action' with respect to the Middle East would never be realised. A powerful competitor appeared on the scene right away: Curzon. As Cecil confessed to Balfour on 8 January, he had attempted 'to smother decorously' the MEC – 'the function of which seems mainly to be to enable George Curzon and

Mark Sykes to explain to each other how very little they know about the subject' – but had been found out by Curzon, who held 'strongly to it'. Cecil's attempt accordingly 'had to be abandoned. They are now to meet regularly on Saturday mornings: a tune fixed with the hope that it may ultimately prove discouraging to their existence'.[66] At the MEC's next meeting, Curzon explained that he 'had latterly found that a number of questions which had been raised and could advantageously have been discussed by the Committee had been dealt with departmentally. He hoped that in the future the position of the Committee would be placed on a more regular footing and that meetings would be held more frequently.' Cecil voiced his agreement, but also mentioned Sykes's appointment in the Foreign Office.[67]

Curzon's position *vis-à-vis* Sykes was strengthened even further by the War Cabinet's decision to merge the MEC with the Persia and the Russia Committee at the beginning of March 1918. This merger originated in a growing dissatisfaction with the way in which Balfour and Cecil were running the Foreign Office. As Hankey noted in his diary on 1 March, 'as long as Balfour and Cecil remain at the F.O. peace is utterly impossible, owing to their ultra-caution and laziness and lack of drive'. One week later, he recorded an interview with Curzon, in which the latter had complained 'about the inefficiency of the Foreign Office under Balfour's régime, which, he said, was losing us the war'. Sir Maurice had replied that 'to the best of [his] knowledge, the P.M. and all his colleagues shared this view'. Curzon had then wanted to know why the Prime Minister did not make a change. When Hankey had answered that there was the difficulty of 'finding a suitable successor without taking someone out of the War Cabinet', Curzon had immediately volunteered to give up his seat. Hankey had reported the conversation to Lloyd George who, until then, 'had always refused to look at Lord Curzon for the post', but this time the Prime Minister had wondered 'what sort of Secretary he would make'?[68] Lloyd George nevertheless did not want Balfour's position undermined. As chairman of the new Eastern Committee it was left to Curzon to draft its terms of reference, but 'care must be taken to safeguard the departmental authority and responsibility of the Secretary of State for Foreign Affairs'.[69]

One of the problems with which the London authorities were confronted in the first half of 1918 was the very familiar one that 'the' Syrians, however internally divided they might be, greatly objected to French pretensions in

Syria, which both Syrians and the French understood to include Palestine. The policy line advocated by Sykes was to try and mediate between the two camps, but Wingate in Cairo and Clayton in Jerusalem took the Syrians' side against the French. They strongly protested against any suggestion coming from London to ameliorate Georges-Picot's awkward position in Palestine. Giving in to French claims would only increase Syrian anxieties, and could lead to the Syrians definitely throwing in their lot with the Turks.

On 15 December 1917, Bertie reported that French foreign minister Stephen Pichon wished that 'General Allenby will, as soon as possible, establish at Jerusalem mixed administration system provided for in Franco–British Agreement'. That same day, Clayton wrote to Sir Mark on 'the question of Picot'. The latter claimed that the French and British governments had agreed that he would be 'the French representative in a joint Anglo–French provisional administration [...] in Palestine until the end of the war'. Clayton had 'heard nothing of it, and I cannot protest too strongly against any such unworkable and mischievous arrangement. The country is under Martial Law and under Martial Law it must remain for a long time to come – probably till the end of the war.'[70] Graham was of the same opinion. He minuted on Bertie's telegram that Pichon's request should be refused 'at once [...] It is without doubt that in the present situation in Palestine with military operations in full swing it would be ridiculous to attempt to institute a mixed administration.' Hardinge fully agreed – 'we should be quite firm in resisting any such claims while military operations are in full progress' – and a telegram in this sense was sent to Bertie on 20 December.[71]

According to Cecil the French were:

> Dreadfully afraid that we are going to oust them from their traditional guardianship of Near Eastern Christianity. Pichon spoke to me about this and asked me to hasten the establishment of civil government, which by our engagement is to be internationalised. I replied soothingly. It would be a good thing if Allenby could appoint French and Italian officers as governors of some of the holy places – pending a final arrangement on the subject.[72]

On 30 December, Bertie telegraphed that the 'French government fully recognise necessity in present circumstances and in view of uncertainty of situation in Palestine of maintaining exclusively military administration', but that they insisted that it might be possible 'to give effect to the agreements of December 1916'. This telegram was submitted to Sykes for his observations. He agreed with Lord Robert that some kind of gesture should be made. It would be wise if Allenby 'of his own accord employed some French officers in civil posts, that it would [serve] at once to calm the French and improve our own position [...] M. Gout [Jean Goût, head of the Asian Department in the French ministry of foreign affairs; R.H.L.] and M. Pichon both said that this would suffice'.[73] Hardinge concurred, and enquired whether the CIGS could assent 'to the participation of French and Italian officers in the administration of Palestine'. Robertson saw no objections, and Clayton and Allenby were instructed accordingly, on the understanding that 'this could only be done if it in no way hampered military operations, nor must we do anything to jeopardise our future political position'.[74] Although the MEC on 12 January were 'unanimously of the opinion that the War Office should press General Allenby to carry out the [...] suggestion for diplomatic reasons',[75] General Macdonogh reported two weeks later that Allenby had replied that it was 'not practicable to appoint any French or Italian officers to administrative posts in Palestine'. The MEC did not challenge Allenby's decision.[76]

The issue of Picot's position subsequently dropped from view, mainly because Picot was not very successful in his efforts to win over the local population to the French cause. On 14 January, Weizmann already wrote to Brandeis that 'the French are making themselves as disagreeable as possible there. They pose as the conquerors of Palestine, as the Protectors of the Christians, as the modern Crusaders',[77] while Clayton gleefully observed to Wingate on 4 February that 'Pro-British feeling in Palestine, especially in Jerusalem is remarkable and is increasing daily. They say openly in many quarters that of course we have come to stay and they welcome it. A tribute to Picot's efforts!!'[78] It seemed that Georges-Picot also gave up trying. On 15 March, Clayton referred to the latter as 'quiescent but disgruntled'.[79]

Two months later, Clayton even went so far as to suggest that, 'unless political considerations forbid, it would be desirable from local point of view to put an end definitely to Anglo–French Mission and thereby dispense with necessity of any French Representative until military operations approach the districts where the French have special interests'.[80] It was precisely in this context that the issue of political desiderata versus military necessities returned to the Eastern Committee's agenda, especially after Sykes had had a 'private and personal conference' with Picot at the beginning of July. According to Sir Mark, Picot had:

> Found himself in an impossible position and [had done] his best to maintain his dignity without provoking a real rupture. The French feel that we have made good politically in Palestine by setting up an all-British administration. They now fear we may extend this all-British provisional administration in Syria if the fortune of war carried us there [...] I regard it as essential to disabuse the French of any idea of our having ulterior motives in Syria.

Sykes proposed that 'it would be a proper and graceful act on our part if we were to inform the French that in all matters concerning political relations between the E.E.F. and inhabitants of the areas of special interest to France that we should use the French mission as our medium', and that Allenby should be instructed to 'regard the French Commissioner as his political adviser on military-political questions which directly concern these regions', and that 'in event of our occupying any part of these areas of special interest to France, we should rely on the French mission to organise and control (with due regard to military decision) any temporary administration which it might be necessary to set up'.[81]

At the Eastern Committee's meeting of 11 July 1918, Sykes defended his proposal, but General Smuts believed that 'it was impossible to agree to this'.[82] The discussion was continued a week later. Sir Mark explained that 'he thought it very necessary to give the French an assurance that if, and when, we get into Syria they will be accorded special privileges'. He 'quite recognised that any administration [...] must be subject to military considerations; but they wanted from us a definite guarantee that we will not treat Syria as we have treated Palestine and take over its government ourselves. If we did not give way on this point he apprehended serious trouble.' Macdonogh however was 'quite certain that General Allenby would strongly object to having a French High Commissioner administering Syria when he got there [...] No General would like to have foreign administrative officers in charge of "back areas".' Where Sykes stressed the vital importance of smoothing French ruffled feelings, Balfour and Montagu emphasised that 'military considerations must outweigh all others', and that Allenby must have 'supreme jurisdiction'. The Committee decided to send a telegram to Allenby 'asking his opinion as to the steps that would require to be taken to meet French views in the event of his forces advancing into Syria'.[83]

On 21 July, Macdonogh submitted a draft telegram to the Foreign Office. It was 'from a political point of view':

Very desirable that we should be able to give the French assurances that, subject to your supreme authority, French advice would be taken and French assistance accepted in regard to purely administrative affairs in areas of special interest to France in event of their occupation by your forces, but of course it is realised that, in war, military considerations are paramount. I should be glad of your personal opinion and views on this question and hope you may be able to meet the French wishes.[84]

The Foreign Office approved the telegram, and it was sent on 25 July. Allenby reacted the very next day. He was ready to accept, 'subject to my supreme authority, French advice and assistance in regard to purely administrative affairs so long as they do not conflict with military requirements'.[85] Curzon was quite satisfied with this reply, as it 'showed that General Allenby was prepared to accept the Committee's suggestion in quite the right spirit',[86] but both Sykes and Cecil, although they had not objected to the draft telegram, were not yet prepared to give up their position that more was required than accepting 'French advice and assistance'. After the French Embassy had inquired on 1 August how matters stood with the administration of the territories in the French sphere of influence, they tried to make Allenby's instructions more specific, and more in line with Sykes's earlier proposals. Sir Mark drew up a brief memorandum on the 'French–Syrian question', as well as two declarations (a third declaration '(C), to the King of the Hijaz' (see next section), was also annexed). These were circulated to the members of the Eastern Committee by Cecil, who expressed his agreement. In the first declaration (A), it was stated that Allenby would recognise Georges-Picot 'as his adviser on matters pertaining to any administration of a civil character which it may be necessary to set up in such areas', and would rely on the latter 'to provide the administrative personnel for the purpose of carrying on the administration', while in the second declaration (B), in full agreement with the original instructions of the Sykes–Picot mission of February 1917 (see Chapter 6, section 'The British Offensive in the Sinai and the Sykes–Picot Mission'), it was stated that Allenby would consider Georges-Picot 'as his direct political adviser in regard to any negotiations which it may be necessary to enter into with the native elements permanently inhabiting Syrian areas of special interest to France but still in Turkish occupation'.

During the subsequent meeting of the Eastern Committee on 8 August, Cecil again put forward that it was accepted policy that 'when we entered

Syria, to place the French civil administration on the same footing as our own administration in Palestine', and that it was desirable to demonstrate to the French 'our disinterestedness'. However, Smuts and Macdonogh would have none of it. In their view, Allenby's formula was 'as far as it was necessary to go', and Cecil had to give in. The Committee decided to request the Foreign Office to re-draft the declarations.[87] This was done personally by Cecil some ten days later. He decided to drop declaration (B), and in declaration (A) Allenby was merely instructed 'in the event of the occupation [...] of Syrian areas which are of special interest to France', to be 'ready to accept French advise and assistance in regard to purely administrative and political affairs so long as they do not conflict with military requirements'.[88] Despite Sykes's repeated warnings of possible dire consequences for Anglo–French relations, military exigencies had again trumped French Syrian susceptibilities.

Syria: Syrian, French and Hashemite Ambitions

In his dispatch of 11 June 1917 (see section 'The Failure of the "Projet d'Arrangement"', above), Wingate had also touched upon the well-known conflict between French and Arab ambitions with respect to Syria, and had argued that Britain was bound to assist 'the Arab peoples [...] in arriving at a solution satisfactory both to the future administrators of the country (i.e. the French) and to its inhabitants'.[89] Sykes naturally saw things differently. Britain should stand by France and they should together search for a solution that would satisfy both French and Arabs. As he explained in a letter to Clayton at the end of July 1917, 'there is only one possible policy, the Entente first and last, and the Arab nation the child of the Entente. Get your Englishmen to stand up to the Arabs on this and never let them accept flattering of the "you very good man, him very bad man" kind.' Clayton assured Sir Mark that he 'need not be afraid of any Fashoda-ism' on his part, and that for him 'the indissoluble Entente is everything', but admitted that 'honestly, I fail to see how the French are ever going to make good their aspirations in Syria (all the indications at present available go to show that they are disliked and distrusted by nearly all sections of the people interested in their proposed sphere)'.[90]

One of the means Sykes considered would ameliorate the situation was that the French government should publicly disavow annexationist designs on Syria and the Lebanon, and declare its support of the Arab nationalist movement. As he wired to Clayton on 26 November, until the idea of France annexing Syria and the Lebanon was 'squashed you cannot expect enthusiasm or real help. Annexation is contrary to democratic spirit now prevailing in all countries.'[91] Clayton concurred: 'lack of any definite pronouncement against annexation especially in Syria, is causing distrust and uneasiness'. He also observed that 'as regards Syria there is an impression that we may be only marking time until our military successes place us in a position to hand Syria over to France with as few pledges as possible'. He particularly urged that the French government make 'a definite pronouncement disclaiming any idea of annexation in Syria (including blue area) and emphasising their intention of assuring liberty of all Syrians and helping them along the path towards independence and government by people'. Graham reacted favourably, 'the importance of reassuring the Syrians and forestalling possible Turkish manoeuvres is considerable. I believe it would be a good thing if we sent Sir M. Sykes to Paris to discuss matters with the French authorities in this sense.'[92] Sykes, for his part, thanked Clayton for his 'illuminating' telegram, and informed him that he, in anticipation of Clayton's suggestion, had already written to Goût in this sense.[93]

In the middle of December, Sykes was sent to Paris to inquire after the fate of the 'projet d'arrangement', and took the opportunity to discuss the matter with Goût. The latter agreed on the desirability of making a declaration, and 'we accordingly met the Syrian Committee and conjointly delivered the enclosed speeches; Monsieur Gouts observations will I make no doubt have a good effect'. Sykes had emphasised the unity of purpose between Great Britain and France. They were 'completely united in their policy regarding the non-Turkish parts of the Ottoman Empire', and there existed no 'points of divergence or dispute between the two countries'. He had also represented to the Syrians that they must 'wish that France renders you her indispensable assistance, which a long oppressed people needs before it can walk by itself'. Goût had impressed upon the audience that:

> The two Allies reject all ideas of colonial domination and are determined, each in its own sphere of action, to guide the Arabic-speaking populations and all those speaking other languages inhabiting the regions extending from the Anatolian Mountains to the Indian Ocean to a regime of autonomy

and civil development with mutual respect between the religions and the nationalities. Guide to a better future, arbiter between religious and ethnic groups, friendly counsellor of civilisation, this is the role that France and Great Britain are prepared to take up, the one in the north and the other in the south.[94]

On 16 February 1918, Wingate wired to London that he had seen a copy of the newspaper *Al Mustakbil*, which was published in France, containing the two speeches. He presumed that he was 'at liberty to make full use of these important pronouncements on Anglo–French policy. Their publication will have good effect on local Syrians.' On the suggestion of Sykes the Foreign Office replied in the affirmative.[95]

Communicating the speeches to leading Syrians in Cairo had, however, not the expected benevolent effect. As Wingate confided to Clayton, 'the apparent coalition of the Moslem and Christian sections against French initiative rather surprised me by its vehemence.'[96] He informed the Foreign Office that the reception had been 'decidedly unfavourable', and explained that the source of the Syrians' 'hostility is almost ineradicable belief that however liberal and rational may be a French programme its execution will be left to capitalists and clericals to the detriment of conception of ambition of greater Syria [...] Many Moslems make no secret of their preference to remain under Turk rather than to come under France.' Harold Nicolson complained of 'the culpability of the Egyptian Intelligence Department', and Sir Mark squarely laid the blame for this fiasco with the Cairo authorities. He minuted that 'Sir R. Wingate has not General Clayton's knowledge and his staff is composed of either purely Hejaz specialists or not the best men'.[97] Sykes also wrote to Clayton that he:

> Might point out to the Syrian Committee in Cairo that it took me all my time to get Gout to repudiate once for all every idea of annexation. You might also tell them that it is not encouraging if one gets the French to adopt a more liberal line than they have ever adopted before, to find that this is not met with any response on their side.

The best way to solve the problem was that 'we should do our utmost to encourage the advance of Faisal in Syria. The moment an opportunity arises, of establishing direct touch with Faisal we should take advantage of the event to recognise Arab independence on Arab soil.' When due publicity was given to this 'fait accompli' this 'should do much to satisfy Arab sentiment, pull the Syrians together force the French into adopting a policy which would do them some good instead of harm'.[98]

This was again wishful thinking on Sykes's part, because the one thing Syrians – Muslims and Christians alike – dreaded just as much as French designs on Syria were Hashemite designs on the country. On 2 November 1917, Wingate informed Balfour that 'progress of revolt has shown very clearly that Shereef is not likely to put up any form of government which would be acceptable in Syria, either to Christians or Moslems, and it appears improbable that such personal aspirations as he may have in that area can ever be realised', and although many Syrians regarded Faysal 'as possible head of a Syrian–Arab State', the 'idea of a pure Sherifian government is distasteful to all classes and whatever Arab government is instituted in Syria can never be more than nominally under Meccan control or Suzerainty'.[99]

Clayton also recognised the difficulty. At the end of November he telegraphed to Sykes that there was 'no doubt' that there existed 'a very real fear amongst Syrians of finding themselves under a government in which patriarchalism of Mecca is predominant. They realise that reactionary principles from which Sherif of Mecca cannot break loose are incompatible with progress on modern lines.' He therefore urged that the British should 'avoid any impression that we intend to force Sherif of Mecca or any Sherifian form of government on peoples who are unwilling to accept him'.[100] Wingate chimed in the next day by stating that 'King Hussein has in no degree abated his original pretensions concerning Syria and apparently still nourishes illusion that through the good offices of His Majesty's Government he may be installed as, at any rate nominally, overlord of greater part of the country', but he was sanguine that the whole problem would never materialise as the 'inefficiency of the Hedjaz Administration is a practical guarantee against the spread of Meccan patriachialism'.[101] Clayton for his part saw light at the opposite end of the tunnel. Fear of Zionist ambitions might induce the Syrians and the Hashemites to unite. As he explained to Gertrude Bell at the beginning of December 1917, 'up to date the Syrian Arab has shown the utmost distaste for any idea of a government in which Meccan patriarchalism has any influence. Hence a lack of real sympathy with the Sherif. Fear of the Jew may cause rapproachment.'[102]

An opportunity to tackle Syrian dislike of the Hashemites and aversion to the French seemed to offer itself in the form of an address by seven 'Syrian Politicians and exiles resident in Egypt' that Wingate received in the first week of May 1918. He reported to Balfour that from his 'knowledge of their personalities and antecedents I should say they were well qualified to represent Syrian Moslem opinion in Egypt', and that they asked 'for a guarantee of the ultimate independence of Arabia – in which term they comprise, besides the Arabian Peninsula, the Gezira, Syria, Mesopotamia, Mosul and a large part of the province of DiarBekr – as a condition to their energetic action with their fellow countrymen on behalf of the Allies and against the Turks'. Sir Reginald realised that Britain could not 'give the far-reaching guarantees they ask for', but he felt 'strongly that we should be ill-advised to ignore the aspirations towards independence and eventual political union'. He also believed – and here Wingate returned to a favourite theme – that 'it would be advantageous to supplement, if possible, the very general – and in native eyes, vague and consequently unsatisfactory – lines of our declared policy in regard to the future of Arab peoples'.

One of the reasons the seven Syrians presented their address was that they wanted to be provided with ammunition to counter the 'sarcastic' reproach made 'by some Egyptians' that their allies France and England 'have concluded amongst themselves an agreement to divide your territory into two zones, the North of which is to be under French influence and the South to be under British'. They therefore inquired whether they could 'assure our people that it is the aim of the British government that the Arabs should enjoy complete independence in Arabia?' Their other worry was the relationship with Husayn, and accordingly they also wished to know whether it was British policy 'to assist the inhabitants of these countries to attain their complete independence and the composing of an Arab government decentralised like the United States of America?' They claimed that 'the Syrians, though only too glad to form part of the Arab Federal government, have […] for a long time previous to the war, been working to apply the principle of decentralisation to Syria', and that although 'the source of the Arab revolution appeared in the Hedjaz its corner stone was Syria and it had the greater share in the intellectual movement'.[103]

The dispatch reached London four weeks later. It was left to Sykes to draw up a reply. This time Sir Mark was prepared to oblige Wingate. On 11 June a telegram was sent to Cairo, approved by Hardinge, but not submitted to the Eastern Committee (it received a copy for its information), which stated that:

The areas mentioned in the memorandum fall into four categories.

1. Areas in Arabia which were free and independent before the outbreak of the war.
2. Areas emancipated from Turkish control by the action of the Arabs themselves during the present war.
3. Areas formerly under Ottoman dominion, occupied by the Allied forces during the present war.
4. Areas still under Turkish control.

In regard to the first two categories, His Majesty's Government recognise the complete and sovereign independence of the Arabs inhabiting these areas and support them in their struggle for freedom.

In regard to the areas occupied by the Allied forces […] It is the wish and desire of His Majesty's Government that the future government of these regions should be based upon the principle of the consent of the governed and this policy has and will continue to have the support of His Majesty's Government.

In regard to the areas mentioned in the fourth category, it is the wish and desire of His Majesty's Government that the oppressed peoples of these areas should obtain their freedom and independence and towards the achievement of this object His Majesty's Government continue to labour.[104]

A fortnight later, Wingate reported that Hogarth had met with two of the seven Syrians. He had read out a statement in which categories one and two, and three and four, had been put together. Regarding the first group, 'Arab lands [that] have long enjoyed or recently attained in arms complete and sovereign independence', Hogarth had proclaimed that the British government fully recognised their sovereignty, while with respect to the second, 'the other Arab lands […] still occupied by the troops of the Allies or by the enemy', he had declared that 'His Majesty's Government hopes and trusts that freedom will be established and that after the war a settlement will be arrived at in accordance with the wishes of the inhabitants'. Hogarth's statement had been well received: 'one of the signatories expressed his great gratification'. The other had wished to know 'if such governments as the Arabs might set up would be recognised by His Majesty's Government?'

Hogarth had replied in the affirmative, provided these were 'properly established and effective'.[105]

The reply to the memorandum of the seven Syrians drafted by Sykes had not addressed the question of the relations between Syria and the Hijaz. This was one of the reasons why Sir Mark and Georges-Picot decided during their private conference at the beginning of July that yet another declaration, this time a joint one to the King of the Hijaz, was needed. The major advantages of a declaration of this kind, so Sykes explained in a memorandum on 3 July 1918, were first that it 'would dispel for good and all the idea that we are endeavouring to secure Syria as a French Colony', and second that 'it will be seen that we in no way commit ourselves to any idea of a Pan Arab Empire which is so detestable to Syrians and others and makes the King of the Hejaz's cause less popular than it would otherwise be'. Sir Mark admitted that the proposed declaration was 'susceptible of amendment', but believed that 'if in substance it is presented to the King of Hejaz and the main lines of it indicated when and where occasion required, our position *vis-à-vis* the Arabic speaking peoples will be improved, and we shall be rid of a constantly recurring difficulty'. They proposed the following declaration:

> The governments of Great Britain and France desire jointly to inform the Government of Hejaz that their policy in regard to the Arabic speaking peoples of Arabia, Syria, Jazirah, and Irak is as follows:
>
> 1. In such areas as were free before the war the governments recognise and re-affirm the existing freedom and independence of the inhabitants.
> 2. In such areas as have been liberated since the war by the efforts of the inhabitants, the two governments recognise the complete and sovereign independence of the inhabitants of those regions.
> 3. With regard to such areas as are now occupied by the Allied forces it is the intention and desire of the two governments that those areas should be permanently delivered from the oppression under which they formerly suffered, and that their future government should be based upon the principle of the consent of the governed.
> 4. With regard to areas still subject to Ottoman oppression it is the desire of the two governments that the inhabitants of these areas should be delivered from the oppression to which they are now subjected, and that the inhabitants should be put into a position to decide upon forms of government which appear most suitable for the various regions with due regard to the maintenance of security and order.

5. The two governments desire to make it clear to the Government of Hejaz and to the Arabic speaking peoples above mentioned, that on the part of neither government has there ever been any intention of annexing these areas nor of disposing of them, nor allowing them to be disposed of by any other party, in any way other than is desired by the populations thereof.[106]

Sykes did not think that 'we are sacrificing anything by making such a declaration, and it is in fact only slightly different from one His Majesty's Government made to the Arab memorialists', but this was not quite true. Paragraph 5 had not figured in the Declaration to the Seven. It was a further attempt by Sykes to push through a 'no annexation' policy, and it was immediately stopped.[107] In yet another memorandum on the subject prepared for the Eastern Committee, Sykes had already foreseen that people might object to 'the no-annexation clause',[108] and sure enough Curzon did not fail to do so at the Committee's meeting on 15 July. He pointed out that 'in the reply which His Majesty's Government had sent on the 11th June to the memorial of seven Syrians in Egypt, no disclaimer of annexation had been made, whereas in Sir Mark Sykes paper [...] the words "no intention of annexing", which had been introduced, appeared gratuitously to raise the question of Basra'.[109] At the Committee's next meeting, Curzon returned to the attack, 'it was quite gratuitous to volunteer pledges now for which no one had asked', and it was decided to delete from paragraph 5 the 'no annexation' clause. The rest of the declaration fared even worse. Smuts thought that 'confusion was bound to be caused by the varying formulae adopted in several paragraphs of the draft declaration', and Cecil agreed. He suggested that 'the first four paragraphs of the declaration might be eliminated'. Sykes stressed the importance of inducing 'the French to associate themselves with us in some such declaration', but in Montagu's opinion a joint declaration on the Middle East should be avoided. He wondered 'whether it was desirable, as proposed in the preamble, to associate ourselves in any way with the French in a declaration that embraced Mesopotamia with which the French had nothing to do'. The Eastern Committee in the end decided to replace the preamble and the five paragraphs with the following formula:

The Governments of Great Britain and France desire to make it clear to the Government of the Hejaz, and Arabic-speaking peoples of Arabia, Syria, Jazirah, and Irak, that on the part of neither government has there ever been any intention of disposing of these areas, or of allowing them to be disposed of by any other party, in any way other than as desired by the population thereof.[110]

Sykes had again suffered a resounding defeat in the Eastern Committee.

Palestine: Syrian, Zionist and Hashemite Ambitions

In August 1917, Clayton had already prophesised in a letter to Sykes that it would 'not help matters if the Arabs – already somewhat distracted between pro-Sherefians and those who fear Meccan domination, as also between pro-French and anti-French are given yet another bone of contention in the shape of Zionism in Palestine as against the interests of the Moslems resident there'.[111] On 6 December 1917, the French embassy in London communicated a telegram from Picot for Sykes in which the former observed that it was evident from: 'all conversations I have had here since my arrival, that Mr Balfour's declarations on the subject of Zionism have provoked considerable emotion among the Syrian Arabs', and warned that whatever demonstrations of Zionist and Arabian cooperation and solidarity were organised in England, 'they do not correspond to any reality here'. Clayton informed Sykes a few days later that he agreed 'in principle' with Picot's telegram, and that 'in spite of all arguments Mecca dislikes Jews [...] while Arabs of Syria and Palestine fear repetition of story of Jacob and Esau'. Sykes would have none of this. The Balfour declaration, so he claimed in a telegram to Picot that Hardinge considered 'a good reply':

> Amply safeguards local Arab interests. Jews at all meetings emphasise necessity, not only of cordial cooperation against common Turkish enemy but emphasise their firm intention and determination of paying scrupulous attention to Arab rights and interests in land matters. I am convinced, from what I have seen, as is every Arab, and they are many, who has come in contact with S. and W. [Sokolow and Weizmann; R.H.L.], that the fears which you inform me of are unfounded.[112]

Picot's and Clayton's warnings seemed only to strengthen the case for a Zionist commission headed by Weizmann to be sent out to Palestine as soon as possible. On 17 December 1917, Weizmann submitted a brief note on the status and the objects of the commission (see Chapter 7, section 'The Capture of Jerusalem and Martial Law'). The commission's status should be that of 'an advisory body to the British Authorities in Palestine in all matters relating to Jews or which may affect the establishment of a National Home for the Jewish people in accordance with the Declaration of His Majesty's Government'. Weizmann distinguished six objectives, the fifth of which was 'to help in establishing friendly relations with the Arabs and other non-Jewish communities'.[113] The MEC discussed the project during its meeting on 19 January. Its members were not so much concerned with the effectuation of the Balfour declaration as with, and in line with Sykes's point of view, 'the necessity of bringing the British authorities in Egypt and Palestine and the Arabs into contact with the responsible leaders of the organisation'. This had the result that, although the committee approved the dispatch of the Zionist Commission, Weizmann's statement on the status of the commission with its explicit link with the Balfour declaration was deleted, and that 'to help in establishing friendly relations between the Jews on the one hand, and the Arabs and other non-Jewish communities on the other' became the commission's first objective. It was also decided that a political officer should be attached to the commission, who would be responsible to Clayton.[114]

Two weeks later, Sir Mark, in view of several letters he had received 'from Palestine showing that the local Zionists and Jews were inclined to complicate matters with their Arab neighbours', urged the commission's early departure, but it was not until the beginning of March that it finally left England for Egypt and Palestine. In the meantime, William Ormsby Gore had been appointed political officer with the commission. His instructions did not contain any reference to the Balfour Declaration. The commission's first task was to get 'in touch with the Arab leaders and representatives of other communities in Palestine'. It should also investigate ways to prevent 'land speculation during the continuance of the war', as well as the 're-opening (of) Zionist banks in Jaffa and Jerusalem subject to the approval of the military authorities'.[115]

The Zionist Commission arrived in Alexandria on 20 March 1918. Kinahan Cornwallis, director of the Arab Bureau, reported a month later that, before the commission's arrival, among 'leading Syrians and Palestinians' there had existed 'a deeply felt fear that the Jews not only intended to assume the reins of Government in Palestine but also to expropriate or buy up during the war large tracts of lands owned by Moslems and others, and gradually to force them from the country'. Naturally, British officers had done 'everything possible' to allay these fears, but it had not helped that they had been ignorant 'of the exact programme of the Zionists'. This unsatisfactory state of affairs had been explained to Weizmann upon his arrival, and the latter had 'lost no time in meeting the leading Syrians and Palestinians', and had elucidated the Zionist aims. It was:

> His ambition to see Palestine governed by some stable government like that of Great Britain, that a Jewish government would be fatal to his plans and that it was simply his wish to provide a home for the Jews in the Holy Land where they could live their own national life, sharing equal rights with the other inhabitants.

Weizmann had also assured them that 'he had no intention of taking advantage of the present conditions caused by the war by buying up land', but merely wished 'to provide for future emigrants by taking up waste and crown lands of which there were ample for all sections of the community'. Cornwallis concluded that 'this frank avowal of Zionist aims has produced a considerable revulsion of feeling amongst the Palestinians, who have for the first time come into contact with Jews of good standing'. Admittedly 'suspicion still remains in the minds of some', but he did not doubt that it would 'gradually disappear if the Commission continues its present attitude of conciliation'.[116] Clayton was also full of praise for Weizmann's performance. He wrote to Sykes on 4 April that 'we are all struck with his intelligence and openness and the Commander-in-Chief has evidently formed a high opinion of him. I feel convinced that many of the difficulties which we have encountered owing to the mutual distrust and suspicion between Arabs and Jews will now disappear.'[117]

Fourteen days later, Clayton assured Sykes that he 'personally' was in favour of Zionism, and that he was 'convinced that it is one of our strongest cards', but that Sykes, with his 'knowledge of all that has taken place in the past in this area', would agree with him on 'the necessity of caution if we are to bring that policy to a successful conclusion', especially since, as Clayton explained to Balfour that same day, British officers experienced 'some difficulties in consequence of the fact that up to date our policy has been directed towards securing Arab sympathy in view of our Arab Commitments. It is not easy therefore to switch over to Zionism all at once in the face of a considerable degree of Arab distrust and suspicion.' He reiterated this point to Wingate three days later. It was 'not an easy thing […] to endeavour to bring together two parties and policies whose aims hitherto have been almost diametrically opposed. It is all very well for people at home to give vent to high-sounding sentiments but we are up against the practical difficulties.' He could only hope that London 'should leave the execution of the policy to us here […] and not rush us'. But there was more. Clayton saw himself first of all as a champion of the Arab cause. He could not 'conscientiously carry out any line of policy which will go against our pledges to the Arabs'. At the same time he felt bound to say that 'so far things have gone excellently well and a "rapprochement" between Arabs and Jews looks far more probable than I had ever anticipated […] Weizmann himself is very tactful and good with them.'[118] This was a conclusion Ormsby Gore could subscribe to. Even though Weizmann at times was 'too fanatical and too partisan and uncompromising', all in all he was 'doing well. He is very fair and reasonable with the Arabs, and rules his own people with a big stick.'[119]

The first high point of Weizmann's attempts to soothe the Palestinian leaders was a speech he delivered at a dinner party organised by Storrs on 27 April. The latter reported three days later that Weizmann:

> Read aloud the speech a copy of which is attached. It will be seen that the document is a frank, and, from the Arab point of view, somewhat drastic exposition of the theme 'back to the land' with the subtle distinction that the land in question is not for the moment the national property of those who propose to go back to it. From an oratorical point of view the speech was not impressive being neither rhetorically nor, as English, accurately pronounced […] It is my opinion, without wishing to over-estimate the results of an evening's enthusiasm, that much good has already been done, and more may follow, as the result of these frank and friendly exchanges of programmes.[120]

Ormsby Gore agreed with Storrs's last observation. He was confident that 'relations between Jews and Arabs show a distinct change for the better', and considered that Weizmann's 'speech exactly fitted the requirements of the local situation and occasion'.[121]

In his report on his interviews with Husayn, Hogarth had already hinted at a possible deal between the Hashemites and the Zionists. According to Hogarth, the king 'probably knows little or nothing of the actual or possible economy of Palestine and his ready assent to Jewish settlement there is not worth very much. But I think he appreciates the financial advantage of

Arab cooperation with the Jews.'¹²² On 2 April, Clayton noted 'a certain distrust of Zionist aims' on the part of Faysal, and stressed the desirability of a meeting with Weizmann so that the Emir could be 'reassured in regard to the scope of the Zionist movement'.¹²³ This meeting finally took place at Faysal's headquarters in the neighbourhood of Akaba on 4 June. According to Clayton, Weizmann was 'much pleased with result'. At first sight this seemed a bit puzzling, because Faysal claimed that he was in no position 'to express definite opinions on political questions as he was merely his father's agent in such matters', and felt unable 'to discuss the future of Palestine', but what counted was that Faysal had twice stressed the 'necessity of close cooperation between Jews and Arabs especially at present time', and 'for mutual benefit of both'.¹²⁴ Colonel P.C. Joyce, who acted as interpreter, gave it as his 'private opinion that Feisal really welcomed Jewish cooperation and considered it essential to future Arab ambitions'. Joyce had also gained the impression that 'Feisal fully realises the future possibility of a Jewish Palestine and would probably accept it if it assisted Arab expansion further north'.¹²⁵

After his meeting with Faysal, Weizmann proceeded to Alexandria, where he had several conversations with Wingate's confidant Major Stewart Symes. At the time, Symes was struggling with the problem that 'the three policies – Zionist, Syrian and Sherifial – [...] present several points of conflict', and that 'until and unless we can find a common basis of agreement between them there is serious danger of their disagreement being exploited to our (British) and Arabs disadvantage at the Peace Conference'. On 9 June, Weizmann had a conversation with Symes during which he 'stigmatised the Palestinian Arabs as a demoralised race with whom it was impossible to treat: and contrasted their type with Feisal – a true Prince and a man "whom one would be proud to have as an enemy and would welcome as a friend"'. Symes subsequently reported to Wingate his 'impression that W. had it in mind to bargain with the Sherifials for a free hand with the Palestinians'. The next day, Weizmann returned to this theme and, finally, 'with all diffidence' put forward 'a suggestion which had occurred to him "as the result of much thought on the subject"', which he had already 'mentioned to General Clayton'. The bargain Weizmann had in mind was:

> Shortly, that, recognising that the King of the Hedjaz was the Head of the Arab Movement, the Zionists, <u>acting as a private organization</u>, should deal direct with him and should offer:

(a) Financial and, if necessary, other assistance for the establishment of the Kingdom of the Hedjaz.
(b) Support in Europe and America of Syrian autonomy, without French or an enemy's power's intervention, but with British assistance as may be desired by the Sherifial and Syrian factions:
In return for:
Recognition of Zionist aims in Palestine.

Weizmann realised that he should 'obtain President Wilson's support', but once he had this, he would convene a Jewish congress in Jerusalem, which 'would ask for a British Protectorate over Palestine and publicly declare their alliance with the Sherifials and their support of the Syrians' aspirations for autonomy, with or without Sherifial Suzerainty, and under British (not French) guidance.

Symes was all in favour of Weizmann's proposed bargain, in particular considering that the main bone of contention 'between the Sherifials and the Syrians may be eliminated by the offer by the latter of their Emirate to Feisal'. This was the common basis he had been looking for, and it seemed that 'a working agreement mutually advantageous and politically efficient might be reached between these three parties'. However, nothing would come of this unless 'our obligations to France under the Sykes–Picot agreement were finally repudiated and all idea of conserving the privileges of the Palestine Arabs abandoned'.[126]

Wingate extensively quoted Symes's note in a long dispatch on the extent to which 'King Hussein's policy can be reconciled with other leading factors in the situation'. His starting point was Weizmann's suggestion that Arab recognition of Zionist aspirations in Palestine was possible if the Zionists for their part gave financial aid and other assistance to the Hijaz, and supported 'Syrian aims and sympathies' in Europe and America. In an attempt not to offend Sykes's well-known sensibilities, Wingate prudently deleted Weizmann's original references to an autonomous Syria without French intervention and with British assistance. He also toned down Symes's verdict that the Sykes–Picot agreement had to be repudiated. According to Sir Reginald, a reconciliation of Syrian, Hashemite and Zionist ambitions could only be attained 'if our formal obligations to France respecting Syria are regarded as no longer binding'. He also did not mention Weizmann's intention of organising a Jewish congress in Jerusalem that would publicly declare support for Syrian autonomy under British guidance. However, all this was of no avail. The only thing that Sir Mark picked up when he read Wingate's dispatch was the anti-French nature of the proposed arrangement. The most ardent advocate of 'the Entente first and last' angrily minuted that:

> Sir R. Wingate's Despatch and Dr Weizmann's indicated policy show a decided anti-French tendency. Dr Weizmann's ideas are naturally based on a Zionist and not a British hypothesis, it is easy to see that he would naturally prefer an all British policy because if Great Britain is behind Zionism and at the same time runs Damascus, Mecca and Baghdad, there is a fine opportunity for the Zionist element to have a preponderating influence in all the countries surrounding Palestine [...] We have to bear in mind that French interest in Syria is no imaginary thing and that it must be reckoned with from an Entente point of view.

The only 'real way' of dealing with the Syrian difficulty was '(a) for the French to come out with a real assurance of Syrian independence [...] (b) for us to assure the Syrians that we concur in and support French policy, that we are not going to quarrel with our Allies to please Syrian politicians.' Everything depended 'on two things (1) the initial sincerity of Great Britain and France (2) Their capacity to resist temptation in the future'.

Hardinge minuted that 'we must certainly take steps to correct some of Sir R. Wingate's ideas and [...] point out our complete detachment from Syria and the danger of encouraging any exclusive pro-British sympathies [...] It would be very advantageous to get from the French a declaration of policy regarding Syria that would satisfy King Hussein, but it would not be easy to obtain'. Cecil concurred: 'we should aim at settling with the French on the basis that they publicly and definitely renounce all idea of annexing or occupying Syria and that we recognise that it is outside our and inside their sphere of interest'. This position 'must be made very clear to Sir R. Wingate [...] Finally we must confine Zionist activities to Palestine. Dr Weizmann is an enthusiast which means that he looks only at one side of the problem and he must be controlled.'

However desirable, a dispatch once again impressing upon Wingate Britain's complete disinterestedness in Syria was not sent, because Cecil first wanted a 'very short memorandum [...] stating in the form of definite propositions our policy'. Sykes subsequently drew up a Memorandum on Eastern Policy on 2 August, containing a list of eight proposals,[127] but the next day this memorandum was replaced by Sykes's very brief memorandum on the 'French–Syrian question' to which the two draft declarations (A) and (B) (see section 'French Participation in the Administration of Palestine', above), as well as the pruned version of the 'declaration to the King of Hedjaz' (see section 'Syria: Syrian, French and Hashemite Ambitions', above) were annexed. After the Eastern Committee had rejected draft declarations (A) and (B), neither Sykes, Hardinge, nor Cecil did return to the subject that Wingate should be told to obliterate from his mind any thought of exploiting Syrian, Zionist and Hashemite anti-French sentiment to Great Britain's advantage.

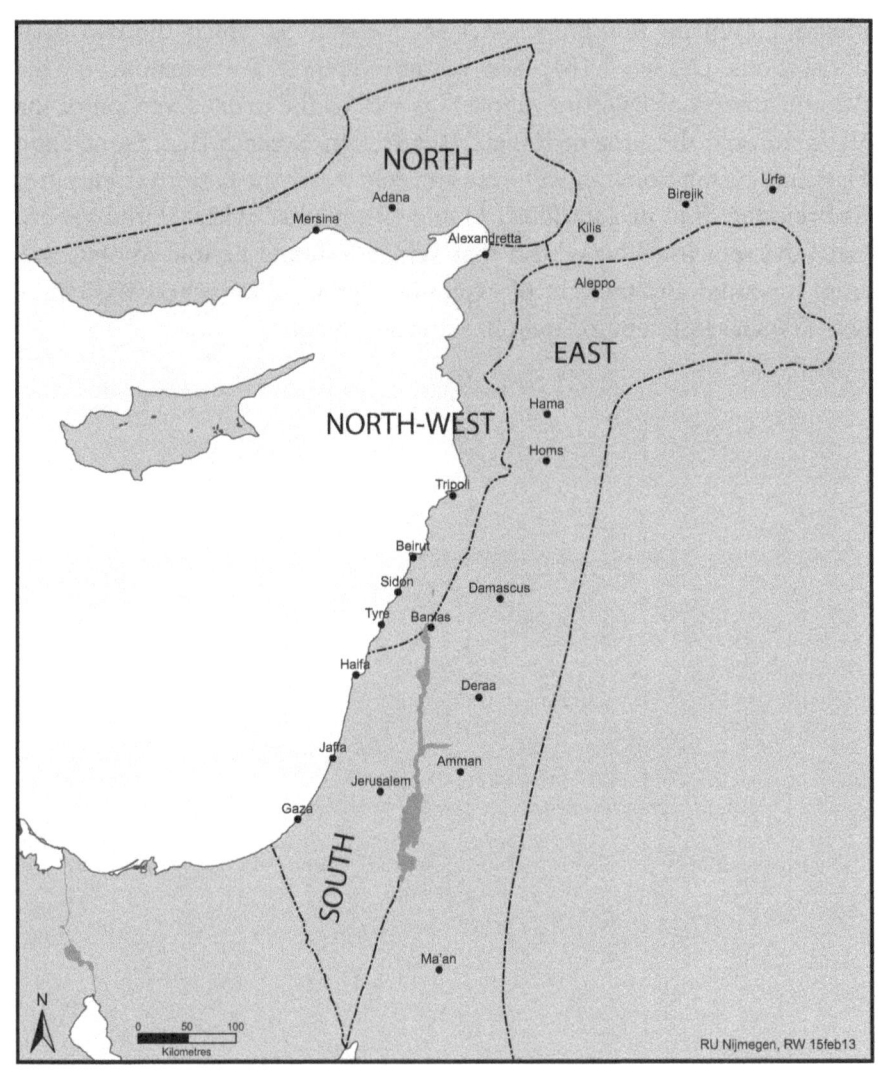

Map 9.1 Occupied Enemy Territory, Administrative Zones
(Source: Falls, *Military Operations* Vol. II)

9 SINCE I AM SO EARLY DONE FOR, I WONDER WHAT I WAS BEGUN FOR!

Introduction

This chapter is for the greater part concerned with the attempts by the British authorities to get their French counterparts to agree that the Sykes–Picot agreement could not stand. These had already started in February 1917, continued right up to the eve of the Paris peace conference, and were singularly unsuccessful. Whatever arguments the British introduced to justify a revision or cancellation of the agreement the French were unreceptive and held fast to it. A second theme is the struggle between Lord George Curzon, the chairman of the Eastern Committee, and Lord Robert Cecil, assistant secretary of state for foreign affairs, for control of British Middle East policy. Curzon generally managed to assert the committee's predominance, but Cecil, thanks to an intervention by Foreign Secretary Arthur Balfour at the end of September 1918, was given the opportunity to pursue his line of policy with respect to the revision of the Sykes–Picot agreement, which, so it turned out in the middle of November 1918, also ended in failure.

Before I start my discussion of the British efforts to get out of the Sykes–Picot agreement, I relate how the authorities in Cairo, Baghdad and London steadily lost their grip on the continuing and deepening rivalry between Husayn and Ibn Sa'ud, in particular regarding the possession of the desert town of Khurma. British warnings of dire consequences if the protagonists did not hold back and settle their differences peacefully had little or no effect. All the British authorities apparently could do was to hope that the question would go away or sink into oblivion.

The Khurma Affair

In the early spring of 1918, Sir Percy Cox travelled to London for consultations with the India Office and the Eastern Committee on the future of Mesopotamia. He made a stopover in Egypt, where on 23 March a conference was held at the Residency to discuss the situation between Husayn and Ibn Sa'ud. Cox explained that 'Ibn Saud was exceedingly jealous and suspicious of King Hussein and he [...] was personally convinced that Ibn Saud would never acknowledge the King as his temporal overlord, though he would always pay him, as he does now, the great respect due to his religious position'. The conference agreed that 'the Imam of Yemen, Idrisi of Asir, and Ibn Saud were unlikely to accept King Hussein as their temporal overlord', but that this might change if Faysal's forces were successful in Syria, although admittedly 'the inhabitants of Syria and Mesopotamia were at one in their determination to allow no direct interference in their affairs from the part of the King'. As far as British policy in Central and South Arabia was concerned, little else could be done than 'to keep the peace between the different Amirs and to fulfil [our] treaty terms with each'.[1]

British policy towards the Arab chiefs remained one of not favouring any one of them at the expense of the others, and preventing their jealousies and rivalries escalating into open warfare. It was to be severely tested as a result of what became known as the Khurma affair. On 9 July, Sir Reginald Wingate wired that 'relations between King Hussein and Ibn Saud are becoming increasingly strained and may lead to hostilities by their respective adherents or even open rupture'. It was 'not possible accurately to appreciate various points at issue between them, but I think warning against giving provocation addressed impartially to each would be salutary'. He proposed a message in the following sense:

> That His Majesty's Government note with regret the ill-feeling between King Hussein and Emir Ibn Saud as shown in their [?recent] correspondence and regard it as seriously prejudicial to their interests and Arab cause. His Majesty's Government would view with great disfavour any action by either party or their followers liable to aggravate situation or to provoke hostilities.

In a further telegram Wingate warned that Husayn was greatly worried about his position *vis-à-vis* Ibn Sa'ud and the other Arab chiefs, and that 'his present state of mind might lead him to a nervous breakdown or ill-considered action'.[2] Sykes was all in favour for making 'the very strongest appeal' to Husayn and Ibn Sa'ud 'to compose their differences and at least agree to a truce for the duration of the war', but he did not believe that a crisis was at hand, since 'the Arab mind always runs to negotiation and compromise. It should not be impossible to get the two to appoint delegates to meet on some neutral ground and there discuss the matter.'[3] The Eastern Committee subsequently reformulated Wingate's proposed message so that it sounded less peremptory, and offered the British government's good offices 'in coming to an agreement by negotiations'.[4]

The town of Khurma was situated some 120 miles to the north-east of Taif, and in Aiteiba territory. It had been part of Husayn's domains, but the governor appointed by the king had gone over to Ibn Sa'ud after a quarrel with Abdullah. The situation escalated when Husayn decided to send troops to Khurma to reassert his authority. Although Husayn assured Wilson that 'matter is purely one of internal administration and that no hostile action of any sort against Bin Saud is intended', and that he expected 'to settle it without fighting', Philby warned that it was 'fairly clear if expedition referred to materialises in Khurma the tension between Ibn Saud and Sharif, already acute, will develop into open hostilities. It would seem desirable therefore to request Sharif to defer action.'[5]

In view of this danger, the Foreign Office decided to send a sterner message to both chiefs. The British government could not 'tolerate dissension between their friends, and they must insist, on pain of their severe displeasure, that neither party shall take any action likely to lead to open breach'. Husayn and Ibn Sa'ud were also requested to send conciliatory messages to one another, and to come to 'amicable exchange of views with object of arriving at settlement of outstanding differences'.[6] After Cyril Wilson had communicated this message to Husayn, it led to the kind of ill-considered action Wingate had warned against. The king requested the British government 'to accept his abdication as he feels he may be regarded as an obstacle to Arab movement and an unwilling obstructor of His Majesty's Government's policy'. According to Sir Reginald, Husayn considered 'his scheme of unification as the only satisfactory solution of Arabian question'. He also suspected the British of 'partiality to Bin Saud', and insisted that 'our attitude towards his action at Khurma is an evidence of this. He would prefer to resign now than to wait and see the collapse of his policy.' Wingate suggested sending a pacifying message to the king.[7] The Foreign Office replied the next day. Wilson was instructed to tell Husayn that the British government could not:

> Regard seriously a decision to abdicate […] under a mistaken impression that Your Highness had lost the confidence of His Majesty's Government […] far from this being the case His Majesty's Government regard your leadership of the Arab movement in the war as vitally necessary for the Arab cause and cannot think that Your Highness will withdraw at such a juncture.[8]

The same day, the India Office informed the viceroy and Cox that Khurma clearly fell 'under King Husain's sphere and outside that in which intervention by Bin Saud is warranted. Philby should impress this view of the case on Bin Saud.' The Indian and Mesopotamian authorities should realise that as far as Ibn Sa'ud was concerned 'neither his services or commitments in the past, nor his potential utility in the future, will bear any comparison with those of King Hussein', and that therefore 'we cannot allow latter's interests to be prejudiced […] by ill-timed activities of Bin Saud'.[9]

On 7 August, Arnold Wilson transmitted a report by Philby, in which the latter explained that Ibn Sa'ud had little room for manoeuvre in the question of Khurma. When he gave in to Husayn, this might fatally weaken his position *vis-à-vis* his Ikhwan warriors.[10] Sir Reginald was receptive to Philby's argument. Although Britain must 'uphold [Husayn's] right to punish a rebel Sheikh', and that 'Mr Philby's ready acquiescence in Bin Saud's assertion that King's action is aggressive' was 'most regrettable and ill-advised', at the same time Wingate fully appreciated 'necessity of returning friendship of Bin Saud whom I understand represents strongest if not only Anglophile element in Nejdean politics'. He therefore agreed that Ibn Sa'ud 'should be treated liberally in the matter of funds which may also exercise a pacifying influence on hostile public opinion referred to by Mr Philby', but he also urged that 'other sinews of war should not be supplied'.[11]

Sir Reginald saw no other option to resolve the Khurma dispute than 'continuing representations to both parties that it is to their common and individual interests to prevent outbreak of hostilities and by trying to induce them to correspond (either direct or through us) with a view to discovering a modus vivendi'.[12] The Foreign Office showed greater creativity. On 28 August it suggested that 'good might result if a meeting between King Hussein and Ibn Saud could be arranged under careful management. A discussion between them, held under our auspices and direction might clear the air and facilitate a settlement.' If these discussions were to fail, then at least time would have been 'gained, as both would be likely to remain quiescent pending the meeting'. A 'strong and impartial' commission – consisting of Philby, Lawrence or Cyril Wilson, with an impartial chairman – should prepare and oversee the negotiations between the two chiefs.[13] Wingate, however, disapproved of the plan. Hardinge suggested that a meeting between Abdullah and Ibn Sa'ud's brother might be a viable alternative. Cecil only regretted that Cairo failed to appreciate that the plan, 'even if it came to no result […] would hang up the controversy for the time being'.[14]

After Allenby's rout of the Turkish forces at Megiddo (see section 'Allenby's Offensive and the Capture of Damascus', below), and the rapid advance of his troops to the north, Sykes hoped that the whole intractable question would sink into oblivion. When Wingate reported on 23 September that Husayn had rejected the proposed meeting between Abdullah and Ibn Sa'ud's brother, Sir Mark noted that 'the great danger has hitherto been that under stress of internal dissensions either the king would abdicate or Ibn Saud would go over to the Turks. There are now no Turks to go over to, and if Medina surrenders the King's position will be much more stable […] In any event central Arabian politics have returned to the normal condition of unimportance.'[15] A few weeks later, Sykes minuted that the Arabian situation after Allenby's victory had 'subsided to its chronic and normal unimportance'.[16] However, the question simply would not go away. On 6 December, Wingate wired that the Ikhwan had attacked a Hashemite supply base some 45 miles north of Taif, and that 'a collision appears imminent'.[17] Four days later, he reported that the Ikhwan were advancing further on Hijaz territory. Sir Reginald therefore strongly recommended 'immediate despatch by His Majesty's Government of peremptory instructions to Bin Saud to withdraw all militant Ikhwan from neighbourhood, making it clear to him that failure or delay in compliance will entail reprisals'.[18]

On 23 December the Army Council made a startling proposal. In a letter to the Foreign Office they explained that they were 'doubtful whether this matter can be settled by putting pressure on Ibn Saud personally, as the latter may be unable to exercise control over the fanatical elements among his subjects, many of whom regard his friendliness towards Europeans as unorthodox and degenerate'. The Army Council therefore believed that 'more open measures are required to shew Arabia definitely that the policy of His Majesty's Government is to support King Hussein, against all aggression'. If the foreign secretary concurred, they were prepared to dispatch 'immediately to Mecca, such equipment as the Sherif may ask for and be able to use, as well as a suitable force of Mohamedan troops'. Shades of Rabegh, although not for Sir Eyre Crowe, who proposed to concur, and the India Office was so informed immediately.[19] The India Office also appeared to have no recollection of the Rabegh crisis. It saw 'no objection to the proposals of the War Office'. George Kidston of the Foreign Office had, however, asked Lawrence for his opinion, and the latter was very much against it. He used the same argument that had been so effective in killing the plans to send a brigade to Rabegh in the autumn of 1916, namely that the deployment of British troops in the Hijaz would fatally discredit Husayn in the eyes of the Arabs. It would be 'regarded as the crowning phase of the policy of which we are accused in hostile Moslem circles in Asia – the gradual reduction of Mecca to the status of a British protectorate'. In view of Lawrence's objections, Kidston thought that it was 'difficult to act as proposed [...] The only thing, therefore, that we can do is to warn the War Office of the danger of offering Hussein Mahommedan troops for Mecca.' It was not until 10 January 1919 that the Foreign Office informed the Army Council that, 'after full consideration', it was 'averse from the proposal to despatch Mohammedan troops to Mecca, since such a step might be made use of by unfriendly persons to spread in Moslem circles the impression that the policy of His Majesty's Government with respect to the Arab State implies undue interference in the holy places of Islam'.[20] That same day, the garrison of Medina finally surrendered to the Hashemite forces. In view of this development, so Montagu wired to Arnold Wilson on 16 January, 'nothing is to be gained by further intervention in dispute between King Hussein and Bin Saud'.[21]

Mitigating or Abolishing the Sykes–Picot Agreement

The very first attempt to persuade the French that the terms of the Sykes–Picot agreement should be reconsidered was made by Sykes (see Chapter 7, section 'Zionist Ambitions and the French Difficulty'). On 28 February 1917, he explained to Georges-Picot that an international administration for the 'brown area' – as laid down in article 3 of the agreement – would 'inevitably drift into a condition of chaos and dissension'. It would be far better if Palestine should become an American protectorate. Picot, however, refused to consider this alternative. Prime Minister Lloyd George was very much in favour of a British protectorate, but at the conference of Saint Jean-de-Maurienne his hints in this direction 'had been very coldly received' by the French and the Italians. When the War Cabinet reviewed the results of the conference on 25 April 1917, they therefore concluded that although they 'inclined to the view that sooner or later the Sykes–Picot Agreement might have to be reconsidered [...] No action should at present be taken in this matter.'[22]

David Hogarth was in London at the beginning of July 1917. He drew up a memorandum in which he advocated 'some reconsideration of the Agreement'. He claimed that it had favoured France, but presumed that there must have been 'sufficient reasons of general policy [...] to so favour France'. These, however, appeared no longer to apply, especially because 'the position of one beneficiary – ourselves – has been very greatly strengthened both by the part we have played among the Arabs in the Hejaz and in Mesopotamia, and by the open and insistent preference declared by the Zionist Jews', while at the same time 'a strong and increasing feeling has manifested itself in opposition to French penetration of any part of the Arab area'.[23] Even though Hogarth observed to Clayton that in London he had 'found no one who both takes the S.P. Agreement seriously and approves of it – except M.S. himself',[24] Sykes could cheerfully report to Clayton some two weeks later that Hogarth 'got trounced by the Foreign Office for meddling in affairs without consulting proper authorities, he being an Admiralty employee. This departmentalism for once served my ends.'[25]

On 13 July, Harold Nicolson completed a memorandum, written at the request of Balfour, on British 'contractual' and 'moral' obligations towards Russia, France, Italy and the Sherif of Mecca with respect to the territory of the Ottoman Empire. Nicolson's observations on the Sykes–Picot agreement made Sir Mark produce a memorandum of his own, in which he submitted that Nicolson had not attributed 'sufficient importance to the moral side of the question and to the ideals for which the best elements in this war are fighting, viz: the liberation of oppressed peoples and the maintenance of world peace'. Sykes admitted that the Sykes–Picot agreement allowed the signatory states to annex certain areas, but claimed that 'formal annexation' was 'quite contrary to the spirit of the time, and would only lay up a store of future trouble'. Two central axioms should guide British action in the Middle East. One was the 'unalterable friendship of Great Britain and France', the other 'the duty of Great Britain and France towards oppressed peoples'. It was Sykes's firm belief that if 'Great Britain and France stick to these two grand principles then we may gain our temporal requirements without endangering our good name or running counter to the ethical sense of mankind as a whole'. What was needed was a 'frank discussion between the British and French governments', in which it was 'essential' to get the French to 'play up to Arab nationalism with loyalty and purpose, and give definite instructions to their local officers to act accordingly'. Sir Mark also reminded his colleagues that France was 'a better neighbour than Turkey or Germany', and that (in a clear snipe at Hogarth) 'no petty consideration that France is getting more than her share should stand between Great Britain and the beating of the enemy'.[26]

In a further memorandum Sykes reiterated that the frank discussion between the allies should concentrate on 'the attitude they intend to adopt towards the populations inhabiting those regions'. First of all, the avenue that had been 'left open to annexation' had to be closed off. Annexation was 'contrary to the spirit of the time, and if at any moment the Russian extremists got hold of a copy they could make much capital against the whole entente'. France and Britain should come to an agreement 'not to annex but to administer the country in consonance with the ascertained wishes of the people and to include the blue and red areas in the areas A and B'. If France boldly came out 'with a recognition of [...] Arab nationality in Syria as a whole they would sacrifice nothing and gain much'. With respect to Palestine, France should agree that Britain was 'appointed trustee of the Powers for the administration' of the country. Naturally, this would 'be very objectionable to the French, but they really must be induced to settle matters up in their own interest'. They also should accept that Syria and the Lebanon became autonomous states, 'under French patronage, but under a national flag'. If the French would 'not agree to such a joint policy', then Britain should abide by the agreement, but then it would be for the French 'to make good – that is to say that if they cannot make a military effort compatible with their policy they should modify their policy'.

George Clerk was rather taken aback by the boldness of Sykes's proposals. He noted that 'the conclusion of this paper seems to be that, having got the Sykes–Picot Agreement [...] we are to propose scrapping the whole thing. "Since I am so early done for, I wonder what I was begun for!"' He also observed that a policy of no annexation would 'make Basra rather a problem'. Although some of Sir Mark's proposals were 'excellent', 'desirable', or 'possibly salutary' they would not 'enhance our popularity'. Sir Ronald Graham agreed that, 'with the possible exception of Basrah, it is preferable for us to "protect" or "influence" rather than formally annex. But it is a delicate matter to approach the French [...] on the subject and we are likely to be misunderstood.' He suggested that Georges-Picot, 'who is now over here and will go further in the direction proposed than any other Frenchman I know of, should be consulted'. Balfour, however, rejected Graham's suggestion. Until the War Cabinet had considered the matter there was 'little use in interesting Picot'.[27]

At Sykes's request, his memorandum was circulated to the War Cabinet, but was not put on the agenda. At the end of September 1917, Clayton nevertheless felt confident enough to reassure Lawrence – who had written a violently anti-French, anti-agreement letter to Sykes that Clayton thought inadvisable to send on[28] – that from all he had heard:

> The S–P agreement is in considerable disfavour in most quarters [...] The change in the Russian situation has wounded it severely and the general orientation of Allied policy towards 'no annexations', 'no indemnities, etc.', militates still further against many of its provisions. I am inclined, therefore, to think that it is moribund. At the same time we are pledged in honour to France to give it the 'coup-de-grace' and must for the present act loyally up to it, in so far as we can.
>
> The S–P agreement was made nearly two years ago. The world has moved at so vastly increased a pace since then that it is now as old and out of date as the battle of Waterloo or the death of Queen Anne. It is in fact dead and, if we wait quietly, this fact will soon be realised. It was never a very workable instrument and is now almost a lifeless monument. At the same time we cannot expect the French to see this yet, and we must therefore play up to it as loyally as possible until force of circumstance brings it home to them.[29]

A further impetus to the idea that the Sykes–Picot agreement was obsolete and could not stand was provided by a flurry of declarations and speeches on war aims by, respectively, the Bolsheviks, the Central Powers, Prime Minister Lloyd George and President Wilson in the last weeks of December 1917 and the first of January 1918. On 22 November 1917, Leon Trotsky, commissary of foreign affairs, had addressed a note to the ambassadors at Petrograd 'containing proposals for a truce and a democratic peace without annexation and without indemnities, based on the principle of the independence of nations, and of their right to determine the nature of their own development themselves'.[30] Peace negotiations with the Quadruple Alliance – Germany, Austria-Hungary, Bulgaria and Turkey – started at Brest-Litovsk one month later. During the opening session of the conference, the Russian delegation read out a declaration on the six principles on the basis of which the negotiations should be conducted. The third of these stated that national groups that had not been independent before the war should be 'guaranteed the possibility of deciding by referendum the question of belonging to one State or another, or enjoying their political independence', and the fourth that minorities should have the right to an autonomous administration. On behalf of the Quadruple Alliance, the Austrian minister for foreign affairs, Count Czernin, replied on 25 December. The Russian principles formed 'a discussible basis [...] for peace'. With respect to principles three and four, Czernin declared that the 'question of State allegiance of national groups which possess no State independence' should be solved by 'every State with its peoples independently in a constitutional manner', and that 'the right of minorities forms an essential component part of the constitutional right of peoples to self-determination'.[31]

Lloyd George and other members of the War Cabinet felt that Czernin's speech could not be left unanswered. At the end of December and during the first days of January there were a series of discussions on the contents of a British declaration on war aims. At a meeting of the War Cabinet on 3 January, the Prime Minister expressed his willingness 'to accept the application of the principle of self-determination to the captured German colonies [...] Mesopotamia [...] and [...] Palestine'.[32] In the final version of Lloyd George's speech, which he delivered on 5 January, there were several references to the right of self-determination. The most important was that a 'permanent peace' could only be secured through a territorial settlement 'based on the right of self-determination or the consent of the governed'. With respect to the non-Turkish parts of the Ottoman Empire, the Prime Minister scoffed at Czernin's third principle, which implied that 'the form of self-government [...] to be given to Arabs, Armenians, or Syrians is [...] entirely a matter for the Sublime Porte'. The British government for their part were agreed that 'Arabia, Armenia, Mesopotamia, Syria, and Palestine are [...] entitled to a recognition of their separate national conditions', but 'what the exact form of that recognition in each particular case should be need not here be discussed, beyond stating that it would be impossible to restore to their former sovereignty the territories to which I have already referred'. Lloyd George could not deny that much had recently 'been said about the arrangements we have entered into with our Allies on this and on other subjects', but that the conditions under which these had been made had changed, and he expressed his readiness 'to discuss them with our Allies'.[33]

Three days later it was President Wilson's turn to answer Czernin's challenge. In a speech to a joint session of the American Congress he stated that:

> What we demand in this war, therefore, is nothing peculiar to ourselves. It is that the world be made fit and safe to live in; and particularly that it be made safe for every peace-loving nation which, like our own, wishes to live its own life, determine its own institutions, be assured of justice and fair dealing by the other peoples of the world, as against force and selfish aggression.

Wilson subsequently enumerated the 14 points on which 'the program of the world's peace must be based'. The 12th of these was that 'the Turkish portions of the present Ottoman Empire should be assured a secure sovereignty, but the other nationalities which are now under Turkish rule should be assured an undoubted security of life and an absolutely unmolested opportunity of autonomous development'. The President did not explicitly invoke the principle of self-determination, but in a further speech to Congress on 11 February, Wilson observed that 'self-determination is not a mere phrase. It is an imperative principle of action which statesmen will henceforth ignore at their own peril.'[34]

Predictably, Sykes was the first to recognise the implications of these declarations and speeches for the Sykes–Picot agreement. He minuted on 16 February that 'the Anglo–French Agreement of 1916 in regard to Asia Minor should come up for reconsideration', and deplored that ministers were placed 'under the necessity of having to uphold agreements which are out of harmony with the expressed policy of the Entente and the United States, and which are based on a state of affairs which no longer exists'. Hardinge, also rather predictably, disagreed. He warned that 'to do this would only open the door to further discussion with the French and Italians, and unless it be necessary from a Parliamentary point of view I would deprecate such action.'[35]

Sykes wrote to Clayton on 3 March 1918 that 'ever since Kerensky's disappearance', he had regarded the agreements 'as completely worn out and that they should be scrapped. When they were made the United States of America was not in the war, Russia existed and the Italians had not been defeated.' He claimed that 'for the time at which it was made the Agreement was conceived on liberal lines', but admitted that 'the world has marched so far since then that the Agreement can only be considered a reactionary measure […] the stipulations in regard to the red and blue areas can only be regarded as quite contrary to the spirit of every ministerial speech that has been made for the last three months.' He enclosed a letter to Georges-Picot in the same vein, and observed that he 'should be very glad if you would talk this matter over with Monsieur Picot. I do not think he quite realises how far things have gone or how little interest outside a very narrow circle in France people take in the question of Syria and Palestine.'[36] Clayton was simply delighted. On 4 April he replied that Sykes's 'clear statement of the state of affairs in regard to this question' had helped him 'greatly'. He confessed that he had always felt this way, but until the receipt of Sir Mark's letter he 'had not been quite sure that H.M.G. had come to a definite decision in the matter'. He presumed that the French government had not yet been informed of it, as he saw 'no sign from Picot that he has any idea that such a policy is in contemplation and he still regards the agreements as his bible'. Clayton assured Sykes that he would 'take an early opportunity of discussing the whole question with him and sounding him on those lines, probably giving it as my own personal opinion that the agreements are out of date, reactionary, and only fit for the scrap heap'.[37] He reported this conversation to Balfour on 19 May 1918. He had intimated to Picot 'my opinion that the Sykes–Picot agreement, if not absolutely dead, is at any rate an impracticable instrument as it stands'. The latter had 'allowed that considerable revision was required in view of changes that had taken place in the situation since agreement was drawn up', but nevertheless considered that 'agreement holds, at any rate principle'.[38]

At the beginning of April, on the eve of Sir Percy Cox's visit to London, the India Office wrestled with the implications of 'the spread of the doctrine of "self-determination" under the powerful advocacy of the President of the United States' for the future status of Mesopotamia. It was not suggested that the government's policy 'should be modified in essence', as it was 'scarcely thinkable that we should suffer the results already achieved to be entirely thrown away', but one could not ignore 'the general change of outlook [...] which the war has brought about'. The India Office therefore proposed to ask Cox 'what elements in the population is it specially desirable to strengthen and encourage, with a view of ensuring that, if and when the moment for "self-determination" arises, there will be a decisive pronouncement in favour of continuing the British connection?' Sir Percy for his part was not disturbed by the principle that 'the peoples of the countries interested or affected should be allowed to determine their own form of government'. He assumed that 'if at the end of the war we find ourselves in a sufficiently strong position, and in effective administrative control, we should still hope to annex the Basrah Vilayet and exercise a veiled protectorate over the Baghdad Vilayet'. At the same time he recognised that 'the question of annexation has become exceedingly difficult *vis-à-vis* the President of the United States, who will presumably exercise the most potent influence at the Peace Conference. Our original proposals must consequently be regarded as a counsel of perfection, and we must be prepared to accept something less.' A policy of an 'Arab façade' should offer 'no insurmountable difficulties'.

Sykes was shocked by Cox's adaptation of the principle of self-determination to the Mesopotamian situation. He angrily noted:

> We should come to a clear decision as to what is the basis of our Mesopotamian policy. Is it to be camouflaged Imperialism or is it a policy of development with Democratic and World objectives? I have always objected to the expression Arab Façade as typifying an out-of-date point of view.

He urged the Eastern Committee not to take Egypt or India as models, as in 'both places our basis of occupation is Imperialistic, and in both places we are going to be confronted with revolutionary democratic movements which will probably have the support of the future governments of this country when the re-action comes after the war'. These difficulties could only be avoided 'if our policy is logical and public and does not conceal a second policy of hidden annexation and ascendancy'.[39] Sir Mark, however, got nowhere at the meeting of the Eastern Committee where the question was discussed in his presence and Cox's on 24 April 1918. Although Curzon agreed that British policy 'might have to be adapted to certain formulae, such as that of "self-determination," increasingly used as a watchword since President Wilson's entry into the war', that was as far as he was prepared to go. In Mesopotamia 'we should construct a State with an "Arab Façade", ruled and administered under British guidance', and where Basra was concerned, 'it might be desirable to keep Basra town and district entirely in British hands'. Balfour believed that:

> President Wilson did not seriously mean to apply his formula outside Europe. He meant that no 'civilised' communities should remain under the heel of other 'civilised' communities: as to politically inarticulate peoples, he would probably not say more than that their true interests should prevail as against exploitation by conquerors. If so, an Arab State under British protection would satisfy him (and with him the American public, though less enlightened), if it were shown that the Arabs could not stand alone. Doubtless the Arabs, if offered the choice, would choose what we wished.

He therefore thought it 'unlikely that President Wilson would oppose the policy suggested'. After Curzon had expressed the hope that 'should the word "annexation" appear too inauspicious (as suggested by Sir Mark Sykes) [...] a terminological variant, such as "perpetual lease," or "enclave," might be found, both to safeguard the reality which we must not abandon, and to save the appearances which the occasion might require', the Eastern Committee 'approved Sir P. Cox's Memorandum, and desired him to proceed with the development of the administration in Mesopotamia on the lines that had been laid down'.[40]

During their conference at the beginning of July 1918 (see also Chapter 8, sections 'Syria: Syrian, French and Hashemite Ambitions' and 'Palestine: Syrian, Zionist and Hashemite Ambitions'), Sykes and Picot also discussed the situation with respect to the agreement. Sykes repeated once more his argument that it 'had been profoundly affected by the exit of Russia, the entrance of the United States and the accentuation of the Democratic nature of allied War Aims in general'. Picot countered by explaining that 'the Agreement could not be abolished, as such an act would raise violent opposition and ill feeling among the Colonials in France, and would give great strength to the financial pro-Turkish elements both of which would be most fatal developments, and helpful to the enemy'. After 'some discussion and careful examination', they drew up two papers. The first of these was a proposal for a joint declaration to the King of the Hijaz (see Chapter 8, section 'Syria: Syrian, French and Hashemite Ambitions'). The second, paper B, concerned a statement of Anglo–French war aims in the Middle East:

1. In the opinion of the governments of Great Britain and France there can be no prospect of a permanent and lasting peace in the Middle East so long as non-Ottoman nationalities, now subject to Ottoman rule, or inhabiting areas hitherto subject to Ottoman rule now occupied by the Allied forces, have no adequate guarantee of social, material, and political security.
2. That the only guarantee of permanent improvement is to be found in the securing of self-government to the inhabitants of such areas.
3. That in view of the condition of these areas arising from misgovernment, devastation, and massacre, it is the opinion of the two Powers, that a period of tutelage must supervene before the inhabitants of the areas are capable of complete self-government, and in a position to maintain their independence.
4. That the Powers exercising such tutelage should exercise it on the sanction of the free nations of the world, and with the consent of the inhabitants of the areas concerned.[41]

Paper B was coolly received in the Foreign Office. Sir Eric Drummond doubted 'very much the wisdom of B. I do not think we ought to bind ourselves definitely to the principles laid down in paragraphs 3 and 4', and Hardinge was 'very doubtful as to the value of such declarations. We have already made several […] and they may, as has often happened in the past, prove inconvenient in the future.'[42]

Paper B was to be discussed at the Eastern Committee's meeting of 15 July, but on Sykes's request the discussion was adjourned. At the next meeting, discussion was again postponed at his request, this time, as it turned out, for good.[43] The idea that it was desirable to publish an Anglo–French declaration on war aims in the Middle East had, however, set. On 6 August, Cecil told the Italian ambassador that 'there was considerable anxiety in Arab circles lest we should be going to annex districts which were populated by Arabs, and it was partly to allay these anxieties that we were considering whether we should formally propose to the French government some declaration of this kind'.[44] At the Eastern Committee's meeting of 8 August, Cecil moreover emphasised that the point of such a declaration 'was to ensure beforehand that the French if and when we entered Syria, should not make use of our military forces in order to carry out a policy which was at variance with our general engagements'.[45]

The next day, Hogarth submitted a memorandum on the Arab question to the Foreign Office in which he again pressed home the point that:

> The belief, amounting, since Bolshevik revelations, to certainty, that we have pledged great part of Syria to France, for her occupation or her exclusive influence, is the greatest stumbling-block we have to encounter [...] Outside a small denationalised minority, which however is more articulate than the majority, the feeling of all classes of Syrians against entry into the French colonial sphere is of the strongest and most irreconcilable sort.[46]

Hogarth's memorandum led to an interview with Lord Robert on 17 August. The next day, Hogarth submitted the draft of an Anglo–French declaration to the King of the Hijaz, as an alternative to the one proposed by Sykes and Picot. Cecil heavily edited Hogarth's draft, which resulted in the following text:

> Great Britain and France undertake severally and jointly to promote and assist the establishment of native governments and administrations in all parts of the Arab-speaking areas of Arabia, Syria, Jazirah and Upper Iraq, and to recognise them as effectively established. Further, they pledge themselves, after the areas have been liberated from the Turks, not to annex any part of them, provided they be not invited expressly to do so by the majority of the inhabitants or by the native government of any of such areas, unless the native governments should become unable or unwilling to prevent annexation, protection, or occupation by any other foreign power.

George Lloyd was also invited to give his views on a joint Anglo–French declaration. He observed that it was 'generally agreed that in view of what has occurred since', the Sykes–Picot agreement was 'a source of embarrassment at the moment', but rather doubted the wisdom of making yet another declaration, especially considering that 'America may well be in a position to disturb and perhaps break any agreements we now make, and if this occurred we should suffer serious damage in regard to Eastern confidence in our undertakings'. He therefore advised that 'fresh declarations made by ourselves and France to the Arabs or made between France and ourselves about the Arabs are undesirable if they can by any means be avoided'. However, in case it was decided that a declaration could not be avoided, then it should be 'clearly understood that it is not made as a rider or an addendum to the Sykes–Picot agreement, but in definite substitution of it and of all those agreements with Italy or others that resulted from it'. Cecil quite agreed, but lamented 'how are we to mitigate or abolish the S.P. agreement? It is I fear impossible to induce the French to agree to its abrogation.'[47]

On 4 September 1918, the French Embassy reminded the Foreign Office of its demarche of 1 August on the administration of occupied enemy territory in the French sphere of influence (see Chapter 8, section 'French Participation in the Administration of Palestine'). Sykes minuted that the best thing was to ask Georges-Picot 'to come over here and put the matter on a settled basis'. He still adhered to his 'original idea that we should do two things together. (A) In return for arrangements as to French position west of Syria being occupied by us, get (B) French statement as to the policy they would follow'.[48] A few days later, Sykes received a letter from Picot complaining that 'the embassy has several times demanded a reply to its demarches on the administration of the territories in our zone; but failed to get one', and warning that in France 'people do not understand this silence at all; malicious spirits see hidden intentions, others are worried. As far as I am concerned, I cannot return before the question is settled and the prolongation of my stay threatens every day to lead to a scandal.'

In his reply, Sir Mark almost pleaded with Picot that France should relent and at last acknowledge 'the spirit of the age'. If French colonialists insisted on 'supporting an annexationist policy', then 'disaster alone' could ensue. France really had no other option than 'to come out with a declaration supporting Syrian and Lebanese independence on national lines. To say that France is ready to give all assistance and protection to Syria, but does not desire to impose institutions on the country, nor to insist on an unsolicited occupation thereof after the war.' Sykes threatened that even he, France's last champion in England, was thinking of giving up on her, and ended his letter on a note of exasperation:

> My point is this, getting France to make a concession in policy is like getting blood out of a stone. I don't ask you to modify the area of your interest, but the extent of it [...] Just as Syrians ask me for a single proof that France means to do other than back minorities, annex Blue Syria, and paralyse the hinterland, so British people ask me for a single proof that Syria is going to be developed on other than ordinary French colonial lines, and any real indication that anything else is to be expected.[49]

The Eastern Committee and the Foreign Office Middle East Department

Cecil chafed under the Eastern Committee's dominant position in the formulation of Middle East policy. He very much resented the Committee's, and especially its chairman's, constant meddling in matters he firmly believed to be the preserve of the Foreign Office. The day-to-day execution of Middle East policy should be in the hands of his department. The Eastern Committee should limit itself to discussing matters of high policy and to arbitrate and coordinate when the policies pursued by the departments concerned – the India Office, the War Office, the Foreign Office and, occasionally, the Treasury – threatened to come into conflict. In the middle of July 1918, Cecil's chances to push through this vision appeared to be greatly increased by his appointment as assistant secretary of state for foreign affairs – a constitutional novelty – with special responsibility for, among other subjects, the Middle East (he continued as parliamentary under-secretary for foreign affairs).

From a memorandum Montagu had submitted on 5 July, it appeared that he thought on the same lines as Cecil. He was sure that action had 'been delayed by the necessity for awaiting decisions of the Eastern Committee'. The committee 'should not attempt actual executive action, but [...] should be a Cabinet Committee, discussing, on behalf of the Cabinet, Cabinet matters, questions of policy, leaving details of the conduct of the policy to the Departments concerned'. Montagu also suggested the establishment of a sub-committee of three, 'consisting of an Under-Secretary of State or an Assistant Under-Secretary of State from the Foreign Office and from the India Office, with the Director of Military Intelligence from the War Office'. This sub-committee would then have the duty 'to thresh out everything, and to give decisions except on matters of high policy or of such great importance as should go before the Ministers of the Committee for decision'.

Sir Henry Wilson also chimed in. The CIGS claimed that 'Mr Montagu's statement that the present organisation inevitably leads to action being frequently delayed cannot be disputed'. Action was not only 'delayed owing to the necessity of obtaining the sanction of the Committee to every step taken in the execution of policy already laid down by the Committee', but also 'a ruling as to important questions of policy has on several occasions been postponed from one meeting to another owing to the fact that the

Committee is overburdened with executive action'. The War Office therefore were 'in general accord' with the changes 'of great importance' suggested by Montagu.

Cecil naturally could not but agree. He noted on 20 July that 'for executive purposes the Eastern Committee is not a convenient instrument. It necessarily meets comparatively seldom, and even so is a great burden on the time of the very busy men who constitute the Committee.' Executive matters therefore should be dealt with, 'as far as possible [...] either by the individual departments immediately concerned or by informal consultations between two or more departments, and I trust that this system will be increasingly adopted in the future'. Only in important matters 'the Chairman of the Committee should be consulted just as the Prime Minister is, or ought to be'.

The Foreign Office, however, did not speak with one voice. On 17 July the department had circulated its own note on the subject, which was far less critical of the Eastern Committee. It admitted that 'action in important matters meets occasionally with some delay', and agreed that 'a considerable number of questions of secondary importance relating to the situation in the East which are now submitted to the Committee are capable of interdepartmental adjustment without recourse to the Committee', but on the whole it could 'hardly be denied that the Eastern Committee in its present form has proved a very useful branch of the War Cabinet', and it was 'doubtful whether the conduct of affairs now under the control of the Committee would either in the present or the future be improved by any material change in its present form of organisation'. Ten days later, Balfour sided with the department. He, too, thought that the critics of the Eastern Committee 'exaggerate its shortcomings'. Balfour moreover completely turned around Montagu's suggestion to set up a small sub-committee that would deal with day-to-day affairs. Instead of the sub-committee deciding which matters should be sent up to the Eastern Committee, it should be Curzon as chairman deciding which questions could be handled by the sub-committee.

Curzon therefore had an easy time in parrying the three-pronged attack by Montagu, Wilson and Cecil. In a memorandum, dated 1 August, he declared that he was not 'aware of any question of importance, the decision of which has been delayed by the procedure or constitution of the Committee'. Certainly there had been delays, 'as, for instance, the discussion of the present subject', but these had been caused not by the Committee, 'but by the slowness of the departments in submitting their views'. Curzon added that:

> In practice the departmental devolution that is recommended in some of these papers already exists [...] Action is taken upon the great majority of the telegrams that come in both to Foreign Office, India Office, and War Office, without any reference to the Committee (or, I may add, to the Chairman) at all. The Departments have found no difficulty in discriminating between what I may call departmental cases and Committee cases.

He also saw 'no reason for the constitution of a Sub-Committee, with powers either of decision or action'. He could only 'concur in Mr Balfour's view that we are dealing not unsuccessfully with a complex situation, and that for the present no substantial changes are required'.[50]

Curzon was not allowed to savour his moment of triumph for very long. He had 'only just completed [his] note on Montagu's proposals' when he received a letter from Cecil in which the latter announced his intention, 'unless you see some objection', to ask 'Oliphant, Shuckburgh, and Macdonogh to meet frequently, so that all routine matters arising out of the Persian and Middle East telegrams and involving more than one of the offices can be rapidly disposed of without interdepartmental correspondence'. These officials would meet in Cecil's room 'two or three times a week, or oftener if necessary, and then I could see that they did not dispose of any really important matter without consulting you, or if necessary the Eastern Committee'. Curzon replied right away. He was shocked that Cecil 'without waiting for any decision' contemplated setting up this committee, and viewed this move 'with considerable suspicion'. The committee would 'almost certainly develop into a little _imperium_ in imperio, whose tendency will be to act on his own account, and to usurp the powers of the Eastern Committee'. Curzon therefore hoped that 'after this explanation [...] you will not think it necessary to pursue the idea'. Lord Robert hastily assured Curzon the same day that 'of course no meeting of the kind to which you object shall take place, pending a discussion of the whole matter by the Eastern Committee'.[51]

The discussion on the Eastern Committee and its functions finally took place on 13 August 1918. Montagu, Cecil and Curzon extensively rehearsed their arguments. At the end of the discussion, Curzon found it necessary to warn that, if the Eastern Committee would overrule him and approve the establishment of 'a formal sub-committee', then he would have 'to ask to be relieved of his present duties'. General Smuts came to his rescue. He had been 'much impressed with the case made out by the Chairman, who had, it was universally admitted exceptional qualifications for his present position as President of their Committee. It would be a very serious matter to set up a smaller body which might encroach upon the functions of the Committee.' He moreover opined that the Eastern Committee was not free to decide this matter; 'if any considerable change were contemplated he thought the matter would have to go before the Cabinet'.[52]

Even though Curzon visited Hankey one week later 'to explain to me his difficulties with Montagu and Lord R. Cecil at the Eastern Committee',[53] this was more or less where the affair ended, also because Montagu decided not to pursue the matter any further. As he explained in a letter to Cecil, he had found that 'you, and I noticed at dinner Eric [Sir Eric Drummond; R.H.L.], are not a little inclined to consider my desire to get a better form of administration in Eastern matters as being personal in their application to Lord Curzon'. This was 'so inaccurate and has caused me such deep concern, that I propose to abandon the matter and to acquiesce, rather than to be further misunderstood [...] I therefore propose to drop the subject and shall inform Lord Curzon of this decision when he returns to London.'[54]

In August 1918, Cecil was also busy setting up a department within the Foreign Office that would deal with the Middle East, Egypt and Persia. Almost three years previously, Sykes had already urged upon him the establishment of such a department (see Chapter 4, section 'The Arab Bureau'), and at the end of July Lord Robert had requested Sir Mark to draw up 'a rough draft of the scheme of organisation for Middle Eastern affairs'.[55] In a note he sent to Hardinge one month later, Cecil explained how he envisaged the new department. He laid particular stress on the fact that the problems Britain confronted in Egypt, Arabia, Palestine and Mesopotamia were 'mainly administrative and not diplomatic [...] they should be dealt with by a special Department of the Office, which should be largely staffed by persons with administrative experience'.[56]

Hardinge supported the idea that a Middle East Department should be established as soon as possible, but disagreed with Cecil on who should be the under-secretary in charge of it. Lord Robert had first considered Sir Arthur Hirtzel, but had reached the conclusion, so he explained to Balfour, that Hirtzel 'for various reasons, including your dislike of I.O. officials [...] would not do'. He had subsequently opted for Crowe.[57] Hardinge agreed that

Hirtzel was 'not at all suitable', but according to him Crowe would not do either, because the latter had neither Middle Eastern expertise nor experience. He proposed Graham instead. The latter had spent many years in Egypt, and was 'the soul of loyalty and would, I am convinced, make the new department a success'.[58] Lord Robert, however, held on to Crowe. He informed Hardinge the next day that he had telegraphed to Balfour, who was away on holiday, on the subject 'telling him what you have suggested and explaining quite definitely my view that I would rather not attempt the scheme at all unless I am permitted to have in charge of the department someone with whom I can work satisfactorily'.[59] Balfour was rather puzzled by Cecil's attitude. He had 'no reason to question your estimate of Crowe – you have seen more of his work than I have. But surely you underestimate Graham? He has industry, good sense, and [...] ability; and though I think Crowe is probably the cleverer man is it so clear that he has the sounder judgment?' Balfour also pointed out that 'so far as actual experience is concerned, Graham is the better man'.[60]

In a long reply written the next day, Lord Robert set out his 'case against Graham'. When Cecil had discussed the matter with him, Graham had been 'against the whole proposal', and he was still 'almost passionately anxious to retain Egypt as part of the ordinary Foreign Office organisation'. Graham really had the 'diplomatic mind' and would 'never be a good administrative official'. He added for good measure that Graham had 'been quite useless to me in Middle Eastern affairs during Hardinge's absence. Indeed he really knows less about them than I do.' What it all amounted to was that Graham did 'not suit [him] as a subordinate', while with Crowe it was the opposite. The 'Hardinge–Graham mind' was no use to him, 'whereas Crowe's suits me exactly'. Cecil observed in conclusion that 'as you have asked me to do this work I do very earnestly beg that I may be allowed to have the assistance which I believe to be essential to me'.[61] Balfour gave in. On 28 August, he informed Drummond that he had telegraphed to Cecil that Crowe should be appointed.[62] Three days later, Cecil reported to Balfour that 'the Crowe incident is closed. I gather the appointment has given very general satisfaction in the Office.'[63]

None of the protagonists in the conflict had thought of making the acting adviser on Arabian and Palestine affairs head of the new Middle East Department. During the greater part of the month of August, Sykes had been away from the Foreign Office. He had stayed for a few weeks at his home at Sledmere to recuperate. When he returned and was confronted with the creation of this new department for which he had drafted a first outline but of which Crowe was in charge, he lodged a feeble protest with Lord Robert. He thought it 'only right that I should point out that under this arrangement I drop down in the scale. I advised Lord Hardinge who passed the stuff on to the Secretary of State. Under the present arrangement I advise Sir Eyre Crowe who advises Lord Hardinge, and when the stuff comes back it will have to go back to Sir Eyre Crowe,'[64] but left it at that.

Allenby's Offensive and the Capture of Damascus

On the morning of 19 September 1918, the EEF opened attack on the Turkish lines in what became known as the battle of Megiddo. As Archibald Wavell, who served on the staff of Allenby's XX Corps, noted in his book on the Palestine campaigns, Allenby 'had massed on a front of some fifteen miles […] 35,000 infantry, 9,000 cavalry and 383 guns. On the same front, the unconscious Turk had only 8,000 infantry with 130 guns […] The battle was practically over before a shot was fired'.[65] The Turkish defeat was complete by 21 September. Five days later, Allenby ordered the advance on Damascus.

The occupation of Damascus offered another opportunity to get the French to accept that changes in circumstances prevented the execution of the Sykes–Picot agreement, this time by creating facts on the ground. If an Arab administration had been established in area 'A' before French officials and soldiers arrived, then France would have no other option but to accept the fait accompli, and to give up her imperialistic designs. On 23 September, Ormsby Gore urged Sykes that Faysal, whose force operated on the right flank of Allenby's army, should be proclaimed 'Emir in the event of our capturing Damascus. We should recognise Arab government there at once.'[66] A first step was to recognise the belligerent status of Faysal's troops. On 24 September, the Director of Military Intelligence was informed that the Foreign Office had wired to Lord Derby – Bertie's successor at the Paris embassy – that 'the time has come for formally recognising the belligerent status of the friendly Arabs operating in the Palestine–Syrian theatre against the Turks'. In a subsequent letter four days later, the Foreign Office went one step further by proclaiming that:

> In pursuance of the general policy approved by His Majesty's Government, and in accordance more particularly with the engagements into which they have entered with the King of Hedjaz, the authority of the friendly and allied

Arabs should be formally recognised in any part of the Areas A and B, as defined in the Anglo–French agreement of 1916, where it may be found established, or can be established, as a result of the military operations now in progress.

This implied that these territories should be treated as 'allied territory enjoying the status of an independent state, or confederation of states, of friendly Arabs which has in consequence of its military successes and the organisation of a government (or governments) established its independence of Turkey'. The Foreign Office also reminded the Director of Military Intelligence that:

If and where the Arab authorities request the assistance or advice of European functionaries, we are bound under the Anglo–French agreement to let these be French in Area A. It is important from this point of view that the military administration should be restricted to such functions as can properly be described as military, so as to give rise to no inconvenient claim to the employment of French civilians where unnecessary. It is equally important to keep our procedure in that part of Area B, which lies East of the Dead Sea and of the Jordan-Valley, on the same lines, so as not to give the French the pretext for any larger demands in Area A.[67]

Allenby could not have agreed more. On the day he had ordered the advance on Damascus, he also issued a 'Special instruction' to the Australian Mounted Division, which spearheaded his offensive, that 'while operating against the enemy about Damascus care will be taken to avoid entering the town if possible. Unless forced to do so for tactical reasons, no troops are to enter Damascus.'[68] Damascus should not surrender to British troops, but to Faysal's Northern Arab Army. Tactical reasons, however, forced the Australian Mounted Division's hands. The attempt 'to pass around Damascus' in pursuit of the retreating Turkish army had to be abandoned because 'the terrain was too rugged'.[69] This had the result that in the early morning of 1 October 1918, the 10th regiment Australian Light Horse entered Damascus on its way to Homs. According to Cyril Falls, the official historian of the campaign:

Once in the streets the horsemen were compelled to pull up to a walk, for they found themselves surrounded by a population gone mad with joy [...]

Major Olden dismounted for a few minutes at the Serai or Town Hall, where he found sitting a committee, under Mohammed Said [Sa'id al-Jazairi; R.H.L.], a descendant of Abd el Kader, the famous Algerian opponent of the French, who declared that he had been installed by Jemal Pasha as Governor the previous afternoon, and formally surrendered the city to him.[70]

Lawrence arrived in Damascus around 9:00 a.m. That same day he sent a telegram to General Headquarters in which he reported his reception 'amid scenes of extraordinary enthusiasm on the part of the local people. The streets were nearly impassable with the crowds, who yelled themselves hoarse, danced, cut themselves with swords and daggers and fired volleys into the air.' He and his companions had been 'cheered by name, covered with flowers, kissed indefinitely, and splashed with attar of roses from the house-tops'. Lawrence also mentioned that Shukri al Ayubi, a local supporter of Faysal, had been installed as military governor, but failed to mention that he had dismissed the Arab administration appointed by Djemal Pasha that had surrendered Damascus to the British troops.[71] Only one week later, the Foreign Office learned from Clayton that he had:

> Ascertained [that] a certain Ammed Sayed and Abd Elara Kader el Jezari [Abd al-Qadir, the brother of Sa'id al-Jazairi; R.H.L.] attempted to usurp civil control in Damascus during Turkish withdrawal on September 30th but were dismissed by Emir Feisal's representative and Abd el Kader imprisoned on October 2nd after his attempt to inflame local Moslem opinion against the Christian and Shereffian occupation which had led to rioting by Moors and Druses in Damascus.

Clayton apologised that he had not reported this incident sooner, but he 'did not consider it advisable to telegraph vague rumours and unsubstantiated reports'.[72]

Allenby wired to the War Office on 6 October that he had visited Damascus three days before, and that 'Sharif Feisal made his entry amid the acclamation of the inhabitants same day'. During an interview he had informed the Emir that he 'was prepared to recognise the Arab administration of occupied territory East of the Jordan from Damascus to Maan inclusive as a military administration under my supreme control' (see also Map 9.1). He had further told Faysal that he would 'appoint two liaison officers, between me and the Arab Administration, one of whom would be British and the other French and that these two officers would communicate with me through my Chief Political Officer'.⁷³ Allenby did not mention that Faysal had 'objected very strongly' to this arrangement, 'as he knew nothing of France in the matter', and that he had felt it necessary to remind Faysal that the latter was under his command and had to obey orders. Faysal had finally 'accepted this decision and left with his entourage'.⁷⁴

On 7 October, Allenby did report that trouble had arisen with respect to Beirut. The French political officer Captain Coulondre had officially protested to Faysal about the latter hurriedly sending Arab troops to occupy that city. Faysal had claimed that he had sent these troops 'for purely military reasons to prevent disturbance', and had 'indignantly denied charge of any ulterior motive and bad faith'. Allenby, however, had no hesitation in pointing out that ulterior motives were involved. The Arab nationalists were intent on exploiting the formula for the second type of areas distinguished in the Declaration to the Seven, which referred to 'areas emancipated from Turkish control by the action of the Arabs themselves during the present war', where Britain recognised 'the complete and sovereign independence of the Arabs inhabiting these areas'. This clause applied to the past. It covered the areas that had been liberated since the beginning of Husayn's revolt. Syria was covered by the fourth type of areas that had been distinguished, those that 'were still under Turkish control', and in respect to which the British government had only expressed their wish and desire that 'the oppressed peoples of these areas should obtain their freedom and independence' (see Chapter 8, section 'Syria: Syrian, French and Hashemite Ambitions'). According to Allenby, the Arab nationalists interpreted the formula adopted for the second type of area as a promise that Britain would recognise the complete and sovereign independence of all areas liberated by the Arabs themselves.⁷⁵ This was the reasoning behind Faysal's rush to Beirut.

After Faysal's troops had reached Beirut, Shukri al-Ayubi had been installed as governor, and the Sherifian flag hoisted. This was unacceptable to Allenby. Beirut was in the blue area and he therefore appointed a French military governor, while Faysal was ordered to withdraw his forces. Faysal initially refused to do so. On 11 October, Clayton wrote to Wingate that he must 'go to Damascus and give Faisal a talking to, as he is getting rather out of hand'. Faysal should understand that he would 'surely prejudice his case before the Peace Conference if he tries to grab'. It would be far better if the latter 'should devote his energies to forming a sound and reliable administration in Damascus and the "A" and "B" areas, so that he may have something tangible to show at the Peace Conference'.[76]

Clayton had his talk with Faysal on 14 October. The latter had tendered his resignation the day before, in protest against the lowering of the Arab flag at Beirut, but had been persuaded to postpone it.[77] Faysal explained to Clayton that he regarded himself as 'a guardian who has pledged his honour to secure the freedom and independence of the Arab people of Syria', and emphasised that 'the people of Beirut and other coastal towns took the first possible opportunity of declaring for Arab government'. He nevertheless acquiesced in Shukri's removal, and when he was informed that 'no flags will be flown in Beirut', he was also 'satisfied regarding the lowering of the Arab flag' there.[78] In a further telegram, Clayton took the opportunity to drive home once more that 'the crux of the situation' still was the 'necessity for definitive declaration of policy by the French and British governments to the effect that there will be no question of annexation whether open or veiled in any part of Syria. Arabs will not wish to accept French assistance without this declaration.'[79] Allenby fully agreed. He warned the War Office that 'the general feeling of uneasiness on the parts of the Arabs can only be dispelled by public declaration of policy by the French and British governments'.[80] Both Clayton and Allenby were not aware that, as Crowe minuted on Clayton's telegram, 'the public declaration of policy desired by General Clayton is being prepared in consultation with the French'.[81]

The Foreign Office's Window of Opportunity and the Joint Declaration

Four days after the launch of Allenby's offensive, Balfour, who substituted for Cecil as the latter was away on holiday, received Paul Cambon. The French ambassador reminded the foreign secretary that Syria was 'by the Sykes–Picot Agreement, within the French sphere of influence, and it was extremely important from the French point of view that this fact should not be lost sight of in any arrangements that General Allenby, as Commander-in-Chief, might make for the administration of the country'. Subsequently, they had 'a conversation of considerable length, in which Sir Mark Sykes, the joint author of the Sykes–Picot Agreement took a part'. In the end, completely bypassing the Eastern Committee, Balfour:

> Drafted for M. Cambon's guidance the following statement of policy, which seemed to me to be required by the letter and spirit of the Agreement:–
> Private.
> The British government adhere to their declared policy with regard to Syria: namely that, if it should fall into the sphere of interest of any European Power, that Power should be France. They also think that this policy should be made perfectly clear both in France and elsewhere.
> The exact course which should be followed by the two governments in case General Allenby takes his forces into Syria should be immediately discussed in Paris or London. But it is understood that in any event, wherever officers are required to carry out civilian duties, these officers should (unless the French government express an opinion to the contrary) be French and not English; without prejudice of course to the supreme authority of the Commander-in-Chief while the country is in military occupation.

Balfour in one stroke regained for the Foreign Office the initiative in formulating British policy towards the Middle East. He also confirmed the policy that Cecil and Sykes had been advocating for months that Britain should without reserve recognise the French claims in Syria and the Lebanon that flowed from the Sykes–Picot agreement, but which had time and again been thwarted by the Eastern Committee. For the moment, however, the Eastern Committee remained unaware of Balfour's initiative. The day after the interview, the Foreign Office did inform the Director of Military Intelligence that Balfour had telegraphed to Derby that 'if General Allenby advances to Damascus it would be most desirable that in conformity with the Anglo–French Agreement of 1916 he should if possible work through an Arab Administration by means of French liaison'. It also suggested that 'this telegram should be repeated to Sir E. Allenby for his guidance'.[82] It was only at the Eastern Committee's meeting of 26 September that Balfour related that he had drawn up 'a brief statement of policy', which 'had been cabled the same evening to our Ambassador in Paris'. He assured the committee that copies of his note would be circulated, but suggested that 'the further discussion of the subject should be postponed until members were in possession of these papers'. Curzon was quite taken aback. He declared that 'he regarded the question as one of the utmost importance. The Foreign Office appeared now to be relying upon the Sykes–Picot Agreement from which the Committee had hitherto been doing their best to escape.'[83]

On 27 September, on the eve of Georges-Picot's visit to London (see section 'Mitigating or Abolishing the Sykes–Picot Agreement', above), Cambon called upon Cecil. The ambassador explained that 'in the existing state of things it would scarcely do to leave the negotiations in the hands of Sir Mark Sykes and M. Picot exclusively', and proposed that 'M. Picot might be accompanied by somebody from the French Embassy, and Sir Mark by someone from this office'. Cecil agreed that 'it was desirable that the negotiations should be rather more formal than they had been', and suggested that Cambon and he should both preside.[84]

The Anglo–French conference took place on 30 September. On the proposition of Lord Robert, and 'subject to the confirmation of the British and French governments', it was agreed that:

> In the areas of special French interest, as described in the Anglo–French Agreement of 1916, which are or may be occupied by the Allied forces of the Egyptian expeditionary force, the Commander-in-Chief will recognise the representative of the French government as his Chief Political Adviser. The functions of the Chief Political Adviser will be as follows:
>
> 1. Subject to the supreme authority of the Commander-in-Chief, the Chief Political Adviser will act as sole intermediary on political and administrative questions between the Commander-in-Chief and any Arab government or governments, permanent or provisional, which may be set up in Area 'A', and recognised under the terms of clause 1 of the Agreement of 1916.
> 2. At the request of the Commander-in-chief, and subject to his supreme authority, the Chief Political Adviser will be charged by the Commander-in-Chief with the establishment of such provisional administration in the towns of the Syrian littoral situated in the blue area, and in the blue area in general.
> 3. Subject to the approval of the Commander-in-Chief, the Chief Political Adviser will provide […] Such European advisory staff and assistants as the Arab government or governments set up in Area 'A' may require under clause 1 of the Anglo–French Agreement of 1916 […] Such personnel as may be necessary for civil duties in the littoral towns or other parts of the blue area.

The conference also decided that the 'above arrangement shall remain in force until such time as the military situation justifies reconsideration of the question of civil administration and political relations', and to recommend to their respective governments that they:

Take an early opportunity to issue a declaration, or declarations, defining their attitude towards the Arab territories liberated from Turkish rule. Such a declaration should make it clear that neither government has any intention of annexing any part of the Arab territories, but that, in accordance with the provisions of the Anglo–French Agreement of 1916, both are determined to recognise and uphold an independent Arab State, or confederation of States, and with this view to lend their assistance in order to secure the effective administration of those territories under the authority of the native rulers and peoples.[85]

The policy urged by Sykes and Cecil of faithfully adhering to the terms of the Sykes–Picot agreement, but at the same time preventing the French from realising their imperialistic plans by binding them through a joint declaration to a policy of no annexation and Arab independence, seemed finally to have been vindicated. When the Foreign Office received Allenby's telegram to the War Office of 30 September, in which he set out his proposed administrative arrangements with respect to the blue area and the areas 'A' and 'B' – appointing 'French Military officers wherever administration may be necessary in the French "Blue" area', and in area 'A' recognising the local Arab administration and appointing a 'French liaison officer as required' – Crowe noted with satisfaction that this was 'practically what we suggested'.[86] A further indication that things at last were going the Foreign Office's way was that the French government concurred in recognising 'the belligerent status of the Arab forces fighting as auxiliaries of the Allies against the common enemy in Palestine and Syria',[87] but Cecil still had to brave the storm in the Eastern Committee.

The committee met on 3 October to discuss the agreement. Curzon immediately opened the attack. The Eastern Committee 'had for a long time been proceeding on the hypothesis that this Anglo–French Agreement of 1916 was out of date and unscientific, and that it was desirable to get rid of it', but he feared that the committee was 'now presented with something like a *fait accompli* in Syria', and that this 'new provisional agreement seemed to fix even more firmly on our shoulders the agreement of 1916, the terms of which he, for one, deplored'. Montagu's first concern was the future status of Baghdad and Basra. He wished to know whether the proposed declaration announcing that 'neither Great Britain nor France has any intention of annexing any part of the Arab territories' also applied to these vilayets. Cecil stated that it 'undoubtedly' did, and that 'the paragraph alluded to by Mr Montagu was specially inserted at our instance, and not very willingly agreed to by the French'. As far as Basra was concerned, he reassuringly added that 'in practice it would always be possible for us to control it, whether we annexed it or established a protectorate'. However, Montagu was not in search of reassurance; on the contrary, he 'urged very strongly that the Committee should accept' the proposed declaration, but he did so for the same disingenuous reason that had previously led Cox to embrace self-determination (see section 'Mitigating or Abolishing the Sykes–Picot Agreement', above). According to Montagu, and Smuts concurred, Britain 'stood to lose nothing by pledging itself not to use the word "annexation". We could maintain the Arab façade and yet ensure British paramountcy.'

Lord Robert informed the committee that the duration of the military administration had been another issue that had involved hard bargaining. General Thwaites, Macdonogh's successor as DMI, explained that the French had been anxious to have in writing that this 'should only last up to the cessation of hostilities', but the War Office had insisted that 'a civil administration should not be established until the cessation of military occupation'. The clause on the subject inserted in the agreement implied that the 'matter, therefore, had been left over without decision'.

Cecil laid great stress on the provisional nature of the agreement, that it 'did not in any way pledge us at the Peace Conference', but he had to admit that 'it would probably be desirable to call the attention of the French government to this fact'. He also promised to suggest to the French government that 'the Agreement of 1916 ought now to be revised'. He further observed that it 'was most important that the French should not be allowed to annex any portion of the blue area', considering that the British 'wished to secure the cooperation of the Americans in settling the future of the occupied territories and in order to do this we must declare against annexation'. What it all boiled down to regarding the proposed joint declaration was that there should be 'no annexation in the red and blue areas, and that in "A" and "B" there should be an independent Arab administration with European advisers'. In the end it was agreed that 'every possible endeavour should be made to induce the French government, in view of the changed circumstances, since the French–Syrian Agreement was signed, viz., the elimination of Russian and the extravagance of Italian claims, to consent to its abrogation outside the limits of Syria proper'.[88]

Curzon resumed his attack on the agreement during a meeting of the War Cabinet – which was attended by Balfour but not by Cecil – that same afternoon. This 'hush' meeting had been called to discuss Turkish peace feelers and Lloyd George's forthcoming conference with his French and Italian colleagues Clemenceau and Orlando at Paris. When it was 'pointed out that in any question of peace discussions with Turkey the French would constantly refer to the Sykes–Picot agreement', Curzon related what had happened since Cambon's visit to Balfour, and criticised the agreement as it 'had been based entirely on the supposition that the Agreement of 1916 still held good'. He stated that Smuts and he were 'greatly concerned' about this because 'the French had received far more out of this Agreement than they had ever hoped for'. The Prime Minister now joined the fray, and introduced yet another argument why the Sykes–Picot agreement could not stand. He explained that he:

> Had been refreshing his memory about the Sykes–Picot Agreement, and had come to the conclusion that it was quite inapplicable to present circumstances, and was altogether a most undesirable agreement from the British point of view. Having been concluded more than two years ago, it entirely overlooked the fact that our position in Turkey had been won by very large British forces, whereas our allies had contributed but little to the result.

Lloyd George, too, was angry with the Foreign Office's handling of the matter: 'the whole question ought to have been discussed at the War Cabinet before the Conference took place at the Foreign Office'. Balfour chose to ignore this criticism, but doubted whether Clemenceau and Orlando would be susceptible to Lloyd George's argument. He reminded the War Cabinet that:

> The original idea had been that any territories that the Allies might acquire should be pooled and should not be regarded as the property of the nation which had won them. The theory had been that the fighting in one theatre of war, where there was little to gain, might be just as important a contribution to the cause of the Allies as much easier fighting in other theatres where great successes were achieved.[89]

Lloyd George left for Paris on 4 October. Cecil joined him two days later. On 5 October, the German government sent a telegram to President Wilson, in which they requested his good offices in bringing about an immediate armistice. They also accepted the Fourteen Points as a basis for peace negotiations. On 6 October, after dinner, so Hankey related in his diary, there was a 'very interesting discussion about the cutting up of Turkey. Ll G. took a very *intransigeant* attitude and wanted to go back on the Sykes–Picot agreement, so as to get Palestine for us and to bring Mosul into the British zone, and even to keep the French out of Syria'. It also became clear that Lloyd George and Cecil disagreed on tactics. Where the Prime Minster was 'anxious to arrange the division of Turkey between France, Italy and G.B. before speaking to America', Lord Robert 'was for sticking to the Americans at all costs, and for bringing them into the controversy at once, as he thought they would pull the chestnuts out of the fire for us with the French and Italians'.[90] From the memorandum Cecil sent to Pichon on 8 October, it appeared that Lloyd George for the moment had accepted Cecil's plan of campaign. The memorandum – 'to which the Prime Minister agrees. It has not yet been approved by the Cabinet, and until that has taken place it must be treated as to that extent provisional' – stated that the British government were 'prepared to accept the arrangement reached at the conference held at the Foreign Office on the 30th September', on the understanding that it only provided 'for the situation caused by the recent advance of General Allenby's force into Syria, and is to be deemed to refer only to the territories occupied, or to be occupied by that force'. Regarding the Sykes–Picot agreement, Cecil observed that its provisions 'do not in all respects appear suitable to present conditions', considering that 'the United States have come into the war and Russia has gone out', and that the 'military position in Mesopotamia, Palestine, and Syria' had completely altered. Lord Robert finally claimed that 'America cannot be ignored in any settlement of the future of these countries, and particularly of Syria and Palestine', and that therefore in the coming months 'fresh conversations' should take place, 'in which the governments of Italy and the United States as well as the French and British governments should be invited to take part'.[91]

That same day, President Wilson replied to the German note. He had not bothered to consult the British, French and Italian governments, something the latter much resented. The President stated that he could not answer the German request until he was sure that the German government really accepted the Fourteen Points, and understood that negotiations on an armistice could only start if the Central Powers consented to withdraw their forces from all invaded territory. On 12 October, the German government confirmed their acceptance of the Fourteen Points,[92] and declared that they were ready to evacuate their troops on foreign soil.

An indication that Cecil was on the right track and that the Americans considered getting involved in the post-war settlement of the Ottoman Empire's territories was that Irwin Laughlin, the American chargé d'affaires in London, called upon Crowe 'to enquire whether it was the case that a secret agreement was in force between us and France for the partitioning of certain Turkish territories, and if so whether we should object communicating the contents of such agreement to the US government'. Sir Eyre told Laughlin that 'at a much earlier stage of the war, long before the US came into it, we agreed with our several allies upon a modus operandi in dealing with the problem of the non-Turkish portion of the Turkish Empire which might in the course of the war succeed in effecting their liberation'. He also explained that 'the withdrawal of Russia, the entry of the US, and the course of our military operations had combined to alter entirely the basis on which the agreement with our Allies had been built up, and that the allies were practically agreed as to the necessity of its fundamental revision'.[93]

Lord Robert received Laughlin on 14 October. He informed the latter of the contents of the memorandum to Pichon, and declared that the Sykes–Picot agreement needed revision considering that 'America had come into the war and Russia had gone out of it', and that 'America should certainly be given an opportunity to intervene in any discussions on that subject if she desired to do so – indeed I rather urged that it was of great importance that she should be consulted about it'.[94] Cecil's triumph seemed complete when that same day the War Cabinet discussed the memorandum to Pichon, this time with Cecil in attendance, and Curzon stated that the Eastern Committee 'had hesitated to recommend' the agreement of 30 September, but now that it was clearly expressed in the memorandum that the agreement only applied to territories occupied by the EEF, and that the British government considered the agreement of 1916 as 'out of date', he approved of it. The War Cabinet agreed, and Cambon was informed of the War Cabinet's decision right away.[95]

Cecil, too, would not savour his moment of triumph very long. The very next day, Sykes reported that Jean Goût had telegraphed the text of a joint declaration. The first part was more or less a translation into French of Cecil's revised version of Hogarth's draft for a declaration to the King of the Hijaz (see section 'Mitigating or Abolishing the Sykes–Picot Agreement', above), which Lord Robert had handed to Georges-Picot at the Conference of 30 September. This was all to the good, but the French had added a seemingly innocuous paragraph, full of rhetorical flourish on the allies' noble intentions in assisting the long oppressed peoples liberated from the Turkish yoke, but which ended with a disquieting explicit reference to the Sykes–Picot agreement, a clear indication that in Paris policy makers did not believe that the agreement no longer applied, however much circumstances might have changed. According to the French addition, the two governments would take up the role assigned to them 'in the zones where they are called upon to act by their agreements of 1916'. This portent of future trouble did not alarm Sir Mark. He merely suggested without further comment to substitute 'in the regions above mentioned' for the French clause.[96]

The French signal also escaped the members of the Eastern Committee's notice when they discussed the joint declaration on 17 October. Crowe, in consultation with Sykes, had prepared a revised version, the main difference being 'the excision of any negative declaration against annexation by inserting in its place a positive statement in favour of the establishment of independent rule'. France and Great Britain were 'agreed to encourage and assist the establishment of indigenous governments and administrations in Syria and Mesopotamia'. Curzon would have preferred that the declaration only applied to Syria, but according to Cecil this was 'impossible, and that unless we made a self-denying declaration in regard to Mesopotamia, the French would not make a similar declaration in regard to Syria', a point that Curzon accepted. The 'important thing' was 'to put Arab independence in the forefront of the declaration, and to bring in any reference to the French and British governments later'. The Foreign Office was requested to prepare yet another draft in the light of the Eastern Committee's discussion.[97]

Cecil submitted the fresh draft to Curzon, and added that Balfour was anxious that the American government 'should be informed of this declaration before it is actually made'. Curzon believed that the new formula was 'very good', and submitted that 'it should satisfy even the critical and democratic taste of President Wilson. Short of an actual disclaimer of annexation I do not see how we could go further.' The British text was communicated to Cambon on 17 October. In the covering letter Balfour explained that the British modifications of the French text had been made 'chiefly with the view of accentuating the desire of the two governments to aid in setting up and recognising in Syria and Mesopotamia national governments resting on the expressed will and consent of the native inhabitants'. He added that the British government believed that it was desirable 'that the text of the declaration should be brought to the notice of President Wilson for his information before it is actually published'.[98]

The French ambassador called upon Lord Robert the next day. Cambon first of all told Cecil that Pichon accepted the memorandum of 8 October, and that the French government agreed that President Wilson should be informed of the Sykes–Picot agreement and 'subsequent arrangements'. He then turned to the subject of the declaration, and introduced a new difficulty, which constituted a further indication that the French were not prepared to give up their rights under the Sykes–Picot agreement without a fight. Pichon's counter-move was that he accepted the British text 'as it stood, except that he wanted it to extend not only to Syria and Mesopotamia, but all territories liberated from the Turks'. The intent of the proposed modification was readily grasped by Cecil. He 'pointed out that there might be a difficulty about Palestine where the present idea was to set up an international government', but he 'promised to consider M. Pichon's proposal'.[99] From the official letter that Cambon delivered the next day, it appeared that Pichon was not above putting things on their head, by explaining that he wanted the more general formula, 'in the territories liberated from the Turkish yoke', because by confining the declaration to Syria and Mesopotamia, the French and British governments ran the risk of 'arousing President Wilson's suspicions'. Lord Robert was quite at a loss how to respond to Pichon's move. He adhered to his view that 'the declaration should be confined to Syria and Mesopotamia'. If it was 'extended beyond the countries named', then it would be 'difficult to square with our declared policy in Palestine'.[100] The French government refused to budge. They kept insisting on a generally worded reference to the territories covered by the declaration.[101]

On 22 October 1918, the French government increased the pressure when the French embassy delivered a note that plainly stated that France did not accept that the altered circumstances to which Cecil had referred in his memorandum of 8 October – America in, Russia out, British military victories in Palestine, Mesopotamia and Syria – implied that the Sykes–Picot agreement could no longer stand. They did allow that there had been momentous changes, and that in view of these the French, British and Italian governments might together re-examine their rights and interests under the existing agreements, and also agreed that, when these negotiations had been brought to a successful conclusion, the results should be communicated to President Wilson, but they were also of the opinion that, as long as this new agreement had not been reached, the Sykes–Picot agreement and the agreement of St Jean-de-Maurienne remained 'good and valid'. It was, moreover, the French government's point of view that Britain and France should first come to an accord before they approached Italy on the matter. This time Sykes *was* alarmed. He regarded 'certain points in the French note as very disquieting. A certain amount may be put down to ordinary diplomatic play, that is to get the utmost and to give way as little as possible. This is not to be objected to, but there are certain insinuations which are indicative of something far more menacing.' Besides, the French proposal 'to enter into conversations "à deux"' was 'manifestly impossible' after President Wilson 'with the approbation of the whole world [had] declared against secret diplomacy'. According to Cecil the question was 'what reply should be made to the French Note', and he believed that it would be best if it was confined to 'the contents of the Note itself', and not to address its wider ramifications. The British reply therefore merely discussed several inaccuracies in the French memorandum, and remained completely silent on the French position that the Sykes–Picot agreement still held good. It also rejected the proposal that France and Britain should first reach an agreement before Italy was approached.[102]

The deadlock on the wording of the joint declaration was finally broken on 30 October. Cecil and Cambon agreed that the declaration would apply to 'Syria and Mesopotamia presently liberated by the Allies and in the territories they continue to liberate'. The declaration was telegraphed to Washington the next day, where French ambassador Jusserand and British chargé d'affaires Barclay would communicate it to Wilson. In view of the difficulties 'with the French government over the wording of the second paragraph giving the areas in which we undertake to encourage and aid in the establishment of native governments and administrations', the Foreign Office instructed Barclay to 'make sure that the version telegraphed to your French Colleague is worded as above'.[103] It was only on 3 November, so Barclay reported, that 'text of Anglo–French declaration was presented to President'. Wilson had praised 'sentiments which had inspired declaration and which he said were the same as those he had expressed so often himself'. Barclay had also verified that 'wording of passage mentioned by you was as stated in your telegram'.[104] The declaration was finally published simultaneously in Great Britain, France and Egypt on 8 November 1918.

Publication had been held up for another few days, because the French insisted that Georges-Picot should personally present the declaration to Faysal.[105] The British and French governments declared that:

> The goal that France and Great Britain envisage while pursuing in the East the war unleashed by German ambition, is the complete and definitive enfranchisement of the peoples so long oppressed by the Turks, and the establishment of national governments and administrations deriving their authority from the initiative and free choice of the indigenous populations.
>
> In order to carry out these intentions, France and Great Britain are agreed to encourage and assist the establishment of indigenous governments and administrations in Syria and Mesopotamia presently liberated by the Allies and in the territories they continue to liberate, and to recognise at once those that will effectively be established. Far from wanting to impose on the populations of these regions this or that institution, they have no other worry than to assure by their support and effective assistance the normal functioning of governments and administrations to which they will freely dedicate themselves. To insure an impartial and equal justice for all, to facilitate the economic development of the country, to realise and encourage local initiatives, to promote the spread of education, to put a stop to the divisions too long exploited by Turkish policy, such is the role the two Allied governments claim in the liberated territories.[106]

It soon became apparent that the declaration, the wording of which had taken up so much time, could be interpreted in ways its advocates, Sykes and Cecil in the first place, had not foreseen. At the Eastern Committee's meeting of 17 October, Lord Robert had stated that 'the main object of the declaration [...] was generally to reassure the Arabs',[107] but only three days after its publication, Hogarth observed that the declaration would not reassure any of the Arab leaders 'by any means. They will see that France can find an easy loophole to protectorate or annexation in the phrase "effectively established", and that wholesale tutelage is assumed in the wording of the last part.'[108] On 16 November, Clayton sent a telegram to London from which it appeared that Cecil's exertions to exclude Palestine from the territories to which the declaration applied had also been to no avail as far as Palestinian Muslims and Christians were concerned. To them, Palestine was part of Syria, and therefore they were 'relieved at what they consider a check to extravagant Zionist aspirations'.[109] Arnold Wilson telegraphed from Baghdad that same day that he had received a deputation of the Jewish community. They had wished 'to express keen apprehension at tenour of Anglo–French Declaration of 8th November'. This was something Wilson could well understand, considering that 'local Mohammedan gentry, whose unbalanced minds have been excited by Anglo–French Declaration, are already announcing to Jews and Christians that they will shortly see themselves once more under Mohammedan domination etc.' This made George Kidston sigh that 'our pet Declaration which was only born after such lengthy pains, does not seem to be an unqualified success'.[110]

The Foreign Office Admits Defeat

On 15 October 1918, Wingate wrote to Allenby that he had:

> Had an interesting talk yesterday with Lawrence who evidently intends to talk plainly when he gets to London – they should welcome the views of such an expert as he is, though I expect our French Allies would find them not exactly palatable and I shall be surprised if H.M.G. go as far as he recommends. There is much ignorance at home in these matters and those who really do understand are not always listened to.[111]

Allenby agreed that Lawrence would 'be able to do much good at home, and he will, no doubt, be listened to as having knowledge and authority to speak'.[112] Lawrence was received by Cecil on 28 October. The latter reported to the department that Lawrence had 'denounced in unmeasured terms the folly (or, as he called it, the levity) of the Sykes–Picot Agreement, the boundaries of which were, he said, entirely absurd and unworkable'. Lord Robert had shown Lawrence 'the proposed joint declaration by the French and the British, which he thought quite satisfactory, but inconsistent with the Sykes–Picot Agreement: as undoubtedly it is'. Cecil also recorded that Lawrence was 'violently anti-French', and that he had 'suggested that, if there were to be fresh conversations, it would be well to have both Arab and Zionist representatives present, as well as Americans and Italians'.[113]

Lawrence attended a meeting of the Eastern Committee the following day in order to enlighten its members on 'the views that were entertained by the Arab chiefs concerning the settlement of the conquered territories and Franco–Arab relations in particular'. Lawrence concentrated on the situation in Syria, the Lebanon and upper Mesopotamia, and claimed that the Arabs 'had deduced from the attitude of the French during this war, wherever they had come into contact with them, that the French were inimical to the Arab movement for national independence'. However, he expected that Faysal 'would probably be content to leave Beirut and the Lebanon to French tutelage provided that there was no question of French annexation', but warned that 'Tripoli is the part the Arabs will make a fight for'. In conclusion, he related that he had met Picot in Rome, and that the latter had made it clear that 'the French intended to impose French advisers upon Feisal', but that the Emir 'took the view that he was free to choose whatever advisers he liked', and 'was anxious to obtain the assistance of British or American Zionist Jews for this purpose'.[114] Curzon was sufficiently impressed to warn the War Cabinet that:

> Serious trouble [...] was likely to arise – if it had not already arisen – in regard to French aspirations in Syria. Syria was likely to be the scene of great anxiety to us in the future. We had conquered the country, and the French wanted the spoils. This would necessarily bring us in as third parties to any dispute between the French and the Arabs.[115]

Lloyd George was not present at the meeting of the War Cabinet. He was in Paris for an informal conference with Clemenceau and Orlando, which was attended by foreign ministers Balfour, Pichon and Sonnino, as well as Edward 'Colonel' House, President Wilson's personal representative. In preparation for the conference, the Prime Minister had a private talk with House, in the course of which he sketched his ideas on the partition of the Arab-speaking parts of the Ottoman Empire. Great Britain 'would have to assume a protectorate over Mesopotamia and perhaps Palestine. Arabia he thought should become autonomous. France might be given a sphere of influence in Syria.'[116] At the conference the next day, Lloyd George experienced how right Balfour had been in warning him that his argument that France and Italy must accept that the terms of an eventual settlement with Turkey should reflect the fact that Great Britain had done all the fighting while France and Italy had done next to nothing, would not get him very far. The bone of contention was that British Admiral Calthorpe had been conducting armistice negotiations with the Turks without consulting French Admiral Gauchet, who was the commanding officer for the Mediterranean. The French demanded that in further negotiations

Calthorpe be joined by Admiral Amet, as Gauchet's representative, and that they together sign the armistice. Lloyd George flatly refused to consider this:

> Except for Great Britain no one had contributed anything more than a handful of black troops to the expedition in Palestine. He was really surprised at the lack of generosity on the part of the French government. The British had now some 500,000 men on Turkish soil. The British had captured three or four Turkish armies and had incurred hundreds of thousands of casualties in the war with Turkey. The other governments had only put in a few nigger policemen to see that we did not steal the Holy Sepulchre. When, however, it came to signing an armistice all this fuss was made.

The French rejected Lloyd George's argument, but in the end, 'in a spirit of conciliation', they accepted the fait accompli. Calthorpe could continue the negotiations and sign the armistice first.[117] The ceremony took place at Mudros the following day.

On the day of the publication of the joint declaration, Cambon asked permission to send Consul Roux and Commander Sciard on a humanitarian mission to Mosul. Crowe would have none of it:

> We should reply to this by reminding M. Cambon that he and his govt. have themselves agreed that the agreement of 1916 requested revision because the conditions on which it rested have entirely changed, and that in accordance with the agreement since arrived at with him we look forward at an early date to the contemplated discussions with the U.S., France and Italy, the purpose of which is to arrive at a revised agreement.
>
> In these circumstances it is to be regretted that the French government apparently demands the immediate putting into force of the old agreement as it stands, just as if the whole discussion respecting revision had never taken place.

A letter in line with Crowe's minute was sent to the French embassy on 14 November.[118] When it was sent, the Foreign Office had already been informed by the DMI that the French had approached the War Office on yet another project, the dispatch of a battalion of the French 'Légion d'Orient' to Mosul. Thwaites assumed that Hardinge would 'consider the possible employment of a French contingent at Mosul as undesirable, as do the War

Office'. Hardinge – who had only recently returned to the Foreign Office, having been away for several weeks after suffering a broken leg – certainly agreed, but warned that 'we had better go steady in this matter. I gathered from M. Cambon that we have not heard the last of the question of relief at Mosul.' Cecil for his part admitted that 'we are undoubtedly on a very awkward position and unless we receive help from the Americans I do not see how we can get out'.[119]

Cecil's policy, enthusiastically supported by Crowe, to get the French to admit that the Sykes–Picot agreement was no longer valid, considering that circumstances had radically changed and that France and Britain were now bound by a declaration in which they expressed their support for self-determination, was on the verge of collapsing with American help nowhere in sight. Cambon administered the coup de grace in his reply to the Foreign Office letter of 14 November. He reminded Balfour that his government had admitted that 'conversations on the subject of the agreements of 1916 were desirable, but, when admitting this, M. Pichon has specified that these arrangements remained "good and valid" until further order'. He therefore insisted that the Roux–Sciard mission 'was authorised immediately'. Hardinge was not above rubbing it in. He minuted that it seemed to him that 'the French have a strong case, especially as M. Pichon seems to have made the condition, while accepting the idea of revision, that the Sykes–Picot agreement remains in force until a new arrangement has been come to. And there is no doubt that Mosul is in the French area, according to that unhappy agreement.' Cecil admitted defeat. He doubted 'whether anything is gained by continuing the controversy and I should simply, with all proper wishes for cooperation with the French, express regret if anything in the previous note has given rise to misunderstanding and add that we have consulted the military authorities and are awaiting their reply'.[120]

On 18 November, Cambon also communicated a note by Pichon, who had felt it necessary 'to state precisely the French views regarding the Anglo–French agreements of 1916 [...] and the provisional arrangement of 30 September 1918'. He declared that France was prepared to discuss with her allies the ways in which the agreement of 1916 should be adapted to the changed circumstances, and noted that the British government had rejected the French suggestion to discuss these matters together before Italy and the United States became involved. He also begged the British government 'to take note that France does not accept at a single point, whether it is at Damascus, Aleppo or Mosul, the diminution of what are her rights under the agreement of 1916'. With respect to the joint declaration Pichon finally observed that 'the French government agree with the general principle that a lasting peace must be based on the satisfaction of the aspirations of the people. But they acknowledge that in the Orient there is reason to assist the populations in order to avoid that they tyrannise one another,' and France therefore counted on 'maintaining her tutelage over the Arab populations living in the zones that have been assigned to her through the agreement of 1916'.

The French simply refused to move even one inch. Crowe dejectedly noted on 21 November that:

> This amounts in fact to the withdrawal of the assent which we thought we had obtained from the French government to the revision of the territorial agreements embodied in the 1916 agreement.
>
> The French government here definitely announces that they refuse to contemplate any arrangement differing substantially from the 1916 agreement.
>
> Our recent discussion and arrangements with M. Cambon and M. Pichon are practically disavowed and consigned to the official paper basket.
>
> I confess that I have always expected this.
>
> All we can do now is to leave the peace conference to go into this matter. If France insists, we cannot easily repudiate our signature at the bottom of the 1916 agreement. We can however use every effort to demonstrate both to France and to the United States that in view of the radically changed situation, we do not see how effect can be given to the agreement without provoking both injustice to the population concerned and grave danger to future peace.
>
> If further controversial correspondence is to be avoided [...] we might restrict ourselves to acknowledging receipt and expressing our sincere regret at the spirit in which the French government have met our desire to adjust the arrangements of 1916 to the entirely changed conditions now prevailing.

Hardinge agreed that 'it would be useless to argue. This note is absolutely uncompromising.' He also approved Crowe's suggested reply, to which Cecil proposed to add that 'we trust the French may not find their Allies equally unaccommodating on points to which the French attach importance'.[121]

That same day, Lord Robert offered his resignation to Lloyd George. This had nothing to do with the utter failure of his policy to get the French government to accept that the Sykes–Picot agreement was no longer 'good and valid', but with the disendowment of the Church of England's property in Wales as a consequence of the Church of Wales Act of 1914, which had been suspended until the end of the war. The trigger had been a letter, published on 2 November 1918, from Lloyd George to the leader of the conservative party Bonar Law, which had been 'the product of extensive drafting between the two'.[122] In this letter the Prime Minister had called for an early general election, and proposed that the existing coalition should campaign on a common platform, one minor element of which was that the Church of Wales Act should come into force. Cecil wrote to Lloyd George that he was:

> Deeply pledged by word and conduct to the defence of the Church in Wales […] If your letter to Bonar Law were the programme of a new government, as in substance it is, I should be clearly precluded from joining it. It seems to me equally clear that I ought not by retaining office in the present government to make myself responsible for a policy which I am unable to approve. With very real regret therefore I must ask you to transmit my resignation to the King.

Lloyd George replied the next day that he 'most unwillingly' complied with Cecil's 'request to submit your resignation to His Majesty',[123] but failed to do so. On 16 December 1918, 'now that the Election is over and Ministers are free to turn to their ordinary business', Balfour urged Lloyd George to put an end to this anomalous situation, and 'to appoint Bob Cecil's successor without delay',[124] but Lloyd George still did not take action. It would be almost another four weeks before, on 10 January 1919, Cecil Harmsworth was appointed parliamentary under-secretary in Lord Robert's place. That same day, Curzon became acting foreign secretary. Two days after 'Bob's most regrettable departure', Curzon had already offered his services to Balfour.[125] At the beginning of January 1919, Lloyd George had finally asked Curzon 'to take over the control of the Foreign Department' during the time that Balfour was away in Paris to attend the peace conference.[126] Curzon was all too happy to oblige. The Eastern Committee ceased to exist as a War Cabinet committee.[127]

On 22 November 1918, Faysal sailed from Beirut for Marseilles. He was on his way to Europe to represent his father at the coming peace conference. His mission was a British initiative. The French had only been informed that Faysal was coming on 19 November. They had not been consulted on the advisability of this mission (see Chapter 10, section 'The Hijaz at the Peace Conference'). The French government naturally resented this very much. On 30 November, Cambon handed in yet another memorandum, in which the French government lodged a strong protest against this fresh example of British disingenuousness. The French government reiterated that they had been prepared to discuss 'a loyal adjustment of the common interests between the two countries alone', but that:

> Even this agreement, which we proposed, has been refused us, and everywhere, in Palestine, in Mesopotamia, in Syria, our agents and rights are treated with little respect; and on top of that, without any conversation with us, not even a prior notice, Emir Faysal is directly sent to France, as the representative of a general Arab kingdom in fact effectively placed under English protection, a clear demonstration of a policy to remove us even from Syria.

In conclusion, the French government once again enjoined the British government to agree that their common interests were best served by 'a direct and completely frank discussion of each other's wishes'. According to Kidston, the memorandum therefore should first of all be seen as 'a renewed appeal to us to come to some arrangement with the French before the Americans can have their say'. Crowe was rather fed up with 'these intemperate notes by M. Cambon', and went on to rehearse all the arguments that had been marshalled in the previous months to convince the French why the Sykes–Picot agreement was obsolete, and that the text of the joint declaration 'promised to the native population concerned arrangements very different from those contemplated in the agreements of 1916'. He also drafted a reply, but could imagine that 'Mr Balfour would prefer to ignore the offensive note and talk the matter over with M. Cambon direct'. Hardinge found 'the tone of the French note [...] irritable and irritating', but he did not think that 'it infringes the recognised rules of diplomatic courtesy'. He agreed, however, that if a reply to the memorandum was made it should be verbal and not a written one. In preparation for this interview, Drummond summed up the situation for Balfour in the following manner:

> I think the United States are going to take the line that all these treaties and

conventions are overridden by the acceptance of the Allies of the 14 points as the basis of peace [...] The French are frightened of the United States combating their claims in the Middle and Near East and are therefore going to try to rule the United States out of the settlement on the ground that they never went to war with Turkey. The United States view, I believe, suits us much better than that of the French, and we should therefore do nothing to commit ourselves against it. The time for international discussion is approaching and I think we ought to try not to send any formal reply to the French Note.

Balfour, however, refrained from discussing the matter with Cambon. On 29 December 1918, Drummond laconically minuted that 'these papers have been slumbering in the S. of S. box for some considerable time. Perhaps the sleep should be continued in the Department.'[128]

All British attempts since the early spring of 1917 to get the French to agree that the Sykes–Picot agreement could not stand had failed. Appeals that circumstances had changed (Russia's collapse, America's entry into the war, Britain practically doing all the fighting in Palestine and Syria), the issue of a joint declaration in which France and Britain embraced the principle of self-determination, as well as the encouragement of Arab nationalists to create facts on the ground had all failed to move the French. They still stood by the terms of the agreement of 1916. With an eye to the approaching peace conference, only two viable options remained. The first was to do what the French wished and to come to a separate agreement on the Middle East before the conference started. The second was to play the American card, to induce the Americans to take up the British case, and when they did, considering France's overwhelming dependence on the United States, the French would finally have to face the fact that in the era of self-determination proclaimed by President Wilson, the Sykes–Picot agreement was obsolete. Prime Minister Lloyd George chose the first option, all other British policy makers involved the second.

10   GETTING OUT OF THIS SYRIAN TANGLE

Introduction

This chapter is concerned with the settlement of the Syrian question. It describes how the British authorities – in London, Paris and the Middle East – gradually came to realise that, in contrast to what they had initially believed, they could not dictate terms to the French with respect to Syria. When the peace conference opened in January 1919, they might have differed among themselves about the best way to secure British interests in the Middle East, but they all shared the presumption that Great Britain could negotiate with the French from a position of strength. It was only a question of time before the latter would understand that they had no other option than to give in to British demands. British forces occupied the country, the USA strongly opposed French imperialistic designs, and if France nevertheless succeeded in pushing through her ambitions and tried to occupy the country, Arab armed resistance would lead to bloodshed on a scale France could scarcely afford. It was only through Britain's good offices that France would be able to secure Syria by peaceful means. By the end of August it had become clear that all this had been an illusion. In January it had already been realised that the costs of occupation constituted an intolerable burden for the British treasury, but there remained the possibility of American intervention and there was still the threat of the Arab nationalists attacking French soldiers. By May, however, everything indicated that the Americans would not take a stand on Syria, and by July the Arab threat more or less evaporated as a result of a more realistic appreciation of the strength of the Arab forces under Faysal's command. Prime Minister David Lloyd George nevertheless thought he could still settle matters in Britain's favour by presenting the French with the fait accompli of a British evacuation of Syria as of 1 November, and handing over the towns of Damascus, Homs, Hama and Aleppo to Faysal's forces in pursuance of the British agreement with the Emir of Mecca. He believed that French prime minister Georges Clemenceau would not dare run the risk of an armed confrontation. Clemenceau did not even blink. He demanded that the British put a stop to their meddling in the Syrian question, and leave it to the French to deal with Faysal and the Arab nationalists. By the middle of October, it was Lloyd George who gave in. Faysal was left to fend for himself.

The major underlying theme of this chapter is the total eclipse of the Foreign Office regarding the handling of the Syrian question. This applies equally to Arthur Balfour and his staff as part of the British delegation at Paris and to Lord Curzon and Foreign Office officials in London. At the end of the period covered in this chapter, the Foreign Office had been reduced to the role of a faithful executioner of Lloyd George's Syrian policy whose advice went mostly unheeded.

The British Delegation to the Peace Conference

On 10 October 1918, Lord Hardinge addressed a letter to Balfour in which he explained that within the Foreign Office during the last 18 months, preparations had been made for the setting up of the necessary administrative machinery for the coming peace conference. These were now 'almost complete', and Hardinge therefore suggested that Balfour would seek Lloyd George's approval of this scheme so that the Foreign Office had the necessary authority to contact the relevant government departments 'to perfect this machinery, which it is the duty of the F.O. to prepare'.[1] Sir Eric Drummond forwarded Hardinge's letter to J.T. Davies, one of the Prime Minister's private secretaries, two days later. Drummond emphasised that the foreign secretary 'would be grateful if the Prime Minister could let him have his opinion as soon as possible'.[2] Lloyd George did not reply. Four days later, Drummond again wrote to Davies, explaining that 'Mr Balfour is most anxious to have a reply as soon as possible. Could you expedite matters?'[3] Although the War Cabinet had a preliminary discussion on the requirements for a peace conference the next day, the Foreign Office did not receive the necessary authorisation to go ahead. On 19 October, Drummond wrote yet another letter to Davies, stressing that Hardinge's proposals only concerned the 'mechanical part' of the matter,[4] but this was to no avail. On 21 October, the War Cabinet decided that General Smuts would prepare 'a British brief for the Peace Conference […] The War Cabinet had thus determined that the Foreign Office was not to be at the centre of the organisation of the Peace Conference'.[5] This also implied that not Hardinge, but Sir Maurice Hankey would be the principal British functionary at the conference. According to James Headlam-Morley, of the Political Intelligence Department in the Foreign Office, this constituted 'a very grave slight to the Foreign Office and to Lord Hardinge'.[6]

It took almost another two months before arrangements were finalised. On 17 January 1919, the day before the official opening of the peace conference, Lloyd George announced that Hardinge would be 'Organising Ambassador', 'in charge of the Administrative organisation of the whole Departmental mission', and that Hankey would act as 'British Secretary to the Peace Conference'. According to Hankey it was all 'very awkward, as it ought to have been Lord Hardinge's job, and he has brought over a huge organisation. However, he has been most charming about it.'[7]

Instead of being in a domineering position at the peace conference, the Foreign Office had been sidelined. At Paris, it took Balfour and the small group of Foreign Office officials in the British peace delegation some months before they finally realised that it was not they, but Lloyd George and whoever for whatever reasons enjoyed his confidence (but never someone from the Foreign Office), who were in on all the major decisions – including those with respect to the settlement of the Syrian question – and that they were mere bystanders, watchers of policy making instead of policy makers. At London, Curzon and the remaining Foreign Office staff from the start understood that their role in the peace process would be confined to that of a spectator, commenting on the events that seemed to be happening in Paris, but it also took them several months before they realised that the members of the Foreign Office section of the British delegation, notwithstanding they were actually there, fulfilled the same role. In the middle of April, Sir Ronald Graham was instructed by Curzon to write privately to Sir Louis Mallet to complain about 'the delay which seems to occur in supplying us with official information on which we can act regarding the decisions arrived at'. At Paris, Robert Vansittart was sympathetic, but it was 'almost impossible to keep the F.O. informed to their satisfaction when we are not informed to ours'. Mallet assured Graham that 'the most stringent instructions for the regular transmission of news' had been issued, but that perhaps 'the conditions under which we are working – which it is difficult to explain in a letter – are more to blame than the officials'. He nevertheless tried his hand at an explanation. The difficulty was that 'so far as individual Sections of the British Delegation at the Astoria [the hotel in which they were staying; R.H.L.] are concerned, we rarely receive, except occasionally through private channels, on which it is not often easy to take prompt action, any official intimation of the decisions reached'. Delays were therefore 'often unavoidable, owing to the complicated machinery which the work of the Conference has obliged it to evolve'.[8]

British Preparations for the Peace Conference

On 17 November 1918, Arnold Wilson continued his campaign against the Anglo–French Declaration of 8 November (see Chapter 9, section 'The Foreign Office's Window of Opportunity and the Joint Declaration'). He telegraphed to the India Office that he 'with experience of my political officers behind' him, could 'confidently declare country as a whole neither expects nor desires any such sweeping scheme of independence as is adumbrated if not clearly denoted in Anglo–French Declaration'. He claimed that the best course of action was 'to declare Mesopotamia to be British protectorate, under which all races and classes will be given forthwith maximum possible degree of liberty and self-rule that is compatible with that good and safe government to which all nations aspire, but so few now enjoy'.[9] In a note on 'Policy in Arabia', Sir Arthur Hirtzel confirmed that is was 'not improbable from such evidence as is available that we might get a British Protectorate, in the sense of Sir P. Cox's first alternative (see Chapter 9, section 'Mitigating or Abolishing the Sykes–Picot Agreement'), accepted in Iraq, if we worked for it at once', but rather doubted its expediency considering 'the effect that this would have on Franco–Arab relations in Syria and the French sphere. A British Protectorate in Iraq would be interpreted by the French as entitling them to a protectorate in Syria.' At the same time, the India Office should take a stand against the 'tendency to sacrifice Mesopotamia and British and local interests there to diplomatic exigencies in Syria', seeing that 'the material interests involved in Mesopotamia are far too great to be jockeyed away merely for the sake of diplomatic convenience'. British pledges to Husayn moreover related:

Only to those areas in which we can act without detriment to French interests, and we ought to take our stand firmly on that ground, and not allow ourselves to be used by the Arabs to secure their interests in Syria at the expense of the French. That, however, is what we are doing at present; and in doing it we risk losing the fruits of the Mesopotamian campaign for the *beaux yeux* of King Hussein and his scheming sons.

Britain therefore 'neither by honour or interest' was bound 'to defend the Arabs against the French'. It was in addition a dangerous illusion to think that the French would 'allow themselves to be eliminated from Syria [...] or that, if they do, they will allow us to take their place'. Syria was 'too deeply graven on the heart of France for that'. Continuing support of Arab nationalist ambitions in Syria could only mean that 'we incur the ill-will of France, and we have to live and work with France all over the world'.[10]

Hirtzel's note was circulated to the Eastern Committee, which held a series of meetings from the end of November until the middle of December to prepare the British case for the peace conference 'in regard to the Turkish territories which had passed into our occupation or under our sway'. The first meeting, on 27 November, was devoted to Mesopotamia. As far as the future administration of the country was concerned, there was consensus that a British-controlled Arab state, 'under an Arab Amir, including Basra, Baghdad, and Mosul, is an ideal solution', but a wide divergence of opinion existed on who should be that Arab emir. Cecil personally favoured Abdullah, because from all he had heard he would do 'tolerably well if we have the right man to control him. He is a cleverish fellow, I understand, and is thought to be the cleverest of the Sherif's sons. He is a sensualist, idle, and very lazy.' Edwin Montagu fully agreed that 'if Abdullah is the lascivious, idle creature he is represented to be, he is the ideal man', but did not think that this needed to be decided before the peace conference started. There was time to consult experts like Gertrude Bell and Sir Percy Cox.

The main topic of discussion was how to get rid of the Sykes–Picot agreement, that 'unfortunate Agreement, which has been hanging like a millstone round our necks', as Curzon put it, and to which 'the French seem disposed to adhere most tenaciously'. Lord Robert held fast to his opinion that 'the French are in an unassailable position. If we cannot induce them in any way to abandon the Agreement, we cannot go back on our signatures,' and that the only way to make the French change their minds was to get the Americans in on the side of the British. However, American support would not be forthcoming unless the British had the Arabs behind them, as 'the Americans will only support us if they think we are going in for something in the nature of a native government'. Although Curzon doubted whether Britain was still bound by her signature in view of the fact that the Sykes–Picot agreement had been 'concluded under conditions wholly different from those existing now', the Eastern Committee found no fault with Cecil's tactics. Smuts concurred that the Americans were 'the only people who can get us out of [...] this impossible situation', and that the best way to achieve this was 'to get the Arabs behind us', while General Macdonogh emphasised that he had already suggested in a paper that 'the only way in which we could get out of the Sykes–Picot Agreement was by a combination of President Wilson and the policy of self-determination'.[11]

The Eastern Committee discussed Syria on 5 December. In his opening statement Curzon declared that 'if we consult our own feelings we should all of us like to get the French out of Syria altogether'. Although he did not fail to mention Hirtzel's position that Britain should 'back the French at the expense of Feisal; after all, the French are a great Power, and you have to be on good terms with her in different parts of the world [...] see her through to the best of your ability, and do not be too much concerned about the Arabs', Curzon clearly favoured the opposite policy. In this connection he questioned Balfour on whether the proposed policy of backing self-determination in order to get the Americans to put pressure on the French would work:

> Is it possible that, when we sit down to the Peace Conference, President Wilson might say, and might get us out of a great difficulty by saying, 'Here we are inaugurating a new era of free and open diplomacy; the various States of Europe have bound themselves by all sorts of unscrupulous secret engagements in the earlier years of the war; before we enter into any arrangements for the future let us sweep all those off the board; let the Sykes–Picot Agreement go, let the Agreement with the Italians go, and let us start with a clean slate?'
>
> If that is impossible, may I suggest that our line of action probably should be this, to back Feisal and the Arabs as far as we can, up to the point of not alienating the French [...] Ought we not to play the policy of self-determination for all it is worth? [...] We ought to play self-determination for all it is worth wherever we are involved in difficulties with the French, the Arabs, or anybody else, and leave the case to be settled by that final

argument knowing in the bottom of our hearts that we are more likely to benefit from it than anybody else.

Balfour confirmed that 'self-determination – the broad principle of self-determination – is the one that we should work for', but warned against the eagerness with which Curzon appeared to be ready to play the card of self-determination. The British:

> Ought to be most careful not to give either the French or the Italians the impression that we are trying to get out of our bargains with them made at an earlier and different stage of the war. If the Americans get us out well and good […] But it is all-important that we should not only not do it ourselves, but that we should not either appear to do it or really do it.

Now that the war was over, 'the price in both cases, so far as we are concerned, must be paid without chicanery. If the Americans choose to step in and cut the knot, that is their affair, but we must not put the knife into their hand.' Cecil, too, cautioned against 'pressing self-determination, quite apart from treaty obligations, too far'. Echoing Hirtzel, he also stressed that, however much the British might wish to get the French out of Syria, it would:

> Be an awful mistake if we think we can get rid of the French out of Syria […] you will never get the French to give up the whole of Syria without the most tremendous convulsion. They would rather give up anything in the world than give up that claim to Syria; they are mad about it, and Cambon is quite insane if you suggest it. I am sure you will never get them out of Syria, and we ought to make up our mind to go for some settlement which will give them some position in Syria, however unpleasant it may be to have them there.[12]

The resolution on Syria adopted by the Eastern Committee one week later nevertheless completely disregarded Cecil's (and Hirtzel's) warning. It contained a maximalist programme, which envisaged British predominance in Syria, and expected the French to give up their rights under the Sykes–Picot agreement in area 'A', and even the Syrian parts of the blue zone, in order that an 'autonomous Arab State, with capital at Damascus' would have access to the sea. In exchange, Britain was magnanimously prepared to 'support the French claims to a special position in the Lebanon and Beirut […] and at Alexandretta', keeping in mind that it was 'essential that no foreign influence other than that of Great Britain should be predominant in areas A and B'.[13]

At the Eastern Committee's next meeting, on 18 December, it seemed that Lord Robert had set aside his scruples about pushing self-determination at the expense of the French, but this time it was Balfour who urged that the French – and the Italians, for that matter – would never accept this. A policy based on self-determination was 'most admirable and logical, and wholly consistent […] It fits in with all the theories, and with the fourteen points of President Wilson, but it does not fit in with the Powers we have to deal with – the French and the Italians. They are not in the least out for self-determination, they are out for getting whatever they can.' When Cecil retorted that the French and Italians were imperialists, Balfour agreed, 'exactly. They are Imperialistic and quite frankly so […] The French may not be quite as frank [as the Italians], but that is exactly what they are thinking of.' It was now Balfour's turn to echo Hirtzel, when he pointed out that the French would say 'By all your arrangements, the Sykes–Picot Agreement of 1915 [sic], and all the rest of it, equality is what we look to'. Cecil naturally could not but admit that 'the French have a good contractual claim', but if the French insisted on equal treatment than they had no other option than to make it their business that the native populations liked them and, if they failed, 'we cannot help that'. To which Curzon gleefully added that the French were bound to fail, as 'none of these nations in any circumstances would ever consent to be protected by the French'.[14]

To the Eastern Committee it was quite clear what Britain's policy in the Syrian question ought to be. It was the policy Cecil had advocated for months, but that still had borne no fruit. The Sykes–Picot agreement was obsolete and had to be cancelled, but because the French refused to contemplate this and Britain was bound by her signature, it should be left to the Americans to bring pressure on the French to give up their Syrian claims. However, the former would only be prepared to do so if Britain was seen to embrace the principle of self-determination. Moreover, taking a stand on self-determination cut both ways. It not only promised an elegant way out of the Sykes–Picot quagmire without Britain having to break her word, but also clearly served British self-interest because, if left the choice, the Syrian population would certainly vote for a British mandate.

What was scarcely considered during these sessions was the alternative policy of coming to an agreement with the French on the Middle East before the peace conference started. On 9 December, Balfour briefly touched upon this possibility, only to reject it right away:

> That is the one thing the French want. If I were to go to the French tomorrow and say, 'Will you make common cause with us against everybody; we will support everything you want which does not affect our interests, and you must support everything which does not affect your interests.' I have not a doubt that we should come to an agreement. We should come to it at the cost of our own principles, probably; at the cost of our obligations to the Arabs, probably; at the cost of our friendship with America, probably; and at the cost of our friendship with Italy, probably; but it could be done. I do not think it ought to be done.[15]

What Balfour and the members of the Eastern Committee were unaware of was that Lloyd George had done precisely that, just eight days before. On 1 December 1918, Clemenceau and Marshal Foch had arrived in London and had received a triumphant welcome. As Hankey related in his diary three days later, 'Clemenceau had been really affected by his welcome. Ll.G. had seized the opportunity to demand first Mosul and then Jerusalem in the peace terms. Clemenceau, in his malleable state, had agreed, but had said "But Pichon will make difficulties about Mosul".'[16] Two days before, after a conversation in which Cambon had reiterated his view that 'England and France should settle all the questions in which they were in any way interested, before the Conference began; so that when the President came over he would find himself face to face with a united opposition and a accomplished fact', Balfour had warned Lloyd George that this would be 'little short of insanity'. According to the foreign secretary, Colonel House, who due to illness was unable to come to London, was 'undoubtedly anxious to work with us as closely as he can and it would be fatal to give him the impression that we were settling, or had at least desire to settle, great questions behind his back',[17] but the Prime Minister did not heed Balfour's advice. He also did not bother to inform his foreign secretary of the deal he had struck with Clemenceau. The policy advocated by the Foreign Office and adopted by the Eastern Committee – playing the card of self-determination in order to induce the Americans to step in and pressurise the French to accept that the Sykes–Picot agreement was obsolete – had been relegated to the dustbin even before the peace conference had started, but it would be some months before the Foreign Office and Eastern Committee would find this out.

For Hankey there remained the delicate problem of how to harmonise the Eastern Committee's resolutions on British desiderata in the Middle East, which had been formulated for adoption during a meeting of the Imperial War Cabinet at the end of December in preparation for the peace conference, with the secret verbal agreement between Lloyd George and Clemenceau. He pointed out to the Prime Minister that it would be 'extremely difficult' to adopt the resolutions with respect to Syria and Palestine 'en bloc', 'involving as they do the cancellation of the Sykes–Picot Agreement' while Lloyd George through his deal had implicitly accepted that it still held good. Sir Maurice suggested that the best way to handle this was 'for the Imperial War Cabinet to take note of these Resolutions and to give a free hand to the Prime Minister and the Foreign Secretary to do the best they can, while freely recognising that the cancellation of the existing agreement can only be effected with the consent of both parties'.[18] Two days later, Hankey reported that he had succeeded. He had 'been very careful to leave a free hand to Mr Balfour and yourself', while the Imperial War Cabinet with respect to Syria 'would support the adoption of some plan in harmony with the Joint Declaration by the French and the British governments, published on the 9th November, 1918, and based on the resolutions of the Eastern Committee rather than on the Sykes–Picot Agreement'.[19]

The Hijaz at the Peace Conference

On 4 November 1918, Sir Edmund Allenby telegraphed to Sir Henry Wilson that he considered 'it very important that King of the Hedjaz should be told immediately that he will have the right and will be invited to send an Arab representative to any Inter-Allied Conference regarding settlement of liberated areas where Arab interests are concerned, and that this representative will attend Peace Conference'.[20] Sir Reginald Wingate for his part expressed the hope that an 'invitation will be sent to King as soon as possible. Presence of a representative might go to mitigate his disappointment at details of final settlement.' He also believed that Faysal, in view of his 'personality and knowledge of Syrian conditions' was 'particularly suitable' as the king's representative, and that 'if and when invitation is transmitted to King I could suggest this if you concur'. Sir Eyre Crowe hesitated to agree with Wingate's proposal because 'we are not […] quite free agent in a matter of this kind and I apprehend the French would raise every kind of objection to having Faisal, whose anti-French sentiments are notorious, admitted to an inter-allied conference'. Cecil did not share Crowe's scruples. He minuted that 'it would be best to ask King Hussein to nominate the Representative letting it be known that we should regard Feisal as the proper man'.

After consultations with Lawrence a telegram was sent to Wingate on 8 November, containing a message from Lawrence to Husayn informing the latter that there would be:

> Conversations in fifteen days' time between the Allies about the question of the Arabs. General Allenby has telegraphed that you will want to have a representative there. If this is so, I hope you will send Feisal, since his splendid victories have given him a personal reputation in Europe which will make his success easier. If you agree please telegraph him to get ready to leave Syria […]
>
> You should meanwhile telegraph to the governments of Great Britain, France, America and Italy telling them that your son is proceeding at once to Paris as your representative.[21]

Wingate held up Lawrence's message pending further instructions, because he feared that 'King Hussein may be somewhat perplexed by this message', as it came from Lawrence and not from the British government. George Kidston reacted that he did 'not see how we can possibly invite any person to be represented at an allied Conference without first consulting the other members of such Conference, and such consultation will not only waste valuable time but the French will probably put up a most determined opposition to Hussein being invited at all', but Lord Robert was undeterred. On 11 November a telegram was sent to Sir Reginald in which he was given to understand that 'the fact that Colonel Lawrence's message was sent to you in official telegram should have made it clear that it was in accordance with considered views of His Majesty's Government', and that it was 'most regrettable that valuable time has been lost by your holding it back. It should go forward at once.'[22] Two days later Wingate informed the Foreign Office that Husayn had instructed Faysal 'at the desire of His Majesty's Government […] to proceed to Paris at once'. Kidston was much embarrassed by Husayn's formula. It unduly compromised the British government as the French 'almost certainly' would find out about it and take offence. Crowe observed that they had better try to make the best of it, and inform the French that in view of Husayn being worried about the peace settlement, the British government had 'suggested that the best course would be for the King to depute Feisal for this purpose'. Telegrams in this sense were finally sent to Paris, as well as Washington and Rome, on 19 November.[23]

On 22 November, Faysal sailed from Beirut for Marseilles. Lawrence was to meet him there and to accompany the Emir throughout his sojourn in Europe. That same day, Lord Derby notified the Foreign Office that the French government had reacted to the news of Faysal's coming in the way that Crowe and Kidston had feared. They desired 'to give their point of view before agreeing to despatch of Emir Feisal or any other delegate of King of the Hedjaz', and maintained that Faysal could only come to Europe after 'the two governments especially interested' had agreed on Faysal's status, which, as far as the French government was concerned, would be that of 'a private envoy of King of Hedjaz in order to plead cause of an Arab group which should only be constituted under respective supervision of English and French in zones where two countries have defined their limits and civilising mission'. From his minute it appeared that Crowe was afraid that the French might even refuse to allow Faysal to land,[24] but the French did not to go as far as that. On arrival and during his stay, Faysal would be treated as a 'distinguished foreigner, son of the King of the Hedjaz', but on disembarking he would be informed straight away that he had 'no recognised official title and that his qualifications for any purpose remains to be discussed between Allies: that in no case before a formal agreement between Allies can he be admitted as representative of Arabs to any meeting of plenipotentiaries'.[25]

Faysal arrived in Marseilles on 26 November. He was first taken by the French authorities on a tour of the battlefields in the north of France, before he was allowed to visit Paris. The Emir reached London on 10 December. The day before, Cambon had left a note with Balfour stating that French foreign minister Pichon hoped that the British authorities would avoid discussing questions relating to Syria during Faysal's sojourn, and that if the Emir brought up this subject, they would point out to him that this was of special interest to the French government and that he therefore should discuss it only with them.[26] This intervention was in vain. Balfour received Faysal and Lawrence on 11 December, and the situation in Syria was freely discussed. Faysal announced that 'if the French showed aggressive designs in Syria he would attack them at once and without hesitation. He well knew that the Arabs could not successfully resist the military power of so great a country as France. But he and his followers would rather perish in the struggle than tamely submit without a blow.'[27]

During the last days of December 1918, Lawrence and Faysal were engaged in drafting a memorandum under Faysal's signature presenting the Arab nationalist case for the peace conference.[28] Faysal proclaimed that it was 'the aim of the Arab nationalist movements [...] to unite the Arabs eventually into one nation', but also admitted that at the present time the economic and social differences between the 'various provinces of Arab Asia – Syria, Irak, Jezireh, Hedjaz, Nejd, Jemen' were such that it was 'impossible to constrain them into one frame of government'. The memorandum was carefully tailored to suit the maximalist programme adopted by the Eastern Committee. As far as Syria was concerned, Faysal claimed that the country was 'sufficiently advanced politically to manage her own internal affairs. We feel also that foreign technical advice and help will be a most valuable factor in our national growth', but warned the powers that the Syrians could not 'sacrifice [...] any part of the freedom we have just won for ourselves by force of arms'. With respect to Mesopotamia, he believed that its government would have 'to be buttressed by the men and material resources of a great foreign Power'. He asked, 'however, that the government be Arab, in principle and spirit'. The Hijaz was 'a tribal area' and its government would 'remain, as in the past, suited to patriarchal conditions. We appreciate these better than Europe, and propose therefore to retain our complete independence there.' Yemen and Nejd were 'not likely to submit their cases to the Peace Conference. They look after themselves, and adjust their own relations with the Hejaz and elsewhere.' In the case of Palestine, Faysal realised that the Arabs could not 'risk assuming the responsibility of holding level the scales in the clash of races and religions that have, in this one province, so often involved the world in difficulties'. The Arabs therefore wished for 'the effective superposition of a great trustee, as long as a representative local administration commended itself by actively promoting the material prosperity of the country'. In the final paragraphs, Faysal appealed to 'the Powers at the Conference' not to consider the Arabs 'only from the low ground of existing European material interests and supposed spheres', and 'lay aside the thought of individual profits, and of their old jealousies'.

At the Foreign Office, people were much taken with the memorandum. Arnold Toynbee considered it an 'extremely moderate and statesmanlike document'. Mallet believed it to be 'eminently reasonable', and did not fail to notice that Faysal's 'claims conflict nowhere with our interests', while Balfour judged it 'a very impressive document'.[29] However, there still remained the problem that Faysal's participation in the peace conference had not been settled. On 16 January 1919, only two days before the conference was to open, Drummond wrote to Balfour that he feared that 'an awkward position is likely to arise as regards the representation of Arabia. The Hedjaz is not included in the published list of States which are to have representation at the Conference.' Lawrence had come to see him, and had 'pointed out that the King of the Hedjaz has been recognised as independent and a belligerent by Great Britain, France and Italy and is therefore on a similar footing to Poland and the Tcheco-Slovaks'. Sir Eric thought that these arguments were 'unanswerable and that we ought to press for two delegates from the King of the Hedjaz. If the French raise the question of Syria our answer should be that Syria does not enter into the question at all. It is for the Hedjaz that two delegates are claimed.'[30] The French gave in at the last moment, and the Hijaz was assigned two seats at the conference table (on a par with countries like China, Poland, Rumania, Czechoslovakia and Portugal). Faysal was on the whole very pleased with the outcome. He drafted a telegram for his brother Zeid at Damascus, which was submitted by Lawrence to the Foreign Office section of the British peace delegation. According to Faysal 'everything is going very well. We have two delegates for the Peace Conference, and hope not to delay much longer.' He further enjoined his brother to 'do all you can to make effective and popular the Arab government in Syria, and follow English advice in all things', and concluded by saying that 'they are helping us magnificently'. Eric Forbes Adam could not let this pass. The telegram that was finally sent on 22 January merely stated: 'Everything is going very well. We have two delegates for the Peace Conference and hope not to delay much longer. Follow advice of British military authorities in all things.'[31]

Impasse: The Council of Ten, January to March 1919

The Paris peace conference opened on 18 January 1919. Strictly speaking, it was a preliminary conference of the Allied and Associated Powers that had fought against the central powers with a view to reach agreement between themselves on the terms of peace to be imposed on Germany, Austria, Hungary, Turkey and Bulgaria. These countries were not represented at the conference. They had to await the outcome of the deliberations at Paris, and were only to be called to the French capital when the participating states had finalised the respective peace treaties. At the end of October 1918, House had reported to Wilson that Lloyd George thought that 'the preliminary conference [...] could be finished in 3 or 4 weeks', while 'the Peace Conference itself need not last longer than 1 week'.[32] This was not to be. When, at the end of June 1919, Lloyd George and Wilson left Paris, only the peace treaty with Germany had been signed. It took another 14 months before the last of the treaties with Germany's allies was signed.

Clemenceau was president of the conference. During the first phase, which lasted until the middle of March 1919, the Supreme Council or Council of Ten was the most important organ. It was during a meeting of the Council of Ten on 30 January that Lloyd George, who had taken responsibility for the Syrian question, broached the subject for the first time. He explained that Great Britain had 1,084,000 soldiers in the non-Turkish territories of the Ottoman Empire. 'It was true that only between 250,000 and 300,000 were British troops, but they had to maintain the lot, and it was an enormous expense'. If the British government had to keep these troops there until the allies:

> Had made peace with Turkey, and until the League of Nations had been constituted and had started business, and until it was able to dispose of this question, the expense would be something enormous, and they really could not face it, especially as they had not the slightest intention of being mandatories of a considerable number of territories they now occupied, such as Syria and parts of Armenia [...] Unless the Conference was prepared to relieve them of that responsibility, he would really have to press very hard for a definite appointment of the mandatories, which he thought would be the most satisfactory way of dealing with it. Then they could clear out, and leave the mandatory to undertake the job.

President Wilson suggested that this was 'chiefly a military question', and that therefore 'the military advisers of the Supreme War Council should have this question [...] referred to them for recommendation'. There were no objections to Wilson's suggestion, although Lloyd George added that 'supposing the British agreed to withdraw from Syria altogether, he would like to know the attitude of the military authorities. This was a point put to him by Mr Balfour'.[33]

In the weeks before, the British military authorities had done their best to drive the message home that relations between the French and the Arab nationalists under Faysal were very tense, and if the French insisted on the execution of the Sykes–Picot agreement this might easily lead to an outburst of violence that would, in the words of the Army Council, 'necessitate the retention of an effective army of occupation in Syria for many years to come'.[34] On 15 January, the War Office telegraphed to Allenby that the French intended to dispatch two regiments 'as reinforcements to their Contingent under your Command. Are you prepared to accept this reinforcement?'[35] Sir Edmund replied three days later that no reinforcements were required, and warned that 'the arrival of increased numbers of French troops in Syria or Cilicia will have very bad political effect as Syrians and Arabs will look on it as sort of annexation'.[36] The War Office readily agreed and informed the French that they should 'defer sending [...] the reinforcements for the present'. General Spears, the head of the British military mission with the French government also accepted Allenby's position, but greatly feared that 'if this question is not very carefully handled it will lead to serious difficulties between the French and ourselves. It is necessary to convince the French we have no political motive in objecting to their reinforcing their detachment in Syria, and this will be difficult to do.'[37]

To convince the French that the British military authorities had no political motives was naturally an uphill battle. On 31 January, Pichon communicated a note to Balfour, which started with the French government deeply regretting that they were:

> Obliged once more to draw the most serious attention of the British government to the unfriendly attitude adopted with regard to French interests by certain officers of the British armies in Syria and Mesopotamia and by a number of officials of the British Civil Service in Egypt, which attitude reveals a spirit entirely opposed to that rightly to be expected from representatives imbued with an idea of the duties imposed by the Alliance.

The note included many pages in which the wrongdoings of British officials were related. No pains had 'been spared by certain officers and officials to humiliate or wound France in the person of her agents'. Among the French complaints were Allenby's refusal to accept French reinforcements and, of course, that Faysal – 'a nomad Chief transformed into the representative of all Arabic-speaking peoples' – had been sent to Europe without first consulting the French. The French government could only conclude that 'the object of all these intrigues, as also their too-evident result, has been each time to confront France with a fait accompli'.

In Paris, the Foreign Office section of the peace delegation believed that London should deal with this note. Forbes Adam was not so much worried by the contents of the note, as many of the complaints had 'already been made in separate notes addressed by M. Cambon to the F.O. and answered at the time', as by its tone. It attacked 'our whole attitude especially as regards the Emir Feisal and the Arab administration in the occupied areas in much stronger terms than yet employed in official correspondence'. Hardinge, too, was not alarmed by the memorandum's contents, 'it should be easy to find a suitable and possibly a crushing reply', but took offence at its tone.[38] As he explained to Graham, 'we must not sit down under it […] It is a big game of bluff the French are playing and we consider here that it is very necessary to reply as quickly and as firmly as possible and without any compromise at all. If we only threaten them with the big stick they will climb down.'[39] At London, George Kidston considered it 'an extraordinarily bitter document and if it reflects the spirit in which discussions are being carried on in Paris the prospect of the Peace Conference and the League of Nations do not seem very rosy'. Sir Ronald thought it 'most regrettable that we should be drawn into a controversial and even acrimonious correspondence of this kind with our Ally', and for what? The British were quarrelling with the French 'on behalf of a future Arab State which, with all deference to Sykes and Lawrence, may never materialise and would, in any case, collapse like a house of cards, the moment our active support and gold subsidies were withdrawn'. Should this question not be 'dealt with in Paris in friendly conversations and not in unpleasant notes?' Curzon, however, shared Hardinge's sentiments. He did 'not at all take the view that we ought to sit down under this sort of ill-tempered fussilade'.[40]

The War Office informed Allenby of Pichon's note right away. It wired on 1 February that the note accused 'some British officers of being animated by spirit not in accord with 1916 agreement', and that officers of the occupation army had encouraged anti-French sentiments. It requested the commander-in-chief 'as regards insinuations against your officers' to 'telegraph categoric refutation and short summary of methods you have adopted to assist French legitimate aspirations in face of considerable local difficulties'.[41] Allenby replied three days later. The French complaints were:

Entirely unfounded not any officers of mine have in word or in deed acted in opposition to agreement of 1916 [...] I have done all in my power to support legitimate aspirations of French [...] There is a strong anti-French party in Syria. I have worked untiringly to promote a better understanding and with some success. This is well known to the French Military administrator and to my political adviser Monsieur Picot with both of whom I am in close touch and constant touch. On all questions of politics and of administration I deal with them openly and frankly and they are fully aware that I and all British officers under me are quite free from political bias.[42]

In a memorandum of 31 January 1919, the Military section of the British Delegation moreover informed the Foreign Office section that the War Office upheld 'General Allenby's objection to the despatch of reinforcements on the grounds that General Allenby is solely responsible for the working of the military administration until such time as the form of administration is changed as a result of territorial allocation decided on by Peace Conference'. The CIGS considered that 'there is danger of serious disturbance if French troops are sent'.[43] Mallet minuted that Sir Mark Sykes, who had returned from the Middle East,[44] had also told him that 'the appearance of French troops in Beyrut will be the signal for bloodshed', and that this was 'confirmed by Colonel Lawrence'. He fully shared the military view that if French troops were admitted to the country 'we shall be held by the Arabs to have facilitated the French landing and, if disturbance occurred, we could not stand aside, as we are responsible for maintaining order'. If Clemenceau persisted, he would 'be placing us in an unfair position and I cannot help thinking that he would see this, if it were put to him'.[45] The French government did not see the British point at all. On 2 February the War Office cabled to Allenby that this time Georges-Picot had 'pressed for reinforcements', and that the French government proposed to send them. Sir Edmund should wire his 'principal reasons distinguishing between military and political reasons against the despatch of French reinforcements'. The latter was quick to oblige:

(A) Military. I have already sufficient troops. (B) Political. If more French troops arrive whilst the Peace Conference is sitting it will convey to the inhabitants who are openly suspicious of French intentions the impression that the French intend to retain that part of Syria included in O.E.T. West and Cilicia permanently. Anti-French feeling among Arabs which has already been excited by French propaganda would thus be stimulated and a peaceful settlement of territorial question in Syria will be prejudiced.[46]

In a conversation with Sir Henry Wilson on 1 February, Lloyd George confirmed that he wanted 'to clear out of Constantinople, Batoum, Baku, Transcaspia and out of Syria', and that he wished to 'to force the pace, and to force President Wilson to take his share in garrisoning, or to name the Mandatory'. He also asked the CIGS to help him to accomplish this. Sir Henry protested that 'all this is Foreign Office work', but immediately realised that 'with A.J.B. here and Curzon in London we have no Foreign Office. So I will see how I can help.'

Wilson spoke with Balfour, and asked him how he 'proposed to tear up the Sykes–Picot agreement', but the latter refused to be drawn. He professed that 'he did not know'.[47] Dr Howard Bliss, the American director of the Syrian Protestant College at Beirut, and Mr Kisbany of the Manchester Syrian Committee were more forthcoming. This could be done by playing the card of self-determination. They were received by Sir Louis Mallet and explained that an international commission should be sent to Syria 'to consult the wishes of the inhabitants on the spot'. If not, and the conference imposed a settlement, then 'there would certainly be serious trouble in the Lebanon and in Syria'. Both men 'were most anxious that any attempt by the French to impose a solution by the Conference without reference to the Syrians themselves in Syria [...] should be strongly objected to by the British and American delegations'.[48]

On 4 February the meeting took place of the military representatives of the Supreme War Council, as suggested by President Wilson. Lloyd George again gave an exposition of Britain's plight. The French military representative, General Belin, subsequently stated that France was 'ready to maintain order in Syria'. This set off yet another round of French–British skirmishing over their respective claims. The British military representative, General Sackville-West, immediately wanted to know 'whether Palestine was included in the zone which the French government wished to take over'. Belin confirmed that it was. Sackville-West thereupon observed that Britain 'desired to continue policing Palestine', and that Palestine extended 'as far as Mount Hermon'. Belin pointed out that this 'was exactly the zone the French were then occupying and it was not part of Palestine', but also indicated that 'if the British government insisted on taking charge of Palestine, the French would accede'. With respect to Syria, Belin claimed that if the French 'were to undertake the policing of Syria, they must have the railways at their disposal as well as the towns of Aleppo, Damascus and Homs'. Then Sackville-West sprang a surprise on him. He ventured the opinion that:

> During the last 4½ years the Arabs had proved themselves to be a nation. It seemed to him that we could leave them to manage their own affairs. Therefore, from an economical point of view, he thought and he suggested, that a great saving both of man-power and of the expense incidental to the maintenance of troops, could be spared if it is recommended that since this country North of Palestine is to all intents and purposes inhabited by Arabs, it be included in Arabia, and Arabia left to settle her own method of administration.

Belin objected that 'at the present time there were European troops maintaining order in those regions and they should continue that European occupation in order to avoid disorder'. According to Sackville-West, however, 'the Arabs were themselves maintaining order in the territory'. The French could take over the Lebanon 'as they had interest in that region either commercial or at least sentimental', but Belin could not accept this, because the French 'had the same interests in Syria as in the Lebanon'. Sackville-West insisted that the status quo, 'where the policing was in the hands of the Arabs', should be maintained. He was afraid that 'if any European troops were put there now there would be severe trouble with the Arabs'.[49] The military representatives left it at that.

Faysal was scheduled to present his case before the conference on 6 February 1919. Just before his presentation, Clemenceau handed Lloyd George a note containing a French proposal for a new Anglo–French agreement on Syria. The note was conciliatory in tone. Although it confirmed that the Sykes–Picot agreement remained 'the basis of our whole policy in the Levant', it also admitted that it was 'necessary to adapt the clauses of this agreement to the new conditions resulting from the unanimous desire of the Allies to organise a League of Nations and from their decision to repudiate any annexation'. The French government accepted that this implied 'the suppression of all distinction between the "Blue zone" and zone A laid down in 1916; the zone of direct sovereignty disappears and is fused in zone A whose regime is to be revised and subsequently defined'. France was, moreover, 'quite disposed to accept at Damascus a regime approximate to that laid down for zone A in 1916 which would ensure for the Emir Feisal the situation in which the Allies desire to place him in the common interest of the Arab peoples and of modern civilisation'. France 'would be willing to give up Mosul', and notwithstanding that Palestine was part of Syria, she accepted that it 'may be detached', because 'of her illustrious past that raises difficulties of which we prefer not to assume the burden alone'. The note emphasised that 'France attaches capital importance only to Syria and its annexes', the Lebanon and Cilicia. With respect to the basin of the upper Tigris France also stated that 'whatever may be the solution of the territorial questions, France insists expressly upon receiving treatment strictly equal to that of the British government and British subjects in all that concerns the exploitation of this great natural wealth'.[50]

The French note had been prepared on Clemenceau's instructions and was based on the deal made with Lloyd George on 1 December 1918,[51] but Toynbee and Mallet did not know that a deal had been struck. They were convinced that self-determination still held the field. They dismissed the note because it ignored 'the principles governing the Conference and of the joint Declaration [...] in which the two Powers have declared that they aim purely at the establishment of national governments derived from the free choice of the native populations'. It was telling that 'no evidence regarding the desires of the population is put forward in the French memorandum', and they 'suggested that the first step should be to ascertain on the spot what these desires are'. They refused to explore the possibilities of a compromise solution based on the Sykes–Picot agreement, and proudly proclaimed that 'His Majesty's Government are ready to take their stand upon the self-determination of the Arabs and to leave to them in every case the free choice of the Power whose assistance they desire'.[52]

In his statement before the conference, Faysal 'asked for the independence of all the Arabic-speaking peoples in Asia, from the line Alexandretta–Diarbekr southward'. This was the ideal of 'all Arab patriots' and Faysal could not imagine that 'the Allies would run counter to their wishes. If they did so the consequences would be grave.' He also stated that 'the Arabs were most grateful to England and France for the help given them to free their country. The Arabs now asked them to fulfil their promises of November, 1918,' and expected that 'the greatest difficulty would be over Syria'. He was willing to admit the independence of the Lebanon and to put Palestine, 'in consequence of its universal character', on one side, and assured his audience that 'the Arabs realised how much their country lacked development'.

They 'wanted to seek help from everyone who wished them well; but they could not sacrifice for this help any of the independence for which they had fought'. He therefore 'asked that the various Provinces, on the principle of self-determination, should be allowed to indicate to the League of Nations the nature of the assistance they required', and if it could not be established at Paris what the precise wishes of the population were, then 'an international enquiry, made in the area concerned, might be a quick, easy, sure, and just way of determining their wishes'.[53]

Lloyd George returned to London on 8 February. Lord Milner became responsible for the Syria file during the Prime Minister's absence. On 11 February 1919, Hankey wrote to his wife that 'we have had rather difficult relations with the French about Syria [...] However Milner has been seeing Clemenceau and Sonnino this morning and I think the difficulty is laid for the moment'.[54] Philip Kerr reported to Lloyd George that Milner had made it clear to Clemenceau that 'we did not want Syria, and that we had not the slightest objection to France being there, but that we were anxious about the peace, if the French rushed to occupy it at once'. What the British wanted 'was an arrangement which both the French and the Arabs could accept, and it was impossible for us to move our troops until that had been arranged'. Clemenceau had been 'greatly mollified',[55] and had agreed, so Kerr added the next day, 'to have a talk with Feisal or Lawrence on his behalf provided a British representative, for instance Lord Milner, was present'.[56] Milner and Balfour therefore would have a talk with Lawrence 'with the object of inducing him to moderate Feisal's demands'. Kerr was on the whole quite sanguine. As he explained to Davies in a further letter, it seemed that the French now realised that 'we are not trying to get them out of Syria, and that the Arab difficulty is a genuine one not fomented by us'. Milner was going to do his best to bring the French and Faysal to an agreement, and Kerr had no doubt that 'if the French will be content with the Lebanon [...] that a settlement with Feisal can be made'.[57] In case the French nevertheless 'try and rush the question', the British could always 'fall back on the American proposal to send a Commission of Enquiry. The President told Mr Balfour at lunch today that he supported this course.'[58]

President Wilson left Paris for a short visit to the USA on 14 February. That day, Gertrude Bell sent a memorandum to Balfour giving Lawrence's and her views on 'the Arab settlement'. They warned that if the French obtained 'the mandate for Syria and prepare to exercise it in such manner as to turn the country into a French province [...] it is inevitable that they will meet with armed opposition which if successful will bring their mandatory authority to an abrupt close, and if unsuccessful will develop into a long period of guerrilla warfare.' They regretted that the French were 'either dangerously unconscious of the hostility to themselves which exists in Syria or no less dangerously determined to ignore it'. There remained 'two possible alternatives. (a) That the French should abandon their ambition to receive the mandate for Syria and consent to see another Power installed there. (b) That they should receive their mandatory authority on terms which will not do violence to Syrian Nationalist hopes.' Naturally, option (a) was the better of the two solutions, but (b) might be more realistic. If the latter were pursued, 'it would be necessary that the French should come to an arrangement with the Syrian Nationalists who are partly represented in Paris by the Emir Feisal'. Unless the Americans stepped in, however, the French would never be prepared 'to make substantial concessions to local opinion'.[59]

Whereas Bell and Lawrence once again prescribed the medicine of self-determination and American pressure to solve the Syrian problem, Hirtzel, in a memorandum of the same date, held fast to his position that a rapprochement with France ought to have the highest priority. The British must realise that 'after the war, as before it, we shall have to live next door to the French all over the world. They may not be pleasant neighbours in detail, but there it is.' Hirtzel strongly disapproved the tendency 'observable in the extreme pro-Arab policy advocated in certain quarters [...] to exaggerate the purely parochial importance of the Arab question at the expense of the ecumenical importance of the maintenance of cordial relations with France'. Instead of putting pressure on the French through the Americans, who in addition might prove to be unreliable, Britain should play the role of 'the honest broker between French and Arabs', and Sir Arthur believed that the French, as they were 'in a weak position [...] would be glad to make terms'.[60]

Milner was quite taken with Hirtzel's 'excellent memo', and gave instructions that the latter should be told that he was 'personally in entire agreement with his main proposition that we should not try to push France out of Syria but seek to act as the honest broker between her and the Arabs'.[61] Mallet, clearly, was less impressed. He minuted that everyone was 'agreed as to the necessity of an understanding with France, in regard to French rights and claims and I do not think that there is any danger of the F.O. overlooking this'. Sir Louis still aimed for the maximalist programme of giving Britain 'a free hand in the Arab countries', which 'would be preferable in many respects to a divided mandate', and also 'more in harmony with Arab wishes'. Mallet was confident that the situation was 'well in hand and we have many cards to play'. As a matter of fact 'an effort is now being made to bring Faisal and M. Clemenceau together with a view to a friendly settlement'.⁶²

The projected meeting between Clemenceau and Faysal did not take place, however. The French prime minister was wounded in an assassination attempt on 19 February. In the week thereafter, Faysal met with Goût, as well as with former prime minister Aristide Briand. Goût had been commissioned by Pichon 'to offer his regrets', and declared that the French foreign minister hoped that 'that an agreement, satisfactory to us both, may be reached'. Briand assured Faysal that the French foreign ministry had 'made a hopeless muddle of its Eastern policy', but steps had 'been taken to correct it'. When Faysal observed that he wanted 'to see some tangible evidence of your good will', Briand replied that he 'must allow us to earn our fares', and that the French intended 'to meet [him] half way'.⁶³

Kerr reported to Lloyd George on 28 February that 'all the larger questions are in suspense pending the return of yourself and Clemenceau',⁶⁴ but only three days later, one day before Lloyd George was to return to Paris, the French tried to force the issue of sending reinforcements to Syria. The French foreign office informed the British peace delegation that the French government had decided to send three battalions of infantry and four squadrons of cavalry. General Allenby had failed to produce any valid strategic argument against their arrival. The French government therefore trusted that the British government would instruct him to cease his opposition.⁶⁵ Balfour was rather shocked. He minuted that 'this afternoon Lord Milner and I were given a paper at the Conference implying that the French proposed sending 3 divisions to Syria at once!! This is, or may become, a very serious matter.'⁶⁶

On his return, Lloyd George resumed responsibility for the Syria file. Milner handed Balfour 'the papers regarding Clemenceau's abrupt announcement of the despatch of French troops to Syria', and observed that 'of course, we are really at cross-purposes. The French pretend that this is only a replacement and if it were only a replacement, it would be in accordance with our views,' but 'in reality what the French are after is an increase of the number of their troops in Syria with a view to strengthening their hold on the country'. According to Milner the matter was 'not sufficiently big to make a great fuss about it', and that some sort of qualified consent should be given. His belief that things were getting serious notwithstanding, Balfour did not follow Milner's advice, and fully backed Allenby's position. On 5 March, he proposed to Curzon that the Foreign Office should reply to the French note that the British government felt 'unable to alter their view on the further despatch of troops to Syria [...] In this they are acting in deference to General Allenby's wishes which, owing to the nature of his responsibility, they feel unable to disregard.'[67]

Lloyd George had a conversation with Clemenceau on Syria on 7 March. The Prime Minister afterwards recorded that he had said that 'France I suppose, will undertake Syria', and that Britain claimed Mosul 'which you agreed to give us'. He then urged the importance of a settlement with Faysal. Clemenceau explained that he had already tried but had failed, and that he was afraid that 'we shall have to fight him'. Lloyd George professed that this 'would be a disaster', and that Faysal was 'a very formidable fighter'. Of course, the French 'would beat him in the end, but it would be a very expensive operation, so I strongly urge that you should arrange things with him. M. Clemenceau said he would do his best.' The Prime Minister finally put to Clemenceau a suggestion made by Kerr in his letter of 28 February that it might help if General Allenby should come to Paris. The French prime minister readily assented. He 'said he had a great opinion of him and he would be very pleased if I would wire for him'.[68]

Lloyd George, clearly, was not pleased with the manner in which the Syrian question had been handled during his absence. In a long letter, Milner tried to justify what he had done, and more especially what he had not done. During his interview with Clemenceau he had told the latter:

> Quite frankly that while we were dissatisfied with the Sykes–Picot scheme which he had himself recognised the necessity of radically altering, we had no desire to play the French out of Syria or to try to get Syria for ourselves. Our interest was confined to an extended Mesopotamia, to Palestine, and to a good connection between them. The Syrian difficulty was not our doing, but was due to the fact that the French had unfortunately fallen foul of the Arabs. This put us in a very awkward position as we were friends with the French but also friends with the Arabs who had fought gallantly on our side against the Turks and contributed materially to our victory. It was therefore

entirely in our interest that the French and the Arabs should get on better terms with one another.

There was at the same time an equal necessity for the French, for if Feisal were to stick his toes into the ground and refuse to have anything to do with them, I did not see how, in view of their and our explicit declarations about complete enfranchisement for the people of Syria and their right to choose their own rulers, the Peace Conference could possibly impose France upon Syria as a mandatory power. The only way out seemed to be that the French should stop continually bullying and irritating Feizal and try to make up to him.

Clemenceau had said that 'if I, or some other responsible British representative were present, he would be willing to talk to Feizal'. As Milner had been just about to leave for London, he had promised that he 'would try and arrange such a meeting on my return', but 'on the day I returned, Clemenceau was shot, and I have not liked to trouble him again in the matter since'.

Milner further explained that he was 'totally opposed to the idea of trying to diddle the French out of Syria. I know that it will be very difficult to get any agreement between them and Feizal, but I do not think it impossible if we [...] bring pressure upon both parties to compromise.' However, he defied 'any human being to get out of this Syrian tangle by any scheme which is not open to many objections, and I want to get out of it somehow without a row'. There was one other thing: 'if we are to play the honest broker between France and Feizal, and especially to get France out of her present difficulty by persuading Feizal to come to terms with her, we must take care that in return the French fulfil their promise to us about Mosul and Palestine, and give it a liberal interpretation'. With the latter he meant that the French should accept that Britain's good offices came at a price. The frontiers laid down in the Sykes–Picot agreement should undergo yet another revision in Britain's favour. The boundary between the French zone of influence (A) and the British zone of influence (B) should be shifted 'considerably towards the north' – bringing for instance the oasis of Palmyra into the British sphere – in order to allow Britain to construct a railway from Mosul to Palestine around the Syrian desert.[69]

Milner's last action with respect to Syria was to hand over to Hardinge a further note by Pichon on the misdoings of British officers in the Middle East. It had been written 'at the request of Clemenceau, who attaches or pretends to attach, importance to these complaints about our treatment of the French in Syria and Mesopotamia'. Altogether the note contained 25 complaints, many of them not new.[70] At the Foreign Office, Kidston first of all wondered why Pichon had handed the note to Milner. He also stated that Curzon had not yet replied to Pichon's previous note, and fancied that 'we should have very good ground for demanding the instant recall of these French agents and officials, who are supposed to be working under General Allenby's orders and as is shown in this document, have lost no opportunity of reporting unfavourably on his administration behind his back'.[71]

The Foreign Office finally replied to Pichon's two notes on 19 March 1919. In the course of his weekly conversation with Ambassador Cambon that same day, Curzon had already warned that the reply was 'couched in somewhat sharp language', but that this had 'only been provoked, and was justified by the very unusual tone of M. Pichon's remarks'.[72] The Foreign Office stood firmly by the British military authorities in the Middle East who, 'far from working against French interests, have done their best to cooperate with their French Allies' under very difficult circumstances that had been produced 'on the one hand by the antagonistic attitude of the Arabs towards the French, and on the other hand by the failure of the French government to supply an administrative personnel possessing the experience and authority necessary to cope with so complex and delicate a situation'. In line with Kidston's suggestion, it was also pointed out that 'a number of these officials find an outlet for their activities in telegraphing home voluminous complaints as to incidents, many of which appear to be quite undeserving of serious consideration, and which in the large majority of cases, ought to admit of local solution'. 'A strong and good note', Hardinge minuted with satisfaction.[73]

House wrote in his diary on 10 March that Clemenceau, Lloyd George and he had 'discussed the Syrian question at considerable length, but no agreement was arrived at'. The French wanted 'all of Syria', but Lloyd George had 'produced a map which Milner had prepared. This gave Lebanon to France, allowing Great Britain and the Arabs an outlet to the Mediterranean. Clemenceau did not like this.' Two days later, the French prime minister confessed in a private conversation with House that 'he was distressed at the turn matters were taking with the British. He said Lloyd George did not keep his promises, that in England he had promised him Syria just as the French now desired.'[74]

Impasse: The Council of Four, March to May 1919

President Wilson arrived back in Paris on 14 March 1919. The official reason for his trip had been that he needed to be in Washington for the closing sessions of Congress, but in reality he had gone back 'to deal with the growing opposition to the League of Nations'. In this he utterly failed. Just before Wilson was to return to Paris, it became clear that more than a third of the senators supported a motion submitted by Henry Cabot Lodge, the leader of the Republican majority in the Senate, that further discussions on the League should be postponed until the peace treaty with Germany had been signed.[75] In Paris, the portents were clear. Harold Nicolson later attributed 'the sudden slump in idealism', which 'overwhelmed the Conference towards the middle of March', to the 'horror-struck suspicion that Wilsonism was leaking badly, that the vessel upon we had all embarked so confidently was foundering by the head'.[76] This also meant that Wilson was in no position to give a definite answer to the question of whether the USA was prepared to become the mandatory power for certain parts of the Ottoman Empire.

A few days after his return, Wilson suggested that Clemenceau, Lloyd George, Orlando and he should meet as a Council of Four in order to speed up the decision-making process on 'the big and infinite number of problems' related to the peace treaties.[77] Wilson's activities in the context of the Council of Four only further undermined his stature. According to John Maynard Keynes, 'there can seldom have been a statesman of the first rank more incompetent than the President in the agilities of the council chamber'. Once Wilson 'stepped down to the intimate quality of the Four, the game was evidently up'.[78] This was a conclusion with which House would have agreed. He felt that Wilson was 'influenced by his constant association with Clemenceau and George'. He reported in his diary on 30 May that there was 'a bon mot going the round in Paris and London, "Wilson talks like Jesus Christ and acts like Lloyd George"', to which he added at the end of June that when the President stepped from his lofty pedestal to wrangle 'with representatives of other states on equal terms, he became as common clay'.[79]

The first meeting of the Council of Four took place on 20 March. The first and most important subject on the agenda was 'Syria and Turkey'. Before this meeting, Balfour in a letter to Curzon gave voice to his anxieties with respect to 'the Middle Eastern problem'. In Paris, they had 'arrived at no satisfactory solution of it, nor do I quite see by what machinery such a solution is to be obtained'. He explained that the negotiations were 'in the hands of the P.M.', and that, while he entirely agreed 'with what I understand to be his main objects, I am by no means sure that he has thought out the question as a whole; or that, in more or less informal conversations with this or that Member of the Conference, he may not give away to one Power what ought to be reserved for another'. In this connection Balfour mentioned quite casually that 'Clemenceau, in London, asked him what he wanted, and he answered "Mosul". Clemenceau replied, "Then you shall have it"'. The foreign secretary believed that 'if "Mosul" can be interpreted to mean the upper regions of Mesopotamia this, in my opinion might give us all we really want; but it by no means gives us what Feisal thinks we ought to have, and leaves Damascus and Aleppo, etc. in the French sphere, which Feisal swears he will on no account tolerate'. The French continued to base their claims on the Sykes–Picot agreement, 'but the Sykes–Picot Agreement has been qualified by the Anglo–French declaration of last November; and Feisal asserts that, if that declaration means what it says, no French official will ever have rights in Damascus'. The result was that there had been 'an "impasse" about Syria'. After the meeting of the Council of Four, Balfour added in a postscript that 'since writing the above the P.M. has declared "ex cathedra" that under no circumstances will Britain accept Syria. A Commission is to be sent there, and also to Mesopotamia and Armenia – to find out who among the Allies would be most welcome as Mandatory in each of these regions!'[80]

Pichon had opened the discussion. After a long exposition of the history of the Syrian question, which according to him had its origins in the Sykes–Picot agreement, he wound up by stating that 'France had strongly protested against any idea of dividing Syria. Syria had geographical and historic unity,' but that the French government 'frankly avowed that they did not want the responsibility of administering Palestine, though they would prefer to see it under an international administration'. What the French government wanted was '(1) That the whole Syrian region should be treated as a unit: and (2) That France should become the mandatory of the League of Nations of this region'. Pichon also mentioned that 'recently Lord Milner had left a map with M. Clemenceau [which] greatly circumscribed the French area'. According to him:

> It was evident that the French government could not look at this scheme […] even though they had the greatest desire to reach an agreement […] French opinion would not admit that France could be even partly excluded

after the sacrifices she had made in the War, even if she had not been able to play a great part in the Syrian campaign. In consequence, the minimum that France could accept was what had been put forward in the French government's Note to Mr Lloyd George.

Lloyd George replied that Pichon 'had opened as though the question of the mandate for Syria was one between Great Britain and France. There was, in fact, no such question as far as Great Britain was concerned.' He therefore 'wished to say at once that just as we had disinterested ourselves in 1912 [see also Chapter 1, section 'Lord Kitchener Intervenes'], so we now disinterested ourselves in 1919. If the Conference asked us to take Syria, we should reply in the negative.' At the same time, Lloyd George reminded Pichon that under the Sykes–Picot agreement France was 'prepared to recognise and uphold an independent Arab State or Confederation of States' in area 'A'. He asked whether France was 'prepared to accept that?' Pichon replied in the affirmative, 'if France was promised a mandate for Syria, she would undertake to do nothing except in agreement with the Arab State or Confederation of States. This is the role which France demanded in Syria. If Great Britain would only promise her good offices, he believed that France could reach an understanding with Feisal.'

At that point, President Wilson intervened. He finally took up the position that the Foreign Office – Cecil in the first place – and the Eastern Committee had worked and hoped for since the autumn of 1918. He explained that the USA were:

> Indifferent to the claims both of Great Britain and France over peoples unless these peoples wanted them. One of the fundamental principles to which the United States of America adhered was the consent of the governed. This was ingrained in the United States of America thought. Hence, the only idea from the United States of America point of view was as to whether France would be agreeable to the Syrians. The same applied as to whether Great Britain would be agreeable to the inhabitants of Mesopotamia. It might not be his business, but if the question was made his business, owing to the fact that it was brought before the Conference, the only way to deal with it was to discover the desires of the population of these regions.

He had been told that, 'if France insisted on occupying Damascus and Aleppo, there would be instant war'. The President asked Allenby, who attended the meeting, 'what would happen if France occupied the region of Syria, "even as narrowly defined"'. The latter replied that 'there would be the strongest possible opposition by the whole of the Moslems, and especially by the Arabs [...] If the French were given a mandate in Syria, there would be serious trouble and probably war.' After an adjournment, Wilson:

> Suggested that the fittest men that could be obtained should be selected to form an Inter-Allied Commission to go to Syria, extending their enquiries, if they led them, beyond the confines of Syria. Their object should be to elucidate the state of opinion and the soil to be worked on by any mandatory [...] If we were to send a Commission [...] it would, at any rate, convince the world that the Conference had tried to do all it could to find the most scientific basis possible for a settlement. The Commission should be composed of an equal number of French, British, Italian and American representatives. He would send it with carte blanche to tell the facts as they found them.

Clemenceau said that 'he adhered in principle to an inquiry', but asked 'for twenty-four hours of reflection before setting up the Commission'. Lloyd George declared that 'he had no objection to an inquiry into Palestine and Mesopotamia [...] Neither would he object to an inquiry into Armenia.' It was decided that the president would undertake 'to draft a Terms of Reference to the Commission'.[81]

At the Foreign Office in London, Archibald Clark Kerr thought it 'strange that we should not have been informed officially of the despatch to the Levant of the Commission'. Personally he was 'disposed to welcome it, even at the risk of further delay, seeing in it considerable chance of the collapse of the bulk of the French pretensions'. Curzon could not disagree more. He considered it 'a fantastic proposal', and 'a confession of hopeless failure at Paris'.[82] In his reply to Balfour's letter, Curzon, however, was less outspoken. Balfour's description of the Middle Eastern problem had caused him 'a good deal of anxiety, which, so far from being diminished has been considerably increased by the information that has since come to hand as to the conclusions arrived at in Paris during the last few days'. He put it to Balfour that 'if the Commission reports in favour of a French Syria, it will have to ignore all the evidence which will be supplied to it. If it reports against a French Syria, are the French prepared to surrender their ambitions?' Curzon was quite unhappy with the way things were going in Paris, but admitted that his observations were 'only the reflections of an outsider who is at some distance from the scene; and it may be that, if I had been upon the spot, my policy would not have been any more sound or effective'.[83]

In the meantime, Faysal threatened to leave for Syria. At the beginning of February he had already written to his father that he 'wished to return (to) Syria when Commission for ascertaining public wish there [was] approved at Paris',[84] and although Briand had assured him that the French wanted to meet him halfway, they still treated him with 'studied contempt'. According to Henry Wickham-Steed, editor of *The Times*, 'in order to avoid this breach, which would probably have led to hostilities between the Arabs and the French in Syria, I made an effort to bring the chief exponents of the British and the French views together'. During a meeting that lasted for 'nearly six hours', the Syrian question was 'discussed in all its aspects'. In the end, the participants 'reached so large a measure of agreement that Colonel Lawrence undertook to advise Feisal not to leave Paris, while the French undertook to get into direct touch with Feisal. In this way it was hoped to avoid the necessity of sending out a special Commission from the Conference to Syria, and to settle the question in Paris.'[85]

Lloyd George had second thoughts about the commission. During a meeting of the Council of Four on 27 March, he reported that one of his administrators from Mesopotamia who had recently arrived in Paris (the Prime Minister referred to Arnold Wilson) held views that quite differed from Allenby's regarding Arab sentiments towards the French, and claimed that the arrival of the proposed commission could only lead to unrest in the region, while the mentality of the people of the East would prevent the commission from being able to establish what they really wished. President Wilson was not impressed. He preferred 'despite everything an inquiry, done with impartiality'. When Lloyd George added that Faysal, too, seemed to have changed his attitude, the President remained unmoved. He insisted that they held fast to their decision. Clemenceau sided with Wilson. He wished them to go through with the inquiry, 'avoiding all loss of time'.[86]

President Wilson drafted the terms of reference for the commission,[87] and appointed two American commissioners – Dr Henry King, the president of Oberlin College, and Charles Crane, a Chicago businessman with strong links to Wilson. During a meeting of the Council of Four on 11 April, Wilson wished to know whether Clemenceau and Lloyd George had appointed theirs. The latter replied he had not, and that he believed that there should be 'a conversation on this subject between M. Clemenceau and me'. The President reminded his colleagues that a formal decision had been taken and that he did not see 'how an agreement between France and England could relieve us from sending this commission to Asia. What we need to know is not whether France and England are agreed, but what is the sentiment of the populations.' Clemenceau did not deny this, but it was useful to know beforehand 'how France and England can reach agreement on the question of the mandates, in order to be able to present proposals that the populations could accept'. After a brief discussion it was decided that the British and French governments would have further talks on the Syrian question. Lloyd George once again stressed Britain's disinterestedness, and declared that he would give Faysal to understand that he should not count on 'discord between France and England'.[88] All this seemed to indicate that the British prime minister had decided to settle the question in Paris, but after the meeting Hankey was instructed to say to Balfour that Lloyd George concurred in the foreign secretary's proposal that Sir Henry McMahon and Commander Hogarth should be the British commissioners, and that Balfour 'should make the necessary arrangements [...] for them to come to Paris immediately, with a view to an early start on their mission'.[89]

The next day, Saturday 12 April, a meeting took place between Lloyd George and Clemenceau, accompanied by Pichon, Berthelot and Goût. According to Mallet the negotiations 'completely failed owing to the extravagance of M. Pichon demands'.[90] The meeting between Clemenceau and Faysal, on Sunday, also ended in failure. As the French prime minister explained to House the following day, 'he and Feisal came to an agreement, but after Feisal had talked with Col. Lawrence [...] he withdrew from what he had said to Clemenceau'.[91] Lloyd George had had enough. On Monday morning, just before he was to leave for London to address the House of Commons, he assured Lawrence that 'the commission would go at once'.[92] However, the commission did not go. Although Balfour telegraphed to Curzon on 18 April that Lloyd George 'desired the arrangements to be expedited, so that it is desirable that MacMahon and Hogarth should come at once',[93] Arnold Toynbee minuted one day later that Albert Lybyer, the secretary of the American commissioners had told him that King had been 'informed by Col. House last night that the Commission would not go, and that he was free to make personal plans'.[94]

Clemenceau and Faysal had agreed on an exchange of letters, 'on the clear understanding that Feisal's reply to [Clemenceau's] letter would be of a satisfactory character'.⁹⁵ On 17 April the French prime minister sent a draft letter, in which the French government declared that they recognised 'the right of Syria to independence in the form of a federation of autonomous governments in agreement with the traditions and wishes of the populations', and claimed that Faysal had recognised 'that France is the Power qualified to render Syria the assistance of various advisors necessary to introduce order and realise the progress demanded by the Syrian populations'.⁹⁶ Faysal's draft reply, according to Lawrence 'a frank statement of what the Syrians wanted from the Powers and were willing to offer France', had been rejected by the French and 'therefore never transmitted'.⁹⁷ On 20 April, Faysal submitted another letter, which proved to be acceptable, even though its wording was highly ambiguous. The Emir assured Clemenceau that he had been:

> Deeply impressed by the disinterested friendliness of your statements to me while I was in Paris, and must thank you for having been the first to suggest the dispatch of the inter-allied Commission, which is to leave shortly for the East to ascertain the wishes of the local peoples as to the future organisation of their country. I am sure that the people of Syria will know how to show you their gratitude.⁹⁸

Faysal left Paris the following day. House recorded in his diary that the Emir had come to bid him goodbye. During their conversation, Faysal had 'insisted that the Syrian Commission should go as soon as possible. If it did not, he would not be responsible for the peace in that part of the world.' House thereupon wrote a letter to Wilson 'asking him if I should stop Dr King [...] who was about to return to America. The President asked me to stop him which I did. I asked King to get in touch with Charles R. Crane and arrange with the French and British Commissioners for their trip.'⁹⁹

At the Council of Four the next day, Clemenceau handed Lloyd George a copy of Faysal's letter, and claimed that the Emir had been satisfied. He 'asked what was to be done about the Commission'. Lloyd George replied that 'he thought the Commission should soon start. It was settled so far as he was concerned.'¹⁰⁰ Four days later Clemenceau returned to the subject. He reminded Lloyd George that the latter had spoken to him about the dangers of sending the commission and that it had been the British prime minister who had proposed that the French and the British should first reach an agreement. Lloyd George answered that all he had to say was that the British government 'absolutely refused to accept a mandate for Syria. To us, the friendship of France is worth ten Syrias.' Wilson for his part repeated that 'the mandates question cannot be simply settled by an arrangement between you two'.[101] The three decided that '(1) The French government should immediately nominate their representatives. (2) The Commission should start as soon as possible.'[102] When Toynbee and Lybyer visited Goût the next day, however, the latter told them that:

> He had received no instructions from either M. Clemenceau or M. Pichon, though he had seen M. Pichon this afternoon; that they had no commissioners in view, and that their appointment would take some time; and that in his opinion the season was so far advanced that it would only be possible now to visit Armenia – leaving all the Arab countries to the autumn and winter![103]

On 4 May Wickham-Steed had an interview with Clemenceau, during which the latter 'complained bitterly that Lloyd George had continually failed to keep his word to him'. He told the editor of *The Times* that:

> At first Lloyd George expressed himself entirely in favour of a French mandate for Syria and said that the only obstacle was Wilson. 'Agree with Wilson,' he added, 'and I will help you in every way, provided that you do not want to conquer Syria, that you give up your claims to Cilicia and that you leave Mosul in the British sphere'.

All this Clemenceau had done, but Lloyd George had done nothing. The latest insult was that the Prime Minister had 'allowed Allenby to send away to Cilicia the regiment of cavalry which the British had asked me to send to Beirut. I really cannot stand this sort of slap in the face.'[104] The French embassy delivered an official protest the next day. Allenby's decision tended to 'remove all French troops from the regions of Syria'. The French government therefore demanded the suspension of Allenby's orders.[105] The officials at the Foreign Office failed to appreciate that Allenby's order was more or less the last straw as far as the French were concerned. The situation in Syria was 'still a military one and as long as General Allenby is in command he will continue to give such orders as he finds necessary to deal with the situation. The question has no political aspect whatsoever.'[106] This was also what Curzon told Cambon. Allenby's orders were 'probably required by military considerations' and to him the question appeared 'to be in the main not political, but military. Through the mouth of our Prime Minister in Paris we had dissociated ourselves in a political sense from Syria. The fact that our troops were in occupation was the result, not of any political design, but of the circumstances of the war.'[107] Clemenceau nevertheless declined to pursue the matter any further. He explained to Wickham-Steed on 11 May that 'he was much bothered with other matters and did not wish to raise another thorny question with Lloyd George at this juncture'.[108]

The next day, Kerr informed Forbes Adam that the Prime Minister was 'anxious that the Syrian Commission should start as soon as possible,'[109] but on 14 May George Montgomery of the American delegation telephoned Vansittart 'to ask if the Commission really was going'. Vansittart replied that he 'supposed so and we were looking about for a ship'. The American then informed him that he had just been told by Goût 'it wasn't going', and that the latter 'seemed so cocksure that he (Mr Montgomery) thought we must have settled something with the French behind their (American) back. I said "nothing of the kind", but it is evident the French are going to resist till the last.'[110] At the Council of Four that same day, Lloyd George and Clemenceau decided on yet another attempt 'to make a clean job' of the Syrian question. The Prime Minister suggested that 'at the moment, the best plan would be to draw up a map of occupation, showing what territories would be occupied by the various Powers concerned'. They appointed André Tardieu and Sir Henry Wilson to examine the question and work out a solution.[111]

Hogarth had come over to Paris in order to make the necessary preparations. He informed Balfour on 20 May that when he had talked with Goût and de Caix:

> Both gentlemen made it quite clear that they have the strongest objection to any international Commission going to Syria at this stage, but would welcome such a Commission as soon as the Mandate for Syria was irrevocably given to France and she was in sole military occupation.
> The commission is, therefore, in a complete impasse from which it can only emerge by such pressure being exercised by the highest authorities.[112]

The foreign secretary agreed. He wrote to Lloyd George that the Commission was 'being blocked by the French who refuse to move. The

F.O. delegation cannot deal with the situation. It must be tackled by the "4".[113] Balfour simply washed his hands of the whole affair. House for his part noted in his diary on 20 May that he had:

> Told the President it was something of a scandal that this Commission had not already gone to Syria as promised the Arabs. The honor of Great Britain, France and the United States were at stake, and I hoped he would insist that the Commission leave at once. The President assured me that he had done everything he could in the direction indicated. I then suggested that he set Monday [26 May; R.H.L.] as the time when our Commission would start regardless of the French and English. He adopted the suggestion and said he would tell Clemenceau and Lloyd George tomorrow.[114]

President Wilson announced at the Council of Four the next day that 'the Delegates whom he had nominated were men of such standing that he could not keep them waiting any longer in Paris, consequently he had instructed them to leave for Syria on Monday'. Lloyd George stated that this also 'applied to the British Delegates and he thought he would give them the same orders'. Clemenceau replied that 'in this case he must drop out', and then gave free rein to his pent-up frustrations with the Syrian question:

> The promises made to him had not been kept [...] [In December] he had come to London and had asked Mr Lloyd George to say exactly what he wanted. Mr Lloyd George had said Mosul and Palestine. He had returned to Paris, and in spite of the objections of M. Pichon and the Quai d'Orsay, he had conceded it. Then Mr Lloyd George had said France and Great Britain would get along all right. Early in the year the proposal had been made for the evacuation of Syria by British troops and the substitution of French troops. Lord Milner had asked him to put this aside for the moment and had undertaken to discuss it with him. He had never done so. Then Lord Milner had promised to help M. Clemenceau with Emir Feisal. He had never carried out his promise. After this, Lord Milner had produced a map by which Syria was divided in order to provide a railway for the British to Mesopotamia [...] He had even agreed to this.

Here Lloyd George interrupted and wanted to know 'what M. Clemenceau's grievance was? What constituted a breach of faith?' Clemenceau, however, ignored him and continued that:

The last phase had concerned the withdrawal of British troops. It had been agreed to arrange for zones of occupation. It had been agreed that M. Tardieu and General Sir Henry Wilson should study the question. After three days of consultation, General Wilson said that there could be no arrangement unless the limits of Syria were fixed. M. Tardieu had quite properly said that this was not a matter he could deal with.

Lloyd George replied that 'as regards the charge of a break of faith, this was without any foundation. On the occasion of the London visit, Mr Lloyd George had promised Syria to France provided that he gave up Mosul.' Respecting the 'proposal that he had made for a redistribution of the forces in Turkey in order to relieve the British Army', he explained that when he was away at London 'for some reason he had never quite understood, the scheme had fallen through'. Furthermore, as far as not keeping one's word was concerned, France had never appointed her delegates to the inter-allied commission. He 'did not say that M. Clemenceau had not kept faith, but he certainly had not carried out the bargain'. Regarding the boundaries that Wilson had submitted to Tardieu, these were 'merely a proposal that was under discussion, and there was no breach of faith here'.

Clemenceau stated that he was ready to send his delegates the moment 'the relief of the occupation forces had begun', but he believed that it was 'useless to send a commission to Syria to make inquiries under the dictatorship of General Allenby'. Lloyd George was very offended. He had done his utmost to help the French in Syria, and it had only brought him the accusation that the British had broken their word. He considered that 'M. Clemenceau would have to make excuses for having brought this accusation against us'.[115] The French prime minister refused and a 'frightful row' ensued. According to Hankey, 'both lost their tempers violently and made the most absurd accusations [...] It was all over the question of the frontier line between Syria and Palestine. We are at rather a deadlock there.'[116]

The next day, Clemenceau and Lloyd George continued their dispute. This time there were no accusations of bad faith. The French prime minister explained that:

He had been very surprised on the previous day to see the map now before him [...] what had surprised him was to find the line across the desert had been moved northwards for a considerable distance. In fact, the new line he saw on this map was the line on the map Lord Milner had shown him, and which Mr Lloyd George had professed at the time not to know anything about. After all that he had previously given up, this new concession was asked for.

Lloyd George replied that 'once Mosul had been conceded to the British, the upper line shown on the map was the only possible line', and threatened that 'unless the map he had presented was agreed to, he would have to await the report of the Commission before withdrawing the British troops'. Clemenceau was not impressed. He was 'not willing [...] to accept the line now proposed', and with regard to Lloyd George's threat, he 'thought that Mr Lloyd George was wrong, but he would take very great care not to push matters so far as to make trouble between the Entente. As for himself, he would say plainly that he would no longer associate in connection with the British in this part of the world, because the harm done to his country was too great.' When President Wilson interjected that he 'had never been able to see by what right France and Great Britain gave [Syria] away to anyone', Lloyd George confirmed that 'he was quite willing to abide by the decision of the inhabitants as interpreted by the Commission'. The British prime minister, however, like his French counterpart, did not want to push matters too far and announced that 'he could not send Commissioners if the French would not send any, but the American Commissioners could go alone'. Sir Henry Wilson thereupon 'asked if General Allenby would remain in command in Syria, and whether he was authorised to refuse to allow French troops to be sent in'. Lloyd George answered in the affirmative: as long as Allenby 'was in command and was responsible for order [he] must have a free hand in the matter until a settlement had been reached'. The impasse regarding Syria remained complete.[117]

Balfour sent Lloyd George a memorandum on the Syrian question the same day. He emphasised that the British position was:

> Not a very logical one. We are garrisoning Syria with British troops [...] while, at the same time, we have explained explicitly, not only to the French but to all the world, that we have no Syrian ambitions. We are thus, to all appearance, doing something which is highly inconvenient to ourselves and, at the same time, highly offensive to the French.

The foreign secretary wondered 'why are we doing it?' As far as he could make out, this was mainly because the British believed that, 'if our forces are withdrawn and if the Arabs and the French come into direct contact with each other, there will probably be bloodshed, and possibly serious Military operations'. However, the fact was, so Balfour pointed out, that the French clearly thought otherwise, and he could not see 'what possible reason we have for preventing them, as it were by force, from putting their convictions to the test'. There existed no doubt 'a real danger of an Arab–French collision. If so, the French might find themselves involved in costly Military operations […] But they will never make this discovery as long as we remain there.' Balfour dismissed another possible explanation of Britain's illogical behaviour, 'that to denude Syria of British troops would be to betray our Arab Ally'. He did not think 'this view can be maintained. The French have in the most explicit terms promised to deal with Syria on the principle of self-determination, and subject to the general control of the League of Nations.' He therefore did 'not see why we should suggest any doubts as to their intentions, or modify our policy to suit Arab prejudices'. The way out of the Syrian morass Balfour saw was to 'withdraw British troops behind the frontier which we think is the proper frontier of Syria', and to 'inform the French that we mean to hold this frontier until the Conference comes to a decision on this vexed question'. Faysal should also be told what the British intended to do, reminding him of 'the French promises contained in the Declaration of November 8th […] on the subject of self-determination', as a way of 'formally notifying him that his interests have not been ignored'.[118]

On 15 May 1919, Clayton had wired the Foreign Office that Faysal had asked that 'he may be given indication whether Britain would accept mandate for Syria if asked by Peace Conference on recommendation of Commission. If possible some answer should be given him.' Mallet minuted on 26 May that 'as the Prime Minister has said that he will not take the mandate for Syria, as discussions are now proceeding with a view to the despatch of French troops in substitution of our own, and as the prospects of an international Commission going are vanishing', it was 'a question whether we ought not frankly to let Feisal know that owing to reasons of which he is probably aware, it is not possible for Great Britain to accept the offer that he makes – and that we recommend him to come to terms with the French – Clayton ought, anyway, to know our policy'. Hardinge agreed, 'in any case it would be well that Feisal should understand that Great Britain will not accept a mandate for Syria', but Balfour warned that it was 'only the Prime Minister' who could do this. Kerr was subsequently consulted to obtain Lloyd George's views. He reported that 'a telegram should be sent to

General Clayton saying that he can only reply to Feisal that, as the Prime Minister has already stated on several occasions in Paris, the British government is determined not to take a Mandate for Syria'. A telegram in this sense was sent on 29 May.[119]

The American President finally decided to send his commissioners alone. They left for the Middle East on 28 May.[120] Lord Eustace Percy informed Hardinge that Lloyd George still hoped that 'the British and French Sections of the Commission may follow shortly',[121] but this was not to be, even though the Prime Minister made a last attempt at the Council of Four on 31 May 1919.

The occasion was a telegram from Allenby, containing two messages from Faysal. In the first, Faysal proclaimed that he considered himself '*irresponsible* for what may occur if the French force is increased even by one soldier'. In the second, Faysal protested that 'we cannot accept to be divided like cattle. We cannot accept any decision except that of the liberty of nations and parties by sending the commission.' According to Allenby the situation was:

> Extremely grave. Unless you can at once enable me to reassure Feisal and tell him that the Commission is coming out and will decide the future of the country it is certain he will raise the Arabs against the French and ourselves. This will jeopardise position of my troops in Syria and will seriously endanger the whole situation in Syria and Palestine. A word from Feisal will bring against us all the warlike Bedouins from the East of the Jordan, on whose friendly attitude depends the safety of Palestine and the security of my long lines of communication.[122]

Balfour also chimed in. He produced another memorandum in which he declared that the British delegation urged 'with the greatest insistence the importance of sending the Commission to the East as soon as possible'.[123] At the Council of Four, Lloyd George read out Allenby's telegram. It indicated that 'the situation in Syria would be extremely grave unless the Commission of the Peace Conference should come to Syria [...] Hence, he felt that the moment had come to decide whether the Commission should proceed at once [...] The situation was so serious that he could not postpone action.' Clemenceau would not budge, 'as long as Syria remained entirely in British military occupation, and Mr Lloyd George's latest proposals held the field, it was useless to send French Commissioners'. The only concession he was prepared to make was that 'he would undertake not to send any more French troops against the wishes of the British government'. The British prime minister reiterated that 'he would not send Commissioners if the French did not'. He subsequently 'read a copy of the telegram he proposed to send to General Allenby. At M. Clemenceau's request he agreed to alter one passage in order to make it clear that the French were not willing to send Commissioners until the relief of British troops by French troops had been arranged.'[124] Sir Edmund was therefore informed that 'as an arrangement to do this cannot be agreed, French Commissioners will not go out. Under these circumstances we think it for obvious reasons inexpedient to send ours,' and authorised 'to state when Americans arrive that the British government will give the fullest weight to the advice which the Council [...] will receive from the American Commissioners'.[125]

Gathering a Breakthrough: June to September 1919

Until the end of May, the British authorities, whether in Paris or London, neither questioned Allenby's assessment that the arrival of French troops in Syria would lead to bloodshed on a large scale, nor his claim that he acted as an impartial arbiter who had to navigate between the irreconcilable Syrian ambitions of the French on the one hand, and Faysal and the Arab nationalists on the other hand, but in the course of June, this gradually began to change. Lieut.-Colonel Gribbon of the General Staff was the first to challenge Allenby's credibility. He observed in a memorandum of 12 June that 'too much weight should not be attached to the contemplated danger from the Arabs' and, according to his calculations, Faysal's 'whole force' during his campaign 'did not exceed 10,000 men'.[126] Britain was confronted with the alternatives 'of bringing her policy as far as possible into line with that of a relatively solid France or of an unstable Arabia. And it may be as well to recognise here, once and for all, that a really united Arabia is an illusion and a dream. Arabs never have combined and never will combine.' It was clear which alternative Gribbon favoured, 'we must not allow our relations with [France] to be displaced by our relations with the unstable Arabs'. The challenge that remained was 'to make the best arrangement for the British Empire between the French and the Arabs'. Such an arrangement would 'enable us to maintain our relations with France without detriment to the strategical position which we have acquired in this war'. Britain 'must retain the possibility of direct air, railway and oil routes between Mesopotamia and the Mediterranean'.[127]

Gribbon had also talked the matter over with Vansittart, who entirely agreed. The latter minuted that 'the only "realpolitik" for us is to take a line in the Near East that will keep in with the French (much as I dislike it) [...] and not to be too nervous of Arab susceptibilities. We cannot sacrifice the reality of France for an Arab unity that will never materialise.'[128]

On 12 June, Allenby sent a telegram to the Foreign Office from which it appeared that he had thought fit in the statement of British policy Faysal had requested, to combine Balfour's telegram of 29 May, in which it had been stated that the British government were determined not to take a mandate for Syria, and Balfour's telegram of 31 May, in which it had been said that the British government would give the fullest weight to the report of the American commissioners. Sir Edmund had declared to Faysal that 'His Majesty's Government have expressed unwillingness to accept a mandate for Syria but will give fullest weight to advice of Commission in the Council of Allied and Associated Powers'. This declaration was not well received at the Foreign Office. Kidston complained that it again hedged 'over the vital question of whether we would accept a mandate or not'. Graham was also critical. He believed that 'our local attitude in this question cannot be said to be altogether above reproach and we run the risk of still further annoying the French while at the same time misleading the Arabs'. He also wondered whether the Foreign Office should not insist 'on Feisal being clearly told', but Curzon refused to contemplate this. It was 'for Paris to put Feisal right, if he is going wrong. As no single piece of advice that we have been given with regard to Syria has been accepted at Paris. They had better paddle their canoe in their own way.'[129]

Allenby's ambiguous wording had precisely the effect on Faysal the Foreign Office officials feared. On 15 June Sir Edmund reported that the Emir had replied that he had:

> Noted Great Britain's expression of unwillingness to take mandate for Syria. Its intention to give the fullest weight to advice Peace Commission however is cheerfully understood by us all. The Syrians will be unanimous in expressing to Commission their wish to have Britain and no other [...] profoundly trusting British honour will never permit those who pray for its assistance to be thrown away into strange arms.

Hubert Young ruefully minuted that Allenby's reply had given Faysal 'an entirely wrong impression, and we shall not only be suspected by the French of playing double (and with some justice), but shall also be accused by Faisal (with equal justice) of letting him down, if and when we finally decline the mandate'.[130] However, this time Paris reacted decisively. On 26 June, a stern telegram drafted by Mallet and amended by Balfour was sent to Allenby. The latter was informed that:

> Feisal has based his message on a misunderstanding of your reply [...] Feisals's view apparently is that while H.M.G. are reluctant to be mandatory for Syria, they would accept position if American Commission advised that this was in accordance with the wishes of the people concerned.
>
> This however is a mistake. H.M.G. have not departed from view expressed orally by Prime Minister, I think in your presence [...] that in no circumstances would Britain become mandatory for Syria.
>
> It is evident he is unwilling to accept even the most direct statement as conclusive, but it is all important that he should be made to understand that whatever happens Great Britain must refuse to take any leading part in guidance or control of Syrian affairs, and that he is quite without justification in thinking that this refusal constitutes an abandonment either of himself or of the Arab cause.

At the Foreign Office, people were relieved. According to Kidston the telegram was 'at least something definite and should prevent any further elusive statements to Feisal'. Sir Ronald was 'very glad that the situation is being made perfectly clear to Faisal at last', while Curzon minuted that 'Paris has paddled to our canoe'.[131]

The peace treaty with Germany was to be signed on 28 June 1919. Wilson and Lloyd George intended to return home immediately after the ceremony. On 26 June, Balfour addressed yet another memorandum to the Prime Minister, in which he expressed his earnest hope that 'the departure of the two most important members of the Supreme Council will not take place until the outlines of the Turkish settlement are more or less agreed to'.[132] However, his hope was dashed. On 2 July, in reaction to a telegram from Allenby in which the latter had explained that he considered it important that 'no decision regarding the future of Syria and Palestine should be published until Commission had made its report', Kidston minuted that Sir Eyre Crowe had told him that 'the consideration of the Turkish Treaty terms in Paris had again been indefinitely postponed. The idea being that time should be given to President Wilson to sound the US people as to whether they would accept a mandate for any part of the Ottoman Empire.'¹³³ Moreover, if Lawrence was to be believed, the prospects that the USA would take a mandate looked very bleak. Kerr wrote to Lloyd George on 16 July that Lawrence had received a letter from Cabot Lodge 'stating that under no circumstances would America accept any mandate in Turkey or its late territories and that he had a majority in the Senate with him on the point'.¹³⁴ Two days later, Henry White of the American delegation informed the Council of Heads of Delegations – the successor to the Council of Four – that Wilson had telegraphed that the delay before the USA would be able to decide whether or not to take a mandate for certain parts of the Ottoman Empire would 'be very considerable'. As far as Clemenceau was concerned, this was just as well. He was 'for certain reasons not ready to talk about Asia Minor'. He did not wish 'to wait indefinitely', but 'for the time being he could make no statement. When other work had been done, the Council would do its best to settle the affairs of Turkey.'¹³⁵

From a conversation with Balfour that same day, it appeared that Clemenceau had forgotten nothing and that he still smarted from the way the British had treated the French with regard to the Syrian question. He stated that Allenby's attitude:

> Inspired him with mistrust. That attitude was anti-French: the General would not permit the French to relieve troops in Asia Minor: he had studiously excluded the French from Syria: he had sent them to Cilicia where France had no interests: he said that the French were unpopular; if that were true, it must be ascribed entirely to the action of British agents […] he had piles of dossiers in regard to the anti-French attitude of British agents and he was prepared to prove everything that he said. If General Allenby were not personally privy to this, at all events his entourage was.

Balfour 'expressed regret that M. Clemenceau should have thought it necessary to bring up the vexed question of Syria', and 'said that he was sure that these charges against General Allenby could not be sustained, and that no responsible British officer could conceivably desire to interfere with the popularity of the French', especially considering that 'Great Britain was not disposed in any circumstances to accept a mandate for Syria'.¹³⁶

A few days later Balfour was no longer so sure. Kerr explained to Lloyd George that:

A certain Major Barker, who was Chief Political Officer at Tripoli, has just passed through Paris on his way to England. He disturbed Mr Balfour a good deal by saying that the British political officers in Syria had no notion that the British government had declared that in no circumstances would it accept a mandate for Syria until early in July. In consequence he had always replied to the many deputations asking him what the British intentions were, that he did not know and that they must express their own preference to the Commission.

The result of this interview is to make Mr Balfour feel that the French have got a certain measure of a case against us.[137]

Balfour clearly failed to realise that part of the confusion had been created by his two telegrams to Allenby of 29 and 31 May, and that only with his telegram of 26 June could there no longer be a shadow of a doubt as to Great Britain's position on a possible Syrian mandate. Barker's statement that it was not until early in July that the British political officers knew about it should not have come as a surprise to the foreign secretary. What mattered, however, was that Balfour, as a result of his conversation with Barker, now also began to lend credence to stories that the British military authorities in Syria had not been acting fairly in their dealings with the French. As he observed to the Foreign Office, this ignorance of British policy towards Syria might well have 'caused suspicion in the French mind as to the genuine intentions of H.M.G., and may possibly even have given rise to action in individual cases of a nature to lend some colour to these repeated French complaints'.[138] It was all very distressing. Balfour remarked to Colonel Meinertzhagen that 'we had not been honest with either French or Arab, but it was now more preferable to quarrel with the Arab rather than with the French, if there was to be a quarrel at all'. When Meinertzhagen opined that 'we must now decide between agreeing to French aspirations and abandoning Arab dreams in Syria, or we must openly oppose the French Syrian Policy and back the Arab', the foreign secretary, however, demurred. He still 'thought a working agreement could be reached between French and Arab'.[139] Kerr was less optimistic. He fully realised the importance of squaring 'our difficulties with France about Syria', but French feeling was 'still very bitter and now that the war is over and everybody is preoccupied with reconstruction it is becoming in some ways more difficult to deal with the situation'.[140]

On 11 August 1919, Balfour completed a long memorandum on the Syrian question. He confessed that the effect this question was having on Anglo–French relations caused him 'considerable anxiety – an anxiety not diminished by the fact that very little is openly said about it, though much is hinted'. As far as the foreign secretary was concerned there was much to be said for the French 'attitude of resentful suspicion'. Not only had Clemenceau made concession after concession, which had only induced the British to come back and ask for more, but at the very moment that Lloyd George announced that England under no circumstances would accept a mandate for Syria, 'and ever since, officers of the British army were occupied in carrying on an active propaganda in favour of England'. Balfour could very well understand that in French eyes these manoeuvres had but one object, 'namely, to make the British mandate, which had been so solemnly, and doubtless, so sincerely, repudiated in Paris, a practical necessity in the East'. The British should face the fact that they had 'made a dramatic renunciation, but it has fallen flat. We have made a *beau geste*, and none have applauded.' Balfour partly blamed, if he was 'rightly informed, the British officers in Syria [who] have not always played up to the British Ministers in Paris'. He acknowledged that this was 'vehemently and most sincerely denied by General Clayton. But friends of mine from Syria confirm the view.' Personally he knew 'one case in which a British officer, though well acquainted with the Prime Minister's pledge, thought himself precluded by his instructions from giving an Arab deputation […] the clear and decisive answer which, by destroying all hopes, would effectually removed all misunderstandings'.

The 'unhappy truth' was that 'France, England, and America have got themselves into a position over the Syrian problem so inextricably confused that no really neat and satisfactory issue is now possible for any of them'. The sending of the commission to Syria was a glaring example. Did the powers really mean:

> To consult principally the wishes of the inhabitants? We mean nothing of the kind. According to the universally accepted view there are only three possible mandatories – England, America, and France. Are we going 'chiefly to consider the wishes of the inhabitants' in deciding which of these is to be selected? We are going to do nothing of the kind. England has refused. America will refuse. So that, whatever the inhabitants may wish, it is France they will certainly have.

Balfour saw only one way out of the Syrian muddle, and that was to retain 'the fundamental conception underlying the Sykes–Picot Agreement […] a French sphere centring round Syria, a British sphere centring round the Euphrates and the Tigris', while the 'blue' and 'red' areas 'should be absorbed in the general body of areas A and B, as ultimately defined'. Regarding the latter, Britain should no longer entertain thoughts of extending its zone of influence northwards. Claims on the town of Palmyra should be given up. It belonged 'naturally to the sphere of Damascus, if it belongs anywhere, and the French will take more trouble to prevent our having it that it will ever be worth, either to them, or to us.'[141]

Unaware of Balfour's memorandum – he only showed it to the Prime Minister at the beginning of September[142] – Lloyd George decided to take action. Hankey wrote to Curzon on 15 August to enquire 'what are the prospects of a Mandate being accepted by the United States government for some part of the former Turkish Empire?' He explained that he asked this because the Prime Minister thought that 'before the Cabinet separate they ought to have a discussion as to the next step in regard to Turkey'.[143] Davies informed Kerr the same day that Lloyd George had heard that Clemenceau was 'very anxious to discuss the question of Syria with Mr Balfour, and he wishes me to tell you that he will be glad if you will discourage this as much as possible'. Lloyd George feared that 'the old "Tiger" thinks that Mr Balfour will be more ready to come to terms with the French on this question than the Prime Minister himself would feel inclined to do'.[144] Kerr assured Lloyd George three days later that 'nothing at all has happened in regard to the reopening of negotiations about the Turkish settlement', but that Balfour was 'writing a memorandum on the whole question, which he will probably send you in a few days'.[145]

Ronald Lindsay, counsellor at the British embassy at Washington, telegraphed to Curzon on 16 August that the 'question of Turkish Mandate is very obscure and I have no authoritative opinion to quote but from general impressions consider acceptance is most unlikely […] In fact public opinion has not yet been formed on the subject but I confidently expect it will be hostile.'[146] Balfour had more or less gained the same impression. On 18 August, he wired Curzon that he had gathered 'from various somewhat obscure hints let fall by Mr Polk [Frank L. Polk, head of the American delegation; R.H.L.] in private conversations […] that probability of American Congress and Senate agreeing to United States accepting mandate for any part of former Turkish Empire is diminishing'.[147]

The War Cabinet discussed 'the question of the future of Turkey' for the first time the next day, 'in the light of information to the effect that the prospects of the United States of America accepting a mandate in Turkey are diminishing'. Against this background, 'various alternatives were discussed', which really meant, so Curzon explained to his wife afterwards, that 'no one knows what ought to be done, and meanwhile, of course, nothing is done, and we go on getting deeper and deeper into the mire'.[148] The War Cabinet also instructed Hankey 'to obtain immediately information as to the size of the garrisons of British and Indian forces in all parts of the former Turkish Empire, and also as to the cost of maintaining those forces'. The following day, the War Cabinet had yet another 'prolonged discussion on the future of Turkey, and the policy to be followed in regard to Syria'. No decisions were taken. Curzon was requested 'to discuss these questions with Mr Balfour', while 'the War Office should examine and report upon the question of how far the oasis of Tadmor (Palmyra) is essential to the construction of a railway and pipe-line between Mosul and the Mediterranean'.[149]

Curzon wrote a long letter to Balfour. He reported that the War Cabinet had explored the 'Eastern Question' in 'all its branches, with results (I am afraid) not much more satisfactory or conclusive than those which have been reached on earlier occasions'. However, one thing stood out: 'the burden of maintaining an English and Indian Army of 320,000 men in the various parts of the Turkish Empire and in Egypt, or of 225,000 men excluding Egypt, with its overwhelming cost, is one that cannot any longer be sustained'. This implied that the 'settlement of the Eastern Question cannot be postponed even till the date at which Wilson may have persuaded, or failed to persuade, the Senate to make up its mind about a Turkish Mandate'. Preparations for the evacuation of British troops from Syria should start as soon as possible, and it was therefore desirable that Allenby should come over, 'in order to ascertain his exact views and proposals about military evacuation'. The War Cabinet also 'agreed that we should go as far as we legitimately could, without breaking our pledges, to help the French in respect of Syria'. It was therefore 'essential to get hold of Feisal, to have a perfectly plain talk with him, to insist on his coming to terms with the French'. It might be that there was 'no alternative but to leave the French and him to fight it out to the end', but Curzon personally could not believe that 'the arrangement Feisal was so near to making three months ago, has now become impossible'. At the same time it should be ascertained 'from the

French what is the exact and irreducible nature of their claim', and so to establish 'the possible basis of a harmonious settlement for the future'. A question that still needed to be cleared up in this connection was the boundary between Syria and Mesopotamia, and 'at this point the Prime Minister attached an importance, which I should be inclined to think excessive, to the necessity of having a railway and a pipeline exclusively in British hands from Mesopotamia to a Mediterranean port'.[150]

It seemed that the Prime Minister was the last remaining obstacle in the way of reaching a settlement with the French. When Kerr arrived from Paris on 23 August, 'evidently impressed with the necessity of making concessions to the French in the Eastern Mediterranean', Lord Riddell noted in his diary that Lloyd George was still 'angry with the French for their attitude concerning Syria. He said that the Syrians would not have the French, and asked how the Allies could compel them to accept mandatories who were distasteful.'[151]

Endgame: September to October 1919

Lloyd George arrived at Hennequeville on the Normandy coast on 8 September in preparation for a visit to Paris from 12 to 15 September. In the next three days he held several conferences on the Syrian question with Allenby, who had become a field-marshal and been created Viscount Allenby of Megiddo.

On 8 September, Colonel Meinertzhagen, who had succeeded General Clayton as chief political officer of the EEF, telegraphed to Curzon that, if the rumour was correct that 'Prime Minister is proceeding to Paris to confer on Syrian question [...] it is urged that Emir Feisal be allowed to go there also without delay'. Kidston had not forgotten what had happened in November 1918. He held 'most strongly that no encouragement should be given to Feisal to come to Paris except with the fullest concurrence of the French. This seems obvious but perhaps it would be as well to telegraph it to Paris and repeat to Col. Meinertzhagen.' He subsequently added that, by Curzon's instructions, he had spoken to Davies. According to the latter the Prime Minister thought Meinertzhagen's suggestion 'an excellent one'. Kidston had told Davies that 'Lord Curzon felt very strongly that the assent of the French government must be obtained before any arrangements are made for facilitating Feisal's journey'. Lloyd George's private secretary had 'promised to communicate with Paris at once in this sense and to arrange that if the

French raised no objections instructions should be sent direct from Paris to Col. Meinertzhagen'.[152] Kerr duly wrote to Lloyd George the same day that Curzon thought 'it would be a mistake to summon [Faysal] without the concurrence of Clemenceau. He suggests that you should consult Clemenceau and if he agrees that a telegram should be sent direct to Feisal.'[153]

The first of the series of conferences with Allenby, which Bonar Law also attended, was held on 9 September. The participants had before them a statement Faysal had made to the military authorities at Damascus, as well as a letter he had written to the Prime Minister. Bonar Law 'remarked that the Emir Feisal seemed to hold that the various pledges made by the British government were inconsistent with one another'. Allenby readily agreed and 'said that it was extremely difficult to harmonise the different pledges which had been made to different people under different circumstances', but Lloyd George thought otherwise. He believed that 'a means could be found of reconciling the various pledges' and that there 'was no doubt from an examination of the Sykes–Picot Agreement that it had been based on these pledges [to Husayn]. The very wording proved this.' It appeared to him that the British 'could keep faith both with the French and with the Arabs if we were to clear out of Syria, handing our military posts there to the French, and, at the same time, clear out of Damascus, Homs, Hama, and Aleppo handing them over to Feisal. If the French then got into trouble with Feisal it would not be our fault.' That the French had already rejected this solution at the end of January apparently did not count; what did count was that Lloyd George wished to tell Clemenceau that the British were 'tired of these accusations of breach of faith and consequently decided to withdraw altogether [...] At the same time he would send for Feisal and notify him.'[154] The Prime Minister's pride, too, had been wounded, and instead of trying to come to an understanding with the French, he still wanted to teach them a lesson by confronting them with a fait accompli. At their next meeting, Hankey 'raised certain questions relating to the invitation to be sent to Feisal. Should the invitation be from the Conference or from the British government?' He pointed out that Allenby had told him that 'it was essential that the French should be communicated with'. The field-marshal's advice was not heeded (and Curzon's not even mentioned). After some discussion it was decided that Clemenceau should only be notified that an invitation had been sent to Faysal 'on the ground that the French and British governments had both promised that Feisal should be present at the Syrian settlement'.

Lloyd George, however, accepted Allenby's point of view that it was 'not essential to include the oasis of Tadmor within the British zone [...] The line can, therefore, be drawn somewhere east of Palmyra, and on this side there should be no special difficulty in meeting the French wishes'.[155] At least on this point there now was room for a compromise, which was just as well because Clemenceau, so Kerr reported after a conversation with the French prime minister on 11 September, 'implied by his manner rather than by his speech that he would never yield in the proposed line'.

During this interview, Clemenceau had emphasised that he attached 'supreme importance [...] to maintaining the unity between Great Britain and France. He thought it even more important than the union with America.' He had also repeated the familiar French position that a settlement of the Syrian question must proceed from the Sykes–Picot agreement. He fully accepted that there 'must be modifications in that Agreement [...] but they must be made as a result of give and take'. Lloyd George's policy of presenting Clemenceau with faits accomplis would give great offence, but Kerr considered that the French prime minister was in a weak position. It was his 'impression [...] that Clemenceau is not at all anxious to tackle the Syrian problem at this moment. No doubt that is partly because he realises the difficulties which would follow for France.'[156] This was an estimate that Lloyd George certainly shared. He had already explained to Allenby and Bonar Law that Clemenceau 'would not wish to send troops to Syria' until after the elections for the French National Assembly, which were scheduled for the middle of November.[157]

On 11 September, Lloyd George wrote to Clemenceau that 'the question of mandates for Turkey would take longer to settle than we had anticipated', and that the burden of garrisoning parts of the Ottoman Empire had become intolerable. This involved 'the question what will happen in the parts of the Turkish Empire we withdraw from. When the Syrian question is discussed, the British government wish to lay certain proposals before the Supreme Council in regard to it.' He hoped that Clemenceau would be able to see him before the planned meeting of the Council of Heads of Delegations on 15 September, and informed the latter that 'as the British and French governments are both pledged to the Emir Feisal that he shall be present when the settlement of Syrian is reached', he had taken 'the responsibility of inviting him to Paris'. Clemenceau reacted the same day. The question of the British troops in Syria only concerned 'the French and British governments, because of their agreements in 1916, and ought to be settled directly between them without any intermediary'. This was moreover 'a purely military question', which did not 'prejudge the final settlement of the Syrian question'. He therefore believed that 'the journey of the Emir Feisal at this moment, and before a previous understanding between ourselves, would not appear to have any definite object in view'.[158]

On the basis of the conferences with Allenby, Hankey and Kerr drew up an aide-mémoire that was to be presented at the meeting of the Heads of Delegations on 15 September. Its main points were the following:

1. Steps will be taken immediately to prepare for the evacuation by the British Army of Syria and Cilicia including the Taurus tunnel.
2. Notice is given both to the French government and to the Emir Feisal of our intentions to commence the evacuation on November 1, 1919.
3. In deciding to whom to hand over responsibility for garrisoning the various districts in the evacuated area, regard will be had to the engagements and declarations of the British and French governments, not only as between themselves, but as between them and the Arabs:
4. In pursuance of this policy the garrisons in Syria west of the Sykes–Picot line and the garrisons in Cilicia will be replaced by a French force, and the garrisons of Damascus, Homs, Hama, and Aleppo will be replaced by an Arab force.[159] […]
5. The territories occupied by British troops will then be Palestine, defined in accordance with its ancient boundaries of Dan to Beersheba, and Mesopotamia, including Mosul, the occupation thus being in harmony with the arrangements concluded in December 1918, between M. Clemenceau and Mr Lloyd George […]
6. Until the boundaries of Palestine and Mesopotamia are determined the British Commander-in-Chief shall have the right to occupy outposts in accordance with the boundary claimed by the British government.[160]

At the meeting of the Heads of Delegations, Lloyd George handed out the aide-mémoire, which he had already given to Clemenceau during their private meeting on 13 September, and summarised its contents. The French prime minister, in reaction, first stated that he was preparing a reply to the aide-mémoire and that he 'reserved the right to discuss [it] more fully'. He then went on to say that he 'could accept no condition in the Aide-Mémoire, other than the occupation by the French troops'. France was prepared to replace British troops in Cilicia and in Syria west of the Sykes–Picot line, 'on the distinct understanding that [...] the French government was not committed to acceptance of any other part of the arrangements proposed in Mr Lloyd George's Aide-Mémoire'.[161]

On 18 September, Meinertzhagen wired to the Foreign Office that he had learned from Reuters that an agreement had been reached between the British and French governments on the evacuation of Syria, and submitted that, 'in view of present state of political feeling in Syria', that 'it should not be left to Reuter News Agency to communicate it', and that he 'should be glad if [he] could be informed in advance of any future decision so vitally affecting political work here'. At the Foreign Office, Kidston had only 'succeeded in securing privately from the W.O. a copy of the Paris resolution regarding Syria' that same day,[162] and Meinertzhagen was therefore informed that they were 'also awaiting official confirmation of the message to which you refer'.[163] The next day, a telegram was sent to Meinertzhagen at the request of Hankey, who also drafted part of it. Meinertzhagen was told that Clemenceau had 'accepted proposal of Prime Minister for evacuation of Syria and Cilicia by British troops and replacement by French troops in Cilicia and in Syria west of the Sykes–Picot line but refused to commit himself to acceptance of more comprehensive programme suggested by Mr Lloyd George'. It was also explained that Faysal had arrived at London, and that he would see the Prime Minister that same afternoon.[164] If still further proof was needed that the Foreign Office did not count for much in the settlement of the Syrian question, then it was Curzon having to ask the Prime Minister that he be allowed 'to be present at the discussions between yourself, Feisal and Allenby'.[165] The request was granted.

The Prime Minister opened the meeting with Faysal with an exposition of the British position. The occupation costs of the territories liberated from the Ottoman Empire constituted an intolerable burden on the British Exchequer, and when it had become apparent that it would take quite some time before it would be clear whether the USA were prepared to take on any mandate or not, the British government had decided to withdraw their troops from Cilicia and Syria, starting on 1 November. In order to honour their obligations to the French and the Arabs, they would hand over the territories west of the Sykes–Picot line to the French, and the towns of Damascus, Homs, Hama and Aleppo to the Arabs. Lloyd George laid particular stress on the provisional nature of these arrangements, as 'the ultimate settlement of these territories the British government were not now attempting to determine', and this was up to the peace conference.

Faysal predicted that 'on the evacuation of the western zone by the British troops and their replacement by French troops [...] there would be a general rising against the French occupation of the coast. In his view, Great Britain would be responsible for any bloodshed that might ensue'. Lloyd George replied that 'he would be greatly distressed but he was in the position of a man who had inherited two sets of engagements, those to King Hussein and those to the French [...] He was trying loyally to interpret his engagements to both.' When the question was raised whether Faysal 'would have the right to ask for assistance where he wished', the Prime Minister 'said it appeared that in the areas opposite the zone, temporarily and provisionally occupied by the French, the Emir Feisal would have to ask for French advisers'. Faysal bitterly commented that 'he himself and the Arab nation were being very badly treated in having a Power thrown on them when it had been promised that they should select for themselves, and he was certain that every Arab would shed his last drop of blood before he admitted the French'.[166]

At their next meeting, on 23 September, Lloyd George explained that the aide-mémoire was 'in no sense an agreement', and that Clemenceau also 'could not accept [it] as a final settlement'. He 'wished the Emir to understand thoroughly that it was not the result of negotiations with the French government behind the back of the Arab representatives'. The Prime Minister declared that the battle for the freedom of the Arabs had been won in the north of France, and that France had greatly suffered. Faysal sympathised with France and 'her sacrifice *for her existence*', but the Arabs 'had also been fighting for their existence'. He was 'astonished that a great nation fighting for its existence should now try to encroach upon a small nation. It was not right that Frenchmen should live and that the Arabs should die.' The Emir told his audience that the aide-mémoire 'seemed to him to be based on the 1916 agreement between the British and the French, which to the Arab nation was a sentence of death. That sentence he hoped would never be pronounced by his friends.'[167]

On 25 September a railway strike broke out in Great Britain. It fully consumed the Prime Minister's attention for ten days. During that time he was 'exclusively occupied with strike matters', and paid 'no attention to anything else'.[168] It was only on 8 October that Lloyd George could again busy himself with the Syrian question. Hankey informed Winston Churchill, the minister for War, that he understood 'that no executive action has yet been taken in regard to the withdrawal of the British troops into Palestine up to the present moment', but that Lloyd George thought that 'the time has come when the necessary orders should be given and he instructed me this morning to write to you in this sense'.[169] Two days later, Ronald Campbell informed Curzon that Kerr had brought over a reply to a letter from Faysal of 21 September, 'which the Prime Minister approved (It is drafted for your signature)'. The Foreign Office proposed some slight alterations, which Lloyd George accepted, in order that 'the French cannot possibly take exception', and according to Kidston there was 'now nothing positively dangerous' in the letter, which was 'ready for Your Lordship's signature'.[170]

In his letter, Faysal had lodged a strong protest against the aide-mémoire, and asked that 'this proposed engagement between the British and French governments shall be entirely cancelled'. He had also warned that the Arabs would 'be obliged to defend their unity and existence with their utmost available power and zeal'.[171] Lloyd George, through Curzon, now replied that:

> His Majesty's Government have not the slightest doubt that the best course for the Arab people is to accept the temporary arrangement proposed, and to enter into friendly working arrangements for its execution [...] As previously suggested, they strongly urge that your Highness should discuss these arrangements at once with the French government. His Majesty's Government will be only too glad to do all in their power to promote a cordial and satisfactory understanding between their two Allies in regard to the occupation during the interim period. They would, however, be failing in their duty to their Arab Ally if they did not declare in the most earnest as well as in the most friendly manner that they can conceive of no policy more fatal to Arab aspirations and prosperity, both at the forthcoming Peace Conference and afterwards, than the method of military resistance hinted at in your Highness's letter. [172]

The French, however, were no longer interested in British good offices. On 10 October, Clemenceau replied to the aide-mémoire. His letter was conciliatory in tone with respect to the border between Syria and Palestine, and on the issues of the railway and the pipeline, but regarding Syria it was uncompromising. He stated that:

> The situation of France in Syria and her relations with the Arabs in her zone cannot be but identical with the situation of England in Mesopotamia and her relations with the Arabs in her zone. This perfect parallel is the result of the agreement under which the two countries have put their signature.

The French prime minister considered Britain's continued protection of Faysal an unacceptable interference in the French zone and the French mandate over Syria.[173] During a discussion between British and French military experts on the technicalities of the British evacuation, it also turned out that Clemenceau 'did not agree to the relief of the British by Arab troops in the four towns and wished British troops to remain until they were relieved by French troops'. Kidston claimed that he had 'anticipated that the French would take this line', but failed 'to see what we can do in the matter, which seems to lie between the Prime Minister and M. Clemenceau'. Curzon could well understand Clemenceau's position, but it took:

No account of the British or the Arab standpoint for

(1) it postpones indefinitely the British withdrawal.
(2) it postulates that we should keep the bed warm for the French to jump into; or to change the metaphor we are to be the stalking horse behind which they are to creep into military occupation of the Syrian towns.
(3) it would provoke the furious hostility of the Arabs and Feisal.

However, he, too, had nothing further to offer than that "the P.M. should see at once".[174]

As a sop, Lloyd George had suggested in a further letter to Faysal that a mixed commission with French, Arab, British and American representatives might be entrusted with the adjustment of 'the problems involved in the impending withdrawal of British troops from Syria on the 1st November'.[175] Faysal eagerly grasped at this last straw. During a third meeting with Lloyd George on 13 October, he expressed 'his gratitude [...] for the suggestion [...] that the British government would be very glad to arrange an immediate meeting between the Emir, a French, an American, and a British representative'. He hoped that discussions would not be confined 'to military questions only. He would particularly like an American representative to be present to hear the discussions, which might bear upon administrative as well as military questions.' Lloyd George already regretted his suggestion, and pointed out that although the British government did not have 'any objection to America being represented', there was the difficulty of getting a properly accredited American representative. Faysal, however, insisted. Had not the Prime Minister 'particularly mentioned an American representative in his letter to him?'[176] It was decided to send a telegram to Clemenceau in which the latter was asked to send General Henri Gouraud – who had just been appointed high commissioner for Syria and commander-in-chief of the French Army of the Levant – to London to discuss with Allenby and Faysal 'the military arrangements for the occupation of Syria from 1st November'. The Prime Minister also informed his colleague that, as the Emir had been 'very anxious that an American representative should be present', he was instructing the British ambassador, 'if the French government has no objection, to communicate with Mr Polk on this subject'.[177]

In a separate telegram, containing a private and personal message, Lloyd George emphasised that 'the negotiations with Feisal have been very difficult' and that it would be much easier to induce the latter 'to accept French occupation of Western Syria if Gouraud were to come over and meet him and Allenby at once'. He urged Clemenceau 'in the interest of peace in Syria' to fall in with his proposal.[178] The latter would have none of it. He replied the next day in quite violent terms. He continued to regret that Faysal had been called to Europe by the British government without previous consultations with the French government. This certainly did not help to find solutions. It was now time to put the question on its proper footing. France must deal with Faysal directly. British protection only encouraged the latter's ambitions and resistance. Clemenceau understood full well 'the difficulty in which the English negotiators find themselves after being driven by political necessities to enter into engagements with the Hedjaz, Nejd and with France that, if not opposed to one to another, are at any rate difficult to adjust', but the way out of this embarrassment could not consist in 'sacrificing the French rights and interests'. The only solution was that the British government told Faysal that he must come to an understanding with France and that he 'could leave without fear the responsibility for the situation to France'. Under these conditions he was prepared to meet Faysal in Paris, if the latter wished to come to an agreement.[179]

According to Hankey this was 'an exceedingly rude refusal, suggesting bad faith on our part'.[180] Lloyd George replied on 15 October. Clemenceau's letter filled him with:

> Surprise and deep regret. Its tone represents a complete change from the friendly attitude you took up on this subject a month ago in Paris, and is one which I could not have believed possible for one Ally to address another after five years of intimate brotherhood in arms. I profoundly regret your

decision because it defeats a sincere and loyal attempt by your Ally to bring about by agreement between all concerned a temporary settlement of the Syrian difficulty which should be in complete accordance with British and French engagements [...] As it is your decision has rendered fruitless our endeavour to bring this about. For the consequences the British government must disclaim all responsibility.[181]

There was nothing for it than to leave Faysal to fend for himself. On 16 October, Curzon telegraphed to Derby that Faysal had accepted Clemenceau's invitation.[182] He explained in a dispatch that Allenby and he had spoken with the Emir that day, and 'urged Feisal to go to Paris without delay, unaccompanied by any Englishman, and with no evidence of British inspiration or backing, to see Clemenceau personally [...] to realise that this was in all probability the last opportunity of coming to a friendly agreement with the French'.[183] Faysal left for Paris on 20 October.

At the beginning of January 1920, the French and Faysal at last came to an understanding. Faysal accepted a French mandate 'for the whole of Syria', while France in return consented 'to the formation of an Arab state that included Damascus, Homs, Hama and Aleppo, and was to be administered by the Emir with the assistance of French advisers'.[184] At the Conference of San Remo four months later, the mandates for the Lebanon and Syria were assigned to France. This cleared the way for a final showdown. On 14 July 1920, Faysal was presented with an ultimatum demanding, among other things, the recognition of the French mandate over Syria. Faysal's last-minute unconditional acceptance of the ultimatum was ignored. Sherifian forces tried to stop the French advance, but were routed. Damascus was occupied on 26 July.[185] A few days later, Faysal was sent into exile.

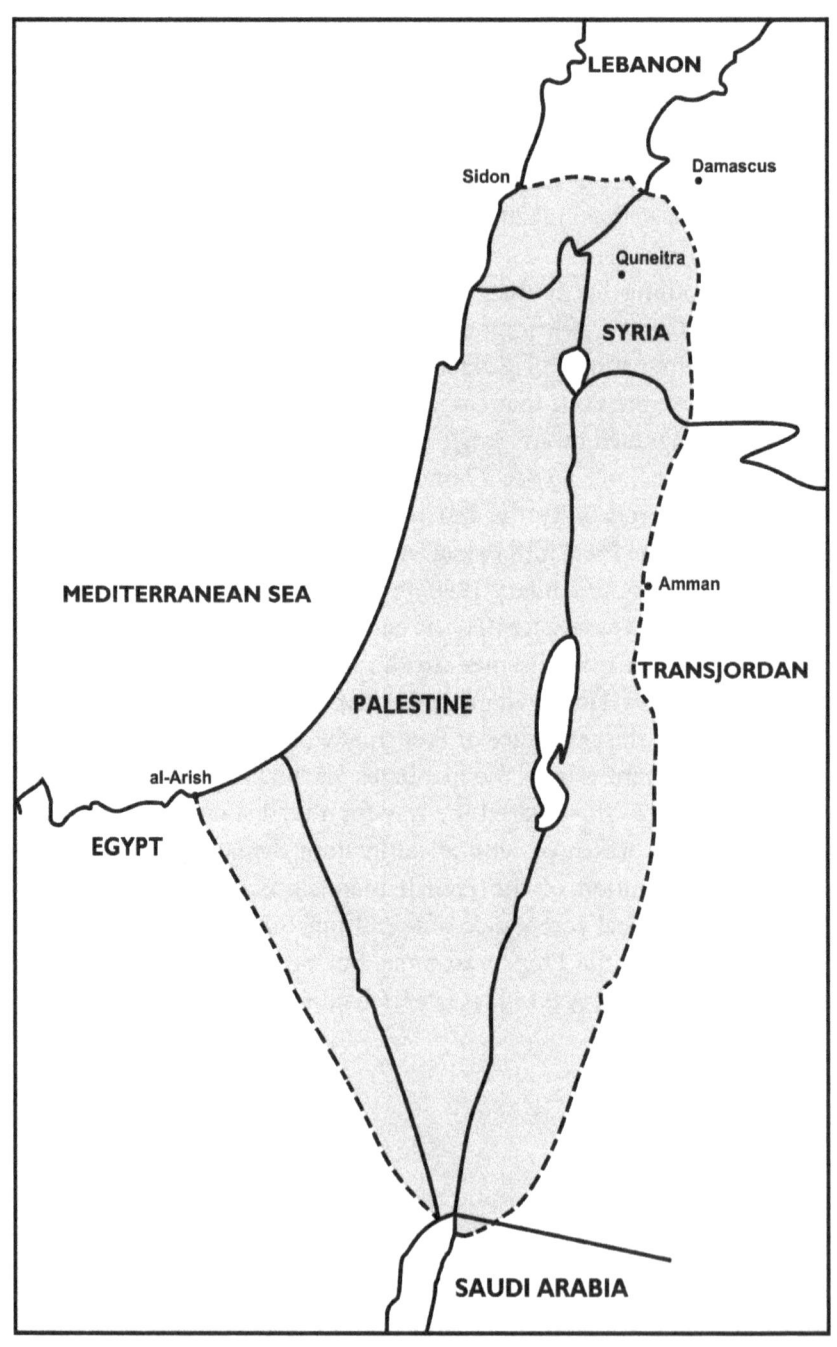

Map 11.1 Palestine, as Claimed by the Advisory Committee on Palestine, November 1918 (Source: Jewish Virtual Library)

11 WE REGARD PALESTINE AS BEING ABSOLUTELY EXCEPTIONAL

Introduction

In this chapter it becomes clear that during the first seven months of 1919 the struggle continued unabated between the British military authorities in Palestine and the Zionists about how the former could use their best endeavours to facilitate the aim of establishing in Palestine a national home for the Jewish people. In London, Lord Curzon and the officials of the Foreign Office sided with the military authorities. In Paris, Arthur Balfour and officials of the British delegation to the peace conference took sides with the Zionists. What tilted the balance in favour of the Zionists was that Curzon, although he deplored Balfour's pro-Zionist policy and warned against its dire consequences, in the end time and again acquiesced in it. Curzon had no qualms about executing a policy to which he was completely opposed as long as he could wash his hands of it, even after Balfour had resigned and Curzon had succeeded him. By the end of 1919 it was generally accepted by the British policy makers concerned, whether eagerly or reluctantly, that Great Britain would be the mandatory power for Palestine, that it would be the mandatory's duty to implement the Balfour Declaration and that this entailed creating the conditions that would give the Zionists the opportunity eventually to establish in Palestine a Jewish state, provided the rights of the existing Muslim and Christian population were respected.

The second topic I deal with in this chapter concerns the northern and eastern boundaries of Palestine. The Zionists claimed that economic necessity required that, in the north, Palestine should include the River Litani as well as Mount Hermon, and in the east extend to a line along and close to the Hijaz railway. Although Balfour supported the Zionist claims, at the Foreign Office it was realised that the Zionist proposals would be unacceptable to the French government, while Prime Minister Lloyd George, true to his vision of a Palestine from Dan to Beersheba, thought their claim on Mount Hermon excessive. French prime minister Clemenceau for his part insisted on the Sykes–Picot line. Another confrontation between Lloyd George and Clemenceau threatened, but after the latter resigned in January 1920, a compromise solution was found that left the River Litani and Mount Hermon in the Lebanon and Syria, respectively, and gave Dan to Palestine, while the River Jordan, in accordance with the Sykes–Picot agreement, became Palestine's eastern frontier.

British and Zionist Preparations for the Peace Conference

It had been laid down in the The Hague Conventions of 1899 and 1907 that the occupying power should 'take all steps in his power to re-establish and insure, as far as possible, public order and safety, while respecting, unless absolutely prevented, the laws in force in the country'. On 23 October 1918, General Sir Edmund Allenby accordingly instructed his military administrators – Colonel Philpin de Piépape (OET North), General Ali Riza Pasha El Rikabi (OET East) and Major-General Sir Arthur Money (OET South) – that 'as far as possible the Turkish system of government will be continued and the existing machinery utilised'. He also reminded them that 'the administration is a military and provisional one and without prejudice to future settlement of areas concerned'.[1] This meant that the 'iron wall of military routine' against which Chaim Weizmann 'had beaten his head' during his sojourn in Palestine remained firmly in place.[2]

On 9 October 1918, Weizmann had been received by Balfour, and obtained assurance, so Ormsby Gore reported to the Foreign Office on 15 November, that 'when questions affecting Palestine came before the Allied Powers for decision the Zionists would be heard thereon'. Ormsby Gore also informed the Foreign Office that 'the breach between Zionists and the League of British Jews has been healed', and that the fruit of this collaboration would be a 'memorandum regarding the definite aspirations of Jews in regard to Palestine'. As he had seen the draft, Ormsby Gore believed he could 'say that the proposals are both wise and practical, though doubtless there will be some difficulty on the question of territorial boundaries'.[3]

Ormsby Gore referred to the Advisory Committee on Palestine, under the chairmanship of Herbert Samuel, in which prominent Zionists and non-Zionists participated, with Ormsby Gore acting as one of the committee's consultants. He handed in the undated memorandum on 19 November. Its main points addressed the questions of the mandatory power, the boundaries of Palestine and the Jewish national home. Great Britain should receive the mandate for Palestine. As to the boundaries, the memorandum stated that (see also Map 11.1):

> The boundaries of Palestine should be as follows:–
> In the North, the northern and southern banks of the Litani River, as far north as latitude 33°45″. Thence in a south-easterly direction to a point just south of the Damascus territory and close to and west of the Hedjaz railway.
> In the East, a line close to and west of the Hedjaz railway.
> In the South, a line from a point in the neighbourhood of Akaba to El Arish.
> In the West, the Mediterranean Sea.

With respect to the national home it was claimed that 'Palestine should be placed under such political, economic, and moral conditions, as will favour the increase of the Jewish population, so that in accordance with the principles of democracy it may ultimately develop into a Jewish Commonwealth'.

Ormsby Gore was no longer sure about the wisdom and the practicability of the Committee's proposals, at least those regarding the boundaries and the national home. The first 'should not be published', and as far as the second was concerned, 'the word "Commonwealth" would be interpreted as "State" and give rise to great uneasiness among the non-Jews of Palestine'. It was better to omit the whole sentence. Sir Eyre Crowe concurred, and submitted that Weizmann should be approached to make the necessary alterations, to which Lord Hardinge added that these 'should be accepted unconditionally'. Lord Robert Cecil feared that, even in its amended form, it contained passages that would 'raise great trouble with the Arabs. As Feisal is here, could not Dr Weizmann talk it over with him?'[4]

Cecil's fears were confirmed by three telegrams from Clayton. In the first, he warned that the Palestinian Arabs were 'strongly anti-Zionist and [...] very apprehensive of Zionist claims', also because 'local Zionists contemplate a much more extended programme than is justified by the terms of Mr Balfour's declaration'.⁵ In the second telegram, Clayton explained that 'Christian and Moslem antipathy to Zionism has been displayed much more openly since armistice the recent Anglo–French declaration has encouraged all parties to make known their wishes by every available means in view of approaching Peace Conference'. He accordingly considered the 'present time [...] particularly unsuitable for special Zionist activity in Palestine which should be delayed until status of country and form of administration has been finally decided upon'.⁶ This equally applied, so Clayton observed in the third telegram a few days later, to 'any further declaration of Zionist policy', which 'should be deferred until future of Palestine has been definitely settled'.⁷

Weizmann had another interview with Balfour on 4 December. He stated that the proposals of the Samuel Committee constituted 'the necessary minimum of the Zionist demands'. They did not contain 'anything new', and merely sketched 'the broad lines of the measures which would have to be taken in order to carry out in practice the policy laid down in the Declaration'. He also stressed once again that the Jewish problem could only rationally and permanently be solved through Zionism, but that this presupposed:

> Free and unfettered development of the Jewish National Home in Palestine – not mere facilities for colonisation, but opportunities for carrying out colonising activities, public works etc. on a large scale so that we should be able to settle in Palestine about four to five million Jews within a generation, and so make Palestine a Jewish country. Such development is possible if sufficient elbow room is allowed to the Jewish people.

When Balfour 'asked whether such a policy would be consistent with the Statement made in his Declaration that the interests of non-Jewish communities in Palestine must be safeguarded', Weizmann replied that in 'a Jewish Commonwealth there would be many non-Jewish citizens, who would enjoy all the rights and privileges of citizenship, but the preponderant influence would be Jewish. There is room in Palestine for a great Jewish community without encroaching upon the rights of the Arabs.' The foreign secretary agreed that 'the Arab problem could not be regarded as a serious hindrance in the way of the development of a Jewish National Home', but like Cecil 'thought that it would be very helpful indeed if the Zionists and Feyzal could act unitedly and reach an agreement on certain points of possible conflict'.⁸

The Eastern Committee took up the question of Palestine the next day. Curzon introduced the subject with an exposition of British commitments and the existing state of affairs. One of the difficulties with which the British were confronted was:

> The fact that the Zionists have taken full advantage – and are disposed to take even fuller advantage – of the opportunity which was then offered to them [...] their programme is expanding from day to day. They now talk about a Jewish State. The Arab portion of the population is well-nigh forgotten and is to be ignored. They not only claim the boundaries of the old Palestine, but they claim to spread across the Jordan into the rich countries lying to the east, and, indeed, there seems to be very small limit to the aspirations they now form.

It was therefore no surprise that the 'Zionist programme, and the energy with which it is being carried out, have [...] had the consequence of arousing the keen suspicions of the Arabs [...] who inhabit the country'. As to the borders of Palestine, Curzon gladly availed himself of the opportunity to point out that in the Sykes–Picot agreement 'the most ridiculous and unfortunate boundaries seem to have been drawn for that area'. It was imperative that the British recovered 'for Palestine, be it Hebrew or Arab, or both, the boundaries up to the Litani on the coast, and across to Banias, the old Dan, or Huleh in the interior'. With regard to the eastern boundary proposed by the Zionists, which included 'trans-Jordan territories where there is good cultivation and great possibilities in the future', Curzon remarked that these had not been part of Palestine 'for many centuries, if [they] ever did', while with respect to the Zionist claims on the lands south of Beersheba, he noticed that there were 'those who say: "Do not complicate the Palestine question by bringing in the Bedouins of the desert, whose face looks really towards Sinai, and who ought not to be associated with Palestine at all"'.

Curzon subsequently explained that an international or French administration of the country was out of the question. The choice was between the USA and Great Britain. Curzon plumped for Britain in view of Palestine's close economic ties with Egypt, its strategic importance for the defence of the Suez Canal, and because 'from all the evidence we have so far, the Arabs and Zionists in Palestine want us. The evidence on that point seems to be conclusive.' Cecil agreed that the French were 'entirely out of the question [...] also because the Italians would really burst if you suggested it – and the Greeks too', but he was not convinced that everything pointed to a British mandate for Palestine. He did not wish 'to rule out the Americans', and as far as Palestine's strategic importance was concerned, he was 'not much impressed by the argument that in order to defend Egypt we had to go to Palestine, because in order to defend Palestine we should have to go to Aleppo or some such place. You always have to go forward; at least, I gather so.'[9]

On 16 December, the Eastern Committee adopted a resolution on Palestine in which an international administration, as well as a French or Italian mandate, was rejected. Great Britain should not object 'to the selection of the United States of America, yet if the offer were made to Great Britain, we ought not to decline'. The choice between the two powers 'should be, as far as possible, in accordance with the expressed desires (a) of the Arab population, (b) of the Zionist community in Palestine'. The British negotiators at the peace conference were finally exhorted to make every effort 'to secure an equitable re-adjustment of the boundaries of Palestine, both on the north and east and south'.[10]

The meeting between Faysal and Weizmann took place on 11 December 1918. It appeared that the basis for a mutual understanding was still there. Both wanted to keep the French out of Syria and Palestine, and in return for Zionist support of Faysal's ambitions in Syria, the latter was prepared to assist Zionist ambitions in Palestine. According to Weizmann's report of the meeting, Faysal had been 'quite sure that he and his followers would be able to explain to the Arabs that the advent of the Jews into Palestine was for the good of the country, and that the legitimate interests of the Arabs would in no way be interfered with'. When Weizmann had observed that 'the country could be so improved that it would have room for four or five million Jews, without encroaching on the ownership rights of Arab peasantry', the Emir had agreed. He 'did not think for a moment that there was any scarcity of land in Palestine. The population would always have enough, especially if the country were developed.'[11] Small wonder, then, that on 17 December Weizmann wired to David Eder, the acting chairman of the Zionist Commission, that his interview with Faysal had been 'most successful'.

Weizmann also informed Eder that the Zionists had formulated new proposals for the effectuation of the Balfour Declaration. The most important were that 'the whole administration of Palestine shall be so formed as to make of Palestine a Jewish Commonwealth under British trusteeship', and that 'Jews shall so participate in the administration as to assure this object'. Clayton was greatly worried when he set eyes on this telegram and wired the Foreign Office on 31 December 1918 that 'in view of the fact that quite 90% of the inhabitants of Palestine are non-Jewish, it would be highly injudicious to impose, except gradually, an alien and unpopular element which up to now has had no administrative experience'. Clayton's telegram was something of a surprise to the Foreign Office, as it had not received a copy of Weizmann's telegram to Eder. It was only on 9 January 1919 that, after 'considerable difficulty', it finally managed to get one. Both telegrams were laid before Curzon on his first working day as acting secretary of state of foreign affairs. He was 'absolutely staggered',[12] especially when read in conjunction with Clayton's earlier telegram of 5 December, in which he had reported that 'non-Jews in Palestine number approximately 573,000 as against 66,000 Jews'.[13] Curzon 'profoundly [pitied] the future Trustee of the "Jewish Commonwealth" which at the present rate will shortly become an Empire with a Hebrew Emperor at Jerusalem'. He had, however, to admit that his 'views on this subject are unpopular'. He gave instructions that when sending the telegrams to the peace delegation at Paris it should be 'stated that I agree with General Clayton and that I view the proposals of the Zionist Commission which so far as I know have no sanction in any undertakings yet given by us, with no small alarm'.[14]

A few days later, Curzon had an interview with General Money. In a letter to Balfour he informed the latter that both Money and Allenby stressed that 'we should go slow about the Zionist aspirations and the Zionist State. Otherwise we might jeopardise all that we have won. A Jewish *Government* in any form would mean an Arab rising, and the nine-tenths of the population who are not Jews would make short shrift with the Hebrews.' He added that he shared the generals' view, and that he had 'for long felt that the pretensions of Weizmann and Company are extravagant and ought to be checked'.[15] Balfour clearly had fewer qualms. He wrote back to Curzon that as far as he knew 'Weizmann has never put forward a claim for the Jewish *Government* of Palestine. Such a claim is in my opinion certainly inadmissible and personally I do not think we should go further than the original declaration which I made to Lord Rothschild.'[16]

On 9 January, Clayton, who had been recalled to London for consultations, telegraphed to Allenby that the Zionists had 'come to definite arrangement with Feisal with whom they are in close cooperation'.[17] Faysal and Weizmann had managed to reach an agreement on 3 January. Its main points were as follows: first, the boundary between Palestine and the Arab state should be determined by a commission after the end of the peace conference; second, the 'constitution and administration of Palestine' should 'afford the fullest guarantees for carrying into effect' the Balfour Declaration; and third:

> All necessary measures shall be taken to encourage and stimulate immigration of Jews into Palestine on a large scale, and as quickly as possible to settle Jewish immigrants upon the land through closer settlement and intensive cultivation of the soil. In taking such measures the Arab peasant and tenant farmers shall be protected in their rights, and shall be assisted in forwarding their economic development.

Faysal, however, added the proviso that 'if the Arabs are established as I have asked in my manifesto of January 4th [actually dated 1 January 1919, see Chapter 10, section 'The Hijaz at the Peace Conference'; R.H.L.] [...] I will carry out what is written in this agreement. If changes are made, I cannot be answerable for failing to carry out this agreement.'[18] Arnold Toynbee minuted that Lawrence had told him that 'in the first draft of the present document, Dr Weizmann used the phrases "Jewish State", "Jewish government", and that the Emir Feisal altered these to "Palestine", "Palestinian government".' Ormsby Gore believed it was 'a very important document and should be compared very carefully with the new demands of the Zionist Organisation contained in their memorandum for the peace conference,'[19] which Nahum Sokolow communicated to Sir Louis Mallet on 20 January.[20]

Two days later, Ormsby Gore completed a note on the latest Zionist proposals. These went:

> Very much further than any demands hitherto put forward by responsible Zionists. The phrase 'Jewish Commonwealth' has been introduced as the result of a resolution passed by the American Jewish Congress of December 16th, 1918. What exactly is meant by the world 'Commonwealth' is not defined, but it is clear that it involves steps towards the creation of what is practically and virtually if not nominally a Jewish government in Palestine.

He further stated that 'the real character of these new proposals can be most readily appreciated by attention to the section dealing with the "Administration" of the future Palestine'. According to the Zionists, the governor of Jerusalem 'must be a man of the Jewish religion', and could only be appointed by the mandatory power after consulting 'the Jewish Council for Palestine, an extra Palestinian body representative of Jews in all countries'. Ormsby Gore could 'imagine few things which would create greater distrust of Zionist aims among both Christian and Moslem inhabitants of Palestine than the insistence upon a racial and religious test' for the governor of Jerusalem. He considered the 'proposals regarding the Executive Council and the Legislative Council [...] even more extreme'. The Zionists proposed that 'on both councils there should be an assured Jewish majority. Thus racial and religious tests are to be introduced and gross over-representation of the Jews in proportion to the rest of the population is to be insisted upon.' There were 'many other smaller points' to which Ormsby Gore took exception, and in conclusion he observed that:

> In general it would seem that Dr Weizmann who has hitherto been moderate and reasonable in his proposals has been pushed along by the Jewish Jingoes of America and neutral countries who having been given an inch want an ell. To my mind such extravagant demands will injure and not assist the cause of Zionism both in Palestine and elsewhere and if these demands are persisted in I presume H.M.G. will make it clear that they cannot be answerable if they lead to disaster and reaction.

Sir Louis Mallet entirely agreed and suggested that Ormsby Gore should be 'authorised to communicate with Dr Weizmann and Mr Sokolov with a view to modifying this document'. Mallet also mentioned the matter to Balfour, 'who agreed that we should point out the unwisdom of putting forward such proposals', and discussed it with Sir Eric Drummond, who 'deprecated our making ourselves, in any way, responsible for this case [...] The less they mention Great Britain the better, except to say that they desire our tutelage.'[21] All these sentiments were reflected in the letter Ormsby Gore sent to Sokolow on 24 January. He had spoken to Mallet and Drummond and both 'wished it to be made quite clear to you that there must be no suggestion that your proposals have been approved by the British government. There is no objection to you asking for Great Britain as Mandatory provided you do this entirely on your own.' He also stated that Mallet had 'made it quite clear that in his opinion the British government would not accept the duties of a Mandatory if the constitution proposed in the printed Memorandum were insisted upon by you and the Conference', and that Sir Louis and he 'certainly both think this Memorandum is far too extreme as well as being much too long and too detailed'. It would be better if the Zionists submitted 'something briefer and less likely to offend the susceptibilities of the majority of the present inhabitants of Palestine'.[22]

The next day, Kidston reported that Weizmann had come 'to see me a couple of days ago and said that he was seriously distressed about the position in Palestine. The Jews were not receiving that consideration which they had expected in a country which was to be their national home.' In reply, Kidston had pointed out that British 'officers had many conflicting interests to reconcile and the Jews were making their task difficult by their importunity. They seemed to think that their national home must be handed over to them ready-made at a moment's notice.' Graham thought 'Mr Kidston's language perfectly correct', and observed that Weizmann had never 'publicly asked for more than a Jewish "national home" in Palestine – with the idea of a Jewish commonwealth always looming in the background'. This induced Curzon to have a second look at Weizmann's telegram to Eder of 17 December, in which the former had stated that Palestine should become 'a Jewish Commonwealth under British Trusteeship'. Curzon wondered:

> Now what is a Commonwealth? I turn to my dictionaries and find it thus defined:– 'A State', 'A body politic,' 'An independent Community'. 'A Republic'. Also read the rest of the telegram. What then is the good of shutting our eyes to the fact that this is what the Zionists are after, and that the British Trusteeship is a mere screen behind which to work for this end?[23]

Curzon decided to devote a further letter to Balfour to this question. He entertained 'no doubt that [Weizmann] is out for a Jewish government, if not at the moment, then in the near future'. He pointed out that Weizmann, in his account of his meeting with Balfour on 4 December, had:

> Deliberately inserted the underlined words: 'all necessary arrangements for the establishment in Palestine of a Jewish National Home or Commonwealth.' You meant the first, but he interpreted it as meaning the second. Again, on December 17, he telegraphed to Eder of the Zionist Commission at Jaffa: 'The best proposal stipulates that the whole administration of Palestine shall be formed as to make Palestine a Jewish Commonwealth.'

Curzon therefore felt 'tolerably sure' that Weizmann contemplated 'a Jewish state, a Jewish nation, a subordinate population of Arabs ruled by Jews, the Jews in possession of the best of the land and directing the Administration', and that he was 'trying to effect this behind the screen and under the shelter of British trusteeship'. Curzon's complaint made no impression whatsoever in Paris. Balfour merely wanted to know when did he talk 'about a Jewish Commonwealth?', while Drummond minuted that 'this hardly requires an answer'.[24]

Ormsby Gore's letter to Sokolow proved to be far more effective. On 30 January, Mallet minuted that Samuel had called on him 'to say that he had revised the Zionist case for the Conference and that the demand for a Jewish Governor, a majority on the Council, had been eliminated and the tone of the document greatly modified'. Samuel had also explained that a 'reference to the development of the country later on into a Jewish Commonwealth' had nevertheless been left in, 'in deference to the views of American Zionists who wanted something more to look forward to than a National Home'.[25]

The 'Statement of the Zionist Organisation Regarding Palestine' was finally submitted to the peace conference on 3 February 1919. The Allied and Associated Powers were asked to 'recognise the historic title of the Jewish people to Palestine and the right of the Jews to reconstitute in Palestine their National Home', to vest the country's sovereignty in the League of Nations, and to appoint Great Britain as the mandatory power. The mandate should be:

> Subject also to the following special conditions:–
>
> (I) Palestine shall be placed under such political, administrative and economic conditions as will secure the establishment there of the Jewish National Home and ultimately render possible the creation of an autonomous Commonwealth, it being clearly understood that nothing shall be done which may prejudice the civil and religious rights of existing non Jewish communities in Palestine or the rights and political status enjoyed by Jews in any other country.
> (II) To this end the Mandatory Power shall inter alia;
> (a) Promote Jewish immigration and close settlement on the land, the established rights of the present non Jewish population being equitably safeguarded.

(b) Accept the cooperation in such measures of a Council representative of the Jews of Palestine and of the world that may be established for the development of the Jewish National Home in Palestine.

The boundaries the Zionist Organisation claimed for Palestine were the same as those indicated in the Advisory Committee's proposals communicated to the Foreign Office in the middle of November.

Whereas Faysal's statement had enthusiastically been received by members of the British delegation at the peace conference, the one by the Zionist Organisation mainly drew critical comments, in particular with respect to the proposed boundaries and Council. Ormsby Gore minuted that the 'northern boundary is a little too far north, the Eastern boundary proposed here [...] too far East and I do not believe that Akaba can be usefully developed as a part of Palestine'. He thought that a Jewish council might be helpful 'to prevent speculation and to facilitate the provisions of funds and land for the development of the Jewish national home', but it 'should have no political functions and the fewer administrative functions it has the better'. Mallet wished to go even further. This 'Jewish Council should [...] be merely a consultative body and have no powers of administration in Palestine. If it has, little by little it will encroach and become very embarrassing for the Governor. It should clearly not be in the Mandate conferred by the Peace Conference.' He also concurred that 'Akaba should certainly not be included in Palestine. We have agreed upon a boundary with the American delegation and I am referring it to the Egyptian experts.'[26]

Zionist Aspirations, Arab Hostility and the British Military Administration

Colonel Richard Meinertzhagen lunched with Balfour on 7 February 1919. Afterwards he noted in his diary that he had bluntly asked the foreign secretary whether the Declaration was 'a reward or bribe to the Jews for past services given in the hope of full support during the war?' Balfour had immediately replied, 'certainly not; both the Prime Minister and myself have been influenced by a desire to give the Jews their rightful place in the world; a great nation without a home is not right'. Meinertzhagen had then asked whether, 'at the back of your mind do you regard this declaration a charter for ultimate Jewish sovereignty in Palestine or are you trying to graft a Jewish population on to an Arab Palestine?' This time Balfour had not answered right away, and when he did, he had chosen 'his words carefully "My personal hope is that the Jews will make good in Palestine and eventually found a Jewish State. It is up to them now; we have given them their great opportunity".'[27]

The ambiguity inherent in the Balfour Declaration was also something that troubled Cardinal Bourne, the archbishop of Westminster, who was visiting Palestine at the time. On 25 January he wrote to Lord Edmund Talbot, the conservative chief whip, that the declaration 'was very vague and is interpreted in many ways'. He related that 'the Zionists here claim that the Jews are to have the domination of the Holy Land under a British Protectorate; in other words they are going to force their rule on an unwilling people of whom they form only 10%', and noted that 'the officials are clearly at a loss how to act for fear of giving offence and being disavowed at home if they withstand Zionist pretensions'. The cardinal therefore begged Talbot 'to urge on the Prime Minister and Mr Balfour the <u>immediate need of a clear and definite declaration on the subject of Zionism</u>'. Talbot had passed on Bourne's letter to the Prime Minister, who on 15 February wrote to Kerr that 'if the Zionists claim that the Jews are to have domination of the Holy Land under a British Protectorate, then they are certainly putting their claims too high'. He also informed Kerr that he had 'heard from other sources that the Arabs are very disturbed about the Zionists' claims'. He warned that 'we certainly must not have a combination of Catholics and Mohammedans against us. It would be a bad start to our government of Palestine.'[28]

In the discussion on how the Balfour Declaration should be interpreted – did it mean that there would be a national home for the Jews in an Arab-dominated Palestine, or that the home constituted the basis on which a Jewish-dominated Palestine would be erected, but with the civil and religious rights of the Arab minority secure? – Kerr and Balfour adhered to the second interpretation. According to Kerr, 'we have promised that Palestine should be treated as the national home of the Jews and that if the Jews migrate there in sufficient numbers they will eventually become the predominant power in the country'. Lloyd George should not be fooled by appeals to self-determination, because these meant that 'as the Jews are now only one tenth of the population they will never get a look in at all'. If the Declaration meant 'anything at all it means that the Jews of the rest of the world through some kind of Zionist Council shall not only have the right to foster immigration and undertake the public work necessary to enable the

Jews to immigrate but that they should have some recognised position in the governmental machinery', if not, then 'local influences will be able to stop Jewish immigration and the development of Palestine as a Jewish home'.[29] Balfour was even more explicit:

> The weak point of our position of course is that in the case of Palestine we deliberately and rightly decline to accept the principle of self-determination. If the present inhabitants were consulted they would unquestionably give an anti-Jewish verdict. Our justification for our policy is that we regard Palestine as being absolutely exceptional; that we consider the question of the Jews outside Palestine as one of world importance, and that we conceive the Jews to have an historic claim to a home in their ancient land; provided that home can be given them without either dispossessing, or oppressing the present inhabitants.[30]

The Zionists presented their case to the peace conference on 27 February 1919. Sokolow was the first to address the Council of Ten. He said that 'the solemn hour awaited during eighteen centuries by the Jewish people had, at length, arrived. The Delegates had come to claim their historic rights to Palestine, the land of Israel.' It was true that there existed 'happy groups of Jews' in the countries of Western Europe and in America, 'but these were, comparatively speaking, only small groups. The great majority of the Jewish people did not live in those countries and the problem of the masses remained to be solved.' Weizmann spoke next. Where Sokolow had made an emotional appeal to the members of the Council of Ten, Weizmann appealed to their self-interest. The disaster that had befallen the six to seven million Jews in Russia implied that 'Jewish emigration [...] would increase enormously, whilst at the same time the power of absorption in the countries of Western Europe and of America would considerably decrease'. The result would be that 'the Jews would find themselves knocking about the world, seeking a refuge and unable to find one. The problem, therefore, was a very serious one, and no statesman could contemplate it without feeling impelled to find an equitable solution.' According to Weizmann, 'the solution proposed by the Zionist organisation was the only one which would in the long run bring peace, and at the same time transform Jewish energy into a constructive force, instead of being dissipated into destructive tendencies or bitterness'. It was also a realistic proposal, because in Palestine 'there was room for an increase of at least 4,000,000 to 5,000,000 people, without encroaching on the legitimate interests of the people already there. The Zionist wished to settle Jews in the empty spaces of Palestine.'

American Secretary of State Robert Lansing asked Weizmann 'to clear up some confusion which existed in his mind as to the correct meaning of the words "Jewish National Home." Did that mean an autonomous Jewish government?' Weizmann directly denied this, but when he continued it became clear that this denial had to be qualified. In the short run the answer was 'no', but in the long run it was 'yes'. What the Zionists wanted for the moment was 'an administration, not necessarily Jewish, which would render it possible [...] [to] make Palestine as Jewish as America is American or England English'. Weizmann ended by stating that 'he spoke for 96 per cent of the Jews of the world, who shared the views which he had endeavoured to express that afternoon'.[31]

The next day, Clayton warned Curzon that in Palestine the 'fear of Zionism among all classes of Christians and Moslems is now widespread, and has been greatly intensified by publications in Zionist journals and utterances of leading Zionists of a far reaching programme greatly in advance of that foreshadowed by Doctor Weizmann'. Zionists conveniently attributed 'local anti-Zionist feeling to influence of "Effendis" who are spoken of as corrupt and tyrannical', but the truth was that 'fear and dislike of Zionism has become general throughout all classes'. Clayton also observed that the increase in Zionist ambitions had resulted in a 'lack of confidence in Great Britain', committed as Britain was to France and the Zionists. In the eyes of the majority 'America is the only power left'.[32] He returned to this theme in a dispatch he sent two days later. There was 'little doubt that in the early days of the occupation British protection or tutelage would have been welcomed universally, and that fear and dislike of Zionism has induced the present attitude in the population of Palestine'.[33]

At the meeting of the Council of Four on 20 March, it was Clemenceau who proposed that the inter-allied commission should not limit its inquiries to Syria, but also visit Palestine, Mesopotamia and Armenia (see also Chapter 10, section 'Impasse: The Council of Four, March to May 1919'). Lloyd George declared that he 'had no objection to an inquiry into Palestine and Mesopotamia, which were the regions in which the British Empire were principally concerned',[34] but Balfour was clearly worried. On 23 March, he wrote a note in which he explained that he had spoken to Wilson and Lloyd George on the inadvisability of including Palestine 'in the sphere of operations to be covered by the Commissioners'. Both, however, had not thought 'the arguments [he] used were sufficiently strong to justify any alteration in the draft already sanctioned'. He therefore wished 'to put on record my objections to the inclusion of Palestine within the area of investigation'. The problem was that the commissioners were 'directed to frame their advice upon the wishes of the *existing* inhabitants of the countries they are going to visit'. If they carried out these instructions, Balfour could 'hardly doubt that their report will contain a statement to the effect that the present inhabitants of Palestine, who in a large majority are Arab, do not desire to see the administration of the country so conducted as to encourage the relative increase of the Jewish population and influence'. This would have the result that 'the task of countries which, like England and America, are anxious to promote Zionism will be greatly embarrassed', and 'the difficulties of carrying out a Zionist policy [...] much increased'.

At the Foreign Office, Clark Kerr considered Balfour's fears 'fully justified'. It would 'be interesting to see when Zionism will awake to the danger of this threat against its aspirations'.[35] The Zionists as a matter of fact had already done so. On 26 March, House noted in his diary that the American Zionist Felix Frankfurter had been 'an excited afternoon caller. The Jews have it that the Inter-allied Commission which is to be sent to Syria is about to cheat Jewry of Palestine.'[36] Hogarth wrote to Clayton four days later that he had dined with Frankfurter and Weizmann, and 'found both singing very low'.[37] To Curzon, however, the possible outcome that the commission might find against a British mandate for Palestine provided the one glimmer of hope in connection with the whole project. He wrote to Balfour on 25 March that he would 'rejoice at nothing more than that the Commission should advise that a mandate be conferred upon anyone else rather than Great Britain'.[38]

On 31 March, Balfour wrote to Samuel that he still had 'great hopes that Palestine will be eliminated from the scope of any Commission', and added, for Samuel's 'personal and confidential information', that the dispatch of the inter-allied commission was 'still an open question and by no means definitely determined'. However, Balfour's main reason for writing his letter was that 'the position in Palestine is giving me considerable anxiety'. He had received reports 'from unbiased sources that the Zionists there are behaving in a way which is alienating the sympathies of all the other elements of the population. The repercussion is felt here and the effect is a distinct set back to Zionism.' He therefore requested Samuel to warn 'the Zionist leaders both here and in Palestine that they would do well to avoid any appearance of unauthorised interference in the administration of the country'.[39] Balfour sent a letter in the same vein to Weizmann three days later.[40]

Samuel replied on 7 April. He was very glad to know that there still was 'a prospect that the question of Palestine may be settled without the long delay involved by a local inquiry by Commission'. Regarding Balfour's worries, he had 'already spoken to one or two of the Zionist leaders here in the sense of the latter part of your letter and am sending a message to Dr Weizmann also', but his sources had told him that there was 'another side to the case'. The Jews in Palestine felt 'a sense of grievance that the military administrators there usually proceed as though the Declaration of November 1917 had never been made'. They were 'unsympathetic military men, from the Soudan and elsewhere, who have never heard of Zionism, who regard all the inhabitants as "natives", and who give preference to the Arabs to the detriment of the Jews [...] because they have been accustomed to deal with similar people and understand them better'. Weizmann in his reply did not mince words. They were 'dealing [...] with purposeful and organised misunderstanding. Indisputably a vigorous agitation is on foot.' He, too, wished to direct Balfour's 'attention to the quality of British officials who are in the administration in Palestine', who 'however well intentioned [...] bring to Palestine an outlook hardened by experience in Egypt or the Sudan. All Zionists [...] know your deep friendliness and that of General Allenby to our cause [...] unfortunately, as we proceed down the line of military and civil officials the spirit is lost in transmission.'[41] Weizmann therefore thought that 'it would be of very great value if an officer from here who knows the East and is acquainted with the questions involved were to go out'. He added that 'the C.I.G.S. concurs in this opinion.'[42] Clayton, however, certainly did not. According to him there was no necessity 'to send an Officer out from England'.[43]

Clayton telegraphed a report by Money to the Foreign Office on 2 May 1919. Like Clayton, the latter claimed that 'in the present state of political feeling there is no doubt that if Zionist's programme is a necessary adjunct to a mandatory the people of Palestine will select in preference the United States or France as the mandatory power'. The idea that 'Great Britain is the main upholder of the Zionist programme will preclude any local request for a British mandate'. Money therefore submitted that 'if a clear and unbiased expression of wishes is required and if a mandate for Great Britain is desired by His Majesty's Government it will be necessary to make an authoritative announcement that the Zionist programme will not be enforced in opposition to the wishes of majority'. Clayton added that he concurred in

Money's appreciation of the situation. According to him, 'fear and distrust of Zionist aims grow daily and no amount of persuasion or propaganda will dispel it […] A British mandate for Palestine on the line of the Zionist programme will mean the indefinite retention in the country of a military force considerably greater than that now in Palestine.'

Kidston believed that Clayton's views were 'particularly sound', but rather doubted whether these were 'shared by the War Office here, for Colonel Gribbon rang me up yesterday on the telephone with the express object of saying that he thought that too much attention should not be paid to this opinion on the situation'. When Kidston had subsequently aired Curzon's point of view that 'it might be a blessing if the mandate were to go elsewhere', Gribbon had been 'profoundly shocked and maintained that Palestine was essential to us strategically for the defence of Egypt'.[44] In Paris, General Thwaites informed Harding that Allenby agreed with Money's assessment that 'if Great Britain desires the people to vote for a British mandate it will be necessary to make an authoritative announcement that the Zionist programme will not be enforced in opposition to the wishes of the majority'. However, in sharp contrast to the way in which the military authorities in London and Paris handled the Syrian dossier, Thwaites proposed not to defer to the military authorities on the spot. If the British government persisted in their policy of backing 'a moderate Zionist policy', it would moreover 'be worthwhile to bring new blood into General Allenby's political administration by sending out an officer, such as Colonel Meinertzhagen, who, with full knowledge of the position in Europe could help General Allenby to overcome the difficulties' he was confronted with. Forbes Adam minuted that Weizmann had told him that a proclamation as advocated by Money, Clayton and Allenby would 'produce a violent disturbance in Eastern Europe the effects of which might be much more disastrous and far reaching than the opposition of the local population (Christian and Moslem) of Palestine to the decisions of the Conference'. Mallet merely observed 'we cannot possibly go back'.[45]

During a meeting of the Samuel Committee on 10 May, Weizmann admitted that lately 'a great deal' had been heard 'about the unrest amongst Arabs and their opposition to Zionism', but mainly blamed this on a lack of support of the Zionist movement 'by the Administration on the spot', in particular 'the lower officials who in some cases have done a great deal of irreparable damage'. The military authorities had apparently lost confidence in 'the possibility or advisability of putting into effect the Balfour Declaration', but nothing could be 'more unjust and short-sighted than that. Jewry is not going to give up its claim to Palestine and Great Britain or America is not going back on a solemnly pledged word.'[46] This was precisely the line Balfour took in a letter to Curzon on the declaration proposed by Money. There could 'of course be no question of making any such announcement as that suggested [...] and in this connection it might be well' to remind Clayton that 'the French, United States and Italian governments have approved the policy set forth in my letter to Lord Rothschild of November 2nd, 1917'. Balfour also informed Curzon that Thwaites had suggested that 'it might be advisable at this stage to send out to Palestine a further advisor on Zionist matters to assist General Clayton', and that Thwaites had 'proposed, in this connection, Colonel Meinertzhagen, D.S.O. as the most suitable person.'[47] The Foreign Office telegraphed Balfour's observations to Clayton without further comment on 27 May 1919.[48] Clayton replied on 9 June: 'your remarks noted. With regard to Colonel Meinertzhagen if you send him out he will be useful to me.'[49] From a later telegram it appeared that he was not a bit impressed by Balfour's reminder that Britain's allies also supported the Zionist cause. He wired on 19 June that 'unity of opinion among the Allied governments on the subject of Palestine', was 'not a factor which tends to alleviate the dislike of non-Jewish Palestinians to the Zionist Policy. Indeed, it rather leads to still further anxiety on their part to express clearly to the world their own point of view.'[50]

In a minute of 3 June, written on a letter that the secretary of the Zionist Commission had sent to Aaron Aaronsohn and Felix Frankfurter at the beginning of May, Meinertzhagen left little doubt as to the side he was on in the struggle between Zionists, Arabs and the British military authorities. The secretary had violently complained about the Palestinian Arabs, who were 'the most cowardly and weak-kneed Moslems', the native Christians, who had joined the anti-Jewish movement 'stimulated by an endless flow of French gold', and the military administration, who it seemed had 'received the mot d'ordre to put the Jew at a disadvantage. With each Governor or sub-Governor there is an Arab or Christian advisor, who influences the British official against the Jews.' The regrettable truth was that Great Britain had 'lost all power and prestige here [...] Only fair and strong action can save Great Britain's position with the Moslems.' Meinertzhagen commented that he knew 'the writer of this letter. He is a moderate, level-headed, and sensible Zionist'. The letter further only confirmed 'which we already know – namely that our administration in Palestine is in a unhappy state and has been signally unsuccessful in getting the sympathy of the Jew and the confidence of the Arab'.[51]

On 31 May, Sir William Tyrrell communicated a part of Clayton's telegram of 2 May to Samuel, and explained that Balfour had suggested that Samuel 'should be consulted […] with a view to ascertaining whether you have any proposals to offer as to how the present hostility to Zionism in Palestine can best be allayed by the administrative authorities on the spot'.[52] In his reply, Samuel presented a complete catalogue of the measures that according to the Zionists should be taken to put an end to the unrest in Palestine. The first was that 'H.M. Government should send definite instructions to the local administration to the effect that their policy contemplates the concession to Great Britain of the Mandate for Palestine', and that 'the terms of the Mandate will certainly embody the substance of the declaration of November 2nd 1917'. The second was that the Arabs should be assured that 'in no circumstances will [they] be despoiled of their land or required to leave the country', and that there would 'be no question of the majority being subjected to the minority'. At the same time they should be reminded that a choice in favour of America or France as the mandatory power for Palestine would bring no solace, since 'the American and French governments are also pledged to favour the establishment in Palestine of the Jewish National Home'. The third measure was that the local authorities should 'be instructed to bring these facts to the attention of the Arab leaders at any convenient opportunity, and to impress upon them that the matter is a chose jugée [the matter is final and not open to appeal; R.H.L.] and that continued agitation could only be to the detriment of the country and would certainly be without result'. Samuel finally suggested that:

> An officer, whether civil or military, who has been in close touch with the British Delegation in Paris or with the Foreign Office in London, who is well acquainted with the policy of H.M. Government in relation to Palestine and is personally in sympathy with it, should be sent to Palestine with the special mission of conveying to the local administration, more fully than can be done by correspondence the views of the government.

Maurice Peterson at the Foreign Office minuted on Samuel's letter that 'something like what Mr Samuel proposes will, I fancy, have to be done after we have received the mandate. But until then, and with the American Commission on its way, I doubt if Paris will be ready for so bellicose a statement.' Kidston related that he had spoken with Samuel Landman of the Zionist Organisation, who had complained that 'either the attitude of H.M.G. towards Zionism had changed or that the Military Administration in Palestine were not acting in accordance with the policy of the Home Government'. Kidston had firmly taken the side of the military administration, and warned Landman that the Zionists:

> Must not forget that Palestine was still enemy occupied territory under military occupation; they, like many were too apt to forget that we were still in a state of war with Turkey; they expected the administration to act as if peace had been signed and the mandate of Palestine already given to Great Britain, we here were called upon to exercise a good deal of patience in these days and I feared that the Zionists must learn to do the same.

Graham believed that 'Mr Kidston's reply met the case very well', and Curzon agreed, 'the Zionists have only themselves to thank'.[53] But where London sided with the military authorities, Paris sided with the Zionists. Forbes Adam hoped that Samuel's proposals would 'be followed up',[54] and when on 24 June Balfour had a conversation with Louis Brandeis on the eve of the latter's visit to Palestine, he 'expressed entire agreement' with Brandeis's understanding that 'the commitment of the Balfour Declaration' entailed that 'Palestine should be the Jewish homeland and not merely [...] a Jewish homeland in Palestine'. Two days later, in the memorandum for Lloyd George in which Balfour expressed the hope that the outlines of the Turkish settlement should be agreed to before the Prime Minister and President Wilson left Paris (see Chapter 10, section 'Gathering a Breakthrough: June to September 1919'), it became clear that he also fully agreed with the two other conditions that according to Brandeis must be fulfilled to enable the successful realisation of the Zionist programme. The first was that there 'must be economic elbow room for a Jewish Palestine', which 'meant adequate boundaries, not merely a small garden within Palestine', and the second that 'the future Jewish Palestine must have control of the land and the natural resources which are at the heart of a sound economic life'.[55] Balfour observed that Palestine's northern frontier 'should give [the country] a full command of the water power which geographically belongs to Palestine and not to Syria; while the Eastern frontier should be so drawn as to give the widest scope to agricultural development on the left bank of the Jordan, consistent with leaving the

Hedjaz railway completely in Arab possession'.[56] On 1 July, Balfour further stated in a dispatch to Curzon that instructions should be sent to Allenby on the lines of the measures Samuel had proposed in his letter. He also again brought up the question of 'the despatch of a further officer to Palestine', which 'might in the first instance be discussed with General Clayton on his forthcoming visit to England on leave'.[57]

At the Foreign Office, a telegram was drafted containing Samuel's suggestions, but this was held up in order to obtain Clayton's views upon it. In the meantime, Samuel and Weizmann continued their attacks on the British military authorities in Palestine. Sir Ronald Graham recorded that he had an interview with each on 2 July. Samuel had 'complained of the attitude of the British Military authorities [...] and declared that they took every opportunity of injuring Zionist interests'. He 'earnestly' hoped that 'in the forthcoming changes which were to be made in the administration of Palestine new officers would be appointed who would possess a better understanding of the intentions of His Majesty's Government'. Weizmann had 'referred in far more violent terms to the present situation in Palestine. He declared that the British Authorities were showing a marked hostility to the Jews and lost no opportunity of not only injuring their interests but of humiliating them.' Weizmann therefore 'earnestly begged that the question should be taken in hand and that a new spirit should animate the direction of affairs in Palestine'. Curzon, however, refused to move: 'to a large extent the Zionists are reaping the harvest which they themselves sowed'.[58]

After his arrival in London, Clayton had two meetings with the Zionist leadership on 8 and 9 July. From his reports of the meetings to the Foreign Office it appeared that he had not wavered under the barrage of Zionist complaints and had stubbornly defended the line of policy adopted by the military authorities. During the first meeting it had become clear that the criticisms 'brought up by Mr Samuel and Dr Weizmann in their interviews with Sir R. Graham' could not be 'illustrated by specific instances, except in the case of one or two incidents of minor importance'. He had:

> Pointed out that the present administration was a temporary and provisional [one] and was not therefore justified in pushing a Zionist policy at a time when the future status of Palestine had not been decided by the Peace Conference. However confident the Zionists might be that the eventual decision would be in their favour, it would be incorrect for the occupying

power to prejudice that decision by acting as though the mandate had already be given to Great Britain.[59]

At the second meeting, Clayton had admitted that 'individual administrators may have appeared to show lack of will', and attributed this 'to the fact that the staff of administrators was collected under great difficulties, and from the material available at the time. Most of the best men were already serving elsewhere.' He had, however, insisted that the military administration was 'not placed there in order to carry out any particular policy, but to maintain security in the country. They were in the position of a trustee awaiting a decision regarding the fate of the country,' and that this implied, 'in the absence of definite instructions from the Home Government', that the administration was 'not justified in doing anything which could be construed as in some way forestalling the mandate'.[60]

It took more than a fortnight after his meetings with the Zionists before the Foreign Office was able to consult Clayton on the draft telegram to his deputy Colonel French containing the instructions based on Samuel's letter of 5 June. According to this draft:

> His Majesty's Government's policy contemplates concession to Great Britain of Mandate for Palestine. Terms of Mandate will embody substance of declaration of November 2, 1917. Arabs will not be despoiled of their land nor required to leave the country. There is no question of majority being subjected to the rule of minority, nor does Zionist programme contemplate this.
>
> American and French governments are equally pledged to support establishment in Palestine of Jewish national home. This should be emphasised to Arab leaders at every opportunity and it should be impressed on them that the matter is a *'chose jugée'* and continued agitation would be useless and detrimental.

When Clayton set eyes on the draft telegram on 25 July, it had been decided that Meinertzhagen would succeed him as chief political officer for Syria and Palestine. He no longer put up a fight. He merely observed that he agreed that 'if the question is a "chose jugée", the sooner General Allenby is given a definite line the better'. However, Curzon was not yet ready to give in. He was afraid that he could not 'see why a policy should be suggested or dictated to us by Mr Herbert Samuel who is not a member of H.M.G.'

Neither did he 'see why we should lay down – in anticipation of the decision of the Peace Conference – (a) that we are going to receive the mandate (b) what its terms are to be'. But this was no more than a token resistance, because he added that this might be 'the policy of H.M.G. and if Mr Balfour so decides I have nothing more to say'. On 4 August, Kidston could accordingly note that Curzon had seen the draft telegram to French and 'agreed to its despatch as it apparently represents Mr Balfour's policy'.[61]

On 23 July 1919, Weizmann wrote to Balfour on the impending resignations by General Clayton and General Money.[62] It was 'essential' that 'these two very important offices should be filled by men who are in complete sympathy [...] with the policy that His Majesty's Government has adopted'. Replacing the chief political officer and the chief military administrator was in Weizmann's eyes not enough. He expected that steps would be taken 'to replace officers, some of them filling positions inferior only to those already mentioned, who, according to all the information we have received, have shown themselves not only unsympathetic but even hostile to the Jewish population of the country'. When he transmitted the letter to the Foreign Office, Balfour confined himself to the observation, on the suggestion of Forbes Adam, that he trusted that Curzon and the War Office would 'endeavour to meet Dr Weizmann's wishes in the matter of new appointments'.[63]

Although nobody in Paris apparently took exception to Weizmann's interfering in the appointment of British officials, Clark Kerr in London certainly did. He could not 'help feeling that this is allowing the Jews to have things too much their own way', but supposed 'we must bow to the ruling of Paris'. He also related that Landman had told him that 'a General Watson [Major-General Harry D. Watson; R.H.L.] was to succeed General Money'. Curzon initially merely minuted that he wished 'the letter had been addressed to me',[64] but subsequently decided to address one more letter to Balfour to give vent to his indignation. He informed the latter 'how much startled' he was:

> At a letter from Dr Weizmann to you dated July 23 in which that astute but aspiring person claims to address me as to the principal politico-military appointments to be made in Palestine and to criticise sharply the conduct of any such officers who do not fall on the neck of the Zionists (a most unattractive resting place) and [...] the 'type of man' whom we might or might not to send.

It seemed that Weizmann would 'be a scourge on the back of the unlucky mandatory, and I often wish you would drop a few globules of cold water on his heated and extravagant pretensions!'[65]

When Curzon's latest complaint arrived in Paris, Balfour was putting the finishing touches to his long memorandum on the Syrian question (see Chapter 10, section 'Gathering a Breakthrough: June to September 1919'). From his observations on Palestine it appeared that Curzon's appeals and Clayton's warnings had failed to make any impression. Balfour took the same position he had taken in his letter to Lloyd George in the middle of February in reaction to Cardinal Bourne's letter, and in his note of the end of March, prompted by the Council of Four's decision to send an inter-allied commission of inquiry to the Middle East. Balfour observed that:

> In Palestine we do not propose even to go through the form of consulting the wishes of the present inhabitants of the country, though the American Commission has been going through the form of asking what they are. The four Great Powers are committed to Zionism. And Zionism, be it right or wrong, good or bad, is rooted in age-long traditions, in present needs, in future hopes, of far profounder import than the desires and prejudices of the 700,000 Arabs who now inhabit that ancient land.
>
> In my opinion that is right. What I have never been able to understand is how it can be harmonised with the declaration, the Covenant, or the instructions to the Commission of Enquiry.
>
> I do not think that Zionism will hurt the Arabs; but they will never say they want it [...] Whatever deference should be paid to the views of those who live there, the Powers in their selection of a mandatory do not propose, as I understand the matter, to consult them.

With respect to Palestine's borders, Balfour repeated what he had stated in his memorandum to Lloyd George of 26 June. It was 'eminently desirable' that Palestine 'should obtain the command of the water-power which naturally belongs to it, whether by extending its borders to the north, or by treaty with the mandatory of Syria', and 'should extend into the lands lying east of the Jordan. It should not, however, be allowed to include the Hedjaz railway.'[66]

When General Watson filed his first report as military administrator on 16 August, he explained that 'on taking over the Administration of O.E.T.A. South I had an open mind with regard to the Zionist movement and was fully in sympathy with the aim of the Jews for a National Home in Palestine – and with that aim I am still in sympathy', but that there was no escaping the fact that 'the feeling of the great mass of the population is very antagonistic to the scheme'. Opposition until now had been more inspired by nationalist than religious sentiments, but he greatly feared that it might 'take a religious turn' and lead to 'a Holy War'. He emphasised, like Clayton and Money had done before him, that the 'antagonism to Zionism of the majority of the population is deep rooted – it is fast leading to hatred of the British – and will result, if the Zionist programme is forced upon them, in an outbreak of a very serious character necessitating the employment of a much larger number of troops that at present located in the country'. He therefore urged 'most strongly', 'for the sake of Zionism, for the sake of the National Home for the Jews [...] that the work of the establishment of the Jews in Palestine be done very very slowly and carefully. Peaceful penetration over a long period of years will bring about the desired result.'[67]

The Draft Declaration on Zionism and the Borders of Palestine

In his long letter to Balfour of 20 August 1919 (see Chapter 10, section 'Gathering a Breakthrough: June to September 1919'), Curzon also devoted a few lines to Palestine. The War Cabinet was divided on the question. Curzon was very much in favour of withdrawing from the country 'while yet we can'. Others had, however, taken Balfour's position that, 'irksome as will be the burden', Britain could not 'now refuse [the mandate] without incensing the Zionist world'. Lloyd George for his part had clung to 'Palestine for its sentimental and traditional value, and [talked] about Jerusalem with almost the same enthusiasm as about his native hills.'[68]

During the first of his series of meetings with Field-Marshal Allenby at Hennequeville (see also Chapter 10, section 'Endgame: September to October 1919'), Lloyd George stated that it 'was essential to acquire the whole of Palestine without any truncation whatever.'[69] At their second meeting the next day, the Prime Minister wanted to know 'whether it was proposed to include Mount Hermon within the boundaries of Palestine', as the Zionists claimed, but to him this seemed 'to be rather excessive'. Allenby concurred and assured Lloyd George that the line he 'would like to draw for Palestine [...] would exclude Mount Hermon'. Because the French insisted on the border agreed in the Sykes–Picot agreement, which meant that Lake

Tiberias would not form part of Palestine, Hankey was instructed to get from London a copy of 'Adam Smith's Atlas (containing the boundaries of Palestine at different periods)' (a reference to George Adam Smith, *Atlas of the Historical Geography of the Holy Land*, which had been published in 1915), because Lloyd George 'wanted a map showing what actually constituted Palestine. He was convinced that this would include Lake Tiberias.' Bonar Law subsequently suggested that 'President Wilson should be asked to arbitrate as to the boundaries of Palestine'. He also wished to know 'what was the value of Palestine?' Allenby replied that 'it had no economic value whatsoever. Its retention by the British would keep our minds active for the next generation or two. He anticipated great trouble from the Zionists.' Lloyd George could not let this pass. He 'pointed out that the mandate over Palestine would give us great prestige', but in Allenby's view it was the other way around, 'we could [not] now give up Palestine without great loss of prestige'. Lloyd George cut off this dispute by proclaiming that 'anyhow it was impossible for us to give up Palestine', and summed up the British position as 'we could neither give up Palestine nor take Syria', to which Allenby agreed.[70]

At their next meeting on 11 September, the Prime Minister started with accepting Bonar Law's plan of 'leaving the arbitration of the northern boundary of Palestine to someone selected by President Wilson'. Hankey subsequently 'produced Adam Smith's Atlas […] and some time was spent in examining [it]'. Lloyd George concluded that 'the maps of different epochs gave Haifa to Palestine, but not Acre', but Gribbon pointed out that this time the Sykes–Picot line worked in Britain's favour, as it 'gave Acre to Palestine'. When the discussion shifted to the border between Syria and Mesopotamia, Gribbon strongly advocated the inclusion of Deir es Zor in the British zone, but Bonar Law was not impressed, 'the French would make out that the English grabbed everything good and left only what was useless'. Allenby, too, was prepared to leave the town to the French, but first Britain should claim it 'as a bargaining asset […] in order to obtain a good line to the north of Palestine'.[71]

With regard to the question of the frontiers between Palestine, Syria and Mesopotamia, it was finally decided 'after a prolonged conversation at the dinner table' in which Frank Polk, the head of the American delegation also took part, that paragraph seven of the aide-mémoire to be presented at the meeting of the Heads of Delegations on 15 September (see also Chapter 10, section 'Endgame: September to October 1919') should merely state that 'in the event of disagreement, the British government was prepared to accept American arbitration in regard to the boundaries of Palestine and Mesopotamia'.[72]

Balfour left Paris before Lloyd George arrived there. On his way to Scotland for an extended holiday, he made a stopover at London on 10 September, and informed Curzon of his plans to resign as secretary of state for foreign affairs. Curzon wrote afterwards to his wife that he had gone 'over everything with him. He is never coming back to the Foreign Office in any capacity.' Balfour had told him that 'he would have resigned at once had not Lloyd George pressed him to stay. He realises that this half-and-half arrangement is hard on me; but says that he is not going to interfere in the smallest degree.'[73] On 23 October, after Balfour had returned to London, Curzon was finally appointed foreign secretary.

Colonel Meinertzhagen sent his first dispatch to the Foreign Office on 26 September. He started, 'as the value of any opinion on controversial matter is enhanced by a knowledge of the personal leanings of the informant', with an exposition of his own position towards Zionism. He explained that his 'inclinations towards Jews in general is governed by an anti-semitic instinct which is invariably modified by personal contact. My views on Zionism are those of an ardent Zionist.' He therefore did not 'approach Zionism in Palestine with an open mind, but as one strongly prejudiced in its favour'. Meinertzhagen continued with an analysis of the situation in Palestine. The existing opposition to Zionism sprang 'from many sources, but they are mainly traceable to a deliberate misunderstanding of the Jew and everything Jewish – this in turn is based on contact with the local Jew, the least representative of Jewry or Zionism'. It was accordingly not 'difficult to understand that in Palestine every man's hand is against Zionism', and that 'to reconcile this mass of opposition to the policy of H.M.G. has been no easy task for our administration', especially considering that the personal views of the British administrators, 'no matter how anxious they are to conceal them, incline towards the exclusion of Zionism in Palestine'. On the whole however, so Meinertzhagen believed, 'our administration has exhibited laudable tolerance towards a subject they dislike and towards a community which is often unreasonable and by nature exacting'.

Ardent Zionist or not, his first weeks in Palestine had taught Meinertzhagen that the Zionist programme could only succeed – and here he sounded very much like Clayton, Money and Watson – if its 'growth is slow and methodical. In its incipient stages Zionism can only be artificial and unpopular and though it is realised that eventual success must depend on its own merits, it is only by careful nursing that it will develop a healthy growth.' He had also reached the conclusion, again in line with the previous warnings by Clayton, Money and Watson, that 'the people of Palestine are not at present in a fit state to be told openly that the establishment of Zionism is the policy to which H.M.G., America and France are committed'. It had therefore 'been found advisable to withhold for the present [...] from general publication' the instructions contained in the Foreign Office telegram to Colonel French of 4 August, which had been based on Samuel's letter of 5 June. He proposed to await Weizmann's arrival in Palestine – the latter was to take up the presidency of the Zionist Commission for a second turn – and to draw up together with him and General Watson:

> A statement giving in the most moderate language what Zionism means, the gradual manner of its introduction [...] its eventual benefits to Palestine and a denial that immigration spells the flooding of Palestine with the dregs of Eastern Europe.
>
> This has never been explained to the people of Palestine and it is the opinion of many officers of the present Administration that if moderately yet frankly put, such a declaration will go far to allay local apprehension.

It drew no comment in London or Paris that Meinertzhagen, the political officer Weizmann and Samuel had so vigorously lobbied for, had decided to withhold the instructions Samuel had proposed at the invitation of Balfour. Peterson merely minuted that Meinertzhagen 'should be thanked for his frank despatch', while Kidston hopefully speculated 'could we not even now resort to the "international solution" and throw the responsibility on the French?'[74]

On 28 October, Major E.G. Waley, who was political officer in Jerusalem, called at the Foreign Office and handed in the text of the draft declaration Meinertzhagen had drawn up. Meinertzhagen stated in his covering letter that the draft had the approval of Watson and Weizmann, and that it would be submitted to Allenby on the latter's return to Egypt. Waley could 'personally explain [...] the extreme necessity of immediately publishing such a document and the reasons underlying the points mentioned therein'. The draft declaration was quite a lengthy document. It first stipulated that in view of the fact that the British, American and

French governments were 'pledged to support the establishment of a Jewish National Home in Palestine', it had to 'be accepted that Zionism is a *chose jugée* and that continued agitation is only to the detriment of the whole community and will certainly be without the result it aims at attaining'. At the same time it admitted that it was 'most desirable clearly to state what Zionism means and what it entails, in order to remove some erroneous and exaggerated impressions which exist'. As far as the holy places were concerned, the declaration stated that there was nothing in the Zionist 'programme or ideals which aims at in any way altering the custody or status of the holy places of all religions in Palestine'. On the subject of Jewish immigration, the declaration assured that 'Zionism does not entail the flooding of Palestine with the poorer class of Jew'. With respect to the 'spoliation and ejection of present landowners in Palestine', the declaration observed that 'no such idea has existed among responsible Zionists' and that 'Zionism is as tolerant and sympathetic towards the sanctity of ownership of property as it is towards religious questions'. It did 'however require and can reasonably demand […] a certain degree of preferential treatment in its initial growth'. Regarding the fear that the majority would be subjected to the minority, the draft declaration proclaimed that 'such a principle [was] entirely opposed to Zionist doctrine of Justice and Freedom, and to the terms of any mandate under which Palestine will be governed'. The draft declaration finally drew attention to the 'material benefits which will fall to the lot of the people of Palestine, by the realisation of Zionist ideals, [which] have never been sufficiently appreciated. The introduction of Jewish brains and money can only lead to scientific progress, and development.'[75]

Although Peterson believed that the draft declaration was 'admirably adapted to its purpose', it was not well received higher up in the Foreign Office's hierarchy. Kidston had apparently quite forgotten that the original purpose of the proposed declaration had been to make clear that a British mandate and the establishment of a Jewish national home were a *chose jugée*, and complained that the draft presupposed 'throughout that Great Britain is to have the mandate for Palestine'. In his view that was still an open question. The declaration should consequently be modified, so that 'the whole document would be rather in the nature of an apologia for Zionism issued by the Power in Occupation for reasons of internal order than a pledge given by the future mandatory'. Tilley added that he also liked to 'tone down the passages which extol Zionist virtues. We should not issue a panegyric on Zionism or Zionists but merely state the aims of Zionism and point out that there is nothing to fear from it.' Hardinge opined that the declaration was 'unnecessarily aggressive towards those who do not see eye to eye with the Zionists, and we have yet to see how the Zionists behave before we issue panegyrics'. Curzon, finally, objected to 'the whole thing' and could not 'see why we should have any more declarations at any rate before the Mandate is given. The voice may be the voice of Jacob. (Col. M.) But the hand is the hand of Esau. (Dr W.).' He also believed that the draft declaration went 'far beyond' the instructions contained in the Foreign Office telegram of 4 August but as he did not 'desire to recede from [...] the policy of Mr Balfour', he asked for an alternative draft.

This draft declaration was far shorter than Meinertzhagen's. It no longer tried to explain what Zionism entailed, but focused on stating what the Balfour Declaration 'does *not* contemplate', namely (a) 'any interference with the custody of the holy places'; (b) 'the flooding of Palestine with Jewish immigrants'; (c) 'spoliation or eviction of present landowners'; and (d) 'the government of a majority by a minority'. Meinertzhagen's exposition of the economic benefits of Zionism was reduced to the statement that 'none can deny the present backward state of industry and agriculture in Palestine. It is in cooperation of the Zionists with the future Mandatory Power that a remedy for this unhappy condition must be sought.'

Curzon minuted on 5 November that he was 'quite willing to accept the amended declaration. But much doubt if the Zionists will like it.' The Foreign Office draft was wired to Cairo two days later. Allenby was also informed that the Foreign Office had felt unable to approve Meinertzhagen's draft, 'since it (a) appears to pre-judge the decision of the Peace Conference as to the mandate; (b) commits His Majesty's Government further than desirable in the direction of endorsing Zionist aspirations and guaranteeing their future conduct'. Allenby was requested to consult Meinertzhagen and to 'telegraph your views as to publication'.[76]

Meinertzhagen replied on 12 November. He refrained from commenting on the Foreign Office's drastic pruning of his draft declaration, and simply stated that Allenby agreed with the Foreign Office text, subject to one minor alteration, and proposed 'publication on receipt of your assent to alteration'. The Foreign Office telegraphed its assent on 18 November.[77] At the beginning of December, the Foreign Office wished to know whether the declaration had 'been published and if so with what results?'

Meinertzhagen wired back on 9 December that the declaration had not yet been published. He explained that the situation had 'improved and it may possibly be undesirable to do so but will report further at early date'. A rather startling outcome, especially considering all the time and effort that had been spent on a declaration of this kind since the beginning of June, and Meinertzhagen's own claim in his letter of 14 October that the early publication of such a declaration was extremely necessary. Tilley, however, was only relieved. He merely minuted that 'Lord Curzon was by no means anxious to make any declaration'.[78]

On 17 November 1919, Meinertzhagen had sent a dispatch to Curzon in which he had informed the foreign secretary that the provisional line to which the British troops were withdrawing, although it passed 'considerably north of the Sykes–Picot line', nevertheless did not satisfy 'the economic interests of Palestine'. If these were:

> To be secured, the northern boundary should [...] run from the sea, just north of the Litany river and following up, and at some distance from, the right bank, cross it from west to east about the Litany gorges. The boundary should thence be guided by including those of the Hermon waters which flow into the Litany or Jordan basins [see also Map 11.2].

With respect to the eastern boundary he had emphasised 'the desirability of Palestine having control over the Jordan valley as a whole, and the lower waters of Jordan tributaries flowing from the east'. When Kidston studied this dispatch on 17 December, he noted that it seemed 'to be based on the most extreme demands ever put forward by the Zionists. Dan to Beersheba is left far behind.' Vansittart added that Meinertzhagen's proposals would be criticised in a memorandum Forbes Adam and he were preparing in reply to a note containing French proposals for the settlement of the outstanding questions in the Middle East that Philippe Berthelot, chief secretary for political and commercial affairs at the French foreign ministry, had submitted on 12 December.[79]

Forbes Adam and Vansittart noted in their memorandum that 'with regard to the northern and eastern frontier of Palestine, the French Memorandum apparently accepts a rectification of the Sykes–Picot frontier', and proclaimed that economic considerations were 'the only really defensible and justifiable basis on which the British proposals for a considerable rectification of the Sykes–Picot line in Palestine in favour of the Zionists can be founded'. The Zionist proposal for the northern frontier, however, went too far. They believed that:

> The Zionist aims in this direction can be substantially met if the frontier, instead of including the whole Litani valley from the sea to the bend northwards, be made to run more or less from the present point of departure of the Sykes-Picot line, north of Acre, north-eastwards so as to include in Palestine the bend of the Litani itself and a small portion of the [?area] to the north of the bend. Thence it might run due east to the southern slopes of Mount Hermon south of Rasheya and cutting the Nahr Hasbani.

In their opinion this line, as it left 'to Syria the coastal area north of Acre and round Tyre, and also the nationalist districts of Hasbeya and Rasheya would be a very fair compromise'. Should the French nevertheless refuse to accept it, they recommended then that 'we should revert to the proposal for American arbitration'.[80]

The question of the northern border of Palestine was one of the subjects discussed during an Anglo–French conference on the Turkish settlement at the Foreign Office on 22 and 23 December 1919. Berthelot began by explaining that Clemenceau stood by the Sykes–Picot line. The French prime minister felt that he had already made enough concessions by giving up Mosul and accepting that Great Britain would be the mandatory for Palestine. He was prepared to come to an economic agreement with the Zionists respecting 'the waters flowing from Mount Hermon southwards' into Palestine, but further than this the French could not go. Vansittart, supported by Gribbon, replied that 'it was essential for economic reasons [...] that the streams flowing south from the Hermon into the Jordan basin, and a bit of the Litani, should fall within the Palestine territory'. He subsequently introduced the compromise he and Forbes Adam had come up with. In reaction, Berthelot merely 'stated that he was not in a position to accept this'. Curzon then intervened. He 'could not understand why the French government insisted on the Sykes–Picot line, even in places where it had been drawn regardless of political, geographical, or economic facts'. Lloyd George had moreover 'spoken publicly of the Palestine of the future as comprising the territory from ancient Dan (represented more or less by Banias) to Beersheba, and he felt sure that he was not prepared to give way on this point'. Berthelot answered that he was 'equally sure that M. Clemenceau was not prepared to yield'. The French prime minister 'thought that he had already made a great cession in respect of Palestine'.

After an adjournment, Curzon reported that he had spoken with Lloyd George about the northern frontier of Palestine. One of the reasons the Prime Minister felt that the French should accept the British compromise was that he 'had publicly committed himself on more than one occasion to the formula of including in Palestine all the ancient territories from Dan to Beersheba. He could not recede from this attitude.' He was, however, 'quite willing that the question should be submitted to arbitration by the United States'. Berthelot was not impressed. Clemenceau 'had never agreed to Mr Lloyd George committing himself in this way'. It was regrettable that 'Mr Lloyd George found himself in a difficult position *vis-à-vis* the British public in this matter', and the French government 'would do what they felt just and possible to help matters'. American arbitration was out of the question; this was 'a matter which the British and French governments ought to settle themselves'. Curzon closed the discussion by concluding that 'no agreement seemed possible at present, and that they must each report to their respective prime ministers and governments how the matter now stood and the arguments used by both sides'.[81]

It seemed that the personal antagonism between Lloyd George and Clemenceau, sparked off by the former's greediness as well as his belief that the British could dictate terms to the French, and fuelled by the latter's accusations of bad faith, which had so greatly hampered the finding of a solution to the Syrian question, had finally come to haunt the settlement of the border between Syria and Palestine, but Clemenceau resigned on 20 January 1920 after he had been defeated in the French Presidential elections.

Great Britain received the mandate for Palestine at the San Remo conference. Curzon telegraphed to Hardinge on 26 April that 'as regards Palestine an Article is [...] to be inserted in Peace Treaty entrusting administration to a mandatory, whose duties are defined by a verbatim repetition of Mr Balfour's declaration of November 1917'.[82] He further stated that the mandatory power for the country was 'not mentioned in Treaty, but by an independent decision of Supreme Council was declared to be Great Britain'. As to Palestine's boundaries, during the conference France and Britain had decided with respect to its eastern frontier to adhere to the line fixed in the Sykes–Picot agreement, where the River Jordan had been the boundary between zone 'B' and the area under international administration,[83] while the border between Palestine and Syria, so Curzon informed Hardinge, would be 'determined at a later date by the principal Allied Powers'.[84] It took France and Great Britain almost three years before they finally managed to settle this boundary. Except for a revision that left the Golan Heights in Syria, it more or less followed the compromise solution formulated by Forbes Adam and Vansittart in December 1919.

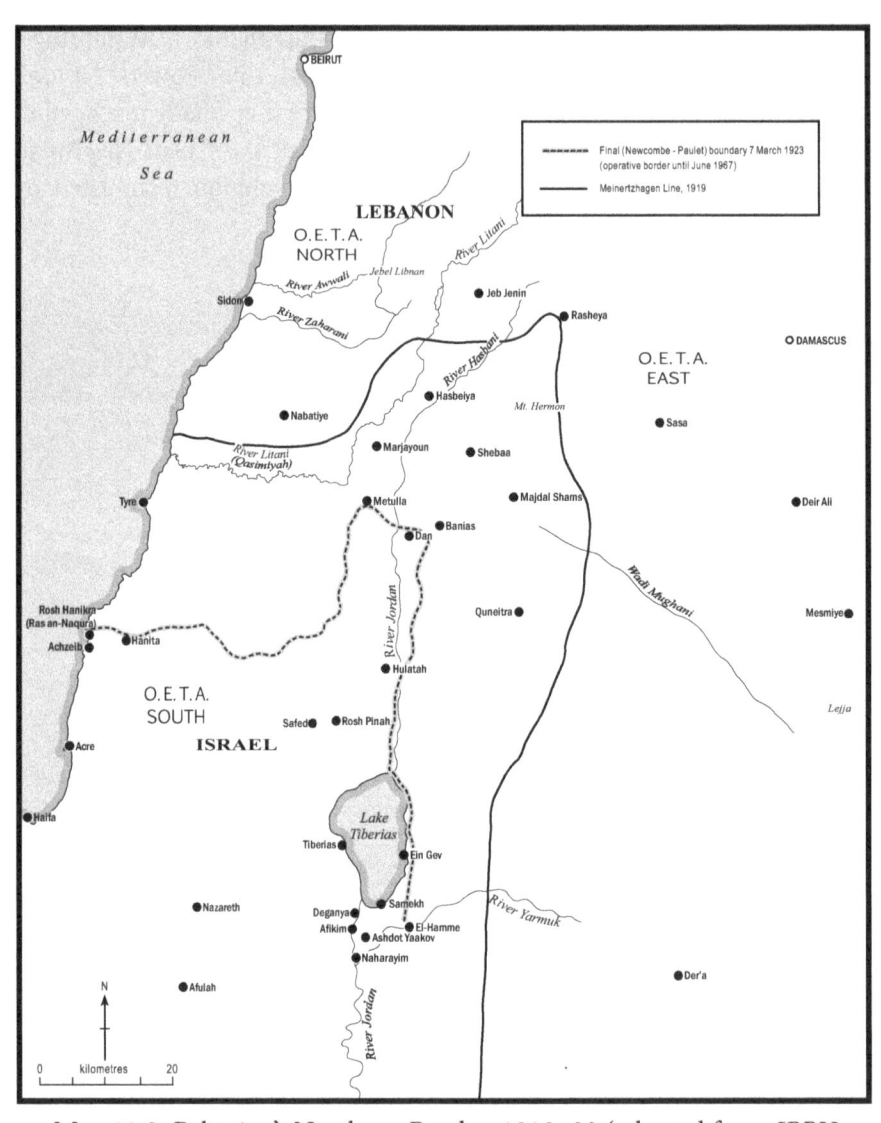

Map 11.2 Palestine's Northern Border, 1919–23 (adapted from *IBRU Boundary Security Bulletin* 2000–1, p. 74)

CONCLUSION

Looking back almost one century later, one may say that the two major events that took place with respect to British foreign policy making towards the Middle East, from the beginning of World War I until the fall of the Asquith coalition government in December 1916, are the Foreign Office authorising Sir Henry McMahon to enter into negotiations with Sharif Husayn, the Emir of Mecca, and the signing of the Sykes–Picot agreement. The crux of my explanation of these events, which now loom so large, is that Sir Edward Grey and his officials were not very much alive to the significance of what they were doing, because for them Middle Eastern affairs were simply not that important. This meant that as long as Grey and his civil servants perceived the advice of various experts not to be inconsistent with the essence of the Foreign Office's policy – to uphold the Entente with France – they were prepared to follow it. This is why they acted without much ado upon recommendations by Lord Hardinge, Lord Kitchener, Sir Reginald Wingate, McMahon and Sir Mark Sykes, even when these contradicted one another. This tendency was especially prominent during the first months of the war, when Cairo was alternately instructed to encourage the Arab movement in every way possible, and to refrain from giving any encouragement. The sudden change in the summer of 1915, from a policy of restraint with regard to the Middle East to an active, pro-Arab policy, may also be explained in this manner. Perhaps Wingate and McMahon were able to outstrip the India Office and the Government of India as the Foreign Office's premier advisors on the Arab question because they were, after all, in the service of the Foreign Office, perhaps because

Austen Chamberlain had succeeded Lord Crewe as secretary of state for India, but the main point is that Sir Edward and his officials need not have had 'good' reasons for thinking that Wingate and McMahon were in a better position to judge how to react to Husayn's opening bid. Wingate's letters and memoranda definitely played a role in the Foreign Office's conversion to a more active, pro-Arab policy, but it is highly improbable that Grey and his officials would have been receptive to Sir Reginald's arguments if they themselves had invested heavily in the policy of restraint advocated by the Indian authorities.

The negotiations that led to the signing of the Sykes–Picot agreement presented to the Foreign Office more a technical problem than a politically sensitive one. Once it was realised that the conflicting claims of Arabs and French regarding Syria were amendable to a settlement – as Wingate, Sir John Maxwell, McMahon, Aubrey Herbert and Sykes, one after the other, had emphasised – the Arab question became something of a routine affair, something that was covered by the rule that nothing should be done that might arouse France's Syrian susceptibilities. The negotiations with the Emir of Mecca could only be brought to a close after those with the French had successfully been concluded. Even though the authorities in Cairo, and Sykes, urged the vital importance of a quick reply to Husayn's overtures, the negotiations with the French, as these entailed consultations with the relevant departments as well as with Russia, simply had to run their course. This also implied that once these negotiations were under way it was very difficult to stop them. Neither the information that the Arabs were in no position to rise against the Turks (which seemed to have knocked the bottom out from under the *raison d'être* of the negotiations) nor that Husayn was not *the* spokesman of the Arabs (which appeared to imply that, perhaps as far as the Arab side was concerned, there was nobody to negotiate with) halted their progress. Regarding the relative importance of the Arab question, it is naturally also very telling that, after the Anglo–French agreement had been signed in the middle of May 1916, nobody in the Foreign Office observed that the way was now clear to finalise the negotiations with the Emir of Mecca, or noticed, at the beginning of June, that he had started his revolt before the negotiations with him had been completed.

For British policy makers, the sending of British troops to Rabegh was unquestionably the most important question as far as the Middle East was concerned during the years of the Asquith governments. They were very much alive to the significance of this question, now completely forgotten.

Some ministers, notably Lord George Curzon, Chamberlain, Grey, Arthur Balfour and David Lloyd George, dissatisfied with the manner in which the war was being conducted, believed that Rabegh provided the opportunity to challenge the dominant view that the war could only be won in France and that sideshows must be avoided at all costs. Although the significance of the Rabegh question was largely symbolic – a small ally, a small force – the stakes in terms of credibility were very high as a result of Sir William Robertson's initial flat refusal even to consider the dispatch of troops. This implied that the protagonists in this controversy were very reluctant to put their credibility at risk. That is why the War Committee's policy with respect to Rabegh amounted to the decision to postpone the decision, even when it had been decided to take a decision, and of course this also applies to Wingate, the strongest advocate of sending troops. In the end, he also refused to put his credibility on the line, and for his part tried to shift the responsibility onto Husayn.

Looking back on the years of the Lloyd George government, the one event that naturally stands out, considering the enduring Israel–Arab conflict, is the decision by the War Cabinet to authorise foreign secretary Balfour to make a declaration of sympathy with Zionist aspirations in November 1917. This time, too, the decision makers concerned realised the significance of what they were doing, if only because of Edwin Montagu's violent protests against such a declaration, but this did not mean that they had any clearly circumscribed notion of why Britain should issue it. It was a curious blend of sentiment (the romantic notion of the Jews returning to their ancient lands after 1,800 years of exile) and anti-Semitism (world Jewry was a force that could vitally influence the outcome of the war) that led them to this decision. When Curzon introduced some factual considerations into the discussion, these were easily swept aside in favour of the 'diplomatic' argument that a declaration of sympathy with Zionism would greatly contribute to the Jews of Russia and the USA siding with the cause of the Entente.

Another major event with far-reaching consequences for the present-day Middle East is of course the private deal between Lloyd George and French prime minister Georges Clemenceau on 1 December 1918, which brought Palestine and Mosul into the British sphere. In the course of 1919, Lloyd George made several attempts to get Clemenceau to accept yet another revision in Britain's favour of the boundaries laid down in the Sykes–Picot agreement. Clemenceau greatly resented these in view of his concessions in December, and started openly to accuse Lloyd George of bad faith. This had the result that the settlement of the Arabic-speaking parts of the Ottoman Empire turned into a highly personal affair between the two prime ministers, in the course of which the credibility stakes became higher and higher. By the autumn of 1919, only the two prime ministers were still prepared to let the Middle East further burden Anglo–French relations. In the end, Lloyd George gave in as far as the south-eastern border of Syria was concerned, and had more or less his way regarding the northern border of Palestine, but this only after Clemenceau had left office.

In my opinion, one of the most striking phenomena as far as British decision making with respect to the Arab question 1914–19 is concerned, is the rapid decline of the Foreign Office's influence, which set in after Balfour had succeeded Grey. During the first years of World War I, British Middle East policy was very much the Foreign Office's own preserve, and Grey, with the support of Prime Minister Henry Asquith, was eager to guard the Foreign Office's preeminence. Moreover, after 11 years as foreign secretary, the Foreign Office had to a very large extent become 'his' department, so that Grey and his officials most of the time spoke with one voice. This altered drastically after the advent of the Lloyd George government in December 1916. Compared to Grey, Balfour could only be an outsider, and continued to be so during the whole period of his tenure of the Foreign Office. His reputation was not bound up with the department, and he ran the office in much the same lackadaisical manner as he had run the Admiralty. This left Lloyd George ample space to intervene in British Middle East policy and to bypass the Foreign Office whenever he felt like it. A first occasion was the conference of St Jean-de-Maurienne in April 1917 to settle Italian claims in the Eastern Mediterranean, where no representative of the Foreign Office was present. The frequency of Lloyd George's interventions increased over time and in 1919, as far as the settlement of the Syrian question was concerned, the Prime Minister was completely in command, and the Foreign Office could only follow.

When he was chairman of the Eastern Committee, Curzon succeeded in curbing the Foreign Office's grip on Middle East policy, which was greatly resented by Lord Robert Cecil, but when Curzon became acting foreign secretary in January 1919, it soon became apparent that he totally lacked the power to reverse the tide and reestablish the Foreign Office's authority in this policy area. I cannot imagine a better illustration of just how low the Foreign Office's reputation had sunk by the autumn of 1919, than Curzon having to request Lloyd George that he be present at the negotiations with Faysal.

The eclipse of the Foreign Office also implied that the basis of its policy towards the Middle East – that nothing must be done that might excite French susceptibilities with respect to Syria – was gradually eroded from 1917 onwards, with the result that in 1919 Lloyd George, confident that he could dictate terms to the French, had no qualms in treating these with contempt. Where traditional Foreign Office policy implied that possible trouble in the Middle East was to be preferred to trouble with the French, Lloyd George's priorities were exactly the opposite. In this connection I should not fail to point out that the policy advocated by Cecil in 1918, although at first glance it might have looked like a return to the Foreign Office's traditional policy, actually was nothing of the kind. It was almost as hostile to French interests as Lloyd George's. Although Cecil accepted that Britain's signature under the Sykes–Picot agreement held good, at the same time he tried to undermine the French position, by creating facts on the ground, trying to bind the French to the principle of self-determination, and to induce the Americans to step in and force the French to recognise that the agreement was inconsistent with the spirit of the times. Where Lloyd George was blunt, Lord Robert was too clever by half, and both failed in their attempts to get the French to give up their acquired rights in Syria under the Sykes–Picot agreement.

What is also striking to me is that whenever 'the men on the spot' did not see eye to eye with the decision makers in London, the former did not succeed in convincing the latter that the policy they advocated should be abandoned, and a different one adopted. Although officials, soldiers and ministers in London readily accepted that their knowledge of Middle Eastern affairs was inferior to that of those who were actually there (except Curzon and Sykes of course), at the same time they did not doubt that their knowledge was superior, because they saw the bigger picture, however vague that picture might be. This equally applied to the Foreign Office's traditional policy that nothing should be done that might arouse French susceptibilities with respect to Syria, and to Balfour's policy to create in Palestine the conditions that would give the Zionists the opportunity to establish a Jewish state (provided that the rights of the existing population were respected). Concrete, practical difficulties did not stand a chance against lofty principles and general notions. At best, such difficulties were acknowledged in London while the men on the spot were encouraged to bear with them. At worst, these were merely seen as attempts by the latter to obstruct agreed policy and yet to have it their way. The insensitivity of the London decision makers to the worries and warnings of the British authorities in the Middle East triggered the latter to depict the consequences if their policy proposals were not adopted in the shrillest terms. Disaster would surely follow if the demands of the Arab nationalists were not met right away, if a brigade was not sent to Rabegh, if the British government insisted on implementing the Balfour Declaration. That same insensitivity, however, also had the result that when these dire consequences failed to materialise, hardly anybody in London noticed this and called to account those who had uttered these apparently empty threats.

More generally speaking, and in line with the bureaucratic-politics perspective I developed in the Introduction (see section 'A Bureaucratic-Politics Perspective'), especially my observations on the role that arguments and facts play in the decision-making process, I should note that gaining the reputation of being an expert does not increase a decision maker's effectiveness. Experts are called in to share their knowledge with ministers, who only pick up whatever suits their own interests. Experts do not take decisions. Sykes's temporary prominence in British Middle East policy was not the result of his testimony before the War Committee after his tour of the Near and Middle East, but of his success in coming to a speedy agreement with François Georges-Picot. From May 1915 onwards, Curzon was the (War) Cabinet's expert on Middle Eastern affairs in residence, so to speak, and although he sometimes managed to thwart the policy initiatives of others, especially Sykes's, he never managed to put his stamp on the main lines of British Middle East policy. Lloyd George, on the contrary, even though he knew next to nothing of the Middle East, certainly did.

To me, Sykes is undoubtedly one of the most fascinating persons figuring in British policy making towards the Middle East 1914–19. At the beginning of 1916, he established a reputation as an effective negotiator. His reputation was further strengthened by his appointment as assistant secretary to the War Cabinet, but it began to wane when in the summer of 1917 there were signs that he had failed to impart to King Husayn a clear understanding of what the Sykes–Picot agreement meant, and it was fatally injured at the end of 1917, when it became clear that the French government would not ratify the projet d'arrangement Sykes had negotiated. What makes Sir Mark fascinating is that he did not hesitate to put the most fantastic, outrageous observations, theories and schemes to paper and circulate them to whomever might be interested. His observations on the influence of the Jews on the war efforts of the belligerents did perhaps not raise too many eyebrows, because these were very common at the time, but this certainly did not apply to his various schemes about how French, Arab, Armenian, Zionist and whoever else's interests could be combined and reconciled, and put to work in support of the British war effort. It is hard to believe that anyone for one moment took these seriously, or was ready to entertain them, but it was very seldom that they were openly ridiculed. People put up with them as long as Sykes was in the ascendant, and simply ignored them after his career had taken a downturn. However, it remains an intriguing thought that someone who loudly proclaimed such fanciful notions, their relationship with reality often being very tenuous and sometimes perhaps even non-existent, was considered to be a force to be reckoned with as far as British Middle East policy was concerned for a period of two years at least.

These observations lead me to another more general point, namely that British policy makers in the main had only hazy notions of what was going on in the world outside. Most of the time they were guided by preconceived notions, underdeveloped theories, and commonplaces – on how the world functioned, what was in the British interest, what the characters of the French, Arabs, Jews, Italians and Americans looked like, how these people operated and what they deemed important and what not. These found ready confirmation almost every day, and were practically never rejected with the realisation that they did not correspond with the facts. 'Facts-in-themselves' had scarcely a role to play. What mattered to British decision makers was who presented certain facts and, more precisely, what was the position of the person who presented these facts – did he matter or not? – and it was on the basis of this assessment they decided whether these facts warranted action being taken, or could safely be ignored. A precise measurement of degrees of knowledgeableness is of course impossible, but in accordance with the bureaucratic-politics perspective, I conjecture that they were more knowledgeable about this internal world than the external one.

One other phenomenon I should finally draw attention to is that British policy makers' relative ignorance went hand in hand with a strong dose of arrogance. They displayed a feeling of superiority towards the outside world, which was particularly manifest in their attitude towards and treatment of the Arabs. British relations with Sharif Husayn, the Emir of Mecca, are a very good case in point. In the eyes of his British interlocutors, Husayn was 'the poor sharif', an Arab potentate buried away in Mecca, who naturally did not understand the fine points of diplomatic negotiations, the working of international power games, or what the fighting of modern wars required. Although Husayn had survived the snake pit of the Sultan's court at Constantinople, which to my mind is a considerable achievement in itself as well as a good indication that he must have had some conception of how things worked in the corridors of power, he was not taken seriously. That the Emir succeeded in getting Great Britain, one of the greatest powers in the world, to support his ambition to establish himself as the supreme ruler in the Arab world while he was not even sure of his own power base in Mecca, must surely rank as one of the most astounding achievements in the annals of diplomatic history. Arrogance prevented his British supporters from seeing a shrewd negotiator who managed to harness them to make good his exorbitant pretensions. They only saw a poor old man to whom it had to be explained that the British subsidy in gold should be spent on bribing tribes and not be kept in his own coffers, who should not be discouraged too much after he had proclaimed himself King of the Arab Nation, whose employment of this title in his correspondence with Ibn Sa'ud was merely an unhappy accident, and whose pretensions to have a say in the future of Palestine, the Lebanon, Syria and Mesopotamia should not firmly be rejected but treated as harmless extravagances. I can very well imagine that Husayn and his sons time and again must have rubbed their eyes in incredulity at all these manifestations of British gullibility.

Way back in 1969, as a second-year student in political and social sciences at the University of Amsterdam, I was greatly struck by David Knowles's dictum, quoted in E.H. Carr's *What is History?*, that 'the historian is not a judge, still less a hanging judge'. Now, some 47 years later, I hope I have been able to do full justice to Knowles's maxim as far as British foreign policy towards the Middle East 1914–19 is concerned. I also hope that the reader, after reading this book, will agree with me that Lord Grey was perfectly right when he claimed in his memoirs that, whatever British foreign ministers were doing – and as far as I am concerned this also applies to all other officials, soldiers and ministers who mattered in British policy making towards the Middle East in these years – the business of the day prevented them from making elaborate calculations for the future.

BIOGRAPHICAL NOTES

British officials, politicians and soldiers connected with British foreign policy towards the Arab Middle East, 1914–19

ALLENBY OF MEGIDDO, Edmund Henry Hyman, Viscount (1861–1936)
Joins the army, 1882; colonel, 1902; major-general, 1909; army corps commander, BEF, 1914–17; lieutenant-general, 1916; general officer commanding-in-chief, EEF, 1917–19; general, 1917; field-marshal, 1919; high commissioner Egypt, 1919–25.

AMERY, Leopold Charles Maurice Stennet (1873–1955)
Fellow of All Souls, 1897; MP for Birmingham South, 1911–45; joins the army; intelligence officer in the Balkans and eastern Mediterranean, 1915–16; assistant secretary, War Cabinet, 1917–18; parliamentary under-secretary, Colonial Office, 1919–21.

ASQUITH, Herbert Henry (1852–1928)
Balliol; MP for East Fife, 1886–1918; home secretary, 1892–5; chancellor of the Exchequer, 1905–8; prime minister, 1908–16.

BALFOUR, Arthur James (1848–1930)
Trinity College, Cambridge; MP for Hertford, 1874–85, East Manchester, 1885–1906, City of London, 1907–22; chief secretary for Ireland, 1887–91; first lord of the Treasury, 1891–2, 1895–1902; prime minister, 1902–5; first lord of the Admiralty, 1915–16; foreign secretary, 1916–19; lord president of the Council, 1919–22.

BELL, Gertrude Margaret Lowthian (1868–1926)
Member of Arab Bureau, 1915; oriental secretary to the civil commissioner Iraq, 1917–20.

BERTIE OF THAME, Francis Leveson, Viscount (1844–1919)
Clerk in the Foreign Office, 1863; assistant clerk, 1882; senior clerk, 1889; assistant under-secretary, 1894; ambassador at Rome, 1903–5; ambassador at Paris, 1905–18.

BUCHANAN, Sir George William (1854–1924)
Attaché, 1875; secretary of Embassy, 1899; agent and consul-general in Bulgaria, 1903; envoy extraordinary and minister plenipotentiary to the Queen of the Netherlands, 1909; ambassador at St Petersburg, 1910–17; ambassador at Rome, 1919–21.

CALLWELL, Sir Charles Edward (1859–1928)
Joins the army, 1878; colonel, 1904; retired, 1909; military correspondent *Morning Post*, 1909–14; temp. major-general and director of military operations, 1914–15.

CECIL, Lord Edgar Algernon Robert (1864–1958)
University College, Oxford; MP for East Marylebone, 1906–10, Hitchin Division of Hertfordshire, 1911–23; parliamentary under-secretary for foreign affairs, 1915–18; minister of blockade, 1916–18; assistant foreign secretary, 1918; member British delegation at the peace conference, 1919.

CHAMBERLAIN, Austen (1863–1937)
Trinity College, Cambridge; MP for East Worcestershire, 1892–1937; chancellor of the Exchequer, 1903–5; secretary of state for India, 1915–17; member of the War Cabinet, 1918; chancellor of the Exchequer, 1919–21.

CHEETHAM, Sir Milne (1869–1938)
Attaché, 1893; first secretary Cairo, 1910; counsellor of the Embassy, 1911; chargé d'affaires, June–December, 1914; acting high commissioner, December 1914–January 1915.

CLAYTON, Sir Gilbert Falkingham (1875–1929)
Woolwich; joins the army, 1895; Egyptian army, 1898; private secretary to Sir Reginald Wingate, 1908–10; Sudan agent and director of intelligence, Egyptian army, 1913–17; head military intelligence at British Headquarters Egypt, 1914–17; colonel, 1914; brigadier-general, 1916; chief political officer, EEF, 1917–19; advisor to the Egyptian Ministry of the Interior, 1919–22.

CLERK, Sir George Russell (1874–1951)
New College, Oxford; clerk in the Foreign Office, 1898; assistant clerk, 1907; senior clerk, 1913.

CORNWALLIS, Kinahan (1883–1959)
Temp. major and director Arab Bureau, 1916–20; assistant political officer, EEF, 1919.

COX, Sir Percy Zachariah (1864–1937)
Sandhurst; joins the Indian army, 1884; British agent and consul in Muscat, 1899–1904; political resident and consul-general at Bushire, 1904–13; secretary, Foreign Department, to the governor-general in Council, 1913–14; chief political officer, Force 'D' and MEF, 1914–17; civil commissioner Mesopotamia, 1917–18; minister to Persia, 1918–20.

CREWE, Robert Offley Ashburton, Marquess of (1858–1945)
Trinity College, Cambridge; lord president of the Council, 1905–8, 1915–16; lord privy seal and secretary of state for the Colonies, 1908–10; secretary of state for India, 1910–15; lord privy seal, 1912–15; president of the Board of Education, 1916.

CROWE, Sir Eyre (1864–1925)
Clerk in the Foreign Office, 1885; assistant clerk, 1900; senior clerk, 1906; assistant under-secretary, 1912; member British delegation at the peace conference, 1919–20.

CURZON OF KEDLESTON, George Nathaniel, Earl (1859–1925)
Balliol; Fellow of All Souls, 1883; MP for Southport, 1886–98; parliamentary under-secretary for India, 1891–2; parliamentary under-secretary for Foreign

Affairs, 1895–8; governor-general and viceroy of India, 1898–1905; lord privy seal, 1915–16; member of the War Cabinet and lord president of the Council, 1916–19; acting foreign secretary, 1919; foreign secretary, 1919–24.

DERBY, Edward Stanley, 17th Earl of (1865–1948)
Postmaster-general, 1903–5; parliamentary under-secretary for War, 1916; secretary of state for War, 1916–18; ambassador at Paris, 1918–20.

DRUMMOND, Sir James Eric (1876–1951)
Clerk in the Foreign Office, 1900; private secretary to parliamentary under-secretary for Foreign Affairs, 1906–10; précis-writer to Sir Edward Grey, 1910–11; private secretary to H.H. Asquith, 1912–15; private secretary to Sir E. Grey, 1915–16; private secretary to A.J. Balfour, 1916–19.

FITZMAURICE, Gerald Henry (1865–1939)
Student interpreter, 1888; 3rd dragoman Constantinople, 1897; chief dragoman, 1907.

FORBES ADAM, Eric Graham (1888–1925)
Clerk in the Foreign Office, 1913; member British delegation at the peace conference, 1919.

GRAHAM, Sir Ronald William (1870–1949)
Attaché, 1892; clerk in the Foreign Office, 1903–7; counsellor of Embassy, 1907; advisor to the Egyptian Ministry of the Interior, 1910–16; assistant under-secretary, 1916–19; acting permanent under-secretary, 1919; envoy extraordinary and minister plenipotentiary at the Hague, 1919–21.

GREY OF FALLODON, Edward, Viscount (1862–1933)
Balliol; MP for North Berwick, 1885–1916; parliamentary under-secretary for Foreign Affairs, 1892–5; foreign secretary, 1905–16; ambassador at Washington, 1919–20.

HANKEY, Sir Maurice Pascal Alers (1877–1963)
Woolwich; Royal Marine Artillery, 1895; secretary to the Committee of Imperial Defence, 1912–38; secretary of the War Cabinet, 1916–18; British secretary to the peace conference, 1919, secretary of the Cabinet, 1919–38.

BIOGRAPHICAL NOTES 429

HARDINGE OF PENSHURST, Charles, Baron (1858–1944)
Trinity College, Cambridge; attaché, 1880; secretary of Embassy, 1898; assistant under-secretary, 1903–4; ambassador at St Petersburg, 1904–6; permanent under-secretary, 1906–10; governor-general and viceroy of India, 1910–16; permanent under-secretary; 1916–20; organising ambassador British delegation at the peace conference, 1919.

HIRTZEL, Sir Arthur (1870–1937)
Trinity College, Oxford; fellow of Brasenose College, 1895–1902; enters India Office, 1894; private secretary to secretary of state, 1903–9; secretary, Political Department, India Office, 1909–17; assistant under-secretary, 1917–21; member British delegation at the peace conference, 1919.

HOGARTH, David George (1862–1927)
Member of Arab Bureau, 1916–18.

HOLDERNESS, Sir Thomas William (1849–1924)
University College, Oxford; Indian Civil Service, 1872; secretary, Revenue and Agricultural Department, to the governor-general in Council, 1898–1901; secretary, Revenue Statistics and Commerce, India Office, 1901–12; permanent under-secretary, 1912–19.

KERR, Philip (1882–1940)
Private secretary to D. Lloyd George, 1916–21.

KIDSTON, George Jardine (1873–1954)
Attaché, 1897; clerk in the Foreign Office, 1916.

KITCHENER OF KHARTOUM, Herbert Horatio, Earl (1850–1916)
Joins the army, 1871; colonel, 1888; sirdar Egyptian army, 1892–9; major-general, 1896; chief of staff South Africa, 1900–2; general, 1902; commander-in-chief, India, 1902–9; field-marshal, 1909; governor Malta, 1910–11; British agent and consul-general Egypt, 1911–14; secretary of state for War, 1914–16.

LAWRENCE, Thomas Edward (1888–1935)
Jesus College, Oxford; joins the army, 1914; member of Arab Bureau, 1916; staff officer, HEF, 1917; staff officer, EEF, 1918.

LLOYD, George Ambrose (1879–1941)
Honorary attaché at Constantinople, 1905–6; MP for West Staffordshire, 1910–18; captain Warwickshire Yeomanry; governor, Bombay, 1918–23.

LLOYD GEORGE, David (1863–1945)
MP for Caernarvon Burroughs, 1890–1945; chancellor of the Exchequer, 1908–15; minister for Munitions, 1915–16; secretary of state for War, 1916; prime minister, 1916–22.

MACDONOGH, Sir George Mark Watson (1865–1942)
Joins the army, 1884; colonel, 1912; General Staff GHQ, BEF, 1914–16; major-general, 1916; director of military intelligence, 1916–18; adjutant-general to the forces, 1918–22; lieutenant-general, 1919.

MALLET, Sir Louis du Pan (1866–1936)
Clerk in the Foreign Office, 1888; précis-writer to the Marquess of Lansdowne, 1903–5; private secretary to Sir Edward Grey, 1905–7; assistant under-secretary, 1907; ambassador at Constantinople, 1913–14; assistant under-secretary, 1918; member British delegation at the peace conference, 1919.

MAURICE, Sir Frederick Barton (1871–1951)
Joins the army, 1892; colonel, 1915; director of military operations, 1915–18; major-general, 1916.

MAXWELL, Sir John Grenfell (1859–1929)
Sandhurst; joins the army, 1879; colonel, 1898; major-general, 1906; general officer commanding-in chief, Egypt, 1908–12 and 1914–16; lieutenant-general, 1912; commander-in-chief, Ireland, 1916; commander-in-chief, Northern Command, 1916–19; general, 1919.

MCMAHON, Sir Arthur Henry (1862–1949)
Joins the army, 1882; Indian army, 1885; Indian Political Department, 1890; secretary, Foreign Department, to the governor-general in Council, 1911–14; high commissioner, Egypt, 1914–16.

MEINERTZHAGEN, Richard (1878–1967)
Joins the army, 1899; Intelligence Section, EEF, 1917–18; colonel, 1918; War Office, 1918–19; member British delegation at the peace conference, 1919; chief political officer, Syria and Palestine, 1919–20.

MILNER OF ST JAMES'S AND CAPE TOWN, Lord Alfred (1854–1925)
Balliol; high commissioner, South Africa, 1897–1905; member of the War Cabinet, 1916–18; secretary of state for War, 1918; secretary of state for the Colonies, 1919–21.

MONTAGU, Edwin Samuel (1879–1924)
Trinity College, Cambridge; MP for Chesterton Division, Cambridgeshire, 1906–22; parliamentary under-secretary for India, 1910–14; financial secretary to the Treasury, 1914–15; chancellor of the Duchy of Lancaster, 1915; minister for Munitions, 1916; secretary of state for India, 1917–22.

MURRAY, Sir Archibald James (1860–1945)
Joins the army, 1879; colonel, 1903; director of Military Training, 1907–12; major-general, 1910; inspector of Infantry, 1912–14; chief of staff, BEF, 1914; lieutenant-general, 1915; deputy chief and chief of the Imperial General Staff, 1915; general officer commanding-in-chief, EEF, 1916–17; general officer commanding-in-chief, Aldershot, 1917–19.

NEWCOMBE, Stewart Francis (1878–1956)
Joins the army, 1898; Egyptian army, 1901–11; general staff, 1914–15; staff officer, HEF, 1917.

NICOLSON, Sir Arthur (1849–1928)
Brasenose College, Oxford; clerk in the Foreign Office, 1870; secretary of Embassy, 1893; envoy extraordinary and minister plenipotentiary to the Sultan of Morocco, 1895–1905; ambassador at Madrid, 1905–6; ambassador at St Petersburg, 1906–10; permanent under-secretary, 1910–16.

NICOLSON, Harold George (1886–1968)
Attaché, 1909; clerk in the Foreign Office, 1914.

OLIPHANT, Lancelot (1881–1956)
Clerk in the Foreign Office, 1903; assistant clerk, 1916.

ORMSBY GORE, William George Arthur (1885–1964)
New College; MP for Denby District, 1910–18, and Stafford, 1918–38; joins the army, 1914; parliamentary secretary to Lord Milner and assistant secretary, War Cabinet, 1917–18.

PETERSON, Maurice Drummond (1889–1952)
Clerk in the Foreign Office, 1913.

ROBERTSON, Sir William Robert (1859–1933)
Joins the army, 1877; colonel, 1903; major-general, 1910; director of Military Training, 1913–14; quarter-master-general, 1914–15; chief of staff, BEF, 1915; lieutenant-general, 1915; chief of the Imperial General Staff, 1915–18; general, 1916; commander-in-chief, Great Britain, 1918.

SAMUEL, Herbert Louis (1870–1963)
Balliol; MP for Cleveland Division, North Riding, Yorkshire, 1902–18; parliamentary under-secretary Home Office, 1905–9; chancellor of the Duchy of Lancaster, 1909–10; postmaster-general, 1910–14; president of the Local Government Board, 1914–15; postmaster-general, 1915; chancellor of the Duchy of Lancaster, 1915; postmaster-general, 1915–16; home secretary, 1916.

SHUCKBURGH, John Evelyn (1877–1953)
King's College; junior clerk India Office, 1900; senior clerk, Political Department, India Office, 1906; assistant secretary, Political Department, India Office, 1912; secretary, Political Department, India Office, 1917.

SMUTS, Jan Christiaan (1870–1950)
General officer commanding-in-chief, East Africa, 1916; member of the War Cabinet, 1917–18, member British delegation at the peace conference, 1919.

STORRS, Ronald (1881–1955)
Pembroke College; oriental secretary to the British agent and consul-general, Egypt, 1908; political officer, EEF, 1917; governor, Jerusalem, 1917–26.

SYKES, Sir Tatton Benvenuto Mark, 6th Baronet (1879–1919)
Jesus College; joins the army, 1899; retires, 1902; honorary attaché at Constantinople, 1905–6; lieut.-colonel Territorial Reserve Force, 1910; MP for Central Hull, 1911–19; assistant secretary, War Cabinet, 1916–18; acting adviser on Arabian and Palestine affairs, Foreign Office, 1918.

SYMES, George Stewart (1882–1962)
Sandhurst; joins the army, 1900; Egyptian army, 1906; private secretary to Sir Reginald Wingate, 1912–16; attached to Staff of High Commissioner, Egypt, 1917–19.

THWAITES, Sir William (1868–1947)
Joins the army, 1887; colonel, 1916; major-general, 1918; director of military intelligence, 1918–22.

TILLEY, John Anthony Cecil (1869–1952)
King's College, Cambridge; clerk Foreign Office, 1893; senior clerk, 1910; chief clerk, 1913; acting assistant under-secretary, 1919.

TOYNBEE, Arnold Joseph (1889–1975)
Political Intelligence Department, Foreign Office, 1918; member British delegation at the peace conference, 1919.

TYRRELL, Sir William George (1866–1947)
Clerk in the Foreign Office, 1889; private secretary to Sir T.H. Sanderson, 1896–1904; assistant clerk, 1903; précis-writer to Sir Edward Grey, 1905–7; senior clerk, 1907; private secretary to Sir Edward Grey, 1907–15; assistant under-secretary, 1918; member British delegation at the peace conference, 1919.

VANSITTART, Robert Gilbert (1881–1957)
Attaché, 1902; second secretary, 1908; assistant clerk, 1914; member British delegation at the peace conference, 1919.

WEAKLEY, Ernest (1861–1923)
Appointed commercial attaché European and Asiatic Turkey and Bulgaria, 1897; Contraband Department, 1914.

WEMYSS, Sir Rosslyn Erskine (1864–1933)
Joins the Navy, 1877; captain, 1901; vice-admiral, 1916; commander-in-chief, East Indies and Egypt Station, 1916–17; deputy first sea lord, 1917; first sea lord, 1917–19; admiral of the Fleet, 1919.

WILSON, Arnold Talbot (1884–1940)
Sandhurst; joins the Indian army, 1903; political department, 1909; deputy chief political officer, Force 'D' and MEF, 1915–17; deputy

civil commissioner, Mesopotamia, 1917; acting civil commissioner, Mesopotamia, 1918–20.

WILSON, Cyril Edward (1873–1938)
Sandhurst; joins the army, 1893; Egyptian army, 1898–9; South Africa, 1900–2; rejoins Egyptian army, 1902; Sudan government, 1902; governor, Sennar, 1902; governor, Khartoum, 1909; governor, Red Sea Province, 1913–22; HM representative at Jedda, 1916–19.

WILSON, Sir Henry Hughes (1864–1922)
Joins the army, 1884; colonel, 1904; director of military operations, 1910–14; major-general, 1913; commander 4th Army Corps, 1915–17; head of Military Mission to Russia, 1917; lieutenant-general, 1917; chief of British Mission to French army, 1917; member Supreme War Council, 1917–18; general, 1918; chief of the Imperial General Staff, 1918–22; field-marshal, 1919.

WINGATE, Sir Francis Reginald (1861–1953)
Woolwich; joins the army, 1880; Egyptian army, 1883; director of military intelligence, Egyptian army, 1889; colonel, 1899; sirdar and governor-general Sudan, 1899–1916; major-general, 1903; lieutenant-general, 1908; general, 1913; general officer commanding, HEF, 1916–19; high commissioner Egypt, 1917–19.

BIBLIOGRAPHY

Official Sources: Printed

Butler, Rohan and J.P.T. Bury (eds), *Documents on British Foreign Policy 1919–1939*, First Series, Vol. VIII (London, 1958: HMSO).
Butler, Rohan and J.P.T. Bury (eds), *Documents on British Foreign Policy 1919–1939*, First Series, Vol. XIII (London, 1963: HMSO).
Gooch, George P. and H. Temperley (eds), *British Documents on the Origins of the War, 1898–1914*, Vol. X, 2 (London, 1936–8: HMSO).
Papers Relating to the Foreign Relations of the United States 1919. The Paris Peace Conference, Vol. I (Washington, 1942: Government Printing Office).
Papers Relating to the Foreign Relations of the United States 1919. The Paris Peace Conference, Vol. III (Washington, 1943: Government Printing Office).
Papers Relating to the Foreign Relations of the United States 1919. The Paris Peace Conference, Vols V and VI (Washington, 1946: Government Printing Office).
Proceedings of the Brest–Litovsk Peace Conference. The Peace Negotiations between Russia and the Central Powers. 21 November, 1917 – 3 March, 1918 (Washington, 1918: Government Printing Office).
Woodward, E.L. and R. Butler (eds), *Documents on British Foreign Policy 1919–1939*, First Series, Vol. I (London, 1947: HMSO).
Woodward, E.L. and R. Butler (eds), *Documents on British Foreign Policy 1919–1939*, First Series, Vol. IV (London, 1952: HMSO).

Official Sources: Unpublished

India Office Records and Private Papers, London:
    India Office Papers
Library of Congress, Washington:
    American Peace Commission to Versailles

The National Archives, Kew:
    Cabinet Papers
    Foreign Office Papers
    War Office Papers

Private Papers

Bodleian Library, Oxford:
    Asquith Papers
    Milner Papers
British Library, London:
    Balfour Papers
    Cecil Papers
    Robertson–Murray Correspondence
Churchill College, Cambridge:
    Hankey Papers
National Archives of Scotland, Edinburgh:
    Lothian Papers
Parliamentary Archives, London:
    Lloyd George Papers
St Anthony's College, Oxford:
    Allenby Papers
    Samuel Papers
    Sykes Papers
The National Archives, Kew:
    Cromer Papers
    Grey Papers
    Hogarth Papers
    Kitchener Papers
    Milner Papers
    Nicolson Papers
University Library, Cambridge:
    Hardinge Papers
University Library, Special Collections, Sudan Archive, Durham:
    Clayton Papers
    Wingate Papers
Yale University Library, Manuscripts and Archives, New Haven (CT):
    House Papers

Literature

Adelson, Roger, *The Formation of British Policy towards the Middle East, 1914–1918* (Ann Arbor, 1973: unpublished dissertation).

―――, *Mark Sykes. Portrait of an Amateur* (London, 1975: Jonathan Cape).
Allison, Graham T., *Essence of Decision. Explaining the Cuban Missile Crisis* (Boston, 1971: Little, Brown and Company).
Amery, Leopold, *My Political Life. Volume Two: War and Peace* (London, 1953: Hutchinson).
Andrew, Christopher M. and A.S. Kanya-Forstner, *France Overseas. The Great War and the Climax of French Imperial Expansion* (London, 1981: Thames and Hudson).
Antonius, George, *The Arab Awakening* (New York, 1965: Capricorn Books).
Baker, Randall, *King Husain and the Kingdom of the Hejaz* (New York, 1979: The Oleander Press).
Barr, James, *Setting the Desert on Fire. T.E. Lawrence and Britain's Secret War in Arabia, 1916-1918* (New York and London, 2008: W.W. Norton & Company).
Beaverbrook, Lord, *Politicians and the War*, Vol. II (London, 1932: Lane Publications).
Bertie, Francis L., *The Diary of Lord Bertie of Thame: 1914-1918*, 2 vols (London, 1924: Hodder & Stoughton).
Bowle, John, *Viscount Samuel: A Biography* (London, 1957: Victor Gollancz).
Brémond, Général E., *Le Hedjaz dans la guerre mondiale* (Paris, 1931: Payot).
Busch, Briton Cooper, *Britain, India, and the Arabs 1914-1921* (Berkeley, 1971: University of California Press).
Callwell, Charles E., *Field-Marshal Sir Henry Wilson Bart. G.C.B. D.S.O.: His Life and Diaries*, Vol. II (London, 1927: Cassell).
Carr, Edward Hallett, *What is History?* (Harmondsworth, 1964: Pelican Books).
Chamberlain, Austen, *Down the Years* (London, 1935: Cassell).
Churchill, Winston S., *Great Contemporaries* (London, 1948: Odhams Press).
Dockrill, Michael L. and Z. Steiner, 'The Foreign Office at the Paris Peace Conference in 1919', *The International History Review*, 2/1 (1980), pp. 55-86.
Egremont, Max, *Balfour: A Life of Arthur James Balfour* (London, 1980: Collins).
Eldar, Dan, 'French Policy towards Husayn, Sharif of Mecca', *Middle Eastern Studies*, 26 (1990), pp. 329-50.
Eshel, David, 'The Israel-Lebanon border enigma', *IBRU Boundary and Security Bulletin*, Winter (2000-1), pp. 72-83.
Falls, Captain Cyril, *Military Operations Egypt & Palestine from June 1917 to the End of the War*, 2 vols (London, 1930: HMSO).
Farr, Martin, 'Waging democracy. The British general elections of 1918 reconsidered', *Cercles*, 21 (2011), pp. 65-94.
Fisher, John, *Curzon and British Imperialism in the Middle East 1916-1919* (London, 1999: Frank Cass).
Friedman, Isaiah, *The Question of Palestine, 1914-1918: British-Jewish-Arab Relations* (London, 1973: Routledge and Kegan Paul).
―――, *Germany, Turkey, and Zionism* (Oxford, 1977: Clarendon Press).
Gilbert, Martin, *Winston S. Churchill*, Companion Vol. III (London, 1972: Heinemann).
Gilmour, David, 'The unregarded prophet: Lord Curzon and the Palestine question', *Journal of Palestine Studies*, 25/3 (1996), pp. 60-8.
Graves, Philip, *The Life of Sir Percy Cox* (London, 1941: Hutchinson).

Grey of Fallodon, *Twenty-five Years, 1892-1916*, 2 vols (London, 1925: Hodder & Stoughton).
Halperin, Morton H., *Bureaucratic Politics and Foreign Policy* (Washington, 1974: The Brookings Institution).
Hankey, Lord, *The Supreme Command*, 2 vols (London, 1961: Allen & Unwin).
Hardinge of Penshurst, *Old Diplomacy: The Reminiscences of Lord Hardinge of Penshurst* (London, 1947: John Murray).
Heller, Joseph, *British Policy towards the Ottoman Empire 1908-1914* (London, 1983: Frank Cass).
Hinsley, Francis H. (ed.), *British Foreign Policy under Sir Edward Grey* (Cambridge, 1977: Cambridge University Press).
Hughes, Matthew, *Allenby and British Strategy in the Middle East 1917-1919* (London, 1999: Frank Cass).
Janis, Irving L., *Groupthink: Psychological Studies of Policy Decisions and Fiascoes* (Boston, 1982: Houghton Mifflin).
Jenkins, Roy, *Asquith* (London, 1978: Collins).
Johnson, Gaynor, 'Preparing for office: Lord Curzon as acting foreign secretary, January–October 1919', *Contemporary British History*, 18/3 (2004), pp. 53–73.
Jones, G. Gareth, 'The British government and the oil companies 1912–1924: the search for an oil policy', *Historical Journal*, 20/3 (1977), pp. 647–72.
Kedourie, Elie, *In the Anglo–Arab Labyrinth* (Cambridge, 1976: Cambridge University Press).
———, *England and the Middle East: The Destruction of the Ottoman Empire 1914–1921* (London, 1987: Mansell).
Keynes, John Maynard, *The Economic Consequences of the Peace* (New York, 1920: Harcourt, Brace and Howe).
Khalidi, Rashid, *British Policy Towards Syria and Palestine 1906-1914: A Study of the Antecedents of the Hussein–McMahon Correspondence, the Sykes–Picot Agreement, and the Balfour Declaration* (London, 1980: Ithaca Press).
Lansing, Robert, *The Peace Negotiations: A Personal Narrative* (Boston and New York, 1921: Houghton Mifflin).
Laqueur, Walter, *The Israel–Arab Reader: A Documentary History of the Middle East Conflict* (New York, 1970: Bantam Books).
Lawrence, T.E., *Seven Pillars of Wisdom: A Triumph* (London, 1977: Penguin).
Liddell Hart, Basil H., *History of the First World War* (London, 1972: Pan Books).
Lieshout, Robert H., 'Keeping better educated Muslims busy: Sir Reginald Wingate and the origins of the Husayn–McMahon correspondence', *Historical Journal*, 27/2 (1984), pp. 120–34.
———, *Without Making Elaborate Calculations for the Future: Great Britain and the Arab Question 1914–1916* (Utrecht, 1984: unpublished dissertation).
———, *Between Anarchy and Hierarchy: A Theory of International Politics and Foreign Policy* (Aldershot and Brookfield, 1995: Edward Elgar).
———, *The Struggle for the Organization of Europe: The Foundations of the European Union* (Cheltenham and Northampton, 1999: Edward Elgar).

Macmillan, Margaret, *Peacemakers. Six Months that Changed the World* (London, 2001: John Murray).
MacMunn, Lieut.-General Sir George and Captain Cyril Falls, *Military Operations Egypt & Palestine from the Outbreak of War with Germany to June 1917* (London, 1928: HMSO).
Mantoux, Paul, *Les Délibérations de Conseil des Quatre (24 mars – 28 juin 1919)*, 2 vols (Paris, 1955: Centre National de la Recherce Scientifique).
Meinertzhagen, Richard, *Middle East Diary, 1917–1956* (London, 1959: The Cresset Press).
Morgan, Kenneth O., *Consensus and Disunity: The Lloyd George Coalition Government 1918–1922* (Oxford, 1979: Clarendon Press).
Morgenthau, Hans, *Politics Among Nations: The Struggle for Power and Peace* (New York, 1978: Alfred A. Knopf).
Murray, Sir Archibald, *Sir Archibald Murray's Despatches* (London, 1920: J.M. Dent & Sons).
Nevakivi, Jukka, *Britain, France and the Arab Middle East, 1914–1920* (London, 1969: Athlone Press).
Nicolson, Harold, *Peacemaking 1919* (London, 1937: Constable).
Popper, Karl R., *The Open Society and Its Enemies*, Vol. II (Princeton, 1971: Princeton University Press).
Reinharz, Jehuda, 'Chaim Weizmann: statesman without a state', *Modern Judaism*, 12/3 (1992), pp. 225–42.
——, *Chaim Weizmann. The Making of a Statesman* (Hanover, NH, 1993: University Press of New England).
Renton, James, *The Zionist Masquerade: The Birth of the Anglo–Zionist Alliance, 1914–1918* (Basingstoke, 2007: Palgrave Macmillan).
Riddell, George A., *Lord Riddell's Intimate Diary of the Peace Conference and After, 1918–1923* (London, 1934: Reynal & Hitchcock).
Robertson, Sir William, *Soldiers and Statesmen, 1914–1918* (London, 1926: Cassell).
Ronaldshay, Earl of, *The Life of Lord Curzon: Being the Authorized Biography of George Nathaniel Marquess Curzon of Kedlestone, K.G.*, Vol. III (London, 1928: Boni and Liveright).
Roskill, Stephen, *Hankey: Man of Secrets*, Vols I and II (London, 1970: Collins).
Rowland, Peter, *Lloyd George* (London, 1975: Barrie and Jenkins).
Samuel, Viscount, *Memoirs* (London, 1945: Cresset Press).
Schimmelfennig, Frank, 'The community trap: liberal norms, rhetorical action, and the Eastern enlargement of the European Union', *International Organization*, 55/1 (2001), pp. 47–80.
Schneer, Jonathan, *The Balfour Declaration: The Origins of the Arab–Israeli Conflict* (London, 2011: Bloomsbury).
Stein, Leonard, *The Balfour Declaration* (London, 1961: Vallentine Mitchell).
—— (ed.), *The Letters and Papers of Chaim Weizmann*, Vol. VII, Series A, August 1914–November 1917 (Jerusalem, 1975: Israel University Press).
Steinbruner, John D., *The Cybernetic Theory of Decision: New Dimensions of Political Analysis* (Princeton, 1974: Princeton University Press).

Storrs, Ronald, *Orientations* (London, 1937: Nicholson & Watson).
Suarez, Georges, *La Vie Orgueilleuse de Clemenceau* (Paris, 1930: Éditions de France).
Thomas, James Paul, *The Sykes-Picot Agreement of 1916: Its Genesis in British Policy* (Ann Arbor, 1971: unpublished dissertation).
Vereté, Mayir, 'The Balfour Declaration and its makers', *Middle Eastern Studies*, 6/1 (1970), pp. 48–76.
Warman, Roberta M., 'The erosion of Foreign Office influence in the making of foreign policy, 1916–1918', *The Historical Journal*, 15/1 (1972), pp. 133–59.
Wasserstein, Bernard, *The British in Palestine: The Mandatory Government and the Arab-Jewish Conflict 1917–1929* (London, 1978: Royal Historical Society).
Wavell, Archibald P., *The Palestine Campaigns* (London, 1931: Constable).
Weizmann, Chaim, *Trial and Error* (London, 1949: Hamish Hamilton).
Wickham-Steed, Henry, *Through Thirty Years, 1892–1922: A Personal Narrative*, Vol. II (Garden City, 1924: Doubleday).
Wilson, Arnold T., *Loyalties, Mesopotamia 1914–1917: A Personal and Historical Record* (London, 1930: Oxford University Press).
Wilson, Jeremy, *Lawrence of Arabia: The Authorised Biography of T.E. Lawrence* (London, 1989: Heinemann).
Wilson, Trevor, *The Political Diaries of C.P. Scott, 1911–1928* (London, 1970: Collins).
Yale, William, 'Ambassador Henry Morgenthau's special mission of 1917', *World Politics*, 1/3 (1949), pp. 308–20.

NOTES

Introduction

1 Sykes to Montagu, 14 August 1917, St Anthony's College, Sykes Papers, box 2.
2 The argument I develop in this section is first based on Chapter 8, 'Decision making and the management of conflict in hierarchical systems' in my *Between Anarchy and Hierarchy: A Theory of International Politics and Foreign Policy* (Aldershot and Brookfield, 1995: Edward Elgar). Major sources of inspiration for that chapter were Graham T. Allison, *Essence of Decision* (Boston, 1971: Little, Brown and Company); Morton H. Halperin, *Bureaucratic Politics and Foreign Policy* (Washington, 1974: The Brookings Institution); Irving L. Janis, *Groupthink* (Boston, 1982: Houghton Mifflin); and John D. Steinbruner, *The Cybernetic Theory of Decision* (Princeton, 1974: Princeton University Press). In recent years, a major influence has been Frank Schimmelfennig's exposition of the concept of 'rhetorical action', as, for instance, in his article 'The community trap: liberal norms, rhetorical action, and the Eastern enlargement of the European Union', *International Organization*, 55/1 (2001), pp. 47–80.
3 Hans Morgenthau, *Politics Among Nations: The Struggle for Power and Peace* (New York, 1978: Alfred A. Knopf), p. 30.
4 Karl Popper, *The Open Society and its Enemies*, Vol. II (Princeton, 1971: Princeton University Press), p. 225 (italics in original).

Chapter 1: I Suppose the I.O. Know How This Can be Done

1 Tel. Grey to Mallet, no. 659, 11 October 1914, FO 371/2142/58203.
2 Tel. Mallet to Grey, no. 692, 4 September 1914, FO 371/2139/46520.
3 Minute Grey, not dated, on Hirtzel to Clerk, 31 August 1914, FO 371/2139/44923.
4 Minute Clerk, 5 September 1914, on Mallet to Grey, no. 692, 4 September 1914, FO 371/2139/46520.
5 Note Crowe on conversation with General Barrow (I.O.) and Vice-Admiral Slade (Admiralty), 26 September 1914, FO 371/2139/53671.

6 Sultan Selim I had usurped the title of caliph in 1515. Since then, Sunni Muslims had regarded the Sultan of Turkey as the caliph. In that capacity, the sultan was the *amir al-mu'minin* (commander of the legions of Islam), and could claim the loyalty of the Sunni Muslims – the majority of the Indian Muslims were Sunnis – in a war between the Ottoman Empire and Great Britain.
7 Tel. Hardinge to Crewe, private, 31 August 1914, FO 371/2139/44923.
8 See tel. Hardinge to Crewe, private, 4 September 1914, FO 371/2139/46490.
9 Hirtzel to Clerk, 31 August 1914, and minute Nicolson, not dated, FO 371/2139/44923.
10 Tel. Hardinge to Crewe, private, 19 September 1914, FO 371/2143/52310.
11 See G. Gareth Jones, 'The British government and the oil companies, 1912–1924', *Historical Journal*, 20/3 (1977): pp. 651–3 and 658, and Briton Cooper Busch, *Britain, India, and the Arabs, 1914–1921* (Berkeley, 1971: University of California Press), pp. 6–8.
12 See tel. Hardinge to Crewe, private, 4 September 1914, FO 371/2139/46490.
13 Note Crowe on a conversation with General Barrow (I.O.) and Vice-Admiral Slade (Admiralty), 26 September 1914, FO 371/2139/53671.
14 Tel. Hardinge to Crewe, private, 7 October 1914, Cab 21/70.
15 Crewe to Hardinge, private, 9 October 1914 (underlining in original) and Hardinge to Crewe, private, 15 October 1914, Hardinge Papers, vol. 120.
16 Roy Jenkins, *Asquith* (London, 1978: Collins): 342.
17 Cheetham to Grey, no. 143, 24 August 1914, FO 371/2140/46261.
18 Mallet to Grey, no. 117, 24 February 1914, FO 371/2131/9033.
19 See Rashid Khalidi, *British Policy Towards Syria and Palestine 1906–1914* (London, 1980: Ithaca Press), pp. 341–6; George Antonius, *The Arab Awakening* (New York, 1965: Capricorn Books), p. 120; Joseph Heller, *British Policy towards the Ottoman Empire 1908–1914* (London, 1983: Cass), pp. 127–8.
20 Tels Cheetham to Grey, no. 76, 9 August 1914, and Grey to Cheetham, no. 87, 11 August 1914, FO 371/1968/37584.
21 Minute Kitchener, not dated, on Cheetham to Grey, no. 143, 24 August 1914, FO 371/2140/46261.
22 See James Paul Thomas, *The Sykes–Picot Agreement of 1916: Its Genesis in British Policy* (Ann Arbor, 1971: unpublished dissertation), pp. 25–37 and 109–29; Khalidi, *British Policy*, pp. 272–80; Christopher M. Andrew and A.S. Kanya-Forstner, *France Overseas: The Great War and the Climax of French Imperial Expansion* (London, 1981: Thames and Hudson), pp. 49–50; Jukka Nevakivi, *Britain, France and the Arab Middle East, 1914–1920* (London, 1969: Athlone Press), pp. 8–9; Leonard Stein, *The Balfour Declaration* (London, 1961: Valentine, Mitchell), p. 46; Antonius, *Arab Awakening*, p. 154.
23 Memorandum Fitzmaurice, 11 October 1914, FO 371/2140/57234.
24 Tel. Mallet to Grey, no. 965, 12 October 1914, FO 371/2140/58669; see also tels Mallet to Grey nos. 966 and 967, 12 October 1914, FO 371/2140/58670 and 58671.
25 Minute Oliphant, 13 October 1914, FO 371/2140/57234.
26 Tels Cheetham to Grey, no. 202, 17 October 1914, and Grey to Cheetham, no. 269, 18 October 1914, FO 371/2140/60661.

27 Tels Cheetham to Grey, no. 264, 13 November 1914, and Grey to Cheetham, no. 347, 14 November 1914, FO 371/2140/70884.
28 Clayton to Cheetham, 30 October 1914, encl. in Cheetham to Grey, 15 November 1914, FO 371/2140/77088.
29 Tels Cheetham to Grey, no. 264, 13 November 1914, and Grey to Cheetham, no. 347, 14 November 1914; minutes Clerk, 14 November 1914, Grey, not dated, FO 371/2140/70884.
30 Tel. viceroy to secretary of state for India (S.S.I.), 20 November 1914, FO 371/2139/75868.
31 See tel. S.S.I. to viceroy, 27 November 1914, FO 371/2140/78239.
32 Tel. Maxwell to Kitchener, no. 331 E, private, 27 November 1914, Kitchener Papers, PRO 30/47/45.
33 Crewe to Kitchener, 27 November 1914 (underlining in original), Kitchener Papers, PRO 30/57/69.
34 Tel. S.S.I. to viceroy, 27 November 1914, FO 371/2140/78239.
35 Minute Hirtzel, not dated, on F.O. to I.O., no. 77088/14, 4 December 1914, L/P&S/10/523, 4774.
36 Tel. viceroy to S.S.I., 8 December 1914, encl. in I.O. to F.O., no. 4780/14, 11 December 1914; minute Oliphant, not dated; tel. Grey to Cheetham, no. 432, 18 December 1914, and initials Grey and Kitchener, FO 371/2140/81700.
37 Tel. Mallet to Grey, no. 191, 27 March 1914/ FO 371/2131/13601.
38 Most of the time Husayn is referred to as 'the Sharif of Mecca', or as 'the Grand Sharif of Mecca', and his fief is accordingly called the 'sharifate', or 'sherifate'. This, however, is not correct. As a direct descendant of the Prophet Muhammad through his daughter Fatima and his son-in-law Ali, Husayn was a 'sharif'. In 1908, he had been appointed Emir of Mecca. Randall Baker, *King Husain and the Kingdom of Hejaz* (Cambridge, 1979: The Oleander Press), pp. 1–3.
39 Kitchener to Grey, no. 22, 6 February 1914; Gooch and Temperley, *British Documents on the Origins of the War, 1898–1914*, Vol. X, 2, p. 827.
40 Mallet to Grey, no. 193, 18 March 1914, Gooch and Temperley, *British Documents*, Vol. X, 2, pp. 828–9.
41 Abdurrahman to Mallet, no. 16, 11 March 1914, encl. in Mallet to Grey, no. 219, 2 April 1914, FO 371/2130/15057.
42 Devey to Mallet, 2 April 1914, encl. in Mallet to Grey, no. 258, 17 April 1914, FO 371/2130/18245.
43 Kitchener to Grey, no. 58, 4 April 1914; Gooch and Temperley, *British Documents*, Vol. X, 2, p. 830.
44 Devey to Mallet, 2 April 1914, encl. in Mallet to Grey, no. 258, 17 April 1914, FO 371/2130/18245.
45 Abdurrahman to Mallet, no. 17, 19 March 1914, encl. in Mallet to Grey, no. 219, 2 April 1914, FO 371/2130/15057.
46 Storrs, *Note*, 19 April 1914, encl. in Cheetham to Grey, no. 204, 13 December 1914, FO 371/1973/87396.
47 Sir Ronald Storrs, *Orientations* (London, 1937: Nicholson and Watson): 172. I have not been able to trace Storrs's letter to Kitchener. I did find a letter from Storrs to

Fitzgerald, Kitchener's private secretary, in which he explained that 'it took me, with Clayton's help, 3 weeks to get the first telegram suggesting action in Mecca and Arabia, sent off'. Storrs to Fitzgerald, 11 November 1914, Kitchener Papers, PRO 30/47/45.
48 *Appreciation of Situation in Arabia*, encl. in Cheetham to Grey, no. 149, 6 September 1914, initials Oliphant, Clerk, 21 September 1914, Nicolson, 22 September 1914, and Kitchener, 24 September 1914, and minute Grey, 24 September 1914, FO 371/2140/51344.
49 Tel. Grey to Cheetham, no. 219, 24 September 1914, FO 371/2139/52598.
50 Tels Cheetham to Grey, no. 233, 31 October 1914, and Grey to Cheetham, no. 303, 31 October 1914, FO 371/2139/65589.
51 Memorandum Ryan, not dated, minute Clerk, 14 October 1914, FO 371/2140/57234.
52 I.O. to F.O., 19 October 1914, FO 371/2140/61238.
53 Kitchener to Grey, private, 11 November 1914, minute Grey, not dated, Grey Papers, FO 800/102.
54 Crewe to Grey, 13 November 1914, minute Grey, 2 December 1914, and tel. Hardinge to Crewe, private, 29 November 1914, Grey Papers, FO 800/98.
55 Crewe to Hardinge, private, 4 December 1914, Hardinge Papers, vol. 120.
56 F.O. to I.O., no. 81133/14, 11 December 1914, minutes Hirtzel, 12 December 1914, Crewe, not dated, and Holderness, 14 December 1914, and tel. Cheetham to Grey, no. 310, 10 December 1914, L/P&S/10/523, 4855.
57 Cheetham to Grey, no. 203, 13 December 1914, minutes Grey, not dated, Oliphant, 4 January 1915, Nicolson, 5 January 1915, and Grey, not dated, FO 371/2140/87395.
58 On 1 December 1914, Kitchener wrote to Grey that 'I have seen Sir H. McMahon, he will be glad to go to Egypt. Can I bring him round to you tomorrow at the FO, what time would be convenient?' That same evening, McMahon, to his utter surprise, so he confided to Hardinge, learned that the Cabinet had decided to ask him 'to go to Egypt as High Commissioner to start the new regime under a protectorate, and (so I understand) carry on until the end of the war when the future status of Egypt will be decided'. Lord Curzon, former viceroy of India, was rather pleased with Sir Henry's appointment. In his opinion, the new high commissioner had 'courage, industry, tenacity and tact, and I think he should do well'. Crewe also was sympathetic. He thought that McMahon's 'appreciation of the Arabian position is likely to be sounder than Kitchener's'. Hardinge for his part was perhaps even more surprised than McMahon. On 6 January he wrote to Nicolson:

> I was surprised when I heard of McMahon's appointment as High Commissioner in Egypt. He is a very nice man and his opinions are generally sound though somewhat reactionary. His fault […] is that he is so dreadfully slow. I could have shaken him over and over again when he was my Foreign Secretary, but I am very fond of him as he is a very straight little man.

Kitchener to Grey, 1 December 1914, Grey Papers, FO 800/102; McMahon to Hardinge, 4 December 1914, Hardinge Papers, vol. 71; Curzon to Cromer, 2 December

1914, Cromer Papers, FO 633/23; Crewe to Hardinge, private, 18 December 1914, Hardinge Papers, vol. 120; Hardinge to Nicolson, private, 6 January 1915, Nicolson Papers, FO 800/377.

Chapter 2: Keeping Better Educated Moslems Busy

1. Lloyd George, *Suggestions as to the Military Position*, 1 January 1915, Cab 42/1/8.
2. Tel. Cheetham to Grey, no. 10, 7 January 1915, minutes Oliphant and Nicolson, 7 January 1915, FO 371/2480/2506.
3. Secretary's Notes of a Meeting of a War Council, 8 January 1915, Cab 42/1/12.
4. McMahon to Grey, no. 23, 15 February 1915, and minutes Clerk, 3 March 1915, and Nicolson, not dated, FO 371/2480/23865.
5. Tel. Grey to McMahon, private, 8 March 1915, Grey Papers, FO 800/48.
6. McMahon to Nicolson, private, 8 March 1915; Nicolson to McMahon, private, 31 March 1915, Nicolson Papers, FO 800/377.
7. Note Clerk on meeting with Hirtzel and Slade, 16 November 1914, FO 371/2139/71465.
8. Tel. Resident Aden to viceroy, 5 January 1915, in tel. viceroy to S.S.I., 7 January 1915; minute Oliphant, 11 January 1915; tel. Grey to McMahon, no. 20, 12 January 1915, FO 371/2478/3573.
9. Wingate to Clayton, private, 9 January 1915, and Wingate to Clayton, very private, 14 January 1915 Clayton Papers, box 469/8.
10. Tel. McMahon to Grey, no. 22, 24 January 1915, FO 371/2478/9057.
11. Clayton to Wingate, private, 5 February 1915, Wingate Papers, box 134/2.
12. I.O. to F.O, no. P. 373/15, 5 February 1915, FO 371/2478/14108; tel. Resident Aden to viceroy, 28 January 1915, FO 371/2478/11414; tel. Resident Aden to S.S.I., 30 January 1915, FO 371/2478/12433; tel. Grey to McMahon, no. 74, 8 February 1915, FO 371/2478/14108.
13. Wingate to Clayton, 13 February 1915, and Wingate to Clayton, very private, 18 February 1915, Clayton Papers, box 469/8.
14. Clayton to Wingate, very private, 3 March 1915, Wingate Papers, box 134/3.
15. Wingate to Clayton, very private, 27 February 1915, Clayton Papers, box 469/8.
16. Clayton to Wingate, private, 5 February 1915, Wingate Papers, box 134/2.
17. See Wingate to Clayton, private, 24 February 1915, and Wingate to Clayton, very private, 27 February 1915, Clayton Papers, box 469/8.
18. Symes, A further note on British policy in Arabia and its relation to British Moslem Policy, 15 February 1915 (underlining in original), encl. in Wingate to Grey, private, 27 February 1915, Grey Papers, FO 800/48.
19. Hardinge to Wingate, private, 28 March 1915, Wingate Papers, box 134/3.
20. Clayton to Wingate, private, not dated, presumably March 1915, Wingate Papers, box 134/4.
21. Wingate to, respectively, Grey, Hardinge and McMahon, private, 11 March 1915, Wingate Papers, box 134/3.
22. Grey to Wingate, private, 30 March 1915, Wingate Papers, box 134/4.

23 See Hardinge to Wingate, private, 30 March 1915, Wingate Papers, box 134/3.
24 See Wingate to, respectively, Grey, Hardinge and McMahon, private, 27 March 1915, Wingate Papers, ibid, and Wingate to Cromer, private 31 March 1915, Wingate Papers, box 134/4.
25 Tel. Grey to McMahon, no. 173, 14 April 1915, FO 371/2486/44598.
26 Grey to Wingate, private, 19 April 1915, Wingate Papers, box 134/5.
27 Wingate to Grey, private, 30 April 1915, Grey Papers, FO 800/48.
28 Hardinge to Wingate, private 21 April 1915, Wingate Papers, box 134/5.
29 Hardinge to Crewe, 2 December 1914, Hardinge Papers, Vol. 120.
30 Hardinge, NOTE ON THE FUTURE STATUS AND ADMINISTRATION OF BASRAH, 24 February 1915, Nicolson Papers, FO 800/377.
31 Hardinge to Wingate, private, 28 March 1915, Wingate Papers, box 134/3.
32 Hardinge to Wingate, private, 21 April 1915, Curzon to Cromer, private, 22 April 1915, encl. in Cromer to Wingate, private, 23 April 1915, Wingate Papers, box 134/5.
33 Wingate to Grey, private, 15 May 1915; Al-Mirghani, *Memorandum*, 6 May 1915, FO 371/2486/77713.
34 Wingate to Cromer, private, 14 May 1915, Wingate Papers, box 134/6.
35 Hardinge to Wingate, private, 10 June 1915, Curzon to Cromer, 9 June 1915, encl. in Cromer to Wingate, private, 11 June 1915, Wingate Papers, box 134/7.
36 Tel. Wingate to Clayton, no. 455, 12 July 1915, FO 882/12.
37 Wingate to Clayton, private, 17 July 1915, Clayton Papers, box 469/10.
38 Wingate to Grey, private, 20 July 1915, note Symes, 19 July 1915, Grey Papers, FO 800/48.
39 Tel. Clayton to Wingate, no. 735, 12 August 1915, Wingate Papers, box 135/2.
40 Draft and revised draft of tel. Wingate to Clayton, no. 528, 12 August 1915, Wingate Papers, ibid.
41 See Roskill, Stephen, *Hankey Man of Secrets*, Vol. I (London, 1970: Allen and Unwin), pp. 151–5.
42 See Sazonof, *Aide Mémoire*, 4 March 1915, encl. in Buchanan to Grey, no. 44, 13 March 1915, FO 371/2449/35812.
43 Secretary's Notes of a Meeting of a War Council, 10 March 1915, Cab 42/2/5.
44 Minute Clerk, 18 March 1915, on Wingate to Grey, private, 27 February 1915, Grey Papers, FO 800/48.
45 Memorandum Morison, not dated, Cab 37/126/8.
46 Minute Clerk, 17 March 1915, on Wingate to Grey, private, 27 February 1915, Grey Papers, FO 800/48.
47 Secretary's Notes of a Meeting of a War Council, 19 March 1915, Cab 42/4/14.
48 Crewe to Grey, private, 13 April 1915, Grey Papers, FO 800/98; minute Asquith, 14 April 1915; tel. Grey to McMahon, 14 April 1915, FO 371/2486/44598. In his letter to the grand kadi conveying this promise, Wingate did not mention that the Shia holy places were specifically excluded. He did mention their exclusion in the letter he wrote to his political officers and provincial governors. See Wingate Papers, box 137/5.

49 Wingate to Grey, private, 30 April 1915, Grey Papers, FO 800/48.
50 Crewe to Grey, 18 May 1915, and tel. Grey to McMahon, no. 262, 20 May 1915, FO 371/2486/63383.
51 Tel. viceroy to S.S.I., 23 June 1915, and minute Oliphant, 24 June 1915, FO 371/2486/83311.
52 Tel. McMahon to Grey, no. 306, 30 June 1915, FO 371/2486/87023.
53 Tel. viceroy to S.S.I., 23 June 1915, FO 371/2486/83311.
54 I.O. to F.O., no. P. 2315/15, 6 July 1915, FO 371/2486/91115.
55 Minutes Clerk, Nicolson and Crewe, 1 July 1915, on tel. McMahon to Grey, no. 306, 30 June 1915, FO 371/2486/87023.
56 Al-Mirghani, *Memorandum*, 6 May 1915, encl. in Wingate to Grey, private, 15 May 1915, and minute Grey, 13 June 1915, FO 371/2486/77713.
57 I.O. to F.O., no. P. 2299/15, 24 June 1915, minute Nicolson, not dated, and Grey to McMahon, no. 84355/15, 30 June 1915, FO 371/2486/84355.
58 Storrs, Note, 19 August 1915, encl. in McMahon to Grey, no. 94, 26 August 1915, FO 371/2486/125293.
59 Abdullah to Storrs, 14 July 1915, George Antonius, *The Arab Awakening* (New York, 1965: Capricorn Books), p. 413.
60 Storrs, Note, 19 August 1915, FO 371/2486/125293, see also Clayton to Wingate, private, 21 August 1915, Wingate Papers, box 135/2.
61 Note, not dated, encl. in Abdullah to Storrs, 14 July 1915; Antonius, *Arab Awakening*, p. 414. There were four other conditions, which McMahon summarised as follows: 'Arab government of Sheriff to guarantee Great Britain economic preference in Arab countries. Conditions of mutual assistance. Great Britain to approve and further abolition of foreign privileges in Arabia. Provisions of renewal of alliance.' Tel. McMahon to Grey, no. 450, 22 August 1915, FO 371/2486/117236.
62 Clayton to Wingate, private, not dated, presumably March 1915, Wingate Papers, box 134/4.
63 Clayton to Wingate, private, 21 August 1915, Wingate Papers, box 135/2.
64 Storrs, Note, 19 August 1915, FO 371/2486/125293.
65 Tel. McMahon to Grey, no. 450, 22 August 1915, FO 371/2486/117236.
66 Minute Clerk, 23 August 1915, on Shuckburg to Oliphant, 13 August 1915, FO 371/2486/112369.
67 See draft Grey for tel. Grey to McMahon, not dated, and minute Oliphant, not dated, FO 371/2486/117236.
68 Minute Oliphant, not dated, FO 371/2486/117236, I.O. to F.O., no. P. 3061, 24 August 1915, minutes Clerk, 25 August 1915 and Nicolson, 25 August 1915, and tel. Grey to McMahon, no. 598, 25 August 1915, FO 371/2486/118580.
69 McMahon to Grey, no. 94, 26 August 1915, FO 371/2486/125293.
70 Initials Nicolson, Grey and Kitchener, on McMahon to Grey, no. 94, 26 August 1915, minutes Holderness and Chamberlain, not dated, on McMahon to Grey, no. 94, 26 August 1915, L/P&S/10/523,3455.
71 Wingate to Clayton, private, 27 August 1915, Clayton Papers, box 469/10.

Chapter 3: We Have Got to Keep in with Our Infernal Allies

1 G.O.C.-in-C., M.E.F. to Secretary, War Office, 25 August 1915, minutes H. Nicolson, A. Nicolson and Grey, 10 and 11 September 1915, FO 371/2490/128226.
2 Minute Clerk, 28 September 1915, on W.O. to F.O., no. DMO/I/174 (M.O.2), 27 September 1915, FO 371/2490/139665.
3 Clayton to Wingate, strictly private, 9 October 1915, Wingate Papers, box 135/4.
4 Tel. Wilson to Clayton, no. 1934, 10 October 1915, FO 141/461, file 1198.
5 Storrs to Fitzgerald, private, 10 October 1915, Kitchener Papers, PRO 30/57/47, quoted in Kedourie, *In the Anglo–Arab Labyrinth* (Cambridge, 1976: Cambridge University Press), p. 77.
6 Tels Maxwell to Kitchener, no. 2012 E, 12 October 1915, and Kitchener to Maxwell, no. 8784, 13 October 1915, minute Clerk, 14 October 1915, FO 371/2486/150309.
7 Tel. Maxwell to Kitchener, no. 2030 E, 16 October 1915, FO 371/2486/152729. According to Kedourie this telegram 'constitutes the first intimation to the government of the alleged demand of the Arab party that the four cities, Homs, Aleppo, Hama and Damascus, should belong to "their sphere". Kedourie argues that Storrs was the author of this 'so far-fetched and so peculiar a suggestion', and that he had been inspired by Gibbon's *The Decline and Fall of the Roman Empire*. Jeremy Wilson claims the formula originated with T.E. Lawrence, who in the beginning of 1915 referred in a report on Syria to 'Damascus, Homs, Hama, and Aleppo [...] the four ancient cities in which Syria takes pride'.
Kedourie, *Anglo–Arab Labyrinth*, p. 80, pp. 86–8, and Jeremy Wilson, *Lawrence of Arabia, The Authorised Biography of T.E. Lawrence* (London, 1989: Heinemann), pp. 184, 214–15.
8 Tel. McMahon to Grey, no. 623, 18 October 1915, and minute Clerk, 19 October 1915, FO 371/2486/152901.
9 Tel. McMahon to Grey, personal, 18 October 1915, FO 371/2486/153045.
10 Grey's draft of tel. Grey to McMahon, not dated, minutes Grey (underlining in original) and Kitchener, not dated, FO 371/2486/155203.
11 Chamberlain to Hardinge, private, 22 October 1915, Hardinge Papers, vol. 121.
12 Note Holderness, 20 October 1915, FO 371/2486/155203.
13 See Chamberlain to Hardinge, private, 10 November 1915, Hardinge Papers, vol. 121.
14 Tel. Grey to McMahon, no. 796, 20 October 1915, FO 371/2486/155203.
15 See Busch, Briton Cooper, *Britain, India, and the Arabs 1914–1921* (Berkeley, 1971: University of California Press), pp. 23–30.
16 Jackson and Murray, *The present and prospective situation in Syria and Mesopotamia*, 19 October 1915, Cab 42/4/15.
17 Secretary's notes of a meeting of Dardanelles Committee, 21 October 1915, ibid.
18 Hankey diary, 21 October 1915, Hankey Papers, vol. 1/1.
19 See tel. S.S.I. to viceroy, 23 October 1915, Cab 21/70. The advance, however, was not successful. At the end of November, the British force was defeated at Ctesiphon, some 15 miles south-east of Baghdad, and had to retreat to Kut.

20 Clayton to Wingate, private, 27 October 1915 (underlining in original), Wingate Papers, box 135/4.
21 Wingate to Clayton, private, 1 November 1915, Wingate Papers, box 135/5.
22 Tel. McMahon to Grey, no. 644, 26 October 1915, FO 371/2486/158561.
23 From McMahon's dispatch of 9 October it appeared that he was under the impression that there existed an Anglo–French agreement 'as to the extent of French interests in the Middle East'. In his reply of 30 October, Grey explained that this was not the case.
McMahon to Grey, no. 117, 9 October 1915, and Grey to McMahon, no. 223, 30 October 1915, FO 371/2486/157736.
24 McMahon to Grey, no. 131, 26 October 1915, FO 371/2486/163832. McMahon accordingly fully realised that he could not even promise that the four towns would become part of the Arab countries. Even if he wished to do so, possible French claims prevented this. The formula he adopted in his letter to Husayn concealed the position to some extent, because it at least created the impression that only the coastal region was excluded and that therefore the four towns were included. Kedourie's observations are very much to the point: 'McMahon's circumlocutions were designed to seem to offer the Sharif a substantial territory, while in fact offering him nothing at all. Even the four Syrian towns [...] were conceded with one hand, only to be taken away with the other.' Kedourie, *Anglo–Arab Labyrinth*, p. 99.
25 McMahon to Hardinge, private, 28 October 1915, Hardinge Papers, vol. 94.
26 Minutes Clerk, 27 October 1915, Kitchener, 28 October, and Grey, not dated, on tel. McMahon to Grey, no. 644, 26 October 1915, FO 371/2486/158561.
27 Tels McMahon to Grey, private, 28 October 1915, Grey to McMahon, private 29 October 1915, McMahon to Grey, private, 29 October 1915, and Grey to Bertie, no. 2464, 30 October 1915, FO 371/2486/161325.
28 Tel. McMahon to Grey, no. 666, 2 November 1915, FO 371/2486/162697.
29 See Herbert to Clayton, 7 November 1915, FO 882/2.
30 Memorandum Herbert, 30 October 1915, FO 371/2486/164659.
31 Grey to Kitchener, 4 November 1915, Grey Papers, FO 800/102.
32 Kitchener to Asquith, 5 November 1915, Kitchener Papers, WO 159/4.
33 The French government had nominated François Georges-Picot, second secretary at the French Legation at Cairo and former consul-general at Beirut.
34 Tel. Grey to McMahon, no. 860, 6 November 1915, FO 371/2486/166421.
35 Tel. McMahon to Grey, no. 677, 7 November 1915, minutes Oliphant, 8 November 1915, and Grey, not dated (underlining in original), FO 371/2486/166819.
36 Minute Chamberlain, 27 October 1915, on F.O. to I.O., no. 158561/15, 27 October 1915, L/P&S/10/523, 3935.
37 Tel. viceroy to S.S.I., 4 November 1915, FO 371/2486/165415.
38 Tel. McMahon to Grey, no. 674, 5 November 1915, and minute Grey, not dated, FO 371/2486/165761.
39 Chamberlain, NEGOTIATIONS WITH GRAND SHAREEF, 8 November 1915, minute Nicolson, 9 November 1915, tel. Grey to McMahon, no. 874, 11 November 1915, minute Chamberlain, 11 November 1915, FO 371/2486/166807.

40 Chamberlain to Hardinge, 10 November 1915, Hardinge Papers, vol. 121.
41 See Grey to Bertie, no. 878, 10 November 1915, FO 371/2486/169450.
42 Chamberlain, Memo on Sir E. Grey's conversation with the French ambassador, 12 November 1915 (underlining in original), and minute Grey, not dated, FO 371/2486/174595.
43 Minute Clerk, 5 November 1915, on tel. McMahon to Grey, no. 674, 5 November 1915, FO 371/2486/165761.
44 Tel. viceroy to S.S.I., no. P.4151, 11 November 1915, and minute Grey, 12 November 1915, FO 371/2486/169399.
45 Nicolson to Grey, 6 November 1915, and minute Grey, not dated, FO 371/2486/167429.
46 Minutes Clerk of an interdepartmental meeting, F.O., I.O. and W.O, 13 November 1915, and minute Grey, not dated, FO 371/2486/171431.
47 Clayton to Wingate, private, 12 November 1915, Wingate Papers, box 135/5.
48 See tel. Clayton to Wingate, no. 992, 13 November 1915, Wingate Papers, box 135/4.
49 Wingate to Clayton, private, 15 November 1915, Clayton Papers, box 469/11.
50 Husayn to McMahon, 5 November 1915, George Antonius, *The Arab Awakening* (New York, 1965: Capricorn Books), p. 422.
51 Storrs, *Statement by messenger O*, 12 November 1915, FO 882/19.
52 Tel. Clayton to Maxwell, private, E.R. 195, 12 November 1915, FO 141/461, file 1198, Storrs, 'Summary', 12 November 1915, FO 882/19, tel. McMahon to Grey, 14 November 1915, and minute Clerk, 15 November 1915, FO 371/2486/170981.
53 Tel. McMahon to Grey, 16 November 1915, minutes Oliphant, not dated, Nicolson and Crewe, 17 November 1915, and tel. Grey to McMahon, no. 887, 17 November 1915, FO 371/2486/172416.
54 Tel. Kitchener to Maxwell, no. 9450, 2 November 1915, WO 33/747/2644A.
55 L. de la Panousse, *Note for General Sir A. Murray*, 13 November 1915, Cab 42/5/10.
56 Secretary's Notes of a Meeting of the War Committee, 13 November 1915, ibid.
57 Tel. Grey to Bertie, no. 2602, 13 November 1915, FO 371/2480/170980.
58 Tel. Kitchener to Asquith, no. 29, 13 November 1915, WO 33/747/2790A.
59 Tel. Kitchener to Asquith, no. 38, 15 November 1915, see Hankey, *The Supreme Command*, Vol. II (London, 1961: Allen and Unwin), p. 448.
60 Ibid., p. 450.
61 Tel. Kitchener to Asquith, no. 91, 22 November 1915, WO 33/747/2927A.
62 Parker to Clayton, private, 19 November 1915, Wingate Papers, box 135/6.
63 Parker, NOTE ON ARAB MOVEMENT, 21 November 1915, encl. in Parker to Clerk, 22 November 1915, FO 371/2486/177016.
64 Minute Clerk, 22 November 1915, on tel. McMahon to Grey, no. 707, 21 November 1915, FO 371/2486/175418.
65 Minute Clerk, 3 December 1915, on Parker to Clerk, 3 December 1915 (underlining in original), FO 371/2486/183416.
66 Minute Grey, not dated, on tel. McMahon to Grey, no. 732, 28 November 1915, Cab 37/138/23.

Chapter 4: The Whole Subject is Becoming Entangled

1 Chamberlain to Hardinge, private, 25 November 1915, Hardinge Papers, vol. 121.
2 Clerk's minutes of meeting Nicolson committee with Georges-Picot, on 23 November 1915, 1 December 1915, and minute Nicolson, 27 November 1915, FO 371/2486/181716.
3 Tel. McMahon to Grey, no. 736, 30 November 1915, and minutes Clerk, 1 December 1915, and Hirtzel, not dated (underlining in original), FO 371/2486/181834.
4 Nicolson to Clerk, 10 December 1915, and tel. Grey to McMahon, no. 961, 10 December 1915, ibid. Without any explanation, Hirtzel's modified proviso was not incorporated into the Foreign Office telegram. A copy of Sir Henry's letter to Husayn arrived in London at the end of December. Chamberlain protested against the passage that was based on point 5 of McMahon's telegram of 30 November. He wrote to Grey that:

> Are we not getting into a great mess with these negotiations of McMahon? He has now informed the Grand Sheriff that 'you may rest assured that Great Britain has no intention of concluding any peace in terms of which the freedom of the Arab peoples from German and Turkish domination does not form an essential condition'. Had he any authority for this pledge?

Chamberlain had apparently forgotten that Hirtzel had agreed to point 5, and that he himself had approved the text of the Foreign Office telegram of 10 December. Chamberlain to Grey, 29 December 1915 (underlining in original), Grey Papers, FO 800/98.
5 McMahon to Hardinge, private, 4 December 1915, Hardinge Papers, vol. 94.
6 McMahon to Wingate, 8 December 1915, Wingate Papers, box 135/7.
7 Clayton, *Note 'C'*, 8 December 1915, FO 882/2.
8 Tel. McMahon to Grey, no. 761, 11 December 1915, minutes Clerk, Nicolson and Crewe, 11 December 1915, and Asquith, 13 December 1915, FO 371/2486/189073.
9 Wingate to Maxwell, private, 9 December 1915, Wingate Papers, box 135/7, Wingate to Clayton, private, 10 December 1915, Clayton Papers, box 469/11, and Clayton to Wingate, private, 6 December 1915, Wingate Papers, box 135/7.
10 See Roger Adelson, *Mark Sykes: Portrait of an Amateur* (London, 1975: Jonathan Cape), pp. 36–9, 63–7, 95–6, 99–102, 108–16.
11 See Sykes to Arthur, private, 12 September 1916, Kitchener Papers, PRO 30/57/91.
12 Quoted in Adelson, *Mark Sykes*, p. 176.
13 Sykes to Arthur, private, 12 September 1916, Kitchener Papers, PRO 30/57/91.
14 *Report of the Committee on Asiatic Turkey*, pp. 2, 4 and 25, Cab 42/3/12.
15 M. Sykes to E. Sykes, 3 or 9 September 1915, quoted in Adelson, *Mark Sykes*, p. 190.
16 Lloyd to Clayton, private, 27 May 1916, FO 882/4, quoted in Briton Cooper Busch, *Britain, India, and the Arabs, 1914–1921* (Berkeley, 1971: University of California Press), p. 70.
17 Arnold T. Wilson, *Loyalties, Mesopotamia 1914–1917* (London, 1930: Oxford University Press), p. 152.
18 Sykes to Callwell, no. 19, in tel. McMahon to Grey, no. 707, 20 November 1915, FO 371/2486/175418.

452 BRITAIN AND THE ARAB MIDDLE EAST

19 Sykes to Callwell, no. 18, in tel. McMahon to Grey, no. 706, 19 November 1915, FO 371/2486/174633.
20 *Evidence of Lieutenant-Colonel Sir Mark Sykes, Bart., M.P., on the Arab Question*, Cab 42/6/10.
21 Secretary's Notes of a Meeting of the War Committee, 16 December 1915, Cab 42/6/9.
22 Crewe to Bertie, private, 17 December 1915, and Bertie to Crewe, 21 December 1915 (italics in original), Cab 42/6/11.
23 See: Secretary Notes of a Meeting of the War Committee, 28 December 1915, Cab 42/6/14.
24 Lord Hankey, *The Supreme Command*, Vol. II (London, 1961: Allen and Unwin), p. 469.
25 *Results of the third meeting of the Committee to discuss the Syrian question*, 21 December 1915, FO 882/16.
26 Foreign Office Note, not dated, FO 371/2486/196223.
27 Nicolson to Hardinge, private, 30 December 1915, Nicolson Papers, FO 800/380.
28 Sykes to Clayton, 28 December 1915, FO 882/2.
29 Sykes and Georges-Picot, *Memorandum*, not dated, and Nicolson, covering letter, 5 January 1916, FO 371/2767/2522.
30 Hirtzel, *Note*, 10 January 1916, encl. in Holderness to Nicolson, 13 January 1916, FO 371/2767/8117.
31 Macdonogh to Nicolson, 6 January 1915, FO 371/2767/3851.
32 Hall, *Memorandum on the Proposed Agreement with the French*, not dated, encl. in Hall to Nicolson, 12 January 1916, FO 371/2767/8117.
33 Macdonogh to Nicolson, 6 January 1915, FO 371/2767/3851. In a letter to Hardinge, Nicolson also doubted whether the negotiations 'will ever fructify into anything really definite'. He was personally convinced that Britain could not 'possibly expect the Arabs to come over to our side unless we are in a position to furnish a considerable British force to give them some stiffening'. Without a British military intervention there was no ground for these negotiations, but such intervention was out of the question in view of the War Committee's decision of 28 December. Why then continue these negotiations? Why this dividing of the bear's skin before it had been killed? Indeed, why this dividing of the bear's skin when proponents of the scheme were convinced that the killing would never take place? In the relevant papers I have not come across a clear-cut answer to these questions. Proponents of the scheme might have argued that in view of French susceptibilities it was necessary to reassure them as to British intentions, and that there was no harm in this exercise of dividing the bear's skin, precisely because it was highly unlikely that the beast would ever be killed. This is also the explanation Curzon came up with during a meeting of the Eastern Committee at the beginning of December 1918 (see also Chapter 10, section 'British Preparations for the Peace Conference'):

> When the Sykes–Picot Agreement was drawn up it was, no doubt, intended by its authors [...] as a sort of fancy sketch to suit a situation that had not then

arisen, and which it was thought extremely unlikely would ever arise; and that, I suppose, must be the principal explanation of the gross ignorance with which the boundary lines in that Agreement were drawn.

Nicolson to Hardinge, private, 16 February 1916, Nicolson Papers, FO 800/381, minutes Eastern Committee, 5 December 1918, Cab 27/24.
34 Sykes to Nicolson, 16 January 1916, FO 371/2767/11844.
35 Negotiations with the Arabs, 21 January 1916, and draft agreement, not dated, Holderness to Nicolson, 23 January 1916, Macdonogh to Nicolson, 24 January 1915 and Hall to Nicolson 23 January 1915, FO 371/2767/14106.
36 Nicolson to Grey, 2 February 1916, FO 371/2767/23579.
37 Secretary's Notes of a Meeting of the War Committee, 3 February 1916, Cab 42/8/1.
38 Note, *Arab question*, 4 February 1916, and Nicolson to Grey, 4 February 1916, FO 371/2767/26444.
39 Nicolson to Grey, 9 February 1916, FO 371/2767/28234.
40 Tel. McMahon to Grey, no. 70, 26 January 1916, FO 371/2771/16451, quoted in Elie Kedourie, *In the Anglo-Arab Labyrinth* (Cambridge, 1976: Cambridge University Press), p. 119.
41 McMahon to Grey, no. 16, 24 January 1916, minutes Oliphant, 4 February 1916, and Nicolson, 5 February 1916, FO 371/2767/20954.
42 Clayton to Wingate, private, 14 January 1916, and Clayton to Wingate, private, 17 January 1916, Wingate Papers, box 136/1.
43 Wingate to Clayton, private, 20 January 1916, Clayton Papers, box 470/1
44 Clayton to Wingate, private, 28 January 1916, Wingate Papers, box 136/1.
45 Minute Grey, not dated, on McMahon to Grey, no. 16, 24 January 1916, FO 371/2767/20954.
46 I.O. to F.O., no. P. 621, 28 February 1916, minute Grey, not dated, FO 371/2767/39490.
47 Nicolson to Grey, 2 March 1916, FO 371/2767/40645.
48 Grey to Buchanan, no. 36, 23 February 1916, FO 371/2767/35529.
49 Tel. Buchanan to Grey, no. 345, 10 March 1916, FO 371/ 2767/47088.
50 Tel. Buchanan to Grey, no. 351, 12 March 1916, FO 371/2767/47950.
51 See tel. Buchanan to Grey, no. 382, 17 March 1916, FO 371/2767/51736.
52 Secretary's Notes of a Meeting of the War Committee, 23 March 1916, Cab 42/11/9.
53 Draft Conclusions of a Meeting of the War Committee, 23 March 1916, FO 371/2768/57783.
54 Tel. Buchanan to Grey, no. 435, 27 March 1916, FO 371/2768/58401.
55 Tel. Buchanan to Grey, no. 471, 3 April 1916, FO 371/2768/63342.
56 Tel. Buchanan to Grey, no. 355, 13 March 1916, minute Oliphant, 14 March 1916, and tel. Grey to McMahon, 15 March 1916, FO 371/2767/48683.
57 Tel. McMahon to Grey, no. 204, 21 March 1916, minute Olpihant, 22 March 1916, minute Grey, not dated, and tel. Grey to McMahon, no. 215, 22 March 1916, FO 371/2767/54229.
58 I.O. to F.O., no. 1076^b, 28 March 1916, minutes Oliphant and Nicolson, 29 March 1916, FO 371/2768/59268.

59 Tel. G.O.C.-in-C., Force 'D' to S.S.I., 1404 B., 30 March 1916, encl. in I.O. to F.O., no. P. 1181, 31 March 1916, FO 371/2768/61639.
60 Tel. McMahon to Grey, no. 232, 1 April 1916, memorandum Chamberlain, 3 April 1916 (underlining in original), Grey to Nicolson, not dated, and tel. Grey to McMahon, no. 263, 5 April 1916, FO 371/2768/62377.
61 Tel. Buchanan to Grey, no. 377, 16 March 1916, FO 371/2767/51288.
62 Tel. Grey to McMahon, no. 287, 14 April 1916, FO 371/2768/70889.
63 Tel. McMahon to Grey, no. 278, 20 April 1916, FO 371/2768/76013.
64 Tel. McMahon to Grey, no. 284, 22 April 1916, minutes Oliphant, 23 April 1916 (underlining in original), Nicolson and Crewe, 24 April 1916, and tel. Grey to McMahon, no. 339, 27 April 1917, FO 371/2768/76954.
65 Tels McMahon to Grey, no. 329, 4 May 1916, and Grey to McMahon, no. 371, 6 May 1916, FO 371/2768/84855.
66 Minute Oliphant, 23 April 1916 (underlining in original), FO 371/2768/76954.
67 Minutes Clerk and Nicolson, 3 May 1916, and Kitchener, not dated, on McMahon to Grey, no. 83, 19 April 1916, FO 371/2768/80305.
68 Memorandum Sykes, 8 May 1916, FO 371/2768/87247.
69 Tel. Grey to Bertie, no. 350, 11 May 1916, FO 371/2768/92354.
70 Grey to Cambon and Cambon to Grey, 15 May 1916, and Grey to Cambon, 16 May 1916, E.L. Woodward and R. Butler (eds), *Documents on British Foreign Policy 1919-1939* (*DBFP*), First Series, Vol. IV (London, 1952: H.M. Stationary Office), pp. 244-7.
71 Minute Clerk, 15 May 1916, on McMahon to Grey, no. 86, 25 April 1916, FO 371/2768/87999.
72 Tel. McMahon to Grey, no. 414, 30 May 1916, FO 371/2768/103983.
73 Report Hogarth, 10 June 1916, FO 141/461, file 1198.
74 Minutes Oliphant and Nicolson, 8 March 1916, Chamberlain to Crewe, 8 March 1916 (underlining in original), minutes Kitchener and Nicolson, 9 March 1916, and tel. Grey to McMahon, no. 173, 9 March 1916, FO 371/2773/44538.
75 Wingate to McMahon, private, 17 March 1916, Clayton Papers, box 470/1.
76 Tel. McMahon to Grey, no. 202, 21 March 1916, minute Olpihant, 22 March 1916, and initials O'Beirne, Nicolson and Grey, FO 371/2767/54177.
77 Tel. McMahon to Grey, no. 388, 24 May 1916, and minute Clerk, 24 May 1916 (underlining in original), and tel. Grey to MacMahon, no. 426, FO 371/2773/99316.
78 Tels McMahon to Grey, no. 402, 28 May 1916 and Grey to McMahon, no. 431, 30 May 1916, FO 371/2773/102192.
79 Tel. McMahon to Grey, no. 436, 8 June 1916, minute Sykes, 9 June 1916, FO 371/2773/111398.
80 Tel. McMahon to Grey, no. 443, 11 June 1916, and minute Clerk, 12 June 1916, FO 371/2773/112684.
81 Nicolson to Hardinge, private, 16 February 1916, Nicolson Papers, FO 800/381.
82 Quoted in Adelson, *Mark Sykes*, p. 203.
83 Sykes to DMO, 23 July 1915, FO 371/2486/114293.

84 Sykes to Clerk, private, 4 September 1915 (underlining in original), FO 371/2491/148549.
85 Sykes to Cecil, private, 4 October 1915, Sykes Papers, box 1.
86 Tel. Sykes to DMO, no. 12, 9 October 1915, and minutes Clerk, 12 October 1915 and Nicolson, 14 October 1915, FO 371/2491/148549.
87 Sykes to Clayton, 28 December 1915, FO 882/2.
88 *Establishment of an Arab Bureau at Cairo*, 7 January 1916, Cab 42/7/4.
89 Hirtzel to Grant, private, 7 January 1916, quoted in Busch, *Britain, India*, p. 101.
90 Hardinge to Nicolson, private, 18 February 1916, Nicolson Papers, FO 800/381.
91 Tel. viceroy to S.S.I., 15 February 1916, encl. in F.O. to I.O., no. P. 570, 24 February 1916, and F.O. to I.O., no. 36955/16, 28 February 1916, FO 371/2771/36955.
92 I.O. to F.O., no. P. 1342, 12 April 1916, FO 371/2771/70419.
93 See tel. viceroy to S.S.I., 15 May 1916, encl. in I.O. to F.O., no. P. 1835, and F.O. to I.O., no. 94961, 26 May 1916, FO 371//2771/94961.
94 On 22 May 1916, Sykes was attached to the secretariat of the Committee of Imperial Defence 'with instructions to make a special study of the coordination of Allied political policy in the Middle East'. This appointment was the result of informal conversations on the problem that there was 'diffusion of control and that cooperation is hampered by the want of a coordinating machine which would bring those engaged in the problem into touch with one another'.
C.I.D. to F.O., 22 May 1916, FO 371/2777/97824, and Hankey to Grey, C.I.D. 444, 5 May 1916, FO 371/2777/85174.

Chapter 5: Rabegh Has Been a Perfect Nuisance

1 McMahon to Grey, no. 134, 10 June 1916, minutes Clerk, 23 June, and Grey, not dated, FO 371/2773/119824.
2 See McMahon to Grey, private, 13 June 1916, Grey Papers, FO 800/48.
3 Tels G.O.C.-in-C., Egypt to C.I.G.S, no. A.M. 652, 15 June 1916, and C.I.G.S. to G.O.C.-in-C., Egypt, no. 17939, 16 June 1916, encl. in McMahon to Grey, no. 262, 13 October 1916, FO 371/2782/213987.
4 Tel. G.I.G.S. to G.O.C.-in-C., Egypt, no. 18899, 28 June 1916, FO 371/2773/125987.
5 General Staff, *The Sherif of Mecca and the Arab Movement*, 1 July 1916, FO 371/2773/131897.
6 Secretary's Notes of a Meeting of the War Committee, 6 July 1916, Cab 42/16/1.
7 Wingate to Robertson, 22 June 1916, Wingate Papers, box 137/5.
8 Tel. Wingate to McMahon, no. 895, 4 July 1916, FO 371/2782/213987.
9 Wingate to Hogarth, private, 5 July 1916, Wingate Papers, box 138/3.
10 Murray to McMahon, 19 June 1916, FO 141/461, file 1198.
11 McMahon to Murray, 20 June 1916, FO 371/2782/213987.
12 Tel. Murray to Wingate, no. I.A. 2155, 25 June 1916, FO 882/4.
13 Tel. McMahon to Wingate, 26 June 1916, FO 371/2782/213987.
14 Tel. Wingate to Murray (rep. to McMahon), no. 832, 26 June 1916, FO 882/4.
15 Tels McMahon to Wingate, no. I.G. 781, 28 June 1916, and Wingate to McMahon, no. 862, 30 June 1916, McMahon to Wingate, 2 July 1916, Wingate to McMahon,

no. 895, 4 July 1916, McMahon to Wingate, 10 July 1916, and Wingate to McMahon, no. 954, 11 July 1916, FO 371/2782/213987.
16 Wingate to McMahon, 8 July, encl. in McMahon to Grey, no, 168, 15 July 1916, FO 371/2774/144050.
17 Wingate to Clayton, private, 30 July 1916, Wingate Papers, box 138/16.
18 Murray to Robertson, 18 August 1916, and Robertson to Murray, 29 August 1916, Robertson–Murray correspondence, Add. Mss. 52461A.
19 Tel. McMahon to Grey, no. 741, 30 August 1916, minutes Clerk, 31 August 1916, Hardinge, not dated, and Oliphant, not dated, FO 371/2774/172299. See in connection with Hardinge's return to the Foreign Office, Zara Steiner, 'The Foreign Office and the War', in Francis H. Hinsley (ed.), *British Foreign Policy under Sir Edward Grey* (Cambridge, 1977: Cambridge University Press), pp. 523–5.
20 Tel. McMahon to Grey, no. 745, 31 August 1916, FO 371/2775/172579.
21 Secretary's Notes of a Meeting of the War Committee, 1 September 1916, Cab 42/19/1.
22 Tel. Grey to McMahon, no. 708, 1 September 1916, FO 371/2775/173744.
23 Tel. Wilson to McMahon, 10 September 1916, Wingate Papers, box 140/2.
24 Minutes of a Conference held at Ismailia, 12 September 1916, FO 882/4.
25 Murray to Robertson, 12 September 1916, Robertson–Murray correspondence, Add. Mss, 52462.
26 Minutes of a Conference held at Ismailia, 12 September 1916, FO 882/4.
27 Tel. McMahon to Grey, no. 778, 13 September 1916, FO 371/2775/182577.
28 Sir Edward Grey had been created Viscount Grey of Fallodon in the middle of July. This had been done to lighten his workload. His duties in the House of Lords were far less burdensome than those in the House of Commons.
29 Robertson to Grey, 14 September 1916, Grey to Robertson, 14 September 1916, and tel Grey to McMahon, no. 742, 14 September 1916, FO 371/2775/182577.
30 Tel. McMahon to Grey, no. 794, 17 September 1916, Cab 42/20/3.
31 On 7 July, Lloyd George had succeeded Kitchener as secretary of state for war. The latter had drowned on 5 June – the day Sharif Husayn started his revolt, as nobody fails to mention – when HMS *Hampshire*, the cruiser that carried him on a mission to Russia, struck a German mine.
32 Secretary's Notes and Draft Conclusions of a Meeting of the War Committee, 18 September 1916, Cab 42/20/3.
33 Robertson, *Assistance to the Shereef*, 20 September 1916, Note by Lieut.-Colonel Sir M. Sykes, 18 September 1916, Cab 42/20/8.
34 Secretary's Notes of a Meeting of the War Committee, 25 September 1916, Cab 42/20/8.
35 Hankey diary, 26 September 1916, Hankey Papers, vol. 1/1.
36 Draft Conclusions of a Meeting of the War Committee, 28 September 1916, Cab 42/20/9.
37 See tels McMahon to Grey, no. 823, 28 September 1916, and McMahon to Grey, no. 834, 1 October 1916, FO 371/2775/195502.
38 Robertson to Murray, 16 October 1916, Robertson–Murray correspondence, Add. Mss. 52462.

39 Secretary's Notes of a Meeting of the War Committee, 3 October 1916, Cab 42/21/1.
40 See tel. Grey to McMahon, no. 787, 3 October 1916, FO 371/2775/197886.
41 Tel. McMahon to Grey, no. 844, 4 October 1916, FO 371/2775/198559.
42 Tel. McMahon to Wingate, no. 'C', personal, 4 October 1916, FO 141/462, file 1198.
43 Tel. Wingate to McMahon, no. 394, 5 October 1916, encl. in tel. McMahon to Grey, no. 853, 6 October 1916, FO 371/2775/200087.
44 Tel. G.O.C.-in-C., Egypt to C.I.G.S., no. I.A. 2451, 5 October 1916, WO 33/905.
45 Tel. McMahon to Grey, no. 853, 6 October 1916, and minute Hardinge, not dated, FO 371/2775/200087.
46 Secretary's Notes of a Meeting of the War Committee, 9 October 1916, Cab 42/21/3.
47 Tel. Wingate to Murray, no. 412, 11 October 1916, FO 141/462, file 1198.
48 Tels McMahon to Grey, no. 884, 12 October 1916, and Grey to McMahon, no. 821, 13 October 1916, FO 371/2775/204128.
49 Tel. McMahon to Grey, no. 889, 14 October 1916, FO 371/2775/205511.
50 Tel. Wingate to McMahon, no. 425, 14 October 1916, in tel. McMahon to Grey, no. 890, 14 October 1916, and minute Clerk, 14 October 1916, FO 371/2775/205512.
51 Secretary's Notes of a Meeting of the War Committee, 17 October 1916, Cab 42/22/1.
52 Tel. Grey to McMahon, no. 836, 19 October 1916, FO 371/2775/209795.
53 Tel. McMahon to Grey, no. 954, 1 November 1916, FO 371/2776/219489.
54 Tel. Wingate to Wemyss, no. 603, 1 November 1916, FO 686/56.
55 Secretary's Notes of a Meeting of the War Committee, 2 November 1916, Cab 42/23/3.
56 Tel. Grey to McMahon, no. 875, 2 November1916, FO 371/2776/219489.
57 Tel. C.I.G.S. to G.O.C.-in-C., Egypt, no. 24574, 2 November 1916, in tel. Murray to Wingate, no. A.M. 1214, 3 November 1916, FO 141/825.
58 Wingate to Clayton, private, 3 November 1916, Clayton Papers, box 470/4.
59 Tel. Wilson to Wingate, no. W. 471, 2 November 1916, FO 686/54.
60 Wingate to Clayton, private, 3 November 1916, Clayton Papers, box 470/4.
61 Tel. McMahon to Grey, no. 964, 3 November 1916, FO 371/2776/221035.
62 Tel. Murray to Wingate, no. A.M. 1214, 3 November 1916, FO 141/825.
63 Wingate to Wilson, private, 6 November 1916, Wingate Papers, box 143/1.
64 Minutes Clerk, 4 November 1916, and Hardinge, not dated, on tel. McMahon to Grey, no. 964, 3 November 1916, FO 371/2776/221035.
65 Tel. Wingate to Grey, no. 9, 7 November 1916, FO 371/2776/224106.
66 Hardinge to Grey, 9 November 1916, FO 371/2776/227139.
67 Three days before, the War Committee had decided to replace McMahon by Wingate, because, as Grey explained to the War Committee:

> Sir Henry did not know Egypt or the French language very well. The fact was that he had been Lord Kitchener's nominee for the appointment, and had been sent to Egypt rather with the idea of keeping the post of High Commissioner open for Lord Kitchener than with a view to his permanent retention [...] Although everything had gone quite satisfactorily in Egypt, he rather gathered that there was no great confidence in Sir Henry McMahon.

Already shortly after Kitchener's death, Grey had taken the first steps to bring about McMahon's removal. Cromer, after Grey had sounded him on the subject, had advised the appointment of Sir Reginald: 'On the whole, thinking over the matter again, I am rather inclined to think that Wingate would be the best appointment [...] He has also done admirably all the work which he has set himself to perform, and which has been of an exceptionally difficult and delicate nature.'
Secretary's Notes of a Meeting of the War Committee, 7 November 1916, Cab 42/23/9, and Cromer to Grey, private, 20 June 1916, Grey Papers, FO 800/106.
68 Robertson, Sir William, *Soldiers and Statesmen*, Vol. II (London, 1926: Cassell), p. 159.
69 Robertson, *Soldiers*, Vol. II, p. 160.
70 Rabegh, Note by Lord Grey, 11 November 1916, Cab 42/24/8.
71 Robertson, *Soldiers*, Vol. II, p. 161.
72 Rabegh, Note by Lord Grey, 11 November 1916, Cab 42/24/8.
73 Tels C.I.G.S. to sirdar, no. 24887, 11 November 1916, and sirdar to C.I.G.S., no. 777, 12 November 1916, WO 158/627.
74 Robertson to Hankey, no. O. 1/43/143A, 13 November 1916, Cab 42/24/8.
75 Robertson, *Despatch of an Expeditionary Force to Rabegh*, no. 01/43/143, 13 November 1916, ibid.
76 Secretary's Notes of a Meeting of the War Committee, 16 November 1916 (underlining in original), ibid.
77 T.E. Lawrence, *Seven Pillars of Wisdom: A triumph* (London, 1978: Penguin), p. 114; also James Barr, *Setting the Desert on Fire. T.E. Lawrence and Britain's Secret War in Arabia* (New York and London, 2008: W.W. Norton & Company), pp. 77–8.
78 Tel. G.O.C.-in-C., Egypt to C.I.G.S, no. A.M. 1272, 17 November 1916, Cab 42/24/13. See also report Lawrence, encl. in tel. G.O.C.-in-C., Egypt to DMI, no. I.A. 2629, 17 November 1916, Cab 42/24/8, and Lawrence's account of this episode – 'the sudden help I had lent to Sir Archibald's prejudices' – in his *Seven Pillars*, pp. 113–15.
79 Tel. Murray to Wingate, no. A.M. 1274, 17 November 1916, WO 158/627.
80 See tel. Admiralty to C.-in-C., East Indies, no. 791, 17 November 1916, Cab 42/24/13.
81 Tel. C.-in-C., East Indies to Admiralty, no. 770, 17 November 1916, ibid.
82 Tel. Wingate to Murray, no. 856, 18 November 1916, WO 158/627.
83 Minute Hardinge, not dated, on note Clerk, 18 November 1916, FO 371/2776/235418.
84 Secretary's Notes of a Meeting of the War Committee, 20 November 1916, Cab 42/24/13.
85 Paraphrase of tel. C.-in-C., East Indies to Admiralty, no. 789, 21 November 1916, Cab 42/25/3.
86 Tel. Wingate to Grey, no. 29, 22 November 1916, FO 371/2776/236128, see also tel. Wingate to Grey, no. 31, 22 November 1916, FO 371/2776/235823.
87 Wingate to Wilson, private, 23 November 1916, Wingate Papers, box 143A/8.
88 Robertson to Murray, 1 December 1916, Robertson–Murray correspondence, Add. Mss. 52462.
89 Tel. Wingate to Grey, no. 61, 6 December 1916, FO 371/2776/246845.
90 Tel. Wilson to Wingate, no. W. 821, 6 December 1916, WO 158/604.
91 Tel. Wingate to Grey, no. 65, 7 December 1916, FO 371/2776/247653.

92 See Roy Jenkins, *Asquith* (London, 1978: Collins), pp. 419–63; Stephen Roskill, *Hankey: Man of Secrets*, Vol. I (London, 1970: Allen and Unwin), pp. 323–32; Lord Beaverbrook, *Politicians and the War*, Vol. II (London, 1932), pp. 328–533; Peter Rowland, *Lloyd George* (London, 1975: Barrie and Jenkins), pp. 350–77; Lord Hankey, *The Supreme Command*, Vol. II (London, 1961: Allen and Unwin), pp, 553–70; Austen Chamberlain, *Down The Years* (London, 1935: Cassell), pp. 107–31.

93 See *Note on the Machinery of the British War Cabinet*, December 1916, and *Note on the Composition of the Secretariat of the War Cabinet*, 13 December 1916, Cab 21/102; see also Roskill, *Hankey*, Vol. I, pp. 327–38 and Hankey, *Supreme Command*, Vol. II, pp. 577–80.

94 That Balfour was prepared to serve under Lloyd George took Asquith completely by surprise. Some years later Asquith's wife Margot observed to Blanche Dugdale, Balfour's niece and biographer, that 'this is what hurt my husband more than anything else. That Ll.G. (a Welshman!) should betray him he [...] could understand but that Arthur should join the enemy (Ll.G.) and help to ruin him he never understood.' In private conversation Balfour explained that Lloyd George was the only man 'who can at this moment break down that wall of military red tape and see that the brains of the country are made use of'. Balfour accepted the post of foreign secretary on the evening of 6 December. According to Austen Chamberlain, who extensively reported on the episode in a private and personal letter to Lord Chelmsford on 8 December, Balfour had replied to the question whether or not he accepted the post, 'you are putting a pistol to my head, but in the circumstances, I say, "Yes".'
Max Egremont, *Balfour: A Life of Arthur James Balfour* (London, 1980: Collins), p. 281; Jenkins, *Asquith* (London, 1978: Collins), pp. 450, 453, 461; Roskill, *Hankey*,Vol. I (London, 1970: Allen and Unwin), p. 325; Chamberlain, *Down the Years* (London, 1935: Cassell), p. 126.

95 See: S.S.I. to Prime Minister, 7 December 1916, encl. in I.O. to F.O., no. P. 5118, 8 December 1916, FO 371/2776/248485.

96 Robertson, *Manpower*, 8 December 1916, Lloyd George Papers, F/191/3/1.

97 See tel. Murray to Wingate, no. A.M. 1364, 7 December 1916, WO 158/627.

98 Minutes War Cabinet, 9 December 1916, Cab 23/1.

99 Tel. Wingate to Balfour, no. 68, 9 December 1916, FO 371/2776/249260.

100 Wingate to Clayton, private, 10 December 1916, Wingate Papers, box 144/3.

101 Tel. Wingate to Wilson, no. 230, 10 December 1916, FO 686/53.

102 Tel. Wingate to Balfour, no. 71, 11 December 1916, FO 371/2776/250155.

103 See tel. Wilson to Wingate, no. W. 869, 11 December 1916, and tel. Wingate to Balfour, no. 73, 11 December 1916, FO 371/2776/250345.

104 Tel. Wingate to Wilson, no. 257, 11 December 1916, encl. in tel. Wingate to Balfour, no. 74, 11 December 1916, FO 371/2776/250986.

105 Minutes War Cabinet, 11 December 1916, Cab 23/1.

106 Minute Hardinge, not dated, and tel. Balfour to Wingate, no. 36, 11 December 1916, FO 371/2776/250345.

107 Minute Clerk, 13 December 1916, on tel. Wingate to Balfour, no. 77, 13 December 1916, FO 371/2776/251855.

108 Tel. Wingate to Balfour, no. 83, 14 December 1916, FO 371/2776/253644.
109 Minutes War Cabinet, 15 December 1916, Cab 23/1, and tel. Balfour to Wingate, no. 45, 15 December 1916, FO 371/2776/251855.
110 Minute Hardinge, not dated, on tel. Wingate to Balfour, no. 84, 15 December 1916, FO 371/2776/253936.
111 Tel. Wingate to Balfour, no. 86, 16 December 1916, FO 371/2776/255018.
112 Wingate to Wilson, private, 17 December 1916, Wingate Papers, box 144/3.
113 Graham had returned to the Foreign Office at Hardinge's request. In August 1918, Cecil explained to Balfour that he believed that Hardinge 'was fully justified in bringing back as his subordinate a man whom he trusts and can work with', but that Graham's appointment had been 'to the considerable indignation of those who were already there' (see further Chapter 9, section 'The Eastern Committee and the Foreign Office Middle East Department'). Cecil to Balfour, 23 August 1918, Balfour Papers, Add. Mss. 49738.
114 Minutes Clerk, 18 December 1916, and Graham, 18 December 1916, on tel. Wingate to Balfour, no. 86, 16 December 1916, FO 371/2776/255018.
115 Minutes War Cabinet, 19 and 20 December 1916, Cab 23/1.
116 Tel. Wingate to Balfour, no. 86, 16 December 1916, FO 371/2776/255018.
117 Husayn to Wingate, 21 December 1916, in tel. Pearson to Wingate, no. W. 004, 27 December 1916, and tel. Arbur to Wilson, no. A.B. 486, 28 December 1916, FO 882/6.
118 Tel. Pearson to Arbur, no. W. 099, 3 January 1917, FO 141/825.
119 Memorandum Wingate, in Clayton's handwriting, not dated, Wingate Papers, box 144/1.
120 Murray to Wingate, 5 January 1917, Wingate Papers, box 145/1.
121 Tel. G.O.C.-in-C., Egypt to C.I.G.S, no. A.M 1475, 5 Jan 1917, WO 33/905.
122 Tel. Wingate to Balfour, no. 15, 6 January 1917, FO 371/3042/5379.
123 See tel. Wilson to Pearson, in tel. Pearson to Arbur, 6 January 1917, FO 141/825.
124 See Wilson to Arbur, no. W. 118, 6 January 1917, in tel. G.O.C.-in-C., Egypt to C.I.G.S., no. A.M. 1482, 7 January 1917, WO 33/905.
125 Tels Arbur to Wilson, no. A.B. 544, 6 January 1917, and Wilson to Arbur, no. W. 142, 7 January 1917, FO 141/825.
126 See tel. G.O.C.-in-C., Egypt to C.I.G.S., no. 1482, 7 January 1917, WO 33/905.
127 Tel. Arbur to Wilson, no. A.B. 552, 7 January 1917, FO 141/825.
128 Tel. Wingate to Balfour, no. 22, 8 January 1917, FO 371/3042/6216.
129 Minutes War Cabinet, 8 January 1917, Cab 23/1.
130 See tel. Balfour to Wingate, no. 19, 8 January 1917, FO 371/3042/6540.
131 Tel. Wilson to Arbur, no. W. 146, 8 January 1917, FO 141/825.
132 Wingate to Murray, private, 9 January 1917, Wingate Papers, box 145/1.
133 See tel. Wingate to Balfour, no. 29, 10 January 1917, FO 371/3042/7674.
134 Tel. Wingate to Balfour, no. 34, 12 January 1917, FO 371/3042/9952.
135 Tel. Wingate to Balfour, no. 58, 19 January 1917, FO 371/3042/15877. Now that the danger that an expeditionary force would have to be sent to Rabegh definitely seemed to have been averted, the time was ripe for the abolishment of the odd arrangement

that the Foreign Office was responsible for military operations in the Hijaz. On 31 January 1917, the War Cabinet decided that Wingate 'should be regarded as General Officer Commanding the Hedjaz, and, as such, should be placed under the orders of the War Office'. Minutes War Cabinet, 31 January 1917, Cab 23/1.
136 Wingate to Hogarth, private, 5 July 1916, Wingate Papers, box 138/3.
137 Tel. Abdullah to Foreign Office, 29 October 1916, and minutes Clerk, 31 October 1916, Hardinge, not dated, and Grey, not dated, FO 371/2782/217652.
138 Tel. McMahon to Grey, no. 945, 31 October 1916, FO 371/2782/218006.
139 Tel. McMahon to Grey, no. 947, 31 October 1916, FO 371/2782/218629.
140 Tel. Wingate to McMahon, no. 628, 2 November 1916, FO 371/2782/221025.
141 Tel. McMahon to Grey, no. 947, 31 October 1916, FO 371/2782/218629.
142 Tel. McMahon to Grey, no. 961, 2 November 1916, FO 371/2782/220339.
143 Tel. Wingate to McMahon, no. 628, 2 November 1916, FO 371/2782/221025.
144 Tels McMahon to Grey, no. 961, 2 November 1916, and Wingate to McMahon, no. 628, 2 November 1916, FO 371/2782/220339.
145 Tel. McMahon to Grey, no. 955, 1 November 1916, and minute Clerk, 2 November 1916, FO 371/2782/219490.
146 Minute Clerk, 3 November 1916, on tel. McMahon to Grey, no. 967, 3 November 1916, and tel. Grey to McMahon, no. 880, 3 November 1916, FO 371/2782/220832.
147 See tel. McMahon to Grey, no. 980, 7 November 1916, FO 371/2782/223715.
148 Tel. Grey to Wingate, no. 6, 6 November 1916, FO 371/2782/221869.
149 Tel. Grey to Wingate, no. 13, 13 November 1916, Wingate Papers, box 143/1.
150 Tel. Grey to Wingate, no. 21, 24 November 1916, FO 371/2782/234461.
151 Tel. Balfour to Wingate, no. 35, 11 December 1916, FO 371/2782/246846; cf. also Dan Eldar, 'French Policy towards Husayn, Sharif of Mecca', *Middle Eastern Studies*, 26 (1990), p. 341.

Chapter 6: Taking the Sherif into the Fullest Confidence Possible

1 Robertson, El Arish Operations, 14 December 1916, and minutes War Cabinet, 15 December 1916, Cab 23/1.
2 Anglo–French conference, minutes of a meeting, 28 December 1916, I.C. 12, Lloyd George Papers, F/120/2.
3 Hankey diary, 11 December 1916, Hankey Papers, vol. 1/1.
4 Tels C.I.G.S. to G.O.C.-in-C., Egypt, no. 26174, 9 December 1916, G.O.C.-in-C., Egypt to C.I.G.S., no. A.M. 1380, 10 December 1916, G.I.G.S to G.O.C.-in-C., Egypt, no. 26289, 12 December 1916, G.O.C.-in-C., Egypt to C.I.G.S, no. A.M. 1389, 13 December 1916, and C.I.G.S. to G.O.C.-in-C., Egypt. no. 26624, 15 December 1916,WO 33/905. See also Murray's discussion of these telegrams in his *Sir Archibald Murray's Despatches* (London, 1920: Dent), pp. 130–1.
5 Robertson, 'NOTE ON A PROPOSAL TO UNDERTAKE A CAMPAIGN IN PALESTINE DURING THE WINTER WITH THE OBJECT OF CAPTURING JERUSALEM', 29 December 1916, WO 106/310.

6 Minutes War Cabinet, 2 January 1917, Cab 23/1.
7 See minutes War Cabinet, 31 January 1917, ibid.
8 *Status and functions of Chief Political Officer and French Commissioner*, encl. in Graham to Hardinge, 13 February 1917, Hardinge to Balfour, 14 February 1917, and minute Balfour, not dated, FO 371/3050/56041.
9 Sykes to Wingate, 22 February 1917, Wingate Papers, box 145/2.
10 Clayton, Note on telegram no. 219 from the Foreign Office to the High Commissioner dated March 6th 1917, 10 March 1917, FO 882/16.
11 Tels Wingate to Balfour, no. 257, 12 March 1917, and Balfour to Wingate, 14 March 1917, FO 371/3045/53249.
12 Clayton to Wilson, 10 March 1917, FO 882/16.
13 See Arbur to Wilson, no. A.B. 003, 16 March 1917, ibid.
14 Tels Wilson to Arbur, no. W. 609, 17 March 1917, Wilson to Arbur, no. W. 610, 17 March 1917, and Arbur to Wilson, no. A.B. 024, 18 March 1917, ibid.
15 Wilson to Clayton, 21 March 1917, and P.S., 22 March 1917, FO 882/12.
16 See tel. G.O.C.-in-C., Egypt to C.I.G.S., no. O.A. 377, 28 March 1917, WO 106/1512.
17 Minutes War Cabinet, 30 March 1917, Cab 23/2, see also Matthew Hughes, *Allenby and British Strategy in the Middle East 1917–1919* (London, 1999: Frank Cass), pp. 19–20.
18 Tels C.I.G.S. to G.O.C.-in-C., Egypt, no. 31854, 30 March 1917, and G.O.C.-in-C., Egypt to C.I.G.S., no. A.M. 1749, 31 March 1917, in Lieut.-General Sir George MacMunn and Captain Cyril Falls, *Military Operations Egypt & Palestine from the Outbreak of War with Germany to June 1917* (London, 1928: H.M. Stationary Office), pp. 322–3.
19 See tel. C.I.G.S. to G.O.C.-in-C., Egypt, no. 31898, 31 March 1917, and tel. G.O.C.-in-C., Egypt to C.I.G.S., no. A.M. 1751, 1 April 1917, WO 106/1512. Lloyd George blamed Murray personally for the EEF's defeat at Gaza. On 5 June, the War Cabinet appointed Lieut.-General Sir Edmund Allenby as Murray's successor. Allenby took over on 29 June 1917. Minutes War Cabinet, 5 April 1917, Cab 23/13, and 5 June 1917, Cab 23/3.
20 Minutes War Cabinet, 2 April 1917, Cab 23/2.
21 A complaint that Curzon time and again voiced in Sykes's presence, witness the latter's complaint that Curzon 'never ceases twitting me with having given everything to France'. Sykes to Drummond, 20 July 1917, Sykes Papers, box 2.
22 Notes of a conference, no. G.T. 372, 3 April 1917, Cab 24/9.
23 Tel. Sykes to Graham, no. 18, 30 April 1917, FO 371/3053/88954.
24 Tel. Wingate to Balfour, no. 464, 27 April 1917, FO 371/3054/86526.
25 Clayton to Wilson, 28 April 1917, FO 882/12.
26 Tel. Wingate to Balfour, no. 464, 27 April 1917, FO 371/3054/86526.
27 Wingate to Graham, private, 28 April 1917, Wingate Papers, box 145/5.
28 Clayton to Wilson, 28 April 1917, FO 882/12.
29 See tel. Balfour to Wingate, no. 442, 28 April 1917, FO 371/3054/86526.
30 See Clayton to Wilson, 28 April 1917, FO 882/12.
31 See Roger Adelson, *The Formation of British Policy towards the Middle East, 1914–1918* (Ann Arbor, 1973: unpublished dissertation), pp. 220–8, 318–19; Briton

Cooper Busch, *Britain, India, and the Arabs 1914–1921* (Berkeley, 1971: University of California Press), pp. 110–20, 135; Basil Liddell Hart, *History of the First World War* (London, 1972: Pan Books), pp. 269–73.
32 Tel. S.S.I. to viceroy, 12 March 1917, FO 371/3042/56627; see also minutes War Cabinet, 12 and 14 March 1917, Cab 23/2.
33 Clayton to Wilson, 28 April 1917, FO 882/12. With respect to Sykes's instructions, see tel. Wingate to Balfour, no. 472, 28 April 1917, and tel. Balfour to Wingate, no. 446, 30 April 1917, FO 371/3054/87289.
34 Tel. Wingate to Balfour, no. 496, 7 May 1917, FO 371/3054/93325.
35 Tel. Sykes to Graham, 24 May 1917, FO 371/3054/104269. Shortly afterwards, Faysal complained to Lieut.-Colonel Stewart Newcombe whether the British government intended 'The Arab Kingdom to be weak and die out? as must be the case if they have no port and was that the reason they allowed all the coast to France? […] certainly the large number of persons hanged in Syria and the Lebanon had not died to liberate their country from the Turks to give it to the French.'
Newcombe, Note, 20 May 1917, encl. in Wilson to Clayton, 24 May 1917, FO 882/16.
36 Sykes and Georges-Picot, 'Observations on Arabian Policy as results of visit to RED SEA PORTS, JEDDAH, YEMBO, WEJH, KAMARAN, and ADEN', 17 May 1917, FO 371/3044/120491.
37 Tel. Sykes to Graham, 24 May 1917, FO 371/3054/104269.
38 Wilson to Clayton, 24 May 1917, FO 882/16.
39 Tel. Sykes to Graham, 24 May 1917, and minute Graham, not dated, FO 371/3054/104269.
40 Wilson to Clayton, 24 May 1917, FO 882/16.
41 NOTE BY SHEIK FOAD EL KHATIB TAKEN DOWN BY LT COL NEWCOMBE, not dated, encl. in Wilson to Clayton, 24 May 1917, ibid.
42 Tel. Wingate to Balfour, no. 472, 28 April 1917, FO 371/3054/87289.
43 See tels Balfour to Wingate, no. 571, 5 June 1917, and Balfour to Bertie, no. 1521, 7 June 1917, FO 371/3056/110589.
44 Hogarth, *Note on the Anglo–Franco–Russian Agreement about the Near East*, 9 July 1917, encl. in D.I.D. to F.O., 13 July 1917, FO 371/3054/138899.
45 Clayton to Sykes, 30 July 1917, FO 882/16.
46 Lawrence, Note, 30 July 1917, encl. in Wingate to Balfour, no. 179, 16 August 1917 (underlining in original), and minutes Clerk, 1 September 1917 and Graham, 13 September 1917, and initials Sykes, FO 371/3054/174974.
47 Tel. McMahon to Grey, no. 517, 30 June 1916, and minutes Hardinge and Grey, not dated, FO 371/2773/126674.
48 Secretary's Notes of a Meeting of the War Committee, 11 July 1916, Cab 42/16/1.
49 Tels Grey to McMahon, no. 549, 6 July 1916, FO 371/2773/126674, and McMahon to Grey, no. 559, 10 July 1916, FO 371/2773/133650, Secretary's Notes of a Meeting of the War Committee, 11 July 1916, Cab 42/16/5, tel. Grey to McMahon, no. 570, 12 July 1916, FO 371/2773/133650.
50 Tel. McMahon to Grey, no. 691, 14 August 1916, and minutes Clerk and Hardinge, not dated, and tel. Grey to McMahon, no. 678, 15 August 1916, FO 371/2774/160155.

51 Clayton to Wingate, private, 24 September 1916, Wingate Papers, box 140/6.
52 Tel. Wingate to Balfour, no. 404, 10 April 1917, minutes Oliphant, 11 April 1917, Hardinge and Cecil, not dated, Nicholson, 11 April 1917 and Graham, not dated, FO 371/3048/74596.
53 Waterfield to Nicolson, 19 April 1917, FO 371/3048/80878.
54 Tel. Wingate to Balfour, no. 459, 23 April 1917, FO 371/3048/83145.
55 Nicolson, Note, 28 April 1917, and minute Hardinge, not dated, minute Drogheda, 7 May 1917, FO 371/3048/94110.
56 Waterfield to Oliphant, 7 May 1917, and F.O. to Treasury, no. 94668/17, 11 May 1917, FO 371/3048/94668, Treasury to F.O., no. 15699/17, 12 May 1917, FO 371/3048/97135.
57 Tel. Wingate to Balfour, no. 729, 12 July 1917, and minutes Nicolson and Clerk, 13 July 1917, FO 371/3048/137930.
58 Minute Clerk, 10 September 1917, on tel. Wingate to Balfour, no. 947, 8 September 1917, FO 371/3048/175896.
59 Tel. Wingate to Balfour, no. 645, 18 June 1917, FO 371/3048/121588, tel. Wingate to Balfour, no. 754, 18 July 1917, FO 371/3048/142636.
60 Treasury to F.O., no. 32359/17, 10 October 1917, FO 371/3048/195477.
61 Tel. Wingate to Balfour, no. 1153, 2 November 1917, and minutes Clerk and Graham, 3 November 1917, FO 371/3048/210013.

Chapter 7: Up Against a Big Thing

1 Viscount Samuel, *Memoirs* (London, 1945: Cresset Press), p. 141.
2 Leonard Stein, *The Balfour Declaration* (London, 1961: Valentine, Mitchell), p. 104.
3 Leonard Stein (ed.), *The Letters and Papers of Chaim Weizmann*, Vol. VII (Jerusalem, 1975: Israel University Press), pp. 77–8.
4 John Bowle, *Viscount Samuel: A Biography* (London, 1957: Victor Gollancz), pp. 170–1.
5 Samuel to Grey, 22 January 1915, Grey Papers, FO 800/100.
6 Bowle, *Viscount Samuel*, p. 171.
7 Francis L. Bertie, *The Diary of Lord Bertie of Thame: 1914–1918*, Vol. I (London, 1924: Hodder and Stoughton), p. 106.
8 Isaiah Friedman, *The Question of Palestine, 1914–1918: British–Jewish–Arab Relations* (London, 1973: Routledge and Kegan Paul), pp. 12–13.
9 Bowle, *Viscount Samuel*, pp. 172–6.
10 Roy Jenkins, *Asquith* (London, 1978: Collins), p. 258.
11 Montagu to Asquith, 16 March 1915, Bodleian Library, Asquith Papers, vol. 27.
12 Martin Gilbert, *Winston S. Churchill*, Companion Vol. III, Part I (London, 1972: Heinemann), p. 690.
13 Secretary's Notes of a Meeting of a War Council, 19 March 1915, Cab 42/2/14.
14 Stein, *Letters and Papers*, Vol. VII, p. 184.
15 Ibid., pp. 181, 187.
16 Wolf to Oliphant, 28 April 1915, and minute Oliphant, not dated, FO 371/2488/51705. Wolf had reported that Rabbi Moses Gaster had said that 'the Zionists intended to go

in, and work for "the whole hog". Nothing less than a Commonwealth would satisfy them'.
17 Weizmann to Sacher, 21 August 1915, Stein, *Letters and Papers*, Vol. VII, p. 232.
18 Wolf to Cecil, 18 February 1916, Stein, *Balfour Declaration*, p. 221.
19 Wolf to Oliphant, 3 March 1916, and minute Nicolson, 6 March 1916, FO 371/2817/42608.
20 Wolf to Oliphant, 6 March 1916, minutes Nicolson and Crewe 7 March 1916, O'Beirne, not dated, Nicolson and Crewe, 8 March 1916, and tels Grey to Bertie and Buchanan, no. 633 and 574, 11 March 1916, FO 371/2817/43776.
21 Tel. Buchanan to Grey, private and secret, 14 March 1916, minutes Nicolson, Oliphant and O'Beirne, 15 March 1916, minute Grey, not dated, and tel. Nicolson to Buchanan, Private and Secret, 16 March 1916, FO 371/ 2767/49669.
22 Tel. Buchanan to Grey, no. 377, 16 March 1916, and minute O'Beirne, 17 March 1916, FO 371/2767/51288. In a private letter to Nicolson of 18 March, Sykes presented his assessment of the situation:

> To my mind the Zionists are now the key of the situation – the problem is how are they to be satisfied? With 'Great Jewry' against us there is no possible chance of getting the things through – it means optimism in Berlin – dumps in London – unease in Paris – resistance to last ditch in Constantinople – dissension in Cairo – Arabs all squabbling among themselves – as Shakespeare says 'Untune that string and hark what discord follows' [Troilus and Cressida, Act 1 Scene 3; R.H.L.] – Assume Zionists satisfied the contrary is the case, of that I am positive.
> If they want us to win they will do their best which means they will (A) calm their activities in Russia (B) pessimise in Germany (C) stimulate in France, England and Italy (D) enthuse in USA.
> I am afraid this sounds rather odd and fantastic, but when we bump into a thing like Zionism, which is atmospheric, international, cosmopolitan, subconscious, and unwritten nay often unspoken, it is not possible to work and think on ordinary lines.

The letter drew no written comment from Sir Arthur. Sykes's observations on the hold the Jews had on the outcome of the war were quite commonplace and acceptable at the time. For instance, Clayton, back from a visit to England in July, reported to Wingate that what had particularly struck him:

> Was the widespread influence of the Jews. It is everywhere and always on the 'moderation' tack. The Jews do not want to see anyone 'downed'. There are English Jews, French Jews, American Jews, German Jews, Austrian Jews and <u>Salonica</u> Jews – but all are JEWS, and moreover practically all are anti-Russian. You hear peace talk and generally somewhere behind is the Jew. You hear pro-Turk talk and desires for a separate peace with Turkey – again the Jew.

Sykes to Nicolson, 18 March 1916, Nicolson Papers, FO 800/381, and Clayton to Wingate, private, 3 August 1916, Wingate Papers, box 139/1.

23 Tel. Buchanan to Grey, no. 361, 14 March 1916, and minute Nicolson, 15 March 1916, FO 371/2817/49273.
24 Tel. Bertie to Grey, no. 343, 22 March 1916, and minutes Oliphant, not dated, and O'Beirne, 22 March 1916, FO 371/2817/54791.
25 Note Oliphant, 27 June 1916, minutes Clerk, 29 June 1916, Hardinge, not dated, Grey, not dated, and Oliphant, 4 July 1916, FO 371/2817/130062.
26 Weizmann to Dorothy de Rothschild, 12 November 1916, Stein, *Letters and Papers*, Vol. VII, p. 314.
27 See also Mayir Vereté, 'The Balfour Declaration and its makers', *Middle Eastern Studies*, 6/1 (1970), p. 53.
28 See Jehuda Reinharz, *Chaim Weizmann. The Making of a Statesman* (Hanover, NH, 1993: University Press of New England), pp. 24, 51, 418.
29 Chaim Weizmann, *Trial and Error* (London, 1949: Hamish Hamilton), pp. 144–5.
30 Stein, *Letters and Papers*, Vol. VII, pp. 81–2 (italics in original).
31 Reinharz, *Chaim Weizmann*, p. 110.
32 Stein, *Letters and Papers*, Vol. VII, p. 543.
33 Gaster to Sykes, 31 January 1917; Reinharz, *Chaim Weizmann*, p. 111.
34 Strictly speaking, this agrees with what had been laid down in Article 3 of the Sykes–Picot agreement (see Chapter 4, section 'Sir Mark Sykes and François Georges-Picot Come to an Agreement').
35 This, strictly speaking, is not true, seeing that under the Sykes–Picot agreement the brown area was to have an international administration.
36 Memorandum of a Conference held on 7th February 1917 at 193 Maida Vale, London, W, St Anthony's College, Samuel Papers.
37 See Jonathan Schneer, *The Balfour Declaration: The Origins of the Arab–Israeli Conflict* (London, 2010: Bloomsbury), p. 199; Reinharz, *Chaim Weizmann*, pp. 118–19.
38 Schneer, *The Balfour Declaration*, p. 201.
39 Sykes to Picot, 28 February 1917, Sykes Papers, box 1.
40 Weizmann to Scott, 20 March 1917, Stein, *Letters and Papers*, Vol. VII, p. 343.
41 Weizmann to Scott, 23 March 1917, ibid., pp. 346–7.
42 Weizmann, *Trial and Error*, p. 241.
43 Weizmann to Scott, 23 March 1917, Stein, *Letters and Papers*, Vol. VII, pp. 346–7.
44 Trevor Wilson, *The Political Diaries of C.P. Scott* (London, 1970: Collins), pp. 273–4.
45 Notes of a Conference, G.T.-372, 3 April 1917, Cab 24/9.
46 Tel. Sykes to Graham, no. 1, 6 April 1917, FO 371/3045/72249.
47 Sykes to Hankey, 7 April 1917, Cab 21/96.
48 Tel. Sykes to Balfour, no. 1, 8 April 1917, Sykes Papers, box 1.
49 Sykes to Balfour, no. 2, 9 April 1917, ibid.
50 Sykes to Graham, no. 3, in tel. Bertie to Balfour, no. 334, 9 April 1917, FO 371/3045/73658.
51 Sykes to Balfour, no. 2, 9 April 1917, Sykes Papers, box 1.
52 Bertie to Graham, private and confidential, 12 April 1917, FO 371/3052/82982.
53 Sykes to Graham, no. 2, 15 April 1917, ibid.

54 Tel. Sykes to Balfour, no. 8, 15 April 1917, minute Graham, 17 April 1917, FO 371/3052/78324.
55 Graham to Sykes, 19 April 1917, Sykes Papers, box 1.
56 MEMORANDUM ON THE ANGLO–FRENCH–ITALIAN CONFERENCE, 19 APRIL 1917, Lloyd George Papers, F/120/2.
57 Bertie, *The Diary*, Vol. II, p. 123.
58 Minutes War Cabinet, 25 April 1917, Cab 23/2.
59 See Friedman, *The Question*, p. 233, and Schneer, *Balfour Declaration*, p. 307.
60 Wolf to Oliphant, 21 April 1917, and minute Graham, 25 April 1917, FO 371/3092/83962.
61 Graham to Hardinge, 21 April 1917, minutes Hardinge and Cecil, not dated, and Cecil to Hardinge, 19 April 1917, FO 371/3052/82982.
62 See tel. Balfour to Buchanan, no. 791, 24 April 1917, FO 371/3053/84256.
63 Tel. Buchanan to Balfour, no. 590, 27 April 1914, FO 371/3053/86906.
64 Minutes Oliphant and Graham on tel. Sykes to Graham, private, 28 April 1917, FO 371/3053/87897.
65 Cecil to Ormsby Gore, 15 May 1917, Cecil Papers, FO 800/198.
66 Scott to Weizmann, 16 April 1917, Stein, *Balfour Declaration*, p. 391.
67 Weizmann to Scott, 26 April 1917, Stein, *Letters and Papers*, Vol. VII, pp. 379–80.
68 Ormsby Gore to Sykes, 8 May 1917, Sykes Papers, box 2.
69 Memorandum Cecil, 25 April 1917, FO 371/3053/87062.
70 Weizmann to Scott, 26 April 1917, Stein, *Letters and Papers*, VII, p. 382.
71 Wolf to Oliphant, 2 May 1917, FO 371/3092/89943.
72 Cecil, note, 8 May 1917, FO 371/3092/94113.
73 Wolf to Oliphant, 18 May 1917, and Foreign Office to Wolf, 24 May 1917, FO 371/3053/101437.
74 Wolf to Hardinge, 25 May 1917, FO 371/3053/105582.
75 D.L. Alexander, C.G. Montefiore, Letter to the Editor, *The Times*, 24 May 1917, FO 371/3053/105250.
76 Wolf to Hardinge, 25 May 1917, Minute Nicolson, 27 May 1917, FO 371/3053/105582.
77 *The Times*, 25 May 1917, FO 371/3053/105250.
78 Wolf to Oliphant, 4 June 1917, FO 371/3053/111685.
79 Montagu to Cecil, 14 September 1917, G.T. 2191, Cab 21/58.
80 Wolf to Oliphant, 18 June 1917, and minute Graham, not dated, FO 371/3053/121745. In a confidential note Graham further added that the vote meant that it would 'no longer be necessary to consult that Body'. Graham to Hardinge, Confidential, Zionism, 13 June 1917, FO 371/3058/123458.
81 Wolf to Oliphant, 10 September 1917, FO 371/3053/177948.
82 Austen Chamberlain resigned on 12 July 1917, in result of the findings of the Mesopotamia Commission, which had been appointed to investigate the causes of the defeat at Ctesiphon and the subsequent surrender of the British force at Kut al-'Amara. The India Office was not Montagu's first choice, but he had already explained to Lloyd George that 'he could never refuse the India Office if you wanted me there', with the result that, when Lloyd George offered him the position on 17 July,

Montagu was 'proud to accept'. Montagu to Lloyd George, personal and private, 1 May 1917, and Montagu to Lloyd George, private, 17 July 1917, Lloyd George Papers, F/39/3/11 and 23.
83 Sykes to Graham, no. 3, 15 April 1917, FO 371/3052/82749.
84 Sykes to Sokolow, 14 April 1917, encl. in Sykes to Graham, no. 3, 15 April 1917, ibid.
85 Sokolow to Weizmann, in tel. Rodd to Balfour, 7 May 1917, FO 371/3053/92646.
86 See Schneer, *Balfour Declaration*, pp. 217-18.
87 Cambon to Sokolow, 4 June 1917, FO 371/3058/123458.
88 Tel. Sokolow to Rosov, 6 June 1917, encl. in Weizmann to Graham, 11 June 1917, initials Nicholson and Oliphant, FO 371/3053/116990.
89 In this section it will become clear that Sir Ronald played a very important role in getting through a public declaration in support of Zionist aspirations. In his memoirs, Weizmann acknowledged that Graham 'was of considerable help in bringing about the Balfour Declaration', but at the same time observed that he did 'not know how deep his sympathies were'. It is my impression that Graham, after initial hesitation, saw in the Zionist issue an excellent opportunity to ingratiate himself with Cecil and so to strengthen his position in the Foreign Office (see Chapter 9, section 'The Eastern Committee and the Foreign Office Middle East Department'). Weizmann, *Trial and Error*, pp. 230-1.
90 Graham to Hardinge, Confidential, 13 June 1917, minute Balfour, not dated, FO 371/3058/123458.
91 Rothschild to Weizmann, 17 June 1917, Schneer, *Balfour Declaration*, p. 313.
92 Graham, minute, 19 June 1917, and minutes Balfour and Cecil, not dated, FO 371/3058/123458.
93 Morgenthau was the former American ambassador at Istanbul. He was on his way to Switzerland on a mission to explore the possibilities of a separate peace with the Ottoman Empire. Weizmann succinctly summed up what happened at Gibraltar in the first days of July in a letter to Scott some weeks later:

> The Americans arrived without any plan, instructions or even knowledge of the great issues involved. Morgenthau had an idea that he could try and influence Talaat or Enver, to detach themselves from their mentors. But how it is going to be done, under what conditions and whether the Turks are really ready for such a step, all that Mr M. did not know. It was therefore not difficult to dissuade him and he has abandoned all his plans.

William Yale, 'Ambassador's Henry Morgenthau's special mission of 1917', *World Politics*, 1/3 (1949), pp. 309-10, and Weizmann to Scott, 30 July 1917, Stein, *Letters and Papers*, Vol. VII, p. 475.
94 Weizmann to Sacher, 20 June 1917, Stein, *Letters and Papers*, Vol. VII, p. 445.
95 Sacher to Sokolow, 10 July 1917, Schneer, *Balfour Declaration*, p. 334.
96 Sokolow to Sacher, 10 July 1917, Reinharz, *Chaim Weizmann*, p. 177.
97 See Reinharz, *Chaim Weizmann*, p. 179, and Schneer, *Balfour Declaration*, pp. 334-5.

98 Rothschild to Balfour, 18 July 1917, Balfour to Rothschild, 19 July 1917, and minute Graham, 1 August 1917, FO 371/3083/143082.
99 Longhurst to Nicolson, 20 August 1917, Cab 21/58.
100 Ormsby Gore to Hankey, 18 August 1917, ibid.
101 I have not been able to find out why the Rothschild formula and the Foreign Office draft reply were circulated to Montagu, who as secretary of state for India was not a member of the War Cabinet. It may have been a matter of bureaucratic routine, as both documents were also circulated to the king and Walter Long, the secretary of state for the colonies, and also outside the War Cabinet.
102 Montagu, The Anti-Semitism of the Present Government, 23 August 1917, G.T.-1868 (italics in original), Cab 21/58.
103 Ormsby Gore to Swinton, 23 August 1917, ibid.
104 The War Cabinet minutes did not mention Cecil and Milner, but according to Montagu they were the ones who used this argument 'with such force'. Montagu to Cecil, 14 September 1917, G.T. 2191, ibid.
105 Minutes War Cabinet, 3 September 1917, Cab 23/4.
106 Tel. Balfour to Bayley, 3 September 1917, Balfour Papers, FO 800/204.
107 Tel. House to Drummond, no. 12, 11 September 1917, Cab 21/58.
108 Tel. Weizmann to Brandeis, 12 September 1917, Stein, *Letters and Papers*, Vol. VII, pp. 505–6.
109 Montagu to Cecil, 14 September 1917, G.T. 2191, Cab 21/58. Two days later Weizmann wrote to Philip Kerr in very bitter terms:

> The 'dark forces' in English Jewry have again been at work and this time they have mobilised their great champion who although a great Hindu nationalist now, thought it his duty to combat Jewish Nationalism. It is – I confess – inconceivable to me, how British statesmen still attribute importance to the attitude of a few plutocratic Jews and allow their opinion to weigh against almost a unanimous expression of opinion of Jewish Democracy.

> Weizmann to Kerr, 16 September 1917, Stein, *Letters and Papers*, Vol. VII, p. 511.

110 Weizmann to Kerr, 19 September 1917, Stein; ibid., p. 516.
111 Oliphant to Hankey, 20 September 1917, and Ormsby Gore to Oliphant, 21 September 1917, Cab 21/58.
112 Rothschild to Balfour, 22 September 1919 (underlining in original), FO 371/3083/171855.
113 Graham to Hardinge, *Zionist aspirations*, 24 September 1917, minutes Hardinge, Balfour and Graham, not dated, FO 371/3083/187210.
114 Tel. Brandeis to Weizmann, CX 166, 26 September 1917, G.T. 2158, Cab 21/58.
115 Weizmann to Sokolow, 30 September 1917, Stein, *Letters and Papers*, Vol. VII, p. 520.
116 Wilson, *Political Diaries*, p. 306.
117 Rothschild and Weizmann, Private and Personal, 3 October 1917, encl. in Rothschild to Balfour, 3 October 1917, FO 371/3083/171885.

118 Curzon to Montagu, 8 September 1917, David Gilmour, 'The unregarded prophet: Lord Curzon and the Palestine question', *Journal Of Palestine Studies*, 25/3 (1996), p. 63.
119 Leopold Amery, *My Political Life. Volume Two: War and Peace* (London, 1953: Hutchinson), p. 116.
120 Minutes War Cabinet, 4 October 1917, Cab 23/4.
121 Montagu to Lloyd George, 4 October 1917, Lloyd George Papers, F/39/3/30.
122 Ormsby Gore to Hankey, 5 October 1917, Cab 21/58.
123 Tel. Balfour to Wiseman, no. 21, 6 October 1917, FO 371/3083/200850.
124 Amery, *Political Life*, p. 117.
125 Weizmann, *Trial and Error*, p. 262.
126 Hankey, 'The Zionist movement', 17 October 1917, containing copies of letters from Herbert Samuel, Hertz, Rothschild, Sir Stuart Samuel, Weizmann, Sokolow, Magnus, Montefiore and Cohen, Cab 21/58.
127 Tel. Wiseman to Drummond, no. 27, 16 October 1917, minute Clerk, 20 October 1917, minute Balfour, not dated, FO 371/3083/200850.
128 Minutes War Cabinet, 25 October 1917, Cab 23/4.
129 Leonard Stein is rather embarrassed by Graham's assertion that 'almost every Jew in Russia is a Zionist', although he dubs this 'a miscalculation': 'the Jews who were playing a significant part in the situation in Russia were those associated with the extreme left-wing elements now coming into the ascendant. Jews of this type, so far from being likely to be impressed by a pro-Zionist declaration, were violently hostile to Zionism'. Graham's claim that 'we might at any moment be confronted by a German move on the Zionist question', is equally untrue. Isaiah Friedman has pointed out that at the end of October 1917, an official of the German ministry of foreign affairs tried to convince his superiors 'of the urgency of a German–Turkish pro-Zionist declaration', but was told that 'the proposed move did not accord with German interests'.
Stein, *Balfour Declaration*, pp. 570–1 and Isaiah Friedman, *Germany, Turkey, and Zionism 1897–1918* (Oxford, 1977: Clarendon Press), p. 336.
130 Graham to Balfour, 24 October 1917, FO 371/3054/207495.
131 Balfour to Lloyd George, 25 October 1917, Lloyd George Papers, F/3/2/34.
132 Curzon, 'The future of Palestine', 26 October 1917, G.T. 2406, Cab 21/58.
133 Sykes, note, not dated, minute Drummond, 30 October 1917, FO 371/3083/207407.
134 Minutes War Cabinet, 31 October 1917, Cab 23/4.
135 Draft Balfour to Rothschild, 2 November 1917, corrections Graham, initials Graham and Hardinge, not dated, FO 371/3083/210332. Weizmann's biographer, Jehuda Reinharz, quotes Harry Sacher, who was emphatic that without Weizmann there would have been no Balfour Declaration. I believe this is certainly true. The question then is what was Weizmann's decisive contribution? I think a convincing answer to this question in the end cannot ignore 'the Anti-Semitism of the Present Government'. It lies in his not having any qualms about exploiting British anti-Semitism. In a letter to Weizmann of 1 May 1915, Leon Simon complained that 'you are committing the fatal mistake of Herzl – that of making anti-Semitism the foundation stone of your building. Like him, you are approaching the problem

from the outside – not essentially as a Jew, but from the standpoint of the Goyim'. Simon quite understood that 'Herzl should take the point of view of the Goyim, for he was a Goy. But you, who comes from Pinsk – what are you doing in that gallery?' But his complaint was completely mistaken. It was precisely by taking the outside perspective – by playing on their firm belief that they were 'up against a big thing' – that Weizmann managed to convince British policy makers of the advisability of a public declaration, however qualified, in support of the Zionist cause.

For a similar type of argument, see James Renton, *The Zionist Masquerade*. It is completely beyond me, however, how Renton, after having studied the relevant archives, could have reached the conclusion that other Zionists were more effective than Weizmann in tapping 'into the imagined concerns of government officials at the right moment', and that Weizmann's contribution 'was of minor significance'. Reinharz, *Chaim Weizmann*, p. 172; Jehuda Reinharz, 'Chaim Weizmann: statesman without a state', *Modern Judaism*, 12/3 (1992), p. 227; James Renton, *The Zionist Masquerade* (Basingstoke, 2007: Palgrave Macmillan), pp. 65 and 70.

136 Captain Cyril Falls, *Military Operations Egypt & Palestine from June 1917 to the End of the War*, Vol. I (London, 1930: H.M. Stationary Office), p. 15.
137 Clayton to Wingate, private, 12 October 1917 (underlining in original), Wingate Papers, box 146/6.
138 Tels Wingate to Balfour, no. 802, 29 July 1917 and Balfour to Wingate, no. 787, 3 August 1917, FO 371/3043/149216.
139 Clayton to Wingate, private, 23 November 1917, Wingate Papers, box 146/10.
140 Tels Wingate to Balfour, no. 1262, Very Urgent, 24 November 1917, Wingate to Balfour, no. 1267, Urgent, 25 November 1917, C.I.G.S. to G.O.C.-in-C., Egypt, no. 46484, 26 November 1917, and Wingate to Hardinge, private, 29 November 1917, Wingate Papers, box 146/10.
141 Clayton to Wingate, private, 8 December 1917, Wingate Papers, box 147/2.
142 Clayton to Bell, 8 December 1917, Clayton Papers, G//S 513.
143 Clayton to Sykes, in tel. Wingate to Balfour, no. 1281, 28 November 1917, FO 371/3054/227658.
144 Tel. Balfour to Wingate, no. 1176, 11 December 1917, FO 371/3054/235200.
145 Tel. Wingate to Balfour, no. 1341, 14 December 1917, FO 371/3054/237384.
146 Clayton to Sykes, private, 15 December 1917, Wingate Papers, box. 147/1. Clayton was rather more outspoken in his letter to Gertrude Bell:

> The Arabs of Syria and Palestine sees the Jew with a free hand and the backing of H.M.G. and interprets it as meaning the eventual loss of its heritage. Jacob and Esau once more. The Arab is right and no amount of specious oratory will humbug him in a matter which affects him so vitally.

Clayton to Bell, 8 December 1917, Clayton Papers, G//S 513.

147 Wingate to Allenby, private, 16 December 1917, Wingate Papers, box 147/4.
148 Weizmann to Graham, 17 December 1917, minutes Clerk, 20 December 1917, and Graham, not dated, FO 371/3054/239129.

Chapter 8: A Whole Crowd of Weeds Growing Around Us

1 T.E. Lawrence, *Seven Pillars of Wisdom: A Triumph* (London, 1977: Penguin), p. 113; cf. also Général E. Brémond, *Le Hedjaz dans la guerre mondiale* (Paris, 1931: Payot), pp. 35–44, and Dan Eldar, 'French policy towards Husayn, Sharif of Mecca', *Middle Eastern Studies*, 26 (1990), pp. 337–8.
2 Tel. Wilson to Wingate, no. W. 394, 24 October 1916, Wingate Papers, box 141/3.
3 G.O.C.-in-C., Egypt to D.M.I, no. I.A. 2629, 17 November 1916, Cab 42/24/8; cf. also Eldar, 'French policy', p. 339.
4 McMahon to Hardinge, 21 November 1916, Hardinge Papers, vol. 27.
5 Murray to Robertson, 28 November 1916, Add. Mss. 52462.
6 Tel. Wingate to Grey, no. 29, 23 November 1916, FO 371/2776/236128.
7 See Grey to Bertie, no. 779, 22 November 1916, FO 371/2776/232712.
8 Minute Clerk, 23 November 1916, FO 371/2776/236128.
9 Sykes to Hardinge, 21 November 1916, minutes Clerk, 22 November 1916, and Hardinge, not dated, and tel. Hardinge to Wingate, private, 24 November 1916, FO 371/2779/233854.
10 Tel. Wingate to Hardinge, private, 27 November 1916, Wingate Papers, box 143/4.
11 Wingate to Balfour, private, 11 February 1917, and minutes Hardinge, not dated, Graham, 24 February 1917, and Balfour, not dated, FO 371/3044/40845.
12 See also Roberta M. Warman, 'The erosion of Foreign Office influence in the making of foreign policy, 1916–1918', *The Historical Journal*, 15/1 (1972), pp. 133–59.
13 Sykes to Wingate, 6 March 1917, Sykes Papers, box 2.
14 Sykes to Graham, no. 23, in tel. Wingate to Balfour, no. 497, 8 May 1917, and tel. Balfour to Bertie, no. 1243, 12 May 1917, FO 371/3051/93348.
15 French Embassy to Foreign Office, 16 May 1917, reprinted in John Fisher, *Curzon and British Imperialism in the Middle East 1916–1919* (London, 1999: Frank Cass), pp. 313–16, tel. Balfour to Wingate, no. 540, 29 May 1917, and minutes Graham, 21 May 1917 and Cecil, not dated, FO 371/3056/100065.
16 Tel. Wingate to Balfour, no. 583, 3 June 1917, minutes Oliphant, 4 June 1917, Graham, not dated, tels Balfour to Wingate, no. 571, 5 June 1917, and Balfour to Bertie, no. 1521, 7 June 1917, FO 371/3056/110589.
17 Wingate to Balfour, no. 127, 11 June 1917, FO 371/3054/125564, and tel. Wingate to Balfour, no. 609, 10 June 1917, FO 371/3054/115603.
18 Wingate to Balfour, no. 127, 11 June 1917, FO 371/3054/125564.
19 Minute Sykes, 22 June 1917, on tel. Wingate to Balfour, no. 609, 10 June 1917, Cab 21/60.
20 Tel. Wingate to Balfour, no. 696, 3 July 1917, minutes Graham and Hardinge, not dated, FO 371/3056/131922.
21 See Nicolson, 'Draft for a Note to the French ambassador', 14 June 1917, FO 371/3056/132784.
22 Drummond to Hankey, 7 July 1917, Cab 21/60.
23 Minutes War Cabinet, 13 July 1917, Cab 23/3.
24 Minutes Hardinge and Cecil, not dated, FO 371/3056/165801.

25 Sykes to Graham, not dated, and Clerk to Hardinge, 28 August 1917, minute Hardinge, not dated, FO 371/3044/168691.
26 Memorandum French Embassy, 18 September 1917, minutes Graham and Hardinge, not dated, and tel. Balfour to Bertie, no. 2387, 26 September 1917, FO 371/3056/181851.
27 Minutes Clerk, 8 October 1917, and Hardinge, not dated, on 'Projet d'Arrangement', 3 October 1917, FO 371/3056/191542.
28 Tel. Balfour to Wingate, no. 1152, 4 December 1917, FO 371/3056/227997.
29 Instructions to Sir Mark Sykes, 17 December 1917, FO 371/3056/239988.
30 See Sykes, Report on visit to Paris, 25 December 1917, FO 371/3056/245878.
31 I.O. to F.O., no. P.74, 15 January 1918, minutes Sykes and Hardinge, not dated, and tel. Balfour to Bertie, no. 140, 18 January 1918, FO 371/3380/9495.
32 Tel. Bertie to Balfour, no. 100, 20 January 1918, FO 371/3380/12438.
33 Lloyd to Wingate, private, 2 Feb 1918, Wingate Papers, box 148/5.
34 Wilson to Clayton, 24 May 1917, FO 882/16.
35 Sykes to Cox, 22 May 1917, in tel. Cox to S.S.I., no. 1837, 24 May 1917, FO 371/3054/108249.
36 Tel. Cox to S.S.I., 2 June 1917, FO 371/3054/119702.
37 G.O.C.-in-C., Force 'D' to C.I.G.S., 5 January 1916, encl. in I.O. to F.O., no. P.72/16, 7 January 1916, FO 371/2769/4650.
38 Lawrence, 'the Politics of Mecca', encl. in McMahon to Grey, no. 25, 7 February 1916, FO 371/2771/30673.
39 Cox to Arbur (Cairo), 9 September 1916, encl. in I.O. to F.O., no. P.365/5, 13 September 1916, FO 371/2769/182436.
40 See Lawrence, note, 29 July 1917, encl. in Wingate to Balfour, no. 179, 16 August 1917, FO 371/3054/174974.
41 Wingate to Balfour, no. 315, 23 December 1917, FO 371/3380/12076.
42 Tel. Cox to viceroy, 30 October 1917, FO 371/3061/209456.
43 Tel. Balfour to Wingate, no. 1037, 5 November 1917, FO 371/3061/205968.
44 Tel. Wingate to Balfour, no. 1198, 12 November 1917, FO 371/3061/216252.
45 Tel. Wingate to Balfour, no. 1241, 21 November 1917, FO 371/3061/222650.
46 Tel. Cox to Wingate, 15 December 1917, FO 371/3061/239273.
47 See Briton Cooper Busch, *Britain, India, and the Arabs 1914–1921* (Berkeley, 1971: University of California Press), p. 254.
48 At the end of December, Storrs was in Jerusalem. Neville Travers Borton, former governor of the Red Sea Province and postmaster-general, Egypt, had been appointed military governor of Jerusalem on the recommendation of Clayton and Wingate. However, he suffered a nervous breakdown and resigned on 25 December. Storrs was appointed in his place a few days later.
49 Tel. Wingate to Balfour, no. 1403, 27 December 1917, FO 371/3061/244397.
50 Wingate to Clayton, Strictly Private & Personal, 3 January 1918, Wingate Papers, box 148/2.
51 Tel. Wingate to Balfour, no. 1418, 31 December 1917, minute Hardinge, not dated, and tel. Balfour to Wingate, no. 24, 4 January 1918, FO 371/3054/245810.

52 Hogarth, REPORT ON MISSION TO JEDDAH, 15 January 1918, FO 371/3383/25577.
53 Tel. Cox to viceroy, no. P. 389, 13 January 1918, FO 371/3383/10166.
54 ARABIAN AFFAIRS, Private note of meeting held at The Residency, Cairo, at 10.30 am on 21st January 1918 (underlining in original), Wingate Papers, box 148/1.
55 Hogarth, REPORT ON MISSION TO JEDDAH, 15 January 1918, FO 371/3383/25577.
56 Tel. Wingate to Balfour, no. 154, 22 January 1918, FO 371/3380/14373.
57 Minutes Middle East Committee, 26 January 1918, Cab 27/23.
58 Tel. Cox to viceroy, 25 January 1918, FO 371/3380/18462.
59 Minutes Middle East Committee, 2 February 1918, Cab 27/23.
60 Tel. Balfour to Wingate, no. 163, 4 February 1918, minute Hardinge, not dated, FO 371/3380/22108.
61 Tel. Wingate to Balfour, no. 281, 11 February 1918, FO 371/3380/26617.
62 Wingate to Bassett, private, 24 February 1918, Wingate Papers, box 148/5.
63 Bassett to Wingate, private, 11 February 1918, encl. in Wingate to Sykes, 19 February 1918, FO 371/3380/42105.
64 Sykes, 'The Palestine and West Arabia situation', 1 January 1918, minutes Hardinge, 4 January 1918, and Cecil, not dated, FO 371/3388/3787. Seven months later, Hardinge would claim that 'Sykes was not my invention, but was imposed upon me'. Hardinge to Cecil, 20 August 1918, Balfour Papers, Add. Mss. 49748.
65 Hankey to Cecil, Confidential, 2 January 1918, Cecil Papers, FO 800/98.
66 Cecil to Balfour, 8 January 1918, Balfour Papers, FO 800/207.
67 Minutes Middle East Committee, 12 January 1918, Cab 27/22.
68 Hankey, diary entries 1 and 8 March 1918, Hankey Papers, vol. 1/3.
69 Minutes War Cabinet, 11 March 1918, Cab 23/5.
70 Clayton to Sykes, 15 December 1917, Clayton Papers, G//S 513.
71 Tel. Bertie to Balfour, no. 1482, 15 December 1917, minutes Graham, 17 December 1917, and Hardinge, not dated, and tel. Balfour to Bertie, no. 3101, 20 December 1917, FO 371/3061/237728.
72 Cecil to Lloyd George, 27 December 1917, Lloyd George Papers, F/6/5/11.
73 Tel. Bertie to Balfour, no. 1556, 30 December 1917, minute Sykes, not dated, FO 371/3061/245443.
74 Hardinge to D.M.I., no. 245878/W/44, 2 January 1918, tel. Balfour to Wingate, no. 5, January 1918, FO 371/3056/245878.
75 Minutes Middle East Committee, 12 January 1917, Cab 27/22.
76 Minutes Middle East Committee, 26 January 1918, Cab 27/23.
77 Weizmann to Brandeis, 14 January 1918, FO 371/3394/21931.
78 Clayton to Wingate, private, 4 February 1918, Wingate Papers, box 148/5.
79 Clayton to Wingate, private, 15 March 1918, Wingate Papers, box 148/6.
80 Clayton to Balfour, no. P. 74, 19 May 1918, Bodleian Library, Milner Papers.
81 Sykes, memorandum, and Annex (A), E.C.-825, not dated, Cab 27/24.
82 Minutes Eastern Committee, 11 July 1918, Cab 27/24.
83 Minutes Eastern Committee, 18 July 1918, ibid.
84 Draft tel. C.I.G.S. to G.O.C.-in-C., Egypt, in DMI to Foreign Office, 21 July 1918, FO 371/3383/127256.

85 G.O.C.-in-C., Egypt to C.I.G.S., no. P. 387, 26 July 1918, Cab 27/29.
86 Minutes Eastern Committee, 29 July 1918, Cab 27/24.
87 Appendix, E.C.–1028, and minutes Eastern Committee, 8 August 1918, ibid.
88 Cecil, Draft (A), not dated, FO 371/3381/143456.
89 Wingate to Balfour, no. 127, 11 June 1917, FO 371/3054/125564.
90 Sykes to Clayton, 23 July 1917 and Clayton to Sykes, 20 August 1917, Sykes Papers, box 2.
91 Sykes to Clayton in tel. Balfour to Wingate, no. 1126, 26 November 1917, FO 371/3054/225623.
92 Clayton to Sykes, in tel. Wingate to Balfour, no. 1281, 28 November 1917, minute Graham, not dated, FO 371/3054/227658.
93 Sykes to Clayton, in tel. Balfour to Wingate, no. 1146, 1 December 1917, FO 371/3054/234304.
94 Sykes, Report on Visit to Paris, 25 December 1917, Sir Mark Sykes' speech at Paris, and M. Gouts speech to the Syrians in Paris, FO 371/3056/245878.
95 Tel. Wingate to Balfour, no. 320, 16 February 1918, minute Sykes, not dated, and tel. Balfour to Wingate, no. 262, 20 February 1918, FO 371/ 3380/30325.
96 Wingate to Clayton, private, 6 March 1918, Wingate Papers, box 148/6.
97 Tel. Wingate to Balfour, no. 399, 1 March 1918, minutes Nicolson, 2 March 1918 and Sykes, not dated, FO 371/3380/38817.
98 Sykes to Clayton, 3 March 1918, FO 800/221.
99 Tel. Wingate to Balfour, no. 1153, 2 November 1917, FO 371/3048/210013.
100 Clayton to Sykes, in tel. Wingate to Balfour, no. 1281, 28 November 1917, FO 371/3054/227658.
101 Tel. Wingate to Balfour, no. 1286, 29 November 1917, FO 371/3054/228069.
102 Clayton to Bell, 8 December 1917, Clayton Papers, G//S 513.
103 Wingate to Balfour, no. 90 (70/333), 7 May 1918, and 'Address Presented by Seven Syrians to H.C. Cairo on May 7th 1918', FO 371/3380/98499.
104 Tel. Balfour to Wingate, no. 753, 11 June 1918, Cab 27/27.
105 Wingate to Balfour, no. 127 (70), 25 June 1918, FO 371/3381/126861.
106 Sykes and Georges-Picot, Declaration to the King of Hejaz, 3 July 1918, Cab 27/28.
107 Sykes, Memorandum, E.C.-766, 3 July 1918, FO 371/3381/117108.
108 Sykes, Memorandum, E.C.–825, not dated, Cab 27/24.
109 Minutes Eastern Committee, 15 July 1918, ibid.
110 Minutes Eastern Committee, 18 July 1918, ibid.
111 Clayton to Sykes, 20 August 1917, Sykes Papers, box 2.
112 Tels Georges-Picot to Sykes, communicated by French embassy, 6 December 1917, and Clayton to Sykes in Wingate to Balfour, no. 1334, 12 December 1917, Sykes to Georges-Picot in tel. Balfour to Wingate, no. 1181, 15 December 1917, minute Hardinge, not dated, FO 371/3054/235780.
113 STATUS OF THE COMMISSION AND OBJECTS OF THE COMMISSION, encl. in Weizmann to Sykes, 16 January 1918, FO 371/3394/14214.
114 Minutes Middle East Committee, 19 January 1918, FO 371/3394/19932.

115 Instructions to Captain Hon. W. Ormsby-Gore on proceeding to Egypt with the Commission of Zionist leaders, 21 February 1918, FO 371/3394/32926.
116 Cornwallis, memorandum, 20 April 1918, FO 371/3394/85169.
117 Clayton to Sykes, 4 April 1918, FO 371/3391/76678.
118 Clayton to Sykes, 18 April 1918, Clayton to Balfour, 18 April 1918, and Clayton to Wingate, Personal, 21 April 1918, Wingate Papers, box 148/8.
119 Ormsby Gore to Hankey, 19 April 1918, Cab 21/58.
120 Storrs, Note by the Military Governor of Jerusalem, 30 April 1918, encl. in Clayton to Balfour, no. 10685/B/14, 7 May 1918, FO 371/3395/98470.
121 Ormsby Gore in Clayton to Balfour, no. I/1083b/10, 7 May 1918, FO 371/3395/99963.
122 Hogarth, REPORT ON MISSION TO JEDDAH, 15 January 1917, FO 371/3383/2577.
123 Tel. Clayton to Balfour, no. I.B. 1055, 2 April 1918, Cab 27/25.
124 In his report to the Zionist Organisation, Weizmann had been more concrete. This paragraph, however, never reached the Zionist Organisation as it was censored by Clayton:

> Dr Weizmann pushed the idea of collaboration a little further. He said that Jews and Arabs have parallel interests and thus it was possible for the Jews who were a great force to help him, to realise his great ambitions. We could help him towards Damascus and the territory to the North, which ought not to be encroached upon by the Powers who had really no interests there. By encroachment he meant France.

> In view of this, it is rather ironic that on 14 June Clayton was instructed to convey to Weizmann Balfour's 'appreciation of the tact and skill shown by him in arriving at a mutual understanding with the Sheikh'.
> Report Zionist Commission to Zionist Organisation, no. Z.C. 263, encl. in Clayton to Balfour, 11 July 1918, FO 371/3395/137853, and tel. Balfour to Clayton, no. 133, 14 June 1918, FO 371/3398/105824.

125 Tel. Clayton to Balfour, no. P. 174, 12 June 1918, Cab 27/27.
126 Symes, SECRET. NOTE, 13 June 1918 (underlining in original), Wingate Papers, box 148/10.
127 Wingate to Balfour, no. 129, 25 June 1918, minutes Sykes, Hardinge and Cecil, not dated, Sykes, MEMORANDUM ON EASTERN POLICY, FO 371/3381/123868.

Chapter 9: Since I Am So Early Done For, I Wonder What I Was Begun For!

1 Account of a Meeting Held at the Residency at 6 p.m. on 23 March 1918, Cab 27/25.
2 Tels Wingate to Balfour, no. 1050 and 1055, 9 July 1918, Cab 27/28.
3 Sykes, minute, 10 July 1918, FO 371/3389/121095.
4 Tel. Balfour to Wingate, no. 885, 15 July 1918, Cab 27/24.
5 Tel. Baghdad to Cairo, no. 6065, 23 July 1918, Cab 27/29.
6 Tel. Balfour to Wingate, no. 938, 27 July 1918, Cab 27/24.
7 Tel. Wingate to Balfour, no. 1156, 1 August 1918, Cab 27/29.

8 Tel. Balfour to Wingate, no. 961, 2 August 1918, FO 371/3390/133790.
9 S.S.I. to viceroy (rep. Cox), no. P. 3327, 2 August 1918, FO 371/3390/135458.
10 See tel. Civil Commisioner to S.S.I., no. 6489, 7 August 1918, Cab 27/30.
11 Tel. Wingate to Balfour, no. 1209, 12 August 1918, FO 371/3390/139940.
12 Tel. Wingate to Balfour, no. 1265, 26 August 1918, Cab 27/31.
13 Tel. Balfour to Wingate, no. 1051, 28 August 1918, FO 371/3390/147594.
14 Tel. Wingate to Balfour, no. 1308, 4 September 1918, minutes Hardinge and Cecil, not dated, FO 371/3390/152559.
15 Tel. Wingate to Balfour, no. 1405, 23 September 1918, and minute Sykes, 25 September 1918, FO 371/3390/161898.
16 Tel. Civil Commissioner to S.S.I., no. 8532, 9 October 1918, minute Sykes, not dated, FO 371/3390/171797.
17 Tel. Wingate to Balfour, no. 1827, 6 December 1918, FO 371/3390/202098.
18 Tel. Wingate to Balfour, no. 1857, 10 December 1918, FO 371/3390/203387.
19 Army Council to Foreign Office, no. 152/4920 (M.I.2), 23 December 1918, minute Crowe, 25 December 1919, FO 371/3390/210939.
20 I.O. to F.O., no. P. 5788, 28 December 1918, minutes Lawrence, not dated, Kidston, 1 January 1919, and Foreign Office to Army Council, 10 January 1919, FO 371/3390/213143.
21 Tel. S.S.I. to Civil Commissioner, no. P. 84, 16 January 1919, FO 371/4144/9966.
22 Minutes War Cabinet, 25 April 1917, Cab 23/2.
23 Hogarth, Note on the Anglo–Franco–Russian Agreement about the Near East, encl. in Director of the Intelligence Division to Foreign Office 13 July 1917, FO 371/3054/138899.
24 Hogarth to Clayton, 11 July 1917, Hogarth Papers.
25 Sykes to Clayton, 22 July 1917, Sykes Papers, box 2.
26 MEMORANDUM BY SIR MARK SYKES ON MR NICHOLSON'S NOTE REGARDING OUR COMMITMENTS, 18 July 1917, FO 371/3044/153075.
27 Sykes, MEMORANDUM ON THE ASIA-MINOR AGREEMENT, 14 August 1917, minutes Clerk, 16 August 1917, Graham, 17 August 1917, and Balfour, not dated, FO 371/3059/159558.
28 See Jeremy Wilson, *Lawrence of Arabia. The Authorised Biography of T.E. Lawrence* (London, 1989: Heinemann), pp. 442–5.
29 Clayton to Lawrence, Strictly Private, 20 September 1917, Clayton Papers, G//S 513.
30 Government Printing Office, *Proceedings of the Brest–Litovsk Peace Conference* (Washington, 1918: Government Printing Office), p. 8.
31 Ibid., pp. 40–1.
32 Minutes War Cabinet, 3 January 1918, Cab 23/5.
33 Minutes War Cabinet, 4 January 1918, ANNEX, 4 January 1918, Cab 23/5.
34 Robert Lansing, *The Peace Negotiations: A Personal Narrative* (Boston and New York, 1921: Houghton Mifflin), pp. 95–6.
35 Sykes, Anglo–French Agreement (Asia Minor) 1916, 16 February 1918, minute Hardinge, not dated, FO 371/3399/31030.
36 Sykes to Clayton, private, 3 March 1918, Sykes Papers, FO 800/221.
37 Clayton to Sykes, private, 4 April 1918, FO 371/3391/76678.

38 Clayton to Balfour, no. P. 74, 19 May 1918, Bodleian Library, Milner Papers.
39 India Office, 'Future of Mesopotamia', Note by Political Department, India Office, on points for discussion with Sir Percy Cox, no. B. 281, 3 April 1918 (underlining in original), Cox, 'The future of Mesopotamia', 22 April 1918, MINUTE BY SIR MARK SYKES ON SIR PERCY COX'S NOTE ON "THE FUTURE OF MESOPOTAMIA", not dated, Cab 27/25.
40 Minutes Eastern Committee, 24 April 1918, Cab 27/24.
41 Sykes, Memorandum, 3 July 1918, FO 371/3381/117108 and Paper B, not dated, annex to minutes Eastern Committee, 18 July 1918, Cab 27/24.
42 Minutes Drummond, 6 July 1918, and Hardinge, not dated, FO 371/3381/117108.
43 See minutes Eastern Committee, 15 and 18 July 1918, Cab 27/24.
44 Cecil, memorandum, 6 August 1918, Cecil Papers, Add. Mss. 51094.
45 Minutes Eastern Committee, 8 August 1918, Cab 27/24.
46 Hogarth, THE ARAB QUESTION, 9 August 1918, FO 371/3381/146256.
47 Hogarth to Cecil, 18 August, Cecil, draft Joint Declaration, not dated, Lloyd, Joint declaration by Great Britain and France to promote and assist the establishment of native independent governments in Arabia, not dated, minute Cecil, not dated, FO 371/3381/143456.
48 Sykes, minute, not dated, FO 371/3383/152395.
49 Georges-Picot to Sykes, 6 September 1918, and Sykes to Georges-Picot, Private and Confidential, 16 September 1918, Sykes Papers, FO 800/221.
50 Montagu, The War in the East, 5 July 1918, Wilson, Note on Mr Montagu's Memorandum 'The War in the East', 15 July 1918, Cecil, Note, 20 July 1918, Foreign Office, Departmental Note, 17 July 1918, Balfour, Note, 27 July 1918, and Curzon, 'The War in the East' (Functions of the Eastern Committee), 1 August 1918, Cab 27/24.
51 Cecil to Curzon, Curzon to Cecil, and Cecil to Curzon, 1 August 1918, Cecil Papers, Add. Mss. 51077.
52 Minutes Eastern Committee, 13 August 1918, Cab 27/24.
53 Hankey, diary entry, 20 August 1918, Hankey Papers, vol. 1/5.
54 Montagu to Cecil, Private & Confidential, 3 September 1918, Cecil Papers, Add. Mss. 51094.
55 Sykes to Hardinge, 29 July 1918, Sykes Papers, box 1.
56 Cecil to Balfour, August 1918, encl. in Cecil to Hardinge, 21 August 1918, Cecil Papers, FO 800/198.
57 Cecil to Balfour, 23 August 1918, Balfour Papers, Add. Mss. 49738.
58 Hardinge to Cecil, 20 August 1918, Balfour Papers, Add. Mss. 49748.
59 Cecil to Hardinge, 21 August 1918, Cecil Papers, FO 800/198.
60 Balfour to Cecil, 22 August 1918, Balfour Papers, Add. Mss. 49738.
61 Cecil to Balfour, 23 August 1918, ibid.
62 See Balfour to Drummond, 28 August 1918, Balfour Papers, Add. Mss. 49748.
63 Cecil to Balfour, 31 August 1918, Balfour Papers, Add. Mss. 49738.
64 Sykes to Cecil, 9 September 1918, Cecil Papers, Add. Mss. 51094.
65 Colonel A.P. Wavell, *The Palestine Campaigns* (London, 1931: Constable), p. 203.
66 Ormsby Gore to Sykes, 23 September 1918, Sykes Papers, FO 800/221.

67 Foreign Office to Director of Military Intelligence, no. 162014/W/44, 28 September 1918, FO 371/3389/162014.
68 Wilson, *Lawrence*, pp. 556, 1103, and Matthew Hughes, *Allenby and British Strategy in the Middle East 1917–1919* (London, 1999: Frank Cass), pp. 97–8.
69 Hughes, *Allenby and British Strategy in the Middle East 1917–1919* (London, 1999: Frank Cass), pp. 98–9.
70 Captain Cyril Falls, *Military Operations Egypt & Palestine from June 1917 to the End of the War*, Vol. II (London, 1930: H.M. Stationary Office), pp. 588–9, see also Elie Kedourie, *England and the Middle East: The Destruction of the Ottoman Empire 1914–1921* (London, 1987: Mansell), pp. 120–1, and Hughes, *Allenby*, p. 102.
71 Tel. Lawrence to General Headquarters, 1 October 1918, Wingate Papers, box 150/1.
72 Tel. Clayton to Balfour, no. 97, 8 October 1918, FO 371/3383/169078.
73 Tel. G.O.C.-in-C., Egypt to C.I.G.S., no. P.690, 6 October 1918, FO 371/3383/169524.
74 Chauvel, 'Meeting of Sir Edmund Allenby and the Emir Feisal at the Hotel Victoria, Damascus, on October 3rd. 1918', 22 October 1929, St Anthony's College, Allenby Papers.
75 Tels G.O.C.-in-C., Egypt to C.I.G.S., nos. P.700 and P.695, 7 October 1918, FO 371/3383/169524.
76 Clayton to Wingate, private, 11 October 1918, Wingate Papers, box 150/2.
77 See tel. Clayton to Balfour, no. 117, 13 October 1918, FO 371/3384/171754.
78 Tel. Clayton to Balfour, no. 122, 14 October 1918, FO 371/3384/172663.
79 Tel. Clayton to Balfour, no. 127, 15 October 1918, FO 371/3384/173729.
80 Tel. G.O.C.-in-C., Egypt to C.I.G.S., no. I 6901/P, 17 October 1918, FO 371/3384/175418.
81 Minute Crowe, 18 October 1918, on tel. Clayton to Balfour, no. 127, 15 October 1918, FO 371/3384/173729.
82 Balfour to Derby, no. 805, 23 September 1918, and Foreign Office to Director of Military Intelligence, 24 September 1918, FO 371/3383/162968.
83 Minutes Eastern Committee, 26 September 1918, Cab 27/24.
84 Cecil, minute, 27 September 1918, FO 371/3381/164551.
85 Foreign Office Memorandum, 30 September 1918, FO 371/3383/164945.
86 Tel. G.O.C.-in-C., Egypt to C.I.G.S., no. E.A. 1707, 30 September 1918, minute Crowe, not dated, FO 371/3383/165376.
87 Tel. Balfour to Wingate, no. 1200, 1 October 1918, FO 608/92/4704.
88 Minutes Eastern Committee, 3 October 1918, Cab 27/24.
89 Minutes War Cabinet, 3 October 1918, Cab 23/14.
90 Hankey, diary entry, 6 October 1918, Hankey Papers, vol. 1/5.
91 Cecil to Pichon, Confidential, 8 October 1918, FO 371/3384/170193.
92 The British government had not accepted Wilson's Fourteen Points. Because the naval blockade was Britain's most powerful weapon, they particularly objected to the Second Point, which demanded 'the absolute freedom of navigation upon the seas, outside territorial waters, alike in peace and in war, except as the seas may be closed in whole or in part by international action for the enforcement of international convenants'.

93 Crowe, minute, 10 October 1918, FO 371/3384/170193.
94 Cecil, note, 14 October 1918, FO 371/3384/172808.
95 Minutes War Cabinet, 14 October 1918, Cab 23/8.
96 Sykes, memorandum, 15 October 1918, Cab 27/34. Sykes's feeble reaction must surely be attributed to his decision that same day to quit the Middle East decision-making game in London. He suggested to Cecil that he better be sent out to Syria to act as a liaison between the British military authorities, the French and the Arabs, and to promote better relations between the three. On 24 October the Eastern Committee approved Sykes's mission. Hogarth explained to Clayton that he should not 'take Mark at his own valuation. His shares are unsaleable here and he has been sent out (at his own request) to get him away [...] you can take what line you like about him without fear of being let down.' Sykes, memorandum, 15 October 1918, Cab 27/34, Minutes Eastern Committee, 24 October 1918, Cab 27/24, and Hogarth to Clayton, private, 1 November 1918, Hogarth Papers.
97 Minutes Eastern Committee, 17 October 1918, Cab 27/24.
98 Cecil to Curzon, not dated, and Curzon to Cecil, not dated, and Balfour to Cambon, 17 October 1918, FO 371/3381/174471.
99 Cecil, note, 18 October 1918, FO 371/3384/176454.
100 French Embassy to Foreign Office, 19 October 1918, minute Cecil, not dated, FO 371/3381/174697.
101 See Cecil, notes, 21 October and 22 October 1918, FO 371/3381/177047.
102 French Embassy to Foreign Office, 22 October 1918, Sykes, Memorandum, not dated, Cecil, minute, not dated, Balfour to Cambon, <u>Confidential</u>, 25 October 1918, FO 371/3384/176523.
103 Tel. Balfour to Barclay, no. 6526, 31 October 1918, FO 371/3384/179246.
104 Tel. Barclay to Balfour, no. 4963, 3 November 1918, FO 371 /3384/182490.
105 Kidston, minute, 6 November 1918, FO 371/3384/183683.
106 *Draft Declaration respecting the Near East*, 30 October 1918, FO 371/3384/180528.
107 Minutes Eastern Committee, 17 October 1918, Cab 27/24.
108 Hogarth, memorandum, 11 November 1918, FO 371/3385/191249.
109 Tel. Clayton to Balfour, no. 185, 19 November 1918, FO 371/3385/189886.
110 Tel. Civil Commissioner to S.S.I., no. 9906, 16 November 1918, minute Kidston, 22 November 1918, FO 371/3385/191847.
111 Wingate to Allenby, private, 15 October 1918, Wingate Papers, box 150/3.
112 Allenby to Wingate, private, 18 October 1918, Wingate Papers, box 150/2.
113 Cecil, note, 28 October 1918, FO 371/3384/181025.
114 Minutes Eastern Committee, 29 October 1918, Cab 27/24.
115 Minutes War Cabinet, 29 October 1818, Cab 23/8.
116 House to Wilson, 30 October 1918, Government Printing Office, *Papers Relating to the Foreign Relations of the United States 1919, The Paris Peace Conference*, Vol. I (Washington, 1942: Government Printing Office), p. 407.
117 Notes of a Conference, 30 October 1918, I.C.-84, Cab 28/5.
118 French Embassy to Foreign Office, 8 November 1918, and minute Crowe, 10 November 1918, FO 371/3385/185939.

119 D.M.I. to Foreign Office, no. 771/13 (M.I.2), 13 November 1918, minutes Hardinge and Cecil, not dated, FO 371/3385/188562.
120 French Embassy to Foreign Office, 16 November 1918, minutes Hardinge and Cecil, not dated, see also Foreign Office to French Embassy, 23 November 1918, FO 371/3385/190910.
121 French Embassy to Foreign Office, 18 November 1918, minutes Crowe, 21 November 1918, and Hardinge and Cecil, not dated, FO 371/3385/191068.
122 Martin Farr, 'Waging democracy. The British general elections of 1918 reconsidered', *Cercles*, 21 (2011), p. 72; see also Kenneth O. Morgan, *Consensus and Disunity. The Lloyd George Coalition Government 1918–1922* (Oxford, 1979: Clarendon Press), p. 34.
123 Cecil to Lloyd George, 21 November 1918, and Lloyd George to Cecil, 22 November 1918, Lloyd George Papers, F/6/5/49 and 50.
124 Balfour to Lloyd George, 16 December 1918, Lloyd George Papers, F/3/3/50.
125 Curzon to Balfour, 23 November 1918, Balfour Papers, Add. Mss. 49734
126 See: minutes Eastern Committee, 7 January 1919, Cab 27/24.
127 Instead of the Eastern Committee, an Inter-Departmental Conference on Middle Eastern Affairs was instituted, in which the Foreign Office, the India Office and the War Office participated. This name was clearly too cumbersome. Within a few months people began to refer to it as the Eastern Committee.
128 French Embassy to Foreign Office, 30 November 1918, minutes Crowe, 4 December 1918 and Hardinge, not dated, Drummond, note, 5 December 1918, and minute Drummond, 29 December 1918, FO 371/3385/199469.

Chapter 10: Getting Out of This Syrian Tangle

1 Hardinge to Balfour, 10 October 1918, Lloyd George Papers, F/3/3/35.
2 Drummond to Davies, 12 October 1918, ibid.
3 Drummond to Davies, 16 October 1918, Lloyd George Papers, F/3/3/37.
4 Drummond to Davies, 19 October 1918, ibid.
5 Michael L. Dockrill and Z. Steiner, 'The Foreign Office at the Paris peace conference in 1919', *The International History Review*, 2/1 (1980), p. 58.
6 Dockrill and Steiner, 'The Foreign Office', p. 59.
7 Stephen Roskill, *Hankey: Man of Secrets*, Vol. II (London, 1970: Collins), p. 47. In his memoirs Hardinge, however, sounds distinctly bitter: 'unfortunately, Mr Lloyd George, whose knowledge of many of the problems involved was non-existent, insisted on employing a staff of his own unofficial creation who had no knowledge of French and none of diplomacy, and the Foreign Office organisation was consequently stillborn'. Hardinge of Penshurst, *Old Diplomacy: The Reminiscences of Lord Hardinge of Penshurst* (London, 1947: John Murray), p. 229.
8 Graham to Mallet, 19 April 1919, minute Vansittart, 29 April 1919, Mallet to Graham, 28 April 1919, FO 608/98/8365.
9 Tel. Civil Commissioner to S.S.I., no. 9926, 17 November 1918, FO 371/3385/192144.
10 Hirtzel, 'Policy in Arabia' (Note by India Office), 20 November 1918, Cab 27/37.

11 Minutes Eastern Committee, 27 November 1918, Cab 27/24.
12 Minutes Eastern Committee, 5 December 1918, ibid.
13 Minutes Eastern Committee, 16 December 1918, ibid.
14 Minutes Eastern Committee, 18 December 1918, ibid.
15 Minutes Eastern Committee, 9 December 1918, ibid.
16 Hankey, diary entry, 4 December 1918, Hankey Papers, Vol. 1/5. Two years later, Hankey added in his diary that 'there was absolutely no record or memorandum made at the time, and I believe my diary of Dec. 4th 1918 contains the only record [...] and that was secondhand from Ll.G. for I was not present [...] Thus and thus is history made!' Hankey, diary entry, 11 December 1920, in Roskill, *Hankey*, Vol. II, pp. 28–9.
17 Balfour to Lloyd George, private, 29 November 1918, Lloyd George Papers, F/3/3/45.
18 Hankey, MESOPOTAMIA, SYRIA, AND PALESTINE. SUGGESTED PROCEDURE, 19 December 1918, Lloyd George Papers, F/23/3/30.
19 Hankey, Secret, 21 December 1918, Lloyd George Papers, F/23/3/31.
20 Tel. G.O.C.-in-C., Egypt to C.I.G.S., no. E.A. 1843, 4 November 1918, Cab 27/36.
21 Tel. Wingate to Balfour, no. 1616, 4 November 1918, minutes Crowe, 6 November 1918, and Cecil, not dated, and tel. Balfour to Wingate, no. 1340, 8 November 1918, FO 371/3384/183445.
22 Tel. Wingate to Balfour, no. 1655, 9 November 1918, minute Kidston, 10 November 1918, and tel. Balfour to Wingate, no. 1351, 11 November 1918, FO 371/3385/186251.
23 Tel. Wingate to Balfour, no. 1686, 13 November 1918, minutes Kidston and Crowe, 14 November 1918, FO 371/3385/187977.
24 Tel. Derby to Balfour, no. 1576, 22 November 1918, minute Crowe, 23 November 1918, FO 371/3385/193622.
25 Tel. Grahame to Balfour, no. 1598, 25 November 1918, FO 371/3385/194171.
26 See French Embassy to Foreign Office, 9 December 1918, FO 371/3418/204157.
27 Balfour, note, 11 December 1918, FO 371/3386/205516.
28 See Jeremy Wilson, *Lawrence of Arabia: The Authorised Biography of T.E. Lawrence* (London, 1989: Heinemann), p. 595.
29 Faysal, Memorandum, confidential, 1 January 1919, minutes Toynbee and Mallet, 17 and 16 January 1919, and minute Balfour, not dated, FO 608/80/158.
30 Drummond to Balfour, 16 January 1918, Balfour Papers, FO 800/215.
31 Tel. Faysal to Zeid, 22 January 1919, FO 608/97/447.
32 House to Wilson, 30 October 1918, *FRUS*, Vol. I: 407.
33 Secretary's Notes of a Meeting, 30 January 1919, Government Printing Office, *Papers Relating to the Foreign Relations of the United States 1919, The Paris Peace Conference (FRUS)*, Vol. III (Washington, 1943: Government Printing Office), pp. 806–8.
34 Army Council to Foreign Office, no. 152/4953, 23 January 1919, FO 608/107/1239.
35 Tel. C.I.G.S. to G.O.C.-in-C., Egypt, no. 73975, 15 Jan 1919, FO 608/107/2443.
36 Tel. G.O.C.-in-C., Egypt to C.I.G.S., no. E.A. 2119, 18 January 1919, FO 608/107/1190.

37 Kirke to Corvisart, no. 0144/5123, 21 January 1919, and British Military Mission with the French Government to D.M.O., no. 4401, 26 January 1919, FO 608/107/2443.
38 Pichon, NOTE UPON THE BRITISH AIMS IN ASIA MINOR, 31 January 1919 (underlining in original), minutes Forbes Adam, 10 February 1919 and Hardinge, not dated, FO 608/107/1589.
39 Hardinge to Graham, private, 21 February 1919, FO 371/4178/21940.
40 Minutes Kidston, 10 February 1919, Graham, 11 February 1918, and Curzon, 13 February 1919, on Derby to Curzon, no. 144, 7 February 1919, ibid.
41 Tel. C.I.G.S. to G.O.C.-in-C., Egypt, no. 74815, 1 February 1919, FO 608/107/1693.
42 Tel. G.O.C.-in-C., Egypt to C.I.G.S., no. E.A. 2180, 4 February 1919, FO 371/4178/21940.
43 Military Section of the British Delegation at the Peace Conference, memorandum, 31 January 1919, FO 608/107/1101.
44 Sykes had arrived at Paris at the end of January. Hardinge had asked him 'to "stand by" for the time being', but on 11 February Sir Mark took to bed, one of the victims of the influenza pandemic that raged through Europe and killed millions of people. He did not recover, and died five days later. After he had heard of Sykes's death, Bertie noted in his diary: 'Poor Mark Sykes! He was a charming creature, a wonderful mimic and caricaturist, and *most* amusing. He was accepted by the War Cabinet as *the* expert on Eastern questions, but he was *roulé* over Syria, the Lebanon and Palestine by the French diplomat Picot.'

Lloyd George also believed that Picot had 'got the better' of Sykes and that the latter fully realised this. In consequence, Sykes had become: 'a worried, anxious man. That was the cause of his death. He had no reserve of energy. He was responsible for the agreement which is causing us all the trouble with the French [...] Sykes saw the difficulties in which he had placed us, and was very worried in consequence.' Minute Hardinge, not dated, FO 608/97/1503; Roger Adelson, *Mark Sykes: Portrait of an Amateur* (London, 1975: Jonathan Cape), pp. 294–5; Francis L. Bertie, *The Diary of Lord Bertie of Thame: 1914–1918*, Vol. II (London, 1924: Hodder and Stoughton), p. 317; and George A. Riddell, *Lord Riddell's Intimate Diary of the Peace Conference and After, 1918–1923* (London, 1934: Reynal and Hitchcock), p. 35.
45 Minute Mallet, not dated, FO 608/107/2443.
46 Tels C.I.G.S. to G.O.C.-in-C., Egypt, no. 74849, 2 February 1919, and G.O.C.-in-C., Egypt to C.I.G.S., no. E.A. 2176, 4 February 1919, FO 371/4178/20988.
47 C.E. Callwell, *Field-Marshal Sir Henry Wilson Bart. G.C.B. D.S.O.: His Life and Diaries*, II (London, 1927: Cassell), pp. 167–8.
48 Forbes Adam, Note, 1 February 1919, FO 608/96/1297.
49 Minutes of the 53rd Meeting of the Military Representatives, 4 February 1919, Cab 21/129.
50 British translation of the French draft of a proposed new Anglo–French agreement on Syria, not dated, FO 608/107/1562.
51 See statement, Pichon, 20 March 1919, Government Printing Office, *Papers Relating to the Foreign Relations of the United States 1919, The Paris Peace Conference (FRUS)*, Vol. V (Washington, 1946), p. 3.

484 BRITAIN AND THE ARAB MIDDLE EAST

52 Comments by the Foreign Office Section on the French memorandum, 6 February 1919, FO 608/107/1562.
53 *Secretary's Notes of a Conversation*, 6 February 1919, Lloyd George Papers, F/121.
54 Roskill, *Hankey*, Vol. II, p. 61.
55 Kerr to Lloyd George, 11 February 1919, Lloyd George Papers, F/89/2/7.
56 Kerr to Lloyd George, 12 February 1919, Lloyd George Papers, F/89/2/9.
57 Kerr to Davies, 13 February 1919, Lloyd George Papers, F/89/2/11.
58 Kerr to Lloyd George, 13 February 1919, Lloyd George Papers, F/89/2/10.
59 Bell and Lawrence, NOTE ON THE SETTLEMENT OF THE ARAB PROVINCES, 14 February 1919, Balfour Papers, FO 800/215.
60 Hirtzel, The French Claims in Syria, 14 February 1919, FO 608/107/2256.
61 Minute Milner, not dated, Milner Papers, PRO 30/30/10.
62 Minute Mallet, not dated, on Hirtzel, The French Claims in Syria, FO 608/107/2256.
63 Lawrence, note of a conversation between Emir Faysal and M. Goût, 24 February 1919, and of a conversation between the former and M. Briand, 25 February 1919, not dated, FO 608/93/3322.
64 Kerr to Lloyd George, 28 February 1919, Lloyd George Papers, F/89/2/24.
65 See French Ministry of Foreign Affairs, NOTE, 3 March 1919, FO 608/107/3486.
66 Minute Balfour, not dated, on tel. Curzon to Balfour, no. 794, 21 February 1919, FO 608/107/2983.
67 Milner to Balfour, not dated (underlining in original), and tel. Balfour to Curzon, no. 424, 5 March 1919, FO 608/107/3486.
68 Lloyd George, Notes of interview, 7 March 1919, Lloyd George Papers, F/147/1/1.
69 Milner to Lloyd George, Confidential, 8 March 1919, Milner Papers, PRO 30/10/10.
70 Milner to Hardinge, 8 March 1919 (underlining in original), FO 608/107/3927.
71 Minute Kidston, 15 March 1919, FO 371/4179/40673.
72 Curzon to Derby, no. 527, 19 March 1919, FO 371/4179/45562.
73 Curzon to Cambon, 19 March 1919, minute Hardinge, not dated, FO 608/107/4961.
74 House, diary entries, 10 and 12 March 1919, House Papers MSS 466.
75 Margaret MacMillan, *Peacemakers: Six Months that Changed the World* (London, 2001: John Murray), pp. 161–3.
76 Harold Nicolson, *Peacemaking 1919* (London, 1937: Constable), p. 70.
77 House, diary entry, 3 March 1919, House Papers, MSS 466.
78 John Maynard Keynes, *The Economic Consequences of the Peace* (New York, 1920: Harcourt, Brace and Howe), pp. 43, 50.
79 House, diary entries, 30 May and 29 June 1919, House Papers, MSS 466.
80 Balfour to Curzon, 20 March 1919, Balfour Papers, FO 800/215.
81 Notes of a Conference, 20 March 1919, *FRUS*, Vol. V, pp. 1–14.
82 Tel. Derby to Curzon, no. 540, 20 March 1919, minutes Clark Kerr and Curzon, 24 March 1919, FO 371/4179/44731.
83 Curzon to Balfour, private and confidential, 25 March 1919, Balfour Papers, FO 800/215.
84 Tel. Cheetham to Curzon, no. 231, 12 February 1919, FO 371/4178/25289.

85 Henry Wickham-Steed, *Through Thirty Years, 1892–1922: A Personal Narrative*, Vol. II (Garden City, 1924: Doubleday), p. 300.
86 Paul Mantoux, *Les Délibérations du Conseil des Quatre*, Vol. I (Paris, 1955: Centre National de la Recherche Scientifique), p. 49.
87 See *Future administration of certain portions of the Turkish Empire under the mandatory system*, not dated, FO 608/86/5314.
88 Mantoux, *Délibérations*, Vol. I, pp. 228–9.
89 Hankey to Balfour, 11 April 1919, FO 608/86/5422.
90 Minute Mallet, not dated, on Curzon to Balfour, no. 2123, 10 April 1919, FO 608/86/7030.
91 House, diary entry, 14 April 1919, House Papers, MSS 466.
92 Minute Mallet, not dated, on Curzon to Balfour, no. 2123, 10 April 1919, FO 608/86/7030.
93 Tel. Balfour to Curzon, no. 718, 18 April 1919, FO 608/86/7537.
94 Minute Toynbee, 19 April 1919, on Curzon to Balfour, no. 2298, 15 April 1919, FO 608/86/7675.
95 Curzon to Balfour, no. 3475, 26 May 1919, FO 608/93/11365.
96 Clemenceau to Faysal, 17 April 1919, encl. in Kerr to Mallet, 28 April 1919, FO 608/93/8653.
97 Lawrence to Kerr, 22 April 1919, Lothian Papers, GD 40/17/37.
98 Feysal to Clemenceau, 20 April 1919, encl. in Lawrence to Kerr, 22 April 1919, ibid.
99 House, diary entry, 21 April 1919, House Papers, MSS 466.
100 Notes of a Meeting, 22 April 1919, *FRUS*, Vol. V, p. 112.
101 Mantoux, *Délibérations*, Vol. I, pp. 378–9.
102 Notes of a Meeting, 25 April 1919, *FRUS*, Vol. V, p. 247.
103 Toynbee to Mallet, 26 April 1919, FO 608/86/8626.
104 Wickham-Steed, *Thirty Years*, Vol. II, p. 224.
105 Cambon to Curzon, 5 May 1919, FO 371/4180/68905.
106 OCCUPATION OF SYRIA BY BRITISH AND FRENCH TROOPS, not dated, ibid.
107 Curzon to Derby, no. 749, 8 May 1919, FO 371/4180/71025.
108 Wickham-Steed, *Thirty Years*, Vol. II, p. 325.
109 Kerr to Forbes Adam, 12 May 1919, FO 608/86/7537.
110 Minute Vansittart, 15 May 1919, on tel. Clayton to Curzon, no. 308, 6 May 1919, FO 608/86/9916.
111 Notes of a Meeting, 14 May, 1919, *FRUS*, Vol. V, p. 616.
112 Hogarth to Balfour, 20 May 1919, FO 608/86/10980.
113 Balfour to Lloyd George, not dated, Lothian Papers, GD 40/17/38.
114 House, diary entry, 20 May 1919, House Papers, MSS 466.
115 Notes of a Meeting, 21 May 1919, *FRUS*, Vol. V, pp. 760–6, and Mantoux, *Délibérations*, Vol. II, p. 143.
116 Hankey, diary entry, 21 May 1919, Hankey Papers, vol. 1/5. According to Sir Henry Wilson, the prime ministers had a 'first-class dog-fight'. Clemenceau's biographer Suarez relates that when Lloyd George had demanded an apology,

Clemenceau had cried that he would have to wait for it just as long as it would take to pacify Ireland! Thereupon, Lloyd George had seized Clemenceau by the collar. After the bystanders had separated the prime ministers, Clemenceau had offered Lloyd George satisfaction by means of a duel, by sword or by pistol, at the latter's choosing. Callwell, *Henry Wilson*, Vol. II, p. 194, Georges Suarez, *La vie orgueilleuse de Clemenceau* (Paris, 1930: Éditions de France), p. 576.

117 Notes of a Meeting, 22 May 1919, *FRUS*, Vol. V, pp. 807–12.
118 Balfour, 'Memo sent to P.M.', 22 May 1919 (underlining in original), Balfour Papers, Add. Mss. 49752.
119 Tel. Clayton to Curzon, no. E.A. 2440, 15 May 1919, minutes Mallet, 26 May 1919, Hardinge and Balfour, not dated, and Percy, 28 May 1919, and tel. Balfour to Clayton, no. 16, 29 May 1919, FO 608/86/11585.
120 The American commissioners first travelled to Constantinople, and subsequently visited Palestine, the Lebanon and Syria. They arrived at Jaffa on 10 June 1919, and returned to Constantinople on 21 July. They submitted their report to President Wilson at the end of August, but he did nothing with it. It was not even transmitted to the British and French governments.
121 Percy to Hardinge, 28 May 1919, FO 608/86/11309.
122 Tel. Allenby to Balfour, no. E.A. 2484, 30 May 1919, *DBFP*, Vol. IV, pp. 256–7.
123 Balfour, MEMORANDUM, 31 May 1919, Cab 21/153.
124 Notes of a Meeting, 31 May 1919, *FRUS*, Vol. VI, p. 132.
125 Tel. Balfour to Allenby, no. 48, 31 May 1919, *DBFP*, Vol. IV, p. 259.
126 In September 1919 Allenby explained that 'Feisal had probably not had more than 3,000 or 4,000 men at any one time'. Matthew Hughes quotes Alan Dawnay, who referred to a 'lightly equipped force of 3,000 men'. Notes of a meeting, 9 September 1919, Cab 21/153, Hughes, *Allenby*, p. 77.
127 Gribbon, memorandum, 12 June 1919, FO 608/96/14908.
128 Minute Vansittart, 19 June, 1919, on tel. Civil Commissioner to S.S.I., no. 6714, 14 June 1919, FO 608/80/13141.
129 Tel. Allenby to Curzon, no. E.A. 2529, 12 June 1919, *DBFP*, Vol. IV, pp. 275–6, minutes Kidston, Graham and Curzon, 23 June 1919, FO 371/4181/91666.
130 Tel. Allenby to Curzon, no. E.A. 2536, 15 June 1919, *DBFP*, Vol. IV, p. 277, minute Young, 25 June 1919, FO 371/4181/92879.
131 Tel. Balfour to Allenby, no. 59, 26 June 1919, FO 608/86/13968, minutes Kidston, Graham and Curzon, 27 June 1919, FO 371/4181/94284.
132 Balfour, memorandum, 26 June 1919, encl. in Balfour to Curzon, no. 1158, 2 July 1919, FO 371/4181/97958.
133 Tel. Allenby to Curzon, no. E.A. 2555, 24 June 1919, minute Kidston, 2 July 1919, FO 371/4181/96247.
134 Kerr to Lloyd George, 16 July 1919, Lloyd George Papers, F/89/3/4.
135 Notes of a Meeting, 18 July 1919, *FRUS*, Vol. VII, p. 193.
136 Balfour, Note, 18 July 1919, Balfour Papers, Add. Mss. 49734.
137 Kerr to Lloyd George, 23 July 1919. Lloyd George Papers, F/89/3/8.
138 Balfour to Curzon, no. 1208, 28 July 1919, FO 371/4182/109238.

139 Richard Meinertzhagen, *Middle East Diary, 1917–1956* (London, 1959: The Cresset Press), p. 26.
140 Kerr to Lloyd George, 6 August 1919, Lloyd George Papers, F/89/3/23.
141 Balfour, memorandum, 11 August 1919, *DBFP*, Vol. IV, pp. 340–9.
142 See Balfour to Curzon, 8 September 1919, Balfour Papers, Add. Mss. 49734.
143 Hankey to Curzon, CONFIDENTIAL, 15 August 1919, FO 371/4234/117065.
144 Davies to Kerr, 15 August 1919, Lloyd George Papers, F/89/4/9.
145 Kerr to Lloyd George, 18 August 1919, Lloyd George Papers, F/89/4/12.
146 Tel. Lindsay to Curzon, no. 1275, 16 August 1919, FO 371/4234/117185.
147 Tel. Balfour to Curzon, no. 1277, 18 August 1919, FO 371/4234/117652.
148 Earl of Ronaldshay, *The Life of Lord Curzon*, Vol. III (London, 1928: Boni and Liveright), p. 203.
149 Minutes War Cabinet, 19 and 20 August 1919, Cab 23/12.
150 Curzon to Balfour, 20 August 1919, Balfour Papers, Add. Mss. 49734.
151 Riddell, *Intimate Diary*, p. 112.
152 Tel. Meinertzhagen to Curzon, no. 422, 8 September 1919, minutes Kidston, 9 September 1919, FO 371/4182/126509.
153 Kerr to Lloyd George, 9 September 1919, Lloyd George Papers, F/89/4/19.
154 Notes of a Meeting, 9 September 1919, Cab 21/153.
155 Notes of a Meeting, 10 September 1919, ibid.
156 Kerr to Lloyd George, 11 September 1919, Lothian Papers, GD 40/17/1342/2
157 Notes of a Meeting, 10 September 1919, Cab 21/153.
158 Lloyd George to Clemenceau and Clemenceau to Lloyd George, 11 September 1919, *DBFP*, Vol. IV, pp. 379–80.
159 It would seem that this reference to the Sykes–Picot line was put in the aide-mémoire in order to humour the French, but it was highly problematic seeing that Fasayl's forces at the time occupied positions to the west of the line, while there were French contingents in Damascus and Aleppo.
160 *Aide-mémoire in regard to the Occupation of Syria, Palestine and Mesopotamia pending the Decision in regard to Mandates*, 13 September 1919, *DBFP*, Vol. I, pp. 700–1.
161 Notes of a Meeting, 15 September 1919, *DBFP*, Vol. I, pp. 691–3.
162 Minute Kidston, 18 September 1919, on tel. Grahame to Curzon, no. 1020, 14 September 1919, FO 371/4182/129835.
163 Tel. Meinertzhagen to Curzon, no. 441, 18 September 1919, and tel. Curzon to Meinertzhagen, 18 September 1919, FO 371/4182/130943.
164 Tel. Curzon to Meinertzhagen, no. 296, 19 September 1919, FO 371/4182/130943.
165 Curzon to Lloyd George, 18 September 1919, Lloyd George Papers, F/12/1/44.
166 Notes of a Meeting, 19 September 1919, *DBFP*, Vol. IV, pp. 395–404.
167 Notes of a Meeting, 23 September 1919, ibid., pp. 413–18.
168 Kidston to Curzon, 3 October 1919, FO 371/4183/132930.
169 Hankey to Churchill, 8 October 1919, Cab 21/154.
170 Campbell to Curzon, and Kidston to Curzon, 10 October 1919, FO 371/4183/132930.

171 Faysal to Lloyd George, 21 September 1919, *DBFP*, Vol. IV, pp. 406–9.
172 Curzon to Faysal, 9 October 1919, *DBFP*, Vol. IV, p. 449.
173 Clemenceau, Note, 10 October 1919, ibid., pp. 452–3.
174 Director of Military Operations to Foreign Office, 11 October 1919, minutes Kidston and Curzon, 11 October 1919, FO 371/4183/140241.
175 Lloyd George to Faysal, 10 October 1919, *DBFP*, Vol. IV, p. 452.
176 Notes of a Meeting, 13 October 1919, ibid., pp. 459–60.
177 Tel. Curzon to Derby, no. 1160, 13 October 1919, ibid., p. 463.
178 Tel. Curzon to Derby, 13 October 1919, ibid.
179 Clemenceau to Derby, 14 October 1919, ibid., pp. 468–9.
180 Roskill, *Hankey*, vol. II, p. 119.
181 Tel. Curzon to Derby, no. 1167, 15 October 1919, *DBFP*, Vol. IV, p. 473.
182 See tel. Curzon to Derby, no. 1170, 16 October 1919, FO 608/106/19691.
183 Curzon to Derby, 16 October 1919, *DBFP*, Vol. IV, p. 475.
184 Tel. Derby to Curzon, no. 33, 8 January 1920, ibid., p. 611.
185 See Derby to Curzon, no. 2394, 27 July 1919, *DBFP*, First Series, Vol. XIII (London, 1963: H.M. Stationary Office), pp. 317–20.

Chapter 11: We Regard Palestine as Being Absolutely Exceptional

1 G.O.C.-in-C., Egypt to C.I.G.S., no. E.A. 1808, 23 October 1918, FO 371/3384/178415, see also Bernard Wasserstein, *The British in Palestine. The Mandatory Government and the Arab–Jewish Conflict 1917–1929* (London, 1978: Royal Historical Society), pp. 18–20.
2 Trevor Wilson, *The Political Diaries of C.P. Scott, 1911–1928* (London, 1970: Collins), pp. 360–1.
3 Ormsby Gore, Memorandum on Zionist representation, 15 November 1918, FO 371/3417/189315.
4 Advisory Committee on Palestine, Proposals Relating to the Establishment of a Jewish National Home in Palestine, not dated, minutes Ormsby Gore, 19 November 1918, Crowe, 22 November 1918, Hardinge and Cecil, not dated, FO 371/3385/191828.
5 Tel. Clayton to Balfour, no. 190, 18 November 1918, FO 371/3385/191229.
6 Tel. Clayton to Balfour, no. 197, 20 November 1918, FO 371/3395/191998.
7 Tel. Clayton to Balfour, no. A.B. 850, 25 November 1918, FO 371/3385/195250.
8 Weizmann, NOTE on the INTERVIEW with Mr BALFOUR, 9 December 1918, FO 371/3385/203091.
9 Minutes Eastern Committee, 5 December 1918, Cab 27/24.
10 Minutes Eastern Committee, 16 December 1918, ibid.
11 Weizmann, INTERVIEW with EMIR FEISAL at the CARLTON HOTEL, December 11th 1918, encl. in Weizmann to Crowe, 16 December 1918, FO 371/3420/207372.
12 Tel. Weizmann to Eder, 17 December 1918, tel. Clayton to Balfour, no. 259, 31 December 1918, minutes Clark Kerr, 9 January 1919 and Curzon, 10 January 1919, FO 371/4170/1051.

13 Tel. Clayton to Balfour, no. 213, 5 December 1918, Cab 27/38.
14 Minute Curzon, 10 January 1919, FO 371/4170/1051.
15 Curzon to Balfour, 16 January 1919 (italics in original), Lloyd George Papers, F/3/4/4.
16 Balfour to Curzon, 20 January 1919 (italics in original), Lloyd George Papers, F/3/4/8.
17 Tel. Clayton to Allenby, no. 10, 9 January 1919, FO 371/4178/5161.
18 Walter Laqueur, *The Israel-Arab Reader: A Documentary History of the Middle East Conflict* (New York, 1970: Bantam Books), pp. 18-20.
19 Minutes Toynbee, 17 January 1919, and Ormsby Gore, not dated, FO 608/98/159.
20 See Ormsby Gore, Note on a conversation between Sir Louis Mallet and Mr Nahum Sokolov, 21 January 1919, FO 608/98/465.
21 Ormsby Gore, PALESTINE. Zionist Proposals regarding future constitution, 22 January 1919, minutes Mallet, not dated, FO 608/98/508.
22 Ormsby Gore to Sokolov, 24 January 1919, FO 608/98/633.
23 Kidston, note, 25 January 1919 and minutes Graham, 25 January 1919, and Curzon, 26 January 1919 (underlining in original), FO 608/99/2017.
24 Curzon to Balfour, 26 January 1919, minutes Drummond and Balfour, not dated (underlining in original) Balfour Papers, FO 800/215.
25 Minute Mallet, 30 January 1919, FO 608/98/1295.
26 *Statement of the Zionist Organisation regarding Palestine*, 3 February 1919, minutes Ormsby Gore, 12 February 1919, and Mallet, not dated, FO 608/99/1627.
27 Richard Meinertzhagen, *Middle East Diary, 1917-1956* (London, 1959: The Cresset Press), pp. 8-9.
28 Bourne to Talbot, 25 January 1919 (underlining in original), encl. in Lloyd George to Kerr, 15 February 1919, Lloyd George Papers, F/89/2/15.
29 Kerr to Lloyd George, 17 February 1919, Lloyd George Papers, F/89/2/22.
30 Balfour to Lloyd George, 19 February 1919, Lloyd George Papers, F/3/4/12.
31 *Secretary's Notes of a Conversation*, 27 February 1919, Lloyd George Papers, F/121.
32 Tel. Clayton to Curzon, no. 162/426, 28 February 1919, FO 608/107/3449.
33 Clayton to Curzon, 2 March 1919, FO 608/98/5171.
34 Notes of a Conference, 20 March 1919, *FRUS*, Vol. V, p. 13.
35 Balfour, note, 23 March 1919 (italics in original), and minute Clark Kerr, 4 April 1919, FO 371/4171/51811
36 House, diary entry, 26 March 1919, House Papers, MSS 466.
37 Hogarth to Clayton, 30 March 1919, Hogarth Papers.
38 Curzon to Balfour, private and confidential, 25 March 1919, Balfour Papers, FO 800/215.
39 Balfour to Samuel, 31 March 1919, Balfour Papers, Add. Mss. 49745.
40 See Balfour to Weizmann, private, 3 April 1919, FO 608/99/6950.
41 Samuel to Balfour, 7 April 1919, and Weizmann to Balfour, 9 April 1919, Balfour Papers, FO 800/216.
42 Weizmann to Drummond, 14 April 1919, FO 608/100/7396.
43 Tel. Clayton to Curzon, no. 140, 30 April 1919, FO 608/100/9208.

44 Tel. Clayton to Curzon, no. C. 155, 2 May 1919, minute Kidston, 6 May 1919, FO 371/4180/68848.
45 Thwaites to Hardinge, 13 May 1919, minutes Forbes Adam, 12 May 1919, and Mallet, not dated, FO 608/99/9567.
46 Advisory Committee on Economic Development in Palestine, 5th Meeting, 10 May 1919, FO 608/100/11752.
47 Balfour to Curzon, no. 760, 19 May 1919, FO 608/99/9567.
48 Tel. Curzon to Clayton, no. 181. Urgent, 27 May 1919, FO 371/4180/76242.
49 Tel. Clayton to Curzon, no. 338, 9 June 1919, FO 608/99/12759.
50 Clayton to Curzon, C.P.O. 190, 19 June 1919, *DBFP*, IV, p. 282.
51 The Secretary, Zionist Commission to Aaronsohn and Frankfurter, 8 May 1919, minute Meinertzhagen, 3 June 1919, FO 608/99/11592.
52 Tyrrell to Samuel, 31 May 1919, *DBFP*, IV, p. 283.
53 Samuel to Tyrrell, 5 June 1919, minutes Peterson, not dated, Kidston, 12 June 1919, Graham and Curzon, 13 June 1919, FO 371/4181/86424.
54 Minute Forbes Adam, 10 June 1919, FO 608/99/12093.
55 Frankfurter, Memorandum of an interview, 24 June 1919, *DBFP*, Vol. IV, pp. 1276–7.
56 Balfour, Memorandum, 26 June 1919, ibid., p. 302.
57 Balfour to Curzon, no. 1132, 1 July 1919, FO 371/4181/96834.
58 Graham, note of conversations with Mr Samuel and Dr Weizmann, 2 July 1919, minute Curzon, 3 July 1919, FO 371/4181/98082.
59 Minute Clayton, 8 July 1919, ibid.
60 Minutes of Meeting with General Clayton, Strictly Confidential, 9 July 1919, encl. in Clayton to Kidston, 23 July 1919, FO 371/4225/107282.
61 Minutes Clayton, 25 July 1919, Curzon, 27 July 1919, and Kidston, 4 August 1919, and tel. Curzon to French, no. 245, 4 August 1919, FO 371/4181/96834.
62 Bernard Wasserstein has pointed out that Money resigned of his own accord, 'mainly for private reasons'. He also quotes a letter Money sent to the editor of the *Daily Mail*, which was published on 12 January 1923, in which he denied that he 'had been recalled from Palestine as a result of Zionist pressure', and declared that he 'resigned for purely private reasons'. Wasserstein, *The British*, pp. 48, 49.
63 Weizmann to Balfour, 23 July 1919, minute Forbes Adam, 29 July 1919, FO 608/99/16465.
64 Balfour to Curzon, no. 1485, 1 August 1919, minutes Clark Kerr, 6 August 1919, and Curzon, not dated, FO 371/4233/111235.
65 Curzon to Balfour, 9 August 1919, Balfour Papers, Add. Mss. 49734.
66 Balfour, memorandum, 11 August 1919, *DBFP*, Vol. IV, pp. 345, 347.
67 Watson, Secret, no. 6145/P., 16 August 1919, encl. in French to Curzon, no. C.P.O. 31/110, 26 August 1919, FO 608/99/17239.
68 Curzon to Balfour, 20 August 1919, Balfour Papers, Add. Mss. 49734.
69 Notes of a Meeting, 9 September 1919, Cab 21/153.
70 Notes of a Meeting, 10 September 1918, ibid.
71 Notes of a Meeting, 11 September 1919, ibid.

72 Notes of a Meeting, 12 September 1919, ibid.
73 Ronaldshay, *The Life of*, Vol. III, pp. 204–5.
74 Meinertzhagen to Curzon, no. C.P.O. 31/1, 26 September 1919, minutes Peterson, 15 October 1919 and Kidston, 16 October 1919, FO 371/4184/141037.
75 Campbell, note, 28 October 1919, *Draft Declaration of [on] Zionism*, encl. in Meinertzhagen to Curzon, no. C.P.O. 31/1, 14 October 1919, *DBFP*, Vol. IV, pp. 470–3.
76 Minutes Peterson, 29 October 1919, Kidston and Tilley, 29 October 1919, Hardinge, not dated, Curzon, 30 October 1919, Tilley and Curzon, 5 November 1919, tel. Curzon to Allenby, no. 1216, 7 November 1919, FO 371/4184/146382.
77 Tels Meinertzhagen to Curzon, no. 495, 12 November 1919, and Curzon to Meinertzhagen, no. 340, 18 November 1919, *DBFP*, Vol. IV, p. 529.
78 Tels Curzon to Meinertzhagen, no. 351, 5 December 1919 and Meinertzhagen to Curzon, no. 513, 9 December 1919; ibid., p. 571; and minute Tilley, 17 December 1919, FO 371/4186/161583.
79 Meinertzhagen to Curzon, no. C.P.O. 181, 17 November 1919, minutes Kidston, 17 December 1919, and Vansittart, 19 December 1919, FO 371/4186/161829.
80 Comments of the Political Section of the British Peace Delegation, not dated, *DBFP*, Vol. IV, pp. 578, 580–2.
81 *Notes of an Anglo–French Meeting*, 23 December 1919, ibid., pp. 595–601. On the basis of her overview of Curzon's functioning during the latter's nine months as acting secretary of state for foreign affairs, Gaynor Johnson reaches the conclusion that 'Curzon's impact on [...] the conduct of British foreign policy was significant'. According to Johnson, 'Curzon effectively and convincingly fought of challenges to his authority at the Foreign Office from within the Cabinet and was looked to for leadership in the discussion of foreign policy by senior members of the British delegation at the peace conference'. After reading Chapters 10 and 11, it will be clear that this conclusion cannot stand as far as Syria and Palestine are concerned. In the case of Syria, Curzon disagreed with Lloyd George, but bowed to his wishes, while with respect to Palestine he disagreed with Balfour, but again bowed to his wishes, even after Balfour had left office. It is my strong impression that with Curzon it was enough if he could argue his case, show off his vast knowledge of the East, and that he refused to be bothered with the political manoeuvres, tactics and sweet talk necessary to convince others that it was also in their interest to adopt the policies he advocated. Winston Churchill in *Great Contemporaries* reached the same conclusion: 'one of Curzon's characteristic weaknesses was that he thought too much about stating his case, and too little about getting things done. When he [...] had brought a question before the Cabinet in full and careful form with all his force and knowledge, he was inclined to feel that his function was fulfilled.'

Gaynor Johnson, 'Preparing for office: Lord Curzon as Acting Foreign Secretary, January–October 1919', *Contemporary British History*, 18/3 (2004), pp. 69–70; Winston S. Churchill, *Great Contemporaries* (London, 1948: Odhams Press), p. 219.
82 Tel. Curzon to Hardinge, no. 38, 26 April 1920, *DBFP*, Vol. XIII, p. 251.
83 *British Secretary's Notes of a Meeting*, 25 April 1920, *DBFP*, Vol. VIII, pp. 172–3.
84 Tel. Curzon to Hardinge, no. 38, 26 April 1920, *DBFP*, Vol. XIII, p. 251.

INDEX OF NAMES

Aaronsohn, Aaron, 399
Abd al-Aziz ibn Rashid, 26, 37, 245
Abd al-Aziz ibn Sa'ud, sultan of Najd, 16, 26, 159, 233, 245–7, 249, 275–9, 424
Abd al-Qadir al-Jazairi, 299
Abdullah, second son of Husayn ibn Ali, 7, 14, 23, 27, 30–1, 52, 54, 77, 113, 115–16, 127, 138, 158, 249–50, 277, 279, 325
Abdurrahman, S., 24–5
Abrahams, Sir Lionel, 222
Ahad Ha'am, 198
Alexander, David L., 209, 211
Ali, eldest son of Husayn ibn Ali, 113, 127, 139, 184
Allenby of Megiddo, Edmund Henry Hyman, Viscount, 8, 227–9, 231, 233, 254–8, 297–302, 313, 330–1, 336–8, 344–5, 350–1, 355, 358–66, 369–72, 374, 378, 382, 387, 397–8, 402–3, 406–7, 409, 411, 462n19
Allison, Graham T., 441n2

Amery, Leopold Charles Maurice Stennet, 199, 218, 221, 223
Amet, Jean-François, 314
Asquith, Herbert Henry, 17, 49, 78, 90, 94–5, 104, 134, 139, 144, 149, 191–2, 198, 420, 459n94
al-Ayubi, Shukri, 299–300

Balfour, Arthur James, 8, 66, 78, 95, 104, 124, 132, 134–5, 145, 149, 169, 189–90, 198, 202–4, 208, 213–15, 217–20, 224, 226–8, 231, 233, 236–7, 240–2, 246, 251–3, 256, 261–2, 268, 275, 281, 283, 286, 288, 293, 295–6, 301–2, 306, 309, 314, 316, 318–20, 322–3, 326–30, 332, 334–6, 339, 342, 344–5, 348–9, 351, 353, 356–7, 359–60, 364–9, 381–2, 384, 387, 389, 391–2, 394–7, 399–402, 404–6, 408–9, 411, 419–20, 459n94, 460n113, 476n124
Barclay, Colville, 311
Bassett, J.R., 248, 252

Belin, Émile, 339–40
Bell, Gertrude Margaret Lowthian, 229, 261, 325, 342–3, 471n146
Berthelot, Philippe, 353, 412–14
Bertie of Thame, Francis Leveson, Viscount, 70, 74, 79, 95–6, 160, 191–2, 195, 197, 204–6, 238, 243–4, 254, 297, 483n44
Bliss, Howard, 339
Bonar Law, Andrew, 101, 134, 144–5, 147, 149, 318, 371–2, 407
Borton, Neville Travers, 473n48
Boselli, Paolo, 212
Bourne, Francis Alphonsus, Cardinal, 393
Brandeis, Louis, 218, 220–1, 255, 401
Brémond, Edouard, 234–8
Briand, Aristide, 69, 71, 96, 197, 344, 352
Buchanan, Sir George William, 104–5, 195–6, 206, 208, 214

Cabot Lodge, Henry, 348, 365
Caix, Robert de, Viscount, 207, 356
Callwell, Sir Charles Edward, 80, 92, 117–19
Calthorpe, Sir Somerset, 314–15
Cambon, Jules, 203, 211
Cambon, Paul, 19, 69, 71, 74–5, 83, 85, 102, 104, 112–13, 195, 203, 242, 301, 303, 308–11, 315–17, 319–20, 327, 329, 332, 337, 347, 355
Campbell, Ronald, 376
Carr, Edward Hallett, 424

Cecil, Lord Edgar Algernon Robert, 117, 149, 166, 185–6, 194, 204, 206–9, 211, 213–14, 217–18, 233, 239, 241–2, 252–5, 257–8, 265, 272–3, 275, 279, 289, 311–13, 316–18, 325, 327–8, 330, 350, 383–5, 420–1, 460n113, 468n89, 469n104, 480n96
Chamberlain, Austen, 54–5, 64–6, 72–5, 84, 87, 101, 104, 106–8, 110, 114, 121, 132, 134, 139–40, 142, 145, 147, 149–50, 156, 418–19, 451n4, 459n94
Cheetham, Sir Milne, 18, 20–1, 30–1, 34, 70
Chelmsford, Frederic John Napier, Viscount, 459n94
Cherchali, Si Mustapha, 238
Chetwode, Sir Philip, 227
Churchill, Winston Spencer, 47, 375, 491n81
Clark Kerr, Archibald, 351, 396, 404
Clayton, Sir Gilbert Falkingham, 18, 21, 26, 34, 37–8, 40, 45–6, 52–3, 55, 58–60, 67, 70, 76–7, 80–1, 88–90, 92–3, 95, 97, 103–6, 109–10, 112–13, 119–20, 127, 129, 145, 151, 154, 170–2, 175–7, 180–4, 228–31, 233, 247, 254–5, 258–61, 266–70, 281, 283, 286, 299–301, 312, 360–1, 367, 370, 383–4, 387, 395–9, 402–4, 406, 408–9, 465n22, 471n146, 473n48, 476n124, 480n96
Clemenceau, Georges, 8, 306, 314, 322, 329–30, 335, 338, 340, 342, 344–9,

351–7, 361–2, 365, 367–8, 370, 372–7, 379, 382, 395, 413–14, 419–20, 486n116
Clerk, Sir George Russell, 14–15, 21, 28, 35, 48, 50, 53–4, 59–60, 62, 69, 75–6, 78, 80, 86, 90, 112–13, 115–17, 119, 124, 128, 138, 141, 152–3, 158, 160, 183–4, 186–7, 197, 224, 231, 235, 241–3, 282
Cohen, L.L., 222–3
Cornwallis, Kinahan, 113, 129, 267–8
Coulondre, Captain, 300
Cox, Sir Percy Zachariah, 1, 22, 65, 120, 245–7, 251, 276, 278, 287, 305, 325
Crane, Charles R., 352, 354
Crewe, Robert Offley Ashburton, Marquess of, 15–16, 22, 29–30, 41, 49, 51, 78, 87, 90, 95–6, 101, 111, 128, 191, 195, 418, 444n58
Cromer, Evelyn, Lord, 41–5, 458n67
Crowe, Sir Eyre, 280, 295–7, 301, 304, 308–9, 315–17, 319, 331–2, 364, 383
Cumberbatch, A.H., 20
Curzon of Kedleston, George Nathaniel, Earl, 8, 42, 45, 132, 134–5, 139–40, 142, 145, 149, 174, 183, 190, 202, 217, 220, 224–6, 233, 237, 241, 251–3, 257, 265, 275, 287–8, 293–5, 302, 304, 306, 308–9, 314, 318, 322, 325–8, 337, 339, 345, 347–8, 351, 353, 355, 363–4, 368–71, 374, 376–7, 379, 381, 385, 387, 390–1, 395–6, 399, 401–4, 406, 408, 411, 413–15, 419–20, 422, 444n58, 452n33, 462n21, 491n81

Czernin, Ottokar, Count, 284

Davies, J.T., 322–3, 342, 368, 370
Dawnay, Alan, 486n126
De Bunsen, Sir Maurice William Ernest, 91
Defrance, Albert, 69
Derby, Edward Stanley, Earl of, 297, 302, 332, 379
Devey, G.P., 25
Djemal Pasha, 148, 250, 299
Drummond, Sir James Eric, 224, 226, 241, 289, 295–6, 319–20, 322–3, 334, 389, 391
Dugdale, Blanche, 459n94

Eder, David, 386–7, 390
Enver Pasha, 17, 111, 468n93

Fakhri Pasha, 127
Falls, Cyril, 298
al-Faruqi, Muhammad Sharif, 58–60, 63, 69, 73–4, 76, 92–3, 105, 107–8
Faysal, third son of Husayn ibn Ali, 113, 127–9, 131, 142, 177–8, 184, 236, 245, 260–1, 270–1, 297, 299–301, 314, 318, 322, 326, 330–4, 336–7, 340–6, 349–50, 352–4, 357, 360, 362–4, 369–79, 383–4, 386–8, 463n35
Fitzgerald, Oswald, 59, 91, 119, 444n47
Fitzmaurice, Gerald Henry, 19, 91, 96
Foch, Ferdinand, 329
Forbes Adam, Eric Graham, 334, 337, 356, 398, 401, 404, 412–13, 415

Frankfurter, Felix, 396, 399
French, John, 403–4, 409
Friedman, Isaiah, 470n129

Gallieni, Joseph, 71
Gaster, Moses, 199, 464n16
Gauchet, Dominique-Marie, 314
Georges-Picot, François, 8, 75–6, 80, 84–5, 89–90, 97–104, 108–9, 112–13, 165, 168, 170, 174, 179–83, 195–6, 200–1, 203–4, 228–9, 236–7, 239, 242–4, 254–5, 257, 264, 266, 280, 283, 286, 288, 290–1, 303, 308, 312, 314, 338, 422, 449n33, 483n44
Gilbert, S., 210
Gouraud, Henry Joseph Eugène, 378
Goût, Jean, 255, 259–60, 308, 344, 353, 355–6
Graham, Sir Ronald William, 153, 170, 174–5, 179, 183, 185, 187, 203–4, 206–8, 211, 213–15, 219–20, 224, 226–7, 230, 236–9, 240–3, 254, 259, 283, 296, 323–4, 337, 363–4, 390, 401–2, 460n113, 467n80, 468n89
Grant, A.H., 120
Graves, Philip, 31
Grey, Sir Edward, 7, 13–14, 17–23, 27–9, 31, 33–4, 36, 38, 40–1, 43–5, 48–9, 51, 53–5, 57, 64–7, 69, 70, 72–6, 78, 80, 83–4, 89, 95, 100–1, 104, 106, 108, 112–13, 115–16, 131–2, 134–40, 142, 144, 147, 149, 158, 160, 183–4, 190–2, 196–8, 236–7, 417–20, 424, 444n58, 449n23, 451n4, 456n28, 457–8n67

Gribbon, Walter H., 362–3, 398, 407, 413

Hall, Sir Reginald, 98–100
Halperin, Morton H., 441n2
Hamilton, Sir Ian, 58–9, 71
Hankey, Sir Maurice Pascal Alers, 66, 96, 135, 143, 149, 167, 185, 203, 215, 219, 222, 224, 241, 252–3, 295, 307, 323, 329–30, 342, 353, 358, 368–9, 371, 373–5, 378, 407, 482n16
Hardinge of Penshurst, Charles, Baron, 15–16, 22, 29, 36, 38, 40–4, 50, 64, 67–8, 72, 74–5, 84, 88, 97, 116, 120, 128, 137, 141–2, 144, 146, 152–3, 158, 183–6, 197, 206–7, 210, 219, 229, 234–6, 238, 240–4, 248, 252, 254–5, 262, 266, 272–3, 279, 285, 289, 295–7, 315–17, 319, 322–3, 337, 346–7, 360–1, 383, 398, 411, 415, 417, 444n58, 452n33, 460n113, 474n64, 481n7, 483n44
Harmsworth, Cecil, 318
Headlam-Morley, James, 323
Henderson, Arthur, 149
Herbert, Aubrey, 70, 91, 418
Herzl, Theodor, 470–1n135
Hertz, Joseph Herman, 222–3
Hirtzel, Sir Arthur, 15, 22, 31, 53, 72, 86–7, 99–101, 110, 119–20, 241, 295–6, 324, 327–8, 343, 451n4
Hogarth, David George, 113, 125, 129, 148, 182, 247–8, 250, 263–4, 269, 281–2, 290, 312, 353, 356, 396, 480n96
Holderness, Sir Thomas William, 55, 64–5, 72, 98, 100–1, 139, 241

House, Edward Mansell, 217–18, 221, 224, 314, 329, 335, 347–8, 353–4, 357, 396
Hughes, Matthew, 486n126
Husayn, Ibn Ali, emir of Mecca, 7–8, 24, 26–7, 31, 43, 45, 57, 67, 73–4, 77, 84, 86, 99, 113–16, 123, 127, 130, 132, 135, 138, 141, 147–8, 151–60, 165, 170–1, 175, 177–84, 233, 235–6, 240, 245–52, 261, 264, 269, 272, 275–80, 325, 331–2, 375, 417–19, 422–4, 443n38, 451n4, 456n31

al-Idrisi, ruler of Asir, 26, 36–8, 245, 276
Islington, John Dickson-Poynder, Baron, 251

Jackson, Sir Henry, 65, 135
Janis, Irving L., 441n42
al-Jazairi, Sa'id, 299
Johnson, Gaynor, 491n81
Jones, Dally, 186
Joyce, Pierce Charles, 270
Jusserand, Jean Jules, 311

Kedourie, Elie, 448n7, 449n24
Kerr, Philip, 218, 342, 344–5, 356, 360, 365–6, 368, 370–3, 376, 393, 469n109
Keynes, John Maynard, 348
al-Khatib, Fu'ad, 154–5, 157, 178–80, 182
Kidston, George Jardine, 280, 313, 319, 331–2, 337, 347, 363–4, 370, 374, 376–7, 390, 398, 401, 404, 409–10, 412
King, Henry, 352–4
Kitchener of Khartoum, Herbert Horatio, Earl, 17–24, 26–9, 54–5, 57, 60, 64, 66, 69–70, 76, 78–9, 81, 90–1, 95–6, 101, 104, 106, 112, 114, 197, 417, 444n58, 457n67
Knowles, David, 424

Lake, Sir Percy, 106, 120, 176
Landman, Samuel, 401, 404
Lansing, Robert, 395
Laughlin, Irwin, 308
Lawrence, Thomas Edward, 141, 145, 147–8, 182, 234, 236, 245–6, 279–80, 283, 299, 313–14, 331–4, 337–8, 342–3, 352–4, 365, 388, 448n7
Lindsay, Ronald, 368
Lloyd, George Ambrose, 91–2, 180, 236–7, 244, 290
Lloyd George, David, 8, 34, 78, 95, 132, 135, 144, 149, 156, 166–8, 174, 178, 189–92, 195, 198, 202–5, 208, 213, 217, 219–20, 222, 224, 237, 253, 281, 283–5, 306–7, 314–15, 317–18, 320, 322–3, 329–30, 335, 339–42, 344–5, 347–8, 350–7, 361, 364–5, 367–8, 370–2, 374–9, 382, 393, 395, 401, 405–8, 414, 419–22, 456n31, 459n94, 462n19, 467n82, 481n7, 483n44, 485–6n116
Long, Walter, 469n101
Longhurst, Cyril, 215

Lybyer, Albert, 353, 355

Macdonogh, Sir George Mark Watson, 98–100, 109, 255–6, 258, 294, 326
Magnus, Sir Philip, 222–3
Malcolm, James, 199, 207
Mallet, Sir Louis du Pan, 18, 23–4, 323–4, 334, 338–9, 341, 343–4, 353, 360, 364, 388–9, 391–2, 398
al-Maraghi, Muhammad M., 41
al-Masri, Aziz Ali, 17–18, 21–2, 31, 58, 69, 105, 107–8, 139
Maude, Sir Frederick Stanley, 176
Maurice, Sir Frederick Barton, 156–7
Maxwell, Sir John Grenfell, 22, 37, 59–61, 63, 70, 76–7, 81, 89–90, 105, 418
McMahon, Sir Arthur Henry, 7, 31, 35–8, 40–1, 43–4, 49–51, 53–5, 57, 60–3, 66–74, 76–8, 80–1, 85–9, 102, 105–8, 110–11, 113–16, 124–6, 128–32, 135–9, 159–60, 183–5, 234, 241, 353, 417–18, 444n58, 447n61, 449n23, 24, 451n4, 457–8n67
Meinertzhagen, Richard, 366, 370, 374, 392, 398–9, 408–9, 411–12
Millerand, Etienne, 69
Milner of St James's and Cape Town, Alfred, Lord, 149, 156, 190, 207, 216–18, 220–1, 241, 342–7, 357, 469n104
al-Mirghani, Ali, 43, 51
Money, Sir Arthur, 382, 387, 397–9, 404, 406, 408–9, 490n62
Monro, Sir Charles, 71

Montagu, Edwin Samuel, 1–2, 189–90, 192, 197, 211, 216–18, 220–2, 226, 256, 265, 280, 292–5, 304–5, 325, 419, 467n82, 469n101, 469n104
Montefiore, Claude Joseph Goldsmid, 209, 222–3
Montgomery, George, 356
Morgenthau, Hans, 4
Morgenthau, Henry, 214, 468n93
Morison, Sir Theodore, 47
Murray, Sir Archibald James, 7, 65, 78, 96, 124–33, 135–8, 140, 145–6, 148, 150, 154–7, 166–7, 171–3, 181, 199, 227, 234, 462n19

Newcombe, Stewart Francis, 180, 463n35
Nicolson, Sir Arthur, 15, 31, 34–6, 50–1, 54–5, 74–5, 78, 84–5, 87, 90, 97–8, 100–2, 104, 106, 108, 110–14, 116, 120, 195, 444n58, 452n33, 465n22
Nicolson, Harold George, 185–6, 196, 210, 215, 241, 260, 281, 348
Nixon, Sir John, 65, 67, 176

O'Beirne, Hugh, 196–7
Olden, Arthur Charles Niquet, 299
Oliphant, Lancelot, 20, 31, 34, 36, 50, 53, 72, 78, 91, 102, 105–6, 110–13, 115, 128, 185–6, 193, 196–7, 205, 207–9, 211, 219, 239, 294
Orlando, Vittorio Emanuele, 306, 314, 348
Ormsby Gore, William George Arthur, 207–8, 215–19, 222, 231, 267, 269, 297, 382–3, 388–9, 392

Pacelli, Eugenio, Archbishop, 211
Paléologe, Maurice, 104, 112
Parker, Alfred Chevalier, 80, 89, 129
Pearson, H., 154–5
Percy, Lord Eustace, 361
Peterson, Maurice Drummond, 400, 409–10
Philby, Harry St John Bridger, 246–9, 277–9
Piépape, Philpin de, 382
Pichon, Stephen, 254–5, 307–8, 310, 314, 316–17, 329, 332, 336, 344, 346–7, 349–50, 353, 355, 357
Poincaré, Raymond, 19
Polk, Frank, 368, 378, 407
Popper, Karl Raimund, 6

Reinharz, Jehuda, 470n135
Renton, James, 471n135
Ribot, Alexandre, 166, 204–5, 211
Rida, Rashid, 38, 235
Ridell, Lord George, 370
Rikabi, Ali Riza Pasha El, 382
Robertson, Sir William Robert, 96, 124, 127–8, 130–2, 134–40, 142–5, 147–50, 155–6, 166–8, 173, 176, 229, 234, 255, 419
Rosov, Israel, 212
Rothschild, Dorothy de, 197
Rothschild, James de, 197, 200–1
Rothschild, Walter, Lord, 189–90, 200, 211, 214–15, 219–20, 222–4, 227, 387, 399

Russell, R.E.M., 17
Ryan, Andrew, 28

Sacher, Harry, 214–15, 470n135
Sackville-West, Charles, 339–40
as-Sa'id, Nuri, 22
Samuel, Herbert Louis, 189–93, 196–200, 222–3, 391, 396–7, 400, 402–3, 409
Samuel, Sir Stuart, 211, 222–3
Sazonov, Sergei, 104–5, 112, 196
Schimmelfennig, Frank, 441n2
Scott, Charles Prestwich, 193, 202, 207–8, 468n93
Selim I, 442n6
Shuckburgh, John Evelyn, 294
Simon, Leon, 470–1n35
Slade, Sir Edmond, 16
Smuts, Jan Christiaan, 256, 258, 265, 295, 305–6, 323, 326
Sokolow, Nahum, 200–1, 203–4, 207, 211–14, 222–3, 266, 388–9, 394
Sonino, Baron Sydney, 205, 314, 342
Spears, Edward, 336
Stanley, Venetia, 192
Stein, Leonard, 470n129
Steinbruner, John D., 441n2
Storrs, Ronald, 25–7, 52–3, 59, 77, 81, 113, 115–16, 124, 129, 246–7, 269, 443n47, 448n7, 473n48
Suarez, Georges, 485n116
Sutherland, William, 220
Swinton, Ernest D., 216
Sykes, Sir Tatton Benvenuto Mark, Baronet, 1–2, 90–100, 102, 104–5,

108–10, 112–13, 116–17, 119–21, 128–9, 133–4, 165–6, 168, 170, 174–83, 195–6, 199–4, 206, 208, 211, 226, 229–31, 233, 235–7, 239–45, 247–8, 251–5, 257–8, 260–2, 264–8, 272, 277, 279–82, 285–8, 290–1, 295–7, 301–4, 308–9, 311–12, 337–8, 417–18, 421–3, 455n94, 459n21, 465n22, 474n64, 480n96, 483n44

Symes, George Stewart, 38–41, 45, 47, 52, 270–1

Talaat Pasha, Mehmet, 468n93
Talbot, Lord Edmund, 393
Tardieu, André, 356, 358
Thwaites, Sir William, 305, 315, 398–9
Tilley, John Anthony Cecil, 410–11
Townshend, Sir Charles Vere Ferrers, 176
Toynbee, Arnold Joseph, 333, 341, 353, 355, 388
Trotsky, Leon, 283
Tyrrell, Sir William George, 400

Vansittart, Robert Gilbert, 323, 356, 363, 412–13, 415
Vehib Bey, 24
Viviani, René, 69

Waley, E.G., 409
Wasserstein, Bernard, 490n62
Waterfield, A.P., 185–6
Watson, Harry D., 404–5, 408–9
Wavell, Archibald, 297

Weakley, Ernest, 133–4
Weizmann, Chaim, 189–91, 193–4, 197–9, 202–3, 207–8, 213–14, 218–20, 222–3, 231, 255, 266–73, 382–4, 386–91, 394–8, 402, 404–5, 409, 411, 468n89, n93, 469n109, 470–1n135, 476n124
Wemyss, Sir Rosslyn Erskine, 129, 135, 139–42, 146–7
White, Henry, 365
Wickham-Steed, Henry, 352, 355–6
Wilson, Arnold Talbot, 92, 278, 280, 312–13, 324, 352
Wilson, Cyril Edward, 59, 115, 128–30, 135, 138, 140, 148, 151–7, 159–60, 171–2, 175–6, 179–80, 184, 234–6, 245, 248, 277–9
Wilson, Sir Henry Hughes, 292–3, 330, 339, 356, 358–9, 485n116
Wilson, Jeremy, 448n7
Wilson, Thomas Woodrow, 217–18, 221–2, 271, 283, 285, 288, 306–7, 309–11, 320, 326, 328, 335, 339, 342, 348, 350–2, 354–5, 357, 359, 364–5, 369, 395, 401, 407, 486n120
Wingate, Sir Francis Reginald, 37–8, 40–6, 49–53, 55, 59, 67, 76–7, 81, 88–90, 93, 103, 115, 123–9, 133, 136–43, 146–8, 150–61, 169–72, 175, 177, 181, 184–7, 228–9, 231, 233–7, 239–40, 244, 246–7, 249–52, 254–5, 258, 260–3, 268, 270–3, 276–9, 300, 313, 330–1, 417–19, 446n48, 457–8n67, 461n135, 465n22, 473n48

Wiseman, Sir William, 224
Wolf, Lucien, 193–5, 197, 205–6, 208–11, 464n16

Young, Hubert, 363

Zeid, fourth son of Husayn ibn Ali, 113, 116, 334

INDEX OF SUBJECTS

Abdullah, second son of Husayn ibn Ali, characterization of, 46, 325
    letter to Storrs, 52
    position *vis-à-vis* his father, 46
    visits to Cairo 23–6
Acre, 97–8, 200, 207, 407, 413
Advisory Committee on Palestine (Samuel Committee), 383–4, 398
aide-mémoire of 13 September 1919, 372–6, 407–8, 487n159
Akaba, 124, 270
Alexandretta, British and French claims to, 48, 75, 98, 328
    landing of troops at, 34–5, 58, 78–80, 86, 89, 92–3, 95, 124
Anglo–Jewish Association, 193, 211
'The Anti-Semitism of the Present Government', 216
Arab Bureau, 113, 117–21, 156, 171, 267
'Arab façade', 287, 305
Arab nationalist movement, 185

Arab nationalist territorial ambitions, 38–44, 47–8, 52–3, 56–7, 62–3, 93, 262, 341
Arabian Peninsula, French recognition of British political predominance in, 238–40, 243
Arabs, dissatisfaction with Ottoman rule, 14
    military value of, 73, 89–90, 95
arguments, role of in bureaucratic decision making, 3–7, 422
Asquith government, breakup of, 149, 459n94

Bagdad, 85, 98, 165, 176–7, 180, 325
    Indian and British ambitions regarding, 42, 247, 287
    British occupation of, 65–6, 176
    Proclamation, 176–7
Balfour, Arthur, interviews with Weizmann, 198–9

memoranda on the Syrian question, 359–61, 367–8, 405
position as foreign secretary, 237
resigns, 408
role in fall Asquith government, 459n94
Balfour Declaration, 227, 247, 266–7, 411, 414, 419, 422, 470n135
ambiguity of, 392–4
British decision making leading to, 213–27, 468n89
effectuation of, 190, 229–31, 248, 266, 381, 384, 386–7, 396, 398
Basra, Indian and British ambitions regarding, 42, 45, 48, 61, 63, 72, 75, 248, 250, 265, 283, 287–8, 305
British occupation of, 17, 65
Beirut, 97, 99, 300–1, 314, 328, 338, 355
Board of Deputies, 193, 210–11
Brémond mission, 234–8
British anti-Semitism, 419, 423, 465n22
Weizmann's exploitation of, 470–1n135
British delegation at the peace conference, organization of, 322–3

caliph, 240, 442n6
caliphate, 28–9, 31, 39–41, 43–4, 51–2, 54–5, 70, 94
Cambon letter, 212
Cecil, Lord Robert, appointed assistant secretary of state for foreign affairs, 292
resignation, 317–18

Chamberlain, Austen, resignation as secretary of state for India 467n80
'Chamberlain's proviso', 73–7, 87
Cherchali, instructions to, 238–9, 241
Christian Holy Places, guardianship of, 254
Clemenceau, Georges, conflict with Lloyd George on Syria, 355, 357–9, 371, 378–9, 414, 419–20, 486n116
resigns as prime minister, 382, 414
visit to London, 329
Committee of Union and Progress (CUP), 14, 19, 62, 94, 110–11, 213
Conjoint Foreign Committee, 193–4, 205, 208–11
demise of, 208, 211
letter to *The Times*, 209–10
Constantinople and the Straits, Russian claims on, 47, 49
coordination, British attempts to strengthen, 36–7, 94, 117–21, 252, 455n94
Council of Four, 348
Council of Heads of Delegations, 365
Council of Ten, 335
credibility, 3–6, 419
Curzon of Kedleston, appointment as acting secretary of state for foreign affairs, 318
appointment as secretary of state, 408
chairman Eastern Committee, 253
chairman Middle East Committee, 241

member War Cabinet, 149
opposition to declaration of sympathy with Zionist movement, 221, 225
relationship with Balfour and Lloyd George, 491n81
rivalry with Sykes, 252–3, 462n19

Damascus, British advance on, 297–8
Damascus, surrender of, 298–9
'Damascus, Homs, Hama and Aleppo', 61, 63, 67–8, 70–1, 75, 97, 101, 172, 322, 371, 373–4, 379, 448n7, 449n24
'Dan to Bersheeba', 225, 373, 382, 412–14
Dardanelles, British expedition to, 35, 47, 58
decision making, in a bureaucratic-political environment, 3–7
Declaration to the Seven, 262–5, 300
De Bunsen committee, 91
Deir es Zor, 85, 97, 407
'The Demands', 199
draft declaration on Zionism, 409–12

Eastern Committee, constitution of, 237, 253
functioning of, 292–4
Egyptian Expeditionary Force (EEF), 165, 168, 172, 227, 297, 308, 370
El Arish, British advance on, 124, 144, 166–8

Faysal, third son of Husayn ibn Ali, agreement with Weizmann, 387–8
attempt to occupy Beirut, 300–1
conversations with Sykes and Picot, 178
entry in Damascus, 299
meetings with the British government, 374–5, 377
meetings with Weizmann, 270, 386
memorandum on Arab demands, 333–4
negotiations with the French, 353–4, 379
presents Arab case to the peace conference, 341–2
representative of Hijaz at peace conference, 318–19, 330–2
strength of his forces, 321–2, 362, 486n126
Force 'D', 17, 92, 121, 176
advance on Baghdad, 65, 67
defeat at Ctesiphon, 176, 448n19, 467n82
Foreign Office, decline of influence on British Middle East policy, 322–4, 374, 420–1
Foreign Office Middle East Department, constitution of, 295–7
Fourteen Points, 285, 307–8, 319, 328, 479n92
'The Future of Palestine', memorandum by Curzon, 225
'The Future of Palestine', memorandum by Herbert Samuel, 191

Gallipoli, evacuation of, 57, 71, 76, 78, 127

Gaza, battles for, 165, 172–4, 185, 227–8, 462n19
Goût, Jean, speech to "the Syrian Committee", 259–60
Graham, Sir Ronald, return to the Foreign Office, 460n113

Haifa, 97–8, 204, 407
Hennequeville, conferences at, 371–2, 406–7
Hermon, Mount, 339, 382, 406, 413
Hijaz, representation at the peace conference, 330–4
Hijaz railway, 25, 383, 402, 405
Hogarth mission, 247–9
Husayn ibn Ali, emir of Mecca, assents to 'the formula', 179–83
  attitude in case of war 26–8, 31
  characterization of, 45–6
  conflict with CUP spring 1914, 23–5
  negotiations with Sir Henry McMahon, 53–4, 59, 61, 63–5, 67–8, 77–8, 85–8, 102–103, 113–14
  position *vis-à-vis* other Arab chiefs, 245, 277
  possible successor to the caliphate, 43–5, 51, 55–6, 241–2
  proclaimed and crowned 'king of the Arab nation', 123, 158, 160, 424
  recognized as king of the Hijaz, 159, 161
  rivalry with Ibn Sa'ud, 245–50, 276, 279–80
  spokesman of the Arab nationalist movement, 53, 60–1, 84–5, 106
  subsidy to, 165–6, 183–7
  territorial ambitions, 46, 52–3
Husayn's revolt, political and military consequences of possible defeat, 116, 127, 130, 132–4, 142, 149, 153
  preparations of, 114–15
  start of, 84, 113, 116, 456n31

Indian Muslims, religious susceptibilities of, 13, 15–16, 21, 29, 33, 91
Inter-Allied Commission to Syria, Palestine, Mesopotamia and Armenia, 349, 351–62, 395–7, 405

Jerusalem, 49, 97–8, 195–6, 200, 229–30, 329
  British occupation of, 173, 228
jihad, 52, 59–60, 84, 89, 92–3, 99
joint declaration of November 1918, 312–13, 315–17, 319, 324, 330, 341, 349, 360, 384
  effect of, 312–13
  preparation of, 289, 301, 304–5, 308–9, 311–12

Khurma affair, 275–8
King–Crane commission, 400, 405, 486n120
Kitchener of Khartoum, appointment as secretary of state for war, 13, 17
  death of, 197, 456n31
  influence on Grey, 20–2
  message to Abdullah, 28, 54
  visit to Gallipoli, 71
Kut al-'Amara, 65–6, 127, 176, 467n82

League of Nations, 335, 337, 340–1, 348–9, 360
Lebanon, 97, 328, 340–2, 347, 379
Litani, river, 381–3, 385, 412–13
Lloyd George, David, conflict with Clemenceau on Syria, 355, 357–9, 371, 378–9, 414, 419–20, 486n116
London, Treaty of, 205

al-Masri, Aziz Ali, conflict with CUP, 17–18
  proposal to send him and Faruqi to Mesopotamia, 105–7
  proposes to go to Mesopotamia, 21–3
McMahon, Sir Henry, appointment as high commissioner, Egypt, 444n58
  letter to Husayn of 24 October 1915, 67–8, 449n23, 24
  negotiations with Husayn, 53–4, 59, 61, 63–5, 67–8, 77–8, 85–8, 102–3, 113–14
  replacement as high commissioner, 457–8n67
  struggle for political and military control of Husayn's revolt, 125–7, 136–7
Medina, siege of, 127
  surrender of, 280
Megiddo, battle of, 279, 297
Meinertzhagen, Richard, appointment as CPO Syria and Palestine, 398–400, 402–3
  position on Zionism, 408
Mesopotamia, Indian and British claims to, 40–2, 44–5, 48, 57, 62, 64–5, 68, 72–5, 78, 85, 88, 92–3, 251, 324–5, 349
Mesopotamia Administration Committee (MAC), constitution of, 241
Mesopotamian Expeditionary Force (MEF), 176
Middle East Committee (MEC), constitution of, 241, 252–3
Milner–Amery formula, 221–3, 226
Milner map, 347, 349, 357–8
Milner–Ormsby Gore formula, 217
Montagu, Edwin, appointment as secretary of state for India, 467–8n82
Morgenthau mission, 468n93
Mosul, 85, 97–8, 307, 315–16, 325, 329, 341, 345–6, 349, 355, 357–9, 373, 413, 419
Murray, Sir Archibald, replacement as GOC-in-C, Egypt, 462n19
  struggle for political and military control of Husayn's revolt, 125–7, 136–7
Muslim Holy Places, 41, 49–50

'no annexation clause', 251, 265
Northern Arab Army, 298

Occupied Enemy Territory Administration (OETA), 299–300, 304–5, 382, 405
Ottoman Empire, partition of, 47–9, 193, 205, 214, 307–8, 314

Palestine, American protectorate, of, 201, 203, 214, 281

Anglo–American condominium of, 202
Arab opposition to Zionist claims to, 266, 383–4, 395, 398–400, 406, 408
as a Jewish Commonwealth, 385, 389–91
as Jewish National Home, 199, 212, 214–17, 221, 227, 231, 266, 268, 381, 383–4, 390–3, 395, 400–1, 403, 410
borders of, 200–1, 207–8, 381–3, 385–6, 388, 392, 401, 405–8, 412–15, 420
British mandate of, 282, 381, 383, 385–6, 389, 391, 396–8, 400–1, 403, 406–7, 410, 413–14
British protectorate of, 191–2, 202–3, 205–6, 208, 213, 281, 314
Eastern Committee's resolution on, 386
French claims to, 189, 194, 200, 204, 206
French participation in the administration of, 227–8, 233, 254–5
international administration of, 201–2, 206–8, 228, 280–1, 310, 349, 386
military administration of, 227–8, 254
strategic value of, 385–6, 398
Zionist attacks on military administration of, 397–9, 402, 404
Zionist claims to, 209, 266
Zionist desire of a British protectorate of, 199–201, 203–4, 206, 213, 271, 281
Palmyra (Tadmor), British and French claims on, 346, 368–9, 372
projet d'arrangement, 243–4, 259, 422

Rabegh, 7, 123, 234–5, 280, 418–19, 422, 460n135
first crisis, 128–36
second crisis, 138–9
third crisis, 139–48
fourth crisis, 148–54
fifth crisis, 154–8
Rothschild formula, 215–16, 218
Roux–Sciard mission, 315–16

Saint Jean-de-Maurienne, agreement of, 301
conference of, 204–5, 208, 281, 420
San Remo, conference of, 379, 414
self-determination, 284–7, 305, 320, 326–9, 339, 341, 345, 360, 393–4, 421
Sokolow mission, 203, 208, 211–13
Storrs, Ronald, appointment as military governor, Jerusalem, 247, 473n48
mission to Ibn Sa'ud, 246
proposes to approach Husayn, 26
Suez Canal, Turkish offensive against, 35
Sultani Road, 127, 139

INDEX OF SUBJECTS 509

Sykes, Sir Mark, appointment as assistant secretary, War Cabinet, 199, 422
appointment as Chief Political Officer, EEF, 169
characterization of, 483n44
death of, 483n44
meeting with Zionist leadership, 199–200
move to the Foreign Office, 233, 252
speech to 'the Syrian Committee', 259
testimony before the War Committee, 93–5, 422
visit to the Near and Middle East, 1915, 91–3
Sykes–Picot agreement, 7, 84, 113, 165–6, 168, 170–1, 174–5, 177–8, 182, 190, 195, 207, 240, 242–4, 250, 271, 281, 283, 285, 290–1, 297–8, 301–2, 304, 309–11, 313, 315–16, 320, 325–30, 336–41, 344, 346, 349–50, 368, 371–2, 375, 382, 385, 406, 415, 417–19, 421–2, 452n33, 466n34, 35
British attempts to unmake the agreement, 275, 281–2, 285–6, 297–8, 304–8, 310–11, 316–17, 319–20, 325–7, 329–30
conditional character of, 100–1, 104, 112
negotiations leading to, 69, 71, 75–6, 84–5, 94–5, 97–8, 100–2, 104–5, 109, 112–13
revelation of, 250, 290
Sykes–Picot line, 373–4, 382, 407, 412–13

Sykes–Picot mission, 7, 165, 172, 174–82, 236, 239, 244, 257
Syria, British military evacuation of, 369, 372–7
Eastern Committee's resolution on, 327–8
Foreign Office deference to French claims to and susceptibilities with regard to 7, 13, 19, 21, 29, 33–6, 50, 57–8, 63–4, 68, 79, 81, 86, 233, 235–7, 272, 418, 421
French administration of, 255–8, 291, 301–3
French claims to, 33–5, 44, 48, 57, 62, 71, 79, 84–5, 87–9, 93, 96, 178, 200, 204, 258, 264, 291, 325, 327, 332, 347
French mandate of, 342, 349, 351, 356, 377, 379
Hashemite ambitions in, 250, 261, 264
Lloyd George's declaration of British disinterestedness, 349–50, 353, 355, 360–1, 363–7
Syrian opposition to French claims, 84, 102–3, 253–4, 258, 260, 262, 265, 332–3, 338–9, 342, 351
Syrian opposition to Hashemite ambitions, 252, 261–2, 264–5, 276

Turkish opposition parties, 110–11

war aims, Lloyd George's speech on British, 284–5
War Cabinet, constitution of, 149

War Cabinet Secretariat, constitution of, 149
Weizmann, Chaim, agreement with Faysal, 387–8
    Chemical Advisor to the Ministry of Munitions, 198
    head, Zionist Commission, 267, 269
    interviews with Balfour, 198–9
    learns of Sykes–Picot agreement, 207–8
    meetings with Faysal, 270, 386
    proposes Zionist–Hashemite deal, 269–71
    speech to Palestinian leaders, 269
Wilson, Woodrow, approves of Milner–Amery formula, 224
    characterization of, 348

Wingate, Sir Reginald, appointment as high commissioner, Egypt, 457–8n67
    correspondence with Cromer, Grey, Hardinge and McMahon, 38, 40–1, 43–5
    struggle for political and military control of Husayn's revolt, 125–7, 136–7
Wolf formula, 193–7
World Zionist Organisation, 200, 401
    presents the Zionist case to the peace conference, 394–5

Zionist commission, 231, 266–8, 390, 409
Zionist movement (Zionism), 189, 194, 198–9, 202, 207, 211–13, 216, 219–20, 225, 230